Consumer Finance Law

Understanding Consumer Financial Services Regulations

EDITORS

J.H. Jennifer Lee and Nathan Viebrock

AMERICAN BAR ASSOCIATION

Business Law Section

Cover design by Catherine Zaccarine

Page layout by Quadrum Solutions

Printed in the United States of America.

25 24 23   5 4 3 2

ISBN: 978-1-64105-871-1

Preface

The reach of consumer financial services regulation has been steadily increasing and will continue to expand. As a result, legal expertise in consumer financial services is in greater demand, especially since new products, novel forms of joint ventures and business relationships, and means of access to consumer credit are evolving at a steady clip.

While many of the consumer financial protection laws have been enshrined in federal law for more than forty years, there has not been a published resource providing a collection of high-level explanations regarding each of the many rules governing this space, until this book.

The need for such a resource was amplified by more recent economic developments in the beginning of the twenty-first century. While consumer financial protection laws date back to the 1960s, they became more fashionable (or at least more focused on) during the aftermath of the Great Recession of 2008. Congress passed dramatic financial reform by enacting the Dodd-Frank Wall Street Reform and Consumer Financial Protection Act (the Dodd-Frank Act) in 2010. Title X of the Dodd-Frank Act put forth a new system of federal consumer finance regulation by creating the Consumer Financial Protection Bureau, which—in turn—caused consumer financial issues to become front and center in our public discourse.

For any business attorney doing deals with consumer-facing financial product lines or advising financial services clients, recent laws have dramatically changed the landscape in which companies can sell financial solutions. While not every law has been amended (far from it), there have been substantial changes in the enforcement, bank (or non-bank) supervision, and rulemaking activity of agencies that are overseen to monitor compliance. As such, in the last ten years following the passage of the Dodd-Frank Act, we have seen rapid change in the regulatory environment for businesses. This has been palpable given the current marketplace marked by robust new technologies and innovation in financial services. And yet there had never been a collection of the most critical consumer financial protection laws covered in a single publication.

Given past history, reading this book will also help you stay relevant, in three ways. First, the book is a practical resource guide for any attorney or stakeholder seeking an introductory, high-level treatment of the consumer-finance laws. The authors have addressed both technical rule requirements and policy underpinnings of salient laws. All of the content is prepared to aid the casual reader with a common-sense overview, with the understanding that agency statements and regulatory actions are always available to readers who seek a deeper dive.

Second, the book is timely. Not only is a global pandemic, and ensuing economic decline, an inevitable harbinger to greater challenges and opportunities in the consumer markets, the federal government has also implemented changes in the last decide, given the transfer of authority that the Dodd-Frank Act mandated. This book provides readers with an explanation of the complex federal agencies that enforce these laws. In doing so, we flag for practitioners the reality in which businesses might be subject to multiple federal investigations or inquiries on a single product or company issue.

Third, this book is politically neutral. Consumer financial services regulations—as opposed to other buckets of financial laws—are most susceptible distortion in the public reporting as a result of conscious (or subconscious) partisan influence. This is no surprise given that consumer financial products touch every person, regardless of wealth or economic status. As lawyers, we have a responsibility to our clients, whether they are corporations, consumers, governments, or trade associations, to advise on the law with objectivity and clinical precision. This book has no "skin in the game" in public debates regarding consumer protection policy. Instead, the authors of each chapter have been faithful to the black letter law and only identified key policy goals where needed, in a dispassionate, neutral manner. Therefore, the book is trustworthy.

On behalf of the individual chapter authors, we would be remiss not to mention that the Committee's and our deepest thanks go to many individuals who worked tirelessly to make this publication a success, including David Beam, Elyssa Evans, Chris Capurso, Jason Cover, Sarah Edwards, Taylor Gess, Tai Shadrick Kluemper, Donna Tillis, and Susan Tran. Without their assistance, this publication would not have been possible. We are delighted to present this treatise to you and watch eagerly to see how the ongoing evolution of consumer financial laws may take place in ensuing years, given the new challenges we face.

After all, there is no American who is untouched by the consumer financial services market, and knowledge of the rules governing these products is fundamental not only to advising our clients, but also to understanding the systems that shape our own lives as consumers.

J. H. Jennifer Lee
Partner, Arent Fox
San Francisco, California

Nathan Viebrock
Partner, Viebrock + De Nittis
Charlotte, North Carolina

About the Authors

David N. Anthony is a partner at Troutman Pepper with a national litigation practice representing companies in highly regulated industries, including consumer financial services companies. He has significant litigation experience defending cases under the Fair Credit Reporting Act, the Fair Debt Collection Practices Act, the Telephone Consumer Protection Act, and numerous other federal and state consumer protection statutes, with particular expertise in matters that often involve companion government investigations.

Karlene A. Archer is a bankruptcy lawyer located in the Syracuse, New York, area. She previously worked in Boston, Massachusetts, for WilmerHale and in Nashville, Tennessee, for Bradley Arant Boult Cummings LLP. She has practiced all aspects of bankruptcy law but currently works with banks and mortgage servicers on consumer bankruptcy compliance.

Allyson Baker is chair of Venable LLP's Financial Services practice and co-chair of the Consumer Financial Services practice. Allyson is a trial attorney, civil litigator, and counselor with significant experience in the federal government and private practice who has worked on some of the most significant and high-profile cases and investigations in the consumer financial services area. She is recognized as a "Litigation Trailblazer" by *The National Law Journal* and was named to the "Top 250 Women in Litigation" by Benchmark Litigation. Before joining private practice, Allyson was a trial attorney at the Department of Justice and served as one of the first dozen enforcement attorneys at the Consumer Financial Protection Bureau, where she led the first enforcement action brought by the CFPB and one of the first actions announced.

David L. Beam is a partner in Mayer Brown's Washington, D.C., office. He is a member of the firm's Financial Services Regulatory and Enforcement group, and a co-leader of the firmwide fintech practice. His practice focuses on payment systems and credit products, with an emphasis on legal issues that arise from the innovative use of technology in financial services.

R. Aaron Chastain is a partner in the Birmingham, Alabama, office of Bradley Arant Boult Cummings LLP and a member of the firm's Banking and Financial Services Practice Group. He represents a number of lenders and servicers in compliance and litigation matters, including individual and class action lawsuits under the TCPA, FCRA, and FDCPA. Mr. Chastain has significant experience at both the trial and appellate levels and has drafted appellate briefs and presented oral argument in courts around the country, including the U.S. Courts of Appeals for the Fifth, Sixth, Seventh, Ninth, and Eleventh Circuits.

Jake Christensen is a member of the Consumer Financial Services team and a complex litigation and regulatory associate at Arent Fox. He specializes in helping clients navigate complex regulatory hurdles at the federal, state, and local levels, and represents companies and individuals in a broad range of complex litigation matters. Jake also regularly counsels clients facing federal agency investigations, particularly those initiated by the Consumer Financial Protection Bureau, the Federal Trade Commission, and the Department of Justice.

Scott A. Coleman is a partner with Ballard Spahr LLP in Minneapolis, Minnesota. Scott advises financial institutions and their affiliates in merger and acquisition transactions and on regulatory matters.

Robert A. Cox, Jr. is a partner in the Charlotte, North Carolina, office of Bradley Arant Boult Cummings LLP, where he focuses his practice on financial restructuring and insolvency, including bankruptcy matters, creditors' rights, commercial workouts, receiverships, bankruptcy-related litigation, and distressed asset acquisitions. Mr. Cox represents banks, servicers, corporate debtors, creditors' committees, unsecured creditors, asset acquirers, lessors, equity holders, and other parties in interest in bankruptcy cases and bankruptcy related litigation throughout the United States. Mr. Cox has been recognized as a Board Certified Specialist in Business Bankruptcy Law by the North Carolina State Bar. Prior to entering private practice, Mr. Cox served as law clerk to the Honorable J. Craig Whitley, U.S. Bankruptcy Judge for the Western District of North Carolina.

Julia Dempewolf is a senior associate in Mayer Brown's Washington, D.C., office and a member of the Financial Services Regulatory & Enforcement group. Julia's practice focuses primarily on payment systems, bank regulation, and consumer financial services. Julia has advised both financial institutions and fintech companies regarding bank partnerships, including regulatory compliance and transaction negotiations. She also has extensive experience advising clients regarding state and federal money services businesses compliance obligations and negotiating vendor agreements on behalf of financial institutions.

Robin L. Dull is Associate General Counsel and Senior Vice President at Bank of America, where he provides enterprise legal support for fair lending, UDAAP, and other consumer protection matters. Before joining Bank of America, Robin was a trial attorney with the Civil Rights Division of the U.S. Department of Justice, leading complex civil enforcement actions on behalf of the United States.

Robin also served as a law clerk in the Eastern District of New York and the District of Columbia Court of Appeals.

Steve Forry is a partner in Ice Miller LLP's Litigation practice and the Director of the firm's Financial Services Litigation and Counseling practice. Steve represents financial services clients in consumer and commercial litigation. He also counsels clients regarding compliance with consumer financial services laws and regulations, with special focus on the Federal Fair Credit Reporting Act and analogous state laws.

Lauren M. Frank is an associate in the Los Angeles office of Buckley LLP. She assists clients on a variety of regulatory and compliance-related consumer financial services matters, and has particular experience advising clients on compliance with state and federal auto-finance laws including Regulation M, state retail installment sales acts, and state consumer lending statutes regulating vehicle-secured loans. She also regularly advises clients on compliance obligations in the context of alternative finance products including factoring, merchant cash advance, and other unique fintech offerings.

Peter Frechette is an associate in Venable LLP's Financial Services Practice Group. He advises financial institutions, financial services providers, and companies that offer consumer and business-to-business credit as they navigate financial regulation, investigation, enforcement, and supervision by various federal and state agencies. He frequently counsels clients on residential mortgage compliance issues involved in origination, brokering, servicing, and secondary market sales.

Lee Gilley represents financial institutions, including banks, mortgage companies, debt collectors, small dollar lenders, and payment systems providers (credit cards, debit cards, prepaid cards, mobile payments, etc.) in litigation and regulatory matters related to compliance with the Card Act, ECOA, EFTA, FCRA, FDCPA, GLBA, HPA, RESPA, TILA, TCPA, CFPB regulations, and numerous other state laws and regulations. Lee frequently represents clients in sensitive internal compliance reviews and investigations where he works closely with business, legal, and compliance leaders to identify process issues and develop workable solutions.

Makalia A. Griffith is an associate in Venable LLP's Financial Services Practice Group. Makalia counsels clients on consumer protections, product development, regulatory, and transactional issues. Makalia frequently advises financial institutions, financial services providers, and companies that offer consumer and business-to-business credit in understanding and obtaining necessary licenses and approvals to conduct mortgage, personal and commercial lending, and lead generation at both the state and federal levels.

Reid F. Herlihy is a partner in the Mortgage Banking Group of Ballard Spahr, LLP. Reid provides regulatory and transactional advice for clients on a range of issues involving state and federal consumer finance laws. Reid regularly counsels clients on issues regarding the CFPB's Mortgage Servicing Rules, advertising, fair debt collection, lending and servicing disclosures, loss mitigation, foreclosure procedures, and business practices. He also assists clients with state and federal examination issues and regulatory actions.

Lynette I. Hotchkiss is of counsel at McGlinchey Stafford, PLLC. She has more than thirty years' experience in many aspects of consumer financial services and banking law, including working as in-house counsel at banks, leading teams at service providers developing regulatory compliance solutions for the financial services industry, and as a senior attorney at the Federal Trade Commission. Much of Lynette's experience has focused on mortgage origination and servicing laws and regulations.

Eric L. Johnson is a partner with Hudson Cook, LLP. He assists banks, lenders, sales finance companies, and motor vehicle dealers in the development and maintenance of nationwide consumer finance programs, remote motor vehicle sales, and electronic payment programs. Eric is listed in the 2021 edition of The Best Lawyers in America in the practice areas of Banking and Finance Law, Commercial Litigation, Financial Services Regulation Law and Litigation-Banking & Finance. He is a member of the American Bar Association (Business Law Section; Banking, Commercial Finance and Consumer Financial Services Committees), the National Association of Dealer Counsel, and the Governing Committee for The Conference on Consumer Finance Law (VP-Membership). Eric was also elected to the American College of Consumer Financial Services Lawyers.

Daniel P. Kearney, Jr. is a partner in the Financial Institutions practice at WilmerHale where he represents financial institution clients in government litigation and enforcement matters and advises on financial regulatory matters. He served as Special Assistant to the Legal Adviser to the Secretary of State in 2007–2009 and as a law clerk to Chief Justice John G. Roberts, Jr. from 2004–2006 on the U.S. Supreme Court and U.S. Court of Appeals for the D.C. Circuit. He is a graduate of Yale Law School.

Riley Key is a partner in Bradley's Birmingham office and is a member of Bradley's Banking and Financial Services Practice Group and is also a member of the firm's Auto Finance and Payments industry teams. Riley's practice focuses on counseling financial services clients facing regulatory and enforcement challenges in the mortgage, auto finance, debt collection, small dollar lending, and payments (credit cards, debit cards, prepaid cards, mobile payments, and cryptocurrencies) industries.

Jonathan R. Kolodziej is a partner in Bradley's Birmingham, Alabama, office. He represents all types of consumer financial service providers in regulatory compliance, examination, and enforcement matters. Through this work, he has assisted bank and non-bank mortgage servicers, mortgage originators, debt collectors, depository institutions, credit card issuers, small dollar lenders, reverse mortgage companies, investment firms, and various industry trade associations.

Erik Kosa is an associate in Hudson Cook's Washington, D.C., office. His practice includes representing banks, licensed lenders, sales finance companies, auto dealers and other creditors in regulatory enforcement actions, including actions before the CFPB, FTC, and other federal and state financial regulatory agencies. He also advises clients concerning their compliance obligations under federal and state laws. He is an active member of the ABA's Consumer Financial Service Committee.

Daniel Laudicina is a partner in the Maryland office of Hudson Cook, LLP. He provides regulatory compliance advice for a variety of consumer credit products, with a focus on Truth in Lending Act and Regulation Z, and credit card lending, retail charge programs, and other open-end credit offerings.

J. H. Jennifer Lee is the leader of the Consumer Financial Services team and co-leader of the FinTech group at Arent Fox. She specializes in defending large bank or non-bank clients in Consumer Financial Protection Bureau, Federal Trade Commission, and state agency matters, and counseling investors, big tech, financial services companies or banks on deals, regulatory matters, or public policy. As a former CFPB enforcement official, Jenny's expertise includes swift resolution of investigations or contentious consumer litigation. Jenny is a highly regarded commentator on financial services developments and is often quoted in national publications such as *The Wall Street Journal*, *American Banker*, *The National Law Journal*, *Forbes*, or *Bloomberg*.

Robert Maddox is a Certified Mortgage Banker and a Fellow of the American College of Mortgage Attorneys and the American College of Consumer Financial Services Lawyers. A thought leader at the forefront of the implications of COVID-19 on the mortgage servicing industry, Robert provides clients with regular updates on federal and state laws, as well as guidance on the CARES Act, forbearances, deferrals, foreclosure, and other servicer-related topics. His national practice, with an emphasis in mortgage litigation and compliance and commercial/real estate litigation, focuses primarily on representing two specific industries: financial institutions and mortgage companies. Robert has litigated all facets of the mortgage industry including origination, warehouse lending, pooling and servicing agreements, loan repurchase disputes, investor disputes, secondary market representations and warranties, servicing matters, commercial mortgages, settlement services issues, and mortgage fraud.

Lucy Morris is a partner with Hudson Cook, LLP and chairs the firm's Government Investigations, Examinations and Enforcement practice. Lucy counsels financial institutions and others in complying with federal consumer financial laws and prohibitions against unfair, deceptive, or abusive trade practices. She is an experienced advocate and litigator, representing clients in government investigations, examinations, and enforcement actions before federal and state agencies, including the CFPB, FTC, U.S. DOJ, and state AG offices. Lucy is honored to be a Fellow of the American College of Consumer Financial Services Lawyers and is a frequent speaker and author on a variety of consumer financial services law topics.

Michael Nonaka is co-chair of the Financial Services Group at Covington & Burling LLP and advises banks, financial services providers, and non-bank companies on a broad range of prudential regulatory and consumer regulatory matters as well as compliance, enforcement, transactional, and legislative matters. He has worked extensively with federal and state banking agencies and with other federal agencies authorized to regulate financial services on policy issues, licensing applications, and supervisory processes. Mr. Nonaka also plays an active role in the firm's Fintech Initiative and works with a number of banks, lending companies, money transmitters, payments firms, technology companies, and service providers on innovative technologies such as blockchain, bitcoin and other cryptocurrencies, big data, cloud computing, same day payments, and online lending.

Jacqueline Parker is Deputy Director of Consumer Fairness Compliance at Citigroup Inc. and an adjunct professor at Pace University Elisabeth Haub School of Law. She has served as a strategic adviser in senior and executive roles at domestic and international financial institutions, and she is a member of the American Law Institute and the Board of Regents of the American College of Consumer Financial Services Lawyers.

Dascher L. Pasco is an associate in Troutman Pepper's government investigations compliance and enforcement group. Her practice focuses on business litigation as well as compliance and regulatory issues at the federal, state, and local levels.

Sarah Pruett represents clients in complex commercial litigation, with an emphasis on defending financial institutions and businesses in consumer finance litigation and government investigations and examinations. She regularly represents clients in litigation involving the Fair Credit Reporting Act, the Fair Debt Collections Practices Act, the Equal Credit Opportunity Act, Title X of the Dodd-Frank Act (UDAAP), and state consumer protection laws. Sarah also assists clients facing examinations and investigations by regulators, including the Consumer Financial Protection Bureau and the Federal Trade Commission.

Clinton R. Rockwell, managing partner of Buckley LLP's Los Angeles and San Francisco offices, advises a wide range of clients on consumer and commercial financial services matters. He represents clients on regulatory issues before the Consumer Financial Protection Bureau, the Federal Housing Administration, and the California Department of Financial Protection and Innovation. Mr. Rockwell is annually ranked in Financial Services Regulation: Consumer Finance (Compliance) by Chambers USA, which described him as "very adept at seeing legal issues from a business perspective and very good at protecting the interests of his client . . . a phenomenal lawyer."

Sherry-Maria S. Safchuk is counsel in the Los Angeles office of Buckley LLP, where she represents clients in regulatory and compliance matters and provides support for complex litigation and government investigations involving the mortgage, consumer, and commercial lending industries. She has significant experience in assisting clients on compliance with the Real Estate Settlement Procedures Act, the Truth in Lending Act, the Equal Credit Opportunity Act, the Home Mortgage Disclosure Act, and the prohibitions against unfair, deceptive, or abusive acts or practices. She also assists clients on privacy issues, including those related to the Gramm-Leach-Bliley Act, the California Consumer Privacy Act, and other similar federal and state laws.

Robert Savoie helps financial institutions attain and maintain regulatory compliance with the ever-changing laws and rules governing consumer financial services so they can avoid pitfalls and expand operations. Robert does this through a unique approach combining sophisticated business structuring, cutting-edge policies and procedures, and agile business rules animated by a sense of fairness that help his clients align with both the spirit and the letter of the financial services laws that apply. Robert has extensive experience advising clients across industries with respect to Servicemembers Civil Relief Act (SCRA) and Military Lending Act (MLA) compliance and litigation, and routinely handles inquiries, examinations, and investigations with respect to SCRA and MLA compliance.

Lori J. Sommerfield serves as of Counsel in Ballard Spahr's Consumer Financial Services practice group, and she has practiced consumer finance law for over twenty-five years in federal government, in-house, and private practice settings. Ms. Sommerfield specializes in regulatory compliance with federal and state fair and responsible lending laws (including the Equal Credit Opportunity Act, Fair Housing Act, and UDAP/UDAAP) and the Americans with Disabilities Act and assists clients with examinations, supervisory issues, investigations and enforcement actions related to those laws.

David A. Stein is of counsel at Covington & Burlington LLP and advises clients on credit reporting, financial privacy, open banking/data access, financial technology, payments, retail financial services, and fair lending issues. He assists a broad range of financial services firms, consumer reporting agencies, financial technology companies, and their vendors with regulatory, compliance, supervision, enforcement, and transactional matters. Mr. Stein is a member of the firm's Fintech and Artificial Intelligence initiatives and works with clients on issues related to innovative technologies, such as blockchain, cryptocurrencies, big data and data analytics, artificial intelligence, online lending, and payments technology.

Matthew O. Stromquist is a partner at Pilgrim Christakis LLP, where he advises consumer financial service providers on a wide variety of state and federal compliance issues and defends them in individual and class actions in state and federal courts and arbitrations around the country. His clients include banks, fintech companies, mortgage lenders and servicers, credit card issuers, debt buyers, auto loan lenders, and third-party service providers, among many others. Matthew is active in a number of professional associations, serving currently as co-vice chair of the Litigation and Arbitration Subcommittee for the American Bar Association's Consumer Financial Services Committee. Matthew graduated with senior honors in anthropology from Haverford College, received a master's degree in ethnomusicology from the University of Texas at Austin, and his J.D. with highest honors, order of the coif, from the University of Iowa College of Law. After graduating, Matthew clerked on the D.C. Court of Appeals for Judge Michael W. Farrell.

David Tallman is a partner in Mayer Brown's Houston office and a member of the firm's Consumer Financial Services group. David's practice includes counseling clients on regulatory compliance obligations under federal and state consumer credit laws; performing due diligence in connection with investments, acquisitions, and other transactions related to consumer financial products and services; structuring operations and developing compliance and risk management systems; handling privacy and information security matters; advising clients on a range of consumer protection, advertising, telemarketing, and social media issues; and helping clients to develop e-commerce platforms to facilitate the electronic delivery of financial services.

Ashley L. Taylor, Jr. joined Troutman Pepper in 2001 after a stint in public service and is currently a partner who focuses his practice on federal and state government regulatory and enforcement matters involving state Attorneys General, the Consumer Financial Protection Bureau, and the Federal Trade Commission, as well as regulatory private litigation. Drawing upon his experience as a Deputy Attorney General in Virginia, Ashley has developed an extensive practice handling consumer protection issues and matters related to marketing and advertising representations, statutory disclosures, unfair or deceptive acts or practices, and data security breach response. Ashley is an active participant in industry organizations, and he founded and currently co-chairs the American Bar Association Committee on State Attorneys General Matter. While maintaining his practice with Troutman Pepper, Ashley was appointed by President Bush to serve as a Commissioner on the U.S. Commission on Civil Rights from 2004–2010. He received his B.A. from Virginia Military Institute and his J.D. from the Washington & Lee University School of Law.

Leah A. Tedford is an associate in Troutman Pepper's consumer financial services practice. With her extensive writing experience, she represents national consumer-facing clients in state and federal courts in matters ranging from banking transaction disputes to national class actions brought under the Fair Credit Reporting Act and Telephone Consumer Protection Act. Her clients include financial institutions and background screening companies.

Heather B. Thayer is a shareholder with Thayer Legal Services, PLLC. She is a senior attorney with nearly thirty years of law firm and in-house experience specializing in consumer lending compliance, including residential mortgage originations, servicing and foreclosure operations, with a focus for much of that time on home equity lines of credit.

Nathan Viebrock is a partner at Viebrock + De Nittis where he represents both consumers and responsible financial services providers. He is an accomplished practitioner in consumer financial services law and has experience guiding clients on state and federal regulatory issues and product development in the areas of mortgage origination and servicing, auto finance, and consumer lending. He is well-versed in counseling clients on matters related to UDAAP, TILA, RESPA, FCRA, TCPA, ECOA, and CARD Act compliance. After beginning his career at the CFPB, he also served as in-house product and regulatory counsel at a nationally recognized FinTech company and advised clients on building innovative financial services products at two of America's largest law firms.

Lauren White is Assistant General Counsel for Regions Bank in Birmingham, Alabama. Lauren advises Regions Bank on legal matters related to its consumer payment products. She is a graduate of Cumberland School of Law.

Christopher Willis is the deputy leader of the Consumer Financial Services Practice Group at Ballard Spahr LLP. He has practiced in the area of consumer financial services for twenty-five years, and he assists clients with regulatory investigations and examinations as well as private litigation and in compliance matters.

Alan D. Wingfield is a partner in Troutman Pepper Hamilton Sanders LLP's consumer financial services practice. He defends class actions brought under state and federal consumer protection laws, gives compliance advice to consumer-facing companies, and advocates to regulators. His particular interests are helping companies navigate the "alphabet soup" of federal consumer protection laws—such as UDAP, UDAAP, TILA, TCPA, FCRA, and ECOA—as well as the myriad and complex panoply of state laws, in the design and defense of business models and products in an increasingly Internet-driven, remote contracting marketplace.

Summary Contents

Contents

CHAPTER

1

The Regulators

CHAPTER

1A

The Consumer Financial Protection Bureau

Allyson Baker and Eric L. Johnson

1. Overview

The Dodd-Frank Wall Street Reform and Consumer Protection Act of 2010 (Dodd-Frank Act), signed into law by President Obama on July 21, 2010, established the Consumer Financial Protection Bureau (CFPB or Bureau).[1] Congress vested the CFPB with supervisory, rulemaking, and enforcement authority, among other powers. The CFPB formally began operation on its designated date of transfer, July 21, 2011. The CFPB is an independent agency housed within the Federal Reserve Board (FRB).[2] It is largely autonomous, and the FRB is generally prohibited from interfering with the affairs of the CFPB. The CFPB is led by a director, who is appointed by the president and confirmed by the Senate, with a five-year term.[3] You will find many pages in this treatise dedicated to some of the most important rulemaking and enforcement actions the CFPB has engaged in since its inception. In this chapter, we will provide an overview of the Bureau's structure so that you can become more familiar with the primary federal regulator charged with overseeing and enforcing the consumer financial laws.

---

1. Dodd-Frank Wall Street Reform and Consumer Protection Act, Pub. L. No. 111-203, 124 Stat. 1376 (2010) (codified in scattered sections of U.S.C.).

2. 12 U.S.C. § 5491.

3. *Id.*

2. Why the CFPB Was Created

The CFPB was created to ensure that "all consumers have access to markets for consumer financial products and services and that [those] markets for consumer financial products and services are fair, transparent, and competitive."[4] The Dodd-Frank Act also charges the CFPB with implementing and enforcing federal consumer financial laws in a consistent manner.[5] The CFPB further promulgates and enforces new consumer financial protection rules, monitors the consumer financial services industry, and supervises certain financial institutions with respect to the consumer financial laws. The Dodd-Frank Act mandated that at the Bureau's inception, seven different federal agencies would transfer their enforcement and implementation authority concerning federal consumer financial laws and regulations to the Bureau.[6]

3. The CFPB's Powers

To carry out its purpose, the Dodd-Frank Act empowered the CFPB to (1) issue rules, orders, and guidance to implement federal consumer financial laws; (2) supervise large banks and certain categories of nonbanks to ensure compliance with federal consumer financial laws; (3) enforce federal consumer financial laws and take action to correct violations of those laws; (4) collect, investigate, and respond to consumer complaints; (5) research and monitor markets for consumer financial products and services to identify risks to consumers; and (6) educate consumers about consumer financial products and related laws.[7]

4. Purpose, Objective, and Functions

The CFPB is authorized to exercise its authorities to ensure that, with respect to consumer financial products and services: (1) consumers are provided with timely and comprehensible information that allows them to make responsible decisions about financial transactions; (2) consumers are protected from unfair, deceptive, or abusive acts or practices and from discrimination; (3) outdated, unnecessary, or unduly burdensome regulations are regularly identified and addressed to reduce unwarranted regulatory burdens; (4) federal consumer financial laws are enforced consistently, without regard to the status of a person or institution to promote fair competition;

4. *Id.* § 5511.
5. *Id.* § 5492.
6. *Id.* §§ 5581–82.
7. *Id.* § 5511.

and (5) markets for consumer financial products and services operate transparently and efficiently to facilitate access and innovation.[8]

5. Funding and Budget

The CFPB's operating budget is funded by the FRB. The director of the CFPB is entitled to request from the FRB up to 12 percent of the FRB's total operating expenses, with adjustments based on an inflation index.[9] The director may request these funds in "the amount determined by the Director to be reasonably necessary to carry out the authorities of the CFPB, taking into account such other sums made available to the CFPB from the preceding year."[10]

6. Entities and Persons Regulated by the CFPB

The CFPB has authority to enforce the consumer financial protection laws, including the Dodd-Frank Act's prohibitions against unfair, deceptive, or abusive acts or practices (UDAAP). The CFPB's UDAAP authority applies to "covered persons" and "service providers."[11] A covered person is any person engaged in offering or providing a consumer financial product or service or an affiliate of such person if it acts as a service provider.[12] A service provider is any person that provides material service to a covered person in connection with a consumer financial product or service.[13] These definitions are fundamental. Unless specifically excluded or exempted, all persons that fall within these definitions are subject to the CFPB's enforcement authority.

The CFPB supervises certain entities subject to its statutory authority, including large banks and credit unions (and their affiliates) with total assets of more than $10 billion, mortgage lenders, private student lenders, payday lenders, "larger participants," certain service providers, and other covered persons when it has "reasonable cause to determine that the covered person's offering or provision of consumer financial products or services conduct poses risks to consumers."[14]

A larger participant, in turn, is a nonbank that is subject to the CFPB's supervision authority, as defined in CFPB rulemaking that the Dodd-Frank Act prescribes.[15] Thus far, the CFPB has issued final larger participant rules for providers in (1) the

8. *Id.*
9. 12 U.S.C. § 5497(a)(2)(A)(iii)-(B).
10. *Id.* § 5497(a)(1).
11. *See* 12 U.S.C. §§ 5481(6), (26), 5512, 5514–16.
12. 12 U.S.C. § 5481(6).
13. *Id.* § 5481(26).
14. *Id.* §§ 5514–16.
15. *Id.* § 5514(a)(1)(B).

consumer reporting market,[16] (2) the consumer debt collection market,[17] (3) the student loan servicing market,[18] (4) the international money transfer market,[19] and (5) the automobile financing market.[20] The CFPB has the authority to promulgate additional rulemakings that define other categories of larger participants.

Finally, the CFPB can supervise a nonbank entity when the CFPB has reasonable cause to determine, by order, and after giving notice to that entity and a reasonable opportunity to respond, that the entity is engaging in or has engaged in conduct that poses risks to consumers around the consumer financial products or services that entity offers.[21] Here, the CFPB determines it has reasonable cause based on its review of consumer complaints or information gathered from other sources.[22]

7. Office of Supervision

The CFPB may conduct periodic risk-based compliance examinations of nonbanks to (1) assess compliance with federal consumer financial laws, (2) obtain information about the activities and compliance systems or procedures of that entity, and/or (3) detect and assess risks to consumers and to markets for consumer financial products and services.[23]

The Nonbank Supervision Risk Analytics and Monitoring team (RAM) will perform a risk-based analysis to determine which nonbank supervised entities should be examined. The relevant risk-based factors include (1) the asset size of the nonbank entity, (2) the volume of transactions involving consumer financial products or services in which the nonbank engages, (3) the risks to consumers created by the provision of such consumer financial products or services, (4) the extent to which such institutions are subject to oversight by state authorities for consumer protection, and (5) any other factors the CFPB determines to be relevant.[24]

The CFPB is tasked with coordinating its supervisory activities with those of prudential regulators, the state banking regulatory authorities, and the state agencies that license, supervise, or examine the offering of consumer financial products or services.[25] The CFPB also periodically publishes Supervisory Highlights to share key

16. 12 C.F.R. § 1090.104.
17. *Id.* § 1090.105.
18. *Id.* § 1090.106.
19. *Id.* § 1090.107.
20. *Id.* § 1090.108.
21. 12 U.S.C. § 5514(a)(1)(C).
22. *Id.*
23. *Id.* § 5514(b)(1).
24. *Id.* § 5514(b)(2).
25. *Id.* § 5514(b)(3).

examination findings, assist the industry in limiting risks to consumers, and apprise about compliance with federal consumer financial laws.

8. Enforcement

The CFPB enforces the enumerated federal consumer financial laws, prohibitions against UDAAP, and rules issued by the Federal Trade Commission (FTC) under the Federal Trade Commission Act (FTC Act).[26] It has concurrent enforcement authority with the FTC with respect to nonbanks.[27] The CFPB has primary enforcement authority as to the consumer financial laws with respect to banks and credit unions (and their affiliates) with total assets of more than $10 billion; the federal prudential regulators have secondary authority.[28] The CFPB cannot bring an enforcement action against banks and credit unions (and their affiliates) with total assets of $10 billion or less; this authority remains exclusively with the federal prudential regulators.[29]

8.1 Investigations by the Office of Enforcement

The Dodd-Frank Act authorizes the CFPB to conduct investigations to ascertain whether "any person" is or has been engaged in conduct that, if proved, would constitute a violation of the federal consumer financial law.[30] Section 1052 of the Dodd-Frank Act governs these investigations.[31] To this end, the CFPB's Office of Enforcement may (1) conduct investigations, which includes the power to issue subpoenas and Civil Investigative Demands (CIDs) for interrogatories or document requests;[32] (2) conduct investigational hearings or require the creation of new reports beyond existing documents subject to the usual discovery requests;[33] and (3) commence civil actions in administrative proceedings or in U.S. district courts, which can culminate in cease-and-desist orders to restrain activity or require affirmative action.[34] The CIDs can include interrogatories, requests for production of documents, requests for "tangible things," and demands for oral testimony.[35]

26. *Id.* §§ 5514(c) 5514(e), 5515(c)–(d), 5516(d)–(e).
27. *Id.* § 5514(c).
28. *Id.* § 5515(c).
29. *Id.* § 5516(d).
30. *Id.* § 5562(c).
31. *Id.* § 5562.
32. *Id.*
33. *Id.* § 5563.
34. *Id.* § 5564.
35. *Id.* § 5562(c).

8.2 Emphasized Areas of Enforcement

Many of the CFPB's enforcement cases have involved mortgage origination and servicing and issues relating to those products and services. Credit card disclosures, including add-on products, were an early focus of the Office of Enforcement.[36] More recently, the CFPB has also initiated actions involving servicemember loans,[37] auto loans,[38] and student loans.[39] For example, some enforcement actions concerning loans that were made to servicemembers include allegations of deceptive marketing of auto loans and add-on products to active-duty servicemembers.[40] The CFPB also brought actions against indirect auto lenders alleging fair lending violations, based on a theory of disparate impact.[41]

8.3 Sources of Enforcement Authority

The CFPB draws its enforcement authority from Subtitle E of the Consumer Financial Protection Act of 2010 (CFPA).[42] In addition, Subtitle C of the CFPA includes sections 5531 and 5536 that authorize the CFPB to pursue enforcement actions for any "unfair, deceptive, or abusive act or practice" involving consumer financial products or services.[43] Under section 1036 of the CFPA, the CFPB also has authority to bring an enforcement action against any person who knowingly or recklessly provides substantial assistance to a covered person or service provider in violation of the act.[44] This standard is akin to an aiding and abetting standard.

36. *See, e.g.*, Synchrony Bank, f/k/a GE Capital Retail Bank, CFPB No. 2014-CFPB-0007 (2014); Bank of America, N.A. CFPB No. 2014-CFPB-0004 (2014); FIA Card Services, N.A., CFPB No. 2014-CFPB-0004 (2014); American Express Travel Related Services Co., Inc., CFPB No. 2013-CFPB-0013 (2013).

37. *See, e.g.*, U.S. Bank Nat'l Ass'n., CFPB No. 2013-CFPB-0003 (2013).

38. *See, e.g.*, Ally Fin., Inc. and Alley Bank, CFPB No. 2013-CFPB-0010 (2013).

39. CFPB v. ITT Educational Servs., Inc., No. 1:14-cv-292 (S.D. Ind. 2013).

40. *See, e.g.*, U.S. Bank Nat'l Ass'n, CFPB No. 2013-CFPB-0003 (2013) (finding the defendant made inaccurate disclosures related to the required use of military pay allotments to pay off installment loans and deceptively marketed the cost and coverage of certain add-on products sold in connection with installment loans).

41. *See, e.g.*, Ally Fin., Inc. and Ally Bank, CFPB No. 2013-CFPB-0010 (2013) (ordering defendants to pay $80 million in damages to harmed African-American, Hispanic, and Asian and Pacific Islander borrowers for discriminatory pricing of indirect auto loans).

42. *See, e.g.*, Bank of America, N.A. CFPB No. 2014-CFPB-0004 (2014); FIA Card Services, N.A., CFPB No. 2014-CFPB-0004 (2014); U.S. Bank Nat'l Ass'n, Cincinnati, Ohio, CFPB No. 2013-CFPB-0003 (2013).

43. 12 U.S.C. §§ 5531, 5536.

44. *Id.* § 5536(a)(3).

9. Judicial Review of CFPB Investigations and Adjudication

If a recipient of a CID fails to comply with the demand, the CFPB may petition any federal district court in which the recipient resides or transacts business for an order enforcing compliance with the demand.[45] Before filing any petition to quash a CID, the parties are required to engage in a meet-and-confer session with enforcement staff.[46] Any issues not raised in these sessions may not be raised in a petition.[47]

The Dodd-Frank Act authorizes the CFPB to bring administrative cease-and-desist proceedings against a covered person or service provider that has violated a law, rule, or any condition imposed in writing on the person by the CFPB.[48] These administrative proceedings are governed by the provisions of the Administrative Procedure Act that apply to formal adjudications[49] and the CFPB's Rules of Practice for Adjudication Proceedings.[50] If the CFPB determines that a violation has occurred, it may issue an order requiring the person to cease and desist from the violation and other remedies.[51]

A respondent in any CFPB administrative adjudication is entitled to seek judicial review of a final decision and order of the director (other than a consent order), within thirty days of its issuance, in the U.S. Court of Appeals for the District of Columbia Circuit, or in any court of appeals of the United States for the circuit in which the principal office of the respondent is located.[52]

A temporary cease-and-desist order is effective immediately upon service and remains in effect unless modified or terminated administratively by the CFPB or set aside on judicial review.[53] The order is appealable in federal district court within ten days.[54]

---

45. *Id.* § 5562(e); 12 C.F.R. § 1080.10.

46. Checksmart Fin. Co., CFPB No. 2014-MISC-Checksmart Financial Company-001, at 2 (Jan. 22, 2014).

47. *Id.*; 12 C.F.R. § 1080.6(c)(3).

48. 12 U.S.C. § 5563(b)(1)(A).

49. *Id.* §§ 5563(b), 5514–16.

50. 12 C.F.R. § 1081.

51. *See* discussion of remedial relief options provided the CFPB by 12 U.S.C. §§ 5563(b), 5565.

52. 12 U.S.C. § 5563(b)(4).

53. 12 C.F.R. § 1081.501(d); 12 C.F.R. § 1081.502.

54. 12 C.F.R. § 1081.502(a).

10. Relief and Penalties

The CFPB may obtain civil money penalties in both administrative and civil proceedings.[55] For any entity or person who violates a law, rule, final order, or condition imposed in writing by the CFPB, the CFPB may seek a penalty of up to $5,781.00 for each day during which such violation or failure to pay continues.[56] For any entity or person that recklessly engages in a violation of a federal consumer financial law, the maximum penalty is $28,906.00 for each day during which such violation continues.[57] Any entity or person who knowingly engages in a violation of a federal consumer financial law, a maximum penalty of $1,156,242.00 may be imposed for each day during which such violation continues.[58] These civil penalty amounts are adjusted annually.[59] The CFPB may also recover its costs in connection with prosecuting any action if the agency prevails in the action.[60]

11. Rulemaking

The Dodd-Frank Act transferred to the CFPB rulemaking authority for certain statutes from several government agencies (the prudential regulators), including the FRB, the Office of the Comptroller of Currency (OCC), the Office of Thrift Supervision (OTS), the Federal Deposit Insurance Corporation (FDIC), and the National Credit Union Administration (NCUA).[61] In addition, the Dodd-Frank Act transferred to the CFPB rulemaking authority vested in the FTC "under an enumerated consumer law,"[62] and the Department of Housing and Urban Development's rulemaking authority under the Real Estate Settlement Procedures Act (RESPA), the Secure and Fair Enforcement for Mortgage Licensing Act, and the Interstate Land Sales Full Disclosure Act (ILSA).[63] The Dodd-Frank Act also vests new rulemaking authority with the CFPB. CFPB rulemakings are subject to judicial review in accordance with the provisions of the Administrative Procedure Act.[64]

The Dodd-Frank Act granted the CFPB exclusive rulemaking authority to implement the federal consumer financial laws.[65] This means that the CFPB's

55. 12 U.S.C. § 5565(c).
56. *Id.* § 5565(c)(2)(A).
57. *Id.* § 5565(a)(2)(B).
58. *Id.* § 5565(c)(2)(C).
59. 12 C.F.R. § 1083.1.
60. 12 U.S.C. § 5565(b).
61. *Id.* § 5581(b)(1)–(4), (6).
62. *Id.* § 5581(b)(5)(A).
63. *Id.* § 5581(b)(7)(A).
64. 5 U.S.C. §§ 701–706.
65. 12 U.S.C. § 5512(b)(4).

interpretation of any provision of a federal consumer financial law will be given substantial deference, as the CFPB is the only agency authorized to apply, enforce, interpret, or administer the provisions of such federal consumer financial law.[66]

12. No-Action Policy, Compliance Sandbox, and Innovations

In 2019, the CFPB issued three policies to promote innovation and facilitate compliance: (1) a revised No-Action Letter (NAL) Policy,[67] (2) a new Compliance Assistance Sandbox (CAS) Policy,[68] and (3) a revised Trial Disclosure Program (TDP) Policy.[69]

NALs provide increased regulatory certainty through a statement that the Bureau will not bring an action against a company for providing a product or service under certain facts and circumstances.[70] Some industry participants felt the revised NAL Policy improved the Bureau's 2016 NAL Policy by creating a more streamlined review process that focuses on the consumer benefits and risks of a product or service.

The new CAS Policy enables testing of a financial product or service where there is regulatory uncertainty. After the Bureau evaluates the product or service for compliance with relevant law, an approved applicant that complies in good faith with the terms of the approval will have a "safe harbor" from liability under the Truth in Lending Act, the Electronic Fund Transfer Act, and/or the Equal Credit Opportunity Act for specified conduct during the testing period.[71]

Under the revised TDP Policy, entities seeking to improve consumer disclosures may conduct in-market testing of alternative disclosures for a limited time upon permission by the Bureau. The revised TDP Policy streamlines the application and review process.

Also in 2019, the CFPB and state regulators from seven states launched the American Consumer Financial Innovation Network, an initiative aimed at enhancing coordination among federal and state regulators to facilitate financial innovation and promote regulatory certainty for innovators.[72]

---

66. *Id.*

67. 84 Fed. Reg. 48229 (Sept. 13, 2019).

68. *Id.* 48246.

69. *Id.* 48260.

70. *Id.* 48229, 48244.

71. *Id.* 48246, 48256.

72. *See* CFPB, *CFPB and State Regulators Launch American Consumer Financial Innovation Network* (Sept. 10, 2019), https://www.consumerfinance.gov/about-us/newsroom/bureau-state-regulators-launch-american-consumer-financial-innovation-network/; *see* CFPB, *American Consumer Financial Innovation Network Charter as of October 15, 2019* (Oct. 15, 2019), https://files.consumerfinance.gov/f/documents/201910_cfpb_ACFIN-charter.pdf.

In June 2020, the CFPB announced its first-ever Tech Sprints, which is a program designed to reduce regulatory burden and improve consumer understanding of financial services.[73] The Bureau's Tech Sprints program will bring together regulators, technologists, software providers, consumer groups, and financial institutions to develop technological solutions to shared compliance challenges. The first Tech Sprint kicked off in October 2020, with another planned for March 2021. The October 2020 Tech Sprint focused on existing consumer disclosures; looking at innovative electronic methods for informing consumers about adverse credit actions, including from the use of algorithms. The March 2021 Tech Sprint will focus on the HMDA (Home Mortgage Disclosure Act).

13. Conclusion

Although this chapter serves as an introduction to two of the CFPB's most-watched functions—rulemaking and enforcement—the CFPB also provides additional critical services to consumers. For example, the CFPB's Office of Servicemember Affairs is dedicated to ensuring that America's servicemembers are educated about the financial products and services that are available to them, and constantly monitors providers that tailor their service offerings to military families to ensure that unscrupulous companies are not taking unfair advantage of servicemembers. The CFPB also produces robust educational tools designed to enhance consumers' knowledge of financial products and inform financial companies about their responsibilities to consumers. As you will see throughout this treatise, in its first decade in existence, the CFPB has dramatically transformed the way in which financial services are regulated in America.

73. *See* CFPB, *CFPB Announces Tech Sprints To Empower Consumers, Reduce Regulatory Burden* (June 29, 2020), https://www.consumerfinance.gov/about-us/newsroom/tech-sprints/; *see* CFPB, *CFPB Tech Sprints*, https://www.consumerfinance.gov/policy-compliance/innovation/cfpb-tech-sprints/ (last visited Sept. 14, 2020).

CHAPTER

1B

Prudential Bank Regulators

Daniel P. Kearney, Jr.

1. Overview

Depository institutions in the United States are subject to prudential (also known as "safety and soundness") regulation by federal regulatory agencies. The four main federal prudential bank regulators—the Federal Reserve Board (FRB), the Office of the Comptroller of the Currency (OCC), the Federal Deposit Insurance Corporation (FDIC), and the National Credit Union Administration (NCUA)—wield broad power to promulgate rules, conduct examinations, and bring enforcement actions against depository institutions and their employees and affiliates. Historically, this authority extended to consumer protection in connection with the provision of consumer financial services and products by depository institutions. For example, the FRB previously had authority to prescribe rules implementing various consumer financial laws (e.g., the Truth in Lending Act, TILA; Equal Credit Opportunity Act, ECOA; Electronic Funds Transfer Act, EFTA). The prudential regulators had authority to enforce those rules as to depository institutions in their respective jurisdictions.

The creation of the Consumer Financial Protection Bureau (CFPB or Bureau) by the Dodd-Frank Act in 2010 significantly changed the regulatory landscape. Consumer-protection powers came to be consolidated, with some exceptions, in a single agency with authority to promulgate rules and enforce consumer-protection laws. The FRB lost the authority to enact rules under federal consumer financial laws, and the prudential agencies now must coordinate with the CFPB on consumer-protection matters. It would be a mistake, however, to conclude that the prudential regulators are no longer relevant to the regulation of consumer financial services. In fact, they continue to play a critical role through their supervisory activities, their regulation of depository institutions' powers, and their general enforcement authorities.

This chapter (1) provides an overview of federal prudential regulatory agencies and their jurisdictions and powers, (2) describes their historical role in regulating consumer financial services, and (3) outlines the areas in which prudential regulators continue to play an important role in regulating consumer financial services.

2. Introduction to the Prudential Regulators

2.1 Office of the Comptroller of the Currency

The OCC is the primary regulator for national banks (i.e., federally chartered commercial banks) and federal savings associations.[1] The agency, which is an independent branch of the U.S. Department of the Treasury, is responsible for "assuring the safety and soundness of, and compliance with laws and regulations, fair access to financial services, and fair treatment of customers by, the institutions and other persons subject to its jurisdiction."[2] A national bank is an organization that is authorized to engage in the business of banking and is established under federal law (as opposed to state law).[3] A federal savings association is a federally chartered thrift institution authorized to accept deposits and to extend credit for homes and other goods and services.[4]

As the primary regulator of these institutions, the OCC has the power to conduct examinations and inspections.[5] The OCC also has authority to promulgate regulations to carry out its statutory authority.[6] The agency can bring enforcement actions (e.g., cease-and-desist orders, civil money penalty orders, and prohibition and removal orders) against regulated institutions and their employees and affiliates for violations of law or regulation, including violations of certain consumer financial laws such as section 5 of the Federal Trade Commission (FTC) Act, 15 USC § 45(a)(1), prohibiting "unfair or deceptive acts or practices in or affecting commerce."[7]

1. 12 U.S.C. §§ 1, 26, 1464. Federal savings associations were previously supervised by the Office of Thrift Supervision, which was merged into the OCC in 2011.

2. *Id.* § 1.

3. *Id.* § 21.

4. *Id.* § 1464(a).

5. *Id.* § 481 (providing the OCC with examination powers over national banks); *id.* § 1820(d) (requiring annual on-site examinations of all insured depository institutions); *id.* § 1464(d) (discussing enforcement and examinations of federal savings associations).

6. *Id.* § 93a.

7. *See id.* § 1818(b), (d); *see also* § 25b(j) (referring to the "ability of the Comptroller of the Currency to bring an enforcement action" under section 5 of the FTC Act). Although the OCC has the power to bring a cease-and-desist action based on a violation of "law, rule, or regulation," *see id.* § 1818(b)(1), the OCC does not have authority to implement the enumerated consumer laws as defined by the Dodd-Frank Act. Rather, when a federal banking agency identifies a violation of an enumerated consumer law, that agency is required to make a referral to the CFPB. *See id.* § 1818(t)(6).

Moreover, the OCC considers compliance with consumer financial laws when assessing an institution's overall safety and soundness.[8]

2.1.1 Federal Deposit Insurance Corporation

The FDIC is responsible for administering the federal deposit insurance program.[9] All national banks and almost all state banks are required to maintain federal deposit insurance.[10] As administrator of the insurance program, the FDIC has principal responsibility for conducting examinations of the state-chartered, non-Federal Reserve member depository institutions that it insures (and their affiliates).[11] The FDIC also requires insured depository institutions to submit reports of conditions.[12] As with the other federal prudential banking regulators, the FDIC considers institutions' compliance with consumer financial laws when conducting examinations.[13] The FDIC is also required by statute to make a referral to the CFPB when it identifies a violation of an enumerated consumer law within the CFPB's jurisdiction.[14]

2.1.2 Federal Reserve Board

The FRB has the authority to regulate state-chartered banks that are Federal Reserve members, bank holding companies, and their nonbank subsidiaries.[15] A "bank holding company is any company that has control over a bank or has elected to become a bank holding company pursuant to the procedures of the Bank Holding Company Act [BHCA]."[16]

In practice, the FRB typically regulates bank holding company parent entities, as opposed to depository institutions themselves, and is authorized to issue regulations and orders to fulfill its oversight responsibilities under the BHCA.[17] Such regulations

---

8. *See, e.g.*, OCC, *Comptroller's Handbook, Bank Supervision Process* 17 (June 2018), https://www.occ.treas.gov/publications/publications-by-type/comptrollers-handbook/bank-supervision-process/pub-ch-bank-supervision-process.pdf (identifying "consumer compliance" as an area of examination for a national bank).

9. 12 U.S.C. § 1811.

10. National banks are required to maintain deposit insurance under federal law; 12 U.S.C. § 222. Most state banking laws require that banks chartered by a state obtain deposit insurance. *See, e.g.*, N.Y. Banking Law Art. 2 § 32.

11. 12 U.S.C. § 1820(b)(2).

12. *Id.* § 1817.

13. *See* FDIC, *Consumer Compliance Examination Manual (June 2019)*, https://www.fdic.gov/regulations/compliance/manual/complianceexaminationmanual.pdf.

14. 12 U.S.C. § 1818(t)(6).

15. *Id.* § 1844(b); *see also* 12 C.F.R. § 225 (2018) (implementing regulations pursuant to this FRB's supervisory authority over bank holding companies).

16. 12 U.S.C. § 1841(a)(1); *but see* § 1841(a)(5) (providing exceptions to the bank holding company definition).

17. *Id.* § 1844(b).

include, for example, capital and liquidity requirements for bank holding companies. The Federal Reserve is also charged with examining the safety and soundness of bank holding companies and their subsidiaries.[18] Pursuant to these responsibilities, the Federal Reserve has historically reviewed entities' compliance with consumer financial laws when evaluating their safety and soundness.[19]

2.1.3 National Credit Union Administration

The National Credit Union Administration (NCUA) charters, supervises, and regulates federally chartered and federally insured credit unions.[20] A credit union is an organization created and owned by members that exists to accept savings and provide credit to those members.[21] NCUA serves as the principal authority for those institutions. NCUA requires reports and conducts examinations of federally chartered credit unions.[22] It also administers a form of insurance for credit union member accounts.[23] NCUA's examination program includes review of an institution's compliance with consumer financial laws.[24]

2.2 Supervisory Powers of Prudential Regulators

Prudential regulators possess extensive supervisory powers over depository institutions. They conduct annual and other scheduled examinations of the institutions within their jurisdiction, and these examinations frequently scrutinize an institution's consumer financial practices. However, the CFPB has the exclusive authority to examine depository institutions with total assets (together with their affiliates) exceeding $10 billion for compliance with federal consumer financial laws.[25] Prudential regulators are responsible for examining compliance with federal consumer financial laws by institutions that (together with their affiliates) have less than $10 billion in assets.[26] Even if the CFPB has primary authority, prudential regulators may identify failures related to compliance with federal consumer financial laws during a safety and soundness examination of

18. *Id.* § 1844(c)(2), (3).

19. *See* FRB Supervision and Regulation Letter SR 03-22 / CA 03-15, *Framework for the Assessment of Consumer Compliance Risk in Bank Holding Companies* (Dec. 23, 2003, revised Jan. 8, 2004), https://www.federalreserve.gov/boarddocs/srletters/2003/sr0322.htm.

20. 12 U.S.C. § 1752a. Federally insured credit unions include state-chartered credit unions with federal deposit insurance through the NCUA.

21. *Id.* § 1752(1).

22. *Id.* § 1756.

23. *Id.* § 1781.

24. *See, e.g.*, NCUA Supervisory Letter 17-01, *Evaluating Compliance Risk—Updated Compliance Risk Indicators* (March 29, 2017), https://www.ncua.gov/files/letters-credit-unions/SL-17-01-evaluating-compliance-risk.pdf.

25. 12 U.S.C. § 5515.

26. *Id.* § 5516.

an institution.[27] Likewise, the Uniform Financial Institutions Ratings System (known as CAMELS) assesses six components of a bank's performance: capital adequacy, asset quality, management, earnings, liquidity, and sensitivity to market risk.[28] An element of the management component includes an assessment of an institution's compliance with laws and regulations. In addition, federal banking regulatory agencies have adopted a Consumer Compliance (CC) Rating System designed to reflect the nature and extent of an institution's compliance with consumer-protection and civil-rights statutes and regulations.[29] Finally, a prudential regulator may choose to conduct specific risk-focused examinations to determine whether specific products or services comply with relevant laws and regulations, including consumer financial laws.[30] If a prudential regulator identifies a violation of consumer financial law through supervision it may designate this violation as a matter requiring attention (MRA), a formal written communication that identifies a deficiency.[31] A prudential regulator may also issue a notice of deficiency[32] or create a memorandum of understanding between the regulator and the institution requiring the institution to take corrective measures.[33] Supervisory actions such as these are typically nonpublic.

Prudential regulators continue to play an active role in consumer financial services compliance pursuant to their broad supervisory examination authority. The FDIC, for example, has recently identified areas of particular concern in its jurisdiction as including overdraft programs and debit card processing,[34] kickback fees paid in violation of the Real Estate Settlement Procedures Act (RESPA),[35] calculations of consumer liability for unauthorized transfers pursuant to Regulation E, and skip-a-payment programs. The OCC has focused on compliance risk management, in particular in implementing changes to consumer-protection regulations. For its part, the FRB's recent guidance in the consumer compliance space has focused on integrated disclosures under RESPA and TILA, preparation for a Federal Reserve consumer compliance

---

27. *E.g.*, Wells Fargo Bank, N.A., AA-EC-2018-15 (Apr. 20, 2018) (OCC consent order), https://www.occ.gov/static/enforcement-actions/ea2018-025.pdf.

28. *See* Federal Financial Institutions Examination Council, *Uniform Financial Institutions Rating System,* 61 Fed. Reg. 67021, 67024 (Dec. 19, 1996), https://www.govinfo.gov/content/pkg/FR-1996-12-19/pdf/96-32174.pdf.

29. *See* Federal Financial Institutions Examination Council, *Uniform Interagency Consumer Compliance Rating System,* 81 Fed. Reg. 79473 (Nov. 14, 2016).

30. *E.g.*, FDIC, *Consumer Compliance Supervisory Highlights 2* (June 2019), https://www.fdic.gov/regulations/examinations/consumercomplsupervisoryhighlights.pdf (discussing examinations for debit card overdrafts).

31. *See, e.g.*, OCC, *Policies and Procedures Manual,* PPM 5310-3 at 4 (Nov. 13, 2018), https://www.ots.treas.gov/news-issuances/bulletins/2018/ppm-5310-3.pdf.

32. 12 C.F.R. § 30 (2019).

33. *See, e.g., id.*; Federal Reserve Board, Supervision and Regulation Letter 13-13.

34. FDIC, *Consumer Compliance Supervisory Highlights 2* (June 2019), https://www.fdic.gov/regulations/examinations/consumercomplsupervisoryhighlights.pdf.

35. *Id.*

examination, and shaping a bank's culture of consumer compliance. In addition, the prudential regulators have initiated new examination procedures relating to prepaid consumer accounts, internal compliance programs, Dodd-Frank Act mortgage rules, and institutions' use of social media. Thus, even where the substance of consumer-protection rules may be within the jurisdiction of the CFPB, prudential regulators remain a crucial part of how those rules are applied and enforced.

2.3 Enforcement Powers of Prudential Regulators

More serious violations of consumer financial laws identified through supervisory examinations may lead to a public enforcement action. Here, too, there is a division of authority between prudential regulators and the CFPB.

For *larger institutions* (i.e., those that, together with their affiliates, have assets in excess of $10 billion), prudential regulators generally must refer potential violations of consumer financial laws to the CFPB for enforcement.[36] As to smaller institutions (assets less than $10 billion, including affiliates), the prudential regulator retains primary enforcement responsibility.[37]

Despite these limitations, prudential regulators have a variety of enforcement mechanisms that may be implicated by violations of consumer financial laws or failures in managing consumer compliance risk, even as to larger institutions.[38] Notably, prudential regulators such as the OCC have also demonstrated an increasing willingness to bring such actions against individual bank executives.[39]

3. The Evolving Role of Prudential Regulators under the Dodd-Frank Act

In addition to the prudential regulators' continuing authority as to smaller depository institutions, the Dodd-Frank Act did not transfer responsibility for certain other laws,

36. *See* 12 U.S.C. § 1818(t)(6); 12 U.S.C. § 5515(c). The "enumerated consumer laws" are the Alternative Mortgage Transaction Parity Act; the Consumer Leasing Act; the Electronic Funds Transfer Act; the Equal Credit Opportunity Act; the Fair Credit Billing Act; the Fair Credit Reporting Act; the Home Owners Protection Act; the Fair Debt Collection Practices Act; the Home Mortgage Disclosure Act; the Home Ownership and Equity Protection Act; the Real Estate Settlement Procedures Act; the S.A.F.E. Mortgage Licensing Act; the Truth in Lending Act; the Truth in Savings Act; the Interstate Land Sales Full Disclosure Act; and elements of the Federal Deposit Insurance Act, the Gramm-Leach-Bliley Act, and 12 U.S.C. § 5538. 12 U.S.C. § 5481(12).

37. 12 U.S.C. § 5516(c).

38. *See, generally*, 12 U.S.C. § 1818.

39. *See* OCC News Release, *OCC Issues Notice of Charges Against Five Former Senior Wells Fargo Bank Executives, Announces Settlement With Others*, January 23, 2020, https://www.occ.gov/news-issuances/news-releases/2020/nr-occ-2020-6.html.

such as the power to enforce violations of nonenumerated consumer financial laws, including the FTC Act.[40] Authority to establish regulations relating to the National Flood Insurance Program, as amended by the Biggert-Waters Flood Insurance Reform Act of 2012, also remains vested with the Federal Emergency Management Agency (FEMA) and the prudential regulators.[41] Likewise, the Fair Housing Act (FHA) programs remain primarily entrusted to the U.S. Department of Housing and Urban Development and, accordingly, prudential regulators may enforce FHA violations.[42]

4. Prudential Agencies' Continuing Role in Consumer Financial Services Regulation

Following the passage of the Dodd-Frank Act, the prudential regulators remain an important presence in the consumer financial regulatory landscape. They continue to possess primary supervisory and enforcement authority with respect to consumer financial laws for *smaller institutions* that together with their affiliates have $10 billion or less in assets.[43] In addition, the prudential regulators retain some narrow rulemaking authority with regard to certain consumer financial laws. Finally, the prudential regulators play a critical role in defining the powers and authorities of regulated depository institutions, which can have significant implications for preemption of state lending and other consumer laws.

Supervision. As discussed above, the prudential regulators continue to play an active role in examining depository institutions (both larger and smaller) for compliance with federal consumer financial protection laws.

Rulemaking. Prudential regulators also continue to maintain enclaves of rulemaking authority in certain consumer financial services areas following the Dodd-Frank Act. For example, the OCC and other prudential regulators possess ongoing authority to make rules related to the National Flood Insurance Program and have recently engaged in rulemaking on this topic.[44] Likewise, the OCC continues to issue guidance relating to how banks should interpret Department of Defense changes to regulations related to the Military Lending Act.[45] The OCC also claims authority

---

40. 15 U.S.C. § 45.

41. *See* 42 U.S.C. § 4128.

42. *Id.* § 3612.

43. *See* 12 U.S.C. § 5515.

44. *See Loans in Areas Having Special Flood Hazards*, 84 Fed. Reg. 4953 (Feb. 20, 2019), https://www.federalregister.gov/documents/2019/02/20/2019-02650/loans-in-areas-having-special-flood-hazards.

45. *See* OCC, *Comptroller's Handbook, Consumer Compliance, Military Lending Act* (May 2018), https://www.occ.treas.gov/publications/publications-by-type/comptrollers-handbook/military-lending-act/pub-ch-mla.pdf.

to define unfair or deceptive credit practices through section 5 of the FTC Act.[46] The FRB, OCC, and FDIC maintain concurrent authority to establish substantive rulemaking related to the Community Reinvestment Act (CRA) for national banks and federal savings associations.[47]

Enforcement. Prudential regulators continue to engage in enforcement activities related to the consumer financial laws in several respects.

First, in certain instances, the prudential regulators refer identified violations of the consumer financial laws to the CFPB.[48] The CFPB has acknowledged particular reliance on prudential regulator referrals in the areas of the Equal Credit Opportunity Act and fair lending compliance.[49]

Second, prudential regulators have continuing primary authority to bring enforcement actions against smaller institutions and have brought public enforcement actions related to the consumer financial laws following the Dodd-Frank Act. For example, the OCC has brought actions related to a bank's failure to safeguard consumer data in violation of Regulation P[50] and properly present ATM and debit card overdraft services.[51] Similarly, the FDIC has been involved in enforcement matters concerning a bank's debt collection and discriminatory lending practices,[52] a bank's deceptive marketing of add-on products,[53] and a bank's procedure for reconciling deposits.[54]

Third, prudential regulators continue to use their broad powers to oversee institutions' safety and soundness as a means of promoting consumer protection.

---

46. OCC Bulletin 2014-42, *Credit Practices Rules: Interagency Guidance Regarding Unfair or Deceptive Credit Practices* (Aug. 22, 2014), https://www.occ.treas.gov/news-issuances/bulletins/2014/bulletin-2014-42.html.

47. *See* 12 C.F.R. § 25 (2019) (applying to national banks); 12 C.F.R. § 195 (2019) (applying to federal savings associations). For more information on the CRA, see chapter 7 on Fair Lending.

48. *See* 12 U.S.C. § 5515(c)(2). Prudential regulators refer such matters to the Bureau because the Bureau has exclusive jurisdiction related to the federal consumer financial laws over institutions with greater than $10 billion in assets, 12 U.S.C. § 5515(b)(1), and concurrent jurisdiction over all other institutions, 12 U.S.C. § 5516(b).

49. *See, e.g.*, CFPB, Fair Lending Report of the Bureau of Consumer Financial Protection 29 (June 2019), https://files.consumerfinance.gov/f/documents/201906_cfpb_Fair_Lending_Report.pdf (identifying areas of referral).

50. Timothy Perry, No. 2017-043 (June 2, 2017) (OCC consent order), https://www.occ.gov/static/enforcement-actions/ea2017-043.pdf.

51. TCF National Bank, No. 2018-063 (Jul. 20, 2018) (OCC consent order), https://www.occ.gov/static/enforcement-actions/ea2018-063.pdf.

52. American Express Centurion Bank, FDIC-12-315b (Oct. 1, 2012) (FDIC and CFPB joint consent order), https://www.fdic.gov/news/news/press/2012/pr12114a.pdf?source=govdelivery.

53. American Express Centurion Bank, FDIC-13-0285b (Dec. 24, 2013) (FDIC consent order), https://www.fdic.gov/news/news/press/2013/pr13124a.pdf.

54. Citizens Bank of Philadelphia, FDIC 14-0336k (Aug. 12, 2015) (FDIC consent order), https://www.fdic.gov/news/news/press/2015/pr15066a.pdf.

For example, the OCC recently brought actions against former Wells Fargo executives stemming from allegations that the bank engaged in widespread misconduct in the sale of consumer deposit and credit products.[55] Given the political attention often paid to consumer financial issues in Congress and elsewhere, it would not be surprising to see regulators such as the OCC and FRB asserting a significant role in policing consumer financial issues in the future.

Bank Powers and Federal Preemption. A final area where prudential regulators continue to be important concerns federal preemption of certain state consumer laws. While the CFPB has primary authority among federal agencies to determine the extent to which federal *consumer* financial laws preempt state consumer laws on the same topics,[56] various nonconsumer federal statutes may preempt state consumer financial laws in certain circumstances. Prudential regulators retain some authority, as the agencies responsible for implementing these federal statutes, to define the extent to which these statutes preempt state laws for institutions under their supervision. The prudential bank regulators also have broad authority to define the powers of depository institutions in their respective jurisdictions, which can have consequences for preemption of state consumer law. In particular, the National Bank Act[57] and the Home Owners' Loan Act[58] preempt some state consumer financial laws for national banks and federal savings associations, respectively.

Despite the significant changes brought about by the Dodd-Frank Act, federal banking regulatory agencies still play a major role in overseeing compliance with consumer law and regulation by federally chartered and insured depository institutions. The CFPB has taken on a leading role in this area—and is the regulatory focus for many larger institutions—but prudential regulators can be expected to continue to exercise their broad regulatory and supervisory powers to shape consumer law and to bring actions against noncompliant institutions.

55. *See* OCC, *OCC Issues Notice of Charges Against Five Former Senior Wells Fargo Bank Executives, Announces Settlement with Others* (Jan. 23, 2020), https://www.occ.gov/news-issuances/news-releases/2020/nr-occ-2020-6.html.

56. *See* 12 U.S.C. § 5551.

57. 13 Stat. 99 (codified at scattered sections of 12 U.S.C.) (2018).

58. 12 U.S.C. §§ 1461–1468.

CHAPTER

1C

The Federal Trade Commission

J. H. Jennifer Lee and Jake Christensen

The Federal Trade Commission (FTC, Commission, or Agency) was created when President Woodrow Wilson signed the Federal Trade Commission Act (FTC Act) into law on September 26, 1914.[1] The FTC formally opened its doors on March 15, 1915.

1. Why Congress Created the FTC

The FTC was created as a final, direct response to the monopolies that were a hallmark of the late 1800s in the United States.[2] Congress therefore charged the FTC with preventing enumerated individuals and entities "from using unfair methods of competition in or affecting commerce and unfair or deceptive acts or practices in or affecting commerce."[3] Thus, at its core, the FTC's mission is to protect consumers and promote competition in the U.S. The FTC oversees a broad swath of existing antitrust and consumer-protection laws, promulgates and enforces new antitrust and consumer-protection regulations, and monitors all sectors of the U.S. economy for anticompetitive conduct. Although the FTC lacks jurisdiction over banks, it is authorized to regulate

1. Sept. 26, 1914, ch. 311, 38 Stat. 717 (codified as amended at 15 U.S.C. §§ 41–58).

2. The FTC replaced the Bureau of Corporations, an investigatory agency within the then-Department of Commerce and Labor. The Cabinet-level Department of Commerce and Labor was created in 1903 during the Theodore Roosevelt administration but would not last. Dep't of Commerce and Labor Act, Feb. 14, 1903, ch. 552, 32 Stat. 825. Within just over a decade, it would be split into the separate Departments of Commerce and Labor, with the new FTC absorbing the staff and duties of the Bureau of Corporations.

3. 15 U.S.C. § 45(a)(2).

entities outside the financial sector, so long as the practices in question are "in or affecting commerce."[4] Further, aside from the pure consumer-protection function of the FTC, the FTC may also oversee the breaking up of companies that occupy an entire field or engage in severe anticompetitive or monopolistic conduct.[5]

2. Powers, Objective, and Functions

The Commission has specific investigative powers that grant it the authority to investigate Commission-regulated individuals and entities and subject them to compulsory process.[6] The FTC Act grants the Agency broad authority to "prosecute any inquiry necessary to its duties in any part of the United States," by which it may "gather and compile information concerning, and to investigate from time to time the organization, business, conduct, practices, and management of any person, partnership, or corporation engaged in or whose business affects commerce."[7]

In carrying out its mandate, the FTC enforces civil antitrust law under the Sherman Antitrust Act of 1890[8] and the Clayton Antitrust Act of 1914,[9] jurisdiction shared with the Department of Justice's Antitrust Division.[10] The Commission also oversees a variety of other consumer-protection laws and regulations, including its enabling statute, the FTC Act, as well as a plethora of business regulation statutes that delegated enforcement to the FTC, which are discussed further in section 6.

3. Organization

The FTC is an independent executive agency led by a bipartisan committee of five commissioners, who are appointed to seven-year terms by the president with the advice and consent of the Senate.[11,12] The president chooses one of the commissioners to serve

4. *Id.*

5. *Id.* § 45(e).

6. *Id.* §§ 46, 49, 57b-1.

7. *Id.* §§ 43, 46(a). Certain enumerated financial institutions and common carriers are exempt from this authority.

8. July 2, 1890, ch. 647, 26 Stat. 209 (codified as amended at 15 U.S.C. §§ 1–38).

9. October 15, 1914, ch. 323, 38 Stat. 730 (codified as amended at 15 U.S.C. §§ 12–27).

10. *See, generally*, 15 U.S.C. §§ 1–38. The Commission may refer "conduct that may constitute a violation of Federal criminal law" to the attorney general for potential prosecution. *Id.* § 46(k); *see also id.* § 56(b).

11. FTC, Organization Chart (Mar. 16, 2020), https://www.ftc.gov/system/files/attachments/about-ftc/ftc_org_chart_mar-16-2020.pdf.

12. 15 U.S.C. § 41.

as the chairman, who acts as the FTC's executive and administrative head.[13] No more than three commissioners may hail from the same political party.[14] Commissioners are somewhat isolated from presidential overreach in that the president may remove a commissioner only "for inefficiency, neglect of duty, or malfeasance in office."[15]

3.1 The Commission's Bureaus and Offices

The Commission is comprised of the following principal units: the Office of the Executive Director, the Office of the General Counsel, the Office of the Secretary, the Office of the Inspector General, the Office of Administrative Law Judges, the Office of International Affairs, the Bureau of Competition, the Bureau of Consumer Protection, the Bureau of Economics, and the Commission's Regional Offices.[16] From an investigatory or enforcement perspective, the most salient of these units are the Bureau of Competition and the Bureau of Consumer Protection, each of which is discussed further below.

3.1.1 The Bureau of Competition

The Bureau of Competition enforces federal antitrust and trade regulations under section 5 of the FTC Act, as well as the Clayton Act and other statutes that the Commission enforces, through its investigation of alleged violations and recommendation to the Commission of further action. Such further action may include cease-and-desist orders, injunctive and other equitable relief in federal court, litigation before the Commission's administrative law judges (ALJs) or federal courts, the negotiation and entry of a formal settlement, the promulgation of new administrative rules, and/or the mandated submission of reports by regulated entities.[17] The Commission may further seek civil penalties in federal court for failure to comply with a final order. The Bureau of Competition also educates businesses and consumers on competition-fostering laws and compliance, and conducts investigations related to individuals and entities' compliance with final Commission orders.[18]

3.1.2 The Bureau of Consumer Protection

The Bureau of Consumer Protection fulfills the FTC's mission of investigating unfair or deceptive acts or practices pursuant to its section 5 authority under the FTC Act, in addition to potential violations of the myriad other statutes that the Commission enforces. The Bureau of Consumer Protection may seek injunctive or other equitable

13. *Id.*
14. *Id.*
15. *Id.; see also* Humphrey's Ex'r v. United States, 295 U.S. 602, 632 (1935).
16. 5 U.S.C. § 552(a)(1); 15 U.S.C. § 46(g).
17. 15 U.S.C. §§ 45, 53.
18. *Id.* § 46(c).

relief, and issues complaints concerning potential violations, prosecutes the same before the Commission's ALJs, and negotiates consent orders, subject to the full Commission's issuance and approval.[19] The Bureau of Consumer Protection similarly investigates compliance with final Commission orders and trade regulations, and educates consumers and businesses on unfair or deceptive acts or practices.[20] The Bureau of Consumer Protection's Division of Credit Practices also oversees the general administration of the Fair Credit Reporting Act (Title VI of the Consumer Credit Protection Act of 1968).[21]

Included in the FTC Act's prohibitions is the restriction on unfair or deceptive advertising. Specifically, the FTC Act prevents a person from disseminating false advertisements in or having an effect on commerce by any means to induce, or which is likely to induce, "the purchase of food, drugs, devices, services, or cosmetics."[22,23] The Commission may similarly enjoin a party from engaging in, or continuing to engage in, the dissemination of a false advertisement.

3.2 Delegation of Commission Functions

The FTC may, via published order or rule, delegate certain functions to a division of the Commission, individual commissioners, administrative law judges, or employees or employee boards.[24] The Commission may, in its discretion, review any actions performed under delegated authority, either of its own volition, or following a party's petition or intervenor's action. The Commission may also delegate its functions to a single commissioner or other delegatee(s) where (1) no party or intervenor would be adversely affected by the function or authority delegated and would be entitled to seek review from the full Commission; or (2) where the party or intervenor has waived this right.[25]

4. Funding and Budget

The FTC Act provides for the authorization of appropriations "to carry out the functions, powers, and duties of the Commission."[26]

---

19. *Id.* §§ 45(b)–(m), 53.

20. *Id.* § 46(c).

21. Pub. L. No. 90-321, tit. VI, as added Pub. L. No. 91-508, tit. VI, Sec. 601, Oct. 26, 1970, 84 Stat. 1128 (codified as amended at 15 U.S.C. §§ 1681–1681x).

22. As used in the FTC Act, "person" means a "partnership[ ], corporation[ ], and association[ ]." 15 U.S.C. § 71.

23. *Id.* § 52.

24. Reorganization Plan No. 4 of 1961, 5 U.S.C. app. 1, § 1(a).

25. 16 C.F.R. § 0.7.

26. 15 U.S.C. § 57c.

5. Supervision and Oversight: Advisory Opinions and Guidance for Regulated Industries

Individuals and entities may request formal guidance from the FTC on a proposed course of action.[27] The Commission will provide its view where the proposed course of action relates to a substantial or novel question of law or fact and no clear precedent exists, or the request and the Commission's publication of its advice will be of significant public interest.[28] Although any advice by the Commission is subject to future rescission, revocation, and enforcement, the Commission generally will not proceed against an individual or entity that, in good faith, relied on the advice the FTC provided and acted in accordance with the proposed course of action.[29]

The Commission, either of its own accord or following a petition or information application, further provides industry guidance for common practices and specific industries concerning the Commission's administrative interpretations of the laws it enforces to facilitate voluntary compliance with the same.[30]

6. Source of Enforcement Authority

The Commission exercises enforcement and administrative authority under the following statutes and regulations: the FTC Act,[31] the Clayton Act,[32] the Robinson-Patman Act,[33] the Webb-Pomerene (Export Trade) Act,[34] the Packers and Stockyards Act,[35] the Wool Products Labeling Act of 1939,[36] the Lanham Trade-Mark Act,[37] the

---

27. 16 C.F.R. § 1.1(a).

28. 15 U.S.C. § 57a; 16 C.F.R. § 1.1(a).

29. 16 C.F.R. § 1.3.

30. 16 C.F.R. §§ 1.5–1.6, 1.73; 15 U.S.C. § 46.

31. 15 U.S.C. §§ 41–58.

32. *Id.* §§ 12–27.

33. June 19, 1936, ch. 592, 49 Stat. 1526 (codified as amended at 15 U.S.C. §§ 13–13b, 21a).

34. The Webb-Pomerene Act (WPA) authorizes the organization and operation of export trade associations, which are granted certain limited exemptions to requirements under the Sherman and Clayton Acts. An export trade association must request and annually renew a request for exemption. The WPA further extends the Commission's FTC Act jurisdiction to unfair competition used in export trade against competitors, even if the relevant acts are outside the physical territories of the United States. Apr. 10, 1918, ch. 50, 40 Stat. 516 (codified as amended at 15 U.S.C. §§ 61–66).

35. Aug. 15, 1921, ch. 64, 42 Stat. 159 (codified as amended at 7 U.S.C. §§ 181–229).

36. Oct. 14, 1940, ch. 871, 54 Stat. 1128 (codified as amended at 15 U.S.C. §§ 68–68j).

37. July 5, 1946, ch. 540, 60 Stat. 427 (codified as amended at 15 U.S.C. §§ 1051–72).

Fur Products Labeling Act,[38] the Textile Fiber Products Identification Act,[39] the Federal Cigarette Labeling and Advertising Act,[40] the Fair Packaging and Labeling Act,[41] the Truth in Lending Act,[42] the Fair Credit Reporting Act,[43] the Fair Credit Billing Act,[44] the Equal Credit Opportunity Act,[45] the Fair Debt Collection Practices Act,[46] the Electronic Fund Transfer Act,[47] the Hobby Protection Act,[48] the Magnuson–Moss Warranty—Federal Trade Commission Improvement Act,[49] the Energy Policy and Conservation Act,[50] the Hart–Scott–Rodino Antitrust Improvements Act of 1976,[51] the Petroleum Marketing Practices Act,[52] the Comprehensive Smokeless Tobacco Health Education Act of 1986,[53] the Telephone Disclosure and Dispute Resolution Act of 1992,[54] the Telemarketing and Consumer Fraud and Abuse Prevention Act,[55] the International Antitrust Enforcement Assistance Act of 1994,[56] the Credit Repair

38. Aug. 8, 1951, ch. 298, 65 Stat. 175 (codified as amended at 15 U.S.C. §§ 69–69j).

39. Pub. L. No. 85-897, 72 Stat. 1717 (1958) (codified as amended at 15 U.S.C. §§ 70–70k).

40. Pub. L. No. 89-92, 79 Stat. 282 (1965) (codified as amended at 15 U.S.C. §§ 1331–40).

41. Pub. L. No. 89-755, 80 Stat. 1296 (1966) (codified as amended at 15 U.S.C. §§ 1451–61).

42. Pub. L. No. 90-321, tit. I, 82 Stat. 146 (1968) (codified as amended at 15 U.S.C. §§ 1601–67f).

43. 15 U.S.C. §§ 1681–81x.

44. Pub. L. No. 93-495, tit. III, 88 Stat. 1511 (1974) (codified as amended at 15 U.S.C. §§ 1666–66j).

45. Pub. L. No. 90-321, tit. VII, as added Pub. L. No. 93-495, title V, Sec. 503, 88 Stat. 1521 (1974) (codified as amended at 15 U.S.C. §§ 1691–91f).

46. Pub. L. No. 90-321, tit. VIII, as added Pub. L. No. 95-109, 91 Stat. 874 (1977) (codified as amended at 15 U.S.C. §§ 1692–92o).

47. Pub. L. No. 90-321, tit. IX, as added Pub. L. No. 95-630, tit. XX, Sec. 2001, 92 Stat. 3728 (1978) (codified as amended at 15 U.S.C. §§ 1693–93r).

48. Pub. L. No. 93-167, 87 Stat. 686 (1973) (codified as amended at 15 U.S.C. §§ 2101–2106).

49. Pub. L. No. 93-637, 88 Stat. 2183 (1975) (codified as amended at 15 U.S.C. §§ 2301–12, 2345–58).

50. Pub. L. No. 94-163, 89 Stat. 871 (1975) (codified as amended at 42 U.S.C. §§ 6201–22).

51. Pub. L. No. 94-435, 90 Stat. 1383 (1976) (codified as amended at 15 U.S.C. § 18a).

52. Pub. L. No. 95-297, 92 Stat. 322 (1978) (codified as amended at 15 U.S.C. §§ 2801–41).

53. Pub. L. No. 99-252, 100 Stat. 30 (1986) (codified as amended at 15 U.S.C. §§ 4401–4408).

54. Pub. L. No. 102-556, 106 Stat. 4181 (1992) (codified as amended at 15 U.S.C. §§ 5701–24).

55. Pub. L. No. 103-297, 108 Stat. 1545 (1994) (codified as amended at 15 U.S.C. §§ 6101–6108).

56. Pub. L. No. 103-438, 108 Stat. 4597 (1994) (codified as amended at 15 U.S.C. §§ 6201–12); *see also* 15 U.S.C. §§ 46, 57b–1, 1311–12, 6201 & note.

Organizations Act,[57] the Children's Online Privacy Protection Act,[58] the Identity Theft Assumption and Deterrence Act of 1998,[59] the Gramm–Leach–Bliley Act,[60] and other federal statutes. Many of the foregoing consumer-protection-related statutes are also enforced by the Consumer Financial Protection Bureau, which is discussed in greater detail in chapter 1A.

7. Investigations

The Commission has the authority to investigate, through the gathering and compilation of information via mandated annual or special written reports or answers, whether submitted under oath or as otherwise specified, "the organization, business, conduct, practices, and management of any person, partnership, or corporation engaged in or whose business affects commerce," as well as "its relation to other persons, partnerships, or corporations."[61] A primary vehicle through which the Commission exercises its investigatory authority prior to its commencement of further proceedings is through the issuance of civil investigative demands (CIDs), which are investigatory subpoenas for documents and information. Recipients of a CID must respond through written responses, the production of documents, and/or oral testimony.[62]

8. Civil Actions for Violations

Persons that violate any provision of the FTC Act related to unfair or deceptive acts or practices are subject to a civil action by the Commission in a federal district court within three years of the alleged violation.[63] Further, the Commission may initiate a civil action against persons that violate final cease-and-desist orders to which they are subject within one year after the order is final.[64] If the Commission satisfies its burden to demonstrate that the act or practice that the cease-and-desist order forbade

57. Pub. L. No. 90-321, tit. IV, as added Pub. L. No. 104-208, div. A, tit. II, Sec. 2451, 110 Stat. 3009-454 (1996) (codified as amended at 15 U.S.C. §§ 1679–79j).

58. Pub. L. No. 105-277, div. C, title XIII, 112 Stat. 2681-728 (1998) (codified as amended at 15 U.S.C. §§ 6501–6506).

59. Pub. L. No. 105-318, 112 Stat. 3007 (1998) (codified as amended at 18 U.S.C. § 1028 note).

60. Pub. L. No. 106-102, 113 Stat. 1338 (1999) (codified as amended at 15 U.S.C. §§ 6801–6809).

61. 15 U.S.C. § 46(b).

62. *Id.* § 57b-1.

63. *Id.* § 57b(d).

64. *Id.*

was one that a reasonable person would know was dishonest or fraudulent under the circumstances, the court may grant relief as provided in section 19.[65]

9. Relief and Penalties

A court that finds that a person violated section 19(B) may "grant such relief as the court finds necessary to redress injury to consumers or other[s] . . . resulting from the rule violation or the unfair or deceptive act or practice."[66] Such relief may include any of the following actions by the court, so long as they do not constitute "the imposition of any exemplary or punitive damages," "rescission or reformation of contracts, the refund of money or return of property, the payment of damages, and public notification respecting the rule violation or the unfair or deceptive act or practice."[67] Many of the FTC's enforcement actions are discussed in further detail in chapter 2A.

The FTC may further seek and obtain civil monetary penalties in both administrative and civil court proceedings.[68] The Commission may seek the imposition of a fine of between $1,000 and $5,000, and/or up to a one-year prison term, against any person who fails or refuses to appear and testify, or otherwise respond to a lawful inquiry by the Commission, including by failing to produce documentary evidence.[69] Similarly, any person who:

- willfully makes, or causes to be made, a false oral or written recorded statement;
- willfully makes, or causes to be made, a false entry in documents requested by the Commission;
- willfully neglects or fails to make, or causes to be made, a correction of such false statement or entry made or submitted to the Commission;
- removes from the United States or willfully alters or falsifies documents requested by the Commission;
- willfully refuses to submit documents or information requested by the Commission; or
- is guilty of a federal crime and may be subject to a fine of between $1,000 and $5,000, and/or could face up to a three-year prison term.[70]

65. *Id.* § 57b(b).
66. *Id.*
67. *Id.*
68. *Id.* § 50.
69. *Id.*
70. *Id.*

Any person who violates section 8 specific to an advertised commodity that "may be injurious to health because of results from such use under the conditions prescribed in the advertisement thereof, or under such conditions as are customary or usual, or if such violation is with intent to defraud or mislead," is guilty of a misdemeanor and is subject to a fine of up to $5,000, six months' imprisonment, or both.[71] Repeat offenders are subject to fines of up to $10,000, up to one year's imprisonment, or both, for each subsequent violation.[72]

10. Rulemaking

The Commission has federal rulemaking authority to promulgate industry-wide regulations that promote competition and protect consumers from unfair and deceptive acts and practices.[73] The Commission publishes such rules in Title 16 of the Code of Federal Regulations. Under section 18(a)(1)(B) of the FTC Act, the Commission has the power to promulgate trade regulation rules that define acts or practices in or affecting commerce that are unfair or deceptive in nature and may include requirements to prevent such acts or practices.[74] A violation of any such rule, unless it states otherwise, is a violation of section 5(a)(1) of the FTC Act.[75]

The Commission is limited to issuing proposed rules concerning *prevalent* unfair or deceptive acts or practices. Such act or practice is prevalent where (1) the Commission has issued cease-and-desist orders concerning the act or practice, or (2) the Commission has information that indicates "a widespread pattern of unfair or deceptive acts or practices."[76]

In promulgating new rules, the FTC follows standard federal administrative notice-and-comment rulemaking procedures and must initially publish an advance notice of proposed rulemaking and submit the same to both the Senate's Committee on Commerce, Science, and Transportation, and the House of Representatives' Committee on Energy and Commerce.[77] The Commission may amend or repeal previously issued rules, and may also entertain and grant entities' or individuals' requested exemptions from its rules.[78] As with all administrative rulemaking, FTC

71. *Id.* § 54(a) (regarding violation of 15 U.S.C. § 52(a)).
72. *Id.*
73. *Id.* §§ 57a(a), 57b-3; 16 C.F.R. §§ 1.7–1.8.
74. 15 U.S.C. § 57a(a)(1); 16 C.F.R. § 1.8.
75. *Id.*
76. 15 U.S.C. § 57a(b)(3).
77. 5 U.S.C. § 553; 15 U.S.C. §§ 57a(b)(1)–(2); 16 C.F.R. §§ 1.10–1.14.
78. 16 C.F.R. §§ 1.15–1.16.

rulemakings are subject to judicial review in accordance with the provisions of the Administrative Procedure Act.[79]

79. 5 U.S.C. § 553; 15 U.S.C. § 57a(e)(1).

CHAPTER

1D

State and Other Agencies with Authority to Enforce Federal Law

David L. Beam

1. State Officials' Enforcement Authority under Title X of the Dodd-Frank Act

1.1 Overview

The Dodd-Frank Act granted state officials broad authority to enforce the provisions of Title X of the Dodd-Frank Act (the Consumer Financial Protection Act) and regulations issued by the Consumer Financial Protection Bureau (CFPB) thereunder. Title X includes the provisions of the Dodd-Frank Act that prohibit unfair, deceptive, and abusive acts or practices (UDAAP), and that authorize the CFPB to issue regulations declaring particular acts and practices to be UDAAP.

The scope of this authority varies depending on whether the target is a state-chartered company or a federally chartered bank (i.e., national bank or federal savings association).

1.2 Authority with Respect to State-Chartered Companies

With respect to entities other than federally chartered banks, a state attorney general may bring a civil action in the name of the state to enforce the provisions of Title X or regulations that the CFPB issues under Title X.[1] This action can be brought in any federal district court in the state, or in any state court located in the attorney

1. 12 U.S.C. § 5552(a)(1).

general's state that has jurisdiction over the defendant.[2] The attorney general may "secure remedies under provisions of [Title X] or remedies otherwise provided under other law."[3]

Additionally, a state regulator may bring a civil action "or other appropriate proceeding" to enforce the provisions of Title X or regulations that the CFPB issues under Title X against "any entity that is State-chartered, incorporated, licensed, or otherwise authorized to do business under State law."[4]

1.3 Authority with Respect to Federally Chartered Banks

The authority of state officials to bring enforcement actions against national banks and federal savings associations is more limited.

Federal law long has limited the exercise of "visitorial powers" of state agencies with respect to national banks. A provision in the National Bank Act says that no "national bank shall be subject to any visitorial powers except as authorized by Federal law, vested in the courts of justice or such as shall be, or have been exercised or directed by Congress or by either House thereof or by any committee of Congress or of either House duly authorized."[5] Prior to 2011, the Office of the Comptroller of the Currency (OCC) regulations had defined the term *visitorial powers* to include "[e]nforcing compliance with any applicable federal or state laws concerning those activities."[6] In *Cuomo v. Clearing House Association,*[7] the U.S. Supreme Court held that this regulation was invalid to the extent that it defined visitorial powers to include the prosecution of enforcement actions by state attorneys general in state courts.[8] Section 1047 of the Dodd-Frank Act codified Cuomo's holding and extended it to federal savings associations. Specifically, section 1047 provides that "no provision of this title which relates to visitorial powers or otherwise limits or restricts the visitorial authority to which any national bank [or federal savings association] is subject shall

2. *Id.*

3. *Id.*

4. *Id.* The provision expressly says that it is subject to the provisions, discussed momentarily, that address a state attorney general's authority to bring an enforcement action against a national bank or federal savings association. This precedence clause addresses any potential conflict or loophole that might arise from the fact that the state laws in many states expressly authorize national banks and federal savings associations to do business in the states, even though this grant of state authority is not technically necessary, since federally chartered banks derive their powers from federal law.

5. 12 U.S.C. § 484(a). There is a further exception that allows state auditors and examiners "at reasonable times and upon reasonable notice to a bank, [to] review its records solely to ensure compliance with applicable State unclaimed property or escheat laws upon reasonable cause to believe that the bank has failed to comply with such laws." *Id.* § 484(b).

6. 12 C.F.R. § 7.4000(a)(2)(iv) (2010).

7. Cuomo v. Clearing House Ass'n, 557 U.S. 519, 519 (2009).

8. *Id.* at 536.

be construed as limiting or restricting the authority of any attorney general (or other chief law enforcement officer) of any State to bring an action against a national bank in a court of appropriate jurisdiction to enforce an applicable law and to seek relief as authorized by such law."[9] The OCC amended its visitorial powers regulations in 2011 to conform them to these provisions. The amendments added an "exclusion," which said that "[i]n accordance with the decision of the Supreme Court in *Cuomo v. Clearing House Ass'n*, an action against a national bank in a court of appropriate jurisdiction brought by a state attorney general (or other chief law enforcement officer) to enforce an applicable law against a national bank and to seek relief as authorized by such law is not an exercise of visitorial powers[.]"[10]

The Dodd-Frank Act's provisions on the authority of state officials to enforce Title X and regulations issued thereunder follow the demarcation of enforcement authority for national banks established by *Cuomo v. Clearing House Ass'n*. These provisions permit a state attorney general to bring a civil action against a national bank or federal savings association to enforce a regulation issued by the CFPB under Title X.[11] They do not, however, permit a state attorney general to bring a civil action against a federally chartered bank to enforce a provision of Title X itself—only a regulation issued under Title X. One result of this distinction is that a state attorney general cannot bring a civil action against a federally chartered bank alleging that the bank's practices are unfair, deceptive, or abusive unless the practices at issue have been proscribed by a CFPB rule that declares them to be unfair, deceptive, or abusive.

1.4 Procedures for State Enforcement Actions

Before bringing a civil action to enforce Title X (or a regulation issued thereunder) pursuant to the foregoing provisions, the state office must "timely" provide the CFPB with a "complete complaint to be filed and a written notice describing such action or proceeding to the Bureau and the prudential regulator, if any, or the designee thereof."[12]

If it is "not practicable" to provide notice prior to filing suit, then the state official must provide the complaint and notice to the Bureau and (if applicable) the defendant's prudential regulator, immediately upon initiating the action or proceeding.[13] CFPB regulations implementing this provision provide that a state official may provide

9. 12 U.S.C. 24b(i)(1) (applicable to national banks); *Id.* § 1465 ("The provisions of [12 U.S.C. § 25b(i)] shall apply to Federal savings associations, and any subsidiary thereof, to the same extent and in the same manner as if such savings associations, or subsidiaries thereof, were national banks or subsidiaries of national banks, respectively.").

10. 12 C.F.R. § 7.4000(b) (internal citations omitted).

11. 12 U.S.C. § 7.4000(b).

12. *Id.* § 5552(b)(1)(A).

13. *Id.* § 5552(b)(1)(B).

notice after initiating an action if the state official is unable to provide timely notice "in order to protect the public interest or prevent irreparable and imminent harm."[14]

CFPB regulations implementing section 1042 provide that an *action* that requires notice is "any adjudicative proceeding before a court or an administrative or regulatory body to determine whether a violation of any provision of title X of the Dodd-Frank Act or any regulation prescribed thereunder has occurred."[15] Initiating an action under this section would include but not be limited to the filing of a complaint, motion for relief, or other document that initiates an action or a proceeding.

The CFPB is authorized to intervene in any action by a state official to enforce Title X pursuant to the foregoing provisions. If the CFPB intervenes in the action, then it may remove the action to federal district court and be "heard on all matters arising in the action."[16] If the CFPB intervenes, then it may also "appeal any order or judgment, to the same extent as any other party in the proceeding may."[17]

1.5 Authority to Enforce Other Consumer Financial Laws

The provisions described in section 1.4 relate to the authority of state officials to bring actions to enforce Title X of the Dodd-Frank Act. They do not supersede, limit, or modify the authority of state officials to enforce the provisions of other federal consumer financial laws pursuant to the provisions of those laws.[18] Provisions in federal consumer financial laws that grant enforcement authority to state officials are discussed throughout this treatise.

14. 12 C.F.R. § 1082.1(b)(1).
15. 12 C.F.R. § 1082.1(a)(1).
16. *Id.* § 5552(b)(2)(B).
17. *Id.* § 5552(b)(2)(C).
18. *Id.* § 5552(a)(3).

CHAPTER

2

Unfair, Deceptive, and Abusive Acts or Practices

CHAPTER

2A

Overview and History

Clinton R. Rockwell, Sherry-Maria S. Safchuk, and Lauren M. Frank

1. Introduction

The primary federal prohibitions on *unfair, deceptive*, and *abusive* acts or practices (UDAAP) are found in two statutes. First, section 1031(a) of the Dodd-Frank Wall Street Reform and Consumer Protection Act (Dodd-Frank Act) provides that the Consumer Financial Protection Bureau (CFPB or Bureau) may use its rulemaking, supervisory, and enforcement authority to prevent a covered person or service provider from committing or engaging in an unfair, deceptive, or abusive act or practice under federal law in connection with any transaction with a consumer for a consumer financial product or service, or the offering of a consumer financial product or service.[1] Second, section 5 of the Federal Trade Commission Act (FTC Act) prohibits persons subject to that act from engaging in "unfair or deceptive acts or practices in or affecting commerce."[2]

This chapter provides an overview of the history of federal prohibitions on unfair, deceptive, and abusive acts and practices, as well as a summary of how each concept has been defined and interpreted by federal regulators, including the CFPB. There is a dedicated chapter for each of these terms following this introduction.

1.1 Unfairness

The Dodd-Frank Act sets forth specific enumerated elements of *unfairness*, and provides that an act or practice may not be deemed unfair unless the evidence considered forms a reasonable basis to conclude that each of the enumerated statutory elements

1. 12 U.S.C. § 5531.
2. 15 U.S.C. § 45(a)(1).

has been met.[3] Notably, the Dodd-Frank Act provides that "[i]n determining whether an act or practice is unfair, the Bureau may consider established public policies as evidence to be considered with all other evidence."[4] However, "[s]uch public policy considerations may not serve as a primary basis for such determination."[5] This language echoes that of the FTC Act.[6]

Prior to 2020, the CFPB had released only one formal guidance bulletin specifically directed toward the interpretation of UDAAP.[7] The bulletin provides that "substantial injury" generally "takes the form of monetary harm" and states as examples "fees or costs paid by consumers."[8] However, the bulletin also notes that "the injury does not have to be monetary," a position consistent with the original FTC Policy Statement on Unfairness, released in 1980, and with various federal court findings.[9]

The CFPB has further noted that, though rare, there are circumstances in which emotional harm may amount to substantial injury.[10] Also, perhaps most far-reaching, that "substantial injury" does not require "actual injury," but merely "a significant risk of concrete harm[.]"[11] Thus, a policy can be unfair without having injured anyone so long as there is a "significant risk"—a term left undefined—of actual harm. These stances are reflected in the *CFPB Supervision and Examination Manual* (CFPB Exam Manual or Manual).[12]

The CFPB Bulletin also elaborates somewhat on what is meant by the phrase "reasonably avoidable by consumers," noting that "[a]n injury is not reasonably

---

3. For a more complete discussion on unfairness, see chapter 2C of this treatise.

4. 12 U.S.C. § 5531(c)(2).

5. *Id.* § 5531(c)(2).

6. 15 U.S.C. § 45(n).

7. *See* CFPB Bulletin 2013-07, *Prohibition of Unfair, Deceptive, or Abusive Acts or Practices in the Collection of Consumer Debts* (July 10, 2013), https://files.consumerfinance.gov/f/201307_cfpb_bulletin_unfair-deceptive-abusive-practices.pdf [hereinafter CFPB Bulletin 2013-07]. In January 2020, as discussed in more detail later in this chapter, the CFPB issued a bulletin addressing "abusive" acts and practices; *see* CFPB, Statement of Policy Regarding Prohibition on Abusive Acts or Practices, 85 Fed. Reg. 6733 (Feb. 6, 2020), https://www.govinfo.gov/content/pkg/FR-2020-02-06/pdf/2020-01661.pdf.

8. *See* CFPB Bulletin 2013-07, 2.

9. *See* CFPB Bulletin 2013-07; FTC Policy Statement on Unfairness (Dec. 17, 1980), http://www.ftc.gov/bcp/policystmt/ad-unfair.htm; FTC v. Accusearch, Inc., No. 06-cv-105-D, 2007 WL 4356786, at *7–8 (D. Wyo. Sept. 28, 2007); F.T.C. v. Cyberspy Software, LLC, No. 608-CV-1872-ORL-31GJ, 2008 WL 5157718, at *1 (M.D. Fla. Nov. 25, 2008); CFPB Bulletin 2013-07, *supra* note 7, at 2; FTC, Policy Statement on Unfairness (Dec. 17, 1980), http://www.ftc.gov/bcp/policystmt/ad-unfair.htm.

10. *See* CFPB Bulletin 2013-07, *supra* note 7, at 2.

11. *See id.*

12. CFPB, *Supervision and Examination Manual V.2, Unfair, Deceptive, or Abusive Acts or Practices* (2012) at UDAAP 2, https://s3.amazonaws.com/files.consumerfinance.gov/f/documents/102012_cfpb_unfair-deceptive-abusive-acts-practices-udaaps_procedures.pdf [hereinafter CFPB Exam Manual, UDAAP].

avoidable by consumers when an act or practice interferes with or hinders a consumer's ability to make informed decisions or take action to avoid that injury."[13] Also, that "[i]njury caused by transactions that occur without a consumer's knowledge or consent is not reasonably avoidable."[14] Further, if the only way to avoid the injury is through the expenditure of significant resources, while the practice may be avoided, it is not "reasonably" so.[15]

The CFPB Exam Manual provides examples of unfair acts or practices from recent enforcement actions.[16] Examples include (1) refusing to release a lien despite a consumer having made the final payment on a mortgage, (2) dishonoring a credit card or convenience check without notice to the consumer, and (3) processing payments for a company engaged in fraudulent activities.[17]

1.2 Abusiveness

The Dodd-Frank Act prohibits *abusive* conduct, which turns on whether an act or practice materially interferes with a consumer's ability to understand the terms and conditions of financial products or services, or takes unreasonable advantage of a consumer's lack of understanding, lack of alternative options, or reliance on a third party to act in the consumer's interests.[18]

The 2013 CFPB guidance bulletin on the subject of UDAAP refrains from elaborating on the meaning of the term *abusive* beyond reproducing the definition provided in the Dodd-Frank Act.[19] The CFPB Exam Manual takes a near-identical approach.[20]

At a 2012 hearing before the House Subcommittee on TARP, Financial Services, and Bailouts of Public and Private Programs, the CFPB's then director, Richard Cordray, stated that enforcing the abusiveness standard must be done on a "fact and circumstances" basis, and noted that the standard was "not something [...] likely to be able to [be] define[d] in the abstract."[21] Thus, it would appear that the CFPB's lack of substantive guidance as to the meaning of the term *abusive* was not an oversight, but deliberate, under the leadership of Director Cordray. This decision mirrors closely

13. *See* CFPB Bulletin 2013-07, *supra* note 7, at 3.

14. *Id.*

15. *Id.*

16. CFPB Exam Manual, *supra* note 12, at 3–5.

17. *Id.*

18. Chapter 2D of this treatise provides a more detailed analysis of abusiveness.

19. *See* 12 U.S.C. § 5531(d); CFPB Bulletin 2013-07, *supra* note 7, at 4.

20. *See* 12 U.S.C. § 5531(d); CFPB Exam Manual, V.2 (2012) at UDAAP 9, *supra* note 12, at 9.

21. *See How Will the CFPB Function Under Richard Cordray, Hearing Before the Subcomm. on TARP, Financial Services and Bailouts of Public and Private Programs of the H. Committee on Oversight and Gov't Reform*, 112th Cong. 69 (2012), https://www.gpo.gov/fdsys/pkg/CHRG-112hhrg73165/html/CHRG-112hhrg73165.htm.

the approach first taken by the FTC with regard to the terms *unfair* and *deceptive*, allowing enforcement actions over time to provide the basis for any substantive guidance, and waiting to release such guidance until a considerable body of law with regard to the standards had been built up.

Then, in January 2020, the Bureau issued a long-awaited policy statement outlining how it intends to approach *abusive* acts or practices in its supervision and enforcement activities.[22] Specifically, the Bureau outlined the following approach going forward: (1) it will deem conduct as abusive when the harm to consumers outweighs the benefit, (2) it will generally avoid *dual pleading* both abusiveness and unfairness or deceptiveness violations that stem from the same or nearly all of the same facts,[23] and (3) it does not intend to seek monetary relief for abusive violations in instances where there is good-faith effort to comply with the abusiveness standard, except to address consumer injuries caused by the conduct.[24]

Courts also have noted that the legislative intent in including the term *abusive* appears to have been to create a "more flexible" prohibition able to "reach forms of misconduct not embraced by the more rigid, cost-benefit standard that ha[s] grown up around the terms 'unfair' and 'deceptive.'"[25]

1.3 Deceptiveness

The Dodd-Frank Act does not provide a statutory definition of *deceptive*.[26] Instead, the CFPB has adopted the *deceptiveness* standard consistent with the FTC's Policy Statement on Deception.[27]

---

22. CFPB, Statement of Policy Regarding Prohibition on Abusive Acts or Practices, 85 Fed. Reg. 6733 (Feb. 6, 2020), https://www.govinfo.gov/content/pkg/FR-2020-02-06/pdf/2020-01661.pdf [hereinafter Policy Statement, Abusive Acts].

23. Dual pleading occurs when the CFPB brings charges for abusive practices against an entity while also bringing charges for unfairness or deception based on the same factual circumstances.

24. Policy Statement, Abusive Acts, *supra* note 22.

25. *See* CFPB v. ITT Educational Services, Inc., 219 F. Supp. 3d 878, 904 2015 WL 1013508, *18–19 (S.D. Ind. Mar. 6, 2015).

26. *See* 12 U.S.C. § 5531. For further explanation of deception, see chapter 2B of this treatise.

27. *See* CFPB Bulletin 2013-07, *supra* note 7, at n.16; FTC, Policy Statement on Deception (1983), https://www.ftc.gov/system/files/documents/public_statements/410531/831014deceptionstmt.pdf [hereinafter Policy Statement, Deception]; *see also* FTC, Statement of Basis and Purpose, Unfair or Deceptive Advertising, and Labeling of Cigarettes in Relation to the Health Hazards of Smoking, 29 Fed. Reg. 8324, 8355 (1964) [hereinafter FTC, Cigarette Advertising]; J. Howard Beales, *The FTC's Use of Unfairness Authority: Its Rise, Fall, and Resurrection* (May 30, 2003), https://www.ftc.gov/public-statements/2003/05/ftcs-use-unfairness-authority-its-rise-fall-and-resurrection. Chapter 2B of this treatise provides a more detailed analysis of deceptiveness.

The CFPB Exam Manual provides the following examples of deceptive acts and practices in the abstract: (1) making misleading cost or price claims, (2) offering a product or service not actually available, (3) using "bait-and switch techniques," (4) failing to note relevant conditions or material limitations when making an offer, and (5) failing to provide promised services.[28] The Manual also provides examples of deceptive acts, practices, representations, or omissions from recent enforcement actions, including (1) inadequate disclosure of the material lease terms in television advertisements and (2) misrepresentation of loan terms.[29]

2. The History of Unfair, Deceptive, and Abusive Acts or Practices: Formulation and Enforcement Prior to the Dodd-Frank Act

2.1 Statutory Origins: The Federal Trade Commission Act of 1914

The subjective nature of the terms *unfair, deceptive*, and *abusive* has always been a source of frustration for those seeking to bring or defend charges of this kind. The modern prohibition on unfair, deceptive, or abusive acts or practices (UDAAP) has its origins in the original FTC Act of 1914, which created the agency.[30] Since the adoption of the FTC Act, the application and interpretation of UDAAP has focused on the concept of *unfairness* which is reflected in legislative history, case law, and guidance issued by the FTC.

In the years prior to the enactment of the FTC Act, the U.S. government was increasingly concerned with regulating and preventing monopolistic practices with the potential to harm consumers. To this end, in 1890, Congress enacted the Sherman Act,[31] the first substantial piece of antitrust legislation in U.S. history, and in 1903, Congress created the Bureau of Corporations within a new cabinet department

28. CFPB Exam Manual, UDAAP, *supra* note 12, at 5.

29. *Id.*, 7–8.

30. *See* Pub. L. No. 63-203, 38 Stat. 717 (1914), as amended, Pub. L. No. 75-447, 52 Stat. 111 (1938) (codified as amended at 15 U.S.C. §§ 41–58). The FTC Act does not include a prohibition on "abusive" acts and practices; *see* 15 U.S.C. § 45(a). The "abusiveness" prong of UDAAP emerged later, with the enactment of the Dodd-Frank Act in 2010; *see* 12 U.S.C. § 5531(a).

31. *See* Pub. L. No. 51-647, 26 Stat. 209 (1890) (codified as amended at 15 U.S.C. §§ 1–7).

to investigate monopolistic practices.[32] With the passage of the FTC Act in 1914, Congress effectively absorbed the Bureau of Corporations into the new FTC, which had investigatory as well as enforcement powers, and which coincided with the passage of the Clayton Antitrust Act.[33]

The FTC Act, which focused primarily on antitrust violations, provided "[t]hat unfair methods of competition in commerce are hereby declared unlawful."[34] Congress did not define the term "unfair methods of competition" in the FTC Act, and shortly after its enactment, the Supreme Court, in *Fed. Trade Comm'n v. Gratz*, 253 U.S. 421, 427 (1920), conceded that the term's "exact meaning is in dispute."[35]

Nevertheless, the court in *Gratz* took the position that "it is for the courts, not the commission, ultimately to determine as matter of law what" the term includes.[36] The court in *Gratz* asserted that the term "unfair method of competition" was

> clearly inapplicable to practices never heretofore regarded as opposed to good morals because characterized by deception, bad faith, fraud, or oppression, or as against public policy because of their dangerous tendency unduly to hinder competition or create monopoly.[37]

---

32. Marc Winerman, *The Origins of the FTC: Concentration, Cooperation, Control, and Competition*, 71 ANTITRUST L.J. 1, 2 (2003). More than a decade later, Congress passed an act creating a new cabinet department, the Department of Commerce and Labor, and within that department, the FTC's precursor, the Bureau of Corporations; *see* Pub. L. 57-87, 32 Stat. 825 (1903). The Bureau of Corporations' investigatory efforts contributed to the enactment of additional antitrust legislation targeting railroads, as well as to the break-up of Standard Oil; *see* The Hepburn Act, Pub. L. 59-337, 34 Stat. 584 (1906); Standard Oil Co. of New Jersey v. United States, 221 U.S. 1 (1911).

33. Pub. L. No. 63-212, 38 Stat. 730 (1914) (codified as amended in at 15 U.S.C. §§ 12–27, 29 U.S.C. §§ 52–53).

34. Pub. L. No. 63-203, 38 Stat. 717, § 5 (1914), as amended, Pub. L. No. 75-447, 52 Stat. 111 (1938).

35. Fed. Trade Comm'n v. Gratz, 253 U.S. 421, 427, (1920), *overruled in part by* Fed. Trade Comm'n. v. Brown Shoe Co., 384 U.S. 316, 320 (1966)); *see also* Sears, Roebuck & Co. v. Fed. Trade Comm'n, 258 F. 307, 308 (7th Cir. 1919).

36. The court in *Gratz* took the position that "it is for the courts, not the commission, ultimately to determine as matter of law what" the term "unfair methods of competition" includes, and defined unfair competition as those practices which are opposed to good morals since they depict deception, bad faith, fraud, and oppression; Fed. Trade Comm'n v. Gratz, 253 U.S. 421, 427, (1920), *overruled in part by* Fed. Trade Comm'n. v. Brown Shoe Co., 384 U.S. 316, 320 (1966).

37. *Id.*

In addition to providing the first test of *unfair* methods of competition, this language also served as one of the first invocations of *deception* in the unfair or deceptive acts or practices (UDAP) context.[38]

During this time, the FTC was active in enforcing the new prohibition on unfair methods of competition, bringing actions involving a variety of industries, many of which included allegations of *deception* pursuant to the *unfairness* standard set in *Gratz*.[39]

A decade later, in 1931, the Supreme Court again reinforced the notion that the term unfairness was difficult to define, noting that it:

> belongs to a class of phrases which do not admit of precise definition, but the meaning and application of which must be arrived at by what this court elsewhere has called "the gradual process of judicial inclusion and exclusion."[40]

At that time, the limitations of the FTC Act's existing *unfairness* standard became apparent when the Supreme Court held that "[u]nfair trade methods are not per se unfair methods of competition."[41] The FTC interpreted the holding in this case to mean, in effect, "that unless a respondent's unfair acts or practices were proved to have injured actual or potential competitors, the Commission was powerless to prevent their use, regardless of their injurious effect upon the public."[42]

In 1937, the FTC issued an annual report noting its recommendation that Congress amend section 5 of the FTC Act to prohibit unfair or deceptive acts or

---

38. Note that the FTC Act refers only to "unfair" and "deceptive" acts and practices, and therefore is referred to as the "UDAP" prohibition; *see* 15 U.S.C. § 45(a). By contrast, the Dodd-Frank Act prohibits "unfair," "deceptive," and "*abusive*" acts and practices, and therefore is referred to as the "UDAAP" prohibition; *see* 12 U.S.C. § 5531(a).

39. *See, e.g.*, Fed. Trade Comm'n v. Standard Education Society, 302 U.S. 112, 114–15 (1937); Fed. Trade Comm'n v. R.F. Keppel & Brother, 291 U.S. 304, 309 (1934); Fed. Trade Comm'n v. Eastman Kodak Co., 274 U.S. 619, 626–30 (1927); Fed. Trade Comm'n v. Beech-Nut Packing Co., 257 U.S. 441, 453–54 (1922); Fed. Trade Comm'n v. Winsted Hosiery Co., 258 U.S. 483, 493–94 (1922); Moir v. Fed. Trade Comm'n, 12 F.2d 22, 27 (1st Cir. 1926).

40. Fed. Trade Comm'n v. Raladam Co., 283 U.S. 643, 648 (1931) (quoting *Davidson v. City of New Orleans*, 96 U.S. 97, 104 (1877)).

41. *See id.* at 649.

42. Hon. R. E. Freer, Commissioner, Fed. Trade Comm'n, Address at the Annual Convention of the Proprietary Association (May 17, 1938), https://www.ftc.gov/system/files/documents/public_statements/676351/19380517_freer_whe_wheeler-lea_act.pdf; *see also* FTC, Cigarette Advertising, *supra* note 27, at 8349 ("the Supreme Court held that the Commission's jurisdiction over unfair trade practices was limited to cases in which such a practice was used as a weapon for diverting business from, or injuring or impairing the business of, a competitor").

practices in addition to the already proscribed unfair methods of competition.[43] Presumably, in response, Congress amended the FTC Act to shift the focus of the unfairness provision from antitrust to consumer protection. The relevant amendment, the Wheeler-Lea Act, enacted in 1938, provided that "[u]nfair methods of competition in commerce, *and unfair or deceptive acts or practices in commerce*, are hereby declared unlawful."[44] This was the first statutory prohibition invoking *both* unfair *and* deceptive acts or practices (i.e., UDAP), and it is the foundation upon which the modern consumer protection regulatory scheme has been built. Further, this addition aimed to broaden the FTC's jurisdiction to embrace deceptive acts or practices that did not affect competition or competitors.[45]

2.2 Federal Trade Commission Guidance and Enforcement Concerning Unfair or Deceptive Acts

For nearly three decades following the enactment of the prohibition on UDAP, little formal guidance emerged as to what acts or practices were encompassed by the terms (although in the FTC's Annual Reports to Congress the FTC identified orders against companies for the use of unfair methods of competition and other violations of law).[46] The FTC issued neither interpretive regulations nor targeted clarifying guidance during this period, and although enforcement actions shed light on various aspects of the prohibition, the value of such actions was limited.[47] According to a former director, during this period, the FTC

43. Fed. Trade Comm'n, Annual Report of the Fed. Trade Comm'n for Fiscal Year Ending June 30, 1937 15 (1937), https://www.ftc.gov/sites/default/files/documents/reports_annual/annual-report-1937/ar1937_0.pdf; *see also* Fed. Trade Comm'n, Annual Report of the Fed. Trade Comm'n for Fiscal Year Ending June 30, 1934 126 (1934), https://www.ftc.gov/sites/default/files/documents/reports_annual/annual-report-1934/ar1934_0.pdf.

44. Pub. L. No. 75-447, 52 Stat. 111, § 5 (1938), as amended, 15 U.S.C. § 45 (1958) (emphasis added).

45. FTC, Cigarette Advertising, *supra* note 27, at 8349.

46. *See, e.g.*, Fed. Trade Comm'n, Annual Report of the Fed. Trade Comm'n for Fiscal Year Ending June 30, 1955 74–79 (1955), https://www.ftc.gov/sites/default/files/documents/reports_annual/annual-report-1955/ar1955_0.pdf; Fed. Trade Comm'n, Annual Report of the Fed. Trade Comm'n for Fiscal Year Ending June 30, 1950 102–08 (1950), https://www.ftc.gov/sites/default/files/documents/reports_annual/annual-report-1950/ar1950_0.pdf; Fed. Trade Comm'n, Annual Report of the Fed. Trade Comm'n for Fiscal Year Ending June 30, 1939 45–78 (1939), https://www.ftc.gov/sites/default/files/documents/reports_annual/annual-report-1939/ar1939_0.pdf.

47. *See, e.g.*, Regina Corp. v. Fed. Trade Comm'n, 322 F.2d 765 (3d Cir. 1963); Sterling Drug, Inc. v. Fed. Trade Comm'n, 317 F.2d 669 (2d Cir. 1963); Charles of the Ritz Distributors Corp. v. Fed. Trade Comm'n, 143 F.2d 676 (2d Cir. 1944); Fed. Trade Comm'n v. R.F. Keppel & Bro., 291 U.S. 304 (1934).

> largely ignored the word "or" in the amendment, and described acts it found to be offensive as "unfair and deceptive" without making any attempt to distinguish between "unfair" on the one hand, and "deceptive" on the other.[48]

It was not until 1964 that the FTC issued its first piece of comprehensive guidance with respect to the *unfair* act or practice standard, the "Statement of Basis and Purpose, Unfair or Deceptive Advertising, and Labeling of Cigarettes in Relation to the Health Hazards of Smoking."[49] This guidance, relying on the body of enforcement actions carried out under the UDAP provision since its inception, marked the FTC's first attempt to clarify the standard for *unfairness*.[50] The FTC statement provided a three-pronged test requiring consideration of the following to determine whether an act or practice was unfair:

1. whether it offends public policy as established by statutes, common law, or otherwise;
2. whether it is immoral, unethical, oppressive, or unscrupulous; and
3. whether it causes substantial injury to consumers (or competitors or other businesspersons).[51]

The FTC statement also recognized the standard for deceptive acts or practices in advertising, a standard that was built up by the FTC and the courts through fifty years of law enforcement: "If the seller attempts to deceive the consumer in any particular which could influence the latter's buying choice—if, in other words, he uses any false inducement—he has committed a deceptive act or practice in violation of Section 5."[52] The test of unlawful deception, which was articulated by many courts, is "whether the advertisement in question is likely to deceive a substantial segment of the purchasing public, or of that part of the purchasing public to whom the representation is directed, and that this likelihood may be inferred by the [FTC], in the exercise of its accumulated administrative knowledge and experience, on the basis of the challenged advertisement itself."[53] The FTC also noted that an advertiser could mislead without misstating a single fact if it uses "exaggeration, innuendo, ambiguity and half-truths," or it fails to disclose material facts.[54]

Courts have broadly addressed the *deceptiveness* standard, holding that the meaning of the term "deceptive practices" ultimately must be determined by way

48. *See* Beales, *supra* note 27.

49. *See* FTC, Cigarette Advertising, *supra* note 27, at 8355; Beales, *supra* note 27.

50. *See* Beales, *supra* note 27; *see also* Fed. Trade Comm'n v. R.F. Keppel & Bro., 291 U.S. 304 (1934).

51. FTC, Cigarette Advertising, *supra* note 27, at 8355; Beales, *supra* note 27.

52. FTC, Cigarette Advertising, *supra* note 27, at 8350 (citations omitted).

53. *Id.* at 8350 (citations omitted).

54. *Id.* at 8351 (citations omitted).

of judicial construction.[55] Courts also have held that a proceeding by the FTC to prevent deceptive acts or practices may only be brought if such proceeding is in the best interest of the public.[56]

Notwithstanding, between 1964 and 1972, the FTC rarely used its unfairness authority, likely due to Congress's "hostile" reaction to the 1964 guidance.[57] However, in 1972, the Supreme Court, in *FTC v. Sperry & Hutchinson Trading Stamp Co.*, 405 U.S. 233 (1972), adopted the *unfairness* test, which was to remain the definitive standard by which courts and regulators evaluated potential UDAP claims until 1980, when new FTC guidance was released.[58] In June 1980, two senators, Wendell H. Ford (D-KY) and John C. Danforth (R-MO), on the Consumer Subcommittee for the Committee on Commerce, Science, and Transportation, wrote to the FTC requesting clarification of the agency's position on the concept of *unfairness*, in preparation for planned oversight hearings on the subject.[59] The FTC responded by issuing a policy statement on *unfairness*.[60]

Relying on a review of decided cases and rules, in drafting the 1980 FTC Policy Statement on Unfairness, the FTC opted to keep the first and third prongs of the original test, articulated in 1964, largely intact.[61] However, the FTC's changes, adding a second prong requiring courts to weigh the benefits of a practice against its harms, and to consider the options available to the consumer under the circumstances, were not insubstantial.[62] The FTC's altered three-prong test required the following elements to establish an unfair act or practice:

1. substantial consumer injury (e.g., monetary harm, purchase of defective goods or services, unwarranted health and safety risks);
2. not outweighed by either competitive or consumer benefits of the practice; and
3. that consumers themselves could not reasonably have avoided.[63]

The guidance also retained violations of public policy (e.g., when the policy is so clear that it will entirely determine the question of consumer injury) as independent

55. F.T.C. v. Colgate-Palmolive Co., 380 U.S. 374, 385 (1965); Fed. Trade Comm'n v. R.F. Keppel & Bro., 291 U.S. 304, 312 (1934).

56. *See, e.g.*, Thomas v. Fed. Trade Comm'n, 116 F.2d 347, 349 (10th Cir. 1940); Nat'l Silver Co. v. Fed. Trade Comm'n, 88 F.2d 425, 427 (2d Cir. 1937).

57. Beales, *supra* note 27.

58. Fed. Trade Comm'n v. Sperry & Hutchinson Trading Stamp Co., 405 U.S. 233, 244 (1972); Beales, *supra* note 27.

59. FTC, Policy Statement on Unfairness, *supra* note 9.

60. *Id.*

61. *Id.*

62. *Id.*

63. *Id.*

grounds for an unfairness action.[64] The FTC articulated a two-part test for determining whether a policy is an "established" public policy for purposes of determining a violation: (1) whether the policy is clear and well established, and (2) whether the policy is widely shared and not an isolated decision.[65]

An FTC policy statement on deception followed in 1983, articulating a similar three-prong test requiring the following elements for a finding of *deceptiveness* in the consumer context:

1. a representation, omission, or practice that is likely to mislead the consumer (e.g., false oral or written representations, misleading prices claims, use of bait-and-switch techniques, failure to perform promised services, and failure to meet warranty obligations);
2. considered from the perspective of the reasonable consumer; and
3. which is material (i.e., to the consumer's detriment).[66]

In 1994, Congress amended the FTC Act to include the three elements of *unfairness* articulated in the FTC policy statement a decade earlier.[67] However, in codifying the standard, Congress added the caveat that "public policy considerations may not serve as a primary basis for such determination."[68]

2.3 Regulatory and Enforcement Authority Beyond the FTC

The FTC has general enforcement and regulatory authority for section 5 of the FTC Act;[69] however, its authority does not extend to banks and certain other financial institutions.[70] The Federal Deposit Insurance Act of 1950 (FDIA)[71] effectively extends the FTC Act's UDAP prohibition to such institutions by providing that the federal banking regulatory agencies may enforce any "law, rule, or regulation" against federally insured depository institutions.[72]

The FTC Improvement Act of 1975, 15 U.S.C. § 57a, amended the FTC Act to provide the federal banking agencies with regulatory authority, in addition to the enforcement authority conferred by the FDIA. Specifically, the act provided that the Federal Home Loan Bank Board (with respect to savings and loan associations), the Federal Reserve Board (FRB—with respect to banks), and the National Credit Union

64. *Id.*

65. *Id.*

66. FTC, Policy Statement, Deception, *supra* note 27.

67. 15 U.S.C. § 45(n) (2018).

68. *Id.*

69. *Id.* § 45(a)(1).

70. *Id.* § 45(a)(2).

71. Pub. L. No. 81-797, 64 Stat. 873 (1950) (codified as amended at 12 U.S.C. §§ 1811–35a).

72. 12 U.S.C. § 1818(b).

Administration (with respect to federal credit unions) "shall prescribe regulations to carry out the purposes of this section, including regulations defining with specificity such unfair or deceptive acts or practices, and containing requirements prescribed for the purpose of preventing such acts or practices."[73] The FRB exercised its rulemaking authority under the FTC Improvement Act in 1985, when it issued Regulation AA to prohibit banks from engaging in certain credit practices that the FTC had previously prohibited for other entities, and the Federal Home Loan Bank issued similar regulations four years later.[74] This regulatory authority was later removed by the Dodd-Frank Act.[75]

In early 2002, the Office of the Comptroller of the Currency (OCC) and the Federal Deposit Insurance Corporation (FDIC) each issued formal guidance with respect to the applicable standards for evaluating whether acts or practices are deceptive or unfair, making reference to, and closely mirroring, the FTC Policy Statements, pursuant to such agencies' authority under the FDIA.[76] The Federal Reserve Board (Federal Reserve or FRB) and FDIC followed suit in 2004 by issuing joint guidance.[77]

The FDIC, FTC, FRB, and OCC each has initiated UDAP enforcement actions.[78] Notably, the OCC has issued several enforcement actions against national banks alleged to have violated UDAP prohibitions.[79] The first such enforcement action was settled in June 2000.[80]

In addition, state UDAP provisions, often heavily modeled on the FTC Act, began to spring up in the 1960s, and by the early 1980s, such statutes, in one form or another, had been enacted in every state.

---

73. 15 U.S.C. § 57a(f)(1) (1996).

74. *See* 12 C.F.R. § 227.1–227.26 (1992); *see also* 12 C.F.R. § 535 (pre-June 30, 2010).

75. Pub. L. No. 111-203, § 1091 (2010).

76. *See* OCC, Advisory Letter AL 2002-3, Guidance on Unfair or Deceptive Acts or Practices (March 22, 2002), https://www.occ.treas.gov/news-issuances/advisory-letters/2002/advisory-letter-2002-3.pdf.

77. FDIC and Federal Reserve, Financial Institution Letter FL-26-2004, Unfair or Deceptive Acts or Practices by State-Chartered Banks (Mar. 11, 2004), https://www.fdic.gov/news/news/financial/2004/fil2604.html.

78. On the FDIC, *see, e.g.*, Northwest Savings Bank, Consent Order, FDIC-11-361b (August 8, 2011), https://www.fdic.gov/bank/individual/enforcement/2011-09-07.pdf; on the FTC, *see, e.g.*, FTC v. Sperry & Hutchinson Co., 405 U.S. 233 (1972); on the FRB, *see, e.g.*, Mid American Bank & Trust Company, Consent Order, No. 17-038-B-SM (October 25, 2017), https://www.federalreserve.gov/newsevents/pressreleases/files/enf20171026a1.pdf; on the OCC, *see, e.g.*, First National Bank of Marin, Consent Order, OCC No. 2004-45 (May 24, 2004), https://www.occ.gov/news-issuances/news-releases/2004/nr-occ-2004-37a.pdf.

79. *See e.g.*, First National Bank of Marin, Consent Order, *supra* note 78; Clear Lake National Bank, Consent Order, OOC No. 2003-135 (Nov. 7, 2003), https://www.occ.gov/news-issuances/news-releases/2003/nr-occ-2003-88a.pdf; Direct Merchants Credit Card Bank, N.A., Consent Order, OCC No. 2001-24 (May 3. 2001), https://www.occ.gov/static/enforcement-actions/ea2001-24.pdf.

80. *See* Providian National Bank, Consent Order, OCC No. 2000-53 (June 28, 2000), https://www.occ.gov/static/enforcement-actions/ea2000-53.pdf.

3. Broadening of Federal Consumer Protection: The Dodd-Frank Act and the Prohibition on *Abusive* Acts or Practices

As noted above, the twentieth century saw the enactment of prohibitions on certain *unfair* and *deceptive* practices, but it was not until the twenty-first century that the new *abusiveness* standard came into play.

3.1 *Abusiveness* Outside the Financial Regulatory Context

Though not applied broadly in the financial regulatory context until the enactment of the Dodd-Frank Act,[81] the *abusiveness* standard had been used in other regulatory schemes for decades prior. One of its earliest appearances occurred in the 1977 Fair Debt Collection Practices Act, which provided a private right of action for abusive debt collection practices.[82] A prohibition on abusive acts and practices was also included in the 1994 Home Ownership and Equity Protection Act, which was part of the Riegle Community Development and Regulatory Improvement Act of 1994.[83]

3.2 The Rise of *Abusiveness* in the Financial Regulatory Context

As early as 2007, discussion regarding adding an abusiveness standard to the existing version of UDAP in the broader financial regulatory framework had begun. FDIC Chair Sheila Bair was one of the earliest public proponents of the addition of *abusiveness*. She suggested the inclusion of such a standard into the Home Ownership and Equity Protection Act.[84]

The first official suggestion to add the term *abusive* to the existing UDAP standard in the financial regulatory space came in the form of a Department of Treasury white paper, issued in June 2009.[85] The white paper proposed the use of the abusiveness standard to protect consumers "across the financial sector" and further proposed a new "Consumer Financial Protection Agency" with the power

81. *See* Dodd-Frank Wall Street Reform and Consumer Protection Act, Pub. L. No. 111-203 (2010).

82. *See* 15 U.S.C. §§ 1692, 1692d, 1692k(a).

83. *See* Pub. L. No. 103-325, 108 Stat. 2160, §§ 151–58 (codified at 15 U.S.C. §§ 1601–1647).

84. *Improving Federal Consumer Protection in Financial Services: Hearing Before the H. Comm. On Fin. Serv's*, 110th Cong. (2007) (statement of Sheila C. Bair, Chairman, FDIC), https://www.fdic.gov/news/news/speeches/archives/2007/chairman/spjun1307.html.

85. Dept. of the Treasury, Financial Regulatory Reform: A New Foundation—Rebuilding Financial Supervision and Regulation (June 2009), https://www.treasury.gov/initiatives/wsr/Documents/FinalReport_web.pdf.

to enforce such standard, widening the potential scope of a new UDAAP scheme.[86] Notwithstanding, the white paper did not provide guidance as to what an *abusiveness* standard might entail, nor did it make any attempt to define just what the term *abusive* might mean in this context.

The new UDAAP standard, still lacking a definition of the term *abusive*, made its first legislative appearance in a 2009 bill introduced by Congressman Barney Frank (D-MA).[87] Though the bill did not pass the House in its 2009 form, it was a clear indication that congressional attitudes toward financial regulation had shifted. On the heels of the recent financial crisis, Congress was demonstrating serious interest in increasing the scope of financial regulatory oversight, and expansion from UDAP to UDAAP was to be a central part of this initiative.

3.3 The Dodd-Frank Act: The Legislative Turning Point

The *abusiveness* standard finally became an enforceable part of the financial regulatory framework when the Dodd-Frank Act was signed into law, in July 2010. The Dodd-Frank Act also created the CFPB and granted the Bureau the power to enforce an *abusiveness* standard.[88] The earliest version of the law, as passed by the House, included a definition of *abusive* acts or practices, providing that acts were abusive only where: (1) the act was reasonably likely to result in a consumer's inability to understand the terms and conditions of a product or service or to protect their own interest in selecting a product or service; and (2) the widespread use of the act or practice is reasonably likely to contribute to instability and increase risk in the financial system. However, this definition was omitted from the Dodd-Frank Act in its final form and a new one was adopted (see immediately below).[89] The House definition indicates that the genesis of the abusiveness standard was a concern over the stability of the financial system as a whole, not concern over protecting individual consumers, *per se*.

Ultimately, Congress included the following definition of an *abusive act or practice* in the Dodd-Frank Act:

> [T]he act or practice: (1) materially interferes with the ability of a consumer to understand a term or condition of a consumer financial product or service; or (2) takes unreasonable advantage of: (A) a lack of understanding on the part of the consumer of the material risks, costs, or conditions of the product or service; (B) the inability of the consumer to protect the interests of the consumer in selecting or using a consumer financial

---

86. *Id.* at 3, 58, 67.

87. *See* The Consumer Financial Protection Agency Act of 2009, H.R. 3126, 111th Cong. (2009), https://www.congress.gov/bill/111th-congress/house-bill/3126.

88. *See* Dodd-Frank Wall Street Reform and Consumer Protection Act, Pub. L. No. 111-203 (2010).

89. H.R. 4173, 111th Cong. § 4301(c)(3) (2009).

product or service; or (C) the reasonable reliance by the consumer on a covered person to act in the interests of the consumer.[90]

Given the somewhat nebulous nature of the term *abusive*, challenges have arisen as to the constitutionality of Congress delegating enforcement and rulemaking authority pursuant to this portion of the UDAAP provision to the CFPB with respect to activities performed by, for example, attorneys licensed to practice law who also offer or provide a consumer financial product or service.[91] However, such arguments have not been successful. Courts have generally taken the position that the definition of *abusive acts or practices* provided in the Dodd-Frank Act is sufficiently limiting to be in compliance with the constitutional prohibition on the delegation of legislative power outside of Congress.[92]

Despite the Dodd-Frank Act's clear focus on prohibiting consumer abuse, and in keeping with the precedent set by the FTC Act, the Dodd-Frank Act does not create any private right of action.[93] The CFPB can sue and bring administrative enforcement actions against banks and other nondepository financial services providers for UDAAP violations, but consumers can only file complaints with the Bureau—not sue a company directly—(pursuant to the Dodd-Frank Act).[94]

4. The Evolving UDAP/UDAAP Landscape

The general UDAAP provisions of the Dodd-Frank Act are not the sole UDAAP provisions under CFPB authority, neither are they applicable to the financial regulatory industry. In addition to the previously mentioned FTC UDAP provisions, which remain valid and existing law, and the UDAP provisions in the "mini-FTC acts" enacted by nearly every state in the nation (generally enforceable by state attorneys general and through private rights of action),[95] provisions with UDAAP concepts in various forms are included in both the Fair Debt Collection Practices Act (FDCPA)[96] and the Truth in Lending Act (TILA).[97]

---

90. 12 U.S.C. § 5531(d) (2018).

91. *See, e.g.*, Consumer Fin. Prot. Bureau v. Morgan Drexen, Inc., 60 F. Supp. 3d 1082, 1096 (C.D. Cal. 2014).

92. *See, e.g.*, *id.* at 1090.

93. *See* Beider v. Retrieval Masters Creditors Bureau, Inc., 146 F. Supp. 3d 465, 471–72 (E.D.N.Y. 2015).

94. *See id.*; CFPB, *Having a problem with a financial product or service?*, https://www.consumerfinance.gov/complaint/.

95. *See, e.g.*, Ala. Code §§ 8-19-1–15; Del. Code Ann. tit. 6, §§ 2531–2536; Idaho Code Ann. §§ 48-601–619; Or. Rev. Stat. §§ 646.605–656; Tenn. Code Ann. §§ 47-18-101–132.

96. *See* 15 U.S.C. §§ 1692e, 1692k.

97. *Id.* §§ 1604(d), 1639(p)(2), (q).

The CFPB enforces the provisions for which it is responsible through both administrative proceedings and civil suits brought in federal district courts across the country, at times in conjunction with state attorneys general or with other federal regulatory agencies with overlapping jurisdiction (e.g., the Federal Reserve or OCC).[98]

For more than a century, the definitions of *unfair, deceptive*, and *abusive* have steadily evolved and both rulemaking and enforcement will continue to shape their meaning and application.

98. *See, e.g.*, Complaint, Consumer Fin. Prot. Bureau v. Aequitas Capital Mgmt., Inc., No. 17-cv-1278 (D. Or. Aug. 17, 2017); Complaint, Consumer Fin. Prot. Bureau v. RD Legal Funding, LLC, 332 F. Supp. 3d 729 (S.D.N.Y. Feb. 7, 2017) (No. 17-cv-890); Complaint, Consumer Fin. Prot. Bureau v. Siringoringo, No. 14-cv-5681 (C.D. Cal. July 22, 2014); Complaint, United States v. SunTrust Mortgage Inc., 14-1028 (E.D. Va. June 17, 2014).

CHAPTER

2B

Deception

Lucy Morris and Erik Kosa

1. Introduction

The primary regulators of deceptive acts or practices at the federal level are the Federal Trade Commission (FTC or Commission) and the Consumer Financial Protection Bureau (CFPB or Bureau).

The FTC investigates and sues people who commit deceptive acts or practices, promulgates regulations to protect consumers, and educates consumers and businesses about the law and the marketplace. Created in 1914, the FTC draws its power to prohibit deceptive practices from section 5 of the Federal Trade Commission Act (FTC Act), which declares unfair or deceptive acts or practices in or affecting commerce to be unlawful.[1] The FTC Act is quite broad, applying to broad swathes of the economy beyond just consumer financial services. However, the FTC's enforcement powers do not apply to banks, savings and loan institutions, and federal credit unions; the federal banking agencies enforce the FTC Act's prohibition against deceptive practices with respect to banks and federal savings associations that are not within the CFPB's jurisdiction.[2]

The CFPB was created by Congress in 2010 to be the first agency whose sole mission was consumer protection in the financial services sector. Under Sections 1031

1. 15 U.S.C. § 45(a)(1).

2. For additional reading on federal enforcement of the prohibitions against unfair, deceptive, or abusive practices, see Susan Manship Seaman's outline prepared for the "Meet the Federal UDA(A)P Regulators" panel presented by the Federal and State Trade Practices Subcommittee of the American Bar Association's Consumer Financial Services Committee, at the Fall 2018 Business Law Section Annual Meeting, https://www.americanbar.org/content/dam/aba/events/business_law/2018/09/annual/materials/udaap-regulators-201809.pdf.

and 1036 of the Dodd-Frank Wall Street Reform and Consumer Protection Act (Dodd-Frank Act), it is unlawful for any covered person or service provider to engage in any unfair, deceptive, or abusive acts or practices (collectively, UDAAP).[3] The CFPB's authority is limited to *consumer financial products and services*. A consumer financial product or service is a financial product or service offered or provided for use by consumers primarily for personal, family, or household purposes.[4] In addition to the FTC Act and the Dodd-Frank Act, most states also have "mini-FTC Acts" that outlaw deceptive practices in some form and give state attorneys general or financial institution regulators the power to enforce the acts.[5]

2. The Basics of Deception Law

All deception cases involve communications conveying a message to consumers that is false or misleading. The same deception standards apply to all kinds of claims made about all kinds of products and services (e.g., mortgages, credit cards, auto sales and leases, and loan servicing). In addition, the same standards apply regardless of the medium in which the communication is made, whether print, oral, broadcast, Internet, or on mobile devices. Deception most often occurs in promotional messages marketing products or services, but can include any communication with consumers, including statements made during the sales process, in contracts, or during the servicing or collecting of an account.

Neither the FTC Act nor the Dodd-Frank Act defines deception. Because of its long history of consumer protection activities, the FTC has shaped deception law more than any other agency. The *FTC Policy Statement on Deception* (Deception Statement) provides the framework for modern deception law.[6] The Deception Statement, case law, and other agency guidance explain that there are three elements common to all deception cases. Deception exists if (1) there is a representation, omission, act, or practice that is likely to mislead the consumer; (2) the consumer's interpretation of the representation, omission, act, or practice is reasonable under the circumstances; and (3) the misleading representation, omission, act, or practice is material.[7]

---

3. 12 U.S.C. §§ 5531(a), 5536(a). In addition, it is unlawful for any person to knowingly or recklessly provide substantial assistance to a covered person or service provider engaged in UDAAP. 12 U.S.C. § 5536(a)(3).

4. 15 U.S.C. § 5481(5).

5. Carolyn L. Carter, Consumer Protection in the States: A 50-State Report on Unfair and Deceptive Acts and Practices Statutes (Nat'l. Consumer Law Ctr. Inc. Feb. 2009), https://www.nclc.org/images/pdf/udap/report_50_states.pdf.

6. *FTC Policy Statement on Deception* (Oct. 14, 1983), *appended to Cliffdale Assocs., Inc.*, 103 F.T.C. 110 (1984).

7. *See, e.g., id.*; CFPB, *Supervision and Examination Manual* (Oct. 2012), https://files.consumerfinance.gov/f/documents/102012_cfpb_unfair-deceptive-abusive-acts-practices-udaaps_procedures.pdf.

2.1 Representation, Omission, or Practice Likely to Mislead the Consumer

The legal standard is whether the representation, omission, or practice (i.e., the claim) is *likely* to mislead; the government does not have to prove that consumers were actually deceived.[8] In addition, a scienter element is not required.[9] Even a literally true statement can be deceptive if the overall net impression of the communication is misleading. For example, a statement that, standing alone, is literally true but misleading without additional information, is deceptive. Regulators will look at the context of the communication and all of its elements when considering what claims have been made and whether they are likely to mislead consumers.

Both express claims and implied claims may be deceptive. An express claim is one that states a fact directly (for example: "Product X prevents colds"). An implied claim allows the consumer to infer the fact, rather than stating it directly (for example: "Product X kills germs that cause colds" would lead a consumer to infer that Product X prevents colds). Implied claims range on a continuum from language that is virtually synonymous with an express claim to language that literally says one thing but strongly suggests something else to language that relatively few consumers would interpret as making the claim. Because express claims unequivocally state the representation, the representation itself establishes the meaning of the claim. No further proof about the meaning of the claim is necessary.[10] When an implied claim is not clear enough to permit the regulator to determine its existence by examining the ad alone, extrinsic evidence (such as a copy test) may be required.[11]

Consumers can also be deceived through omissions. A deceptive omission occurs when a communication fails to include information in such a way that a consumer would be left with a material misimpression about the communication.

Not all omissions are deceptive, however, even if providing the information would benefit consumers. As the Commission has noted, "the question whether an advertisement requires affirmative disclosure would depend on the nature and extent of the . . . claim made in the advertisement."[12] In other words, context matters. Whether an omission is deceptive will depend on the overall impression created. For example, as the FTC has noted, offering a product for sale creates an implied representation that it is fit for its intended purpose, and not disclosing that it is unfit for this purpose would constitute a deceptive omission.[13]

---

8. *See* Fed. Trade Comm'n v. Algoma Lumber Co., 291 U.S. 67, 78 (1934); Fed. Trade Comm'n v. Verity Int'l, 443 F.3d 48, 63 (2d Cir. 2006).

9. *See, e.g.*, Fed. Trade Comm'n v. Network Servs. Depot, Inc., 617 F.3d 1127, 1138 n.9 (9th Cir. 2010) (holding the FTC Act does not have mental state requirement for injunctive relief for individual liability).

10. 103 F.T.C. 176 (1984).

11. Stouffer Foods Corp., 118 F.T.C. 746, 798–99 (1994).

12. ITT Cont'l Baking Co. Inc., 83 F.T.C. 865, 965 (1976).

13. *See* International Harvester Co., 104 F.T.C. 949, 1058–59 (1984).

Ordinarily, deceptive omissions arise when there are significant qualifications, exclusions, limitations, or conditions on an offer that are not sufficiently disclosed to the consumer. Not all information anyone might want to know must be disclosed, but information should be disclosed if it is necessary to correct a misimpression that a reasonable consumer might otherwise take away from a communication.

Written disclosures may be insufficient to correct a misleading statement or representation, particularly if the disclosure appears in fine print at the bottom of the page, in a footnote, or on a separate page altogether. Disclosures are appropriate to *qualify* a claim, not *contradict* it. It is deceptive to claim one thing in the headline or text of an advertisement, while saying the opposite in the fine print.

Disclosures that add to the meaning of claims made must be clear and conspicuous. To accomplish this, advertisers must place the disclosure as close as possible to the headline claim, ensuring that the various devices consumers may use to view the advertising are capable of displaying the disclosure. The disclosure must be prominent, unavoidable, and understandable to the intended audience.[14] A disclosure is more effective if it is placed near the claim it qualifies. In considering these issues, remember that if a disclosure necessary to prevent an advertisement from being deceptive cannot be made clearly and conspicuously, that advertisement should simply not be disseminated.

Whether a disclosure is sufficiently **clear and conspicuous** will be determined by the following **"Four P's"**:[15]

- **Prominence**—Display disclosures so that they are noticeable to consumers.[16] Evaluate the size, color, and graphics of the disclosure in relation to other parts of the advertisement.[17] Be sure any disclosures are viewable on other devices such as smartphones. If a disclosure is too small to be read on a smartphone, it is not clear and conspicuous.[18]
- **Presentation**—Disclosures must be worded in a way that consumers can easily understand.[19] Do not bury important information in a dense block of text that discourages consumers from reading it.[20]

14. *See* FTC, *.com Disclosures: How to Make Effective Disclosures in Digital Advertising* 1, 7 (Mar. 2013), https://www.ftc.gov/sites/default/files/attachments/press-releases/ftc-staff-revises-online-advertising-disclosure-guidelines/130312dotcomdisclosures.pdf.

15. *See* Lesley Fair, FTC, *Full Disclosure* (Sept. 23, 2014), https://www.ftc.gov/news-events/blogs/business-blog/2014/09/full-disclosure.

16. *.com Disclosures*, *supra* note 14, at 17–18.

17. *Id.*

18. *Id.*

19. *Id.* at 19–21.

20. *Id.*

- **Placement**—Disclosures must be where consumers are likely to look.[21] The best practice is always to place a disclosure immediately next to the claim it supplements.[22]
- **Proximity**—The disclosure must be close to the claim it modifies, in a place a consumer is likely to see it.[23] On a website, additional information may be included in hyperlinks directing consumers to a page with more detailed explanations.[24] However, disclosures that are an integral part of a claim should not be communicated through a hyperlink, but rather placed on the same page and immediately next to the claim.[25] Hyperlinks should be appropriately labeled to make sure it is obvious to the consumer what information is available through the link and why it is important.[26]

The "clear and conspicuous" standard is not a specific set of rules governing font size and type, but a performance standard. **A disclosure is clear and conspicuous if a reasonable consumer notices, reads, and understands it.** The key is the overall net impression of the ad, meaning whether the claims consumers take from the ad are truthful and substantiated. If a disclosure is made but not seen or understood, it will not change the net impression that consumers take from the advertisement and therefore cannot qualify the claim to avoid leaving a misleading impression.[27] A disclosure does not meet these standards if it is in tiny print, or otherwise too removed from the claim it qualifies to do the consumer any good. For example, a disclosure on a web page that is only reachable through a series of click-throughs is not clear and conspicuous.

2.2 A Consumer Acting Reasonably under the Circumstances

In determining whether an act or practice is misleading, one also must consider whether the consumer's interpretation of the representation, omission, act, or practice is reasonable under the circumstances.[28] Whether an act or practice is deceptive depends on how a reasonable member of the target audience would interpret the representation.[29] When representations or marketing practices target a specific audience, such as older

21. *Id.* at 8.
22. *Id.*
23. *Id.* at 8.
24. *Id.* at 10–13.
25. *Id.*
26. *Id.*
27. *See id.* at 6.
28. 103 F.T.C. at 177–79.
29. *Id.*

Americans or financially distressed consumers, the communication must be reviewed from the point of view of a reasonable member of that group.[30]

Representations can often be interpreted in different ways by different consumers. A representation may be deceptive even if the majority of consumers in the target class do not share the deceptive interpretation, so long as a significant minority of such consumers would be misled.[31] When a representation conveys more than one meaning to reasonable consumers, one of which is false or misleading, the person making the representation is liable for the false or misleading interpretation.[32]

2.3 The Misleading Effect Is Material

A representation, omission, act, or practice is material if it is likely to affect a consumer's choice of, or conduct regarding, the product or service. Information that is important to consumers is material.[33]

Certain categories of information are presumed to be material. In general, information about the central characteristics of a product or service—such as costs, benefits, or restrictions on its use or availability—is presumed to be material.[34] For example, the fees and interest rate that apply to a credit card relate to the central characteristics of the product and would be important to consumers in shopping for a credit card. In contrast, whether the color of the credit card is gold, or yellow, is not likely material.

If a representation or claim is not presumed to be material, it still would be considered material if it is shown to be important to consumers in purchasing or using a product or service.[35]

2.4 Examples

Below are some examples of deceptive acts or practices identified by regulators:

- Claiming a credit score a credit bureau markets to consumers is the same score used by lenders to make credit decisions when that is not the case.[36]

---

30. *Id.*

31. *Id.* at 177 n.20.

32. *Id.* at 178.

33. *Id.* at 182.

34. *Id.*; Fed. Trade Comm'n v. Freecom Comm'ns, 401 F.3d 1192, 1203 (10th Cir. 2005) (finding misrepresentations about income that would be made from business opportunity would generally be material and thus likely to mislead).

35. 103 F.T.C. at 182; *Fed. Trade Comm'n v. Freecom Comm'ns.*

36. Experian Holdings, Inc., 2017-CFPB-0012 (Mar. 23, 2017); Equifax, Inc., 2017-CFPB-0001 (Jan. 3, 2017); TransUnion Interactive, Inc., 2017-CFPB-0002 (Jan. 3, 2017).

- Advertising that credit is available to everyone when in fact lenders use credit information from consumer reporting agencies or other sources to determine whether or not to extend credit.[37]
- Misrepresenting that a communication is from a government source or that the source of the communication is affiliated with the government.[38]
- Advertising rates that are available only to a small fraction of consumers, unless that limitation is clearly and conspicuously disclosed.[39]
- Misrepresenting whether information about a payment or nonpayment would be furnished to a consumer reporting agency.[40]
- Telling a consumer that paying a delinquent debt will improve her credit rating because the extent to which paying the debt will materially improve any particular consumer's credit score is seldom known.[41]

3. Common Deception Issues

Below we discuss important deception concepts that frequently arise in the consumer financial services space.

3.1 Substantiation

Before an advertiser can make an objective (factual) claim to consumers, it must have a reasonable basis for the claim.[42] The kind of evidence the advertiser must have depends on the kind of claim made.[43] If the advertiser states that it has a certain level of evidence for a claim, such as "tests" or "surveys," the advertiser must actually have that type and amount of evidence.[44]

---

37. Fed. Trade Comm'n v. Universal City Nissan, Inc. et al., No. 2:16-cv-07329 (C.D. Cal. Mar. 22, 2017).

38. CFPB v. Nat'l Corrective Grp., Inc., et al., No. 1:15-cv-899 (D. Md. Mar. 31, 2015); Flagship Fin. Grp., LLC, 2015-CFPB-0006 (Feb. 12, 2015).

39. Timonium Chrysler, Inc., No. C-4429 (FTC Jan. 28, 2014).

40. Am. Express Centurion Bank, 2012-CFPB-0002 (Sept. 21, 2012).

41. CFPB Bulletin 2013-08, *Fair Debt Collection Practices Act and the Dodd-Frank Act* (July 10, 2013), https://files.consumerfinance.gov/f/201307_cfpb_bulletin_collections-consumer-credit.pdf; *see also* Am. Express Centurion Bank, *supra* note 40.

42. *FTC Policy Statement Regarding Advertising Substantiation* [hereinafter "Substantiation Statement"], FTC (Nov. 23, 1984), https://www.ftc.gov/public-statements/1983/03/ftc-policy-statement-regarding-advertising-substantiation.

43. *Id.*; Pfizer, 81 F.T.C. 23 (1972).

44. Substantiation Statement, *supra* note 42.

When the claim does not expressly reference a specific kind or amount of support, the advertiser must have a "reasonable basis" for the claim.[45] What constitutes a "reasonable basis" depends on a number of factors, most importantly the type and amount of evidence experts in the field believe is necessary to substantiate the claim.[46] For example, if an advertiser claims that "X% of our customers prefer our products to the competition," this should be based on an objective and properly conducted survey, not anecdotal evidence.[47]

The substantiation doctrine has its origin in FTC advertising cases requiring empirical support for objective health and safety claims. The FTC and CFPB have extended this theory in cases involving mortgage servicing and debt collection, among other areas. For example, in a case against a mortgage servicer, the FTC alleged that the company misrepresented that it could substantiate what they told consumers about amounts owed, due dates, and other aspects of the consumer's account; the FTC alleged that, in fact, the servicer could not substantiate their claims because of faulty loan data.[48]

3.2 Testimonials and Endorsements

When using endorsements to advertise a product, advertisers must ensure the advertisement accurately conveys the content of what the endorser said.[49,50] If an advertisement represents that the endorser used a certain product, the endorser must have actually used the product at the time the endorsement was given. Importantly, if an individual customer's experience is presented in the endorsement and the advertiser does not have substantiation to show that experience is representative of what typical consumers will achieve, the statement must be supported by a statement of the average or typical experience.[51] Simply using a "results not typical" disclaimer is not enough.[52]

Moreover, if there is any material connection between the advertiser and the endorser, that is, one not reasonably expected by the audience that might affect the weight or credibility of the endorsement, that fact must be disclosed in the

45. *Id.*

46. *Id.*

47. *Id.*

48. *See, e.g.*, Complaint, Fed Trade Comm'n v. EMC Mortg. Corp., No. 4:08-cv-00338 (E.D. Tex. Sept. 9, 2008).

49. An "endorsement" is any advertising message that consumers are likely to believe reflects the opinions, beliefs, findings, or experiences of a party other than the sponsoring advertiser.

50. Guides Concerning Use of Endorsements and Testimonials in Advertising, 16 C.F.R. § 255 (2009).

51. *Id.* § 255.5, Example 3.

52. *Id.* § 255.2 n.105.

advertisement.[53] One clear example of this would be compensation given to the speaker in connection with the endorsement: any such connection must be disclosed in the ad along with presentation of the endorser's statement.[54]

3.3 "Up To" and Similar Claims

One very common claim that advertisers make is that a product or service will provide a benefit "up to," "as much as," or "as low as" a specified figure.[55] Typically, the advertiser means to imply that results may vary, and the specified figure is a best-case scenario. For example, an advertisement may claim "up to $4,000 savings" or rates "as low as 5 percent APR." Research conducted by the FTC has indicated that this is not the message most consumers take from such claims and the FTC will view such claims skeptically if most consumers will not achieve the stated result.[56]

On June 29, 2012, the FTC published a report summarizing the results of a copy test it conducted on how consumers interpret "up to" claims.[57] A copy test is a type of consumer survey in which consumers are shown an advertisement and asked questions to elicit how they interpret its messages.[58] The study describes what a test group of consumers thought about ads for replacement home windows that purportedly would provide "up to 47 percent" savings in energy costs.[59] About half of the consumers tested took the claim to mean that users of the window could generally expect to achieve the full 47 percent savings.[60]

In releasing the report, the FTC provided the following guidance: "The FTC believes the report will help guide advertisers to avoid the use of misleading 'up to' claims. It reinforces the FTC's view that advertisers using these claims should be able to substantiate that *consumers are likely to achieve the maximum results promised under normal circumstances.*"[61] This is a tougher standard than the FTC had applied to

53. *Id.* § 255.5; Numex Corp., 116 F.T.C. 1078 (1993); TrendMark Int'l, Inc., 126 F.T.C. 375 (1998).

54. 16 C.F.R. § 255.5.

55. We refer to such claims collectively as "up to claims" here. This is not a legal definition; rather it is created here as a convention for ease of understanding this chapter.

56. For an in-depth analysis of the FTC's report, see Joel Winston, *"Up To" Advertising Claims: The FTC Weighs In*, The Antitrust Source, Oct. 2012, 1, 3, https://www.americanbar.org/groups/antitrust_law/publications/the_antitrust_source/.

57. *See* Press Release, Fed. Trade Comm'n, FTC Report: Many Consumers Believe "Up To" Claims Promise Maximum Result (June 29, 2012), http://www.ftc.gov/opa/2012/06/uptoclaims.shtm.

58. *Supra* note 56, at 2 n.6.

59. *Id.* at 2–3.

60. *Id.*

61. *See id.* (emphasis added).

"up to" claims in the past.[62] Although the FTC has not issued formal, legally binding guidance on "up to" claims, advertisers should heed the FTC's warnings and conform their practices to the FTC's views where possible.[63] Taken literally, the FTC's use of the word "likely" is a synonym for "most," which means that to comply with this standard, an advertiser would need to show that most (more than 50 percent) of its customers would achieve the specified, maximum result.[64]

4. Digital Advertising

With online advertising playing a crucial role in reaching consumers, the FTC issued guidance specifically addressing issues that arise when advertising on the Internet. The guide—*.com Disclosures*—applies the basic principles of deception law to special issues presented by digital advertising.[65] It encompasses all advertising online, which the FTC defines broadly to encompass the Internet and other electronic networks, as well as mobile devices such as tablets and smartphones.[66] Although the guide is not a safe harbor from liability, it outlines an important regulator's approach to claims made within this space. The important themes to remember when advertising online are the following:

- **The same laws apply** to digital advertising as print advertising. Both the FTC Act's and the CFPA's prohibitions on deceptive acts apply in the online and mobile marketplaces. In addition, many FTC and CFPB guides are not limited to any particular medium, and therefore apply to online advertising as well as print and other media.
- Advertisers should always be looking for ways to **incorporate important information into the underlying claim wherever possible**, rather than rely on disclosures to cure any potentially misleading claims. Space and consumer attention are limited, and advertisers often do not get a second chance at the reader's attention to supply more information in the fine print.
- Disclosures must remain **clear and conspicuous**. Remember the "Four P's" discussed in section 2.1. If you must use a disclosure, the closer you place it to the claim it modifies, the better. As always, advertisements should be written in language that is easy to understand for a general

62. *Id.* at 3. At various times, the FTC has allowed "up to" claims if "an appreciable number of consumers" would achieve the maximum result. Some advertising watchdogs have considered 10 percent to be an appreciable number; *id.* at 5 (citing Plaskolite, Inc., 101 F.T.C. 344 (1983); Cynex Mfg. Corp., 104 F.T.C. 464, 475 (1984); GCS Elecs., 108 F.T.C. 158 (1986)).

63. *Winston*, *supra* note 56, at 6.

64. *Id.* at 8–11.

65. *.com Disclosures*, *supra* note 14.

66. *Id.* at 1, n.1.

audience. Space and consumer attention are limited, especially on mobile devices, making the clear and conspicuous standard all the more important.

- Because the digital marketplace changes so rapidly, everyone subject to deception law should keep abreast of empirical research on where consumers look while using different digital devices, and keep in mind any technological limitations of a particular means of communication when considering where to place disclosures.[67]

4.1 General Considerations

A disclosure is more effective if it is near the claim it modifies because it increases the chances a consumer will read and understand it. As with print advertisements, proximity can be assessed according to whether the disclosure is separated from the claim by text or graphics. Digital advertising presents special challenges, however; it is more interactive, and multiple pages may be linked together, or pop-ups may play a role in disseminating information, making an assessment of whether a disclosure is sufficiently proximate to its claim more complicated.

Where possible, all material information should be incorporated into the headline claim. This is especially true for information on what a product costs.[68] Where that is not possible, the disclosure should be as close as possible to the claim, taking into account the various devices and platforms consumers may be using to view the advertisement. Scrolling down a web page to view important information should be kept to a minimum because varying screen sizes may result in advertisements displaying differently on different devices, and some consumers may not scroll enough, or in the right direction, to view important qualifying information. When it is necessary, advertisers should use visual cues to get the reader's attention that additional important information is further down. The FTC has said that prompts to the effect of "see below for more information" on the product may help consumers get to the information they need.

Where a web page is particularly lengthy, or claims are repeated often in a digital advertisement, take care to repeat any disclosures proportionately. Do not relegate disclosures to pages consumers would not expect to have important information on the product, such as by burying them in links that normally signify the end of a web page, including "terms of use," "contact us," "privacy policy," and "copyright."[69]

If scrolling is necessary for a consumer to reach a disclosure, the disclosure should be unavoidable. That is, the consumer should be forced to look at the disclosure before reaching other parts of the web page. Websites should be optimized for viewing

67. *Id.* at 8.

68. *Id.* at 10.

69. *Id.* at 9.

on mobile devices so that consumers do not miss important information. For example, if a disclosure appears in an adjacent column on a website, a reader on a laptop-sized screen may see it whereas a reader using a mobile device may miss it, depending on whether the website condenses information such that it is all easy to scroll through on a mobile device.

A disclosure's size, color, and graphics will determine whether it is sufficiently prominent.[70] The FTC has stated that a disclosure that is in font as large as the claim it qualifies is likely to be effective.[71] Further, making a disclosure in a color that contrasts with the background in such a way that emphasizes its text is more likely to be effective.[72] Disclosures should not be buried inside a long paragraph of text that addresses a subject different from that of the disclosure and the claim to which it relates.[73] The FTC has specifically pointed out that consumers are unlikely to read disclosures contained in "terms of use" and similarly, an insufficient disclosure cannot be made effective by forcing a consumer to click that they "agree" to a term or condition.[74]

Further, digital ads also present distracting factors that may take the consumer's attention away from the disclosure. Moving visuals behind important text makes the message of the text more difficult to digest and should be avoided when making disclosures.[75]

Advertisers may overcome some of the constraints inherent in digital advertising by using certain techniques:

- **Repetition**—If disclosures are lengthy, advertisers should repeat them to increase their effectiveness.[76] This is particularly important where consumers access a website through links that take them past the homepage somewhere deeper into the website where they may miss earlier information.[77] Advertisers should also repeat the disclosure each time the claim itself is repeated.[78]
- **Use the same medium for the disclosure as the claim**—For example, an audio claim should be supported by an audio disclosure, a written claim should be supported by a written disclosure, and so on.[79]

70. *Id.* at 17.
71. *Id.*
72. *Id.*
73. *Id.* at 18.
74. *Id.* at 18.
75. *Id.* at 19.
76. *Id.* at 19–20.
77. *Id.*
78. *Id.*
79. *Id.* at 20.

- **Length**—Where a disclosure is made visually, advertisers must allow consumers sufficient time to read it.[80] A disclosure that flashes by on a screen before a reader can reasonably absorb it is not clear and conspicuous.[81]

4.2 Space Constraints in Digital Ads

Many digital advertisements are inherently space-constrained because they are teasers, banner ads, sliders, tweets, and the like, and simply cannot provide much information about the product or service. Often, a consumer has no choice but to click through the ad to get more information. However, even if the ad is constrained like this, it is not exempt from disclosure requirements if it makes a claim that requires qualification.

Where possible, it is best to incorporate the disclosure into the ad itself, though sometimes a disclosure must be too detailed to make effectively with constrained space and may be communicated by linking to another web page. In determining whether to incorporate the disclosure into the main ad itself, the FTC has said advertisers should consider the following factors:

- how important the information is to prevent deception;
- the amount of information that needs to be disclosed;
- the burden of disclosing the information in the ad itself;
- how much information the consumer will be able to absorb from the ad; and
- how effective the disclosure would be if it were made on the website.[82]

4.3 Hyperlinks

Sometimes information will be too complicated to integrate into the same page as the headline claim. For example, a disclosure might say "Service plan required. Get service plan prices," where the underlined portion represents a hyperlink to details about additional fees that are impossible to make part of the main page.

The FTC has set forth the following guidelines for using hyperlinks to lead to a disclosure:[83]

- make the link obvious;
- label the hyperlink appropriately to convey the importance, nature, and relevance of the information it leads to;
- use hyperlink styles consistently, so consumers know when a link is available;

80. *Id.*
81. *Id.*
82. *Id.* at 15.
83. *Id.* at 10–14.

- place the hyperlink as close as possible to the relevant information it qualifies and make it noticeable;
- take consumers directly to the disclosure on the click-through page; and
- assess the effectiveness of the hyperlink by monitoring click-through rates and other information about consumer use and make changes accordingly.[84]
- The key considerations for evaluating the effectiveness of all hyperlinks are the following:[85]
- the labeling or description of the hyperlink;
- consistency in the use of hyperlink styles;
- the placement and prominence of the hyperlink on the web page or screen; and
- the handling of the disclosure on the click-through page or screen.[86]

The clear and conspicuous standard applies to hyperlink labels too, so care must be taken to choose an appropriate label for the hyperlink so that consumers understand what information they are being directed to. The FTC recommends the following:[87]

- make it obvious (consumers must understand they can click the link to get more information);
- label the link to convey the importance, nature, and relevance of the information to which it leads;
- don't hide the ball (i.e., obfuscate why a claim is being qualified);
- don't be subtle (symbols or icons are not enough; use plain language to describe the link);
    - o The FTC has stated that links that simply say "disclaimer," "more information," "details," "terms and conditions," or "fine print" do not convey the importance and relevance of the information they lead to and are thus inadequate.[88]
- account for technological limitations and differences by considering how your linking technique will work on various devices.[89]

Other important considerations to ensure that hyperlinks are clear and conspicuous include:[90]

---

84. *Id.* at ii.
85. *Id.* at 10–14.
86. *Id.* at 11.
87. *Id.* at 10–14.
88. *Id.* at 12.
89. *Id.* at 11–12.
90. *Id.* at 12–13.

- being consistent in hyperlink styles across a website so consumers recognize what it is;
- placing the link near relevant information and making it noticeable;
- making it easy to get to the disclosure on the click-through;
- being mindful of technical limitations in that some browsers or devices may not support certain techniques for displaying hyperlinks; and
- refraining from disclosure of necessary information in pop-ups, which may be blocked by pop-up blocking software.

5. CFPB Regulation of Deceptive Practices

Although for the past several decades the FTC has played the largest role in defining the parameters of deception law, the passage of the Consumer Financial Protection Act as part of the Dodd-Frank Act in 2010 established the Consumer Financial Protection Bureau as a major new force in regulating deceptive acts or practices.

5.1 Unfair, Deceptive, or Abusive Acts and Practices Exam Procedures

The CFPB's exam procedures manual for UDAAP outlines the Bureau's views on deceptive acts or practices.[91] The procedures specifically cite the FTC Deception Statement in outlining the Bureau's definition of what constitutes a deceptive act or practice, namely:

> A representation, omission, act, or practice is deceptive when
>
> (1) the representation, omission, act, or practice misleads or is likely to mislead the consumer;
>
> (2) the consumer's interpretation of the representation, omission, act, or practice is reasonable under the circumstances; and
>
> (3) the misleading representation, omission, act, or practice is material.[92]

The Bureau cites specific examples that stem from federal enforcement actions to illustrate the CFPB's views on what constitutes deception.

- **Inadequate disclosure of material lease terms in television advertising.**[93] The FTC brought actions against vehicle leasing

---

91. *Supervision and Examination Manual, supra* note 7, at 5, 7.

92. *Id.* at 5.

93. *See* Press Release, Fed. Trade Comm'n, FTC Drives to End the Blur in Car Leasing Ads (Nov. 21, 1996), https://www.ftc.gov/news-events/press-releases/1996/11/ftc-drives-end-blur-car-leasing-ads.

companies alleging that their television advertisements represented that consumers could lease vehicles for "$0 down" when advertising a monthly lease payment. Buried in the fine print, however, was a disclosure of costs of at least $1,000, which the FTC alleged was deceptive. The FTC required that if the companies make any representation about the amounts due at lease signing, or that there is "no down payment," the companies must make an equally prominent (readable and audible) disclosure of the total amount of all fees due when consumers sign the lease. The representation of "$0 down" was likely to mislead because the disclosure of the costs flashed by too quickly for a consumer to read it. A reasonable consumer would believe they would not have to put any money down.

- **Misrepresentation about loan terms.**[94] In 2004, the FTC sued a mortgage broker advertising mortgage refinance loans at "3.5% fixed payment 30-year loan" or "3.5% fixed payment for 30 years," implying that the offer was for a 30-year loan with a 3.5 percent fixed interest rate. Instead, the FTC claimed that the broker offered adjustable rate mortgages (ARMs) with an option to pay various amounts, including a minimum monthly payment that represented only a portion of the required interest. As a result, unpaid interest was added to the principal of the loan, resulting in negative amortization. The claims were deceptive because they compared apples to oranges, that is, payments on a fully amortized mortgage to payments on a nonamortizing loan with payments increasing after the first year.

Although a change to the underlying facts could alter the deception analysis, the Bureau's discussion of these cases in its exam procedures manual indicates that the Bureau adheres to the long-standing principles of deception followed by the FTC and fleshed out through the past several decades of enforcement actions.

5.2 Supervisory Highlights

The CFPB periodically releases Supervisory Highlights to share key examination findings and to help supervised entities limit risks to consumers and comply with federal consumer financial laws. The Bureau's Supervisory Highlights provide examples of areas the Bureau is scrutinizing for deceptive acts or practices, such as the following:

- With respect to ancillary products in the auto finance space, applying the total number of miles a financed vehicle was driven to calculate

94. Fed. Trade Comm'n v. Chase Fin. Funding, Inc., No. SACV04-549 (C.D. Cal. May 28, 2004) (order granting stipulated preliminary injunction).

a rebate for extended-warranty cancellations, rather than the net number of miles driven since the borrower purchased the vehicle.[95]

- Representing that payments made through an institution's online bill-pay service would be debited on the date selected by the consumer while failing to disclose that where a payee only accepts a paper check, the debit may occur earlier.[96]
- Misrepresenting mortgage insurance cancellation denial reasons.[97]

5.3 Unfair, Deceptive, or Abusive Acts or Practices Bulletins

The CFPB has issued a small number of guidance bulletins touching on deception. Guidance bulletins address the Bureau's concerns with problematic practices at a broad level, typically without identifying the problematic practices as violations of the CFPA.[98] Guidance bulletins are directed at institutions the CFPB supervises and can be helpful to identify acts or practices the Bureau believes are violations.

- **Prohibition of Unfair, Deceptive, or Abusive Acts or Practices in the Collection of Consumer Debts:**[99] In 2013, the CFPB issued a bulletin on debt collection describing general UDAAP standards, providing a list of examples of conduct that could constitute unfair, deceptive, or abusive acts or practices. Although the CFPB did not specify which legal theories applied to which conduct—that is, unfairness, deception, or abusiveness—it pointed to the following misrepresentations that could constitute a deceptive act:
  - o Misrepresenting the character, amount or legal status of a debt;
  - o Misrepresenting that a communication is from the government or an entity affiliated with the government;
  - o Misrepresenting whether information will be reported to a reporting agency;
  - o Misrepresenting that a debt will be forgiven if a settlement offer is accepted; and
  - o Threatening actions that are not intended or the person does not have authorization to pursue, including false threats of lawsuits, arrest, prosecution, or imprisonment.

---

95. *CFPB Supervisory Highlights*, CFPB (Winter 2019), 3–4, https://www.consumerfinance.gov/policy-compliance/guidance/supervisory-highlights/.

96. *Id.* at 5.

97. *Id.* at 7–8.

98. The CFPB's guidance bulletins may be found at https://www.consumerfinance.gov.

99. CFPB Bulletin 2013-07, *Prohibition of Unfair, Deceptive, or Abusive Acts or Practices in the Collection of Consumer Debts* (July 10, 2013), https://files.consumerfinance.gov/f/201307_cfpb_bulletin_unfair-deceptive-abusive-practices.pdf.

- **Marketing of Credit Card Add-On Products:**[100] The guidance bulletin addresses deceptive marketing and sales practices with respect to credit cards. Credit card issuers market various add-on products to consumers, including credit score tracking, debt protection, and identity theft protection products. The Bureau is concerned with issuers failing to disclose important terms and conditions about these products when they are sold. According to the Bureau, its supervisory experience uncovered instances where consumers were enrolled in such programs without their consent or without realizing they were required to pay for the programs, as well as being billed for services that were not actually performed. It notes that marketers of credit card add-on products should take steps to avoid deceptive acts, such as:
    - Ensuring marketing materials reflect the actual terms of the product; and
    - With respect to scripts for telemarketers, directing customer service representatives to state the terms and conditions of the products, prohibiting enrollment of consumers without clear affirmative consent, and making clear that the purchase of add-on products is not required as a condition of obtaining credit unless there actually is such a requirement.
- **Marketing of Credit Card Promotional Offers:**[101] The bulletin warns credit card issuers of the risk of deceptive practices regarding certain promotional offers, warning that offers providing for zero or low interest rates for balance transfers or other advances without clear disclosures to consumers that accepting the offer may lead to the consumer losing the grace period to make payments on a new purchase may constitute a deceptive act or practice. Specifically, the Bureau remarked:

> Card issuers often market these promotional offers as a chance for the consumer to save money. Many solicitations emphasize the promotional rate associated with the offer, and that the promotional rate will last for a certain period of time—in some cases, well over a year. Depending on the facts and circumstances, the impression conveyed by these materials may be that the only cost of obtaining the promotional interest rate is the transaction fee set forth in the tabular disclosure required by Regulation Z, or that the promotional rate is the only rate at which the consumer will incur interest charges.

100. CFPB Bulletin 2012-06, *Marketing of Credit Card Add-on Products* (July 18, 2012), https://files.consumerfinance.gov/f/201207_cfpb_bulletin_marketing_of_credit_card_addon_products.pdf.

101. CFPB Bulletin 2014-02, *Marketing of Credit Card Promotional APR Offers* (Sept. 3, 2014), https://files.consumerfinance.gov/f/201409_cfpb_bulletin_marketing-credit-card-promotional-apr-offers.pdf.

The Bureau pointed to the following specific practices as deceptive:

Card issuers not adequately conveying that promotional rate offers come with an additional contingent cost that would be important to consumers who maintain a grace period on purchases; and

Issuers not including any information about the loss of the grace period for affected consumers in promotional rate marketing materials.

- **Additional Fees for Paying Bills by Telephone:**[102] The Bureau has warned about charging extra fees when a creditor wishes to pay his or her amount owed over the telephone. The bulletin warns that the following practices may be deceptive:
    - o Failing to disclose the prices of all available phone pay fees when different phone pay options carry materially different fees;
    - o Misrepresenting the available payments options or that a fee is required to pay by phone; and
    - o Failing to disclose that a phone pay fee would be added to a consumer's payment could create the misimpression that there was no service fee.

Furthermore, lack of employee monitoring or service provider oversight may lead to misrepresentations or failure to disclose available options and fees.

6. Recent Deception Cases

In *FTC v. Avant, LLC*, the FTC announced a settlement with an online lender agreeing to settle charges it engaged in deceptive and unfair loan servicing practices.[103] The complaint alleges the lender engaged in deceptive practices by:

- Representing that it would accept payments by credit or debit cards where in fact it in numerous instances rejected such payment methods;[104] and
- Representing that if consumers paid a specified amount, their loan would be paid off where in numerous instances after making this representation, after consumers paid the specified amount, the lender insisted the loan had not been paid off.[105]

102. CFPB Compliance Bulletin 2017-01, *Phone Pay Fees* (July 31, 2017), https://files.consumerfinance.gov/f/documents/201707_cfpb_compliance-bulletin-phone-pay-fee.pdf.

103. Press Release, Fed. Trade Comm'n, Online Lending Co. Agrees to Settle FTC Charges (Apr. 15, 2019), https://www.ftc.gov/news-events/press-releases/2019/04/online-lending-company-agrees-settle-ftc-charges-it-engaged.

104. Complaint ¶¶ 35–37, Fed. Trade Comm'n v. Avant, LLC 1:19-cv-02517 (N.D. Ill.).

105. Id. ¶¶ 41–43.

This case reflects the FTC's view that the same deception standards apply to online lending and other new forms of financial technology.

In *FTC v. LendingClub*, the Commission targeted a lender who allegedly falsely promised consumers that they would receive a specific loan amount with "no hidden fees," when, in actuality, the company deducted hundreds or even thousands of dollars in hidden up-front fees from the loans.[106] The FTC also alleged that after consumers completed loan applications and the lender conducted its front-end review of their applications, but before it had made a final decision whether to approve their loans, the lender represented that those consumers would receive loans when in many instances the lender later made a final decision not to approve the loans.[107]

In *FTC v. SoFi*, the FTC demonstrated why lenders must be careful not to omit important information when making claims, and be aware that burying important information in the fine print cannot cure an omission. The FTC brought an enforcement action against one student lender for claiming "Refinancing student loans saves $22,359 on average," and urging readers to "Start saving on your student loans. Average monthly savings $292."[108] The FTC alleged the savings touted in the advertisements inflated the actual average savings because they omitted large categories of consumers from the calculations. For example, the FTC alleged the lender excluded borrowers whose loans had a longer term than the previous loans those students refinanced. While these exclusions were disclosed, the FTC found they were insufficient because they were only listed in fine print.[109]

In *FTC v. LeadClick Media*, the Second Circuit found a company liable for the deceptive acts of affiliate marketers in its network advertising weight loss products even though the company itself did not disseminate the deceptive materials.[110] Because LeadClick played an active role in the scheme by hiring the affiliate marketers, approving fake news sites about the product, buying advertising space, and providing content for the advertising, the court found the company's actions in furtherance of the deceptive scheme sufficiently material to hold LeadClick primarily liable, to the same extent as the parties that actually made the deceptive statements, not just vicariously.[111] The court explained:

> As the manager of the affiliate network, LeadClick had a responsibility to ensure that the advertisements produced by its affiliate network were not deceptive or misleading. By failing to do so and allowing the use of fake news sites on its network, despite its knowledge of the deception,

106. First Amend. Complaint ¶¶ 16–24, 56–58, Fed. Trade Comm'n v. LendingClub Corp. 3:18-cv-02454-JSC (N.D. Cal. Apr. 25, 2018).

107. *Id.* ¶¶ 59–61.

108. Complaint ¶¶ 5–12, Soc. Fin., Inc. 162-3197 (F.T.C. Oct. 29, 2018).

109. *Id.* ¶ 10.

110. Fed. Trade Comm'n v. LeadClick Media, Inc. 15-1009-cv, 15-1014-cv (2d Cir. Sept. 23, 2016).

111. *Id.* slip op. at 29–33.

> LeadClick engaged in a deceptive practice for which it may be held directly liable under the FTC Act.[112]

The Second Circuit essentially held that a company can be held directly liable for the deceptive acts of another if it could have controlled the practices or knew or should have known they were unlawful.

In *BCFP et al. v. Sterling Jewelers, Inc.*, the Bureau announced a settlement with a nationwide jewelry retailer, alleging the company engaged in deceptive practices by:[113]

> "[R]epresent[ing] to consumers that they were completing a survey, enrolling in a rewards program, or checking to see how much they would qualify to spend in the store when, in fact, the consumers were completing credit-card applications or Sterling's employees were completing applications for consumers without their knowledge or consent."

The Bureau alleged that these misrepresentations were likely to mislead consumers acting reasonably under the circumstances because consumers believed they were providing personal information for other purposes and consumers relied on store employees' representations that consumers were doing something other than applying for a credit card.[114] The Bureau alleged the misrepresentations were material because many consumers likely would not have provided their personal information and signature if they knew they were applying for credit, given that they may not have wanted an extension of credit or the potential negative impact it could have on their credit file or ability to obtain credit in the future.[115]

In *CFPB v. Progrexion Marketing, Inc.* the Bureau sued credit service organizations who contacted consumers across the country through telemarketing campaigns, where a credit service organization's subsidiary would call consumers and transfer them to another defendant who signed them up for credit repair services.[116] The core of the deception theories here is that the defendants promised consumers would receive certain products or services when they had no reasonable basis to make that claim. The complaint alleged:

112. *Id.* slip op. at 32.

113. Complaint ¶ 55, Bureau Consumer Fin. Protection et al. v. Sterling Jewelers, Inc. 1:19-cv-00448 (S.D.N.Y. Jan. 16, 2019).

114. *Id.* ¶ 56.

115. *Id.* ¶ 57.

116. Complaint ¶¶ 74–85, Bureau Consumer Fin. Protection v. Progrexion, 2:19-cv-00298-DBP (D. Utah May 2, 2019).

- One of the defendants' websites stated that enrolling in its service guaranteed any consumer "a 0–3.5% down" mortgage "no matter how bad their Credit is when we start";
- Another defendant's website represented that the company had helped "over 15,000 people buy a home that started with under a 500 Credit Score when they came to [defendant]";
- One of the defendants' ads offered housing that was not actually available and instead routed interested consumers to another defendant;
- Defendants' Facebook advertisements often referenced a "90-day Blitz" program offering home financing in a very short timeframe with express promises such as: "BUY A HOME IN THE NEXT 30–90 DAYS NO MATTER WHERE YOUR CREDIT IS NOW"; and
- Other advertisements said: "Are you tired of dead ends? Games? Gimmicks? Bad Houses and Fake Ads? Would You like to END all that? We know you would. . . . We … have helped over 12,000 people get homes who NEVER thought they could."

The Bureau alleged defendants engaged in deceptive acts because they told consumers, without any review of their credit history or other eligibility factors, that their credit score was the only thing keeping them from their desired product. For example, one telemarketing script told consumers "you'd be the perfect candidate for rent-to-own, but your credit is the only thing holding you back—this makes you a great match for credit repair."[117] However, the Bureau found that the product or service was not available and determined the claims were deceptive.

In *FTC v. Equifax, Inc.*, Equifax, Inc. agreed to pay at least $575 million as part of a global settlement with the FTC, CFPB, and United States and territories to settle allegations that, among other things, it committed deceptive acts by representing it safeguarded consumer personal information when in fact it did not.[118] The FTC alleged that Equifax failed to secure its information network systems, resulting in a data breach that exposed the personal information of millions of consumers, including names, dates of birth, social security numbers, and addresses.[119] The FTC alleged that the company failed to fix flaws in its security systems after becoming aware of them before the breach, although t its privacy policy at the time stated that it limited access to consumers' personal information and implemented "reasonable physical, technical and procedural safeguards" to protect consumer data.[120] The deceptive acts turned specifically on the fact that the company allegedly represented

117. *Id.* at ¶ 85.

118. Complaint ¶¶ 39–41, Fed. Trade Comm'n v. Equifax, Inc. 1:19-cv-03297-TWT (N.D. Ga.); *see also* Press Release, Fed. Trade Comm'n, Equifax to Pay $575 Million as Part of Settlement (July 22, 2019), https://www.ftc.gov/news-events/press-releases/2019/07/equifax-pay-575-million-part-settlement-ftc-cfpb-states-related.

119. Equifax, Inc., *supra* note 118.

120. *Id.*

that it limited access to personal information to employees having a reasonable need to access this information, and that it had reasonable physical, technical, and procedural safeguards to protect personal information for its direct-to-consumer offerings, including credit monitoring and identity theft management services, when this was not in fact the case.[121]

121. *Id.*, Complaint ¶ 39.

CHAPTER

2C

The Unfairness Prong

Matthew O. Stromquist and Robin L. Dull

This chapter provides an overview of the statutory framework and recent federal agency action involving allegations of unfair conduct with respect to consumer financial products and services, pursuant to the Consumer Financial Protection Bureau's (CFPB's or Bureau's) authority under the Consumer Financial Protection Act of 2010 (CFPA) and the Federal Trade Commission's (FTC's) authority under the Federal Trade Commission Act (FTC Act).[1,2] Broadly speaking, the prohibition against unfair acts and practices aims to protect consumers from suffering material and unavoidable injuries that do not make the market more competitive. Although the CFPA was only recently enacted, federal authority to prohibit *unfair* acts or practices was originally enshrined in the FTC Act in 1938, and thus has been interpreted by and applied in case law and policy memoranda for decades. In interpreting and applying this concept, federal agencies and the courts routinely refer to and draw from a long history that has given rise to a "well-developed and long-established" definition.[3]

1. Pub. L. No. 111-203, tit. X, 124 Stat. 1376, 1955 (codified as amended at 12 U.S.C. §§ 5481–5603).

2. *See* Pub. L. No. 109-455, 120 Stat. 3372 (2006) (codified as amended at 15 U.S.C. § 45(a)(1)).

3. Consumer Fin. Prot. Bureau v. ITT Educ. Servs., Inc., 219 F. Supp. 3d 878, 902 (S.D. Ind. 2015).

1. The Statutory Standard

Section 1036(a)(1)(B) of the CFPA makes it unlawful for a covered entity to engage in any unfair practice.[4] An act or practice is unfair under the CFPA where:

> (A) the act or practice causes or is likely to cause substantial injury to consumers;
> (B) which is not reasonably avoidable by consumers; and
> (C) such substantial injury is not outweighed by countervailing benefits to consumers or to competition.[5]

The prohibition on unfairness focuses on a likely and substantial injury that is not avoidable or outweighed by other benefits, and thus, given its scope, arguably has the potential for a broader application as compared to its *deceptive* and *abusive* counterparts.[6]

The FTC has historically rooted the substantial injury analysis in determining whether, objectively, there has been substantial monetary harm, or at least substantial risk of such harm.[7] This also constitutes the starting point for the approach by the CFPB, but the Bureau has stated that emotional harm alone may constitute substantial injury in certain circumstances.[8] Substantial injury may include severe injury to a relatively small number of people, or, conversely, a relatively smaller injury, but

4. For a discussion of covered entities, see chapter 2A.

5. 12 U.S.C. § 5531(c)(1). The FTC Act contains the identical standard. *See* 15 U.S.C. § 45(n).

6. *See* chapters 2B and 2D on deception and abusiveness, respectively; *see also In re* Int'l Harvester Co., 104 F.T.C. 949, 1984 WL 565290, at *88 (Dec. 21,1984) ("[The unfairness] part of our jurisdiction is broader than that involving deception . . . ."). Yet agencies and courts have long recognized that facts relevant to unfairness and deception claims frequently overlay. *See, e.g.*, Orkin Exterminating Co. v. FTC, 849 F.2d 1354, 1367 (11th Cir. 1988) ("[A] practice may be both deceptive and unfair . . . ."); Am. Fin. Servs. Ass'n v. FTC, 767 F.2d 957, 980 n.27 (D.C. Cir. 1985) ("The FTC has determined that . . . making unsubstantiated advertising claims may be both an unfair and a deceptive practice.").

7. Letter to Wendell H. Ford, Chairman, Consumer Subcommittee, Committee on Commerce, Science, and Transportation, et al., from Michael Pertschuk, Chairman, CFPB, et al., on FTC Policy Statement on Unfairness (Dec. 17, 1980) [hereinafter FTC Policy Statement], https://www.ftc.gov/public-statements/1980/12/ftc-policy-statement-unfairness. Outside the financial world, substantial injuries may also include threats to health or safety. *Id.*

8. CFPB Bulletin, *Prohibition of Unfair, Deceptive, or Abusive Acts or Practices in the Collection of Consumer Debts* 2 [hereinafter CFPB UDAAP Bulletin] (July 10, 2013), https://files.consumerfinance.gov/f/201307_cfpb_bulletin_unfair-deceptive-abusive-practices.pdf.; CFPB, *Supervision and Examination Manual* 174 n.2 (2d version 2012) [hereinafter Supervision and Examination Manual], http://files.consumerfinance.gov/f/201210_cfpb_supervision-and-examination-manual-v2.pdf.

which impacts a large class of people.[9] For the second element, an injury generally is "reasonably avoidable" where "consumers had a free and informed choice;"[10] that is, where consumers "have reason to anticipate the impending harm and the means to avoid it," or if consumers are aware of, and are reasonably capable of pursuing, potential avenues toward mitigating the injury after the fact.[11] This element seeks to assure that consumers have information necessary to make informed choices, or, as the FTC calls it, "the free exercise of consumer decision making."[12] The CFPB has clarified that an injury is not reasonably avoidable if the consumer can avoid the injury only by expending significant money or other resources.[13]

The third element then measures whether the net negative effects (the substantial injury) is outweighed by potential net positive effects (the countervailing benefits). Generally, the unfairness of the practice is not outweighed when it "produces clear adverse consequences for consumers that are not accompanied by an increase in services or benefits to consumers or by benefits to competition . . ."[14]

In order to declare that an act or practice is unfair, the agency must have a reasonable basis to conclude that these standards are met.[15] The CFPA also provides that the Bureau, in determining whether an act or practice is unfair, "may consider established public policies as evidence to be considered with all other evidence," but that such public policy considerations "may not serve as a primary basis for such determination."[16] Additionally the CFPB Supervision and Examination Manual provides that the interpretation and application of the unfairness standard by the FTC and federal banking regulators, "through case law, official policy statements, guidance, examination procedures, and enforcement actions" may inform CFPB in its own interpretation, application, and enforcement of the standard.[17]

Therefore, any interpretation or application of the unfairness standard, while always beginning with the statutory text itself, almost never ends there because that somewhat amorphous definition has been "given concrete shape by successive generations of interpretation and refinement."[18] That is not to say that the unfairness standard has been static—it has not—but it has long been rooted in a concern that

---

9. *See Orkin Exterminating*, 849 F.2d 1365 (11th Cir. 1988); FTC v. Windward Mktg., Ltd. No. Civ.-A. 1:96-CV-615F, 1997 WL 33642380, at *11 (N.D. Ga. Sept. 30, 1997).

10. FTC v. Neovi, Inc., 604 F.3d 1150, 1158 (9th Cir. 2010).

11. *Orkin Exterminating*, 849 F.2d at 1365–66.

12. FTC Policy Statement, *supra* note 7. The CFPB's Bulletin provides that an injury is not "reasonably avoidable" when it "interferes with or hinders a consumer's ability to make informed decisions or take action to avoid that injury"; CFPB UDAAP Bulletin, *supra* note 8, at 3.

13. *Id.*

14. *Windward Mktg.*, 1997 WL 33642380, at *11.

15. *Id.*

16. 12 U.S.C. § 5531(c)(2).

17. Supervision and Examination Manual, *supra* note 8.

18. *ITT Educ. Svcs*, 2015 WL 1013508, at *17.

the act or practice causes or is likely to cause substantial injury to consumers.[19] For that reason, at least in part, courts have largely rejected arguments that the unfairness standard is unconstitutionally vague.[20]

2. Recent Application

On the federal level, unfairness claims exert force through governmental actions. As noted above, throughout most of its history, the unfairness claims have been enforced by the FTC, but the enactment of the CFPA vested enforcement authority with the CFPB with respect to consumer financial products and services. However, the FTC retains some unfairness enforcement authority, as do other regulators, including the federal bank regulatory agencies.[21,22] There is no private right of action to bring an unfairness claim under the federal unfair, deceptive, and abusive acts or practices (UDAAP) laws.[23] The Bureau's unfairness authority extends to three areas: rulemaking, supervision, and enforcement. These authorities are discussed in turn below.

2.1 Rulemaking

The Dodd-Frank Act vests with the CFPB the authority to engage in rulemaking to interpret the statute's unfairness provisions.[24] Despite calls from advocates, the private sector, and Congress, the Bureau has thus far declined to exercise that authority. Echoing Congress's early refusal to enumerate unfair practices, the Bureau has rejected promulgating a definitive list of prohibited acts or practices that would be deemed unfair. Instead, the Bureau has made its view of unfair practices known through supervisory activities and enforcement actions.

---

19. *See* FTC v. Sperry & Hutchinson Co., 405 U.S. 233, 250 n.5 (1972) (describing the FTC's criteria for whether a practice is unfair as whether the practice is immoral, unethical, oppressive, or unscrupulous, and whether it causes substantial injury to consumers); *accord Spiegel, Inc. v. FTC*, 540 F.2d 287, 293 (7th Cir. 1976)).

20. *ITT Educ. Servs.*, 2015 WL 1013508, at *18 (finding that the argument that the unfairness standard is unconstitutionally vague "falters in the face of a century's worth of legislative and judicial guidance establishing and refining the term's meaning").

21. 15 U.S.C. § 45.

22. *See* 12 U.S.C. §§ 1818(b) and (i).

23. Moore v. N.Y. Cotton Exchange, 270 U.S. 593, 603 (1926).

24. 12 U.S.C. § 5531(b).

2.2 Supervision

In exercising its supervisory authority, the Bureau has issued a Supervision and Examination Manual.[25] The manual helps on-the-ground examiners advance the Bureau's supervisory examinations, including regularly scheduled company-specific exams (which look at all activities of a particular lender or servicer), targeted reviews (which look at a specific product or service at a single institution, generally arising from a particular concern from the Bureau), horizontal reviews (reviewing a product or practice, such as mortgage servicing, for example, across multiple institutions in the industry), or limited-scope exams (for example, reviewing an institution's compliance management system).[26]

The Supervision and Examination Manual includes a section on UDAAP with a focus on unfairness claims.[27] In addition to setting forth the elements of the claim and providing additional commentary on the contours of the elements, the manual offers several examples of unfairness claims based on federal enforcement actions. For instance, the manual explains that refusing to release a lien after the consumer makes final payments on a mortgage may be unfair.[28] In this example, the consumer sustained economic injury when the mortgage servicer did not release the liens on properties after the consumer had paid the total amount owing on the mortgages. There were no countervailing benefits from the servicer's alleged failure to properly service the loan and promptly release the lien, and consumers had no way of knowing in advance that the servicer would fail to release the lien. In addition, because particular loan servicers are selected by the mortgage holder and imposed on consumers, consumers could not reasonably avoid the injury.[29] The manual provides additional exemplars of unfairness with respect to dishonoring credit card convenience checks without notice and processing payments for companies engaged in fraudulent activities.[30]

In the Examination Procedures section of the manual, the Bureau provides general guidance for examiners to consider, as well as specific exam procedures related to unfairness issues in management, policy, and transactions.[31] As with other areas of Bureau supervision, the manual directs examiners to consider consumer complaints that may be helpful in revealing unfair practices by an institution and notes that a high volume of charge-backs or refunds for a product or service may also be an indicator of an unfair practice.

In addition to the Supervision and Examination Manual, the Bureau has reported supervisory findings of unfairness in its semiregular *Supervisory Highlights*

25. *See, generally*, Supervision and Examination Manual, *supra* note 8.
26. *Id.*
27. *Id.* at pt. II.C.
28. *Id.*, pt. II.C at UDAAP 3.
29. *Id.*, pt. II.C at UDAAP 3–4.
30. *Id.*, pt. II.C at UDAAP 4–5.
31. *Id.* at pt. III.

publication.[32] The CFPB has found unfairness in numerous aspects of consumer financial products and services, including those shown in the table.

Industry	Practice identified as unfair by CFPB
Automobile loan servicing[33]	(i) Incorrect calculation of rebates for ancillary products, (ii) repossessions, (iii) repossessions of borrower vehicles after borrowers make catch-up payments or enter agreements to avoid repossession, (iv) broad waivers in short sale and cash-for-keys agreements, (v) repossession fees and refusal to return property.
Mortgage servicing[34]	(i) Charging consumers unauthorized amounts, (ii) converting trial modifications to permanent status, (iii) paying the wrong consumer's insurance premiums with escrow funds, (iv) loss mitigation, (v) foreclosure process, (vi) servicing transfers, (vii) waivers of rights in loss mitigation agreements, (viii) payment processing.
Payday lending	Debiting consumers' accounts without valid authorization by using account information previously provided for other purposes.[35]
Deposits[36]	(i) Freezing of deposit accounts, (ii) switched balance-calculation methods, (iii) overdraft processing logic.
Mortgage origination	Failure to reimburse unused portions of a required service deposit where certain disclosure language was used constituted an unfair practice.[37]

32. The publication has been less frequent in the post-Cordray era.

33. Findings related to automobile loan servicing include (i) CFPB, *Supervisory Highlights,* Winter 2019, 1, 4; (ii) *Supervisory Highlights,* Summer 2018, 1, 4; (iii) *Supervisory Highlights,* Summer 2017, 1, 5; (iv) *id.* at 22; *Supervisory Highlights,* Fall 2016, 1, 5.

34. *See* (i) CFPB, *Supervisory Highlights,* Winter 2019, 6, and Summer 2018, 1, 4; (ii) *Supervisory Highlights,* Summer 2018, 1, 4, and Fall 2014, 1, 13; (iii) *Supervisory Highlights,* Spring 2017, 1, 11; (iv) *Supervisory Highlights,* Summer 2015, 1, 15; (v) *id.* at 18; (vi) *Supervisory* Highlights, Winter 2013, 1, 5, and Summer 2013, 1, 12; (vii) *Supervisory Highlights,* Winter 2013, 1, 6; (viii) *Supervisory Highlights,* Summer 2013, 1, 12.

35. CFPB, *Supervisory Highlights,* Summer 2018, at 10.

36. *See* (i) CFPB, *Supervisory Highlights,* Summer 2017, 14; (ii) *Supervisory Highlights,* Winter 2015, 1, 8; (iii) *id.* at 9.

37. CFPB, *Supervisory Highlights,* Summer 2017, 19.

Industry	Practice identified as unfair by CFPB
Short-term, small-dollar lending[38]	(i) Workplace collection calls and visits, (ii) repeated collection calls to third parties, (iii) unauthorized debits and overpayments, (iv) inadequate compliance management systems, (v) improper collections calls.
Student loan servicing[39]	(i) Failing to reverse adverse consequences of erroneous deferment terminations, (ii) income-driven repayment plan applications, (iii) borrower choice for payment allocation, (iv) system errors, (v) auto default, (vi) failure to disclose impact of forbearance on co-signor release eligibility, (vii) servicing conversion errors costing borrowers money, (viii) allocating partial payments in a way that maximizes late fees, (ix) charging improper late fees, (x) failure to provide accurate tax information, (xi) improper telephone communications.
Debt collection	Miscoding of accounts unsuitable for sale by debt sellers,[40] overstatement of APRs in account documents.[41]

Supervisory observations often shed additional light on the Bureau's interpretation of unfairness. For example, the Bureau provided further definition to the concept of "substantial injury" when looking at mortgage servicers who charged consumers late fees greater than the amount permitted by mortgage notes. The Bureau noted that the injury was "substantial" both because: (1) consumers paid more in late fees than required by their mortgage notes (the Bureau neither specified nor gave a range of the excess amount) and (2) thousands of customers were affected, making the aggregate injury substantial.[42]

2.3 Enforcement

The CFPB has filed enforcement actions to address unfairness concerns during the administrations of Directors Richard Cordray and Kathleen L. Kraninger and Acting

38. *See* (i) CFPB, *supra* note 54, at 26–27, *and Supervisory Highlights*, Spring 2014, 1, 18; (ii) *Supervisory Highlights,* Summer 2017, 27; (iii) *id.* at 31; (iv) *Supervisory Highlights*, Spring 2014, 1, 15–16; (v) *id.* at 17–18.

39. *See* (i) *Supervisory Highlights*, Spring 2017, 12; (ii) *Supervisory Highlights,* Fall 2016, 16; (iii) *id.*, and Fall 2015, 1, 22; (iv) *Supervisory Highlights,* Fall 2016, 19, and Fall 2015, 1, 22; (v) *Supervisory Highlights,* Winter 2016, 1, 16; (vi) *id.* at 17; (vii) *id.* at 18; (viii) *Supervisory Highlights*, Fall 2014, at 1, 15; (ix) *id.* at 16; (x) *id.*; (xi) *id.* at 17.

40. CFPB, *Supervisory Highlights,* Summer 2016, 1, 6.

41. CFPB, *Supervisory Highlights*, Fall 2014, 8.

42. CFPB, *Supervisory Highlights*, Winter 2019, 6–7.

Director Mick Mulvaney, although researchers have reported that CFPB enforcement activity has "plummeted" following the resignation of Director Cordray in November 2017.[43] The Bureau has most frequently filed enforcement actions alleging deceptive claims, whereas unfairness claims have been the Bureau's second most-frequent grounds for UDAAP claims. Although claims for abusive acts also may be unfair—indeed, abusive claims are sometimes referred to as unfair "plus" claims—the legal standards for abusive and unfair are separate, and abusive claims have been the subject of enforcement actions far less frequently than claims of deception or unfairness.

Some of the Bureau's enforcement activities have grown out of supervisory observations discovered at particular institutions. For example, the Bureau issued a consent order with EZCORP, Inc., a short-term, small-dollar lender, for illegal debt collection practices that were discovered, in part, during the course of a Bureau examination.[44] The procedures for the Bureau moving from supervisory to enforcement activity, termed the ARC process, are covered elsewhere in this treatise.

The CFPB's enforcement activities for unfairness claims have also arisen from matters outside of supervision. For example, the Bureau joined with work started by the Office of the Comptroller of the Currency in issuing a consent order against JPMorgan Chase Bank and Chase Bank to refund an estimated $309 million for unfair billing practices in its credit card business.[45] Enforcement actions may also originate from internal Bureau research, marketplace observations, or complaints.

The Bureau has also exercised its unfairness authority under UDAAP against nonfinancial institutions engaged in consumer financial services transactions, arguably encroaching on territory traditionally overseen by the FTC exercising its authority under section 5 of the FTC Act. For example, the Bureau filed an enforcement proceeding against wireless carriers in which it alleged that the carriers were unfairly allowing third-party merchants to place unauthorized charges on customers' phone bills and ignoring complaints about the charges. The Bureau alleged that the wireless carrier

43. Christopher L. Peterson, Consumer Fed'n of Am., Dormant: The Consumer Financial Protection Bureau's Law Enforcement Program in Decline § 3 (Mar. 12, 2019).

44. *In re* EZCORP, Inc., et al., Consent Order, CFPB No. 2015-CFPB-0031 (Dec. 16, 2015), https://files.consumerfinance.gov/f/201512_cfpb_ezcorp-inc-consent-order.pdf.

45. *In re* JPMorgan Chase Bank, N.A. and Chase Bank USA, N.A., Consent Order, 2013-CFPB-0007 (Sept. 19, 2013), https://files.consumerfinance.gov/f/201309_cfpb_jpmc_consent-order.pdf.

was a "covered person" under the Bureau's jurisdiction based on the company's alleged payment processing and credit extension activities for consumers.[46]

The Bureau has used its unfairness authority to root out industry practices that it views as particularly harmful. For example, beginning around 2012 the Bureau brought multiple enforcement actions against banks and third-party vendors to address credit card add-on services. During that time, credit card companies often offered their customers "add-on" services. Customers were charged annual or monthly fees for these services, which typically included credit monitoring or identity theft protection services. These products were generally sold directly by the bank or through a bank-authorized third-party vendor.[47] The practices were unfair because customers were charged without or before having written authorization for monitoring services, for example, or because customers were charged for services they did not receive.[48]

3. Conclusion

The life of the unfairness claim has shown its malleability. It has grown from a narrow focus on ensuring fair competition between business competitors to keeping consumers safe from undue burdens. It has grown from enforcement by a single federal agency to having a robust role in the quiver of multiple agencies. It is the lens through which several banking regulators conduct supervisory activity. Moreover, it is likely to undergo additional mutations to address regulatory needs in the future.

---

46. Complaint ¶ 10, CFPB v. Verizon Wireless, 3:15-cv-03268 (D.N.J. May 12, 2015), ECF No. 1; Complaint ¶ 9, CFPB v. Sprint Corp., 1:14-cv-09931 (S.D.N.Y. Dec. 17, 2014), ECF No. 1; *see also* Press Release, CFPB, CFPB Takes Action to Obtain $120 Million in Redress from Sprint and Verizon for Illegal Mobile Cramming (May 12, 2015), https://www.consumerfinance.gov/about-us/newsroom/cfpb-takes-action-to-obtain-120-million-in-redress-from-sprint-and-verizon-for-illegal-mobile-cramming/ (last updated Sept. 16, 2015). The FTC filed similar actions against other telecoms. *See, e.g.*, Complaint ¶ 38, FTC v. T-Mobile Wireless, 2:14-cv-967 (W.D. Wa. 2014) ECF No. 1.

47. When the CFPB took action against Santander Consumer USA for engaging in similar practices with respect to add-on products for auto loans, it included only claims of deceptive acts and practices. *See In re* Santander Consumer USA Inc., 2018-BCFP-0008 (Nov. 20, 2018), https://files.consumerfinance.gov/f/documents/bcfp_santander-consumer-usa_consent-order_2018-11.pdf.

48. *See, e.g.*, Consent Order ¶¶ 8–9, CFPB v. JPMorgan Chase Bank, N.A. et al., 2013-CFPB-0007 (Sept. 19, 2013).

CHAPTER

2D

Abusive Acts or Practices

David N. Anthony, Ashley L. Taylor, Jr., and Alan D. Wingfield[1]

1. Introduction

For decades, the primary federal standard governing unfair or deceptive conduct was drawn from section 5 of the Federal Trade Commission Act (FTC Act),[2] which prohibits "unfair or deceptive acts or practices in or affecting commerce" (collectively, UDAP).[3] This UDAP prohibition became the standard for consumer protection and has been adopted by all fifty states in some form through their consumer-protection laws. The federal consumer-protection landscape shifted in 2010 with the enactment of the Dodd-Frank Wall Street Reform and Consumer Protection Act (Dodd-Frank Act) and its creation of the Consumer Financial Protection Bureau (CFPB or Bureau).[4] Through the Dodd-Frank Act, Congress not only gave the Bureau and state regulators the authority to enforce federal consumer-protection laws, but it also gave the Bureau the authority to prohibit unfair, deceptive, *or abusive* acts or practices (collectively, UDAAP).[5] It is important to note that states also have the power to enforce provisions of the Dodd-Frank Act and related implementing regulations, including the power to bring actions to prevent UDAAP.[6] However, state-led enforcement actions have not provided insight into the meaning of the term *abusive*.

---

1. This chapter was written with assistance from Dascher L. Pasco and Leah. A. Tedford.
2. Federal Trade Commission Act, 15 U.S.C. §§ 41–58.
3. *Id.* § 45(a)(1).
4. 12 U.S.C. § 5301–5641.
5. *Id.* § 5531 (emphasis added).
6. *Id.* § 5552.

Although the *unfairness* and *deception* standards carried over from the FTC Act,[7] the *abusiveness* standard was something of an innovation, as the Dodd-Frank Act was the first federal law to prohibit "abusive acts or practices with respect to consumer financial products and services generally."[8] Since the passage of the Dodd-Frank Act in 2010, the *abusiveness* standard has not been formally clarified by regulation. However, on January 24, 2020, the Bureau issued a Statement of Policy Regarding Prohibition on Abusive Acts or Practices providing new insight into the meaning of *abusiveness*.[9] This chapter provides context for how regulators have applied the *abusiveness* standard and examines how the Policy Statement affects future enforcement.

2. The Foundation: The Dodd-Frank Act and Its Text

The legislation that became the Dodd-Frank Act was first introduced in Congress in 2009 in the wake of what the Department of Treasury labeled "the most severe financial crisis since the Great Depression."[10] Although myriad factors caused that economic recession, the Department of Treasury's report on financial and regulatory reform concluded that "[g]aps and weaknesses in the supervision and regulation of financial firms presented challenges to our government's ability to monitor, prevent, or address risks as they built up in the system."[11] This report, one of the earliest documents Congress considered in adopting the Dodd-Frank Act, states that a "key objective" of future legislation is the protection of consumers and investors from "financial abuse" through increased supervision of financial firms.[12] Congress passed the Dodd-Frank Act and created the Bureau to address these concerns.[13]

7. Courts interpreting the "unfair" and "deceptive" prohibitions of the Dodd-Frank Act have generally acknowledged that the FTC Act's use of those terms informs the meaning of the Dodd-Frank Act; *e.g.*, Consumer Fin. Prot. Bureau v. ITT Educ. Servs., Inc., 219 F. Supp. 3d 878, 903 (S.D. Ind. 2015).

8. Consumer Financial Protection Bureau, Statement of Policy Regarding Prohibition on Abusive Acts or Practices, 85 Fed. Reg. 6733 (Feb. 6, 2020), https://www.govinfo.gov/content/pkg/FR-2020-02-06/pdf/2020-01661.pdf [hereinafter, "Policy Statement"].

9. *Id.*

10. Dep't of the Treasury, *Financial and Regulatory Reform: A New Foundation* 2 (2009), http://www.treasury.gov/initiatives/Documents/FinalReport_web.pdf.

11. *Id.*

12. *See id.* at 3 ("We propose: a new Consumer Financial Protection Agency to protect consumers across the financial sector from unfair, deceptive, and abusive practices.").

13. *See* Pub. L. No. 111-203, 124 Stat. 1376 (codified at 12 U.S.C. § 5301–5641 (2010)), http://www.govinfo.gov/content/pkg/PLAW-111publ203/pdf/PLAW-111publ203.pdf.

2.1 Dodd-Frank's Abusiveness Standard and Statutory Interpretation

Basic principles of statutory interpretation require that *abusive* mean something different than *unfair* and *deceptive* in the Dodd-Frank Act.[14] Even the Bureau has said that "[a]lthough abusive acts also may be unfair or deceptive, . . . the legal standards for abusive, unfair, and deceptive each are separate."[15] Nevertheless, the text of the statute provides limited guidance. That is not to say the term is undefined. Rather, Congress stated in section 1031(d) of the Dodd-Frank Act that the Bureau cannot declare an act or practice *abusive* unless that act or practice:

> (1) materially interferes with the ability of a consumer to understand a term or condition of a consumer financial product or service; or
> (2) takes unreasonable advantage of—
> (A) a lack of understanding on the part of the consumer of the material risks, costs, or conditions of the product or service;
> (B) the inability of the consumer to protect the interests of the consumer in selecting or using a consumer financial product or service; or
> (C) the reasonable reliance by the consumer on a covered person to act in the interest of the consumer.[16]

The plain language of the disjunctive statute indicates that an act or practice may be *abusive* if it meets the criteria set forth in any single prong of section 1031(d). However, the statute provides no additional guidance as to the meaning of this broad language. Therefore, we look to basic canons of statutory interpretation and the Bureau's enforcement actions to gain clarity on the meaning of *abusive*.

2.2 *"Abusive"* Is Distinct from *"Unfair"* and *"Deceptive"*

Applying the canon of *expressio unius alterius exclusio*, or, "to express or include one thing implies the exclusion of the other,"[17] reveals three primary differences between *abusive*, *unfair*, and *deceptive* as defined in the Dodd-Frank Act.[18]

---

14. Corley v. United States, 556 U.S. 303, 314 (2009) ("[O]ne of the most basic interpretive canons [is] that a statute should be construed so that effect is given to all its provisions, so that no part will be inoperative or superfluous, void or insignificant.") (internal quotations omitted).

15. CFPB, *Supervision and Examination Manual,* at UDAAP 9 (Sept. 2020), https://www.consumerfinance.gov/documents/6370/cfpb_supervision-and-examination-manual.pdf.

16. 12 U.S.C. § 5531(d).

17. *Black's Law Dictionary* (11th ed. 2019).

18. These principles of interpretation mirror those discussed by eight panelists at the Bureau's Symposium: Abusive Acts or Practices. *See infra* nn.20, 72.

2.2.1 Abusiveness Requires No Proof of Harm

First, *unfairness* in the Dodd-Frank Act must cause, or likely cause, injury rising to the level of *substantial injury*.[19] In contrast, the definition of *abusive* does not have a proof-of-harm requirement. It simply prohibits acts that "materially interfere[ ] with the ability of a consumer to understand a term or condition of a consumer financial product or service" or "take[ ] unreasonable advantage of" certain attributes of the consumer.[20]

2.2.2 Abusiveness Requires Fewer Reasonableness Inquiries

Second, *abusive* does not have *reasonableness* qualifiers in two crucial places. The first is the absence of a *reasonable* basis to ground the Bureau's conclusion that an action is *abusive*. To determine that an action is *unfair*, the Bureau need only have "a reasonable basis to conclude" that the act or practice meets the definition of *unfairness*.[21] In contrast, the definition of *abusive* has no *reasonable basis* language. That omission implies that the Bureau may not declare an act *abusive* "unless the act or practice" undoubtedly meets the definition provided.[22]

The second qualifier missing in *abusive*, but present in *unfair*, modifies the consumer's actions. Although the Bureau may prosecute *unfair* actions only where those actions are likely to cause consumers injury that is not *reasonably avoidable*,[23] the lack of a similar reasonableness qualifier in *abusive* means an action may be *abusive* even where the consumer's "lack of understanding" or "inability . . . to protect [his] interests" was *unreasonable*.[24] The statute simply prohibits a *covered person*[25] from "tak[ing] unreasonable advantage" of a consumer under these circumstances without reference to whether the consumer's circumstances must be reasonable.[26] However, in the final clause of *abusive* in section 1031(d), Congress did include a *reasonableness*

---

19. 12 U.S.C. § 5531(c).

20. *Id.* § 5531(d)(1) (emphasis added); *see also* Adam J. Levitin, *"Abusive" Acts and Practices: Towards a Definition?* 18 (June 19, 2019) (written submission prepared for CFPB Symposium on "Abusive") ("Read literally, neither 'material interference' nor 'taking unreasonable advantage' inherently requires any legally cognizable harm to consumers."), https://www.consumerfinance.gov/documents/7776/cfpb_levitin-written-statement_symposium-abusive.pdf.

21. 12 U.S.C. § 5531(c)(1).

22. *Id.* § 5531(d).

23. *Id.* § 5531(c)(1)(A) (emphasis added); *see also* CFPB *Supervision and Examination Manual*, *supra* note 15, at UDAAP 6 (explaining that *deceptive* acts are assessed "from the perspective of the reasonable consumer").

24. 12 U.S.C. § 5331(d)(2)(A)–(B).

25. The term "covered person" is defined as "any person that engages in offering or providing a consumer financial product or service; and any affiliate of [such person] if such affiliate acts as a service provider to such person." 12 U.S.C. § 5481(6).

26. *Id.* § 5331(d)(2).

inquiry. That prong prohibits "tak[ing] unreasonable advantage of . . . the *reasonable* reliance by the consumer on a *covered person* to act in the interests of the consumer."[27]

2.2.3 Abusiveness Has No Express Cost-Benefit Analysis

The final difference between *unfair* and *abusive* is the cost-benefit analysis embedded in the definition of *unfair* but omitted from *abusive*. The Bureau may not prosecute an act as *unfair* unless it causes, or is likely to cause, injury which "is not outweighed by countervailing benefits to consumers or to competition."[28] The definition of *abusive* includes no express cost-benefit analysis, which suggests that none is intended.[29] In other words, businesses providing financial products or services to consumers may be accused of *abusive* acts even if their acts provide more benefit than confusion to consumers.

3. Regulatory Guidance and Enforcement Actions

In practice, it is unclear whether the Bureau has placed any import on these canons of statutory interpretation. The Bureau states that it has applied the *abusiveness* standard since it began operating in 2011, but only two Bureau enforcement actions contain a stand-alone *abusiveness* claim.[30] The remaining thirty actions alleging an *abusiveness* claim also include an "unfairness" or "deception" claim and, therefore, provide little insight into what behavior constitutes abusiveness.[31] A brief overview of the actions that best illustrate the meaning of *abusiveness* follows.

3.1 American Debt Settlement Solutions, Inc.

In May 2013, the Bureau brought its first action under *abusiveness*. In that action, the Bureau filed a complaint against American Debt Settlement Solutions, Inc. (ADSS) in connection with its provision of debt-relief services.[32] "In exchange for a fee," ADSS offered debt-relief services such as the renegotiation, settlement, reduction, or other

27. *Id.* § 5531(c)(2)(C) (emphasis added).

28. *Id.* § 5531(c)(1)(B).

29. *Id.* § 5531(d).

30. Policy Statement, *supra* note 8, at 6734.

31. *Id.*; *see also* Levitin, *supra* note 20, at 10 ("[G]iven the high degree of overlap between 'abusive' and 'unfair' and 'deceptive,' most products that would raise compliance concerns due to 'abusive,' would also raise concerns regarding 'unfair or deceptive,' such that 'abusive' is not the issue preventing the rollout of such products.").

32. Press Release, CFPB, CFPB Takes Action to Stop Florida Company from Engaging in Illegal Debt-Relief Practices (May 30, 2013), https://www.consumerfinance.gov/about-us/newsroom/cfpb-takes-action-to-stop-florida-company-from-engaging-in-illegal-debt-relief-practices/.

alteration of terms of debts between consumers and their creditors or debt collectors.[33] The fee included "an 'enrollment' fee in an amount calculated as a percentage . . . of the amount of the consumers' enrolled debts" as well as "a 'service' fee that [was] assessed on a monthly basis for the duration of the debt relief program."[34] However, ADSS "failed to renegotiate, settle, reduce, or otherwise alter the terms of a single debt for approximately 89 percent of the consumers who enrolled in its debt-relief programs," and "had reason to know it was nearly impossible" to do so with respect to debts under $700.[35] Importantly, in connection with the consumer-enrollment process, ADSS reviewed worksheets describing consumers' monthly income, expenditures, and debts.[36]

Based on these practices, the Bureau alleged that ADSS's conduct was *abusive* and *deceptive*. Specifically, the Bureau alleged that ADSS's practices were *abusive* because ADSS knew the financial conditions of the consumers and "knew that ADSS was unlikely to settle consumers' debts within the first three to six months of enrollment."[37] The Bureau further alleged that ADSS's practices were *abusive* because they collected enrollment fees "[d]espite receiving financial information showing that some consumers could not afford the monthly payments."[38]

In the Bureau's complaint, the alleged *deceptive* acts were based on the fact that, despite representations to the contrary, "ADSS [was] not likely to renegotiate, settle, reduce, or otherwise alter the terms of debts for consumers who enroll[ed] in its debt-relief programs."[39] The Bureau's *deceptive* claim was based on false representations, but its *abusiveness* claim was centered on ADSS's knowledge regarding the financial circumstances of the consumer. The Bureau noted as much in its statement that "the defendants engaged in abusive acts or practices by signing up and charging fees to vulnerable consumers who the defendants knew had inadequate income to complete the debt-relief programs in which they were enrolled."[40] This suggests that a *covered person*'s knowledge of the consumer may play a key role in *abusiveness*.

---

33. Stipulated Final Judgment and Order, CFPB v. Am. Debt Settlement Solutions, Inc., Case No. 9:13-cv-80548-DMM at 2 (S.D. Fla. June 7, 2018), ECF No. 5, https://files.consumerfinance.gov/f/201306_cfpb_finalorder_adss_signed-judgment.pdf.

34. *Id.*

35. *Id.* at 4.

36. *Id.* at 2.

37. Compl., CFPB v. Am. Debt Settlement Sols., Inc., Case No. 9:13-cv-80548-DMM ¶ 58 (S.D. Fla. June 7, 2018), ECF No. 1, https://files.consumerfinance.gov/f/201305_cfpb_complaint_adss.pdf.

38. *Id.* ¶ 59.

39. *Id.* ¶ 53; *see id.* ¶¶ 41, 47.

40. CFPB Press Release, *supra* note 32.

3.2 *Zero Parallel, LLC*

In September 2017, the Bureau filed one of the two actions based solely on allegedly *abusive* practices. In the matter of Zero Parallel, LLC, the Bureau filed a Consent Order against Zero Parallel in connection with its lead aggregation practices.[41] Zero Parallel "was in the business of receiving Leads from Lead Generators[42] and selling the Leads to small-dollar and installment lenders and to remarketing companies."[43] Zero Parallel's business obtaining and selling these leads spanned forty-six states. In some of those states, the implicated loans were wholly or partially void under the states' consumer-protection laws, "meaning that the lender has no legal right to collect, and the borrower is not obligated to pay, some or all of the principal or interest on the loan."[44] Consumers who submitted their information on a lead generator's web page were directed to a lender's web page through an automated process, "and the consumer [was] not informed that his or her information [had] been filtered through Zero Parallel or sold by Zero Parallel."[45] Zero Parallel was aware that some consumers were residents of states where the loans were void or the lender was prohibited from collecting certain amounts.

Because of these practices, the Bureau alleged that Zero Parallel committed an *abusive* act or practice by steering consumers towards lenders who offered loans that were wholly or partially void under state law.[46] The Bureau found that this practice was *abusive* pursuant to section 1031(d)(2)(A), which prohibits "tak[ing] unreasonable advantage of . . . a lack of understanding on the part of the consumer of the material risks, costs, or conditions of a product or service." In connection with this alleged violation, Zero Parallel and its owner were ordered to pay $350,000 and stop their "illegal abusive practices."[47] The Bureau did not explain why Zero Parallel's action constituted an *abusive* practice, but simply restated the language of section 1031(d)(2)(A).[48] Additionally, it is unclear why the practices described would not be *unfair* or *deceptive* practices under section 1031 or why the Bureau chose to assert only the *abusive* claim.

---

41. Zero Parallel, LLC, 2017-CFPB-0017 (Sept. 6, 2017), https://files.consumerfinance.gov/f/documents/201709_cfpb_zero-parallel-llc_consent-order.pdf.

42. Leads are defined as "a consumer's personal information received, transmitted, or otherwise used in connection with a consumer-financial product or service," and Lead Generators are defined as "Persons that obtain Leads and transmit the Leads to Lead Aggregators or other Persons." *Id.* ¶¶ 3c and 3e.

43. *Id.* ¶ 4.

44. *Id.* ¶ 16.

45. *Id.* ¶ 18.

46. *Id.* ¶¶ 17, 20–25.

47. Press Release, CFPB, CFPB Takes Action Against Zero Parallel for Steering Consumers Toward Bad Deals (Sept. 6, 2017), https://www.consumerfinance.gov/about-us/newsroom/cfpb-takes-action-against-zero-parallel-steering-consumers-toward-bad-deals/.

48. Zero Parallel, *supra* note 41, at ¶¶ 22–23.

3.3 *CFPB v. Aequitas Capital Management Inc.*

In another action based solely on *abusive* practices, Aequitas Capital Management Inc. was subject to a stipulated final judgment and order for alleged *abusive* practices.[49] In that action, the Bureau filed a complaint alleging that Aequitas funded and maintained a private loan program offered to students of Corinthian Colleges, Inc. that allowed Corinthian to "present a façade of compliance with federal law."[50] Until 2014, Corinthian was one of the largest for-profit, post-secondary education companies in the United States.[51] Nearly all of Corinthian's revenue was derived from federal student aid, largely Title IV loans.[52] However, during the relevant period, the federal government required that schools like Corinthian obtain 10 percent of their revenue from sources outside Title IV funds.[53] Because its generally low-income students could not afford out-of-pocket tuition, Corinthian established a private loan program and presented it to Aequitas as a means of attracting Aequitas's investment. But beginning in 2012, "such a loan program could no longer be financed by the school in order to qualify as an outside source of revenue for the purposes of obtaining Title IV funding."[54] Accordingly, Corinthian and Aequitas allegedly came to an arrangement that made it appear as if Corinthian were not funding the loans. Central to the alleged arrangement was an agreement by Corinthian to purchase the loans that became delinquent more than 90 days, "essentially shifting the risk of the program from Aequitas back to Corinthian."[55]

Based on these facts, the Bureau alleged Aequitas engaged in *abusive* acts or practices while lending to Corinthian students. The Bureau asserted that Aequitas "took unreasonable advantage" of student borrowers who were not aware of the schemes associated with the loan program.[56] The Bureau's single claim against Aequitas stated that its conduct in connection with Corinthian's loan program was an "abusive act" as defined by section 1031(d)(2)(B), which prohibits "tak[ing] unreasonable advantage of . . . the inability of the consumer to protect the interest of the consumer in selecting or using a consumer financial product or service."[57] The Bureau claimed that Aequitas knew the loan program was a sham but disregarded the harm it would

---

49. Press Release, CFPB, CFPB Takes Action Against Aequitas Capital Management for Aiding Corinthian Colleges' Predatory Lending Scheme (Aug. 17, 2017), https://www.consumerfinance.gov/about-us/newsroom/cfpb-takes-action-against-aequitas-capital-management-aiding-corinthian-colleges-predatory-lending-scheme/.

50. Complaint CFPB v. Aequitas Capital Mgmt. Inc., Case No. 17-cv-1278 ¶ 1 (D. Or. Sept. 1, 2017) ECF No. 1, https://www.consumerfinance.gov/policy-compliance/enforcement/actions/aequitas-capital-management-inc-et-al/.

51. *Id.* (Compl. ¶ 2).

52. *Id.* (Compl. ¶ 3).

53. *Id.* (Compl. ¶ 4).

54. *Id.*

55. *Id.*

56. *Id.* (Compl. ¶ 123).

57. *Id.* (Compl. ¶¶ 110–26).

cause to consumers.[58] However, as with its claim against Zero Parallel, the Bureau did not further elaborate why this activity was *abusive*, simply concluding that Aequitas violated the "prohibition on abusive practices."[59]

3.4 *CFPB v. Navient Corp. et al.*

In August 2017, the Bureau filed a complaint against Navient Corporation, Navient Solutions, Inc. (collectively, Navient), and Pioneer Credit Recovery, Inc. The Bureau alleged that Navient, the largest loan servicer in the United States, "deterred numerous borrowers from obtaining access to some or all of the benefits and protections associated with" federal student loan payment plans through *unfair*, *abusive*, and *deceptive* acts.[60] Specifically, the Bureau alleged that Navient violated the prohibition on *abusive* acts and practices by "steer[ing] [ ] borrowers experiencing financial hardship" into inappropriate and costly payment plans.[61]

In response, Navient filed a motion to dismiss for failure to state a claim, arguing that, among other things, the *abusiveness* count was not properly pled because, "as a matter of law, borrowers cannot reasonably rely on a loan servicer to serve as a fiduciary."[62] Navient argued the complaint alleged only omissions based on Navient's failure to "provide adequate financial counseling."[63] According to Navient, these allegations were not sufficient to plead *abusiveness* because "borrowers could not reasonably rely on Navient to counsel them into alternative payment plans unless Navient had an affirmative duty to provide such individualized financial counseling."[64]

Navient's arguments led the court to examine the reasonable prong of the *abusiveness* standard, and ultimately reject Navient's position. First, the court noted that "the statutory language does not state that a duty is an element of an abusive act or practice," but that the covered person cannot take "unreasonable advantage of the reasonable reliance by the consumer."[65] Reasonable reliance, the court continued, "is not always paired with a legal duty" and "it is therefore enough that a borrower's reliance that a loan servicer will act in their interest is reasonable, irrespective of whether a

58. *Id.* (Compl. ¶¶ 123–26).

59. *Id.* (Compl. ¶ 126).

60. Compl., CFPB v. Navient Corp. et al., No. 3:17-cv-101 ¶ 4 (M.D. Pa. Jan. 18, 2017), ECF No. 1, https://files.consumerfinance.gov/f/documents/201701_cfpb_Navient-Pioneer-Credit-Recovery-complaint.pdf. This overview focuses on the allegations and defenses related to *abusive* acts and practices, and does not discuss additional claims by the Bureau or other defenses raised by Navient.

61. *Id.*

62. Mem. of Law in Supp. of Defs.' Mot. to Dismiss Pl.'s Compl., CFPB v. Navient Corp. et al., No. 3:17-cv-101 at 20 (M.D. Pa. Jan. 18, 2017) ECF No. 29.

63. CFPB v. Navient Corp. et al., No. 3:17-cv-101, 2017 WL 3380530, at *19 (M.D. Pa. Aug. 4, 2017).

64. *Id.* (internal quotations and alterations omitted).

65. *Id.* at *20.

legal duty actually exists on the part of the loan servicer."[66] Second, the court found that the complaint alleged more than omissions, stating "that Navient placed reliance inducing statements on their webpage."[67] Accordingly, even if Navient was correct that there must be an underlying legal duty in order for a borrower's reliance to be reasonable, "the Court [was] satisfied that Navient's active conduct created a duty to act in accordance with their own statements."[68]

Based on the court's reasoning, the reasonable prong of the *abusiveness* inquiry should be understood from the consumer's prospective and does not require the existence of a legal duty. However, a legal duty may exist where a *covered person* provides "reliance inducing statements."[69]

3.5 Takeaways

As mentioned above, the Bureau's enforcement actions neither support nor undermine any interpretation of section 1031(d) that can be gleaned from the application of basic statutory interpretation principles. Although the Bureau's enforcement actions suggest that *covered persons*' knowledge of consumers is particularly relevant to abusiveness, they do not fully clarify the differences between an *abusive* practice and an *unfair* or *deceptive* one.[70] Although the court's opinion in *Navient* offered some insight, the Bureau acknowledged in the 2020 Policy Statement that "[i]t is difficult to discern from those actions unique fact patterns to which only the abusiveness standard would apply."[71]

66. *Id.*

67. *Id.*

68. *Id.*

69. *Id.*

70. Similarly, the Bureau's other publications provide no additional guidance regarding the definition of *abusive*. *See, e.g.*, CFPB, *Supervision and Examination Manual*, *supra* note 15, at UDAAP 9 (stating *unfair*, *deceptive*, and *abusive* have different legal standards but not further defining *abusive*) (October 2012); CFPB Bulletin 2013-07, *Prohibition of Unfair, Deceptive, or Abusive Acts or Practices in the Collection of Consumer Debts*, at *4 (July 10, 2013), https://files.consumerfinance.gov/f/201307_cfpb_bulletin_unfair-deceptive-abusive-practices.pdf (same) (citing CFPB, *Supervision and Examination Manual*). The only additional narrative provided regarding abusiveness simply restates the language of the Dodd-Frank Act and does not explain why that practice would not also be considered *deceptive*. *See, e.g.*, CFPB Bulletin 2014-02, *Marketing of Credit Card Promotional APR Offers*, at *4 (Sept. 4, 2014), https://www.consumerfinance.gov/policy-compliance/guidance/supervisory-guidance/bulletin-marketing-credit-card-promotional-APR-offers/ (stating that conditions surrounding grace periods may result in the issuer "tak[ing] unreasonable advantage" by exploiting consumers' "lack of understanding").

71. Policy Statement, *supra* note 8, at 4.

4. The 2020 Policy Statement

On June 25, 2019, the CFPB convened a "Symposium on Abusive Acts and Practices" to gather information and perspectives on the meaning and import of *abusiveness* in the marketplace. Eight consumer protection academics and practitioners drafted written statements before the symposium then dialogued about the meaning of the term, expressing their opinions on whether the Bureau should attempt to eliminate any uncertainty through rulemaking or other guidance.[72] While there was significant disagreement among the panelists, the Bureau ultimately concluded that agency guidance was necessary. The Policy Statement is best understood within the context of its creation, beginning with the symposium.

4.1 The Divergent Views of the Symposium Panelists

The panelists' written statements touched on one or more of the following areas: whether the financial services marketplace has been hampered by uncertainty about the definition of *abusiveness*; what a proper definition of the term includes; whether applying the term requires a cost-benefit analysis; and whether the Bureau should engage in rulemaking or issue other guidance to formally define the term. The panelists' wide experience and viewpoints provided a snapshot of the ambiguity in the consumer protection arena surrounding the meaning of *abusiveness*.

---

72. *See* J. Howard Beales III, *What Does It All Mean? "Abusive" Acts or Practices and the CFPB* (2019) (written submission prepared for CFPB Symposium on "Abusive"), https://www.consumerfinance.gov/documents/7777/cfpb_beales-written-statement_symposium-abusive.pdf; Levitin, *supra* note 20; William MacLeod, *Interpreting Abusive Practices* (2019) (written submission prepared for CFPB Symposium on "Abusive"), https://www.consumerfinance.gov/documents/7775/cfpb_macleod-written-statement_symposium-abusive.pdf; Patricia A. McCoy, *The Question of a General Rulemaking to Define the "Abusive" Standard* (June 19, 2019) (written submission prepared for CFPB Symposium on "Abusive"), https://www.consumerfinance.gov/documents/7772/cfpb_mccoy-written-statement_symposium-abusive.pdf; Eric J. Mogilnicki, *CFPB Symposium: Abusive Acts or Practices* (June 25, 2019) (written submission prepared for CFPB Symposium on "Abusive"), https://www.consumerfinance.gov/documents/7771/cfpb_mogilnicki-written-statement_symposium-abusive.pdf; Lucy E. Morris, *Re: Abusive Acts or Practices Symposium* (June 17, 2019) (written submission prepared for CFPB Symposium on "Abusive"), https://www.consumerfinance.gov/documents/7770/cfpb_morris-written-statement_symposium-abusive.pdf; Nicholas F.B. Smyth, *Statement Submitted to the Consumer Financial Protection Bureau for the Symposium on Abusive Acts or Practices* (June 25, 2019) (written submission prepared for CFPB Symposium on "Abusive"), https://www.consumerfinance.gov/documents/7774/cfpb_smyth-written-statement_symposium-abusive.pdf; Todd Zywicki, *Statement Prepared for Consumer Financial Protection Bureau Abusive Acts or Practices Symposium* (June 25, 2019) (written submission prepared for CFPB Symposium on "Abusive"), https://www.consumerfinance.gov/documents/7773/cfpb_zywicki-written-statement_symposium-abusive.pdf.

First, although some panelists urged the Bureau to define *abusiveness* because the fear of ambiguous enforcement actions stifles financial services innovation, others were very skeptical of this premise.[73] The latter group reasoned that the *unfair* and *deceptive* UDAAP prongs likely stifle innovation just as much as the *abusiveness* prong does.[74] To these panelists, any uncertainty about the meaning of *abusive* causes no further harm.

The panelists diverged on another point: whether the definition of *abusiveness* requires the Bureau to focus on the perspective of the service provider or the consumer during the transaction at issue.[75] In other words, was the service provider's conduct *abusive* on its face, or did the condition or understanding of the particular consumer in the transaction make the conduct *abusive*?

A third point of divergence concerned whether enforcement of *abusiveness* actions requires a cost-benefit analysis. Several panelists explained that if the costs to consumers balanced the harms to a particular consumer, the business's action could not be *abusive* in light of the policy objective of promoting business innovation.[76] In addition, if the costs to comply with the Bureau's *abusiveness* standard do not include a cost-benefit analysis, the cost will ultimately be passed on to the consumers "in the form of higher prices or reduced availability of valuable financial products and services."[77] Other panelists stated that under the doctrine of *expressio unius alterius exclusio*, the Bureau may not assess the *abusiveness* of service providers' actions through

---

73. *Compare* MacLeod, *supra* note 72, at 8 ("[T]he ambiguity surrounding the authority contributes to regulatory uncertainty that results in certain products and services being curtailed or not offered to certain populations altogether."), *and* Zywicki, *supra* note 72, at 3–4 ("Distinguishing abusiveness clearly from unfairness and deception will create predictability for providers and consumers of financial products in entering into transactions."), *with* Levitin, *supra* note 72, at 6 ("The terms 'unfair' and 'deceptive' have never been formally defined, yet have existed for over eighty years without impairing American innovation."), *and id.* at 7 ("[L]eaving 'abusive' undefined is not creating any particular problems or uncertainty for the businesses regulated by the Bureau."), *and* McCoy, *supra* note 72, at 7 ("[T]here is no problem needing solving. For vast swaths of the consumer financial services industry, the 'abusiveness' standard is a non-issue."), *and* Smyth, *supra* note 72, at 1 ("[T]he purported cloud of uncertainty created by the prohibition on 'abusive' acts or practices has been exaggerated. The 'abusive' prohibition does not stifle innovation any more than the prohibitions on unfairness or deception do.").

74. *E.g.*, Levitin, *supra* note 20, at 6; Smyth, *supra* note 72, at 1.

75. *Compare* Beales, *supra* note 72, at 5–6 (focusing on the *covered person*'s conduct), *and* Levitin, *supra* note 20, at 17–18 (same), *and* McCoy, *supra* note 72, at 1 (same), *with* Mogilnicki, *supra* note 72, at 5 (focusing on the consumer), *and* Zywicki, *supra* note 72, at 21 (same).

76. Beales, *supra* note 72, at 7; MacLeod, *supra* note 72, at 8.

77. Beales, *supra* note 72, at 7.

a cost-benefit analysis because the textual definition of *abusiveness* does not include a cost-benefit requirement, whereas the definition of *unfairness* does.[78]

Fourth, the panelists disagreed about whether the Bureau should conduct rulemaking or otherwise further define *abusiveness*. Several panelists stated that the text of section 1031 prohibits the Bureau from conducting such rulemaking and that only Congress may further define the term. Those panelists argued that the routine process of judicial interpretation of terms should take its course so *abusiveness* could be defined organically rather than definitively and "prematurely."[79] They also stated that no-action letters should be used to enforce this portion of the statute until a definition is fleshed out.[80] Other panelists disagreed, urging the Bureau to issue guidance to promote certainty for businesses and consumers, particularly because the *common law* process of defining terms through litigation and judicial decisions would take years, and the Bureau could sooner prevent needless litigation over the term's meaning.[81]

5. The Policy Statement's Text and Weight

The Bureau ultimately decided to clarify its goals and procedures for preventing *abusive* acts or practices by issuing its Policy Statement in January 2020. In doing so, the Bureau accepted and rejected various proposals from the panelists. Although the Bureau did not define the term *abusive*, it identified three guiding policies for its ongoing enforcement of *abusiveness*, some of which expressly reject the statutory constructions explained above and during the symposium.

> First, the Bureau added a cost-benefit analysis element to its enforcement approach:
>
> [C]onsistent with the priority it accords to the prevention of harm, the Bureau intends to focus on citing conduct as abusive in supervision or challenging conduct as abusive in enforcement if the Bureau concludes that the harms to consumers from the conduct outweigh its benefits to consumers.[82]

---

78. *Compare* 12 U.S.C. § 5531(c)(1)(B), *with id.* § 5531(d). *See* McCoy, *supra* note 72, at 16; *cf.* MacLeod, *supra* note 72, at 8; *see also* Loughrin v. United States, 573 U.S. 351, 358 (2014) ("[W]hen Congress includes particular language in one section of a statute but omits it in another[,] . . . this Court presumes that Congress intended a difference in meaning." (internal quotation marks omitted)).

79. *See* Levitin, *supra* note 20, at 6; McCoy, *supra* note 72, at 4.

80. *See* Levitin, *supra* note 20, at 12; McCoy, *supra* note 72, at 10; Smyth, *supra* note 72, at 5.

81. *See* Beales, *supra* note 72, at 9; MacLeod, *supra* note 72, at 8; Mogilnicki, *supra* note 72, at 4; Morris, *supra* note 72, at 3; Zywicki, *supra* note 72, at 3–4.

82. Policy Statement, *supra* note 8, at 6736.

Next, it stated its objective to allege claims of *abusive* acts or practices with specificity:

> [T]he Bureau will generally avoid challenging conduct as abusive that relies on all or nearly all of the same facts that the Bureau alleges are unfair or deceptive. Where the Bureau nevertheless decides to include an alleged abusiveness violation, the Bureau intends to plead such claims in a manner designed to clearly demonstrate the nexus between the cited facts and the Bureau's legal analysis of the claim. In its supervision activity, the Bureau similarly intends to provide more clarity as to the specific factual basis for determining that a covered person has violated the abusiveness standard.[83]

This objective was likely a response to an issue the panelists highlighted—the Bureau almost always alleged *abusiveness* claims alongside claims of *unfairness* or *deceptiveness*—a tactic one panelist called a "kitchen-sink pleading strategy."[84]

Finally, for its third objective, the Bureau suggested that scienter is an element of *abusiveness*, but only for damages purposes:

> [T]he Bureau generally does not intend to seek certain types of monetary relief for abusiveness violations where the covered person was making a good-faith effort to comply with the abusiveness standard.[85]

Alongside this explanation of what the Bureau did do, it is important to note what the Bureau did not do: issue a binding rule. The Policy Statement, an effort to clarify the Bureau's enforcement strategy on *abusive* practices, falls within the Administrative Procedure Act's definition of a *rule*,[86] but it is not an enforceable agency rule because it was not subject to notice-and-comment procedures.[87] Thus, it is not a "legislative-type rule," and it lacks the force of law.[88] Rather than stating a "binding norm,"[89] the Bureau in the Policy Statement has "advise[d] the public prospectively of the manner in which the agency proposes to exercise a discretionary power."[90]

---

83. *Id.*

84. Zywicki, *supra* note 72, at 30.

85. Policy Statement, *supra* note 8, at 6736 (footnote omitted).

86. 5 U.S.C. § 551(4) (defining "rule" in relevant part as "the whole or a part of an agency statement of general or particular applicability and future effect designed to implement, interpret, or prescribe law or policy").

87. *See id.* § 553(b)(A) (excluding "statements of policy" from notice-and-comment requirements).

88. *See* Chrysler Corp. v. Brown, 441 U.S. 281, 302 (1979).

89. Pac. Gas & Elec. Co. v. Fed. Power Comm'n, 506 F.2d 33, 38 (D.C. Cir. 1974) (internal quotation marks omitted).

90. Chrysler Corp., 441 U.S. at 301 (quoting Attorney General's Manual on the Administrative Procedure Act 30, n.3 (1947)).

In doing so, the Bureau retained a measure of flexibility for future interpretations of *abusiveness* and discretion in applying its policy goals to individual cases. Providers of financial service products and services should be aware of this purposeful action and its implications.

6. Post-Policy Statement Interpretation of *Abusiveness*

The Policy Statement provides guidelines that may be useful in predicting the CFPB's enforcement behavior, but the Policy Statement has not provided answers to critical questions such as the following:

- Is the focus of *abusiveness* on the condition and knowledge of the consumer at issue?
- Is the focus instead on the conduct of the business providing the financial product or service?
- Will every *abusive* enforcement action also carry *unfair* or *deceptive* allegations?[91]
- Can the Bureau "bring an enforcement action based on a single consumer's experience?"[92]
- Will the Bureau exercise its discretion to decline prosecuting *abusive* acts when the *covered person* acted without *scienter* (guilty knowledge), although section 1031(d) allows such enforcement actions?

Despite the remaining confusion about *abusiveness*, the Symposium panelists generally agreed that a *covered person*'s act is *abusive* if it would harm a particularly *vulnerable* consumer, not an average consumer.[93] The *covered person*, the panelists concluded, must have specialized knowledge about the vulnerabilities or condition of the particular consumer engaging in a transaction for the practice to be *abusive* to that vulnerable

91. In *Navient*, for example, which was pending when the CFPB issued the Policy Statement, the CFPB continued to press both *abusive* and *unfair* claims based on the same predicate facts.

92. Morris, *supra* note 72, at 2.

93. Beales, *supra* note 72, at 8 (focusing on the vulnerable consumer); Levitin, *supra* note 20, at 38–39 (same); McCoy, *supra* note 72, at 17–18 (same); Mogilnicki, *supra* note 72, at 5 (same); Zywicki, *supra* note 72, at 7.

consumer.[94] For providers of financial services and products, this can provide some solace amidst the ambiguity. The Bureau is unlikely to prosecute *covered persons* for *abusive* acts apart from an obviously harmful effect on consumers the *covered persons* know are vulnerable.

7. Why the Meaning of *Abusiveness* Matters

Determining the meaning of *abusiveness* is not an academic exercise.[95] Although Congress and the Bureau have the authority to legislate and interpret *abusiveness*, they have chosen not to do so. Until the Bureau provides clearer guidance on *abusiveness* or the courts help to refine the interpretation, it is critical for financial institutions and businesses subject to the UDAAP provision of the Dodd-Frank Act to have a strategic plan to prevent UDAAP. Businesses, consumers, and courts are forced to grapple with the complexities of a broad term with a great deal at stake, as civil monetary penalties can cost businesses up to $5,000 per day for any violation, $25,000 per day for a *reckless* violation, and $1 million per day for a *knowing* violation.[96]

For companies free from current Bureau enforcement actions, "the best way [to] avoid litigation is by developing a robust compliance management system . . . that monitors consumer complaints, tests internal systems, and carefully reviews all product features before they are rolled out to customers."[97] With careful consumer-facing literature and policies, businesses taking a proactive approach to compliance "need not fear the 'abusive' prohibition."[98]

---

94. This conclusion is consistent with the Bureau's understanding of its long-held mission to protect vulnerable populations. *See* Consumer Financial Protection Bureau, Empowering Low Income and Economically Vulnerable Consumers: Report on a National Convening 2 (November 2013), https://files.consumerfinance.gov/f/201311_cfpb_report_empowering-economically-vulnerable-consumers.pdf ("When establishing the CFPB, Congress recognized that vulnerable populations are frequently unable to fully access the benefits of financial products and services. Congress therefore directed the CFPB to pay particular attention to the issues faced by traditionally underserved Americans. At the CFPB, we take this mission very seriously.").

95. Indeed, Senator Elizabeth Warren and the Senate Committee on Banking, Housing and Urban Affairs wrote to the Director of the CFPB on March 12, 2020, highlighting concerns about the Policy Statement and the Bureau's enforcement plans regarding *abusive* auto lending. *See* Letter from Sen. Elizabeth Warren to the Hon. Kathleen Kraninger, Director of the Consumer Financial Protection Bureau ¶ 4 (Mar. 12, 2020), http://ct.symplicity.com/t/wrn/a124e9ff616f07efd89710e19dd0c0f6/4262265609/realurl=https:/www.warren.senate.gov/download/20200312-letter-to-cfpb-re-auto-lending ("Please describe how the Bureau will evaluate whether or not an auto lender is engaging in an abusive practice. How will the Bureau measure 'harm' and 'benefit'? Will these be monetary thresholds? If so, please include them.").

96. 12 U.S.C. § 5565(c)(2).

97. Smyth, *supra* note 72, at 10.

98. *Id.*

CHAPTER

3

Truth in Lending

CHAPTER

3A

General Principles

Eric L. Johnson

1. Scope of This Chapter

This chapter covers the general principles of the Truth in Lending Act (TILA) and its implementing regulation, CFPB Regulation Z, which require creditors to make certain disclosures when originating and servicing consumer credit and provide for certain substantive protections.[1,2]

2. Regulatory Overview

The purpose of the TILA and Regulation Z is to protect consumers in credit transactions by requiring clear disclosure of credit terms to allow consumers to compare more readily the various credit terms available to them and avoid the uninformed use of credit.[3] Regulation Z is issued by the Consumer Financial Protection Bureau (CFPB),

---

Editor's Note: the authors of the TILA chapters have provided a comprehensive introduction to this important statute that governs many origination and servicing transactions in consumer financial law, but it would not be possible to discuss every important aspect of TILA compliance in these limited pages. For a more thorough discussion of TILA, please see *The Law of Truth in Lending* (Alvin C. Harrell ed. 2013), *The Law of Truth in Lending 2018 Supplement* (John L. Ropiequet and Lynette I. Hotchkiss eds. 2018).

1. Pub. L. No. 90-321, 82 Stat. 146 (1968) (codified as amended at 15 U.S.C. §§ 1601–1667f (2020)).

2. 12 C.F.R. pt. 1026 (2020).

3. 15 U.S.C. § 1601(a) (2020); 12 C.F.R. § 1026.1(b) (2020).

which is charged with TILA rulemaking authority.[4] The CFPB publishes the "official interpretations" of Regulation Z.[5] Good faith compliance with the official interpretations provides a safe harbor from TILA liability.[6]

TILA and Regulation Z provide a standardized method for disclosing the total dollar cost of credit as an amount (finance charge) and the annualized rate of that finance charge (annual percentage rate or APR).[7] TILA and Regulation Z also require disclosure of other terms of credit transactions, such as default charges and security interests.[8]

The disclosure requirements of Regulation Z differ, depending on whether the credit is open-end (e.g., credit cards and home equity lines)[9] or closed-end (e.g., motor vehicle financing).[10] Disclosures may be required in advertising,[11] in an oral discussion of the credit transaction,[12] in writing prior to consummation of the transaction,[13] and in some instances after consummation of the transaction.[14]

3. Purpose

The purpose of the TILA and Regulation Z is to promote the informed use of consumer credit by requiring disclosures about its terms and cost, to ensure that consumers are provided with greater and more timely information on the nature and costs of the residential real estate settlement process, and to effect certain changes in the settlement process for residential real estate that will result in more effective advance disclosure to home buyers and sellers of settlement costs.[15] Regulation Z also includes substantive protections.[16] For instance, it gives consumers the right to cancel certain credit transactions that involve a lien on a consumer's principal dwelling,[17] regulates certain credit card practices,[18] and provides a means for fair and timely resolution

4. 15 U.S.C. § 1604(a) (2020).

5. 12 C.F.R. pt. 1026, supp. I (2020). "Official interpretations" is not a legally defined term and is only a definition created here as a convention for ease of understanding the chapter.

6. 15 U.S.C. § 1640(f) (2020).

7. 12 C.F.R. §§ 1026.6, 1026.18 (2020).

8. *Id.* §§ 1026.6, 1026.18.

9. *Id.* §§ 1026.5–1026.16.

10. *Id.* §§ 1026.17–1026.24.

11. *See, e.g., id.* §§ 1026.16, 1026.24 (2020).

12. *Id.* §§ 1026.4(d)(4), 1026.9, 1026.26, 1026.46(d)(1)(ii).

13. *Id.* §§ 1026.6, 1026.18.

14. *Id.* §§ 1026.19, 1026.20.

15. 15 U.S.C. § 1601(a) (2020); 12 C.F.R. § 1026.1(b) (2020).

16. 12 C.F.R. § 1026.1(b) (2020).

17. *Id.* §§ 1026.15, 1026.23.

18. *Id.* §§ 1026.12, 1026.51–1026.61.

of credit billing disputes.[19] Regulation Z also imposes special rules for certain home mortgage transactions,[20] regulates certain practices of creditors who extend private education loans,[21] and imposes special rules for credit card accounts and open-end credit offered to college students.[22]

4. Applicable Transactions

TILA and Regulation Z apply to a transaction when four conditions are met:

1. the credit is offered or extended to consumers;
2. the offering or extension of credit is done regularly;
3. the credit is subject to a finance charge or is payable by a written agreement in more than four installments; and
4. the credit is primarily for personal, family, or household purposes.[23]

If a credit card is involved, certain provisions apply even if the credit is not subject to a finance charge or is not payable by a written agreement in more than four installments, or if the credit card is to be used for business purposes.[24]

5. Exempt Transactions

The following transactions are exempt from TILA and Regulation Z:

1. credit extended primarily for a business, commercial, or agricultural purpose;
2. credit extended to other than a natural person (including credit to government agencies or instrumentalities);
3. credit in excess of $58,300 (as of January 1, 2020, adjusted annually) not secured by real property, or personal property used or expected to be used as the consumer's principal dwelling;
4. public utility credit;
5. credit extended by a broker-dealer involving securities or commodities accounts;
6. home fuel budget plans;

---

19. *Id.* § 1026.13.
20. *Id.* § 1026.31.
21. *Id.* § 1026.46.
22. *Id.* § 1026.51.
23. *Id.* § 1026.1(c)(1).
24. *Id.* § 1026.1(c)(2).

7. certain student loan transactions; and
8. extension of credit to a participant in certain employer-sponsored retirement plans or eligible governmental deferred compensation plan.[25]

6. Important Definitions

Regulation Z contains some important definitions:

1. *Closed-end credit* means consumer credit other than *open-end credit.*
2. *Consumer* means a cardholder or natural person to whom consumer credit is offered or extended.
3. *Consumer credit* means credit offered or extended to a consumer primarily for personal, family, or household purposes.
4. *Consummation* means the time that a consumer becomes contractually obligated on a credit transaction.
5. *Credit* means the right to defer payment of debt or to incur debt and defer its payment.
6. *Creditor* means a person who regularly extends consumer credit that is subject to a finance charge or is payable by written agreement in more than four installments (not including a down payment), and to whom the obligation is initially payable either on the face of the note or contract, or by agreement when there is no note or contract.
7. *Open-end credit* means consumer credit extended by a creditor under a plan in which (i) the creditor reasonably contemplates repeated transactions; (ii) the creditor may impose a finance charge from time to time on an outstanding unpaid balance; and (iii) the amount of credit that may be extended to the consumer during the term of the plan is generally made available to the extent that any outstanding balance is repaid.[26]

7. Finance Charge

The TILA and Regulation Z specify what fees and charges imposed in a credit transaction are considered finance charges.[27] The distinction between fees and charges that are finance charges, and those that are not, is important to the uniform disclosure of the cost of credit—fees that are finance charges, for instance, affect the APR and,

25. *Id.* § 1026.3.
26. *Id.* § 1026.2.
27. *Id.* § 1026.4.

thus, the cost of credit disclosed to the consumer. A fee treated as a finance charge will increase the APR applicable to the transaction.

Regulation Z defines the *finance charge* as the cost of consumer credit expressed as a dollar amount. It includes any charge payable (directly or indirectly) by the consumer and imposed (directly or indirectly) by the creditor, as an incident to or a condition of the extension of credit. It does not include any charge of a type payable in a comparable cash transaction.[28] Thus, if a charge is imposed equally in both cash and credit transactions, the charge is not a finance charge for purposes of TILA and Regulation Z.

The finance charge includes fees and amounts charged by someone other than the creditor, unless otherwise expressly excluded, if the creditor:

1. Requires the use of a third party as a condition of, or an incident to, the extension of credit, even if the consumer can choose the third party.
2. Retains a portion of the third-party charge, to the extent of the portion retained.

7.1 Examples of Finance Charges

The finance charge includes the following types of charges, except for charges specifically excluded as described in section 7.2:

1. interest, time price differential, and any amount payable under an add-on or discount system of additional charges;
2. service, transaction, activity, and carrying charges;
3. points, loan fees, assumption fees, finder's fees, and similar charges;
4. appraisal, investigation, and credit report fees;
5. premiums or other charges for any guarantee or insurance protecting the creditor against the consumer's default or other credit loss;
6. charges imposed on a creditor by another person for purchasing or accepting a consumer's obligation (e.g., discount fee) if the consumer is required to pay the charges in cash, as an addition to the obligation, or as a deduction from the proceeds of the obligation;
7. premiums or other charges for credit life, accident, health, or loss-of-income insurance, written in connection with a credit transaction;
8. premiums or other charges for insurance against loss of or damage to property, or against liability arising out of the ownership or use of property, written in connection with a credit transaction;
9. discounts for the purpose of inducing payment by a means other than the use of credit; and

28. *Id.* § 1026.4(a).

10. charges or premiums paid for debt cancellation, or debt suspension coverage, written in connection with a credit transaction, whether or not the coverage is insurance under applicable law.[29]

7.2 Exclusions from Finance Charge

The following charges are not considered finance charges:

1. application fees charged to all applicants for credit, whether or not credit is actually extended;
2. charges for actual unanticipated late payment, for exceeding a credit limit, or for delinquency, default, or a similar occurrence;
3. charges imposed by a financial institution for paying items that overdraw an account, unless the payment of such items and the imposition of the charge were previously agreed upon in writing;
4. fees charged for participation in a credit plan, whether assessed on an annual or other periodic basis;
5. seller's points;
6. interest forfeited as a result of an interest reduction required by law on a time deposit used as security for an extension of credit;
7. certain fees in a transaction secured by real property or in a residential mortgage transaction, if the fees are bona fide and reasonable in amount; and
8. discounts offered to induce payment for a purchase by cash, check, or other means.[30]

7.3 Voluntary Credit Insurance Premiums

Premiums for credit life, accident, health, or loss-of-income insurance may be excluded from the finance charge if the following conditions are met:

1. the insurance coverage is not required by the creditor, and this fact is disclosed in writing;
2. the premium for the initial term of insurance coverage is disclosed in writing. If the term of insurance is less than the term of the transaction, the term of insurance must also be disclosed; and
3. the consumer signs, or initials, an affirmative written request for the insurance after receiving the disclosures specified above. Any consumer in the transaction may sign or initial the request.[31]

29. *Id.* § 1026.4(b).
30. *Id.* § 1026.4(c).
31. *Id.* § 1026.4(d)(1).

7.4 Property Insurance Premiums

Premiums for insurance against loss of or damage to property, or against liability arising out of the ownership or use of property, including single interest insurance if the insurer waives all right of subrogation against the consumer, may be excluded from the finance charge if the following conditions are met:

1. The insurance coverage may be obtained from a person of the consumer's choice, and this fact is disclosed (a creditor may reserve the right to refuse to accept, for reasonable cause, an insurer offered by the consumer).
2. If the coverage is obtained from or through the creditor, the premium for the initial term of insurance coverage must be disclosed. If the term of insurance is less than the term of the transaction, the term of insurance must also be disclosed.[32]

7.5 Voluntary Debt Cancellation or Debt Suspension Fees

Charges or premiums paid for (1) debt cancellation coverage for amounts exceeding the value of the collateral securing the obligation or for (2) debt cancellation or debt suspension coverage in case of accident or in the event of the loss of life, health, or income may be excluded from the finance charge, whether or not the coverage is insurance, if the following conditions are met:

1. The debt cancellation or debt suspension agreement or coverage is not required by the creditor, and this fact is disclosed in writing.
2. The fee or premium for the initial term of coverage is disclosed in writing. If the term of coverage is less than the term of the credit transaction, the term of coverage must also be disclosed.
3. The following are disclosed, as applicable, for debt suspension coverage: that the obligation to pay loan principal and interest is only suspended, and that interest will continue to accrue during the period of suspension.
4. The consumer signs or initials an affirmative written request for coverage after receiving the disclosures specified above. Any consumer in the transaction may sign or initial the request.[33]

7.6 Certain Security Interest Charges

Finally, if itemized and disclosed, the following charges may be excluded from the finance charge:

---

32. *Id.* § 1026.4(d)(2).
33. *Id.* § 1026.4(d)(3).

1. Taxes and fees prescribed by law that actually are, or will be, paid to public officials for determining the existence of or for perfecting, releasing, or satisfying a security interest;
2. The premium for insurance in lieu of perfecting a security interest, to the extent that the premium does not exceed the taxes and fees described immediately above, that otherwise would be payable; and
3. Any tax levied on security instruments, or on documents evidencing indebtedness, if the payment of such taxes is a requirement for recording the instrument securing the evidence of indebtedness.[34]

8. Model Disclosures

Regulation Z contains model clauses and disclosures for the required disclosures. These model clauses and sample disclosures are found in appendices G and H to Regulation Z. These forms provide safe harbor to those creditors that choose to use them.[35]

9. Relation to State Laws

State law requirements that are inconsistent with the requirements contained in TILA chapter 1 (General Provisions), chapter 2 (Credit Transactions), or chapter 3 (Credit Advertising), and Regulation Z are preempted to the extent of the inconsistency. A state law is inconsistent if it requires a creditor to make disclosures or take actions that contradict the requirements of the TILA. A state law is contradictory if it requires the use of the same term to represent a different amount or a different meaning than the federal law, or if it requires the use of a term different from that required in the federal law to describe the same item.[36]

Any state may apply to the CFPB to exempt a class of transactions within the state from the requirements of TILA chapter 2 (Credit Transactions) or chapter 4 (Credit Billing) and the corresponding provisions of Regulation Z. The Bureau must grant an exemption if it determines that: (1) the state law is substantially similar to the federal law or, in the case of chapter 4, affords the consumer greater protection than the federal law; and (2) there is adequate provision for enforcement.[37] Exemptions from portions of TILA have been granted to the states of Maine, Connecticut, Massachusetts, Oklahoma, and Wyoming.[38]

---

34. *Id.* § 1026.4(e).
35. 15 U.S.C. § 1604(b) (2020).
36. 12 C.F.R. § 1026.28(a) (2020).
37. *Id.* § 1026.29(a).
38. 12 C.F.R. pt. 1026, supp. I, cmt. 29(a)-4 (2020).

10. Penalties

Noncompliance with the requirements of the TILA and Regulation Z can result in administrative action, civil liabilities, and/or criminal liability. Administrative actions based on inaccurate (understated) disclosures of finance charges or APRs may result in a requirement that the creditor reimburse affected consumers. Regulation Z carries several penalties for violations, which include actual damages and civil damages and criminal penalties. Assignees may also be liable for certain violations.

The TILA creates a private cause of action for violations. A person injured as a result of a TILA violation may sue for actual damages,[39] plus statutory damages of twice the amount of the finance charge; in the case of a consumer lease, 25 percent of the total amount of monthly payments under the lease, with a minimum of $200 and a maximum of $2,000 for certain disclosure violations.[40] In the case of an individual action relating to an open-end credit plan not secured by real property or a dwelling, twice the amount of the finance charge, with a minimum of $500 and a maximum of $5,000; or in the case of an individual action not under an open-end credit plan secured by real property or a dwelling, not less than $400 or greater than $4,000.[41] The maximum award in a class action is the lesser of $1,000,000 or 1 percent of the creditor's net worth.[42] A successful plaintiff may also recover costs and attorney's fees.[43]

TILA also provides for criminal penalties. Whoever willfully and knowingly (1) gives false or inaccurate information or fails to provide information that is required to be disclosed; (2) uses any chart or table authorized by the CFPB in such a manner as to consistently understate the APR; or (3) otherwise fails to comply with any requirement imposed under TILA, will be fined not more than $5,000 or imprisoned not more than one year, or both.[44]

TILA also imposes liability on assignees of a consumer contract. Any civil action for actual or statutory damages may be brought against an assignee for TILA violations that are apparent on the face of the document, except where the assignment was involuntary.[45] A violation apparent on the face of the disclosure statement includes, but is not limited to (1) a disclosure that can be determined to be incomplete or inaccurate from the face of the disclosure statement or other documents assigned, or (2) a disclosure that does not use the terms required to be used by TILA.[46]

Claims for TILA violations must be brought within one year from the date of the occurrence of the violations; however, consumers may use a TILA violation as a

39. 15 U.S.C. § 1640(a)(1) (2020).
40. *Id.* § 1640(a)(2)(A).
41. *Id.*
42. *Id.* § 1640(a)(2)(B).
43. *Id.* § 1640(a)(3).
44. *Id.* § 1611.
45. *Id.* § 1641(a).
46. *Id.*

defense to collection by recoupment or setoff, in the collection action by the creditor.[47] An action with respect to a violation of TILA for certain mortgages may be brought before the end of the three-year period beginning on the date of the occurrence of the violation.[48] The CFPB has enforcement authority over the provisions and requirements of the TILA and Regulation Z.

47. *Id.* § 1640(e).

48. *Id.*

CHAPTER

3B

The Truth in Lending Act and Open-End Credit Disclosures

Daniel Laudicina

1. Scope of This Chapter

This chapter covers the core provisions in the Truth in Lending Act[1] (TILA) and the Consumer Financial Protection Bureau's (CFPB's) Regulation Z[2] that require creditors to make certain disclosures when originating and servicing open-end consumer credit,[3] and that impose certain substantive requirements upon creditors in connection with open-end consumer credit, but does not cover special rules that apply to mortgages and student loans. Thus, this chapter addresses only those requirements applicable to open-end consumer credit that is either (1) unsecured or (2) secured by personal property that is not used as a dwelling. This chapter addresses the content of the required disclosures and certain related requirements, and substantive requirements unique to open-end nonmortgage credit, but does not cover advertising or liability and cure issues.

1. 15 U.S.C. §§ 1601–1667f (2020).

2. 12 C.F.R. pt. 1026 (2020).

3. Note, however, that the prohibition on issuance of unsolicited credit cards and the unauthorized use protections also apply to commercial-purpose credit cards. 12 C.F.R. pt. 1026, supp. I, cmt. 2(a)(8)-2 (2020).

2. Account-Opening Disclosure Requirements

Generally, Regulation Z requires the creditor to make account-opening disclosures before the first transaction is made under the plan.[4] Regulation Z allows creditors to delay making the disclosures under certain conditions if an account is opened by telephone by a merchant to finance the cost of consumer goods and services.[5]

The creditor must make the required account-opening disclosures clearly and conspicuously in writing, in a form that the consumer may keep.[6] Certain account-opening disclosures must be presented in a tabular format and these disclosures must also be readily noticeable to the consumer.[7] The "readily noticeable" standard requires that the disclosures be in at least 10-point font, except the disclosure of the annual percentage rate (APR) for purchases (which must be in 16-point font).[8] The disclosures may be provided to the consumer in electronic form, subject to compliance with the consumer consent and other applicable provisions of the federal E-SIGN Act.[9]

The disclosures must reflect the terms of the legal obligation between the parties.[10] The legal obligation is determined by applicable state law or other law.[11] The disclosures need be made only as applicable.[12]

If there is more than one consumer, the disclosures may be made to any consumer who is primarily liable on the obligation.[13]

Creditors must provide certain account-opening disclosures in the form of a table (or in the case of the balance computation method, billing error rights reference, and circumstances in which a consumer may lose an introductory rate, immediately below the table[14]), with the headings, content, and format substantially similar to any of the applicable tables in G-17 in appendix G to Regulation Z.[15] In the table, any APR, introductory rate, or any rate that will apply after a premium initial rate expires, and any fee or percentage amounts or maximum limits on fee amounts must be disclosed in bold text.[16]

---

4. 12 C.F.R. § 1026.5(b)(1)(i) (2020).
5. *Id.* § 1026.5(b)(1)(iii) (2020).
6. *Id.* § 1026.5(a)(1) (2020).
7. *Id.*
8. 12 C.F.R. pt. 1026, supp. I, cmt. 5(a)(1)-3 (2020).
9. 12 C.F.R. § 1026.5(a)(1)(iii) (2020).
10. 12 C.F.R. § 1026.5(c) (2020).
11. 12 C.F.R. pt. 1026, supp. I, cmt. 5(c)-1 (2020).
12. 12 C.F.R. § 1026.6(b)(2).
13. *Id.* § 1026.5(d) (2020).
14. *Id.* § 1026.6(b)(1)(ii) (2020).
15. *Id.* § 1026.5(b)(1) (2020). Appendix G is available at https://www.consumerfinance.gov/policy-compliance/rulemaking/regulations/1026/G/.
16. *Id.* § 1026.5(b)(1)(i) (2020).

The tabular disclosures must include the APR for purchases, cash advances, or balance transfers.[17] The APR is computed by multiplying each periodic rate by the number of periods in a year.[18] The APR for purchases must be in at least 16-point type.[19] If the APR for any particular class of transactions is a variable rate, the creditor must also disclose the fact that the rate may vary and how the rate is determined.[20] If the initial rate is an introductory rate, the creditor must disclose the rate that would otherwise apply to the account.[21] Except with respect to credit card accounts, the creditor is not required to disclose the introductory rate in the table, but may do so, along with the rate that would otherwise apply to the account, if the creditor also discloses the period during which the introductory rate will remain in effect, and uses the term "introductory" or "intro" in immediate proximity to the introductory rate.[22] For credit card accounts, creditors must disclose any introductory rate that would apply to the account.[23] For disclosed introductory rates, creditors must briefly disclose directly beneath the table the circumstances under which the introductory rate may be revoked, and the rate that will apply after the introductory rate is revoked.[24] If a rate may increase as a penalty for one or more events specified in the account agreement, the creditor must disclose the increased rate that may apply, a brief description of the event or events that may result in the increased rate, and a brief description of how long the increased rate will remain in effect.[25] Regulation Z permits creditors to disclose a range of rates if rates vary by state or based on the consumer's creditworthiness and disclosures are provided in-person at the point of sale of goods and services.[26]

Creditors must disclose in the account-opening table any annual or other periodic fee that may be imposed for the issuance or availability of the plan, including any fee based on account activity or inactivity, how frequently it will be imposed, and the annualized amount of the fee.[27] Creditors must also disclose any nonperiodic fee that relates to opening the plan.[28] A creditor must disclose that the fee is a one-time fee.[29]

17. *Id.* § 1026.6(b)(2)(i) (2020).

18. *Id.* § 1026.14(b) (2020).

19. *Id.* § 1026.6(b)(2)(i) (2020).

20. *Id.* § 1026.6(b)(2)(i)(A) (2020).

21. *Id.* § 1026.6(b)(2)(i)(B) (2020). An "introductory rate" is any APR applicable to one or more balances or transactions for a specified period that is lower than the APR that will be in effect at the end of that period on such balances or transactions, which rate is offered in connection with the opening of an account. *Id.* § 1026.16(g)(2)(i)–(ii) (2020).

22. *Id.* § 1026.6(b)(2)(i)(B) (2020).

23. *Id.* § 1026.6(b)(2)(i)(F)(1) (2020).

24. *Id.* § 1026.6(b)(2)(i)(D)(2) (2020).

25. *Id.* § 1026.6(b)(2)(i)(D)(1) (2020).

26. *Id.* § 1026.6(b)(2)(i)(E)(2) (2020).

27. *Id.* § 1026.6(b)(2)(ii)(A) (2020).

28. *Id.* § 1026.6(b)(2)(ii)(B) (2020).

29. *Id.*

Creditors must disclose in the account-opening table any fixed finance charge and a brief description of the charge.[30] In addition, creditors must disclose any minimum interest charge that exceeds one dollar that could be imposed during a billing cycle, and a brief description of the charge.[31]

Creditors must disclose in the account-opening table any transaction charge imposed by the creditor for use of the plan for purchases.[32]

The account-opening table must include the date by which or the period within which any credit extended may be repaid without incurring a finance charge due to a periodic interest rate and any conditions on the availability of the grace period.[33]

Creditors must disclose any fee imposed for (1) an extension of credit in the form of cash or its equivalent,[34] (2) a late payment,[35] (3) exceeding a credit limit,[36] (4) transfer of an outstanding balance,[37] and (5) a returned payment.[38] If a creditor requires the consumer to purchase credit insurance, debt cancellation coverage, or debt suspension coverage, the creditor must disclose in the account-opening table the fee for such products and a cross-reference to any additional information provided by the coverage.[39]

If the total amount of those required fees and/or security deposit that will be imposed and charged to the account when the account is opened is 15 percent or more of the minimum credit limit for the plan, a creditor must disclose the available credit remaining after these fees or security deposit are debited to the account and that the consumer has a right to reject the plan.[40]

---

30. *Id.* § 1026.6(b)(2)(iii) (2020).

31. *Id.* Note that the one-dollar threshold amount is adjusted periodically by the CFPB to reflect changes in the consumer price index. Each year, the Bureau calculates a price level adjusted minimum interest charge using the consumer price index in effect on June 1 of that year. When the cumulative change in the adjusted minimum value derived from applying the annual consumer price level to the current minimum interest charge threshold has risen by a whole dollar, the minimum interest charge will be increased by one dollar.

32. *Id.* § 1026.6(b)(2)(iv) (2020).

33. *Id.* § 1026.6(b)(2)(v) (2020).

34. *Id.* § 1026.6(b)(2)(vii) (2020).

35. *Id.* § 1026.6(b)(2)(viii) (2020).

36. *Id.* § 1026.6(b)(2)(ix) (2020).

37. *Id.* § 1026.6(b)(2)(x) (2020).

38. *Id.* § 1026.6(b)(2)(xi) (2020).

39. *Id.* § 1026.6(b)(2)(xii) (2020).

40. *Id.* § 1026.6(b)(2)(xiii) (2020).

For issuers of credit cards that are not charge cards,[41] the account-opening table must include a reference to the website established by the CFPB[42] and a statement that consumers may obtain information on the website about shopping for and using credit cards.[43]

Creditors must disclose, directly below the account-opening table, the name of the balance computation method used to determine the balance on which the finance charge is computed, or an explanation of the method used if it is not one of the following: the average daily balance (including new purchases), average daily balance (excluding new purchases), adjusted balance, previous balance, or daily balance.[44]

Creditors must include immediately below the account-opening table a statement that information about consumers' right to dispute transactions is included in the account-opening disclosures (typically, the account agreement).[45]

In addition to the highlighted disclosures that must appear in the account-opening table described above, creditors must disclose the circumstances under which charges may be imposed, including the amount of the charge or an explanation of how the charge is determined.[46] For finance charges, the disclosures must include a statement of when the charge begins to accrue and an explanation of whether or not any time period exists within which any credit that has been extended may be repaid without incurring the charge.[47] For each periodic rate that may be used to calculate interest, creditors must disclose the rate (expressed as a periodic rate and a corresponding APR),[48] the range of balances to which the rate is applicable,[49] the type of transaction to which the rate applies (if different rates apply to different types of transactions),[50] and an explanation of the method used to determine the balance to which the rate is applied.[51]

For variable rates tied to an index or formula, the account agreement must set forth the fact that the APR may increase,[52] how the rate is determined, including the

41. "Credit card" means any card, plate, or other single credit device that may be used from time to time to obtain credit. *Id.* § 1026.2(15)(i) (2020). "Charge card" means a credit card on an account for which no periodic rate is used to compute a finance charge. *Id.* § 1026.2(15)(iii) (2020).

42. https://www.consumerfinance.gov/learnmore/.

43. *Id.* § 1026.6(b)(2)(xiv) (2020).

44. *Id.* § 1026.6(b)(2)(vi) (2020), § 1026.60(g) (2020), 1026.6(b)(1)(ii) (2020).

45. *Id.* § 1026.6(b)(2)(xv) (2020), § 1026.6(b)(1)(ii) (2020).

46. *Id.* § 1026.6(b)(3)(i) (2020).

47. *Id.*

48. *Id.* § 1026.6(b)(4)(i)(A) (2020).

49. *Id.* § 1026.6(b)(4)(i)(B) (2020).

50. *Id.* § 1026.6(b)(4)(i)(C) (2020).

51. *Id.* § 1026.6(b)(4)(i)(D) (2020).

52. *Id.* § 1026.6(b)(4)(ii)(A) (2020).

margin,[53] the circumstances under which the rate may increase,[54] the frequency with which the rate may increase,[55] any limitation on the amount the rate may change,[56] and the effect(s) of an increase.[57] A variable rate disclosure is accurate if it is a rate as of a specified date and this rate was in effect within the last thirty days before the disclosures are provided.[58]

A creditor also must disclose the following, to the extent applicable: the information required to exclude charges for optional credit insurance, debt cancellation or debt suspension coverage from the finance charge;[59] the fact that the creditor has or will acquire a security interest in the property purchased under the plan, or in other property identified by item or type;[60] and a statement that outlines the consumer's rights and the creditor's responsibilities under the billing rights and unauthorized use rules that is substantially similar to the statement found in Model Form G-3(A) in appendix G.[61]

3. Periodic Statement

Creditors must mail or deliver a periodic statement for each billing cycle at the end of which an account has a debit or credit balance of more than one dollar or on which a finance charge has been imposed.[62] A periodic statement need not be sent for an account if the creditor deems it uncollectible, if delinquency collection proceedings have been instituted, if the creditor has charged off the account in accordance with loan-loss provisions and will not charge any additional fees or interest on the account, or if furnishing the statement would violate Federal law.[63]

Creditors must adopt reasonable procedures designed to ensure that, if a grace period applies to the account, periodic statements are mailed or delivered at least twenty-one days prior to the date on which the grace period expires, and the creditor does not impose finance charges as a result of the loss of the grace period if a payment that satisfies the terms of the grace period is received by the creditor within

53. *Id.* § 1026.6(b)(4)(ii)(B) (2020).
54. *Id.* § 1026.6(b)(4)(ii)(C) (2020).
55. *Id.* § 1026.6(b)(4)(ii)(D) (2020).
56. *Id.* § 1026.6(b)(4)(ii)(E) (2020).
57. *Id.* § 1026.6(b)(4)(ii)(F) (2020).
58. *Id.* § 1026.6(b)(4)(ii)(G) (2020).
59. *Id.* § 1026.6(b)(5)(i) (2020).
60. *Id.* § 1026.6(b)(5)(ii) (2020).
61. *Id.* § 1026.6(b)(5)(iii) (2020). Model Form G-3(A) is available at https://www.consumerfinance.gov/policycompliance/rulemaking/regulations/1026/G/#515bc4d9b6f15d9978534410a29bea8683cd4101d2343175bc2e15c4.
62. *Id.* § 1026.5(b)(2)(i) (2020).
63. *Id.*

twenty-one days after mailing or delivery of the periodic statement.[64] "Grace period" means a period within which any credit extended may be repaid without incurring a finance charge due to a periodic interest rate.[65] Further, regardless of whether a grace period applies to the account, creditors must adopt reasonable procedures designed to ensure that periodic statements are mailed or delivered at least fourteen days prior to the date on which the required minimum periodic payment must be received to avoid being treated as late for any purpose, and the creditor does not treat as late for any purpose a required minimum periodic payment received by the creditor within fourteen days after mailing or delivery of the periodic statement.[66]

For credit card accounts, a card issuer must adopt reasonable procedures designed to ensure that periodic statements are mailed or delivered at least twenty-one days prior to the payment due date disclosed on the statement, and that the issuer does not treat as late for any purpose a required minimum periodic payment received by the card issuer within twenty-one days after mailing or delivery of the periodic statement disclosing the due date for that payment.[67]

Creditors must disclose the account balance outstanding at the beginning of the billing cycle ("previous balance");[68] each credit transaction during the cycle;[69] any credit to the account during the billing cycle, including the amount and the date of crediting;[70] each periodic rate that may be used to compute the interest charge expressed as an APR, along with the range of balances to which it is applicable;[71] the balance(s) subject to interest rates;[72] charges (interest and fees), grouped together, in proximity to transactions and in a format substantially similar to sample G-18(A) in appendix G;[73] the grace period;[74] the address to be used for notice of billing errors (alternatively, the address may be provided on a billing rights notice included in the periodic statement);[75] the closing date of the billing cycle and the account balance outstanding on that date ("new balance");[76] and, for any deferred interest or similar programs, the date by which that outstanding balance must be paid in full to avoid the obligation to pay finance charges on such balance.[77] The statement must also

64. *Id.* § 1026.5(b)(2)(ii)(B)(1) (2020).
65. *Id.* § 1026.5(b)(2)(ii)(B)(3) (2020).
66. *Id.* § 1026.5(b)(2)(ii)(B)(2) (2020).
67. *Id.* § 1026.5(b)(2)(ii)(A) (2020).
68. *Id.* § 1026.7(b)(1) (2020).
69. *Id.* § 1026.7(b)(2) (2020).
70. *Id.* § 1026.7(b)(3) (2020).
71. *Id.* § 1026.7(b)(4)(i) (2020).
72. *Id.* § 1026.7(b)(5) (2020).
73. *Id.* § 1026.7(b)(6)(i) (2020).
74. *Id.* § 1026.7(b)(8) (2020).
75. *Id.* § 1026.7(b)(9) (2020).
76. *Id.* § 1026.7(b)(10) (2020).
77. *Id.* § 1026.7(b)(14) (2020).

include separate totals of interest charged and fees charged for the billing cycle, as well as separate totals of interest charged and fees charged for the year.[78] Creditors also have the option to disclose a significant change in account terms in the periodic statement.[79]

If the account is a credit card, the periodic statement must also include the due date for payment,[80] the amount of any late payment fee or penalty rate for failure to pay by the due date,[81] and repayment disclosures that highlight the costs of making only minimum payments and length of repayment if only minimum payments are made.[82] Regulation Z imposes specific format requirements for these credit card disclosures.[83]

4. Subsequent Disclosure Requirements

4.1 Statement of Billing Rights

Creditors must mail or deliver a billing rights statement at least once each calendar year, at intervals of not less than six months nor more than eighteen months, either to all consumers or to each consumer entitled to receive a periodic statement.[84] Alternatively, the creditor may mail or deliver, on or with each periodic statement, a notice substantially similar to model form G-4(A) in appendix G.[85]

4.2 Disclosures for Supplemental Credit Access Devices and Additional Features

If a creditor, within thirty days after mailing or delivering the account-opening disclosures adds a credit feature to the consumer's account or mails or delivers to the consumer a credit access device, including but not limited to checks that access a credit card account, for which the finance charge terms are the same as those previously disclosed, no additional disclosures are necessary.[86] After thirty days, if the creditor adds a credit feature or furnishes a credit access device (other than as a renewal, resupply, or the original issuance of a credit card) on the same finance charge terms, the creditor must disclose, before the consumer uses the feature or device for the

78. *Id.* § 1026.7(b)(6)(ii)–(iii) (2020).

79. *Id.* § 1026.7(b)(7) (2020); *see also id.* § 1026.9(c)(2)(iv)(D)(2) (2020).

80. *Id.* § 1026.7(b)(11)(i)(A) (2020).

81. *Id.* § 1026.7(b)(11)(i)(B) (2020).

82. *Id.* § 1026.7(b)(12) (2020).

83. *Id.* § 1026.7(b)(13) (2020).

84. *Id.* § 1026.9(a)(1) (2020).

85. *Id.* § 1026.9(a)(2) (2020). Model form G-4(a) is available at https://www.consumerfinance.gov/policy-compliance/rulemaking/regulations/1026/G/#G4-A.

86. 12 C.F.R. § 1026.9(b)(1) (2020).

first time, that it is for use in obtaining credit under the terms previously disclosed.[87] Whenever a credit feature is added or a credit access device is mailed or delivered to the consumer, and the finance charge terms for the feature or device differ from disclosures previously given, Regulation Z requires creditors to make disclosures of the costs of the feature or device before the consumer uses the feature or device for the first time.[88]

Notwithstanding the above, for credit card accounts, if checks that can be used to access a credit card account are provided more than thirty days after account-opening disclosures are mailed or delivered, or are provided within thirty days of the account-opening disclosures and the finance charge terms for the checks differ from the finance charge terms previously disclosed, the creditor must disclose on the front of the page containing the checks specific cost terms in the form of a table with the headings, content, and form substantially similar to sample G-19 in appendix G.[89]

4.3 Change in Terms

Generally, when a significant change in account terms is made, a creditor must provide a written notice of the change at least forty-five days prior to the effective date of the change to each consumer who may be affected.[90] A "significant change in account terms" means a change to a term required to be disclosed in or directly below the account-opening summary table, an increase in the required minimum periodic payment, a change to a term required to be disclosed under section 1026.6(b)(4) (information related to periodic interest rates), or the acquisition of a security interest.[91]

If a creditor makes a significant change in account terms, the notice of change in terms must include the following:

1. A summary of the changes, a description of any increase in the required minimum periodic payment, and a description of any security interest being acquired by the creditor;
2. A statement that changes are being made to the account;
3. For accounts other than credit card accounts, a statement indicating the consumer has the right to opt out of these changes, if applicable, and a reference to additional information describing the opt-out right provided in the notice, if applicable;
4. The date the changes will become effective;

---

87. *Id.*

88. *Id.* § 1026.9(b)(2) (2020).

89. *Id.* § 1026.9(b)(3) (2020). Sample G-19 is available at https://www.consumerfinance.gov/policy-compliance/rulemaking/regulations/1026/G/#eba50aa775146f7ef4ef6327fdb62c61bb02c8de9505f07b75e9c8a3.

90. 12 C.F.R. § 1026.9(c)(2)(i) (2020).

91. *Id.* § 1026.9(c)(2)(ii) (2020).

5. If applicable, a statement that the consumer may find additional information about the summarized changes, and other changes to the account, in the notice;
6. If the creditor is changing a rate on the account, other than a penalty rate, a statement that if a penalty rate currently applies to the consumer's account, the new rate described in the notice will not apply to the consumer's account until the consumer's account balances are no longer subject to the penalty rate;
7. If the change in terms being disclosed is an increase in an APR, the balances to which the increased rate will be applied and a statement identifying the balances to which the current rate will continue to apply; and
8. If the change in terms being disclosed is an increase in an APR for a credit card account, a statement of no more than four principal reasons for the rate increase, listed in their order of importance.[92]

If a card issuer makes a significant change in account terms on a credit card account, the consumer has a right to reject the change (subject to a few exceptions) and the notice must include a reference to this right, how to exercise it, and, if applicable, that rejecting the change will result in a loss of the ability to use the account.[93] In addition, if the change in terms is an increase in rates or fees for failure to make a minimum periodic payment within sixty days of its due date, the notice must also state that the increase will cease to apply to transactions that occurred prior to or within fourteen days of provision of the notice, if the creditor receives six consecutive required minimum periodic payments on or before the payment due date, beginning with the first payment due following the effective date of the increase.[94]

A change in terms notice must be made in a specific format that is substantially similar to any of the account-opening tables found in G-17 in appendix G to this part.[95]

4.4 Renewal of Credit or Charge Card

A card issuer that imposes any annual or other periodic fee to renew a credit or charge card account, including any fee based on account activity or inactivity, or any card issuer that has changed or amended any term of a cardholder's account required to be disclosed in or directly below the account-opening table that has not previously been disclosed to the consumer, must mail or deliver written notice of the renewal to the

92. *Id.* § 1026.9(c)(2)(iv)(A) (2020).

93. *Id.* § 1026.9(c)(2)(iv)(B) (2020).

94. *Id.* § 1026.9(c)(2)(iv)(C)(1) (2020).

95. *Id.* § 1026.9(c)(2)(iv)(D)(1) (2020). The G-17 model form and samples are available at https://www.consumerfinance.gov/policy-compliance/rulemaking/regulations/1026/G/.

cardholder.[96] If the card issuer imposes any annual or other periodic fee for renewal, the notice must be provided at least thirty days or one billing cycle, whichever is less, before the mailing or the delivery of the periodic statement on which any renewal fee is initially charged to the account.[97] If the card issuer has changed or amended any term required to be disclosed in or directly below the account-opening table, and such changed or amended term has not previously been disclosed to the consumer, the notice must be provided at least thirty days prior to the scheduled renewal date of the consumer's credit or charge card.[98] The notice must include specific information about the cost of the account and how and when the cardholder may terminate credit availability under the account to avoid paying the renewal fee, if applicable.[99]

4.5 Change in Credit Card Account Insurance Provider

If a credit card issuer plans to change the provider of insurance for repayment of all or part of the outstanding balance of an open-end credit card account, the card issuer must mail or deliver to the cardholder written notice of the change not less than thirty days before the change in provider occurs.[100] The notice must include any increase in the rate that will result from the change, any substantial decrease in coverage that will result from the change, and a statement that the cardholder may discontinue the insurance.[101] If a change occurs, the card issuer must provide the cardholder with a written notice no later than thirty days after the change, including the name and address of the new insurance provider, a copy of the new policy or group certificate containing the basic terms of the insurance, including the rate to be charged, and a statement that the cardholder may discontinue the insurance.[102]

4.6 Increase in Rates Due to Delinquency, Default, or as a Penalty

A creditor must provide a written notice to each consumer who may be affected when a rate is increased due to the consumer's delinquency or default, or as a penalty for one or more events specified in the account agreement.[103] The notice must be provided after the default and at least forty-five days prior to the increase.[104] The notice must include the following:

---

96. *Id.* § 1026.9(e)(1) (2020).
97. *Id.*
98. *Id.*
99. *Id.*
100. *Id.* § 1026.9(f)(1) (2020).
101. *Id.*
102. *Id.* § 1026.9(f)(2) (2020).
103. *Id.* § 1026.9(g)(1) (2020).
104. *Id.* § 1026.9(g)(2) (2020).

1. A statement that the delinquency or default rate or penalty rate, as applicable, has been triggered;
2. The date on which the delinquency or default rate or penalty rate will apply;
3. The circumstances under which the delinquency or default rate or penalty rate, as applicable, will cease to apply to the consumer's account, or that the delinquency or default rate or penalty rate will remain in effect for a potentially indefinite time period;
4. A statement indicating to which balances the delinquency or default rate or penalty rate will be applied;
5. If applicable, a description of any balances to which the current rate will continue to apply as of the effective date of the rate increase, unless a consumer fails to make a minimum periodic payment within sixty days from the due date for that payment; and
6. For a credit card account, a statement of no more than four principal reasons for the rate increase, listed in their order of importance.[105]

For a credit card account, if the rate increase required to be disclosed is an increase based on the consumer's failure to make a minimum periodic payment within sixty days from the due date for that payment, the notice must also state that the increase will cease to apply to transactions that occurred prior to or within fourteen days of provision of the notice, if the creditor receives six consecutive required minimum periodic payments on or before the payment due date, beginning with the first payment due following the effective date of the increase.[106]

Regulation Z imposes specific format requirements for this notice.[107]

4.7 Rejection of Significant Changes in Account Terms

If a creditor is notified of a rejection of a significant change to an account term, the creditor must not apply the change to the account, impose a fee or charge, or treat the account as in default solely as a result of the rejection, or require repayment of the balance on the account using a method that is less beneficial to the consumer than one of the methods permitted by Regulation Z.[108] These provisions do not apply when the creditor has not received the consumer's required minimum periodic payment within sixty days after the due date for that payment.[109]

105. *Id.* § 1026.9(g)(3)(i)(A) (2020).
106. *Id.* § 1026.9(g)(3)(i)(B) (2020).
107. *See id.* § 1026.9(g)(3)(ii) (2020).
108. *Id.* § 1026.9(h)(1)–(2) (2020); *see also id.* § 1026.55(c)(2) (2020).
109. *Id.* § 1026.9(h)(3) (2020).

5. Payments

Creditors must credit payments to the consumer's account as of the date of receipt, except when a delay in crediting does not result in a finance or other charge.[110] However, a creditor may specify reasonable requirements for payments that enable most consumers to make conforming payments.[111] Reasonable requirements for making payment may include, for example:

1. Requiring that payments be accompanied by the account number or payment stub;
2. Setting reasonable cut-off times for payments to be received by mail, by electronic means, by telephone, and in person (provided that such cut-off times shall be no earlier than 5:00 p.m. on the payment due date at the location specified by the creditor for the receipt of such payments);
3. Specifying that only checks or money orders should be sent by mail;
4. Specifying that payment is to be made in U.S. dollars; or
5. Specifying one particular address for receiving payments, such as a post office box.[112]

A card issuer that is a financial institution may impose a cut-off time earlier than the close of business for any such payments made in person at any branch or office of the card issuer at which such payments are accepted.[113] A card issuer may impose a cut-off time earlier than 5:00 p.m. for such payments, if the close of business of the branch or office is earlier than 5:00 p.m.[114]

If a creditor accepts a payment that does not conform to their reasonable requirements, the creditor must credit the payment within five days of receipt.[115] If a creditor does not receive or accept payments by mail on the due date for payments, the creditor may generally not treat a payment received the next business day as late for any purpose.[116] If a creditor accepts or receives payments made on the due date by a method other than mail, such as electronic or telephone payments, the creditor is not required to treat a payment made by that method on the next business day as timely, even if it does not accept mailed payments on the due date.[117]

For credit card accounts, a creditor may not impose a separate fee to allow consumers to make a payment by any method, such as mail, electronic, or telephone

---

110. *Id.* § 1026.10(a) (2020).

111. *Id.* § 1026.10(b)(1) (2020).

112. *Id.* § 1026.10(b)(2) (2020).

113. *Id.* § 1026.10(b)(3)(i) (2020). "Financial institution" means a bank, savings association, or credit union. *Id.* § 1026.10(b)(3)(ii) (2020).

114. *Id.* § 1026.10(b)(3)(i) (2020).

115. *Id.* § 1026.10(b)(4)(i) (2020).

116. *Id.* § 1026.10(d)(1) (2020).

117. *Id.* § 1026.10(d)(2) (2020).

payments, unless such payment method involves an expedited service by a customer service representative of the creditor.[118]

6. Treatment of Credit Balances; Account Termination

When a credit balance in excess of one dollar is created on a credit account (through transmittal of funds to a creditor in excess of the total balance due on an account, through rebates of unearned finance charges or insurance premiums, or through amounts otherwise owed to or held for the benefit of the consumer), the creditor must credit the amount of the credit balance to the consumer's account, refund any part of the remaining credit balance within seven business days from receipt of a written request from the consumer, and make a good faith effort to refund to the consumer by cash, check, or money order, or credit to a deposit account of the consumer, any part of the credit balance remaining in the account for more than six months.[119] No further action is required if the consumer's current location is not known to the creditor and cannot be traced through the consumer's last known address or telephone number.[120]

A creditor may not terminate an account prior to its expiration date solely because the consumer does not incur a finance charge.[121] This limitation does not preclude creditors from closing an account that is inactive for three or more consecutive months.[122] An account is inactive if no credit has been extended (such as by purchase, cash advance, or balance transfer) and if the account has no outstanding balance.[123]

7. Special Credit Card Provisions

7.1 Prohibition on Unsolicited Cards

No credit card (including those issued for business or commercial use) may be issued to any person except in response to an oral or written request or application for the card, or as a renewal of, or substitute for, an accepted credit card.[124]

---

118. *Id.* § 1026.10(e) (2020).
119. *Id.* § 1026.11(a) (2020).
120. *Id.*
121. *Id.* § 1026.11(b)(1) (2020).
122. *Id.* § 1026.11(b)(2) (2020).
123. *Id.*
124. *Id.* § 1026.12(a) (2020).

7.2 Liability of Cardholder for Unauthorized Use

The unauthorized use provisions of Regulation Z apply both to consumer and commercial purpose credit cards.[125] The liability of a cardholder for unauthorized use of a credit card may not exceed the lesser of fifty dollars or the amount of money, property, labor, or services obtained by the unauthorized use before notification to the card issuer.[126] "Unauthorized use" means the use of a credit card by a person, other than the cardholder, who does not have actual, implied, or apparent authority for such use, and from which the cardholder receives no benefit.[127] A cardholder may be liable for unauthorized use of a credit card only if the credit card is an accepted credit card, the card issuer has provided adequate notice of the cardholder's maximum potential liability and of means by which the card issuer may be notified of loss or theft of the card,[128] and the card issuer has provided a means to identify the cardholder on the account or the authorized user of the card.[129]

Notification to a card issuer is given when steps have been taken as may be reasonably required in the ordinary course of business to provide the card issuer with the pertinent information about the loss, theft, or possible unauthorized use of a credit card, regardless of whether any particular officer, employee, or agent of the card issuer does, in fact, receive the information.[130] Notification may be given, at the option of the person giving it, in person, by telephone, or in writing.[131] Notification in writing is considered given at the time of receipt or, whether or not received, at the expiration of the time ordinarily required for transmission, whichever is earlier.[132]

7.3 Right of Cardholder to Assert Claims or Defenses against Issuer

When a person who honors a credit card fails to resolve satisfactorily a dispute as to property or services purchased with the credit card in a consumer credit transaction, the cardholder may assert against the card issuer all claims (other than tort claims) and defenses arising out of the transaction and relating to the failure to resolve the dispute.[133] The cardholder may withhold payment up to the amount of credit outstanding

125. *See* 12 C.F.R. pt. 1026, supp. I, cmt. 2(a)(8)-2 (2020).

126. 12 C.F.R. § 1026.12(b)(1)(ii) (2020).

127. *Id.* § 1026.12(b)(1)(i) (2020).

128. The notice must state that the cardholder's liability may not exceed fifty dollars (or any lesser amount) and that the cardholder may give oral or written notification, and must describe a means of notification (for example, a telephone number, an address, or both). 12 C.F.R. § 1026.12(b)(2)(ii) (2020).

129. *Id.* § 1026.12(b)(2) (2020).

130. *Id.* § 1026.12(b)(3) (2020).

131. *Id.*

132. *Id.*

133. *Id.* § 1026.12(c)(1) (2020).

for the property or services that gave rise to the dispute and any finance or other charges imposed on that amount.[134] The card issuer may not report that amount so withheld as delinquent until the dispute is settled or judgment is rendered.[135]

The right to assert claims and defenses against the issuer is available only if the cardholder has made a good-faith attempt to resolve the dispute with the person honoring the credit card, the amount of credit extended to obtain the property or services that result in the assertion of the claim or defense by the cardholder exceeds fifty dollars, and the disputed transaction occurred in the same state as the cardholder's current designated address or, if not within the same state, within one hundred miles from that address.[136]

7.4 Offsets Prohibited

A card issuer may not take any action, either before or after termination of credit card privileges, to offset a cardholder's indebtedness arising from a consumer credit transaction under the relevant credit card plan against funds of the cardholder held on deposit with the card issuer.[137] This limitation does not prohibit a creditor from obtaining or enforcing a consensual security interest in the funds, attaching or otherwise levying upon the funds, or obtaining or enforcing a court order relating to the funds.[138] Further, creditors may, if authorized in writing by the cardholder, periodically deduct all or part of the cardholder's credit card debt from a deposit account held with the card issuer.[139]

7.5 Prompt Notification of Returns and Crediting of Refunds

When a creditor other than the card issuer accepts the return of property or forgives a debt for services that is to be reflected as a credit to the consumer's credit card account, that creditor must, within seven business days from accepting the return or forgiving the debt, transmit a credit statement to the card issuer through the card issuer's normal channels for credit statements.[140] The card issuer must, within three business days from receipt of a credit statement, credit the consumer's account with the amount of the refund.[141]

---

134. *Id.*
135. *Id.* § 1026.12(c)(2) (2020).
136. *Id.* § 1026.12(c)(3)(i) (2020).
137. *Id.* § 1026.12(d)(1) (2020).
138. *Id.* § 1026.12(d)(2) (2020).
139. *Id.* § 1026.12(d)(3)(i) (2020).
140. *Id.* § 1026.12(e)(1) (2020).
141. *Id.* § 1026.12(e)(2) (2020).

7.6 Discounts and Tie-In Arrangements

Card issuers are prohibited, by contract or otherwise, from precluding any person who honors a credit card from offering a discount to a consumer to induce the consumer to pay by cash, check, or similar means rather than by use of a credit card or its underlying account for the purchase of property or services.[142] Further, issuers may not require any person who honors the card issuer's credit card to open or maintain any account or obtain any other service not essential to the operation of the credit card plan from the card issuer or any other person, as a condition of participation in a credit card plan.[143] If maintenance of an account for clearing purposes is determined to be essential to the operation of the credit card plan, it may be required only if no service charges or minimum balance requirements are imposed.[144]

8. Billing Error Resolution

Regulation Z establishes procedures creditors must follow when a consumer alleges a billing error.[145] A billing error is:

- A reflection on or with a periodic statement of an extension of credit that is not made to the consumer or to a person who has actual, implied, or apparent authority to use the consumer's credit card or open-end credit plan.[146]
- A reflection on or with a periodic statement of an extension of credit that is not identified in accordance with Regulation Z.[147]
- A reflection on or with a periodic statement of an extension of credit for property or services not accepted by the consumer or the consumer's designee, or not delivered to the consumer or the consumer's designee as agreed.[148]
- A reflection on a periodic statement of the creditor's failure to credit properly a payment or other credit issued to the consumer's account.[149]
- A reflection on a periodic statement of a computational or similar error of an accounting nature that is made by the creditor.[150]

---

142. *Id.* § 1026.12(f)(1) (2020).
143. *Id.* § 1026.12(f)(2) (2020).
144. *Id.*
145. *See id.* § 1026.13 (2020).
146. *Id.* § 1026.13(a)(1) (2020).
147. *Id.* § 1026.13(a)(2) (2020); *see also* § 1026.7(b)(2) (2020); § 1026.8 (2020).
148. *Id.* § 1026.13(a)(3) (2020).
149. *Id.* § 1026.13(a)(4) (2020).
150. *Id.* § 1026.13(a)(5) (2020).

- A reflection on a periodic statement of an extension of credit for which the consumer requests additional clarification, including documentary evidence.[151]
- The creditor's failure to mail or deliver a periodic statement to the consumer's last known address if that address was received by the creditor, in writing, at least twenty days before the end of the billing cycle for which the statement was required.[152]

For purposes of the procedures for responding to billing errors, "billing error notice" is a written notice from a consumer that: (1) is received by a creditor at the address disclosed for such purpose no later than sixty days after the creditor transmitted the first periodic statement that reflects the alleged billing error; (2) enables the creditor to identify the consumer's name and account number; and (3) to the extent possible, indicates the consumer's belief and the reasons for the belief that a billing error exists, and the type, date, and amount of the error.[153]

The creditor must mail or deliver written acknowledgment to the consumer within thirty days of receiving a billing error notice, unless the creditor has complied with the appropriate resolution procedures within the thirty-day period.[154] The creditor must comply with the resolution procedures within two complete billing cycles (but in no event later than ninety days) after receiving a billing error notice.[155]

Until a billing error is resolved, the consumer need not pay (and the creditor may not try to collect) any portion of any required payment that the consumer believes is related to the disputed amount (including related finance or other charges).[156] If the cardholder has enrolled in an automatic payment plan offered by the card issuer and has agreed to pay the credit card indebtedness by periodic deductions from the cardholder's deposit account, the card issuer may not deduct any part of the disputed amount or related finance or other charges if a billing error notice is received any time up to three business days before the scheduled payment date.[157] The creditor or its agent may not (directly or indirectly) make or threaten to make an adverse report to any person about the consumer's credit standing, or report that an amount or account is delinquent, because the consumer failed to pay the disputed amount or related finance or other charges.[158] Further, a creditor may not accelerate any part of the consumer's indebtedness or restrict or close a consumer's account solely because the consumer has exercised in good faith rights to allege a billing error.[159]

---

151. *Id.* § 1026.13(a)(6) (2020).
152. *Id.* § 1026.13(a)(7) (2020).
153. *Id.* § 1026.13(b) (2020).
154. *Id.* § 1026.13(c)(1) (2020).
155. *Id.* § 1026.13(c)(2) (2020).
156. *Id.* § 1026.13(d)(1) (2020).
157. *Id.*
158. *Id.* § 1026.13(d)(2) (2020).
159. *Id.* § 1026.13(d)(3) (2020).

While the alleged error is investigated, the creditor is not prohibited from taking action to collect any undisputed portion of the item or bill, from deducting any disputed amount and related finance or other charges from the consumer's credit limit on the account, or from reflecting a disputed amount and related finance or other charges on a periodic statement, provided that the creditor indicates on or with the periodic statement that payment of any disputed amount and related finance or other charges is not required pending the creditor's investigation of the alleged billing error.[160]

If a creditor determines that a billing error occurred as asserted, it must, within the time limits noted above, correct the billing error and credit the consumer's account with any disputed amount and related finance or other charges, as applicable, and mail or deliver a correction notice to the consumer.[161]

If, after conducting a reasonable investigation, a creditor determines that no billing error occurred or that a different billing error occurred from that asserted, the creditor must within the time limits noted above, mail or deliver to the consumer an explanation that sets forth the reasons for the creditor's belief that the billing error alleged by the consumer is incorrect in whole or in part, furnish copies of documentary evidence of the consumer's indebtedness, if the consumer so requests, and if a different billing error occurred, correct the billing error and credit the consumer's account with any disputed amount and related finance or other charges, as applicable.[162]

If a creditor, after complying with all of the above requirements, determines that a consumer owes all or part of the disputed amount and related finance or other charges, the creditor:

- Must promptly notify the consumer in writing of the time when payment is due and the portion of the disputed amount and related finance or other charges that the consumer still owes;
- Must provide any grace period disclosed to the consumer at account opening or in a periodic statement;
- May report an account or amount as delinquent because the amount due remains unpaid after the creditor has provided any applicable grace period for that amount, or ten days (whichever is longer), during which the consumer can pay the amount;
- May not report that an amount or account is delinquent because the amount due remains unpaid, if the creditor receives (within the time allowed for payment as noted in the bullet immediately above), further written notice from the consumer that any portion of the billing error is still in dispute, unless the creditor also:
  (i) Promptly reports that the amount or account is in dispute;

160. *Id.* § 1026.13(d)(4) (2020).

161. *Id.* § 1026.13(e) (2020).

162. *Id.* § 1026.13(f) (2020).

(ii) Mails or delivers to the consumer (at the same time the report is made) a written notice of the name and address of each person to whom the creditor makes a report; and

(iii) Promptly reports any subsequent resolution of the reported delinquency to all persons to whom the creditor has made a report.[163]

A creditor that has fully complied with the billing error requirements has no further responsibilities if a consumer reasserts substantially the same billing error.[164]

9. Additional Rules Applicable to Consumer Credit Cards (CARD Act Rules)

Congress passed the Credit Card Accountability Responsibility and Disclosure Act of 2009 (the CARD Act),[165] which was signed into law by President Obama on May 22, 2009, to provide additional substantive limitations on credit card lending. Regulation Z includes the following rules applicable to consumer credit card lending that implement the CARD Act.

9.1 Ability to Pay

A card issuer must not open a credit card, or increase any credit limit applicable to such account, unless the card issuer considers the consumer's ability to make the required minimum periodic payments under the terms of the account based on the consumer's income or assets and the consumer's current obligations.[166] Card issuers must establish and maintain reasonable written policies and procedures to consider the consumer's ability to make the required minimum payments under the terms of the account based on a consumer's income or assets and current obligations.[167] Reasonable policies and procedures include treating any income and assets to which the consumer has a reasonable expectation of access as the consumer's income or assets, or limiting consideration of the consumer's income or assets to the consumer's independent income and assets.[168] Reasonable policies and procedures also include consideration of at least one of the following: the ratio of debt obligations to income, the ratio of debt obligations to assets, or the income the consumer will have after

---

163. *Id.* § 1026.13(g) (2020).

164. *Id.* § 1026.13(h) (2020).

165. Credit Card Accountability Responsibility and Disclosure Act of 2009, Pub. L. No. 111-24, 123 Stat. 1734 (2009).

166. 12 C.F.R. § 1026.51(a)(1)(i) (2020).

167. *Id.* § 1026.51(a)(1)(ii) (2020).

168. *Id.*

paying debt obligations.[169] It would be unreasonable for a card issuer not to review any information about a consumer's income or assets and current obligations, or to issue a credit card to a consumer who does not have any income or assets.[170]

Regulation Z includes additional rules applicable to applications for credit cards made by consumers who are less than twenty-one years of age.[171] The rules include a requirement that the consumer's application be in writing, and prohibit opening an account unless the issuer has financial information indicating the consumer has an independent ability to make the required minimum periodic payments or a signed agreement of a cosigner, guarantor, or joint applicant who is at least twenty-one years old to be either jointly or secondarily liable for the debt.[172]

9.2 Limitations on Fees

The total amount of fees a consumer is required to pay with respect to a credit card account during the first year after account opening must not exceed 25 percent of the credit limit in effect when the account is opened.[173] Late payment fees, over-the-limit fees, returned-payment fees, and fees that the consumer is not required to pay with respect to the account are not included in the calculation.[174]

In addition, a card issuer must not impose a fee for violating the terms or other requirements of a credit card account under a credit plan unless the dollar amount does not exceed the costs of the violation to the issuer or safe harbor amounts set forth in Regulation Z (which are adjusted annually).[175]

A card issuer must not impose a fee for violating the terms or other requirements of a credit card account when there is no dollar amount associated with the violation.[176]

Finally, card issuers may not impose more than one fee for violating the terms or other requirements of a credit card account based on a single event or transaction.[177] For example, if a returned payment causes the account to become delinquent, the issuer may not impose both a returned payment fee and a late payment fee.

9.3 Allocation of Payments

When a consumer makes a payment in excess of the required minimum periodic payment for a credit card account, the card issuer must allocate the excess amount

---

169. *Id.*
170. *Id.*
171. *See id.* § 1026.51(b)(1) (2020).
172. *Id.*
173. *Id.* § 1026.52(a)(1) (2020).
174. *Id.* § 1026.52(a)(2) (2020).
175. *Id.* § 1026.52(b) (2020).
176. *Id.* § 1026.52(b)(2)(i)(B) (2020).
177. *Id.* § 1026.52(b)(2)(ii) (2020).

first to the balance with the highest APR and any remaining portion to the other balances in descending order based on the applicable APR.[178] Regulation Z provides exceptions to this rule for accounts with balances subject to deferred interest or similar programs, and for accounts with secured balances.[179]

9.4 Limitations on Imposition of Finance Charges

A card issuer must not impose finance charges as a result of the loss of a grace period on a credit card account under an open-end (not home-secured) consumer credit plan if those finance charges are based on balances for days in billing cycles that precede the most recent billing cycle, or any portion of a balance subject to a grace period that was repaid prior to the expiration of the grace period.[180]

9.5 Limitations on Increasing Annual Percentage Rates, Fees, and Charges

Regulation Z prohibits card issuers from increasing APRs or fees on credit card accounts, except under certain limited circumstances.[181] The limited circumstances under which an issuer may raise rates are:

- In connection with temporary rates and fees in effect for six months or longer (provided the issuer satisfies certain notice and other requirements).[182]
- Pursuant to rates that vary based on an index not under the card issuer's control and that is available to the general public.[183]
- With advanced notice (such as a change in terms notice required by section 9(c)(2) of Regulation Z), and so long as the increased rate or fee does not apply to transactions that occurred prior to or within fourteen days after provision of the notice.[184]
- When a consumer fails to make a required minimum periodic payment within sixty days after the due date for the payment (subject to notice from the issuer). If the issuer receives six consecutive required minimum periodic payments on or before the payment due date, beginning with the first payment due following the effective date of the increase, the card issuer must reduce any APR, fee, or charge increased pursuant to this

178. *Id.* § 1026.53(a) (2020).
179. *See id.* § 1026.53(b) (2020).
180. *Id.* § 1026.54(a) (2020).
181. *Id.* § 1026.55(a) (2020).
182. *Id.* § 1026.55(b)(1) (2020).
183. *Id.* § 1026.55(b)(2) (2020).
184. *Id.* § 1026.55(b)(3) (2020).

exception to the APR, fee, or charge that applied prior to the increase with respect to transactions that occurred prior to or within fourteen days after notice.[185]

- In connection with a temporary hardship or workout arrangement (provided the issuer satisfies certain notice and other requirements).[186]
- In accordance with an increase after protections afforded under the Servicemembers Civil Relief Act no longer apply (provided the issuer satisfies certain notice and other requirements).[187]

The rule also includes limitations on accelerating repayment of balances on which an increased rate or fee may not be imposed.[188]

9.6 Requirement for Over-the-Limit Transactions

Card issuers are precluded from charging fees for exceeding the credit limit on a credit card account unless the issuer provides notice to the consumer and an opportunity for the consumer to affirmatively opt in to allowing such fees (in return for honoring transactions that would cause the balance to exceed the credit limit).[189] Consumers who opt in may revoke their election at any time and the creditor must provide notice of this right to the consumer.[190]

A card issuer may not impose more than one over-the-limit fee or charge on a consumer's credit card account per billing cycle, and, in any event, only if the credit limit was exceeded during the billing cycle.[191] In addition, except under certain conditions, a card issuer may not impose an over-the-limit fee or charge on the consumer's credit card account for more than three billing cycles for the same over-the-limit transaction where the consumer has not reduced the account balance below the credit limit by the payment due date for either of the last two billing cycles.[192]

A card issuer may not condition the amount of a consumer's credit limit on the consumer affirmatively consenting to the card issuer's payment of over-the-limit transactions if the card issuer assesses a fee or charge for such service.[193]

185. *Id.* § 1026.55(b)(4) (2020).
186. *Id.* § 1026.55(b)(5) (2020).
187. *Id.* § 1026.55(b)(6) (2020).
188. *See id.* § 1026.55(c) (2020).
189. *Id.* § 1026.56(b)(i)–(ii) (2020).
190. *Id.* § 1026.56(b)(iv)–(v) (2020).
191. *Id.* § 1026.56(j)(1)(i) (2020).
192. *Id.* § 1026.56(j)(1)(ii) (2020).
193. *Id.* § 1026.56(j)(3) (2020).

A card issuer may not impose an over-the-limit fee or charge for a billing cycle if a consumer exceeds a credit limit solely because of fees or interest charged by the card issuer to the consumer's account during that billing cycle.[194]

9.7 Marketing Rules for College Student Credit

No card issuer or creditor may offer a college student any tangible item to induce such student to apply for or open an open-end consumer credit plan offered by such card issuer or creditor, if such offer is made on the campus of an institution of higher education, near the campus of an institution of higher education (within 1,000 feet of the border of the campus of an institution of higher education),[195] or at an event sponsored by or related to an institution of higher education.[196] The rule also imposes reporting requirements upon issuers.[197]

9.8 Internet Posting of Credit Card Agreements

Except in certain limited circumstances, a card issuer must post and maintain on its publicly available website the credit card agreements related to its credit card program.[198] Agreements must be placed in a location that is prominent and readily accessible by the public and must be accessible without submission of personally identifiable information.[199]

With respect to any open credit card account, a card issuer must either post and maintain the cardholder's agreement on its website or promptly provide a copy of the cardholder's agreement to the cardholder upon the cardholder's request.[200] If the card issuer makes an agreement available upon request, the issuer must provide the cardholder with the ability to request a copy of the agreement both by using the issuer's website (such as by clicking on a clearly identified box to make the request) and by calling a readily available telephone line, the number for which is displayed on the issuer's website and clearly identified as to purpose.[201] The card issuer must send to the cardholder or otherwise make available to the cardholder a copy of the cardholder's agreement in electronic or paper form no later than thirty days after the issuer receives the cardholder's request.[202]

194. *Id.* § 1026.56(j)(4) (2020).
195. 12 C.F.R. pt. 1026, supp. I, cmt. 57(c)-3 (2020).
196. 12 C.F.R. § 1026.57(c) (2020).
197. *See id.* § 1026.57(d) (2020).
198. *Id.* § 1026.58(d)(1) (2020).
199. *Id.* § 1026.58(d)(3) (2020).
200. *Id.* § 1026.58(e)(1) (2020).
201. *Id.*
202. *Id.*

An issuer that does not maintain a website from which cardholders can access specific information about their individual accounts may make agreements available upon request by providing the cardholder with the ability to request a copy of the agreement by calling a readily available telephone line, the number for which is displayed on the issuer's website and clearly identified as to purpose or included on each periodic statement sent to the cardholder and clearly identified as to purpose.[203] The issuer must send to the cardholder or otherwise make available to the cardholder a copy of the cardholder's agreement in electronic or paper form no later than thirty days after the issuer receives the cardholder's request.[204]

Regulation Z also requires credit card issuers to submit card agreements and other information (including pricing information) to the CFPB periodically, and includes detailed rules related to these submissions.[205]

9.9 Reevaluation of Rate Increases

If a card issuer increases an APR that applies to a credit card account plan, based on the credit risk of the consumer, market conditions, or other factors, and forty-five days' advance notice of the rate increase is required, the card issuer must evaluate the factors on which the increase was originally based or the factors that the card issuer currently considers when determining the APRs applicable to similar new credit card accounts, and, based on its review, reduce the APR, if appropriate.[206]

If a reduction is required, the card issuer must reduce the rate not later than forty-five days after completion of the evaluation.[207]

A card issuer must have reasonable written policies and procedures in place to conduct the review and must conduct the review no less frequently than once every six months after the rate increase.[208]

If an issuer increases a rate applicable to a consumer's account based on the card issuer not receiving the consumer's required minimum periodic payment within sixty days after the due date, the issuer is not required to perform the review prior to the sixth payment due date after the effective date of the increase.[209] However, if the APR applicable to the consumer's account is not reduced at that time, the first review must occur no later than six months after the sixth payment due following the effective date of the rate increase.[210]

203. *Id.* § 1026.58(e)(2) (2020).
204. *Id.*
205. *See id.* § 1026.58(c).
206. *Id.* § 1026.59(a), (d) (2020).
207. *Id.* § 1026.59(a)(2) (2020).
208. *Id.* § 1026.59(b)–(c) (2020).
209. *Id.* § 1026.59(e) (2020).
210. *Id.*

The obligation to review the accounts ceases to apply: (1) if the issuer reduces the APR to the rate applicable immediately prior to the increase, or, if the rate applicable immediately prior to the increase was a variable rate, to a variable rate determined by the same formula (index and margin) that was used to calculate the rate applicable immediately prior to the increase; or (2) If the issuer reduces the APR to a rate that is lower than the rate (or formula for variable rate accounts) applicable immediately prior to the increase.[211]

Special rules for rate reevaluations and adjustments apply to accounts acquired from other creditors.[212] The reevaluation rules do not apply to increases as a result of loss of the protections afforded under the Servicemembers Civil Relief Act or to accounts that the issuer has charged off.[213]

10. Credit and Charge Card Applications and Solicitations

Card issuers must provide disclosures very similar to (but not exactly mirroring) the account-opening disclosures on or with a solicitation or an application to open a credit or charge card account.[214] A card issuer may provide the account-opening summary table in lieu of the application and solicitation disclosures, if the issuer provides the account-opening disclosures on or with the application or solicitation.[215]

Issuers should consult Regulation Z for further information on these disclosure requirements.

11. Hybrid Prepaid-Credit Cards

Regulation Z includes specific rules governing hybrid prepaid credit cards, which are prepaid accounts with credit features.[216] Issuers should consult Regulation Z for further information.

211. *Id.* § 1026.59(f) (2020).
212. *See id.* § 1026.59(g) (2020).
213. *Id.* § 1026.59(h) (2020).
214. *See id.* § 1026.60(a) (2020).
215. 12 C.F.R. pt. 1026, supp. I, cmt. 60-2 (2020).
216. *See, generally,* 12 C.F.R. § 1026.61 (2020).

CHAPTER

3C

The Truth in Lending Act and Closed-End Credit Disclosures

David Tallman

1. Scope of This Chapter

This chapter covers the core provisions in the Truth in Lending Act[1] (TILA) and Regulation Z[2] that require creditors to make certain disclosures when originating closed-end consumer credit, but does not cover special rules for mortgages and student loans. Thus, this chapter effectively only addresses those requirements applicable to closed-end consumer credit that is either (1) unsecured or (2) secured by personal property not used as a dwelling. This chapter addresses the content of the required disclosures and certain related requirements, but does not cover liability or cure issues. It also does not address TILA advertising or record retention requirements, or certain requirements that apply with respect to the treatment of credit balances.

2. General Disclosure Requirements

2.1 Timing

Regulation Z requires the creditor to make the disclosures described below before consummation of the transaction.[3]

---

1. Pub. L. No. 90-321, 82 Stat. 146 (1968) (codified as amended at 15 U.S.C. §§ 1601–1667f (2020)).

2. 12 C.F.R. pt. 1026 (2020).

3. 12 C.F.R. § 1026.17(b) (2020).

2.2 Form of Disclosures

The creditor must make the required disclosures clearly and conspicuously in writing, in a form that the consumer may keep.[4] This standard requires that disclosures be in a reasonably understandable form.[5] No minimum type size is mandated, but the disclosures must be legible.[6] The disclosures may be provided electronically, subject to compliance with the E-SIGN Act.[7] The disclosures must be grouped together, segregated from everything else, and not contain any unrelated information.[8]

The disclosures may include an acknowledgment of receipt, the date of the transaction, and the consumer's name, address, and account number.[9] The following disclosures may be made together with or separately from other required disclosures: the creditor's identity, the variable-rate example, the insurance or debt cancellation disclosures, and the disclosure regarding certain security interest charge.[10] The itemization of the amount financed must be separate from the other disclosures.[11]

The terms *finance charge* and *annual percentage rate* (APR), when required to be disclosed together with a corresponding amount or rate, must be more conspicuous than any other disclosure except the creditor's identity.[12] The terms must be more conspicuous only in relation to the other disclosures.[13] The terms need not be more conspicuous except as part of the finance charge and APR disclosures themselves, but they may be highlighted wherever used in the required disclosures.[14] The terms need not be more conspicuous than figures.[15] The terms may be made more conspicuous in any way that highlights them in relation to the other disclosures.[16]

---

4. *Id.* § 1026.17(a).
5. 12 C.F.R. pt. 1026, supp. I, cmt. 17(a)(1)-1 (2020).
6. *Id.*
7. Pub. L. No. 106-229, 114 Stat. 464 (1968) (codified as amended at 15 U.S.C. §§ 7001–7031 (2020)).
8. 12 C.F.R. § 1026.17(a)(1) (2020).
9. *Id.*
10. *Id.* If a creditor chooses to include the security interest charges in the amount financed itemization, it need not list these charges elsewhere. 12 C.F.R. pt. 1026, supp. I, cmt. 17(a)(1)-4 (2020).
11. 12 C.F.R. § 1026.17(a)(1) (2020).
12. *Id.* § 1026.17(a)(2).
13. 12 C.F.R. pt. 1026, supp. I, cmt. 17(a)(2)-1 (2020).
14. *Id.*
15. *Id.*
16. *Id.* cmt. 17(a)(2)-2.

2.3 Basis of Disclosures and Use of Estimates

2.3.1 General

The disclosures must reflect the terms of the legal obligation between the parties.[17]

2.3.1.1 Legal Obligation

The disclosures must reflect the terms to which the consumer and creditor are legally bound at the outset.[18] The legal obligation is determined by applicable law.[19] Disclosures based on the assumption that the consumer will abide by the terms of the obligation throughout the transaction comply with this standard.[20] The fact that a term later may be unenforceable does not mean that disclosures based on that term did not reflect the legal obligation.[21]

2.3.1.2 Modification of Obligation

The legal obligation normally is presumed to be contained in the note or other contract between the parties.[22] This presumption is rebutted if another agreement legally modifies that note or contract.[23] If the parties informally agree to a modification, the modification should not be reflected in the disclosures unless it rises to the level of a change in the legal obligation.[24]

2.3.1.3 Variable-Rate Transactions

The disclosures for a variable-rate transaction must be given for the full term of the transaction, based on the terms in effect at the time of consummation.[25] Creditors should base the disclosures only on the initial rate and should not assume that this rate will increase.[26]

When creditors use an initial interest rate that is not calculated using the index or formula for later adjustments, the disclosures should reflect a composite APR based on the initial rate for as long as it is charged and then the rate that would have been applied using the index or formula at consummation.[27] The rate at consummation

---

17. 12 C.F.R. § 1026.17(c)(1) (2020).
18. 12 C.F.R. pt. 1026, supp. I, cmt. 17(c)(1)-1 (2020).
19. *Id.*
20. *Id.*
21. *Id.*
22. *Id.* cmt. 17(c)(1)-2.
23. *Id.*
24. *Id.*
25. *Id.* cmt. 17(c)(1)-8.
26. *Id.*
27. *Id.* cmt. 17(c)(1)-10(i).

need not be used if there is a delay in the implementation of index changes.[28] For example, if the contract specifies that rate changes are based on the index value in effect forty-five days before the change date, creditors may use any value in effect during the forty-five-day period before consummation.[29] The effect of the multiple rates also must be reflected in the calculation and disclosure of the finance charge, total of payments, and the payment schedule.[30] If a loan contains a rate or payment cap that would prevent the initial rate or payment from changing to the fully indexed amount, the effect of the cap should be reflected in the disclosures.[31]

2.3.1.4 Rebates and Loan Premiums

Premiums and rebates must be reflected in accordance with the terms of the legal obligation between the consumer and the creditor.[32] Thus, if the creditor is legally obligated to provide the premium or rebate to the consumer as part of the credit transaction, the disclosures should reflect its value in the manner the creditor is obligated to provide it.[33]

2.3.2 Basis for Estimates

If any information necessary for an accurate disclosure is unknown to the creditor, the creditor must make the disclosure based on the best information reasonably available at the time the disclosure is provided, and state clearly that the disclosure is an estimate.[34] Information is unknown if it is not reasonably available to the creditor at the time the disclosures are made.[35] This standard requires that the creditor, acting in good faith, exercise due diligence in obtaining information.[36] The creditor normally may rely on the representations of other parties in obtaining information.[37] The creditor may use estimates even though the creditor knows that more precise information will be available by consummation,[38] but new disclosures may be required under section 1026.17(f) in those circumstances.

Estimates must be designated as such in the segregated disclosures.[39] Even though they are based on the same assumption on which a specific estimated disclosure

28. *Id.*
29. *Id.*
30. *Id.* cmt. 17(c)(1)-10(ii).
31. *Id.* cmt. 17(c)(1)-10(iii).
32. *Id.* cmt. 17(c)(1)-19.
33. *Id.*
34. 12 C.F.R. § 1026.17(c)(2)(i) (2020).
35. 12 C.F.R. pt. 1026, supp. I, cmt. 17(c)(2)(i)-1 (2020).
36. *Id.*
37. *Id.*
38. *Id.*
39. *Id.* cmt. 17(c)(2)(i)-2.

was based, the creditor has flexibility in labeling the estimates.[40] Generally, only the particular disclosure for which the exact information is unknown is labeled as an estimate.[41] When several disclosures are affected because of the unknown information, the creditor has the option of labeling either every affected disclosure or only the disclosure primarily affected.[42] When many disclosures are estimates, the creditor may use a general statement, such as "all numerical disclosures except the late payment disclosure are estimates," as a method to label those disclosures.[43]

2.3.3 Per Diem Transactions

For a transaction in which a portion of the interest is determined on a per diem basis and collected at consummation, any disclosure affected by the per diem interest will be considered accurate if the disclosure is based on the information known to the creditor at the time that the disclosure documents are prepared for consummation of the transaction.[44]

2.3.4 Minor Variations

The creditor may disregard the effects of the following in making calculations and disclosures: (1) that payments must be collected in whole cents, (2) that dates of scheduled payments and advances may be changed because the scheduled date is not a business day, (3) that months have different numbers of days, and (4) the occurrence of leap years.[45]

Because payments cannot be collected in fractional cents, it is often difficult to amortize exactly an obligation with equal payments; the amount of the last payment may require adjustment to account for the rounding of the other payments to whole cents.[46]

Creditors may base their disclosures on calculation tools that assume that all months have an equal number of days, even if their practice is to take account of the variations in months for purposes of collecting interest.[47]

---

40. *Id.*
41. *Id.*
42. *Id.*
43. *Id.*
44. 12 C.F.R. § 1026.17(c)(2)(ii) (2020).
45. *Id.* § 1026.17(c)(3).
46. 12 C.F.R. pt. 1026, supp. I, cmt. 17(c)(3)-1(i) (2020).
47. *Id.* cmt. 17(c)(3)-1(ii).

2.3.5 Demand Obligations

If an obligation is payable on demand, the creditor must make the disclosures based on an assumed maturity of one year. If an alternate maturity date is stated in the legal obligation between the parties, the disclosures must be based on that date.[48]

2.3.6 Series of Advances

A series of advances under an agreement to extend credit up to a certain amount may be considered as one transaction,[49] or each advance may be disclosed separately.[50]

2.4 Multiple Creditors/Consumers

If a transaction involves more than one creditor, only one set of disclosures must be given.[51] A single, complete set of disclosures must be provided, rather than partial disclosures from several creditors.[52] All disclosures for the transaction must be given, even if the disclosing creditor would not otherwise have been obligated to make a particular disclosure.[53] If there is more than one consumer, the disclosures may be made to any consumer who is primarily liable on the obligation.[54] If one consumer is merely a surety or guarantor, the disclosures must be given to the principal debtor.[55]

2.5 Subsequent Events

If a disclosure becomes inaccurate because of an event that occurs after the creditor delivers the required disclosures, the inaccuracy is not a violation, although new disclosures may be required under certain circumstances.[56]

2.6 Correction of Early Disclosures

If the disclosures are given before the date of consummation of a transaction and a subsequent event makes them inaccurate, the creditor must disclose before consummation:

48. 12 C.F.R. § 1026.17(c)(5) (2020).
49. *Id.* § 1026.17(c)(6)(i).
50. 12 C.F.R. pt. 1026, supp. I, cmt. 17(c)(6)-1 (2020).
51. 12 C.F.R. § 1026.17(d) (2020).
52. 12 C.F.R. pt. 1026, supp. I, cmt. 17(d)-1 (2020).
53. *Id.*
54. 12 C.F.R. § 1026.17(d) (2020).
55. 12 C.F.R. pt. 1026, supp. I, cmt. 17(d)-2 (2020).
56. 12 C.F.R. § 1026.17(e).

- Any changed term unless the term was based on an estimate in accordance with section 1026.17(c)(2) and was labeled an estimate; and
- All changed terms, if the APR at the time of consummation varies from the APR disclosed earlier by more than ⅛ of 1 percentage point in a regular transaction, or more than ¼ of 1 percentage point in an irregular transaction, as defined in section 1026.22(a).[57]

If redisclosure is required, the creditor has the option of either providing a complete set of new disclosures or providing disclosures of only the terms that vary from those originally disclosed.[58]

2.7 Mail or Telephone Orders

If a creditor receives a purchase order or a request for an extension of credit by mail, telephone, or facsimile machine without face-to-face or direct telephone solicitation, the creditor may delay the disclosures until the due date of the first payment, if the following information for representative amounts or ranges of credit is made available in written form or in electronic form to the consumer or to the public before the actual purchase order or request:

- the cash price or the principal loan amount;
- the total sale price;
- the finance charge;
- the APR and, if the rate may increase after consummation, the following disclosures: (i) the circumstances under which the rate may increase, (ii) any limitations on the increase, and (iii) the effect of an increase;
- the terms of repayment.[59]

When the creditor receives a mail or telephone request for credit, the creditor may delay making the disclosures until the first payment is due if (1) the credit request is initiated without face-to-face or direct telephone solicitation (creditors may, however, use the special rule when credit requests are solicited by mail); and (2) the creditor has supplied the specified credit information about its credit terms either to the individual consumer or to the public through advertisements, catalogs, brochures, special mailers, etc.[60]

---

57. *Id.* § 1026.17(f). Section 1026.22(a) defines an "irregular transaction" as one that includes one or more of the following features: multiple advances, irregular payment periods, or irregular payment amounts (other than an irregular first period or an irregular first or final payment).

58. 12 C.F.R. pt. 1026, supp. I, cmt. 17(f)-3 (2020).

59. 12 C.F.R. § 1026.17(g) (2020).

60. 12 C.F.R. pt. 1026, supp. I, cmt. 17(g)-1 (2020).

The location requirements for the insurance disclosures under section 1026.18(n) permit them to appear apart from the other disclosures.[61] Thus, a creditor may mail an insurance authorization to the consumer and then prepare the other disclosures to reflect whether or not the authorization is completed by the consumer.[62] Creditors also may disclose the insurance cost on a unit-cost basis, if the transaction meets the preceding requirements.[63]

2.8 Series of Sales

If a credit sale is one of a series made under an agreement providing that subsequent sales may be added to an outstanding balance, the creditor may delay the required disclosures until the due date of the first payment for the current sale if (1) the consumer has approved in writing the APR or rates, the range of balances to which they apply, and the method of treating any unearned finance charge on an existing balance; and (2) the creditor retains no security interest in any property after the creditor has received payments equal to the cash price and any finance charge attributable to the sale of that property.[64]

In the case of items purchased on different dates, the first purchased is deemed the first item paid for; in the case of items purchased on the same date, the lowest priced is deemed the first item paid for.[65] Creditors structuring disclosures for a series of sales may compute the total sale price as either (1) the cash price for the sale plus that portion of the finance charge and other charges applicable to that sale; or (2) the cash price for the sale, other charges applicable to the sale, and the total finance charge and outstanding principal.[66]

3. Content of Disclosures

The following section addresses the specific disclosures that Regulation Z requires a creditor to make. The disclosures need be made only as applicable.[67]

61. *Id.* cmt. 17(g)-2.
62. *Id.*
63. *Id.*
64. 12 C.F.R. § 1026.17(h) (2020).
65. *Id.*
66. 12 C.F.R. pt. 1026, supp. I, cmt. 17(h)-2.
67. *Id.* cmt. 18-1.

3.1 Creditor

The creditor must disclose its identity to the consumer.[68] When there are multiple creditors, any one of them may make the disclosures; the one doing so must be identified.[69]

3.2 Amount Financed

The creditor must disclose the *amount financed*, using that term, and a brief description such as "the amount of credit provided to you or on your behalf."[70] The amount financed is calculated by (1) determining the principal loan amount or the cash price (subtracting any down payment), (2) adding any other amounts that are financed by the creditor and are not part of the finance charge, and (3) subtracting any prepaid finance charge.

A down payment may include, at the creditor's option, certain deferred down payments or pick-up payments.[71] Deferred down payments that are not treated as part of the down payment (either because they do not meet the definition or because the creditor simply chooses not to treat them as down payments) are included in the amount financed.[72]

Fees or other charges that are not part of the finance charge and that are financed rather than paid separately at consummation are included in the amount financed.[73]

3.3 Itemization of Amount Financed

The creditor must disclose a separate written itemization of the amount financed, including (1) the amount of any proceeds distributed directly to the consumer,[74] (2) the amount credited to the consumer's account,[75] (3) any amounts paid to other

68. 12 C.F.R. § 1026.18(a) (2020).

69. *Id.*

70. *Id.* § 1026.18(b).

71. 12 C.F.R. pt. 1026, supp. I, cmt. 18(b)(1)-1.

72. *Id.*

73. *Id.* cmt. 18(b)(2)-1.

74. This encompasses funds given to the consumer in the form of cash or a check, including joint proceeds checks, as well as funds placed in an asset account. It may include money in an interest-bearing account even if that amount is considered a required deposit. *Id.* cmt. 18(c)(1)(i)-1.

75. The term *consumer's account* refers to an account in the nature of a debt with that creditor. It may include, for example, an unpaid balance on a prior loan, a credit sale balance, or other amounts owing to that creditor. It does not include asset accounts of the consumer, such as savings or checking accounts. *Id.*

persons on the consumer's behalf (and the identities of those persons), and (4) the prepaid finance charge.[76]

The creditor need not comply with this requirement if the creditor provides a statement that the consumer has the right to receive a written itemization of the amount financed, with a space for the consumer to indicate whether it is desired, and the consumer does not request it.[77] Whether given as a matter of course or only on request, the itemization must be provided at the same time as the other required disclosures, although separate from those disclosures.[78]

The regulation establishes only a minimum standard for the material to be included in the itemization of the amount financed.[79] Creditors have flexibility to revise or supplement the information, although no changes are required.[80] When an amount may appropriately be placed in any of several categories and the creditor does not wish to revise the categories shown, the creditor may choose where to show the amount.[81]

3.4 Finance Charge

The creditor must disclose the *finance charge*, using that term, and a brief description such as "the dollar amount the credit will cost you."[82] The creditor may further modify the descriptor for variable-rate transactions with a phrase such as "which is subject to change."[83] The finance charge must be shown on the disclosures only as a total amount; the elements of the finance charge must not be itemized in the segregated disclosures.[84]

The amount disclosed as the finance charge is treated as accurate in a transaction involving an amount financed of $1,000 or less if it is not more than $5 above or below the amount required to be disclosed; or, in a transaction involving an amount financed of more than $1,000, it is not more than $10 above or below the amount required to be disclosed.[85]

---

76. 12 C.F.R. § 1026.18(c)(1) (2020). The prepaid finance charges must be shown as a total amount but may, at the creditor's option, also be further itemized and described. Commentary para. 18(c)(1)(iv)-1. All amounts must be reflected in this total, even if portions of the prepaid finance charge are also reflected elsewhere. 12 C.F.R. pt. 1026, supp. I, cmt. 18(c)(1)(iv)-1 (2020).

77. 12 C.F.R. § 1026.18(c)(2) (2020).

78. 12 C.F.R. pt. 1026, supp. I, cmt. 18(c)-1 (2020).

79. *Id.* cmt. 18(c)-2.

80. *Id.*

81. *Id.* cmt. 18(c)-3.

82. 12 C.F.R. § 1026.18(d) (2020).

83. 12 C.F.R. pt. 1026, supp. I, cmt. 18(d)-1 (2020).

84. *Id.*

85. 12 C.F.R. § 1026.18(d) (2020).

When a finance charge error results in a misstatement of another dollar amount for which the regulation provides no specific tolerance, the misstated disclosure does not violate TILA if the finance charge error is within the permissible tolerance.[86]

3.5 Annual Percentage Rate

The creditor must disclose the APR, using that term, and a brief description such as "the cost of your credit as a yearly rate."[87] For variable-rate transactions, the descriptor may be further modified with a phrase such as "which is subject to change."[88] For any transaction involving a finance charge of $5 or less on an amount financed of $75 or less, or a finance charge of $7.50 or less on an amount financed of more than $75, the creditor need not disclose the APR.[89]

3.6 Variable-Rate Disclosures

If the APR may increase after consummation, the creditor must make the following disclosures: (1) the circumstances under which the rate may increase, (2) any limitations on the increase, (3) the effect of an increase, and (4) an example of the payment terms that would result from an increase. This requirement applies to all transactions in which the terms of the legal obligation allow the creditor to increase the rate originally disclosed to the consumer.[90] It includes not only increases in the interest rate but also increases in other components, such as the rate of required credit life insurance.[91] It does not apply to increases resulting from delinquency, default, assumption, acceleration or transfer of the collateral.[92]

In describing the variable-rate feature, the creditor need not use any prescribed terminology (although model language is provided).[93] For example, limitations and hypothetical examples may be described in terms of interest rates rather than APRs.[94]

In transactions that permit consumers to convert to a fixed-rate transaction, the conversion option is a variable-rate feature that must be disclosed.[95] Creditors should disclose the fact that the rate may increase upon conversion, identify the

---

86. 12 C.F.R. pt. 1026, supp. I, cmt. 18(d)(2)-1 (2020).
87. 12 C.F.R. § 1026.18(e) (2020).
88. 12 C.F.R. pt. 1026, supp. I, cmt. 18(e)-1 (2020).
89. 12 C.F.R. § 1026.18(e) (2020).
90. 12 C.F.R. pt. 1026, supp. I, cmt. 18(f)-1 (2020).
91. *Id.*
92. *Id.*
93. *Id.* cmt. 18(f)(1)-1.
94. *Id.*
95. *Id.* cmt. 18(f)(1)-2.

index or formula used to set the fixed rate, and state any limitations on and effects of an increase resulting from conversion that differ from other variable-rate features.[96]

The circumstances under which the rate may increase include identification of any index to which the rate is tied, as well as any conditions or events on which the increase is contingent.[97] When no specific index is used, any identifiable factors used to determine whether to increase the rate must be disclosed.[98] When the increase in the rate is purely discretionary, the fact that any increase is within the creditor's discretion must be disclosed.[99] When the index is internally defined, the creditor may comply with this requirement either by a brief description of that index or a statement that any increase is in the discretion of the creditor.[100] An externally defined index must be identified.[101]

The requirement to disclose any limitations on the increase includes any maximum imposed on the amount of an increase in the rate at any time, as well as any maximum on the total increase over the life of the transaction, but not usury ceilings.[102] The creditor may disclose that fact.

Disclosure of the effect of an increase refers to an increase in the number or amount of payments or an increase in the final payment.[103] The creditor may make a brief reference to resulting negative amortization.[104] If the effect cannot be determined, the creditor must provide a statement of the possible effects.[105] For example, if the exercise of the variable-rate feature may result in either more or larger payments, both possibilities must be noted.[106]

3.7 Payment Schedule

The creditor must disclose the number, amounts, and timing of payments scheduled to repay the obligation.[107] The schedule should reflect all components of the finance charge except the prepaid finance charge.[108]

---

96. *Id.*
97. *Id.* cmt. 18(f)(1)(i)-1.
98. *Id.*
99. *Id.*
100. *Id.*
101. *Id.*
102. *Id.*
103. *Id.* cmt. 18(f)(1)(iii)-1.
104. *Id.*
105. *Id.*
106. *Id.*
107. 12 C.F.R. § 1026.18(g) (2020).
108. 12 C.F.R. pt. 1026, supp. I, cmt. 18(g)-1 (2020).

3.8 Total of Payments

The creditor must disclose the *total of payments*, using that term, and a descriptive explanation such as "the amount you will have paid when you have made all scheduled payments."[109] In a transaction involving a single payment, the creditor need not disclose the total of payments.[110] The explanation may be revised to reflect a variable-rate feature with a brief phrase such as "based on the current APR which may change."[111] The total of payments must be the sum of the payments disclosed in the payment schedule.[112]

3.9 Demand Feature

If the obligation has a demand feature, the creditor must disclose that fact.[113] When the disclosures are based on an assumed maturity of one year, that fact also must be disclosed.[114] This requirement applies not only to transactions payable on demand from the outset, but also to transactions that convert to a demand status after a stated period.[115]

3.10 Total Sale Price

In a credit sale, creditor must disclose the *total sale price*, using that term, and a descriptive explanation (including the amount of any down payment) such as "the total price of your purchase on credit, including your down payment of $____."[116] The total sale price is the sum of the cash price, the items described in section 1026.18(b)(2), and the finance charge.

3.11 Prepayment

When an obligation includes a finance charge computed by application of a rate to the unpaid principal, the creditor must indicate whether or not a charge may be

109. 12 C.F.R. § 1026.18(h) (2020).

110. *Id.* § 1026.18(h). This exception does not apply to a transaction calling for a single payment of principal combined with periodic payments of interest. 12 C.F.R. pt. 1026, supp. I, cmt. 18(h)-2 (2020).

111. 12 C.F.R. pt. 1026, supp. I, cmt. 18(h)-1 (2020).

112. *Id.* cmt. 18(h)-2.

113. 12 C.F.R. § 1026.18(i) (2020).

114. *Id.*

115. 12 C.F.R. pt. 1026, supp. I, cmt. 18(i)-1 (2020).

116. 12 C.F.R. § 1026.18(j) (2020).

imposed for paying all or part of the loan's principal balance before the date on which the principal is due.[117]

3.12 Late Payment

The creditor must disclose any dollar or percentage charge that may be imposed before maturity due to a late payment, other than a deferral or extension charge.[118]

3.13 Security Interest

The creditor must disclose the fact that it has or will acquire a security interest in the property purchased as part of the transaction, or in other property identified by item or type.[119]

3.14 Insurance and Debt Cancellation

The creditor must disclose the items required by section 1026.4(d) in order to exclude certain insurance premiums and debt cancellation fees from the finance charge.[120] This disclosure may appear apart from the other disclosures.[121] When included with the other segregated disclosures it may not appear with additional explanatory material.[122]

3.15 Certain Security Interest Charges

The creditor must make the disclosures required by section 1026.4(e) in order to exclude from the finance charge certain fees prescribed by law or certain premiums for insurance in lieu of perfecting a security interest.[123]

3.16 Contract Reference

The creditor must include a statement that the consumer should refer to the appropriate contract document for information about nonpayment, default, the right to accelerate the maturity of the obligation, and prepayment rebates and penalties.[124] The statement

117. *Id.* § 1026.18(k)(1).
118. *Id.* § 1026.18(l).
119. *Id.* § 1026.18(m).
120. *Id.* § 1026.18(n).
121. 12 C.F.R. pt. 1026, supp. I, cmt. 18(n)-1 (2020).
122. *Id.*
123. 12 C.F.R. § 1026.18(o) (2020).
124. *Id.* § 1026.18(p).

may include a reference to the contract for further information about security interests and the creditor's policy regarding assumption.[125]

3.17 Required Deposit

If the creditor requires the consumer to maintain a deposit as a condition of the transaction, the disclosures must include a statement that the APR does not reflect the effect of the required deposit.[126] A required deposit does not include (1) an escrow account for items such as taxes, insurance, or repairs; (2) a deposit that earns not less than 5 percent per year; or (3) payments under a Morris Plan,[127] although the creditor may include the disclosure when there is doubt as to whether a deposit constitutes a required deposit.[128]

4. Post-Consummation Events

4.1 Refinancing

A refinancing is considered a new transaction that requires new disclosures.[129] A refinancing occurs when an existing obligation is satisfied and replaced by a new obligation undertaken by the same consumer.[130] The new finance charge includes any unearned portion of the old finance charge that is not credited to the existing obligation.[131]

Whether a refinancing has occurred is determined by reference to whether the original obligation has been satisfied or extinguished and replaced by a new obligation, based on the contract and applicable law.[132] The refinancing may involve the consolidation of several existing obligations, disbursement of new money to the consumer or on the consumer's behalf, or the rescheduling of payments under an existing obligation. In any form, the new obligation must completely replace the prior one.[133] Changes in the terms of an existing obligation, such as the deferral of individual installments, will not constitute a refinancing unless accomplished by the cancellation of that obligation and the substitution of a new obligation.[134] A substitution

---

125. *Id.*
126. 12 C.F.R. § 1026.18(r).
127. *Id.*
128. 12 C.F.R. pt. 1026, supp. I, cmt. 18(r)-1 (2020).
129. 12 C.F.R. § 1026.20(a) (2020).
130. *Id.*
131. *Id.*
132. 12 C.F.R. pt. 1026, supp. I, cmt. 20(a)-1 (2020).
133. *Id.*
134. *Id.*

of agreements that meets the refinancing definition will require new disclosures, even if the substitution does not substantially alter the prior credit terms.[135]

The following circumstances are not treated as a refinancing, even if they are accomplished by cancellation of the old obligation and substitution of a new one:

- A renewal of a single payment obligation with no change in the original terms. This exception applies both to obligations with a single payment of principal and interest and to obligations with periodic payments of interest and a final payment of principal.[136] In determining whether a new obligation replacing an old one is a renewal of the original terms or a refinancing, the creditor may consider it a renewal even if: (i) accrued unpaid interest is added to the principal balance, (ii) changes are made in the terms of renewal resulting from the factors listed in section 1026.17(c)(3), or (iii) the principal at renewal is reduced by a curtailment of the obligation.[137]
- A reduction in the APR with a corresponding change in the payment schedule. A reduction in the APR with a corresponding change in the payment schedule is not a refinancing.[138] If the APR is subsequently increased (even though it remains below its original level) and the increase is effected in such a way that the old obligation is satisfied and replaced, new disclosures must then be made.[139] A corresponding change in the payment schedule to implement a lower APR would be a shortening of the maturity, or a reduction in the payment amount or the number of payments of an obligation.[140] The exception does not apply if the maturity is lengthened, or if the payment amount or number of payments is increased beyond that remaining on the existing transaction.[141]
- An agreement involving a court proceeding.[142]
- A change in the payment schedule or a change in collateral requirements as a result of the consumer's default or delinquency, unless the rate is increased, or the new amount financed exceeds the unpaid balance plus earned finance charge and premiums for continuation of insurance of the types described in section 1026.4(d). A workout agreement is not

135. *Id.*
136. *Id.* cmt. 20(a)(1)-1.
137. *Id.*
138. *Id.*
139. *Id.*
140. *Id.* cmt. 20(a)(2)-2.
141. *Id.*
142. *Id.* cmt. 20(a)(3)-1.

a refinancing unless the APR is increased or additional credit is advanced beyond amounts already accrued plus insurance premiums.[143]

- The renewal of optional insurance purchased by the consumer and added to an existing transaction, if disclosures relating to the initial purchase were provided as required.[144]

If a variable-rate feature was properly disclosed, a rate change in accord with those disclosures is not a refinancing.[145] Even if it is not accomplished by the cancellation of the old obligation and substitution of a new one, a new transaction subject to new disclosures results if the creditor either (1) increases the rate based on a variable-rate feature that was not previously disclosed, or (2) adds a variable-rate feature to the obligation.[146] A creditor does not add a variable-rate feature by changing the index of a variable-rate transaction to a comparable index.[147]

In a transaction involving precomputed finance charges, the creditor must include in the finance charge on the refinanced obligation any unearned portion of the original finance charge that is not rebated or credited against the underlying obligation.[148]

5. Determination of Annual Percentage Rate

The APR is a measure of the cost of credit, expressed as a yearly rate, that relates the amount and timing of value received by the consumer to the amount and timing of payments made.[149] The APR is determined in accordance with either the actuarial method or the U.S. Rule method.[150] Instructions for determining the APR in accordance with the actuarial method are set forth in appendix J to Regulation Z. An error with respect to the APR or finance charge is not a violation if (1) the error resulted from a corresponding error in a calculation tool used in good faith; and (2) upon discovery of the error, the creditor promptly discontinues use of that calculation tool for disclosure purposes and notifies the Consumer Financial Protection Bureau in writing of the error.[151]

---

143. *Id.* cmt. 20(a)(4)-1.
144. 12 C.F.R. § 1026.20(a) (2020).
145. 12 C.F.R. pt. 1026, supp. I, cmt. 20(a)-3 (2020).
146. *Id.*
147. *Id.*
148. *Id.* cmt. 20(a)-4.
149. 12 C.F.R. § 1026.22(a)(1) (2020).
150. *Id.*
151. *Id.*

When a transaction involves "step rates" or "split rates"—that is, different rates applied at different times or to different portions of the principal balance—a single composite APR must be calculated and disclosed for the entire transaction.[152]

As a general rule, the APR is considered accurate if it is not more than ⅛ of 1 percentage point above or below the actual APR.[153] In an irregular transaction, however, the APR is considered accurate if it is not more than ¼ of 1 percentage point above or below the actual APR.[154] An irregular transaction is one that includes one or more of the following features: multiple advances, irregular payment periods, or irregular payment amounts (other than an irregular first period or an irregular first or final payment).[155]

152. 12 C.F.R. pt. 1026, supp. I, cmt. 22(a)(1)-4 (2020).

153. 12 C.F.R. § 1026.22(a)(2) (2020).

154. *Id.* § 1026.22(a)(3).

155. *Id.*

CHAPTER

3D

The Truth in Lending Act and Dwelling-Secured Lending

Lynette I. Hotchkiss and Heather B. Thayer

Few areas of consumer lending are more regulated than credit transactions secured by a consumer's *dwelling* or real property.[1] The Truth in Lending Act and its implementing regulation, Regulation Z (collectively, TILA) govern many aspects of dwelling-secured lending and servicing, not only disclosures but also loan originator compensation and licensing, underwriting, product features, and servicing. This area of the law becomes even more complex when one considers the many nuances surrounding the type of property securing the credit transaction. Some requirements apply to all consumer dwellings, others apply only to the consumer's principal dwelling, still others apply only to real property, and some depend on whether the loan is or is not being used to purchase the secured property.

Given the comprehensive and detailed nature of the TILA requirements governing loans secured by a dwelling or real property, the following is, by necessity, a high-level overview. For a more in-depth analysis, consult *The Law of Truth in Lending* and its 2018 Supplement.[2] This chapter concentrates on TILA provisions specifically applicable to dwelling and real property lending; for general provisions of TILA that are also applicable to dwelling and real property lending, consult chapters 3A, 3B,

---

1. Dwelling means a residential structure that contains one to four units, whether or not that structure is attached to real property. The term includes an individual condominium unit, cooperative unit, mobile home, and trailer, if it is used as a residence. 12 C.F.R. § 1026.2(a)(19).

2. *The Law of Truth in Lending* (Alvin C. Harrell ed. 2013), *The Law of Truth in Lending 2018 Supplement* (John L. Ropiequet and Lynette I. Hotchkiss eds. 2018).

and 3C. However, remain vigilant because even laws of general applicability often have minor nuances for dwelling and real property loans.[3]

1. Closed-End Mortgage Loans

1.1 Introduction

There are unique requirements for closed-end consumer credit transactions secured by a dwelling (mortgage loans).[4] Although the requirements for mortgage loans always have been complex, they have become significantly more so since the 2008 financial crisis. Due to the perceived bad practices and poor controls in the mortgage industry prior to the crisis, Congress, in the Dodd-Frank Act,[5] made several amendments to TILA with regard to mortgage lending and servicing and instructed the Consumer Financial Protection Bureau (CFPB) to write numerous complex mortgage regulations, most of which were directed at the closed-end mortgage market. This section will review a bit of the history of closed-end mortgage lending and servicing requirements and provide a high-level overview of the basic requirements that now apply to this area of lending.

1.2 Mortgage Origination

TILA includes many requirements for what needs to happen during the origination phase of a mortgage loan—the period between when the consumer contacts the creditor about obtaining the loan and the date the loan is consummated. This section will review the requirements during this origination phase.

1.2.1 Mortgage Loan Originators

Following the 2008 financial crisis, Congress amended TILA, adopting new provisions to establish qualification requirements for mortgage loan originators, limit mortgage loan originator compensation, and prohibit steering in mortgage loans.[6] In 2013, the CFPB issued its Loan Originator Compensation rule,[7] amending Regulation Z to

3. This overview only covers the most common kinds of real estate secured loans and does not cover construction loans, timeshares, bridge loans, or reverse mortgages.

4. For ease of reference, these loans will be referred to simply as mortgage loans throughout this section.

5. Dodd-Frank Wall Street Reform and Consumer Protection Act, Pub. L. No. 111-203, 124 Stat. 1376 (2010).

6. Dodd-Frank Act §§ 1401–03.

7. Loan Originator Compensation Requirements under the Truth in Lending Act (Regulation Z), 78 Fed. Reg. 11279 (Feb. 15, 2013).

implement these new TILA requirements. These rules apply to closed-end consumer credit transactions secured by a dwelling.[8]

For purposes of the Regulation Z loan originator compensation and qualification provisions, a *loan originator* is a person who, for compensation or monetary gain (direct or indirect) or the expectation of such compensation or gain, performs any of the following activities: takes an application, offers, arranges, assists a consumer in obtaining or applying to obtain, negotiates, or otherwise obtains or makes an extension of consumer credit for another person; or through advertising or other communication represents to the public that the person can or will perform any of these activities.[9] It does not include a person who performs purely administrative or clerical tasks.[10] Regulation Z distinguishes between an *individual loan originator* (a natural person)[11] and a *loan originator organization* (any loan originator that is not an individual loan originator).[12] The Regulation Z Official Interpretations (Commentary) are a good source of information, providing examples and scenarios to assist in determining whether an individual or an organization is a *loan originator* for purposes of these rules.[13]

1.2.1.1 Loan Originator Qualifications and Identification

In general, loan originators must be registered or licensed in accordance with applicable state and federal laws,[14] including the Secure and Fair Enforcement for Mortgage Licensing Act of 2008 (SAFE Act)[15] and the federal regulations and state laws that implement the SAFE Act.

A loan originator organization must ensure that its individual loan originators are licensed or registered as required by the SAFE Act or state law. An individual

---

8. 12 C.F.R. § 1026.36(b) (2020).
9. *Id.* § 1026.36(a)(1)(i).
10. *Id.* § 1026.36(a)(1)(i)(A).
11. *Id.* § 1026.36(a)(1)(ii).
12. *Id.* § 1026.36(a)(1)(iii).
13. 12 C.F.R. pt. 1026, supp. I, cmt. 36(a)-1 to -4 (2020).
14. 12 C.F.R. § 1026.36(f) (2020).
15. Secure and Fair Enforcement for Mortgage Licensing Act of 2008, Pub. L. No. 110-289, 122 Stat 2654 (codified as amended at 12 U.S.C. §§ 5101–1516 (2008)). The SAFE Act establishes minimum standards for the registration or licensing of *mortgage loan originators* (the term used in the SAFE Act and its implementing regulations) with the Nationwide Mortgage Licensing System and Registry (NMLSR). The CFPB has implemented two separate regulations for compliance with the SAFE Act. In general, Regulation G (12 C.F.R. pt. 1007) includes registration and administrative requirements for national banks, member banks, insured state nonmember banks, savings associations, Farm Credit System institutions, and credit unions. Regulation H (12 C.F.R. pt. 1008) covers minimum standards that states must adopt for licensing and administration of mortgage loan originator requirements primarily under state jurisdiction.

loan originator who is not required to be licensed but must be registered[16] may not act as a loan originator until the loan originator organization has obtained a criminal background check, a credit report, and information about any administrative, civil, or criminal findings by any government jurisdiction regarding the individual.[17] Based on this information, the organization must determine that the individual loan originator has not been convicted of or pled guilty or nolo contendere to a felony involving fraud, dishonesty, a breach of trust, or money laundering at any time, or to any other felony in the preceding seven years.[18] The organization also must determine that the individual has demonstrated financial responsibility, character, and general fitness.[19]

The organization also must provide periodic training on federal and state law requirements that apply to the individual loan originator's activities.[20]

Each loan originator organization and each individual licensed or registered under the SAFE Act is assigned a number by the NMLSR. This NMLSR ID helps facilitate electronic tracking and uniform identification of loan originators and provides public access to loan originators' employment history and any public disciplinary and enforcement actions against them.[21] Whenever the credit application, loan estimate (LE) form, closing disclosure (CD), promissory note, and security instrument[22] are provided to a consumer or presented to a consumer for signature, the loan originator organization must include on those documents its name and its NMLSR ID and the name and NMLSR ID of the individual loan originator with primary responsibility for the origination of the loan.[23]

1.2.1.2 Loan Originator Compensation

Loan originators may not receive (and no person may pay a loan originator) compensation in an amount that is based on a term of a transaction, the terms of multiple transactions, or a proxy for a term of a transaction.[24] For purposes of this rule, *compensation* includes

---

16. Individual loan originators who are not subject to SAFE Act licensing generally include employees of depository institutions and their federally regulated subsidiaries and employees of bona fide nonprofit organizations that a state has exempted from licensing. 12 C.F.R. pt. 1026, supp. I, cmt. 36(f)(3)-1 (2020). However, individual loan originators employed by depository institutions are required to be registered with the NMLSR. 12 C.F.R. § 1007.103(a) (2020).
17. 12 C.F.R. § 1026.36(f)(3)(i) (2020).
18. *Id.* § 1026.36(f)(3)(ii)(A).
19. *Id.* § 1026.36(f)(3)(ii)(B).
20. *Id.* § 1026.36(f)(3)(iii).
21. *Id.* § 1026.36(g)(3).
22. *Id.* § 1026.36(g)(2).
23. *Id.* § 1026.36(g)(1).
24. *Id.* § 1026.36(d).

salaries, commissions, and any financial or similar incentive.[25] It also includes bonuses and awards of merchandise, services, trips, or similar prizes.[26]

To determine whether compensation is prohibited in a specific instance, it is necessary to first determine whether the amount paid is based on a term of a transaction or a proxy for a term of a transaction. For purposes of this determination, a *term of a transaction* is any right or obligation of the parties, including but not limited to, the rights and obligations under the promissory note and the security instrument for the loan.[27] This could include, among other things, the interest rate, APR, length of the loan term, collateral type, or the existence of a prepayment penalty.[28] If objective facts and circumstances indicate that compensation would have been different if a transaction term had been different, then the compensation is likely prohibited as based on a term of the transaction.[29]

The regulation specifically provides, however, that the amount of credit extended is not considered a term of a transaction for these purposes, provided the compensation, which may be subject to a minimum or maximum dollar amount, is based on a fixed percentage of the credit extended that does not vary with the amount of credit extended.[30] For example, a loan originator may receive 1 percent of the amount of credit extended for all loans, subject to a $1,000 minimum and $5,000 maximum compensation. However, the loan originator may not receive a different percentage based on differing dollar amounts of credit extended, such as 1 percent of the amount of the credit extended for loans of more than $300,000, 2 percent for loans between $200,000 and $300,000, and 3 percent for loans of less than $200,000.

The rule also prohibits compensation that is based on a factor that is a proxy for a term of the transaction. A factor is considered to be a proxy for a term of the transaction if that factor varies consistently with that term over a significant number of transactions and the loan originator is able to add, drop, or change that factor.[31] The Commentary provides the following example to illustrate the proxy rule:

> Assume a creditor pays a loan originator a higher commission for transactions to be held by the creditor in portfolio than for transactions sold by the creditor into the secondary market. The creditor holds in portfolio only extensions of credit that have a fixed interest rate and a five-year term with a final balloon payment. The creditor sells into the secondary market all other extensions of credit, which typically have a

---

25. *Id.* § 1026.36(a)(3).

26. 12 C.F.R. pt. 1026, supp. I, cmt. 36(a)-5 (2020). This comment includes additional helpful information on what is and is not considered *compensation* for purposes of this rule.

27. 12 C.F.R. § 1026.36(d)(1)(ii) (2020); 12 C.F.R. pt. 1026, supp. I, cmt. 36(d)(1)-1(iii) (2020).

28. 12 C.F.R. pt. 1026, supp. I, cmt. 36(d)(2) (2020).

29. *Id.* at cmt. 36(d)(1)-1.

30. 12 C.F.R. § 1026.36(d)(1)(ii) (2020); 12 C.F.R. pt. 1026, supp. I, cmt. 36(d)(9) (2020).

31. 12 C.F.R. pt. 1026, supp. I, cmt. 36(d)(1)-2.ii (2020).

> higher fixed interest rate and a 30-year term. Thus, whether an extension of credit is held in portfolio or sold into the secondary market for this creditor consistently varies with the interest rate and whether the credit has a five-year term or a 30-year term (which are terms of the transaction) over a significant number of transactions. Also, the loan originator has the ability to change the factor by, for example, advising the consumer to choose an extension of credit [with] a five-year term. Therefore, under these circumstances, whether or not an extension of credit will be held in portfolio is a proxy for a term of a transaction.[32]

Specific complex rules apply to permit compensation to a loan originator in the form of a contribution to certain designated tax-advantaged defined contribution plans or defined benefit plans, or to nondeferred profits-based plans, as long as those contributions are not based, directly or indirectly, on the terms of the individual loan originator's transactions.[33]

The rules also prohibit dual compensation when the loan originator receives compensation directly from the consumer. If the consumer, or a person (such as a seller or real estate agent) has paid the loan originator directly, the loan originator may not also receive compensation, directly or indirectly, from any other person (including the lender), and no person who knows or has reason to know of the consumer-paid compensation is allowed to pay any compensation to the loan originator, directly or indirectly.[34]

1.2.1.3 Steering Prohibition

Regulation Z prohibits a loan originator from *steering* a consumer to a transaction that will result in the loan originator receiving greater compensation than the loan originator would receive for other transactions the originator could offer the consumer, unless the transaction actually consummated is in the consumer's interest.[35] Steering means advising, counseling, or otherwise influencing a consumer to accept a particular transaction.[36] Under the regulation, steering occurs only if the consumer actually consummates the transaction.[37]

---

32. 12 C.F.R. pt. 1026, supp. I, cmt. 36(d)(1)-2.ii.A (2020).

33. 12 C.F.R. § 1026.36(d)(1)(iii), (iv) (2020). These provisions also include further definitions of what qualifies as a *designated tax-advantaged plan* and the Commentary for these provisions includes examples and other helpful information for understanding the parameters for this type of compensation. Additional conditions apply to nondeferred profits-based plans.

34. *Id.* § 1026.36(d)(2).

35. *Id.* § 1026.36(e)(1). The Commentary includes guidance and examples for help in determining whether the consummated transaction is in the consumer's interest.

36. 12 C.F.R. pt. 1026, supp. I, cmt. 36(e)(1)-1 (2020).

37. *Id.*

The regulation includes a safe harbor for loan originators who present the consumer with a number of loan options for each type of transaction in which the consumer has expressed an interest.[38] *Type of transaction* refers to whether (1) a loan has an APR that cannot increase after consummation, (2) a loan has an APR that may increase after consummation, or (3) a loan is a reverse mortgage.[39] The options presented must be loans for which the loan originator, in good faith, believes the consumer will likely qualify,[40] and must be obtained from a significant number of creditors with which the originator regularly does business.[41] For each type of transaction, the loan options presented must include:[42]

1. The loan with the lowest interest rate;
2. The loan with the lowest interest rate without negative amortization, a prepayment penalty, interest-only payments, a balloon payment in the first seven years of the life of the loan, a demand feature, shared equity, or shared appreciation; and
3. The loan with the lowest total dollar amount of discount points, origination points, or origination fees.[43]

1.2.1.4 Policies and Procedures

Regulation Z requires depository institutions to establish and maintain written policies and procedures regarding loan originator qualifications, identification, compensation, and the prohibition on steering.[44] These policies and procedures must be reasonably designed to ensure and monitor that the depository institution, its employees, its subsidiaries, and its subsidiaries' employees are in compliance with the regulation's loan originator requirements.

---

38. 12 C.F.R. § 1026.36(e)(2) (2020). The Commentary and section 1026.36(e)(4) include information on how to determine how many options for each type of transaction to present to the consumer under the safe harbor provisions.

39. *Id.*

40. *Id.* § 1026.36(e)(3)(ii).

41. *Id.* § 1026.36(e)(3)(i).

42. *Id.*

43. If two or more loans have the same total dollar amount of discount points, origination points or origination fees, the loan with the lowest interest rate that has the lowest total dollar amount of discount points, origination points, or origination fees must be included in the loan options. *Id.* § 1026.36(e)(3)(i)(C).

44. *Id.* § 1026.36(j).

1.2.2 Origination Disclosures

1.2.2.1 Disclosures for Loans Secured by Real Property

Perhaps the biggest change in disclosure requirements in more than thirty years was the radical new approach to disclosures for most mortgage loans that went into effect in 2015.[45] For many years, four separate disclosures were required for consumer loans secured by residential real property. The consumer was entitled to two disclosures at the application stage: an "early disclosure" required by TILA that disclosed estimated finance charges and payments, and a Good Faith Estimate required by the Real Estate Settlement Procedures Act (RESPA) that disclosed the estimated closing fees. At the consummation stage the consumer received two additional disclosures: the final TILA disclosure with finance charges and the payment schedule, and the RESPA HUD-1 settlement statement that disclosed the final fees and charges. These disclosures were promulgated by different federal agencies: the Federal Reserve Board for the TILA disclosures and the Department of Housing and Urban Development (HUD) for the RESPA disclosures. The language and disclosures in the forms were overlapping and not entirely consistent. Over the years there was talk of combining these forms, but no real progress was made. This changed with the Dodd-Frank Act's mandate that the CFPB integrate the TILA and RESPA disclosures.[46] As a result, in November 2013,[47] the CFPB issued the "2013 Integrated Mortgage Disclosure Rule Under the Real Estate Settlement Procedures Act (Regulation X) and the Truth in Lending Act (Regulation Z),"[48] often called TRID (shorthand for TILA-RESPA Integrated Disclosures) or the "Know Before You Owe" rule,[49] which went into effect on October 3, 2015.[50]

TRID fundamentally changed the way in which both initial and closing disclosures are provided for mortgage loans secured by real property or a cooperative unit.[51] Rather than the TILA disclosures required for other consumer credit transactions,

45. The disclosures discussed in this section apply to closed-end consumer credit transactions secured by real property or a cooperative unit, regardless of whether a cooperative unit is treated as real property under state law. 12 C.F.R. pt. 1026, supp. I, cmt. 19(e)(1)(i)-2 (2020).

46. *See* Dodd-Frank Act §§ 1032(f), 1098, 1100A.

47. Although not published in the Federal Register until December 31, 2013, the TILA-RESPA Integrated Disclosures (TRID) rule was issued by the CFPB on November 20, 2013.

48. 78 Fed. Reg. 79730 (Dec. 31, 2013). The CFPB issued a number of amendments after the initial issuance of the TRID rule, leading to the disclosure rules in Regulation Z today for closed-end consumer mortgage loans secured by real property or a cooperative unit.

49. Although most practitioners use TRID, "Know Before You Owe" is the terminology commonly used by the CFPB on its website for these requirements.

50. Although TRID was originally supposed to become effective on August 1, 2015, the CFPB extended the effective date to October 3, 2015. 2013 Integrated Mortgage Disclosures Rule Under the Real Estate Settlement Procedures Act (Regulation X) and the Truth in Lending Act (Regulation Z) and Amendments; Delay of Effective Date, 80 Fed. Reg. 43911 (July 24, 2015).

51. See 12 C.F.R. § 1026.19(e) and (f), 12 C.F.R. § 1026.37, and 12 C.F.R. § 1026.38, and accompanying Commentary for more specific details on these requirements.

for mortgage loans secured by real property or cooperative units, the consumer must be provided a LE at the application stage of the loan and a CD prior to consummation.[52,53] The requirements for these disclosures are extremely complex, requiring detailed and specific information, in specific required formats, with specific timing requirements, and specific rules on what, when, and how changes in pricing or costs at various stages of the process are allowed (or prohibited) and how such changes impact the disclosure requirements. A complete discussion of these requirements would merit an entire treatise of its own. For a more thorough (yet still decidedly brief) overview of these requirements, refer to chapter 15.[54]

1.2.2.2 TILA Disclosures for Dwellings Not Subject to TRID

TRID does not apply to certain closed-end dwelling-secured transactions, for example, closed-end reverse mortgages and loans secured by dwellings that are personal property (but not cooperative units), such as mobile homes.[55] Such transactions are subject to the closed-end account opening disclosures detailed in chapter 3B, with some revisions. The payment schedule required for other closed-end loans[56] is replaced for these dwelling-secured loans with a table showing an interest rate and payment summary.[57] Sample tables showing these disclosures are provided in appendices H-4(E) to H-4(H) to Regulation Z.[58] The table must show the initial interest rate and corresponding payment.[59] If the account has a variable or step rate the creditor must disclose the period of time until the first rate adjustment may occur;[60] the maximum rate that could apply during the first five years,[61] and the earliest date on which that payment could apply, along with the corresponding payment;[62] and the maximum rate that may apply during the life of the loan and the corresponding payment.[63] Any

---

52. See 12 C.F.R. § 1026.37 and accompanying Commentary for details on the content required for the LE.

53. See 12 C.F.R. § 1026.38 and accompanying Commentary for details on the content required for the CD.

54. You also may wish to consult *The Law of Truth in Lending* and its 2018 Supplement, *supra* note 2.

55. 12 C.F.R. § 1026.18(s) (2020); 12 C.F.R. pt. 1026, supp. I, cmt. 18(s)-1 (2020).

56. 12 C.F.R. § 1026.18(g) (2020).

57. *Id.* § 1026.18(s).

58. *Id.* § 1026.18(s)(1).

59. *Id.* § 1026.18(s)(2)(i), (s)(3)(i). There are special disclosures for loans that do not have amortizing payments and loans with special introductory rates. *Id.* § 1026.18(s)(2)(ii)–(iii).

60. *Id.* § 1026.18(s)(2)(i)(B).

61. The five-year period is measured from the date on which the first regular periodic payment will be due, not from account opening. *Id.* § 1026.18(s)(2)(i)(B)(2).

62. *Id.* § 1026.18(s)(2)(i)(B)(2), (s)(3)(i).

63. *Id.* § 1026.18(s)(2)(i)(B)(3), (s)(3)(i).

escrow component of the payment must be separately disclosed.[64] If the account has nonamortizing payment features, such as interest-only,[65] negative amortization,[66] or a balloon payment[67] there are additional required disclosures.

1.2.3 Adjustable-Rate Mortgage Loan Disclosures

TILA requires specific disclosures for closed-end *adjustable-rate mortgage* (ARM) loans,[68] both before and after consummation.[69] The following disclosures must be provided to the consumer at the time an application is provided or before the consumer pays a nonrefundable fee, whichever is earlier:[70]

1. The booklet titled *Consumer Handbook on Adjustable Rate Mortgages*, commonly called the "CHARM Booklet," available on the CFPB's website,[71] or a suitable substitute.

2. A loan program disclosure for each variable-rate program in which the consumer expresses an interest. The regulation includes a list of the detailed specific information that must be contained in the disclosure for each such variable-rate loan program. Model clauses for these required disclosures are provided in appendix H-4(C) of Regulation Z.[72]

As further discussed below, additional disclosures must be provided to the consumer throughout the term of the ARM loan.

1.2.4 Ability to Repay Requirements

Another factor seen as contributing to the 2008 financial crisis was lax underwriting standards used by some mortgage lenders when making mortgage loans, resulting in

64. *Id.* § 1026.18(s)(3)(i)(C).

65. *See Id.* § 1026.18(s)(3)(i)(B), (s)(3)(ii).

66. *See Id.* § 1026.18(s)(3)(i)(B), (s)(4), (s)(6).

67. *See Id.* § 1026.18(s)(3)(i)(B), (s)(5).

68. An ARM loan is a closed-end consumer credit transaction secured by the consumer's principal dwelling in which the annual percentage rate may increase after consummation. *Id.* § 1026.20(c)(1).

69. The disclosures discussed here are in addition to the general variable-rate disclosures required for closed-end loans. See chapter 3B for a discussion of the more generally applicable closed-end variable rate disclosure requirements.

70. 12 C.F.R. § 1026.19(b) (2020). These disclosure requirements apply to all closed-end variable-rate transactions that are secured by the consumer's principal dwelling and have a term greater than one year.

71. CFPB, *Consumer Handbook on Adjustable-Rate Mortgages* (last visited Sept. 15, 2020), files.consumerfinance.gov/f/documents/cfpb_charm_booklet.pdf.

72. 12 C.F.R. pt. 1026, app. H-4(C) (2020).

loans being made to consumers without regard to whether the consumer truly had the ability to repay the loan. As the CFPB put it when issuing its Ability to Repay rule:[73]

> Loose underwriting practices by some creditors—including failure to verify the consumer's income or debts and qualifying consumers for mortgages based on "teaser" interest rates that would cause monthly payments to jump to unaffordable levels after the first few years—contributed to a mortgage crisis that led to the nation's most serious recession since the Great Depression.[74]

To address this concern, Congress included amendments to TILA in the Dodd-Frank Act to require creditors to determine, based on verified and documented information, that the consumer has a reasonable ability to repay the mortgage loan.[75] The CFPB implemented these requirements in its Ability to Repay rule, effective January 10, 2014, with additional amendments to Regulation Z over the years that followed. These rules apply to a *covered transaction*—a consumer credit transaction that is secured by a dwelling, including any real property attached to a dwelling, subject to certain exceptions.[76] Today, at or before consummation, a creditor must make a reasonable and good faith determination that the consumer will have a reasonable ability to repay the loan according to its terms.[77]

1.2.4.1 Determining Repayment Ability

Except for qualified mortgages, discussed below, Regulation Z does not dictate the underwriting standards that creditors must adopt to make the determination of whether a consumer has the ability to repay a mortgage loan. However, the regulation does provide that a creditor must include the following eight factors in its underwriting standards for determining repayment ability.

---

73. Ability-to-Repay and Qualified Mortgage Standards under the Truth in Lending Act ("Ability to Repay rule"), 78 Fed. Reg. 6407 (Jan. 30, 2013). This CFPB rule became effective January 10, 2014.

74. *Id.* at 6408.

75. Dodd-Frank Act § 1411.

76. Congress excluded open-end credit plans, timeshare plans, reverse mortgages, and temporary loans from these requirements. *Id.* The CFPB subsequently excluded certain other creditors and certain loan programs from the requirements. See 12 C.F.R. § 1026.43(a) for a complete list of creditors and loan programs that are not subject to the ability-to-repay requirements. Although certain products are excluded from the Ability to Repay rule, there may be underwriting requirements outside of TILA that are applicable to such products. *See, e.g.*, Interagency Credit Risk Management Guidance for Home Equity Lending (May 16, 2005) (underwriting requirements for home equity lines of credit), https://www.federalreserve.gov/boarddocs/press/bcreg/2005/20050516/attachment.pdf.

77. 12 C.F.R. § 1026.43(c)(1) (2020). The Commentary to this section includes helpful information in considering whether the creditor's determination was reasonable and in good faith.

1. *Income and assets.* The consumer's current or reasonably expected income or assets must be considered.[78] Any type of current or reasonably expected income[79] and any of the consumer's assets[80] may be considered, except that the value of the dwelling securing the loan (including any attached real property) may not be considered.

Only the income and assets necessary to support the determination that the consumer can repay the mortgage loan need to be considered and verified.[81] If multiple consumers apply for a mortgage loan, if the income or assets of one applicant are sufficient to support the repayment ability determination, the other applicants' income and assets do not have to be considered.[82]

The income and assets the creditor relies on to make the determination must be verified by third-party records that provide reasonably reliable evidence of the consumer's income or assets.[83] For example, the following third-party records are acceptable: tax returns, tax-return transcripts, W-2 forms, payroll statements, financial institution records, records from the consumer's employer, and government agency records confirming the consumer's income from benefits.[84]

2. *Employment status.* If income from the consumer's employment is relied on for making the determination, the consumer's current employment status must be verified and documented.[85] If the creditor relied wholly on other income, such as from the consumer's investments, the current employment status need not be considered.[86]

3. *Monthly payment on the mortgage loan.* The creditor must consider the consumer's monthly payment on the mortgage loan.[87] Generally,[88] this payment

---

78. *Id.* § 1026.43(c)(2)(i).

79. 12 C.F.R. pt. 1026, supp. I, cmt. 43(c)(2)(i)-1 (2020). This comment includes the following examples of income that may be considered: salary; wages; self-employment income; military or reserve duty income; bonus pay; tips; commissions; interest payments; dividends; retirement benefits or entitlements; rental income; royalty payments; trust income; public assistance payments; and alimony, child support, and separate maintenance payments.

80. *Id.* The comment includes the following examples of assets that may be considered: funds in a savings or checking account, amounts vested in a retirement account, stocks, bonds, certificates of deposit, and amounts available to the consumer from a trust fund.

81. *Id.* at cmt. 43(c)(2)(i)-2.

82. *Id.* at cmt. 43(c)(2)(i)-5. If the creditor relies on expected income, over and above the consumer's current income, that expectation must be verified with third-party records. *Id.* at cmt. 43(c)(2)(i)-3. Examples include records of past annual bonuses and written confirmation from a future employer that the consumer will, indeed, be employed as the consumer has represented.

83. 12 C.F.R. § 1026.43(c)(4) (2020).

84. *Id.*

85. *Id.* § 1026.43(c)(2)(ii); 12 C.F.R. pt. 1026, supp. I, cmt. 43(c)(2)(ii)-1 (2020).

86. 12 C.F.R. pt. 1026, supp. I, cmt. 43(c)(2)(ii)-1 (2020).

87. 12 C.F.R. § 1026.43(c)(2)(iii) (2020).

88. The regulation includes special calculation rules for loans with balloon payments, and for interest-only and negative amortization loans. *Id.* § 1026.43(c)(4)(2).

must be calculated using (1) the fully indexed rate or any introductory interest rate, whichever is greater; and (2) substantially equal, fully amortizing, monthly payments.[89]

If the loan terms require a payment schedule with something other than monthly payments, then for purposes of the repayment ability calculation, the scheduled payments must be converted to monthly payments to meet the requirement that the determination is based on "substantially equal monthly payments."[90] Likewise, if the loan agreement does not require fully amortizing payments, then for purposes of the repayment ability calculation, any nonamortizing payments must be converted to fully amortizing payments.[91] The monthly payments must be "substantially" equal, but do not need to be exactly equal; minor variations, such as a long or short first or last payment, may be disregarded.[92]

4. *Monthly payment on simultaneous loan.* The creditor must consider and verify the consumer's monthly payment on any *simultaneous loan* that the creditor knows or has reason to know will be made.[93] A *simultaneous loan* is any other *covered transaction* or home equity line of credit (HELOC)[94] that will be secured by the same dwelling securing the mortgage loan, made to the same consumer, at or before consummation of the mortgage loan.[95] The calculation of the monthly payment on the simultaneous loan must take into account any mortgage-related obligations for the simultaneous loan.

If the simultaneous loan is another covered transaction, the payment calculation method is the same as the calculation method discussed above for the mortgage loan for which the repayment ability determination is being made.[96] If the simultaneous loan is a HELOC, the payment calculation must be made using the periodic payment under the terms of the HELOC and the amount of credit to be drawn on the HELOC at or before consummation of the mortgage loan.[97]

If the simultaneous loan is being made by a third-party creditor, the creditor for the mortgage loan may verify the monthly payment on the simultaneous loan by obtaining the necessary information from the third-party creditor.[98]

---

89. *Id.* § 1026.43(c)(5)(i).

90. 12 C.F.R. pt. 1026, supp. I, cmt. 43(c)(5)(i)-3 (2020).

91. *Id.*

92. *Id.* at cmt. 43(c)(5)(i)-4.

93. 12 C.F.R. § 1026.43(c)(2)(iv) (2020).

94. The monthly payments for a HELOC must be considered for purposes of the repayment ability determination, even though HELOCs are not otherwise subject to the closed-end TILA ability to repay requirements. 12 C.F.R. pt. 1026, supp. I, cmt. 43(c)(2)(iv)-1 (2020).

95. 12 C.F.R. § 1026.43(b)(12) (2020). The term also includes a separate loan made after consummation to cover closing costs of the mortgage loan.

96. *Id.* § 1026.43(c)(6)(i).

97. *Id.* § 1026.43(c)(6)(ii).

98. 12 C.F.R. pt. 1026, supp. I, cmt. 43(c)(3)-4 (2020).

5. *Monthly payment for mortgage-related obligations.* The creditor must consider the consumer's monthly payment on mortgage-related obligations,[99] regardless of whether the amounts are included in the monthly payment and whether or not there is an escrow account established.[100] Only payments that occur on an ongoing or recurring basis need to be considered.[101] If the recurring payments for mortgage-related obligations are not made on a monthly basis, the payments should be converted to monthly payments for purposes of the repayment ability analysis.[102]

The mortgage-related obligation payment amounts must be verified with reasonably reliable records from third parties, such as taxing authorities, insurance companies, or homeowners' associations.[103]

6. *Current debt obligations.* The consumer's current debt obligations and obligations to pay alimony or child support must be considered.[104] If multiple consumers apply for the mortgage loan, with the intent that all will be jointly obligated on the loan, the creditor must consider the debt, alimony, and child support obligations of all joint applicants. These current obligations must be verified by reasonably reliable third-party records. For many of the debt obligations, a credit report from a credit reporting agency should suffice for this verification,[105] but other third-party verification may be needed for some obligations, such as alimony or child support.

7. *Monthly debt-to-income ratio.* The consumer's monthly debt-to-income ratio or residual income must be considered.[106] Either or both may be used for the repayment ability determination. If the creditor uses the debt-to-income ratio,[107] the calculation must consider the ratio of the consumer's total monthly debt obligations[108]

---

99. 12 C.F.R. § 1026.43(c)(2)(v) (2020). Mortgage-related obligations include property taxes; premiums and similar charges for credit loss insurance, credit life, accident, health, or loss-of-income insurance, liability insurance and insurance against loss of or damage to property, and debt cancellation or debt suspension insurance, that are required by the creditor; fees and special assessments imposed by a condominium, cooperative, or homeowners association; ground rent; and leasehold payments. *Id.* § 1026.43(b)(8). (See Commentary to § 1026.43(b)(8) for more information and examples of what constitutes a mortgage-related obligation.)

100. 12 C.F.R. pt. 1026, supp. I, cmt. 43(c)(5)(v)-1 (2020).

101. *Id.* cmt. 43(c)(2)(v)-1.

102. See the Commentary for section 1026.43(c)(2)(v) for a more complete discussion of monthly payment pro ration and other considerations for the mortgage-related obligations analysis.

103. 12 C.F.R. pt. 1026, supp. I, cmt. 43(c)(3)-5 (2020).

104. 12 C.F.R. § 1026.43(c)(2)(vi) (2020).

105. 12 C.F.R. pt. 1026, supp. I, cmt. 43(c)(3)-3, -6 (2020).

106. 12 C.F.R. § 1026.43(c)(2)(vii) (2020).

107. *Id.* § 1026.43(c)(7)(ii)(A).

108. Total monthly debt obligations means the sum of: the monthly payment on the mortgage loan, the monthly payment on simultaneous loans, the monthly payment on the mortgage-related obligations for the mortgage loan and simultaneous loans, and current debt obligations, alimony, and child support. *Id.* § 1026.43(c)(7)(i)(A).

to the consumer's total monthly income.[109] If the creditor uses residual income, the calculation must consider the consumer's remaining income after subtracting the consumer's total monthly debt obligations from the consumer's total monthly income.[110]

Regulation Z does not prescribe a specific debt-to-income ratio or residual income threshold that must be used but leaves it to each creditor to determine what threshold to apply in making a reasonable and good faith determination of a consumer's ability to repay.

8. *Credit history.* The consumer's credit history must be considered, including such factors as the number and age of credit lines, payment history, and any judgments, collections, or bankruptcies.[111] If multiple consumers apply for the mortgage loan, with the intent that all will be jointly obligated, the creditor must consider the credit history of all joint applicants.

The regulation does not specify which aspects of the credit history must be considered or how they should be weighed, and does not require use of a consolidated credit score or prescribe a minimum credit score that must be applied.[112] As with the other factors in the ability-to-repay analysis, the specific parameters of the credit history and any applicable minimum credit score threshold are up to the creditor, but must lead to a reasonable and good faith determination of the consumer's repayment ability.

1.2.4.2 Standard Mortgage Refinance Exception

If a creditor refinances a nonstandard mortgage[113] into a standard mortgage,[114] the ability-to-repay requirements do not apply if the following conditions are met:[115]

---

109. Total monthly income means the sum of the consumer's current or reasonably expected income, including any income from assets. *Id.* § 1026.43(c)(7)(i)(B).

110. *Id.* § 1026.43(c)(7)(ii)(B).

111. *Id.* § 1026.43(c)(2)(viii).

112. 12 C.F.R. pt. 1026, supp. I, cmt. 43(c)(2)(viii)-1 (2020).

113. A nonstandard mortgage means a covered transaction that is an ARM loan with an introductory fixed interest rate for a period of one year or longer, an interest-only loan, or a negative amortization loan. 12 C.F.R. § 1026.43(d)(1)(i) (2020).

114. A standard mortgage means a covered transaction that provides for regular periodic payments that do not: (1) cause the principal balance to increase, (2) allow the consumer to defer repayment of principal, or (3) result in a balloon payment; for which the total points and fees do not exceed the amounts specified for a qualified mortgage; for which the term does not exceed forty years; for which the interest rate is fixed for at least the first five years after consummation; for which the proceeds from the loan are used solely to pay off the outstanding principal balance on the nonstandard mortgage and pay closing or settlement charges required to be disclosed under RESPA. *Id.* § 1026.43(d)(1)(ii).

115. *Id.* § 1026.43(d)(2), (d)(3)(i).

1. The creditor for the standard mortgage is the holder of the existing nonstandard mortgage or the servicer acting on behalf of the current holder.
2. The monthly payment for the standard mortgage is materially lower than the monthly payment for the nonstandard mortgage. The regulation prescribes a particular calculation method that must be used to make this determination.[116]
3. The creditor receives the consumer's written application for the standard mortgage no later than two months after the nonstandard mortgage has recast.
4. The consumer has made no more than one payment more than thirty days late on the nonstandard mortgage during the twelve months immediately preceding the creditor's receipt of the consumer's written application for the standard mortgage.
5. The consumer has made no payments more than thirty days late during the six months immediately preceding the creditor's receipt of the consumer's written application for the standard mortgage; and
6. If the nonstandard mortgage was consummated on or after January 10, 2014, the nonstandard mortgage was made in accordance with the ability-to-repay requirements or the qualified mortgage requirements.

In addition to these conditions, the creditor must consider whether the standard mortgage will likely prevent a default by the consumer on the nonstandard mortgage once the loan is recast.

1.2.4.3 Qualified Mortgages

Regulation Z provides that compliance with the ability-to-repay requirements will be presumed if the loan is a qualified mortgage (QM),[117] as discussed below. For most QMs, this is a conclusive presumption that may not be rebutted by the consumer.[118] However, if the loan is a higher-priced covered transaction,[119] a consumer may rebut

---

116. *Id.* § 1026.43(d)(5).

117. *Id.* § 1026.43(e). The factors that go into determining whether a mortgage loan is a QM are detailed and complex, and the space limitations of this treatise allow only the highest-level overview of the QM definitions, presumptions, and exceptions.

118. *Id.* § 1026.43(e)(1)(i).

119. Higher-priced covered transaction means a covered transaction with an APR that exceeds the average prime offer rate for a comparable transaction as of the date the interest rate is set by 1.5 or more percentage points for a first-lien covered transaction, other than a QM under § 1026.43(e)(5)(certain small creditor portfolio loans), (e)(6) (certain balloon-payment loans for which the application was received before April 1, 2016), or (f) (balloon-payment QMs made by certain creditors); by 3.5 or more percentage points for a first-lien covered transaction that is a QM under § 1026.43(e)(5), (e)(6), or (f); or by 3.5 or more percentage points for a subordinate-lien covered transaction. *Id.* § 1026.43(b)(4).

the presumption by proving that, despite meeting all of the QM requirements, the creditor did not make a reasonable and good faith determination of the consumer's ability to repay the loan.[120]

In general,[121] to be considered a QM, the loan must meet the following specific criteria:

1. The loan must provide for regular substantially equal periodic payments. For ARM or step-rate mortgages,[122] payment changes due to an interest rate change are considered substantially equal for purposes of this requirement.[123] The required payments:
   (i) Must not result in an increase of the principal balance.[124] This means the payment schedule must require payments of principal and interest, on a monthly or other periodic basis, that will fully repay the loan amount over the loan term. Negative amortization will prevent the loan from being a QM.[125]
   (ii) Must not allow the consumer to defer repayment of principal.[126] If the terms of the loan permit payments that are applied solely to accrued interest and not to principal, or payments that are applied to both interest and principal, but are insufficient to fully repay the loan over the loan term, the loan is not a QM.

---

120. *Id.* § 1026.43(e)(1)(ii)(B). The consumer may do this by showing that the consumer's income and debt obligations of which the creditor was aware at consummation would leave the consumer with insufficient residual income or assets to meet living expenses.

121. The Ability-to-Repay rule as issued by the CFPB included special rules for certain federally backed mortgage loans, including loans eligible to be insured or guaranteed by HUD, the U.S. Department of Veterans Affairs, the U.S. Department of Agriculture, and the Rural Housing Service. Because each of these agencies has issued its own QM rule, those rules, rather than the special rules in the Ability-to-Repay rules, now apply. Special rules also apply to loans eligible for purchase or guarantee by the government-sponsored enterprises (GSEs)—Fannie Mae or Freddie Mac—while they are operating under conservatorship. The GSE exception had been set to expire on January 10, 2021, but as of this writing, the GSEs still are under conservatorship and the CFPB has extended the expiration date for the GSE exception (85 Fed. Reg. 67938) to correspond to the date amended QM rules are issued (unless the GSEs exit conservatorship prior to that date), as proposed in a separate NPRM (85 Fed. Reg. 41716), which would remove the debt-to-income ratio QM criterion, discussed below, and add a new price-based QM criterion.

122. A step-rate mortgage is a mortgage secured by real property or a dwelling for which the interest rate will change after consummation, and the rates that will apply and the periods for which they will apply are known at consummation. 12 C.F.R. § 1026.18(s)(7)(ii) (2020).

123. *Id.* § 1026.43(e)(2)(i).

124. *Id.* § 1026.43(e)(2)(i)(A).

125. 12 C.F.R. pt. 1026, supp. I, cmt. 43(e)(2)(i)-1 (2020).

126. 12 C.F.R. § 1026.43(e)(2)(i)(B) (2020).

(iii) Must not result in a balloon payment.[127] Note, however, that there is an exception to this limitation for balloon-payment loans made by certain small creditors[128] who have made a first lien covered transaction on a property located in a rural or underserved area[129] within the preceding calendar year.[130,131]

2. The loan term may not exceed thirty years.[132]
3. The points and fees payable in connection with the loan may not exceed the following thresholds, with the dollar amounts being subject to annual adjustment:[133]

---

127. *Id.* § 1026.43(e)(2)(i)(C).

128. To qualify as a small creditor, the creditor must satisfy the requirements in 12 C.F.R. § 1026.35 (b)(2)(iii)(B) and (C), which measures the number of covered transactions made, retained, and sold, and the creditor's asset size for a given period.

129. See 12 C.F.R. § 1026.35(b)(2)(iv) for a description of what constitutes a rural or underserved area.

130. If the loan application was received before April 1 of the current calendar year, the credit meets this requirement if it made such a loan on rural or underserved property during either of the two preceding calendar years. 12 C.F.R. § 1026.35(b)(2)(iii)(A) (2020).

131. *Id.* § 1026.43(f). Under this exception, the balloon-payment loan must provide for substantially equal scheduled payments, calculated using a thirty-year amortization period (regardless of the loan term), use an interest rate that does not increase over the loan term, and have a loan term of five years or more. The creditor must determine that the consumer can make all of the scheduled payments on the loan, excluding the balloon payment, together with the consumer's monthly payments for all mortgage-related obligations, from the consumer's current or reasonably expected income or assets (other than the dwelling that secures the loan). The balloon-payment QM will lose its QM status, however, if it is sold or transferred unless the sale or transfer (1) occurs three years or more after consummation, (2) is made to another small creditor who also meets the rural or underserved covered transaction requirement, (3) is deemed necessary by the creditor's supervisory agency, or (4) is the result of a merger or acquisition. *Id.* § 1026.43(f)(2).

132. *Id.* § 1026.43(e)(2)(ii).

133. *Id.* § 1026.43(e)(2)(ii), (e)(3). The dollar amounts are indexed for inflation. The amounts stated in the regulation are the amounts for 2014, when the Ability-to-Repay rule went into effect. The CFPB announces adjustments for these dollar amounts each year. To illustrate, the threshold amounts for 2021 are 3 percent of the total loan amount for a loan amount greater than or equal to $110,260; $3,308 for a loan amount greater than or equal to $66,156 but less than $110,260; 5 percent of the total loan amount for loans greater than or equal to $22,052 but less than $66,156; $1,103 for a loan amount greater than or equal to $13,783 but less than $22,052; or 8 percent of the total loan amount for loans less than $13,783.

(i) For a loan amount greater than or equal to $100,000, 3 percent of the total loan amount;[134]

(ii) For a loan amount greater than or equal to $60,000 but less than $100,000, $3,000;

(iii) For a loan amount greater than or equal to $20,000 but less than $60,000, 5 percent of the total loan amount;

(iv) For a loan amount greater than or equal to $12,500 but less than $20,000, $1,000;

(v) For a loan amount less than $12,500, 8 percent of the total loan amount.

Points and fees are defined as:[135]

(i) All items included in the finance charge,[136] but excluding the following:
   a) interest;[137]
   b) the premium for any state or federal guaranty or insurance, premiums for nonstate or federal guaranty or insurance that meet certain requirements;[138]
   c) bona fide third-party fees not retained by the creditor, unless another section specifically requires that such fees be included in the points and fees calculation;[139]
   d) up to one or two bona fide discount points so long as the APR does not exceed certain triggers.[140]

(ii) Mortgage broker fees, whether paid by the consumer or the creditor.[141]

---

134. The total loan amount is not necessarily equal to the loan amount stated in the promissory note, but is based on a specific calculated amount. For QMs the total loan amount is calculated in the same way as it is for high-cost loans, further discussed below (see 12 C.F.R. § 1026.32(b)(4)). The Commentary for section 1026.32(b)(4) provides several examples for how to calculate the total loan amount.

135. This QM criterion uses the same definition of points and fees as that used for closed-end high-cost mortgages, further discussed below (see 12 C.F.R. § 1026.32(b)(1) and 12 C.F.R. § 1026.43(a)(9)). The Commentary for section 1026.43(e)(3)(i) provides several examples for how to calculate the points and fees for QM purposes. This description of points and fees is, by necessity, high level. For a more comprehensive discussion of the requirements and nuances, consult *The Law of Truth in Lending* and its 2018 Supplement, *supra* note 2.

136. 12 C.F.R. § 1026.32(b)(1)(i), (b)(2)(i) (2020).

137. *Id.* § 1026.32(b)(1)(i)(A), (b)(2)(i)(A).

138. *Id.* § 1026.32(b)(1)(i)(B), (C), (b)(2)(i)(B), (C).

139. *Id.* § 1026.32(b)(1)(i)(D), (b)(2)(i)(D).

140. *Id.* § 1026.32(b)(1)(i)(E), (F), (b)(2)(i)(E), (F), (b)(3).

141. *Id.* § 1026.32(b)(1)(ii), (b)(2)(ii).

(iii) All real-estate-related fees excluded from the finance charge paid to the creditor or an affiliate of the creditor other than amounts held for the future payment of taxes.[142]

(iv) Credit insurance premiums payable at or before consummation of the loan.[143]

(v) The maximum prepayment penalty payable under the new loan and the total prepayment penalty incurred by the consumer if the new loan is a refinance by the same lender or servicer or an affiliate of either.[144]

If all of the other QM criteria are met, and the creditor discovers, after consummation, that the total points and fees exceeded the applicable threshold, the creditor may preserve the QM status of the loan if, within 210 days after consummation (and prior to certain other events occurring),[145] the creditor pays the consumer the amount by which the points and fees exceeded the applicable threshold amount, plus interest on that amount at the contract interest rate.[146] The creditor also must maintain and follow policies and procedures for post-consummation review of points and fees and for making the corrective payments to consumers.[147]

4. The loan must be underwritten using both of the following calculations (and taking into account the monthly payment for mortgage-related obligations):
   (i) The maximum interest rate that may apply during the first five years after the date on which the first regular periodic payment will be due.[148] For fixed-rate mortgage loans, this will be the interest rate in effect at consummation.[149] For ARM loans, the maximum interest rate to apply must be determined by assuming the interest rate will increase as rapidly as possible, taking into account any periodic or lifetime adjustment caps.[150]

---

142. *Id.* §§ 1026.32(b)(1)(iii), (b)(2)(iii), 1026.4(c)(7).

143. *Id.* § 1026.32(b)(1)(iv), (b)(2)(iv), (b)(6).

144. *Id.* § 1026.32(b)(1)(v), (vi), (b)(2)(v), (vi).

145. The date by which this amount must be paid to the consumer also must be prior to: (1) the institution of any action by the consumer in connection with the loan, (2) the creditor's receipt of a written notice from the consumer stating that the total points and fees exceeded the applicable threshold, or (3) the consumer becoming past due on the mortgage loan. *Id.* § 1026.43(e)(3)(iii)(B).

146. *Id.* § 1026.43(e)(3)(iii).

147. *Id.* § 1026.43(e)(3)(iii)(C).

148. *Id.* § 1026.43(e)(2)(iv)(A).

149. 12 C.F.R. pt. 1026, supp. I, cmt. 43(e)(2)(iv)-2 (2020).

150. *Id.* cmt. 43(e)(2)(iv)-3. The Commentary for this section includes additional helpful information for determining the applicable maximum interest rate, including for ARM loans with an initial fixed-rate period and for step-rate mortgage loans.

(ii) Periodic payments of principal and interest that will repay either (1) the outstanding principal balance over the remaining term of the loan as of the date the interest rate adjusts to the maximum interest rate discussed above, or (2) the loan amount over the loan term.[151]

If the principal and interest payment are calculated using the first option, the creditor must determine what the outstanding principal balance will be on the date the applicable maximum interest rate will be reached, and underwrite the loan by applying a principal and interest payment (using the applicable maximum interest rate) that will repay that balance by the end of the remaining loan term. If the second option is used, the loan amount at consummation is used, and the loan is underwritten by applying a principal and interest payment (using the applicable maximum interest rate) that will repay that original loan amount by the end of the full loan term.[152]

5. The creditor must consider and verify the consumer's current or reasonably expected income or assets[153] and the consumer's current debt obligations, alimony, and child support.[154] As of this writing, the regulation requires the creditor to use the standards in appendix Q of Regulation Z to verify this information.[155] Small creditors[156] are not required to use the standards in appendix Q, but must consider the consumer's monthly debt-to-income ratio or residual income and verify the debt obligations and income used to determine that ratio

---

151. 12 C.F.R. § 1026.43(e)(2)(iv) (2020).

152. The Commentary for section 1026.43(e)(2)(iv) includes several examples and other useful information to help explain how to apply this criterion.

153. 12 C.F.R. § 1026.43(e)(2)(v)(A) (2020).

154. *Id.* § 1026.43(e)(2)(v)(B).

155. See 12 C.F.R. Part 1026, Appendix Q for the standards required to fulfill this verification requirement. Note, however, that on June 22, 2020, the CFPB issued a notice of proposed rulemaking proposing to remove appendix Q and, to prevent any resulting uncertainty, to amend Regulation Z to clarify the requirements for considering and verifying a consumer's income, assets, debt obligations, alimony, and child support in the absence of appendix Q. Qualified Mortgage Definition Under the Truth in Lending Act (Regulation Z): General QM Loan Definition, 85 Fed. Reg. 41716 (July 10, 2020).

156. To qualify as a small creditor for purposes of this exception, the creditor must satisfy the requirements provided for in 12 C.F.R. § 1026.35 (b)(2)(iii)(B) and (C), which measures the number of covered transactions made, retained, and sold, and the creditor's asset size for a given period.

in accordance with the calculation requirements in the special QM definition for small creditor portfolio loans.[157]

6. As of this writing, for the loan to qualify as a QM, the regulation provides that the ratio of the consumer's total monthly debt to total monthly income must not exceed 43 percent, which must be determined in accordance with the standards in appendix Q of Regulation Z.[158] Pursuant to the special QM definition for small creditor portfolio loans, small creditors are not required to apply this debt-to-income ratio criterion.[159]

1.2.4.4 Prepayment Penalty Restrictions

Prepayment penalties are prohibited in covered transactions unless the loan has an APR that cannot increase after consummation, is a QM, is not a higher-priced mortgage loan, and the prepayment penalty is otherwise permitted by law.[160] Even if the loan meets these qualifications, any prepayment penalty may not apply after the three-year period following consummation and may not exceed 2 percent of the amount prepaid during the first two years and 1 percent of the amount prepaid during the third year.[161]

If the creditor offers a consumer a loan with a prepayment penalty, the creditor also must offer the consumer an alternative loan without a prepayment penalty.[162] The alternative loan must have an APR that cannot increase after consummation and the same type of interest rate and the same loan term as the loan with the prepayment penalty, must satisfy the payment conditions and points and fees conditions for a QM, and must be a loan for which the creditor has a good faith belief the consumer likely qualifies. Special rules apply for the offer of an alternative loan through a mortgage

157. 12 C.F.R. § 1026.43(e)(5) (2020). A QM loan that relies on the special small creditor portfolio loans QM definition will lose its QM status if it is sold or transferred, unless the sale or transfer (1) occurs three years or more after consummation, (2) is made to another small creditor, (3) is deemed necessary by the creditor's supervisory agency, or (4) is the result of a merger or acquisition. *Id.* § 1026.43(e)(2).

158. *Id.* § 1026.43(e)(2)(vi). Note that on June 22, 2020, the CFPB issued a notice of proposed rulemaking to amend Regulation Z to remove this criterion and instead add a new price-based criterion measured by comparing the APR to the average prime offer rate. Qualified Mortgage Definition Under the Truth in Lending Act (Regulation Z): General QM Loan Definition, 85 Fed. Reg. at 41716.

159. 12 C.F.R. § 1026.43(e)(5(i)(A) (2020).

160. *Id.* § 1026.43(g)(1). See the higher-priced mortgage loan discussion in section 1.2.5 for a definition.

161. *Id.* § 1026.43(g)(2).

162. *Id.* § 1026.43(g)(3).

broker[163] or when a creditor presents a loan offered by a person to which the creditor will assign the loan after consummation.[164]

1.2.5 Higher-Priced Mortgage Loans

Regulation Z includes special rules for higher-priced mortgage loans. A higher-priced mortgage loan is a closed-end consumer credit transaction secured by the consumer's principal dwelling with an APR that exceeds the average prime offer rate[165] (APOR) for a comparable transaction as of the date the interest rate is set:

1. By 1.5 percent or more for loans secured by a first lien with a principal loan amount that does not exceed the conforming loan limit[166] in effect as of the date the transaction's interest rate is set;
2. By 2.5 percent or more for loans secured by a first lien with a principal loan amount that exceeds the conforming loan limit in effect as of the date the transaction's interest rate is set; or
3. By 3.5 percent or more for loans secured by a subordinate lien.

Note that the APR is compared to the APOR "as of the date the transaction's interest rate is set" or "locked." If the interest rate is set initially and then is reset at a different level before consummation, the last date the interest rate is set must be used.

1.2.5.1 Escrow Accounts Required

A creditor may not make a higher-priced mortgage loan secured by a first lien on the consumer's principal dwelling unless an escrow account is established before consummation for payment of property taxes and premiums for mortgage-related

163. *Id.* § 1026.43(g)(4).

164. *Id.* § 1026.43(g)(5).

165. Average prime offer rate means an annual percentage rate that is derived from average interest rates, points, and other loan pricing terms currently offered to consumers by a representative sample of creditors for mortgage transactions that have low-risk pricing characteristics. *Id.* § 1026.35(a)(2).

166. Regulation Z uses the language "the limit . . . for the maximum principal obligation eligible for purchase by Freddie Mac." This is commonly known as the "conforming loan limit." This limit is established and adjusted annually by the Federal Finance Housing Agency.

insurance that the creditor requires.[167] The escrow account may be cancelled only upon the earlier of the termination of the debt obligation or receipt of the consumer's request to cancel the escrow account, if that request is received no earlier than five years after consummation.[168] The escrow account may not be cancelled based on the consumer's request unless the unpaid principal balance is less than 80 percent of the original value of the property securing the debt and the consumer is not delinquent or in default at the time of the request.[169]

1.2.5.2 Appraisal Required

The creditor must obtain a written appraisal, performed by a certified or licensed appraiser, before consummation of a higher-priced mortgage loan. Except for a loan secured by a new manufactured home and land,[170] the appraiser must conduct a physical visit of the interior of the property.[171] The regulation provides a safe harbor under which the creditor will be deemed to have complied with the appraisal requirement if the appraisal meets specific standards and conditions,[172] and there are a number of exemptions from this appraisal requirement.[173] There also are appraisal notice

167. 12 C.F.R. § 1026.35(b)(1) (2020). There are exemptions from the escrow requirement for small creditors who meet certain conditions, for loans secured by shares in a cooperative, for temporary or "bridge" loans with a term of twelve months or less, and reverse mortgage transactions. Loans to finance the initial construction of a dwelling also are exempt, but the permanent phase of a construction-permanent loan is subject to the escrow requirement. There also are special rules for loans secured by a dwelling in a condominium, planned unit development, or other common-interest community, for which the insurance premiums do not need to be included in the escrow account if the governing association has the obligation to maintain a master insurance policy for the community.

168. *Id.* § 1026.35(b)(3)(i).

169. *Id.* § 1026.35(b)(3)(ii).

170. *Id.* § 1026.35(c)(2)(viii)(A) provides an exemption from this element of the appraisal requirement for a loan secured by a new manufactured home and land.

171. *Id.* § 1026.35(c)(3)(i).

172. See 12 C.F.R. § 1025.35(c)(3)(ii) for the safe harbor provisions.

173. 12 C.F.R. § 1026.35(c)(2) (2020). The following loans are exempt: QMs; a loan in an amount less than or equal to the applicable threshold published by the CFPB for this purpose; a loan secured by a mobile home, boat, or trailer; a loan to finance the initial construction of a dwelling; a "bridge" loan of twelve months or less connected with the acquisition of a dwelling intended to become the consumer's principal dwelling; a reverse mortgage transaction; a refinancing secured by a first lien that meets certain specific requirements; loans secured by a manufactured home and not land that meet certain conditions.

requirements and requirements to provide a copy of the appraisal that largely mirror the appraisal notice and provision requirements in Regulation B.[174]

Two separate written appraisals must be obtained if the higher-priced mortgage loan will finance the purchase of the consumer's principal dwelling and the seller acquired the property recently, but the price the consumer has agreed to pay is significantly higher than the price the seller paid for the property.[175]

Each of the two appraisals must meet the general requirements for an appraisal,[176] must be performed by two different appraisers,[177] and one of the two appraisals must include an analysis of additional specific information that might account for the price increase.[178] The creditor may charge the consumer for only one of the two appraisals.[179] There are several exemptions from this two-appraisal rule.[180]

1.2.6 Counseling Required for Negative Amortization Loans

A creditor may not make a loan that may result in negative amortization[181] to a first-time borrower,[182] unless the consumer has received counseling from a counselor certified or approved by HUD.[183] The required counseling must include information about the risks and consequences of negative amortization. Before extending credit, the creditor must have received documentation showing that the first-time borrower

---

174. *Id.* § 1026.35(c)(5)(i). Compliance with the valuation disclosure requirement in Regulation B (12 C.F.R. § 1002.14(a)(2)) satisfies this disclosure requirement. However, note that the Regulation B requirements apply only to loans to be secured by a first lien, whereas the higher-priced mortgage loan provisions apply to junior-lien loans as well. If the loan is not a higher-priced mortgage loan at the time of application, but becomes a higher-priced mortgage loan after application, the disclosure must be provided no later than the third business day after the creditor determines that the loan is a higher-priced mortgage loan. *Id.* § 1026.35(c)(5)(ii).

175. *Id.* § 1026.35(c)(4). This two-appraisal rule applies if (1) the seller acquired the property 90 days or less prior to the date the consumer agreed to purchase the property and the consumer's purchase price is more than 10 percent above the price the seller paid; or (2) the seller acquired the property 91–180 days prior to the date the consumer agreed to purchase the property and the consumer's purchase price is more than 20 percent above the price the seller paid.

176. *Id.* 1026.35(c)(4)(iii).

177. *Id.* § 1026.35(c)(4)(ii).

178. *Id.* § 1026.35(c)(4)(iv).

179. *Id.* § 1026.35(c)(4)(v).

180. See 12 C.F.R. § 1026.35(c)(4)(vii) for a full list of exemptions.

181. Negative amortization means a payment schedule with regular periodic payments that cause the principal balance to increase. 12 C.F.R. § 1026.36(k)(2)(ii) (2020).

182. A first-time borrower is a consumer who has not previously received a credit transaction secured by a dwelling. *Id.* § 1026.36(k)(2)(i).

183. *Id.* § 1026.36(k). There are exceptions to this prohibition for reverse mortgage loans and loans secured by an interest in a timeshare plan.

has received the required counseling. The creditor may not steer a consumer to choose a particular counselor or counseling organization.[184]

1.3 Post-Consummation Requirements

Regulation Z also includes many requirements for interacting with the consumer after the mortgage loan closes, commonly referred to as the mortgage servicing phase of the loan. This section will review the TILA and Regulation Z requirements during this servicing phase.

1.3.1 Periodic Statements

Periodic statements must be provided for closed-end loans secured by a dwelling (not just the principal dwelling).[185] The periodic statement must be sent within a reasonably prompt time after the payment due date or the end of any grace period provided in the preceding billing cycle.[186] This requirement extends to accounts currently in an active bankruptcy or when personal liability for the debt has been discharged in bankruptcy, with limited exceptions.[187] There is also a limited exemption with respect to sending statements on charged-off loans.[188]

The required disclosures must be made clearly and conspicuously, and many of the disclosures must be grouped together.[189] Sample forms have been provided by the CFPB in appendix H-30 to Regulation Z and use of these forms provides a safe harbor.[190]

The periodic statement must include the following:

1. The amount due, along with the payment due date, the amount of any late charge and when a late charge would be imposed if the payment is not received.[191]
2. An explanation of the amount due, including a breakdown of the monthly amount due showing the amount of the monthly payment that

---

184. *Id.* § 1026.36(k)(3).

185. *Id.* § 1026.41(a).

186. *Id.* § 1026.41(b).

187. *Id.* § 1026.41(e)(5).

188. *Id.* § 1026.41(e)(6). A servicer can stop sending statements on a charged-off loan, but only if no additional fees or interest will be charged. Critically, if a servicer wishes to take advantage of this exemption, the servicer must send a specific notice to the borrower within thirty days after the charge off. If the servicer misses the thirty-day window after the charge off, the servicer must continue to send statements on that charged-off account.

189. *Id.* § 1026.41(c).

190. *Id.* § 1026.41(c).

191. *Id.* § 1026.41(d)(1).

will be applied to principal, interest, and escrow; the total of any fees imposed since the last statement; and any past due amount.[192]

3. A breakdown of all payments received since the last statement, itemized to show how the payment was applied, including the amount held in a suspense or unapplied fund account; a similar disclosure and breakdown showing the total of all payments received since the beginning of the current calendar year;[193] and if the statement shows a partial payment, an explanation of what must happen for the funds to be applied.[194]
4. A list of all transactions causing a credit or debit to the amount due since the last statement.[195]
5. Contact information for the servicer, including a toll-free telephone number, and if applicable, an email address.[196]
6. General account information, including the principal balance, the current interest rate, the date after which the rate may change, any prepayment penalty, and the CFPB or HUD website and toll-free number to access a list of HUD-approved homeownership counselors.[197]
7. If the account is more than forty-five days delinquent, a disclosure regarding the delinquency, including the length of the delinquency, a notification of delinquency risks, an account history showing the amount past due from each billing cycle since the account was last current (not to exceed six months), a notice of the loss mitigation and the foreclosure status if applicable, the amount needed to bring the account current, and a reference to the homeownership counseling information.[198]

The periodic statements for accounts in an active bankruptcy or that have been discharged in bankruptcy may be modified.[199] The periodic statement for bankruptcy customers may omit the late payment fee and some of the information required in the delinquency box. The requirement to show the amount due more prominently than other disclosures does not apply. The periodic statement must also include a statement identifying the consumer's status as a debtor in bankruptcy or the discharged nature of the debt, and a statement that the periodic statement is for informational purposes only.[200] The periodic statements for a debtor in an active Chapter 12 or 13 bankruptcy must bifurcate the debt between the pre-petition amount due (to be paid by the trustee

---

192. *Id.* § 1026.41(d)(2).
193. *Id.* § 1026.41(d)(3).
194. *Id.* § 1026.41(d)(5).
195. *Id.* § 1026.41(d)(4).
196. *Id.* § 1026.41(d)(6).
197. *Id.* § 1026.41(d)(7).
198. *Id.* § 1026.41(d)(8).
199. Although TILA frames the bankruptcy changes as permissive, many of the changes are necessary to comply with bankruptcy requirements.
200. 12 C.F.R. § 1026.41(f)(1), (2) (2020).

through plan payments) and the ongoing contractual post-petition payments.[201] The active Chapter 12 or 13 bankruptcy periodic statements must also include a number of disclosures explaining the bifurcation of payments, how the trustee's involvement may impact payments, and other bankruptcy-specific disclosures.[202]

1.3.2 TILA Servicing Requirements for Loans Secured by Principal Dwelling

TILA imposes specific servicing requirements on closed-end loans secured by the consumer's principal dwelling.[203]

1.3.2.1 Application of Payments

A servicer must credit full contractual payments as of the date of receipt.[204] A full contractual payment is an amount sufficient to cover principal, interest, and any applicable escrow for the applicable billing cycle.[205] This remains the rule even if the loan is under a temporary loan modification; the temporary loss mitigation program payment does not meet the definition of the full contractual payment for the purposes of this requirement.[206] A payment is considered a full contractual payment even if it does not include amounts needed to cover late fees, other fees, or nonescrow advances by the servicer on behalf of the consumer.[207] A servicer may specify in writing reasonable requirements a consumer must follow in making a payment.[208] If the servicer accepts a nonconforming payment, it must credit that payment within five days of receipt.

Upon receipt of a partial payment, if allowed by applicable law and the contract, the servicer may (1) credit the partial payment, (2) return the partial payment to the consumer, or (3) hold the partial payment in a suspense or unapplied funds account.[209] If the servicer retains partial payments (payments less than a full contractual payment) in a suspense or unapplied funds account, the servicer must (1) disclose the total amount of funds held in such account to the consumer on the periodic statement if one is required, and (2) promptly apply the suspense account funds to the oldest outstanding payment when sufficient funds accumulate to cover a full contractual payment.[210]

---

201. *Id.* § 1026.41(f)(3).
202. *Id.* § 1026.41(f)(3)(vi).
203. *Id.* § 1026.36(b).
204. *Id.* § 1026.36(c)(1)(i).
205. *Id.* § 1026.36(c)(1)(i).
206. 12 C.F.R. pt. 1026, supp. I, cmt. 36(c)(1)(i)-4 (2020).
207. 12 C.F.R. § 1026.36(c)(1)(i) (2020).
208. *Id.* § 1026.36(c)(1)(iii); 12 C.F.R. pt. 1026, supp. I, cmt. 36(c)(1)(iii) (2020).
209. 12 C.F.R. pt. 1026, supp. I, cmt. 36(c)(1)(ii)-1 (2020).
210. 12 C.F.R. § 1026.36(c)(1)(ii) (2020).

1.3.2.2 No Pyramiding of Late Fees

A servicer may not charge a late fee with respect to a current payment if the payment is a full contractual payment except for nonpayment of a late fee due to a prior outstanding late charge (no "pyramiding" of late fees).[211]

1.3.2.3 Adjustable-Rate Mortgage Loan Disclosures

For ARM loans, disclosures must be provided to the consumer throughout the loan term to inform the consumer of approaching changes to the interest rate and payment. Prior to the initial interest rate adjustment, the consumer must be provided with detailed disclosures about the current and new interest rate and payments and the due date of the first new payment.[212] Other specific content and formatting requirements apply. These disclosures must be provided at least 210 days,[213] but no more than 240 days, before the due date of the first payment at the adjusted level. They must be provided in a separate document from any other documents provided to the consumer but may be included in the same envelope as other information. Model and sample forms are provided in appendix H-4(D) of Regulation Z.[214]

Adjustment notices also must be provided on an ongoing basis to inform the consumer of interest rate changes and corresponding payment changes.[215] Like the initial adjustment disclosure, these disclosures must contain detailed information about the current and new interest rate and payments and the due date of the first new payment. Other specific content and formatting requirements apply. In general, these disclosures must be provided at least 60, but no more than 120, days before the first payment at the adjusted level is due.[216] Unlike the initial adjustment disclosures, the ongoing disclosures do not have to be in a separate document, but if they are included in a document containing other information, the disclosures must be segregated from the other information. Model and sample forms for the ongoing adjustment disclosures are provided in appendix H-4(D) of Regulation Z.[217]

1.3.3 Escrow Closing Notice

Before cancelling an escrow account established in connection with a closed-end mortgage loan secured by a first lien on real property or a dwelling, the creditor must

---

211. *Id.* § 1026.36(c)(2). This requirement had previously been in Regulation AA.

212. *Id.* § 1026.20(d).

213. If the first adjusted payment is due within the first 210 days after consummation, the disclosures must be provided at consummation. *Id.*

214. 12 C.F.R. pt. 1026, app. H-4(D)(3), H-4(D)(4) (2020).

215. 12 C.F.R. § 1026.20(c) (2020).

216. For certain ARM loans, the disclosures must be provided between 25 and 120 days prior to the adjustment. *Id.* § 1026.20(c)(2).

217. 12 C.F.R. pt. 1026, app. H-4(D)(1), H-4(D)(2) (2020).

provide an Escrow Closing Notice to the consumer.[218] Regulation Z specifies the format and content that must be used and provides a model form in appendix H-29 for this purpose. If the escrow account is cancelled at the consumer's request, the creditor or servicer must ensure that the consumer receives the notice no later than three business days before the escrow account is closed. If the cancellation is not at the consumer's request, the creditor or servicer must ensure that the consumer receives the notice no later than thirty business days before the escrow account is closed.

1.3.4 Other Post-Consummation Considerations

1.3.4.1 Refinancing

If a creditor refinances a mortgage loan, the creditor must provide a complete new set of disclosures to the consumer.[219] A refinancing occurs when the original obligation has been satisfied or extinguished and completely replaced by a new obligation. The regulation provides a list of several subsequent events that do not constitute a refinancing,[220] and provides examples of changes in a loan that will be considered a refinancing.[221]

1.3.4.2 Assumptions

If a new consumer assumes a residential mortgage transaction,[222] then before the assumption occurs, the creditor must make new disclosures to this subsequent consumer.[223] An assumption occurs when the creditor expressly agrees in writing with a subsequent consumer to accept that consumer as a primary obligor on an existing residential mortgage transaction. The disclosures must be given regardless of whether the assumption is accompanied by changes in the terms of the obligation.[224]

---

218. 12 C.F.R. § 1026.20(e) (2020).

219. *Id.* § 1026.20(a).

220. *Id.*

221. 12 C.F.R. pt. 1026, supp. I, cmt. 20(a)-3(ii) (2020).

222. Residential mortgage transaction means a transaction in which a mortgage, deed of trust, purchase-money security interest arising under an installment sales contract, or equivalent consensual security interest is created or retained in the consumer's principal dwelling to finance the acquisition or initial construction of that dwelling. 12 C.F.R. § 1026.2(a)(24) (2020).

223. *Id.* § 1026.20(b).

224. 12 C.F.R. pt. 1026, supp. I, cmt. 20(b)-1(ii) (2020). To determine whether these disclosure requirements apply, the creditor must look to whether the transaction is a residential mortgage transaction with respect to the assuming consumer. For example, if the loan was not for the purchase of the original consumer's principal dwelling, but the assuming consumer will use the home as a principal dwelling, then the loan is a residential mortgage transaction with respect to the assuming consumer, and the disclosures must be provided. *Id.* cmt. 20(b)-2.

2. Open-End Real Estate Loans (Home Equity Lines of Credit)

There are special rules for open-end credit[225] secured by a dwelling, called home equity plans in Regulation Z,[226] but more commonly called home equity lines of credit or HELOCs.

2.1 Origination Disclosures

There are special origination disclosure requirements for open-end credit plans secured by the consumer's dwelling, including disclosures at application and then when the account is opened.[227]

2.1.1 *Application Disclosures*

The creditor must provide disclosures at the time an application is provided to the consumer that include:[228]

1. Statements that the consumer should keep a copy of the disclosure, that the creditor will acquire a security interest in the home, and that the home may be lost in the event of default;[229]
2. A warning that under certain conditions the creditor may terminate the plan and require repayment or may restrict or reduce the line or make other allowed changes;[230]
3. The payment terms of the account (including the length of the draw period and any repayment period), how the minimum payment will be determined, the timing of the payments, warnings (including balloon payment warnings if applicable) if the payments will not amortize the account, and an example based on a $10,00 balance and a recent APR showing the minimum payment and the time to repay the account;[231]

---

225. 12 C.F.R. § 1026.2(a)(20) (2020).

226. *Id.* § 1026.40(a).

227. 12 C.F.R. §§ 1026.6(a), 1026.40(b).

228. *Id.* § 1026.40(b). The listed items are not all of the disclosures required. Review the applicable sections carefully for all required disclosures.

229. *Id.* § 1026.40(d)(1), (3).

230. *Id.* § 1026.40(d)(4)(i). In addition to the warnings about terminations, restrictions, and other allowed changes, the disclosure must also either state that the consumer may request information about the conditions under which such actions may occur or simply just state the conditions in the disclosures. *Id.* § 1026.40(d)(4)(ii), (iii).

231. *Id.* § 1026.40(d)(5).

4. For fixed-rate plans the creditor must disclose a recent APR imposed within the previous twelve months;[232]
5. The fees imposed by the creditor and an estimate of any third-party fees to open the plan;[233]
6. A statement regarding negative amortization if negative amortization may occur;[234]
7. Any transaction requirements, including minimum balances and minimum draw requirements;[235]
8. A statement regarding the tax implications of the plan;[236] and
9. For variable rate plans, there must be an explanation that the APR may vary, that the APR does not include costs other than interest, how the rate will be calculated and a description of the index, special disclosures about introductory rates, a statement that the consumer should ask about the current index, margin and rates, rules relating to any limitations on the APR changes and the maximum APRs, the minimum payment that would be required at the maximum APR for each payment option if there is a $10,000 balance, a chart showing a historical example based on a $10,000 extension of credit showing how the APR and payments would have been affected by changes in the index over the most recent fifteen years of index values, and a statement that rate information will be provided on or with each periodic statement.[237]

Although there is no particular format requirement for the application disclosures,[238] certain disclosures must precede the other required disclosures.[239] The creditor must also provide the home equity brochure "What You Should Know About Home Equity Lines of Credit" that the CFPB has made available on its website.[240]

Because the home equity application disclosures are largely static—only needing to be updated if the product changes or once a year to update the fifteen-year historical chart or fixed-rate APR—most creditors compile the application disclosures, including the CFPB brochure, into a convenient booklet. The disclosures must include a statement of the time by which the consumer must apply to receive the terms disclosed, an identification of any term that may change before account opening, and a statement that if a term changes before account opening (other than interest rate changes due

232. *Id.* § 1026.40(d)(6).

233. *Id.* § 1026.40(d)(7), (8).

234. *Id.* § 1026.40(d)(9).

235. *Id.* § 1026.40(d)(10).

236. *Id.* § 1026.40(d)(11).

237. *Id.* § 1026.40(d)(12)(xi).

238. *Id.* §§ 1026.6(a), 1026.40.

239. *Id.* § 1026.40(a)(2).

240. *Id.* § 1026.40(a), (e); https://files.consumerfinance.gov/f/201401_cfpb_booklet_heloc.pdf.

to a variable rate) and the consumer decides not to open the plan as a result, all fees paid in connection with the application will be refunded.[241]

2.1.2 Account Opening Disclosures

When the account is opened, account opening disclosures must be provided before the first transaction is made under the plan.[242] The account opening disclosures are in large part the contractual terms controlling the account; therefore, they usually are part of the credit agreement itself.[243] The account opening disclosures must:

1. Disclose how finance charges[244] will be calculated and applied to the account, including:[245]
    - (i) a statement of when finance charges will begin to accrue and any grace period during which the balance may be repaid without a finance charge;
    - (ii) details of each periodic rate that may be used, the range of balances to which it is applicable, and the corresponding APR;
    - (iii) if the account has a variable rate, the circumstances under which the rate may increase, any limitations on the increase, and the effects of an increase;
    - (iv) when different rates apply to different types of transactions, the types of transactions to which the rates apply;
    - (v) an explanation of the method used to determine the balance on which the finance charge may be computed; and
    - (vi) an explanation of how the amount of any finance charge will be determined;
2. The fees to use or maintain the plan and other fees that may be imposed as part of the plan;[246]
3. The terms under which the creditor may terminate the plan and require repayment or may restrict or reduce the line or make other allowed changes;[247]

---

241. *Id.* § 1026.40(d)(2). Section 1026.40(g) requires the refund as described in the disclosure.

242. *Id.* § 1026.5(b)(1).

243. The listed items are not all of the disclosures required. Review the applicable sections carefully for all required disclosures.

244. 12 C.F.R. § 1026.4 (2020).

245. *Id.* § 1026.6(a)(1).

246. *Id.* § 1026.6(a)(2).

247. *Id.* § 1026.6(a)(3)(i).

4. Payment information for both the draw period and any repayment period, including the length of the draw period and repayment period and the payment requirements for each;[248]
5. A statement of any transaction requirements;[249]
6. Many of the same warnings as in the application disclosures regarding negative amortization, taxes, that the APR does not include costs other than interest, and the security interest;[250] and
7. A statement of billing rights.[251]

2.2 Fees at Application

No nonrefundable fee may be imposed on the consumer until three days after the consumer receives the required disclosures. If the disclosures are mailed, the disclosures are deemed to have been received three business days after mailing.[252] Although it is acceptable to collect a fee after the consumer has received the disclosures but before the three-day waiting period has expired, any such fee must be fully refundable for three days after the disclosures are provided (six days if the disclosures are mailed), and a separate, clear and conspicuous disclosure must be provided stating the period during which the fees are refundable.[253]

2.3 Home Equity Line of Credit Servicing Requirements

2.3.1 Periodic Statements

Like all open-ended accounts, periodic statements are required for home equity plans.[254] The statement requirements for home equity plans share many elements with other open-end statements; however, certain requirements that are applicable to credit card statements, including specific formatting requirements, do not apply to home equity periodic statements.[255] A periodic statement for a home equity plan must include the following:

---

248. *Id.* § 1026.6(a)(3)(ii).

249. *Id.* § 1026.6(a)(3)(iv).

250. *Id.* § 1026.6(a)(3)(iii)–(vii), (4).

251. *Id.* § 1026.6(a)(5).

252. *Id.* § 1026.40(h).

253. 12 C.F.R. pt. 1026, supp. I, cmt. 40(h)-1, -2 (2020).

254. 12 C.F.R. § 1026.5(b)(2) (2020). There is an exception for charged-off accounts that will no longer incur fees or interest. There is also an exception if furnishing the statement "would violate Federal law" that has been widely read as excluding active or discharged bankruptcy accounts from the statement requirement.

255. *See id.* § 1026.7(b).

1. the account balance at the start of the billing cycle;[256]
2. each transaction during the billing cycle;[257]
3. any credit to the account during the billing cycle;[258]
4. each periodic rate, the range balances to which the rate is applicable, the corresponding APR and, for variable rates, the fact that the rate may vary;[259]
5. the balance to which each periodic rate was applied and an explanation of how that balance was calculated;[260]
6. the amount of the finance charge and other charges;[261]
7. an optional disclosure of the APR;[262]
8. any grace period during which a payment may be made to avoid additional finance charges;[263]
9. the address for notice of billing errors;[264] and
10. the closing date of the billing cycle and the balance on that date.[265]

There is an option under TILA for home equity servicers to follow the credit card provisions for periodic statements,[266] but because the credit card requirements are significantly more difficult and because some of the credit card disclosures are likely to be inapplicable or confusing with respect to a home equity plan, most servicers opt to abide by the periodic statement requirements that are specifically applicable to home equity plans.

2.3.2 Other Open-End Servicing Requirements

HELOCs are subject to all of the servicing requirements that are generally applicable to open-end accounts. See chapter 3B for provisions regarding crediting of payments, treatment of credit balances, and billing error resolution.

2.4 Limitations on Home Equity Plan Changes

Unlike other open-end credit plans, TILA places heavy restrictions on the creditor's ability to make any changes to home equity plans after account opening. Credit

256. *Id.* § 1026.2(a)(4); § 1026.7(a)(1).
257. *Id.* § 1026.7(a)(2).
258. *Id.* § 1026.7(a)(3).
259. *Id.* § 1026.7(a)(4).
260. *Id.* § 1026.7(a)(5).
261. *Id.* § 1026.7(a)(6).
262. *Id.* § 1026.7(a)(7).
263. *Id.* § 1026.7(a)(8).
264. *Id.* § 1026.7(a)(9).
265. *Id.* § 1026.7(a)(10).
266. *See id.* § 1026.7(a).

restrictions, pricing adjustments, and other post-closing actions that restrict or reduce access to the home equity plan are limited.

2.4.1 Change in Terms

After the account is opened, TILA prohibits making changes to home equity plans other than the changes specifically allowed in Regulation Z.[267] A creditor may not change any term, except a creditor may:

1. Change the APR if the change is based on a publicly available index not under the creditor's control;[268]
2. Change the index and margin if the original index is no longer available and other requirements are met;[269]
3. Make a specified change if the consumer specifically agrees to it in writing at that time. Explicit written consent is required; the creditor may not assume the consumer's agreement through continued use of the account;[270]
4. Make a change that will unequivocally benefit the consumer throughout the remainder of the plan;[271]
5. Make an insignificant change in terms;[272] and
6. Provide in the initial agreement that specified changes will occur if a specified event takes place, for example, that the APR will increase by a specified amount if the consumer is no longer employed by the creditor.[273]

2.4.2 Terminating the Line of Credit

A creditor may terminate (permanently end) the ability to draw on a home equity line of credit or declare the full balance due before the maturity date only if:

1. There is fraud or material misrepresentation by the consumer in connection with the account;[274]

267. *Id.* § 1026.40(f).
268. *Id.* § 1026.40(f)(1).
269. *Id.* § 1026.40(f)(3)(ii).
270. *Id.* § 1026.40(f)(3)(iii); 12 C.F.R. pt. 1026, supp. I, cmt. 40(f)(3)(iii)-2 (2020).
271. 12 C.F.R. § 1026.40(f)(3)(iv) (2020).
272. *Id.* § 1026.40(f)(3)(v).
273. *Id.* § 1026.40(f)(3)(i).
274. *Id.* § 1026.40(f)(2)(i).

2. The consumer fails to meet the repayment terms of the agreement;[275]
3. Any action or inaction by the consumer adversely affects the collateral or any right of the creditor in such collateral;[276] or
4. Federal law dealing with credit to executive officers of a depository institution specifically requires that the agreement have a provision making the account payable on demand.[277]

These TILA provisions are part of the account opening disclosures and need to be a binding part of the agreement with the consumer. To ensure that the creditor is in full compliance with and has the benefit of the limited rights granted in TILA, creditors routinely include the default provisions from Regulation Z in the agreement with the consumer without making any edits or changes as part of the account opening disclosures.[278]

2.4.3 Reducing or Restricting a Home Equity Line of Credit

Servicers and credit risk professionals are often surprised by how difficult it is to suspend or reduce a HELOC, even when credit risk principles indicate that such an action would be prudent. However, TILA does not allow suspensions or reductions of HELOCs except in limited circumstances, usually supported by loan-specific data. In addition, the creditor must reinstate the borrowing rights when the reason supporting the restriction no longer applies. If the account meets the requirements for termination listed above, the line can be suspended or reduced without any reinstatement requirement.[279] As with terminations, to be able to claim the full benefit of what is allowed by TILA, it is important to include the full TILA suspension and reduction provisions in the agreement.

Unless the account qualifies for termination, the line may only be suspended or reduced during any period in which:[280]

1. The maximum APR has been reached;[281]
2. The value of the dwelling declines significantly below the value at origination;[282]

---

275. *Id.* § 1026.40(f)(2)(ii). The failure to make payments may be minor. *See* Cunningham v. Nat'l City Bank, 588 F.3d 49, 53 (1st Cir. 2009) (ruling that National City Bank complied with the agreement and with TILA when it terminated lines of credit for payment defaults of only a few days).

276. 12 C.F.R. § 1026.40(f)(2)(iii) (2020).

277. *Id.* § 1026.40(f)(2)(iv).

278. *See id.* § 1026.6(a)(3)(i).

279. 12 C.F.R. pt. 1026, supp. I, cmt. 40(f)(3)(vi)-1 (2020).

280. *Id.*

281. 12 C.F.R. § 1026.40(f)(3)(i) (2020).

282. *Id.* § 1026.40(f)(3)(vi)(A).

3. The creditor reasonably believes that the consumer will be unable to meet their payment obligations because of a material change in the consumer's financial circumstances;[283]
4. The consumer is in default of any material obligation under the agreement;[284]
5. The creditor is precluded by government action from imposing the APR provided for in the agreement;[285]
6. The priority of the creditor's security interest is adversely affected by government action to the extent that the value of the security interest is less than 120 percent of the credit line;[286] or
7. The creditor is notified by its regulatory agency that continued advances constitute an unsafe and unsound practice.[287]

In addition, a HELOC may be suspended or reduced at the request of the borrower and most credit agreements provide that any borrower has the right to suspend borrowing rights. TILA specifically allows, and most creditors require, that all borrowers agree in writing to a reinstatement after a borrower-requested suspension.[288]

2.4.3.1 Imposing a Suspension or Reduction on a Home Equity Line of Credit

Imposition of line suspensions and reductions on home equity plans has been the subject of much regulatory commentary and litigation and must be conducted with care. If access to a HELOC is being suspended or reduced, the creditor must provide a written notice no later than three business days after the action is taken.[289] The notification must include the reason for the restriction, and if the creditor requires the consumer to request reinstatement, the notice must also include the reinstatement instructions.[290] If the creditor is reducing the credit limit, the creditor may not reduce

283. *Id.* § 1026.40(f)(3)(vi)(B).

284. *Id.* § 1026.40(f)(3)(vi)(C).

285. *Id.* § 1026.40(f)(3)(vi)(D).

286. *Id.* § 1026.40(f)(3)(vi)(E).

287. *Id.* § 1026.40(f)(3)(vi)(F).

288. 12 C.F.R. pt. 1026, supp. I, cmt. 40(f)(3)(vi)-5 (2020).

289. 12 C.F.R. § 1026.9(c)(1)(iii) (2020). Interestingly, TILA requires notice only for suspensions or reductions under 12 C.F.R. § 1026.40(f)(3)(i) and (vi) and notice is technically not required for other restrictions, reductions, or terminations. However, as a best practice, it is customary to provide notice of all such actions.

290. *Id.* § 1026.9(c)(1)(iii).

the credit limit below the amount of the outstanding balance if that would result in a higher payment.[291]

The two reasons most commonly considered for suspension or reduction are decline in property value and material change in financial circumstances.

Restricting a HELOC based on a decline in the property value must be based on the value of that particular home. The Commentary provides that what constitutes a significant decline in property value will vary according to individual circumstances, but in any event, if the value of the dwelling declines such that the available equity is reduced by fifty percent from what it was at origination, that would be a significant decline for the purposes of this section.[292] Although a full appraisal prior to restricting the line is not required, some kind of valuation, usually an automated valuation, is.[293] In addition, in determining the equity at the time of the suspension or reduction, some courts have held that the creditor should also take into account the balance of any senior liens, if known.[294] Thus, if the consumer has paid down senior liens, a suspension or reduction may not be allowed even if the property value has decreased.[295]

To be able to restrict a HELOC due to a material change in the consumer's financial circumstances, two criteria must be met: first, there must be a material change in the consumer's financial circumstances from origination;[296] and second, that change must cause the creditor to reasonably believe that the consumer will be unable to make the payments on the HELOC.[297] Use of a decline in the consumer's credit

291. 12 C.F.R. pt. 1026, supp. I, cmt. 40(f)(3)(vi)-1 (2020). Most HELOC credit agreements require immediate repayment of any over-limit amount; therefore, reducing the credit limit to an amount less than the outstanding balance could result in the next payment including the amount over the new, reduced, credit limit. That result is prohibited by this provision.

292. *Id.* cmt. 40(f)(3)(vi)-6.

293. *Id. See In re* JPMorgan Chase Bank Home Equity Line of Credit Litig., 794 F. Supp. 2d 859, 874 (N.D. Ill. 2011).

294. *See In re* JPMorgan Chase Bank at 874 ("Plaintiffs here have seen their HELOCs reduced, allegedly not for legitimate reasons like a decline in home values, but instead mostly to insulate the lender from risk. According to Plaintiffs, Defendant's arbitrary reductions, unrelated to the actual value of the home or the home's equity, contravene TILA's purposes of 'economic stabilization' for consumers and informed credit usage and potentially compromise the borrower's credit score"); *but see* Raeth v. Nat'l City Bank, 755 F. Supp. 2d 899, 903 (W.D. Tenn. 2010). As a practical matter, many creditors take into account the senior lien balances shown on a recent credit report in determining the equity for restriction purposes.

295. *See In re* JPMorgan Chase Bank, at 874; *Raeth*, at 903.

296. The change must be to the consumer's financial circumstances, not a change in the creditor's credit criteria. *See* 12 C.F.R. pt. 1026, supp. I, cmt. 40(f)(3)(vi)-7 (2020).

297. Note that these criteria come into play only if the payments on the HELOC are current. If the borrower is not making payments on time, the criteria to use would be failure to make payments, which allows the creditor to terminate the right to borrow under the line. 12 C.F.R. § 1026.40(f)(2)(ii) (2020).

score alone has long been understood to not support restriction under this section.[298] In addition, even if a material change in the consumer's financial circumstances can be demonstrated, the requirement to show that the change means that the consumer will be unable to pay the HELOC has proven challenging and needs to be supported by modeling and data.[299]

2.4.3.2 Reinstatement

TILA only allows the line to be suspended or reduced for these reasons during any period in which the reason exists. Once the condition no longer exists, the line must be reinstated unless some other circumstance permitting termination, suspension, or reduction exists.[300] TILA provides: "Creditors are responsible for ensuring that credit privileges are restored as soon as reasonably possible after the condition that permitted the creditor's action ceases to exist."[301] A creditor may monitor the line on an ongoing basis to determine when the condition ceases, or, as an alternative to monitoring, may shift the duty to the consumer to request reinstatement.[302] To shift the duty to the consumer, the creditor must include the consumer's obligation to request reinstatement in the suspension or reduction notice.[303]

If the creditor has shifted the burden to request reinstatement to the consumer, then upon receiving the request the creditor must promptly investigate to determine if grounds for the restriction still exist.[304] A creditor may collect bona fide and reasonable appraisal or credit report fees if such fees are actually incurred in investigating whether the conditions allowing the action still exist; however, a creditor may not impose a fee to reinstate the credit line once it has been determined that the conditions allowing the restriction no longer exist.[305]

---

298. For a discussion of the problems in using credit scores, see the preamble to the Federal Reserve Board proposed rule for a comprehensive rewrite of the TILA rules governing open-end home-secured accounts. Truth in Lending, 74 Fed. Reg. 43427, 43493–43494 (Aug. 26, 2009).

299. *See id.*

300. 12 C.F.R. pt. 1026, supp. I, cmt. 40(f)(3)(vi)-2 (2020).

301. *Id.*

302. *Id.*

303. *Id.*

304. *Id.*

305. *Id.* cmt. 40(f)(3)(vi)-3. As a practical matter, most creditors who have imposed restrictions due to a reduction in property value will obtain an automated valuation at their own expense if the consumer requests reinstatement. If the automated valuation will not support reinstatement, the consumer is given the option of paying for a full appraisal, and if the full appraisal supports reinstatement the appraisal fee is refunded to the consumer.

3. Requirements for All Dwelling-Secured Loans

There are some TILA and Regulation Z requirements that apply to all loans secured by a consumer's dwelling, whether open-end or closed-end. As with the requirements unique to open-end or closed-end lending, some of these requirements apply to any dwelling-secured credit transaction, while others apply only if the secured dwelling is the consumer's principal dwelling. This section will explore these requirements.

3.1 Right of Rescission

Certain open-end plans and closed-end loans secured by a dwelling, or when a dwelling is added as security to an existing transaction, are rescindable by each consumer (not necessarily a borrower) whose ownership interest in the property will be subject to the lender's security interest.[306] The right of rescission only applies to refinances; it does not apply to transactions to finance the acquisition of the property or the initial construction of the dwelling.[307] If the refinance is a refinancing or consolidation of an existing credit by the same lender, then the right of rescission only applies to the extent that the proceeds of the new loan exceed the payoff amount of the previous debt plus the costs attributable solely to the refinance.[308] If the account is an open-end account, the right of rescission does not apply to each advance under the plan if the advance is within the previously established credit limit. However, the right to rescind would apply to any increase of the security interest in the dwelling, including in connection with credit limit increases.[309]

The creditor must provide each person who has a right to rescind[310] with two copies of the notice of right to rescind, which describes, among other things, the right to rescind, how to exercise the right, the effects of rescission, and when the right to rescind expires.[311] In addition, each person with a right to rescind must receive a copy of the material TILA disclosures, which vary depending on whether the account is open-end or closed-end.[312] The right to rescind expires on midnight of the third business day after the later of (1) the consummation of the event that gives the right to rescind,[313] (2) delivery of the notices of the right to rescind, or (3)

306. 12 C.F.R. § 1026.15 (2020) (rescission section for open-end); *id.* § 1026.23 (2020) (rescission section for closed-end).

307. *Id.* §§ 1026.2(a)(24), 1026.15(f)(1), 1026.23(f)(1).

308. 15 U.S.C. § 1635(e) (2020); 12 C.F.R. § 1026.23(f)(2) (2020).

309. 12 C.F.R. § 1026.15(a)(2) (2020).

310. Each consumer who has an ownership right in the dwelling must receive the notice of right to rescind and the material disclosures. The right to rescind is not limited to borrowers. *Id.* §§ 1026.15(a), 1026.23(a).

311. *Id.* §§ 1026.15(b), 1026.23(b).

312. *Id.* §§ 1026.15(3), 1026.23(3).

313. Essentially, the loan closing, or the addition or increase of the security interest.

delivery of the material disclosures.[314] If the creditor fails to take the necessary actions to trigger the three-day rescission period, for example, the creditor fails to provide accurate TILA material disclosures, the right to rescind expires the earlier of (1) three years after consummation of the transaction, (2) transfer of the consumer's interest in the property, or (3) sale of the consumer's interest in the property.[315] Unless the right to rescind is waived, the creditor must not disburse any funds other than to the settlement agent's escrow until the rescission period has expired and the creditor is reasonably satisfied that the consumer has not rescinded.[316]

Regulation Z states that upon rescission, the security interest becomes void and the consumer "shall not be liable for any amount, including any finance charge."[317] This is an accurate description of what happens if rescission occurs before any amounts have been disbursed. However, if rescission occurs later, for example if the three-day period was not triggered and the rescission does not occur until after the loan funds are disbursed, courts have generally held that the person rescinding must tender the principal balance of the loan to the creditor (less any finance charges or costs related to the transaction) before the security interest will be voided. Rescission is not a means to obtain a free house.[318]

3.2 Home Ownership and Equity Protection Act

In 1994 Congress enacted the Home Ownership and Equity Protection Act (HOEPA) to address concerns with closed-end refinance loans that had high interest rates or fees.[319] Loans that meet the interest rate or fee triggers in the regulation are

314. 12 C.F.R. §§ 1026.15(a)(3), 1026.23(a)(3)(i) (2020).

315. *Id.* The transfer or sale of the property need not be voluntary, for example, a foreclosure sale terminates the right to rescind. 12 C.F.R. pt. 1026, supp. I, cmt. 15(a)(3)-4(ii), -3(ii) (2020).

316. 12 C.F.R. §§ 1026.15(c), 1026.23(c) (2020). Although this section references waiver of the right to rescind, such waivers are difficult and should be rare. *Id.* §§ 1026.15(e), 1026.23(e).

317. *Id.* §§ 1026.15(d)(1), 1026.23(d)(1). Although these sections state that the security interest is void, the lender must still take steps within twenty days to terminate the security interest and return any money or property given in connection with the transaction, for example, any costs paid by the borrower in connection with the application. *Id.* §§ 1026.15(d)(2), 1026.23(d)(2).

318. "TILA allows rescission 'to protect borrowers. It is not meant to provide borrowers with a free house or other financial windfall,' which is why rescission is conditioned 'on the borrower's tender of the loan proceeds to the lender." John F Gross v. DLI Properties, LLC., No. B292319, 2020 WL 2781619, at *3 (Cal. Ct. App. May 29, 2020). For a more complete analysis of the practical implications of rescission, consult *The Law of Truth in Lending* and its 2018 Supplement, *supra* note 2.

319. *See* High-Cost Mortgage and Homeownership Counseling Amendments to the Truth in Lending Act (Regulation Z) and Homeownership Counseling Amendments to the Real Estate Settlement Procedures Act (Regulation X); Proposed Rule, 77 Fed. Reg. 49090, 49090 (Aug. 15, 2012).

commonly called "HOEPA" or "Section 32" loans, but are defined in the regulation as "high-cost mortgages."[320] In 2010 the Dodd-Frank Act expanded the coverage of HOEPA to include purchase money loans and open-end loans (HELOCs) secured by a dwelling.[321] If the transaction qualifies as a high-cost mortgage, there are significant requirements imposed, including but not limited to additional disclosures, increased underwriting standards, required pre-transaction credit counseling and a certification from a HUD-approved credit counselor, late charge and other fee limits, and limits on financing points and fees.[322]

HOEPA loans are disfavored by the regulators,[323] the GSEs will not purchase high-cost mortgages,[324] and the origination requirements are onerous; therefore, most lenders comply with HOEPA by ensuring that the loans they make do not meet the definition of a high-cost mortgage.[325]

A high-cost mortgage is any consumer credit transaction that is secured by the consumer's principal dwelling in which:

1. The APR[326] will exceed the APOR[327] for a comparable transaction by more than (i) 6.5 percent for a first lien transaction, (ii) 8.5 percent for a first lien transaction where the dwelling is personal property and the loan amount is less than $50,000, or (3) 8.5 percent for a subordinate lien transaction;[328] or

---

320. 12 C.F.R. § 1026.32(a)(1) (2020).

321. 12 CFR § 1026.32(a). Reverse mortgages and construction loans are excluded from the scope of HOEPA. *Id.* § 1026.32(a)(2).

322. *Id.* § 1026.34.

323. The Office of the Comptroller of Currency (OCC) refers to lenders offering HOEPA loans as unscrupulous: "Borrowing from an unscrupulous lender, especially one that offers a high-cost loan using the home as security, could result in the loss of the borrower's home and money." OCC, *Mortgages*, https://www.occ.gov/topics/consumers-and-communities/consumer-protection/mortgages/index-mortgages.html (last visited August 24, 2020).

324. "A loan that is subject to the Home Ownership and Equity Protection Act of 1994 (HOEPA), as described in Section 32 of Regulation Z, is not eligible for delivery to Fannie Mae." Fannie Mae, Selling Guide § B2-1.5 (Feb. 5, 2020), https://selling-guide.fanniemae.com/; "For Primary Residences, purchase transaction Mortgages and refinance Mortgages that exceed the thresholds under the Home Ownership and Equity Protection Act of 1994 (HOEPA) and its implementing regulations are ineligible for purchase by Freddie Mac." Freddie Mac, Single-Family Seller/Servicer Guide § 4202.4 (Mar. 2, 2016), https://sf.freddiemac.com/tools-learning/sellerservicer-guide/overview.

325. Because compliance with HOEPA usually consists of avoiding the applicability of HOEPA, this chapter will not detail the requirements if HOEPA is triggered.

326. For variable rate loans there is a specific method for determining the APR. 12 C.F.R. § 1026.32(a)(3) (2020).

327. *Supra* note 165.

328. 12 C.F.R. § 1026.32(a)(1)(i) (2020).

2. The transaction's points and fees[329] will exceed 5 percent of the total loan amount for a transaction with a loan amount of $20,000 or more, or the lesser of 8 percent or $1,000 for transactions with a loan amount of less than $20,000;[330] or
3. There is a prepayment penalty that can be charged more than thirty-six months after consummation or account opening, or prepayment penalties that can exceed more than 2 percent of the amount prepaid.[331]

3.3 Payoff Statements

The TILA payoff statement requirements apply to all consumer credit transactions secured by a dwelling, including HELOCs.[332] Upon receiving a written request for a payoff statement from a consumer or a person acting on the consumer's behalf, a payoff statement must be provided within a reasonable time but no more than seven business days after the request.[333] If because of bankruptcy, foreclosure, or natural disaster, a payoff statement cannot be provided in this time frame, the lender must provide it within a reasonable time.[334]

3.4 Disclosure of Maximum Rate

TILA provides that in any consumer credit transaction secured by a dwelling, if the interest rate may increase after consummation, the contract must state a maximum interest rate.[335] Therefore, every dwelling-secured loan subject to TILA must have a ceiling rate.

---

329. *Id.* § 1026.32(b)(2)(vii), (viii). See QM discussion, above, for a definition of points and fees. However, there are two additional elements of the points and fees definition used to determine whether a HELOC is a high-cost mortgage: (1) any fee charged for participation in the plan payable at or before account opening, and (2) any transaction fees that will be charged for a draw on the credit line, assuming that the consumer will make at least one draw on the credit line.

330. *Id.* § 1026.32(a)(1)(ii). The $20,000 and $1,000 figures adjusted annually based on the Consumer Price Index; for example, the figures will be $22,052 and $1,103, respectively, on January 1, 2021.

331. *Id.* § 1026.32(a)(1)(iii), (b)(6). Interestingly, one of the requirements once a loan qualifies as a HOEPA loan is that no prepayment penalty is allowed at all. *Id.* § 1026.32(d)(6). Thus, if the loan qualifies as a HOEPA loan solely due to excess prepayment penalties, the prepayment penalty will have to be removed in its entirety, thus taking the loan out of the HOEPA definition.

332. 12 C.F.R. § 1026.36(b).

333. *Id.* § 1026.36(c)(3).

334. *Id.* § 1026.36(c)(3).

335. *Id.* § 1026.30.

3.5 Prohibited Loan Terms

3.5.1 Arbitration and Waiver Prohibition

Arbitration agreements or other agreements that require a nonjudicial procedure to resolve controversies or claims are prohibited in consumer contracts secured by a dwelling, including HELOCs secured by the debtor's principal dwelling.[336] In addition, such contracts cannot be applied or interpreted to bar a consumer from pursuing any claim in court for an alleged violation of any federal law.[337] After a dispute or claim has arisen, the consumer and creditor may agree to settle or use arbitration or other nonjudicial process to resolve the dispute.[338]

3.5.2 No Financing Credit Insurance

A creditor may not directly or indirectly finance any credit insurance premiums or fees in connection with a consumer contract secured by a dwelling, including HELOCs secured by the debtor's principal dwelling.[339] A creditor finances fees or premiums if it provides the consumer the right to defer payment of a credit insurance premium beyond the monthly period in which the premium is due.[340]

3.6 Mortgage Transfer Disclosures

A person who becomes the owner of an existing mortgage loan ("covered person") must mail or deliver disclosures about the transfer of ownership of the loan to the consumer on or before the thirtieth calendar day following the date of transfer. For purposes of this disclosure requirement, a mortgage loan is (1) an open-end consumer credit transaction that is secured by the principal dwelling of a consumer, or (2) a closed-end consumer credit transaction secured by a dwelling or real property.

The mortgage transfer disclosures must include:

1. The covered person's name, address, and telephone number;
2. The date of transfer;
3. The name, address, and telephone number of an agent or party authorized to receive notice of the right to rescind and resolve issues concerning the consumer's payments on the loan, unless the consumer can use the covered person's contact information for these purposes;
4. Where transfer of ownership of the debt to the covered person is or may be recorded in public records, or, alternatively, that the transfer

---

336. *Id.* § 1026.36(h)(1).
337. *Id.* § 1026.36(h)(2).
338. *Id.* § 1026.36(h).
339. *Id.* § 1026.36(g).
340. *Id.* § 1026.36(g)(2).

of ownership has not been recorded in public records at the time the disclosure is provided; and

5. If the transferred mortgage loan is a closed-end mortgage loan, the disclosures must also include the information about the covered person's partial payment policy, under the heading "Partial Payment."

3.7 Valuation Independence

Another product of the Dodd-Frank Act was an amendment to TILA adding appraisal independence requirements.[341] As a result, Regulation Z also was amended to add a new valuation independence section related to the valuation of a consumer's principal dwelling in connection with a consumer credit transaction.[342]

These rules prohibit creditors and settlement service providers ("covered persons") from attempting to cause a valuation of the secured dwelling to be based on anything other than the independent judgment of the person preparing the valuation. More specifically, the regulation prohibits making such an attempt, directly or indirectly, through coercion, extortion, inducement, bribery, intimidation, compensation, instruction, or collusion. The regulation provides examples of actions that violate this prohibition.[343]

The regulation also prohibits a person who prepares valuations from materially misrepresenting the value of the dwelling; prohibits covered persons from falsifying or materially altering a valuation; prohibits covered persons from inducing such a misrepresentation, falsification, or alteration; and provides examples of actions that do not violate these prohibitions.[344]

If a creditor knows, at or before consummation, that any of these prohibitions have been violated, the creditor is prohibited from extending credit based on the valuation unless the creditor documents that it acted with reasonable diligence to determine that the valuation does not materially misstate or misrepresent the value.[345]

Conflicts of interest in preparing valuations also are addressed, prohibiting persons who prepare valuations or perform valuation management functions[346] from

---

341. 15 U.S.C. § 1639e (2020).

342. 12 C.F.R. § 1026.42 (2020).

343. *Id.* § 1026.42(c)(1).

344. *Id.* § 1026.42(c)(2), (3).

345. *Id.* § 1026.42(c)(1).

346. Valuation management functions means (1) recruiting, selecting, or retaining a person to prepare a valuation; (2) contracting with or employing a person to prepare a valuation; (3) managing or overseeing the process of preparing a valuation, including by providing administrative services, such as receiving orders for and receiving a valuation, submitting a completed valuation to creditors and underwriters, collecting fees from creditors and underwriters for services provided in connection with a valuation, and compensating a person that prepares valuations; or (4) reviewing or verifying the work of a person who prepares valuations. *Id.* § 1026.42(b)(4).

having a direct or indirect interest, financial or otherwise, in the property or the transaction for which the valuation is performed. Certain exceptions are provided for employees or affiliates of the creditor and for settlement service providers that provide other settlement services, in addition to providing the valuation, for the credit transaction. The regulation addresses the conditions under which these exceptions apply.[347]

Regulation Z also addresses appraiser compensation, requiring the creditor and its agents to compensate the appraiser[348] at a rate that is customary and reasonable for comparable appraisal services performed in the geographic market of the property being appraised. The regulation includes conditions that, if met, create a presumption that the creditor or its agent has complied with these compensation requirements.[349]

If a covered person reasonably believes that an appraiser has materially failed to comply with the Uniform Standards of Professional Appraisal Practice or ethical or professional requirements for appraisers under applicable state or federal statutes or regulations, the covered person must report the matter to the appropriate state agency.[350] The Commentary includes examples of what may constitute a material failure to comply with these standards.

---

347. *Id.* § 1026.42(d).

348. This requirement applies to a *fee appraiser*, defined as (1) a natural person who is a state-licensed or state-certified appraiser who receives a fee for performing an appraisal, but who is not an employee of the person engaging the appraiser; or (2) an organization that, in the ordinary course of business, employs state-licensed or state-certified appraisers to perform appraisals, and receives a fee for performing appraisals.

349. 12 C.F.R. § 1026.42(f) (2020).

350. *Id.* § 1026.42(g).

CHAPTER

4

Consumer Privacy

David Tallman

1. Scope of This Chapter

This chapter covers the provisions in Title V of the Gramm-Leach-Bliley Act (GLBA) and the Consumer Financial Protection Bureau's (CFPB's or Bureau's) Regulation P that (1) regulate a financial institution's ability to use and disclose *nonpublic personal information* (NPPI) and (2) require a financial institution to provide certain privacy notices to consumers. This chapter does not cover the following topics:

- *Information security*: Title V of the GLBA,[1] as implemented by regulations issued by the Federal Trade Commission (FTC) and other federal regulators, also imposes information security requirements on financial institutions. This topic is discussed in chapter 5.
- *Other agencies' GLBA privacy regulations*: Regulation P[2] applies only with respect to financial institutions over which the CFPB has rulemaking authority. Substantially similar regulations have been issued by the Securities and Exchange Commission, the Commodity Futures Trading Commission, the FTC, and state insurance regulators with respect to

---

The views expressed in this chapter are not necessarily the views of Mayer Brown LLP.

1. Pub. L. No. 106-102, title V, § 501, 113 Stat. 1436 (1999) (codified as amended at 15 U.S.C. §§ 6801–6809).

2. Privacy of Consumer Financial Information (Regulation P), 12 C.F.R. §§ 1016.1–1016.17 (2020).

financial institutions that are subject to their respective jurisdictions.[3] For the sake of convenience, this chapter cites only to Regulation P.

- *Right to Financial Privacy Act*: The Right to Financial Privacy Act[4] limits the circumstances in which an agency of the federal government can access financial records held by certain types of financial institution.
- *Fair Credit Reporting Act*: The Fair Credit Reporting Act,[5] which is addressed in chapter 6, regulates the activities of consumer reporting agencies, users of consumer reports, and furnishers of information to consumer reporting agencies. Certain provisions protect consumer privacy by ensuring that sensitive consumer report information is disseminated only by regulated consumer reporting agencies to users who intend to use such information for a permissible purpose. The law also gives consumers the right to opt out of certain disclosures and uses of personal information.
- *Unfair or deceptive acts or practices (UDAP)/unfair, deceptive, or abusive acts or practices (UDAAP) principles*: The CFPB and the FTC also enforce consumer privacy expectations through their UDAP/UDAAP enforcement authority, which is discussed in chapters 2A to 2D.
- *Consumer outreach laws and regulations*: Some federal laws and regulations, such as the CAN-SPAM Act,[6] the Telephone Consumer Protection Act,[7] and the Telemarketing Sales Rule,[8] occasionally are characterized as consumer privacy laws because they limit the circumstances and manner in which a person may contact a consumer, but these broadly applicable laws are beyond the scope of this volume, which focuses on financial regulation.
- *State and international privacy laws*: This chapter also does not cover state privacy laws, including, for example, the California Consumer Privacy Act,[9] the California Financial Information Privacy Act,[10] the Massachusetts Regulations for the Protection of Personal Information,[11]

---

3. The rulemaking authority of the various agencies is set forth in section 504 of the GLBA.
4. Pub. L. No. 95-630, 92 Stat. 3697 (1978) (codified as amended at 12 U.S.C. §§ 3401–3423).
5. Pub. L. No. 90-321, 82 Stat. 146 (1968) (codified as amended at 15 U.S.C. §§ 1681–1681x).
6. Controlling the Assault of Non-Solicited Pornography and Marketing Act of 2003, Pub. L. No. 108-187, 117 Stat. 2699 (2003) (codified as amended at 15 U.S.C. §§ 7701–7713).
7. Pub. L. No. 102-243, § 3, 105 Stat. 2394 (1991) (codified as amended at 47 U.S.C. § 227) (implemented by 47 C.F.R. § 64.1200 (2019)).
8. 16 C.F.R. §§ 310.1–310.9 (2019).
9. Cal. Civ. Code § 1798.100 *et seq.*
10. Cal. Fin. Code § 4050 *et seq.*
11. 201 C.M.R. 17.00.

or the Vermont Financial Privacy Regulations.[12] It also does not cover international privacy laws, such as the European Union (EU) General Data Protection Regulation.[13]

2. Authority, Purpose, and Coverage

Title V of the GLBA was enacted because Congress intended to impose upon each financial institution an "affirmative and continuing obligation to respect the privacy of its customers."[14] To that end, subject to certain exceptions, the GLBA prohibits a financial institution from disclosing NPPI to a nonaffiliated third party without first providing the consumer with a reasonable opportunity to opt out of such disclosure.[15] It also requires a financial institution to provide initial, annual, and revised notices to consumers that describe the institution's privacy policies and practices.[16]

The GLBA applies only with respect to NPPI about individuals who obtain financial products or services primarily for personal, family, or household purposes from a financial institution.[17] For this purpose, the term *financial institution* includes any institution in the business of "engaging in activities that are financial in nature or incidental to such financial activities as described in section 4(k) of the Bank Holding Company Act of 1956 (12 U.S.C. § 1843(k))."[18]

NPPI generally includes any information: (1) that a consumer provides to a financial institution to obtain a financial product or service from that institution, (2) about a consumer resulting from any transaction involving a financial product or service between the financial institution and a consumer, or (3) that a financial institution otherwise obtains about a consumer in connection with providing a financial product or service to that consumer.[19] The term also includes any list, description, or other grouping of consumers (and publicly available information pertaining to them) that is derived using any such information that is not publicly available.[20] However, NPPI does not include (1) "[p]ublicly available information"; (2) "[a]ny list, description,

12. Regulation B-2018-01, *Privacy of Consumer Financial and Health Information Regulation.*

13. *EU General Data Protection Regulation (GDPR):* Regulation (EU) 2016/679 of the European Parliament and of the Council of April 27, 2016, on the protection of natural persons with regard to the processing of personal data and on the free movement of such data, and repealing Directive 95/46/EC (General Data Protection Regulation), OJ 2016 L 119/1.

14. 15 U.S.C. § 6801(a).

15. *Id.* § 6802.

16. *Id.* § 6803.

17. 12 C.F.R. § 1016.1(b).

18. *Id.* § 1016.3(l)(1).

19. *Id.* § 1016.3(p), (q).

20. *Id.* § 1016.3(p)(1).

or other grouping of consumers (and publicly available information pertaining to them) that is derived without using any personally identifiable financial information that is not publicly available"; (3) "[a] list of names and addresses of customers of an entity that is not a financial institution"; or (4) "[i]nformation that does not identify a consumer, such as aggregate information or blind data that does not contain personal identifiers such as account numbers, names, or addresses."[21]

For these purposes, the term *consumer* means an individual who obtains or has obtained a financial product or service that is to be used primarily for personal, family, or household purposes, or that individual's legal representative.[22] In turn, a *customer* is a consumer who has a continuing relationship with the institution under which the institution provides one or more financial products or services to the consumer that are to be used primarily for personal, family, or household purposes.[23]

3. Notices

3.1 Initial, Annual, and Revised Notices

Regulation P requires a financial institution to provide initial, annual, and revised privacy disclosures to its customers (and in some cases, to noncustomer consumers). These notices must include each of the following items of information:

- The categories of NPPI that the institution collects;
- The categories of NPPI that the institution discloses;
- The categories of affiliates and nonaffiliated third parties to which the institution discloses NPPI (other than nonservice providers to which the institution discloses NPPI under an opt-out exception);
- The categories of NPPI about former customers that the institution discloses and the categories of affiliates and nonaffiliated third parties to which it discloses NPPI about its former customers (other than nonservice providers to which the institution discloses NPPI under an opt-out exception);
- If the institution discloses NPPI to a nonaffiliated third party under the service provider opt-out exception (and no other exception applies), a separate statement of the categories of information it discloses and the categories of third parties with which it has contracted;
- An explanation of the consumer's right to opt out of the disclosure of NPPI to nonaffiliated third parties, including the method(s) by which the consumer may exercise that right at that time;

21. *Id.* § 1016.3(p), (q).
22. *Id.* § 1016.3(e)(1).
23. *Id.* § 1016.3(i)(j).

- Any disclosures that the institution makes pursuant to the provisions of the Fair Credit Reporting Act regarding the ability to opt out of disclosures of information among affiliates;
- The institution's policies and practices with respect to protecting the confidentiality and security of NPPI; and
- To the extent that the institution discloses NPPI to nonservice providers under an opt-out exception, a statement that it makes disclosures to other nonaffiliated companies: (i) for its everyday business purposes, such as to process transactions, maintain account(s), respond to court orders and legal investigations, or report to credit bureaus or (ii) as permitted by law.[24]

An institution's notice may (but is not required to) include (1) categories of NPPI that it reserves the right to disclose in the future, but does not currently disclose; and (2) categories of affiliates or nonaffiliated third parties to which it reserves the right in the future to disclose, but to which it does not currently disclose, NPPI.[25]

Appendix A to Regulation P contains model forms that an institution may use to satisfy the notice requirements. Use of the model forms is not required, but if an institution uses the forms exactly as promulgated, it will benefit from a safe harbor from an administrative claim that its privacy notice is less than clear or conspicuous, or otherwise does not satisfy the regulatory requirements.[26]

3.1.1 Initial Notice: When Required

An institution is required to provide an initial privacy notice to an individual who becomes its customer, no later than when it establishes a customer relationship with that individual.[27] An institution also must provide an initial notice to a noncustomer consumer, before it discloses any NPPI about the consumer to any nonaffiliated third party, if it makes such a disclosure: (1) in a manner that gives the consumer an opt-out right or (2) pursuant to the service provider opt-out exception.[28]

Note, however, that Regulation P allows an institution to provide the initial notice within a reasonable time *after* it establishes a customer relationship with a consumer if (1) establishing the customer relationship was not at the customer's election (e.g., in the event of the transfer of ownership of a loan or the associated servicing rights) or (2) providing the notice at or before the time that the customer relationship is established would substantially delay the customer's transaction and the customer agrees to receive the notice at a later time.[29]

---

24. *Id.* § 1016.6(a)–(b).
25. *Id.* § 1016.6(e).
26. 12 C.F.R. pt. 1016 app. at A.
27. 12 C.F.R. § 1016.4(a).
28. *Id.*
29. *Id.* § 1016.4(e).

If an existing customer obtains a new consumer-purpose financial product or service from an institution, the institution does not need to provide a new initial privacy notice to the customer as long as the initial, revised, or annual notice most recently provided to that customer was accurate with respect to the new product or service.[30] Otherwise, the institution may comply with the initial notice requirement by providing a revised privacy notice to the customer.

An institution may satisfy the initial notice for a consumer who is not a customer by providing a short-form initial notice at the same time as it delivers an opt-out notice. A short-form initial notice must be clear and conspicuous, state that the institution's privacy notice is available upon request, and explain a reasonable means by which the consumer may obtain that notice.[31]

3.1.2 Annual Notice: When Required

An institution must provide a privacy notice to each of its customers no less than annually during the continuation of the customer relationship. For this purpose, *annually* "means at least once in any period of 12 consecutive months during which that relationship exists."[32] An institution may define the 12-consecutive-month period, but must apply it to the customer on a consistent basis. For example, an institution provides a notice annually if it defines the 12-consecutive-month period as a calendar year and provides the annual notice to the customer once in each calendar year following the calendar year in which it provided the initial notice.[33] An institution is not required to provide an annual notice to a former customer.[34]

Regulation P provides that a financial institution establishes a customer relationship with a consumer when it originates or acquires the servicing rights to a loan to the consumer for personal, family, or household purposes. If it subsequently transfers the servicing rights to that loan to another financial institution, the customer relationship transfers with the servicing rights.[35] If an institution subject to Regulation P (other than a credit union), does not have a customer relationship with a consumer under this special rule for loans, then it is not required to provide an annual notice to that consumer.[36]

An institution also is not required to deliver an annual privacy notice if it provides NPPI to nonaffiliated third parties only in accordance with an opt-out exception, and it has not changed its policies and practices with regard to disclosing NPPI since the most recent privacy notice that it provided to the customer.[37] However,

30. *Id.* § 1016.4(d).
31. *Id.* § 1016.6(d).
32. *Id.* § 1016.5(a)(1).
33. *Id.* § 1016.5(a)(2).
34. *Id.* § 1016.5(b)(1).
35. *Id.* § 1016.4(c)(2).
36. *Id.* § 1016.5(c).
37. *Id.* § 1016.5(e)(1).

if the institution's policies or practices subsequently change in such a manner that it no longer qualifies for the exception, it must once again comply with the annual notice requirement.[38] If the change is such that the institution is required to provide a revised privacy notice (discussed below in section 3.1.3), it must provide an annual privacy notice in accordance with the standard annual notice timing requirements, treating the revised notice as an initial notice.[39] If the change in policies or practices is such that it does not require a revised notice, the institution must provide an annual notice within one hundred days of the change.[40]

3.1.3 Revised Notice: When Required

An institution may not disclose NPPI about a consumer to a nonaffiliated third party other than as described in the initial notice provided to the consumer, unless (1) the institution has provided to the consumer a clear and conspicuous revised notice that accurately describes its policies and practices; (2) it has provided to the consumer a new opt-out notice (discussed below in section 3.2); (3) it has given the consumer a reasonable opportunity, before it discloses the information to the nonaffiliated third party, to opt out of the disclosure; and (4) the consumer does not opt out.[41]

3.2 Opt-Out Notice

Regulation P requires a financial institution to provide an opt-out notice to a consumer if it intends to disclose that consumer's NPPI to a nonaffiliated third party outside of an opt-out exception.[42] The notice must state: (1) that the institution discloses or reserves the right to disclose NPPI to a nonaffiliated third party, (2) that the consumer has the right to opt out of that disclosure, and (3) a reasonable means by which the consumer may exercise the opt-out right.[43]

An institution provides a reasonable means to exercise an opt-out right of it (1) designates check-off boxes in a prominent position on the relevant forms with the opt-out notice; (2) includes a reply form together with the opt-out notice that (for most institutions) includes the address to which the form should be mailed; (3) provides an electronic means to opt out, such as a form that can be sent via electronic mail or a process at its website, if the consumer agrees to the electronic delivery of information; or (4) provides a toll-free telephone number that consumers may call to opt out.[44] An institution does not provide a reasonable means of opting out

38. *Id.* § 1016.5(e)(2).
39. *Id.* § 1016.5(e)(2)(i).
40. *Id.* § 1016.5(e)(2)(ii).
41. *Id.* § 1016.8(a).
42. *Id.* § 1016.7(a)(i).
43. *Id.*
44. *Id.* § 1016.7(a)(ii).

if (1) the only means of opting out is for the consumer to write his or her own letter to exercise that opt-out right or (2) the only means of opting out as described in any notice subsequent to the initial notice is to use a check-off box that the institution provided with the initial notice but did not include with the subsequent notice.[45] An institution may, however, require each consumer to opt out through a specific means, as long as that means is reasonable for that consumer.[46]

An institution may provide the opt-out notice together with or on the same written or electronic form as the initial notice.[47] The model forms in appendix A to Regulation P accordingly combine the initial and opt-out forms into a single document. However, if an institution provides the opt-out notice later than required for the initial notice, it must also include a copy of the initial notice with the opt-out notice in writing (or, if the consumer agrees, electronically).[48]

For most financial institutions (other than credit unions and those institutions subject to FTC enforcement authority, for which slightly different rules apply), if two or more consumers jointly obtain a financial product or service from the institution, the institution is allowed to provide a single opt-out notice, which must explain how the institution will treat an opt-out direction by a joint consumer.[49] Any of the joint consumers may exercise the right to opt out.[50] The institution may either (1) treat an opt-out direction by a joint consumer as applying to all of the associated joint consumers or (2) permit each joint consumer to opt out separately.[51] If the institution permits each joint consumer to opt out separately, it must permit one of the joint consumers to opt out on behalf of all of the joint consumers.[52] It may not require *all* joint consumers to opt out before it implements *any* opt-out direction.[53]

An institution must comply with a consumer's opt-out direction as soon as reasonably practicable after the institution receives it.[54] A consumer may exercise the right to opt out at any time.[55] A consumer's opt-out election is effective until the consumer revokes it in writing (or, if the consumer agrees, electronically).[56] When a customer relationship terminates, the customer's opt-out direction continues to apply to the NPPI that the institution collected during or related to that relationship. If the individual subsequently establishes a new customer relationship with the institution,

45. *Id.* § 1016.7(a)(iii).
46. *Id.* § 1016.7(a)(iv).
47. *Id.* § 1016.7(b).
48. *Id.* § 1016.7(c).
49. *Id.* § 1016.7(d)(1).
50. *Id.* § 1016.7(d)(2).
51. *Id.*
52. *Id.* § 1016.7(d)(3).
53. *Id.* § 1016.7(d)(4).
54. *Id.* § 1016.7(g).
55. *Id.* § 1016.7(h).
56. *Id.* § 1016.7(i).

the opt-out direction that applied to the former relationship does not apply to the new relationship.[57]

3.3 Delivering Privacy and Opt-Out Notices

A financial institution must provide initial, annual, revised, and opt-out notices so that each consumer can reasonably be expected to receive actual notice in writing or, if the consumer agrees, electronically.[58]

An institution may reasonably expect that a consumer will receive actual notice if it (1) hand-delivers a printed copy of the notice to the consumer; (2) mails a printed copy of the notice to the last known address of the consumer; (3) for the consumer who conducts transactions electronically, posts the notice on the electronic site and requires the consumer to acknowledge receipt of the notice as a necessary step to obtaining a particular financial product or service; or (4) for an isolated transaction with the consumer, such as an ATM transaction, posts the notice on the ATM screen and requires the consumer to acknowledge receipt of the notice as a necessary step to obtaining the particular financial product or service.[59] An institution may *not,* however, reasonably expect that a consumer will receive actual notice of its privacy policies and practices if it (1) only posts a sign in its branch or office or generally publishes advertisements of its privacy policies and practices or (2) sends the notice via electronic mail to a consumer who does not obtain a financial product or service from the institution electronically.[60]

With respect to annual privacy notices, an institution may reasonably expect that the customer will receive actual notice if (1) the customer uses the institution's website to access financial products and services electronically and agrees to receive notices at the website, and the institution posts its current privacy notice continuously in a clear and conspicuous manner on the website; or (2) the customer has requested that the institution refrain from sending any information regarding the customer relationship, and the current privacy notice remains available to the customer upon request.[61]

Notices may not be provided solely by orally explaining the notice, either in person or over the telephone.[62]

With respect to customers, an institution must provide initial, annual, and revised notices so that the customer can retain them or obtain them later in writing (or, if the customer agrees, electronically).[63] An institution provides a privacy notice to the

---

57. *Id.*
58. *Id.* § 1016.9(a).
59. *Id.* § 1016.9(b)(1).
60. *Id.* § 1016.9(b)(2).
61. *Id.* § 1016.9(c).
62. *Id.* § 1016.9(d).
63. *Id.* § 1016.9(e).

customer so that the customer can retain it or obtain it later if it (1) hand-delivers a printed copy of the notice to the customer; (2) mails a printed copy of the notice to the last known address of the customer, or, in the case of credit unions, mails a printed copy of the notice to the last known address of the customer upon request of the customer; or (3) makes its current privacy notice available on a website (or a link to another website) for the customer who obtains a financial product or service electronically and agrees to receive the notice at the website.[64]

A financial institution may provide a joint notice from the institution and one or more of its affiliates or other financial institutions, as identified in the notice, as long as the notice is accurate with respect to each of the institutions.[65]

Other than with respect to credit unions and institutions subject to FTC enforcement jurisdictions, for which slightly different rules apply, if two or more consumers jointly obtain a financial product or service from an institution, the institution may satisfy the initial, annual, and revised notice requirements by providing one notice to those consumers jointly.[66]

4. Limits on Disclosures of Nonpublic Personal Information

4.1 Disclosure to Nonaffiliated Third Parties (Opt Out)

Unless an exception applies, a financial institution may not, directly or through any affiliate, disclose any NPPI about a consumer to a nonaffiliated third party unless (1) it has provided an initial notice to the consumer; (2) it has provided an opt-out notice to the consumer; (3) it has given the consumer a reasonable opportunity, before it discloses the information to the nonaffiliated third party, to opt out of the disclosure; and (4) the consumer does not opt out.[67]

An institution provides a consumer with a reasonable opportunity to opt out if (1) it mails the notices to the consumer and allows the consumer to opt out by mailing a form, calling a toll-free telephone number, or any other reasonable means within thirty days from the date it mailed the notices; (2) a customer opens an online account and agrees to receive the notices electronically, and the institution allows the customer to opt out by any reasonable means within thirty days after the date that the customer acknowledges receipt of the notices in conjunction with opening the account; or (3) for an isolated transaction, such as the purchase of a cashier's check by a consumer, the institution provides the notices at the time of the transaction and

64. *Id.*
65. *Id.* § 1016.9(f).
66. *Id.* § 1016.9(g).
67. *Id.* § 1016.10(a)(1).

requests that the consumer decide, as a necessary part of the transaction, whether to opt out before completing the transaction.[68]

A financial institution must comply with the opt-out requirements, regardless of whether the institution and the consumer have established a customer relationship.[69] An institution may allow a consumer to select certain NPPI or certain nonaffiliated third parties with respect to which the consumer wishes to opt out.[70]

4.1.1 Opt-Out and Notice Exceptions

4.1.1.1 Service Provider Exception (Including Joint Marketing)

The opt-out requirements do not apply when a financial institution provides NPPI to a nonaffiliated third party to perform services for the institution or functions on its behalf, if the institution: (1) provides the initial notice and (2) enters into a contractual agreement with the third party that prohibits the third party from disclosing or using the information other than to carry out the purposes for which the information was disclosed, including use under an opt-out exception (other than the service provider exception) in the ordinary course of business to carry out those purposes.[71]

The services that the third party may perform can include marketing of the institution's own products or services, or marketing of financial products or services offered pursuant to a joint agreement between the institution and one or more financial institutions.[72] The joint agreement must consist of a written contract pursuant to which the financial institution and one or more other financial institutions jointly offer, endorse, or sponsor a financial product or service.[73]

4.1.1.2 Exceptions for Processing and Servicing

The opt-out, initial notice, and service provider requirements do not apply when an institution discloses NPPI as necessary to effect, administer, or enforce a transaction that a consumer requests or authorizes, or in connection with (1) servicing or processing a financial product or service that a consumer requests or authorizes; (2) maintaining or servicing the consumer's account with the institution, or with another entity as part of a private-label credit card program or other extension of credit on behalf of such entity; or (3) a proposed or actual securitization, secondary market sale (including sales of servicing rights), or similar transaction related to a transaction of the consumer.[74]

---

68. *Id.* § 1016.10(a)(1).
69. *Id.* § 1016.10(b).
70. *Id.* § 1016.10(c).
71. *Id.* § 1016.13(a).
72. *Id.* § 1016.13(b).
73. *Id.* § 1016.13(c).
74. *Id.* § 1016.14(a).

A disclosure will be considered necessary to effect, administer, or enforce a transaction if it is required, or is one of the lawful or appropriate methods, to enforce the financial institution's rights or the rights of other persons engaged in carrying out the financial transaction or providing the product or service.[75] A disclosure also will be considered necessary if it is required, or is a usual, appropriate, or acceptable method:

- To carry out the transaction or the product or service business of which the transaction is a part, and record, service, or maintain the consumer's account in the ordinary course of providing the financial service or financial product;
- To administer or service benefits or claims relating to the transaction or the product or service business of which it is a part;
- To provide a confirmation, statement, or other record of the transaction, or information on the status or value of the financial service or financial product to the consumer or the consumer's agent or broker;
- To accrue or recognize incentives or bonuses associated with the transaction that are provided by the institution or any other party;
- To underwrite insurance at the consumer's request or for reinsurance purposes, or for any of the following purposes as they relate to a consumer's insurance: account administration, reporting, investigating, or preventing fraud or material misrepresentation, processing premium payments, processing insurance claims, administering insurance benefits (including utilization review activities), participating in research projects, or as otherwise required or specifically permitted by federal or state law; or
- In connection with (i) the authorization, settlement, billing, processing, clearing, transferring, reconciling, or collection of amounts charged, debited, or otherwise paid using a debit, credit, or other payment card, check, or account number, or by other payment means; (ii) the transfer of receivables, accounts, or interests therein; or (iii) the audit of debit, credit, or other payment information.[76]

4.1.1.3 Additional Exceptions

The opt-out, initial notice, and service provider requirements also do not apply when a financial institution discloses NPPI:

- With the consent or at the direction of the consumer, provided that the consumer has not revoked the consent or direction;
- To protect the confidentiality or security of the institution's records pertaining to the consumer, service, product, or transaction;

75. *Id.* § 1016.14(b)(1).
76. *Id.* § 1016.14(b)(2).

- To protect against or prevent actual or potential fraud, unauthorized transactions, claims, or other liability;
- For required institutional risk control or for resolving consumer disputes or inquiries;
- To persons holding a legal or beneficial interest relating to the consumer;
- To persons acting in a fiduciary or representative capacity on behalf of the consumer;
- To provide information to insurance rate advisory organizations, guaranty funds or agencies, agencies that are rating the institution, persons that are assessing the institution's compliance with industry standards, and the institution's attorneys, accountants, and auditors;
- To the extent specifically permitted or required under other provisions of law, and in accordance with the Right to Financial Privacy Act, to law enforcement agencies (including the CFPB, a federal functional regulator, the Secretary of the Treasury, with respect to 31 U.S.C. chapter 53, subchapter II (Records and Reports on Monetary Instruments and Transactions) and 12 U.S.C. chapter 21 (Financial Recordkeeping), a state insurance authority, with respect to any person domiciled in that insurance authority's state that is engaged in providing insurance, and the FTC), self-regulatory organizations, or for an investigation on a matter related to public safety;
- To a consumer reporting agency in accordance with the Fair Credit Reporting Act;
- From a consumer report reported by a consumer reporting agency;
- In connection with a proposed or actual sale, merger, transfer, or exchange of all or a portion of a business or operating unit if the disclosure of NPPI concerns solely consumers of such business or unit;
- To comply with federal, state, or local laws, rules, and other applicable legal requirements;
- To comply with a properly authorized civil, criminal, or regulatory investigation, or subpoena or summons by federal, state, or local authorities; or
- To respond to judicial process or government regulatory authorities having jurisdiction over the institution for examination, compliance, or other purposes as authorized by law.[77]

4.2 Limits on Redisclosure and Reuse of Information

Although most of the requirements of GLBA and Regulation P apply only to financial institutions, they also restrict the ability of any person who has received NPPI from a financial institution to reuse and/or redisclose such information.

77. *Id.* § 1016.15.

4.2.1 *Information Received or Disclosed under an Opt-Out Exception (Other than the Service Provider Exception)*

If a person receives NPPI from a nonaffiliated financial institution under an opt-out exception (other than the service provider exception), that person's disclosure and use of that information is limited as follows: (1) the person may disclose the information to the affiliates of the financial institution from which it received the information; (2) the person may disclose the information to its affiliates, but its affiliates may, in turn, disclose and use the information only to the extent that the person may disclose and use the information; and (3) the person may disclose and use the information pursuant to an opt-out exception (other than the service provider exception) in the ordinary course of business to carry out the activity covered by the exception under which it received the information.[78]

If a person discloses NPPI to a nonaffiliated third party under such authority, the third party may disclose and use that information only as follows: (1) the third party may disclose the information to that person's affiliates; (2) the third party may disclose the information to its affiliates, but its affiliates may, in turn, disclose and use the information only to the extent that the third party may disclose and use the information; and (3) the third party may disclose and use the information pursuant to an opt-out exception (other than the service provider exception) in the ordinary course of business to carry out the activity covered by the exception under which it received the information.[79]

4.2.2 *Information Received or Disclosed in Other Circumstances*

If a person receives NPPI from a nonaffiliated financial institution under authority other than the exceptions covered in section 4.2.1 (e.g., pursuant to the service provider exception, or under the authority of the opt-out mechanism), the person may disclose the information only: (1) to the affiliates of the financial institution from which it received the information; (2) to the person's own affiliates, but its affiliates may, in turn, disclose the information only to the extent that it can disclose the information; and (3) to any other person, if the disclosure would be lawful if made directly to that person by the financial institution from which it received the information.[80]

If a person discloses NPPI to a nonaffiliated third party in such circumstances, the third party may disclose the information only (1) to the person's affiliates; (2) to its affiliates, but its affiliates, in turn, may disclose the information only to the extent the third party can disclose the information; or (3) to any other person, if the disclosure would be lawful if the person who originally disclosed the information made it directly.[81]

---

78. *Id.* § 1016.11(a)(1).
79. *Id.* § 1016.11(c).
80. *Id.* § 1016.11(b)(1).
81. *Id.* § 1016.11(d).

4.3 Sharing Account Numbers for Marketing Purposes

A financial institution may not, directly or through an affiliate, disclose, other than to a consumer reporting agency, an account number or similar form of access number or access code for a consumer's credit card account, deposit account, share account, or transaction account to any nonaffiliated third party for use in telemarketing, direct mail marketing, or other marketing through electronic mail to the consumer.[82] For this purpose, a transaction account is an account other than a deposit account, a share account, or a credit card account.[83] A transaction account does not include an account to which third parties cannot initiate charges.[84]

This restriction does not apply if the institution discloses an account number or similar form of access number or access code: (1) to its agent or service provider solely in order to perform marketing for its own products or services, as long as the agent or service provider is not authorized to directly initiate charges to the account; or (2) to a participant in a private-label credit card program or an affinity or similar program where the participants in the program are identified to the customer when the customer enters into the program.[85]

An account number, or similar form of access number or access code, does not include a number or code in an encrypted form, as long as the financial institution does not provide the recipient with a means to decode the number or code.[86]

82. *Id.* § 1016.12(a).
83. *Id.* § 1016.12(c)(2).
84. *Id.*
85. *Id.* § 1016.12(b).
86. *Id.* § 1016.12(c)(1).

CHAPTER

5

Information Security

Michael Nonaka and David A. Stein

This chapter addresses the three primary sources of federal information security law. Section 1 addresses the data security provisions of Title V of the Gramm-Leach-Bliley Act and their implementing regulations, guidelines, and guidance. Section 2 addresses the requirements under the Fair Credit Reporting Act and related regulations and guidelines for the proper disposal of consumer information derived from consumer reports. Section 3 focuses on data security enforcement actions brought by federal regulatory agencies with emphasis on general standards of data enforcement derived from Federal Trade Commission (FTC) enforcement actions.

1. The Gramm-Leach-Bliley Act: Safeguards Rule, Information Security Guidelines, and Data Breach Response Guidance

1.1 Title V of the Gramm-Leach-Bliley Act

The Gramm-Leach-Bliley Act (GLBA), which is also known as the Financial Services Modernization Act of 1999, imposes general information security standards on financial institutions.[1] Although the primary purpose of the GLBA was to remove barriers between commercial and investment banks that had been created by

---

The authors gratefully acknowledge the contributions of their former Covington & Burling LLP colleagues Sam Adriance and Tyler Sines in preparing this chapter.

1. Pub. L. No. 106-102, 113 Stat. 1338 (1999) (codified as amended at 15 U.S.C. §§ 6801–6827 (2018)).

the Glass-Steagall Act of 1933,[2] Title V of the GLBA established a comprehensive regulatory scheme designed to protect the privacy and security of customers' nonpublic personal information held by financial institutions from unauthorized or inappropriate access and use by private parties.[3] The term *financial institution* generally means any institution the business of which is engaging in financial activities as described in section 4(k) of the Bank Holding Company Act of 1956, including extending credit, processing payments, and providing financial advice.[4] The term is not limited to banking organizations.

Title V and its implementing regulations generally require financial institutions to establish standards or "safeguards" for ensuring the security and confidentiality of confidential customer information and records. The statutory text on information security sets forth concise, high-level standards. Specifically, section 501(b) of the GLBA directs the agencies responsible for implementing, enforcing, and overseeing Title V to "establish appropriate standards . . . relating to administrative, technical, and physical safeguards" that financial institutions must follow to:

> (1) insure the security and confidentiality of customer records and information; (2) protect against any anticipated threats or hazards to the security or integrity of such records; and (3) protect against unauthorized access to or use of such records or information which could result in substantial harm or inconvenience to any customer.[5]

1.2 Overview of Implementing Regulations

The agencies responsible for implementing, enforcing, and overseeing the information security provisions of Title V are the Office of the Comptroller of the Currency (OCC), Board of Governors of the Federal Reserve System (FRB), Federal Deposit Insurance Corporation (FDIC—collectively, the federal banking agencies),[6] and the

2. *See* Cong. Res. Serv., *The Glass Steagall Act: A Legal and Policy Analysis* 15–16 (David H. Carpenter, Edward V. Murphy, & M. Maureen Murphy, Jan. 19, 2016), https://fas.org/sgp/crs/misc/R44349.pdf.

3. Prior to the enactment of the GLBA, federal laws imposed restrictions on the disclosure of personal financial information under only limited circumstances. For example, the Right to Financial Privacy Act protected financial data from certain disclosures to federal government entities, Pub. L. No. 11-203, 124 Stat. 2105 (2010) (codified as amended at 12 U.S.C. §§ 3401–3423 (2018)), and the Fair Credit Reporting Act limited the use and disclosure of consumer reports and the information contained in consumer reports. Pub. L. No. 90-321, 84 Stat. 1128 (1970) (codified as amended at 12 U.S.C. §§ 1681–1681x (2018)).

4. 15 U.S.C. § 6809(3)(A).

5. 15 U.S.C. § 6801(b).

6. "Federal banking agencies" is not a legally defined term but is used throughout this chapter for ease of reference.

Federal Trade Commission (FTC), the National Credit Union Administration (NCUA), and the Securities and Exchange Commission (SEC).[7] The Commodity Futures Trading Commission (CFTC) was subsequently added as an agency responsible for Title V implementation and enforcement with respect to certain entities engaged in commodities activities pursuant to the Commodity Futures Modernization Act of 2000.[8] Final regulations were adopted by the SEC on June 29, 2000;[9] the NCUA on January 30, 2001;[10] the federal banking agencies jointly on February 1, 2001;[11] the CFTC on April 27, 2001;[12] and the FTC on May 23, 2002.[13] This section focuses on the regulations, guidelines, and guidance issued by the federal banking agencies, the NCUA, and the FTC, each of which have responsibilities related to consumer financial services.

Each regulation applies to financial institutions subject to the jurisdiction of the agency that promulgated it. For example, the OCC's regulation applies to national banks, savings associations, and other entities subject to the OCC's jurisdiction; the FRB's regulations apply to bank holding companies, state member banks, and other entities subject to the FRB's jurisdiction; the FDIC's regulation applies to state nonmember banks; and the NCUA's regulation applies to federally insured credit unions.[14] All other financial institutions—for example, debt collectors, mortgage and other nonbank lenders, consumer reporting agencies, and state-insured credit unions—are subject to FTC jurisdiction and the FTC's rule.[15]

---

7. The Office of Thrift Supervision (OTS) originally had such responsibility as well, but the agency was abolished in 2011 following the enactment of the Dodd-Frank Wall Street Reform Act of 2010.

8. Pub. L. No. 106-554 § 124 (2000) (codified as amended at 7 U.S.C. §§ 1–27f (2018)).

9. Privacy of Consumer Financial Information (Regulation S-P), 65 Fed. Reg. 40334 (June 29, 2000) (to be codified at 17 C.F.R. §§ 248.1–248.100).

10. Guidelines for Safeguarding Member Information, 66 Fed. Reg. 8152 (Jan. 30, 2001) (to be codified at 12 C.F.R. § 748.0).

11. Interagency Guidelines Establishing Standards for Safeguarding Customer Information and Rescission of Year 2000 Standards for Safety and Soundness, 66 Fed. Reg. 8616 (Feb. 1, 2001) (to be codified at 12 C.F.R. pts. 30, 208, 211, 225, 263, 308, 364, 568, 570) [hereinafter "Interagency Guidelines"].

12. Privacy of Consumer Financial Information, 66 Fed. Reg. 21236 (Apr. 27, 2001) (to be codified at 17 C.F.R. pt. 160). In 2014, the CFTC issued guidance that elaborates on the information security expectations applicable to CFTC-regulated institutions under the GLBA. *See* CFTC, Staff Advisory No. 14-21, *Gramm-Leach-Bliley Act Security Safeguards* (Feb. 26, 2014), https://www.cftc.gov/sites/default/files/idc/groups/public/@lrlettergeneral/documents/letter/14-21.pdf.

13. Standards for Safeguarding Customer Information, 67 Fed. Reg. 36484 (May 23, 2002) (to be codified at 16 C.F.R. pt. 314).

14. *See, generally*, Cong. Res. Serv., *Who Regulates Whom? An Overview of U.S. Financial Supervision* (Mark Jickling & Edward V. Murphy, Dec. 8, 2010), https://fas.org/sgp/crs/misc/R40249.pdf.

15. *See* Standards for Safeguarding Customer Information, *supra* note 13.

The relevant federal agencies have followed two separate regulatory models for implementing the statutory requirements and developing standards that address appropriate safeguards required under Title V. The federal banking agencies and the NCUA promulgated high-level regulatory amendments that reference and incorporate a uniform set of guidelines titled the "Interagency Guidelines Establishing Information Security Standards" (the Guidelines).[16] The Guidelines contain the information security standards mandated by section 501(b) of the GLBA. In contrast, the FTC promulgated a stand-alone, multisection regulation implementing section 501(b) titled "Standards for Safeguarding Customer Information."[17] Despite following different regulatory models, the agencies were required to "consult and coordinate" with each other to ensure, to the extent possible, that each agency's regulations were consistent and comparable to the regulations of the other agencies.[18] The resulting regulations, while broadly similar, are not identical, as discussed below.

The regulations generally define *customer information* to mean any record containing nonpublic personal information, as defined in the GLBA privacy rule, about a customer of a financial institution.[19]

1.3 The Federal Banking Agencies' Interagency Guidelines Establishing Information Security Standards

The federal banking agencies promulgated a substantively identical set of guidelines implementing the information security requirements of the GLBA collectively under a single Federal Register notice.[20] As noted above, under this approach, the federal banking agencies each promulgated a short rule or rules that refer covered entities to an appendix containing the Interagency Guidelines for safeguarding customer information.[21]

The guidelines require each regulated institution to "implement a comprehensive written information security program."[22] This program must include "administrative, technical, and physical safeguards appropriate to the size and complexity of the [institution] and the nature and scope of its activities."[23] Further, the program must be designed to further the objectives articulated in the GLBA's statutory text, as

16. *See* 12 C.F.R. pt. 30, App. B (interagency guidelines as promulgated by the OCC); 12 C.F.R. pt. 208, app. D-2 (as promulgated by the FRB); 12 C.F.R. pt. 364, app. B (as promulgated by the FDIC). Throughout, we cite to the guidelines as promulgated by the OCC. The NCUA guidelines are slightly different but substantively similar. *See* 12 C.F.R. pt. 748, app. A.

17. 16 C.F.R. pt. 314.

18. 15 U.S.C. § 6804(a)(2).

19. 12 C.F.R. pt. 30, app. B, at I.C.c.; 16 C.F.R. § 314.2(b).

20. *See* Interagency Guidelines, *supra* note 11.

21. *See* 12 C.F.R. §§ 30.1(a-b), 30.2, 30.3(a); 12 C.F.R. pt. 30, app. B.

22. 12 C.F.R. pt. 30, app. B, at II.

23. *Id.*

explained above,[24] as well as to ensure "the proper disposal of customer and consumer information."[25]

The Interagency Guidelines impose six categories of requirements in connection with the development and implementation of this comprehensive program:

- *Involve the board.* A covered institution must involve its board of directors (or an appropriate committee of the board) in the development and ongoing oversight of the program, including initial approval of the written program.[26]
- *Assess risk.* A covered institution must conduct a risk assessment that identifies "reasonably foreseeable internal and external threats that could result in unauthorized disclosure, misuse, alteration, or destruction of customer information or customer information systems."[27] This assessment must also consider the likelihood and potential damage from these threats, considering the sensitivity of the customer information, as well as the sufficiency of current policies, procedures, systems, and other arrangements in place to control these risks.[28]
- *Manage and control risk.* Following this risk assessment, a covered institution must design its information security program to control identified risks, commensurate with the sensitivity of the customer information and the complexity and scope of the institution's activities. In so doing, the institution should consider, among other things, the following potential features of the program: (i) access controls; (ii) physical access restrictions; (iii) encryption of customer information in transit and in storage; (iv) procedures designed to ensure that system modifications are consistent with the program; (v) employee controls (such as dual control procedures, segregation of duties, and employee background checks); (vi) intrusion detection and monitoring systems and procedures; (vii) response programs; and (viii) measures to protect against potential environmental hazards.[29] In addition, the institution should train staff to implement the program, regularly test key aspects of the program, and develop appropriate measures to dispose of customer information.[30]
- *Oversee service provider arrangements.* A covered institution must exercise due diligence in selecting service providers, contractually require them to

24. *See* note 5, *supra*, and accompanying text.
25. *Supra* note 22.
26. *Id.* at III.A.
27. *Id.* at III.B.
28. *See id.*
29. *See id.* at III.C.
30. *See id.*

maintain adequate information security programs, and monitor them for compliance with their obligations.[31]

- *Adjust the program.* A covered institution must adjust the program as appropriate to respond to changes in technology, the sensitivity of the customer information it possesses, internal or external threats, and business arrangements.[32]
- *Report to the board.* A covered institution must report to its board of directors or an appropriate committee of the board at least annually regarding the overall status of the information security program.[33]

Although the Interagency Guidelines impose several specific requirements, they are best understood as establishing a general requirement that financial institutions develop and maintain a comprehensive information security program reasonably designed to protect customer information.[34] The Federal Financial Institutions Examination Council (FFIEC), which is an interagency council of regulators that includes as members the federal banking agencies, has promulgated more detailed guidance regarding the agencies' expectations for information security compliance.[35]

The overall "reasonableness" standard in the Interagency Guidelines contrasts with more specific industry-based information security standards. For example, the Payment Card Industry Data Security Standard (PCI DSS)—a private standard imposed by the major credit card associations—has many specific requirements for protecting the security of cardholder data.[36] The PCI DSS requires, for example, all holders of cardholder data to install and maintain firewalls and encrypt the transmission of cardholder data.[37] The Interagency Guidelines employ more general, less prescriptive standards, which has the benefit of providing great flexibility with regard to differently situated financial institutions and allowing rapid adaptation to changes in technology, threats, and other relevant factors.

31. *See id.* at III.D.

32. *See id.* at III.E.

33. *See id.* at III.F.

34. *See* 12 C.F.R. pt. 30, app. B. "Customer information" is defined to mean "any record containing nonpublic personal information . . . about a customer, whether in paper, electronic, or other form, that is maintained by or on behalf of" the covered financial institution. *See* 12 C.F.R. pt. 30, app. B, at I.C.e.

35. *See* FFIEC, Information Technology Examination Handbook Infobase, [hereinafter "IT Handbook"], https://ithandbook.ffiec.gov/.

36. *See* Payment Card Industry Security Standards Council, *Prioritized Approach for PCI DSS, Version 3.2.1* (June 2018), https://www.pcisecuritystandards.org/documents/Prioritized-Approach-for-PCI-DSS-v3_2_1.pdf?agreement=true&time=1596565206216.

37. *Id.* at 5.

1.4 The Federal Trade Commission Safeguards Rule

In contrast to the Interagency Guidelines, the FTC Safeguards Rule takes the form of a traditional, stand-alone regulation.[38] Aside from this formal difference, however, the FTC rule is substantively similar to the Interagency Guidelines. The FTC Safeguards Rule follows the same "reasonableness" approach to information security as the guidelines. Like the guidelines, it requires covered institutions to implement a written information security program tailored to their size and complexity, the nature and scope of their activities, and the sensitivity of the relevant customer information.[39] It also requires such institutions to identify foreseeable internal and external risks, train staff, and oversee their service providers by ensuring that they also employ reasonable cybersecurity programs.[40] Generally, the FTC Safeguards Rule describes the factors covered institutions should consider in less detail than the Interagency Guidelines, but imposes similar substantive requirements.

In a few specific areas, however, the Interagency Guidelines and the FTC Safeguards Rule substantively differ. For example, the guidelines require that a covered institution involve its board of directors in the development and oversight of the information security program, while the FTC Safeguards Rule has no such requirement. Instead, the FTC Safeguards Rule requires that a financial institution designate a specific employee to coordinate the information security program, often known as a "GLBA officer."[41] The guidelines do not impose such a requirement,[42] although in practice, many banking institutions designate their Chief Information Security Officer (or CISO) to fill this role, as recommended under other regulatory guidance for supervised financial institutions.[43] Further, the FTC Safeguards Rule does not include a provision regarding the disposal of customer information, which is instead governed by the FTC's Disposal Rule, discussed later in this chapter.[44]

1.5 Data Breach Response Program

The most significant difference between the Interagency Guidelines and the FTC Safeguards Rule relates to data breach response and notification. The federal banking agencies published supplemental guidance specifying uniform standards that covered financial institutions should follow in the event of unauthorized access to customer

38. *See* 16 C.F.R. §§ 314.1–314.5.

39. 16 C.F.R. § 314.3(a).

40. *See* 16 C.F.R. § 314.4(d); 12 C.F.R. pt. 30, app. B, at III.D.

41. *See* 16 C.F.R. § 314.4(a).

42. *See* Interagency Guidelines, *supra* note 11, at 8620 (Feb. 1, 2001) (determining that it would be unnecessary and unduly burdensome to require by regulation that banks designate a specific employee to oversee the program, such as a CISO).

43. *See* FFIEC, IT Handbook, Management (discussing the proper role of a CISO), https://ithandbook.ffiec.gov/it-booklets/management.aspx.

44. *See* 16 C.F.R. pt. 682.

information.[45] This guidance follows the general approach of the Interagency Guidelines in that it adopts general, flexible standards.

Financial institutions covered by the guidelines must develop and implement a risk-based response program to address data breaches tailored "to the size and complexity of the institution and the nature and scope of its activities."[46] The guidance requires covered institutions to notify their primary federal regulator as soon as possible when "sensitive customer information" has been compromised, and to notify law enforcement consistent with the requirements of the Suspicious Activity Report regulations.[47] "Sensitive customer information" includes "a customer's name, address, or telephone number, in conjunction with the customer's social security number, driver's license number, account number, credit or debit card number."[48] It also includes any information that would allow access to the customer's account, for example, a user name and password combination.[49]

Further, if a covered financial institution determines that misuse of sensitive customer information "has occurred or is reasonably possible," the institution must notify affected or potentially affected customers "as soon as possible."[50] The guidance requires that the customer notice be clear and conspicuous, describe the incident and the type of information compromised, and provide a phone number to obtain more information.[51] The notice also must be delivered in a manner by which there is a reasonable expectation that the customer will receive it.[52]

The FTC, by contrast, has not promulgated a rule with respect to data breach notification, and there is no general federal data breach notification standard for financial institutions that are not subject to the Interagency Guidelines.[53] When an FTC-covered financial institution suffers a breach, the institution is generally not subject to federal breach response requirements.[54]

---

45. *See* 12 C.F.R. pt. 30, app. B, supp. A.

46. 12 C.F.R. pt. 30, app. B, supp. A at II.

47. *See id.* at II.A.

48. *Id.* at III.A.1.

49. *See id.*

50. *Id.* at III.A.

51. *Id.* at III.B.

52. *See id.* at III.C.

53. *See, generally,* Cong. Res. Serv., *Data Security and Breach Notification Legislation: Selected Legal Issues* (Dec. 28, 2015), https://fas.org/sgp/crs/misc/R44326.pdf.

54. With the exception of certain exemptions for institutions regulated by the federal banking agencies, financial institutions are also subject to state breach notification rules. All fifty states, the District of Columbia, Guam, Puerto Rico, and the U.S. Virgin Islands have breach notification statutes. *See* Nat'l Conf. of State Legis., Security Breach Notification Laws (March 8, 2020), http://www.ncsl.org/research/telecommunications-and-information-technology/security-breach-notification-laws.aspx.

1.6 Enforcement

The GLBA does not provide for a private right of action,[55] but is enforced through administrative action by the agencies responsible for implementing its information security requirements. As a general rule, the federal banking agencies tend to resolve GLBA violations through the supervisory process, while the FTC typically brings public enforcement actions to enforce the FTC Safeguards Rule. However, FTC enforcement of the Safeguards Rule is less common than FTC data security enforcement actions under section 5 of the Federal Trade Commission Act (FTC Act), which applies to a broader range of entities.[56] Enforcement is discussed in more detail in section 3 below.

2. Disposal Rule

2.1 Introduction

Section 216 of the Fair and Accurate Credit Transactions Act (FACT Act)[57] amended the Fair Credit Reporting Act (FCRA)[58] in 2003 with the goal of "ensur[ing] proper disposal of consumer information and records derived from consumer reports."[59] To implement this statutory provision,[60] the FACT Act mandated that certain financial regulatory agencies issue regulations requiring their respective regulated entities to "properly dispose" of such consumer information. The implementing regulations generally are referred to as the Disposal Rule or the Disposal Rules.[61]

The FACT Act required the FTC, the federal banking agencies, NCUA, SEC, and CFTC to "consult and coordinate" with one another to ensure that the implementing regulations were "consistent and comparable" across the agencies.[62]

---

55. 15 U.S.C. § 6805; *see, e.g.*, Dunmire v. Morgan Stanley DW, Inc., 475 F.3d 956, 960 (8th Cir. 2007) ("[n]o private right of action exists for an alleged violation of the GLBA").

56. 15 U.S.C. § 45; *see, generally*, Cong. Res. Serv., *The Federal Trade Commissions' Regulation of Data Security Under Its Unfair or Deceptive Acts or Practices (UDAP) Authority* (Gina Stevens, Sept. 11, 2014), https://fas.org/sgp/crs/misc/R43723.pdf.

57. Pub. L. No. 108-159, 117 Stat. 1952 (2003) (codified as amended at 15 U.S.C. §§ 1681–1681x (2018)).

58. 15 U.S.C. §§ 1681–1681x (2018).

59. Cong. Rec. S13889 (Nov. 4, 2003) (amendment introduced by Sen. Shelby on behalf of Sen. Nelson).

60. 15 U.S.C. § 1681w.

61. This chapter uses the plural "Disposal Rules" when referring to the rules of multiple agencies.

62. *Id.* at § 1681w(a)(2)(A).

The agencies followed two approaches to the form of their Disposal Rules, but the content is substantively consistent.[63] The FTC promulgated a stand-alone regulation that explicitly adopted a flexible standard requiring "reasonable measures" to protect consumer information and provided several illustrative examples, as discussed later in this chapter.[64] The federal banking agencies and the NCUA each issued a regulation that incorporated the disposal of records provisions into their existing guidelines implementing the information security provisions of section 501(b) of the GLBA.[65] Accordingly, the federal banking agencies and the NCUA amended their guidelines to incorporate the new objective of ensuring proper disposal of consumer information.[66]

Two statutory provisions address how the FACT Act's disposal of records provision interacts with other laws. First, the statute's rule of construction provides that the disposal of records provision shall not be construed "to require a person to maintain or destroy any record pertaining to a consumer that is not imposed under other law" or "to alter or affect any requirement imposed under any other provision of law to maintain or destroy such a record."[67] As a result, the Disposal Rule was not intended to alter any requirement under any other provision of law to maintain or destroy consumer records.[68]

Second, the FCRA's general preemption provision states, in relevant part, that "[n]o requirement or prohibition may be imposed under the law of any State . . . with respect to the conduct required by" the disposal of records provision.[69] The extent to which state law is preempted by the FCRA depends on how broadly the "conduct" required by the rule is interpreted, which remains unsettled.[70]

---

63. Disposal of Consumer Report Information and Records, 69 Fed. Reg. 68690 & fn. 5 (Nov. 24, 2004) (to be codified at 16 C.F.R. pt. 682).

64. *See* 16 C.F.R. § 682.3.

65. *See* 12 C.F.R. § 41.83 (OCC); 12 C.F.R. § 222.83 (FRB); 12 C.F.R. § 334.83 (FDIC); 12 C.F.R. § 717 (NCUA). The GLBA Safeguards Rule required the establishment of appropriate standards for financial institutions relating to safeguarding customer information. 15 U.S.C. § 6801(b).

66. *See* Standards for Safeguarding Customer Information, *supra* note 13. The NCUA guidelines, although promulgated separately, are "substantially identical" to the federal banking agencies' information security guidelines.

67. 15 U.S.C. § 1681w(b).

68. 69 Fed. Reg. 68694.

69. 15 U.S.C. § 1681t(b)(5)(I).

70. *Compare* Willey v. J.P. Morgan Chase, N.A., No. 09 CIV. 1397(CM), 2009 WL 1938987, at *12 (S.D.N.Y. July 7, 2009) (holding that the FCRA preempts any state law claim—including negligence, negligence per se, breach of contract, and breach of implied contract—relating to the failure to safeguard customer data) *with* Spencer v. Nat'l City Mortg., 831 F. Supp. 2d 1353, 1364 (N.D. Ga. 2011) (holding that breach of contract claims are not preempted by the FCRA).

The rest of section 2 addresses the entities and information covered by the Disposal Rule, the compliance obligations applicable to covered entities, and the consequences of noncompliance.

2.2 Scope of Coverage

2.2.1 Covered Entities

The FCRA's disposal of records provision extends the requirement to protect consumers' credit information to a broader range of entities than the financial institutions already covered by the GLBA information security provisions.[71] The provision broadly applies to "any person that maintains or otherwise possesses consumer information, or any compilation of consumer information, derived from consumer reports for a business purpose."[72]

The FCRA gives the FTC authority over the broadest range of entities, including "consumer reporting agencies, resellers of consumer reports, lenders, insurers, employers, landlords, government agencies, mortgage brokers, automobile dealers, waste disposal companies, and any other business that possesses or maintains consumer information."[73] Any entity, regardless of industry, that obtains a consumer report for a business purpose is subject to the disposal of records provision.[74] The FCRA gives other agencies authority over entities they regulate.[75] For example, the federal banking agencies' Disposal Rules apply, respectively, to the financial institutions regulated by each agency;[76] the NCUA's Disposal Rule applies to federal credit unions, whereas state-chartered credit unions are subject to the FTC's Disposal Rule.[77]

2.2.2 Types of Information Covered

The FCRA's disposal of records provision was enacted to protect "consumer information," which the Disposal Rule defines as "any record about an individual,

71. *See* Cong. Rec. S13889 (Nov. 4, 2003) (statement by Sen. Nelson) (explaining that the amendment will "close the loophole" by applying to more businesses than the Safeguards Rule, including, for example, rental property companies, cell phone companies, and utilities previously not covered).

72. 15 U.S.C. § 1681w(a)(1).

73. *See* 15 U.S.C. § 1681s(a)(1); 69 Fed. Reg. 68696.

74. 69 Fed. Reg. 68696.

75. 15. U.S.C. § 1681s(b).

76. 12 C.F.R. § 41.83(a)(1)–(2) (OCC); 12 C.F.R. § 222.83(a)(1) (FRB); 12 C.F.R. § 334.1(b) (FDIC).

77. *See* 12 C.F.R. § 717.1(a); 15 U.S.C. § 1681s(b)(1)(B); *see also* Fair Credit Reporting—Proper Disposal of Consumer Information Under the Fair and Accurate Credit Transactions Act of 2003, 69 Fed. Reg. 69269 (Nov. 29. 2004) (to be codified at 12 C.F.R. pts. 717 & 748).

whether in paper, electronic, or other form, that is a consumer report or is derived from a consumer report."[78] It also includes any compilation of such records.[79]

The Disposal Rule's protection of "consumer information" overlaps to some extent with the protection of "customer information" under the Safeguards Rule, but the information covered by the two rules is not identical.[80] The primary difference is that "consumer information" under the Disposal Rule is limited to information on or derived from a consumer report.[81] By contrast, "customer information" under the Safeguards Rule or the Interagency Guidelines means any record containing nonpublic personal information, as defined in the GLBA privacy rules,[82] about a customer. [83] Further, the term "consumer information" used in the Disposal Rule refers to information about *any* individual, unlike "customer information," which is limited to individuals who have obtained a financial product or service and have an ongoing relationship with a financial institution.[84]

2.3 Disposal Rule Requirements

2.3.1 Federal Banking Agencies and the National Credit Union Administration

The federal banking agencies and the NCUA each formulated a short regulation[85] directing their respective regulated entities to "properly dispose" of consumer information in accordance with the Interagency Guidelines,[86] which were amended

78. 16 C.F.R. § 682.1(b) (FTC definition); 12 C.F.R. pt. 30, app. B, at I.C.2.b (OCC definition). The term "consumer report" is defined broadly as "any written, oral, or other communication of any information by a consumer reporting agency bearing on a consumer's credit worthiness, credit standing, credit capacity, character, general reputation, personal characteristics, or mode of living" used to establish the consumer's eligibility for credit, insurance, employment, or other authorized purposes under section 1681b of the FCRA. 15 U.S.C. § 1681a(d)(1).

79. 16 C.F.R. § 682.1(b). Consumer information does not include information that does not identify an individual, such as aggregate information or blind data. *Id.*

80. Proper Disposal of Consumer Information Under the Fair and Accurate Credit Transactions Act of 2003, 69 Fed. Reg. 77610-01, 77612 (Dec. 28, 2004) (to be codified at 12 C.F.R. pts 30, 41, 208, 211, 222, 225, 334, 364, 568, 570, 571).

81. 69 Fed. Reg. 77612–13.

82. *See* 12 C.F.R. § 1016.3(p).

83. 12 C.F.R. pt. 30, app. B, at I.C.c.; 16 C.F.R. § 314.2(b).

84. 69 Fed. Reg. 77612–13.

85. 12 C.F.R. § 41.83 (OCC); 12 C.F.R. § 222.83 (FRB); 12 C.F.R. § 334.83 (FDIC); 12 C.F.R. § 717.83 (NCUA).

86. *See* Standards for Safeguarding Customer Information, *supra* note 13. As noted previously, for the purposes of this chapter, specific cites to the Interagency Guidelines are to the OCC's version (12 C.F.R. pt. 30, app. B).

to incorporate the substantive Disposal Rule requirements.[87] The federal banking agencies' aim was to give financial institutions "sufficient latitude" to adopt controls suitable for each institution's particular circumstances.[88] The federal banking agencies expected "minimal" changes to an institution's existing information security program as a result of the Disposal Rule because many of the measures used to dispose of *customer* information pursuant to the Safeguards Rule could be adapted to the disposal of *consumer* information.[89]

The general requirements of the federal banking agencies' and NCUA's Disposal Rules are summarized as follows:

- *Incorporate the disposal of* consumer information *into the entity*'s *existing information security program.* The Interagency Guidelines require covered entities to "implement a comprehensive written information security program that includes . . . safeguards appropriate to the size and complexity of the bank and the nature and scope of its activities."[90] The federal banking agencies and the NCUA amended their guidelines to incorporate the Disposal Rule by adding that information security programs should "[e]nsure the proper disposal of customer information and consumer information."[91] The entity's board should approve of and oversee the development and implementation of such a program.[92] The federal banking agencies' Final Rule also refers to the FFIEC Information Security Booklet for further guidance.[93] The FFIEC Information Security Booklet provides that covered entities should designate a single individual, department, or function to be accountable for disposal methods and compliance with

87. *See* 69 Fed. Reg. 77611 (discussing the addition of the consumer information definition, an objective for the proper disposal of consumer information, and a provision requiring "appropriate measures" be taken for the disposal of such information); 69 Fed. Reg. 69269 (discussing similar amendments to the NCUA Safeguards Rule).

88. 69 Fed. Reg. 77611.

89. *Id.* In fact, the federal banking agencies explained that because "segregating particular records" may entail "considerable cost," many institutions are likely to use the same measures to properly dispose of both customer and consumer information. *Id.* at 77615.

90. Interagency Guidelines, *supra* note 11, at II.A.

91. *Id.* at II.B.4.

92. *Id.* at III.A.

93. *See* 69 Fed. Reg. 77611 ("[T]he Agencies . . . already have issued guidance regarding their expectations concerning the proper disposal of all of an institution's paper and electronic records. *See* FFIEC Information Technology Examination Handbook, Information Security Booklet, December 2002, p. 63.").

disposal policies.[94] Further, policies, procedures, and training should inform employees of how to dispose of sensitive media properly, including media containing consumer information.[95]

- *Incorporate the disposal of* consumer information *into the risk assessment process.* The Interagency Guidelines, as amended, provide that covered entities should implement "appropriate measures" for the disposal of consumer information.[96] The amended guidelines also provide that the disposal of consumer information should be incorporated into the institution's information security risk assessment process, and that appropriate risk-based controls should be implemented to ensure proper disposal.[97] These controls should include logging the disposal of sensitive media.[98]
- *Use appropriate risk-based disposal methods for paper-based media.* Covered entities are expected to tailor their disposal policies based on the sensitivity of the consumer information.[99] The guidelines are not prescriptive in terms of method of disposal. The FFIEC Information Security Booklet, however, provides guidance on regulatory expectations for disposal of "all" types of institution records, including consumer information.[100] It suggests, for instance, shredding or disposing of paper-based media containing consumer information in a manner that ensures such media is "unreadable and unlikely to be reconstructed."[101]
- *Use appropriate risk-based disposal methods for electronic-based media.* The FFIEC Information Security Booklet states that electronic-based media presents "distinct disposal challenges" because residual data often remains even after deletion.[102] Suggested methods for disposing

94. FFIEC IT Handbook, Information Security Booklet [hereinafter "FFIEC Information Security Booklet"] (Sept. 2016), 28, https://www.ffiec.gov/press/PDF/FFIEC_IT_Handbook_Information_Security_Booklet.pdf.

95. *Id.*

96. Interagency Guidelines, *supra* note 11, at III.C.4.

97. *Id.* at III.B. & C.

98. FFIEC, Information Security Booklet, *supra* note 94, at 28.

99. *See id.* ("The institution should base its disposal policies on the sensitivity of the information.").

100. *See* 69 Fed. Reg. at 77611.

101. FFIEC, Information Security Booklet, *supra* note 94, at 28.

102. *Id.*

of electronic-based media include overwriting,[103] degaussing,[104] or physical destruction, but management is responsible for determining the most effective method to make data "non-recoverable."[105] Although the Disposal Rule does not provide examples of improper disposal methods, the FFIEC Information Security Booklet suggests that covered entities should avoid allowing employees to throw away consumer information "using the same disposal system as regular garbage."[106]

- *Implement measures to ensure compliance by service providers.* The Disposal Rule permits covered entities to engage third parties for disposal services, but covered entities remain responsible for ensuring compliance by service providers. Covered entities should conduct appropriate due diligence in selecting such providers.[107] In addition, service providers should be required "by contract to implement appropriate measures designed to meet the objectives" of the Interagency Guidelines.[108] Accordingly, covered entities should contractually require their service providers to develop appropriate measures to comply with the Disposal Rule, and should monitor them, when warranted, to ensure they have satisfied those contractual obligations.[109]

2.3.2 The FTC

The FTC promulgated a stand-alone regulation for its version of the Disposal Rule, rather than incorporating the Disposal Rule into its Safeguards Rule.[110] Covered entities, however, are expected to incorporate the proper disposal of consumer information into their information security programs, as required by the Safeguards Rule.[111] The FTC noted that the coverage of the Disposal Rule and the Safeguards Rule are different both in terms of the entities covered and the types of information protected, but also

---

103. Overwriting destroys data by replacing it with new, random data, which is the preferable method when the media will be reused. FFIEC, Information Security Booklet, *supra* note 94, at 28. The federal banking agencies advise, however, that overwriting may need to be performed many times to be effective. *Id.*

104. Degaussing is a method that scrambles data recorded on media with "powerful, varying magnetic fields." *Id.*

105. *Id.*

106. *Id.*

107. Interagency Guidelines, *supra* note 11, at III.D.1.

108. *Id.* at III.D.2 (emphasis added).

109. *Id.* at III.D.2 & D.3; *see also* 69 Fed. Reg. 77613.

110. *See* 16 C.F.R. § 682.3.

111. 16 C.F.R. § 682.3(b)(5).

acknowledged that the "substantive requirements of both rules are consistent with respect to disposal."[112]

Accordingly, the FTC adopted a flexible, risk-based standard in its Disposal Rule that requires "reasonable measures" to protect against unauthorized access to or use of consumer information.[113] This standard is similar to the standard set forth in the FTC Safeguards Rule. Recognizing that there are "few foolproof methods of record destruction,"[114] the FTC expects covered institutions to consider a variety of factors when determining what measures are reasonable, including "the sensitivity of the consumer information, the nature and size of the entity's operations, the costs and benefits of different disposal methods, and relevant technological changes."[115]

The FTC's Disposal Rule provides several illustrative examples of reasonable measures, depending on the context of the disposal.[116] These examples include "burning, pulverizing, or shredding" paper-based media containing consumer information so that the information "cannot practicably be read or reconstructed."[117] For electronic-based media, the FTC's Disposal Rule provides that reasonable methods include "destroying" or "erasing" electronic media so that the information "cannot practicably be read or reconstructed."[118]

The FTC's Disposal Rule allows covered entities to engage third-party service providers for disposal services provided that the covered entity first conducts appropriate due diligence.[119] Such due diligence could include reviewing an independent audit of the service provider's operations and compliance, obtaining information about the service provider through reliable references, requiring the service provider to have a recognized trade association certification, reviewing and evaluating the service provider's information security policies and procedures, or taking other measures to determine the competency and integrity of the service provider.[120]

Covered entities also should notify the service provider when transferring consumer information and contractually require the service provider to dispose of such information properly.[121] If the service provider receives such notification, the FTC considers the service provider, in addition to the covered entity, to be responsible for the proper disposal of consumer information that it maintains or otherwise possesses.[122] The FTC does not provide examples of what it considers an unreasonable measure

112. 69 Fed. Reg. 68693.
113. 16 C.F.R. § 682.3(a); *see also* 69 Fed. Reg. 68693.
114. 69 Fed. Reg. 68690.
115. *Id.* at 68693.
116. *See* 16 C.F.R. § 682.3(b).
117. *Id.* § 682.3(b)(1).
118. *Id.* § 682.3(b)(2).
119. *Id.* § 682.3(b)(3).
120. *Id.*
121. 69 Fed. Reg. 68694.
122. 16 C.F.R. § 682.3(b)(4); *see also* 69 Fed. Reg. 68694.

of disposal, but FTC enforcement actions make clear that discarding consumer information in public dumpsters is not acceptable.[123]

2.4 Consequences of Noncompliance with the Disposal Rule

The consequences of noncompliance with the Disposal Rule include agency enforcement and private rights of action. The FTC is authorized to use its procedural, investigative, and enforcement powers to ensure covered entities comply with the Disposal Rule; noncompliance is deemed an "unfair or deceptive act or practice in commerce" in violation of section 5(a) of the FTC Act.[124] The FTC has used its enforcement authority to allege violations of the Disposal Rule, typically in situations where an entity has disposed of consumer information in publicly accessible dumpsters.[125] The FTC actions generally result in a consent order mandating that the entity pay civil penalties and implement various remedial measures to improve its information security program, such as annual, independent third-party reviews.[126]

The federal banking agencies have authority over their regulated entities to examine and enforce compliance with the rule pursuant to section 8 of the Federal Deposit Insurance Act.[127] The NCUA has comparable authority over federal credit unions pursuant to the Federal Credit Union Act.[128] The federal banking agencies

123. *See, e.g.*, Press Release, FTC, Mortgage Broker Who Dumped Consumer Records Settles FTC Charges (Jan. 10, 2010), https://www.ftc.gov/news-events/press-releases/2010/01/mortgage-broker-who-dumped-consumer-records-settles-ftc-charges.

124. 15 U.S.C. § 1681s(1).

125. *See* Compl., United States v. Am. United Mortg. Co., No. 07-cv-7064 (N.D. Ill. Dec. 17, 2007), https://www.ftc.gov/sites/default/files/documents/cases/2007/12/071217americanunitedmrtgcmplt.pdf; Comp., *In re* Nation's Title Agency, No. C-4161 (FTC June 19, 2006), https://www.ftc.gov/sites/default/files/documents/cases/2006/06/0523117nationstitle_complaint.pdf; Compl., FTC v. Navone, No. 2:08-cv-01842 (D. Nev. Dec. 30, 2009), https://www.ftc.gov/sites/default/files/documents/cases/2009/01/090121navonecmpt.pdf; Compl., United States v. PLS Financial Servs., Inc., No. 1:12-cv-8334 (E.D. Ill. Oct. 17, 2012), https://www.ftc.gov/sites/default/files/documents/cases/2012/11/121107plspaydaycmpt.pdf.

126. *See* United States v. Am. United Mortgage Co., No. 07-cv-7064 https://www.ftc.gov/sites/default/files/documents/cases/2007/12/071217americanunitedmrtgstipfinal.pdf; *In re* Nation's Title Agency, No. C-4161 (FTC June 19, 2006), https://www.ftc.gov/sites/default/files/documents/cases/2006/06/0523117nationstitledecisionandorder.pdf; FTC v. Navone, No. 2:08-cv-01842 (D. Nev. Dec. 30, 2009), https://www.ftc.gov/sites/default/files/documents/cases/2010/01/100120navonestip.pdf; United States v. PLS Financial Servs., Inc., No. 1:12-cv-8334 (E.D. Ill. Oct. 26, 2012), https://www.ftc.gov/sites/default/files/documents/cases/2012/11/121107plspaydaystip.pdf.

127. 15 U.S.C. § 1681s(b) & (d). Section 8 of the Federal Deposit Insurance Act enumerates the banking agencies' broad range of enforcement powers over depository institutions, including termination of insurance, cease-and-desist orders, and removal powers, among others. 12 U.S.C. § 1818.

128. 15 U.S.C. § 1681s(b)(1)(B).

and the NCUA generally ensure compliance through their respective supervision functions.[129]

The FCRA also provides for private rights of action.[130] Plaintiffs generally may bring suit within two years of the plaintiff's discovery of the violation.[131] Successful plaintiffs in a private action may recover actual, statutory, and punitive damages for willful violations of the FCRA.[132] Negligent violations, on the other hand, permit the recovery of actual damages.[133] Although several individuals have filed complaints alleging violations of the Disposal Rule, each complaint has been dismissed due to insufficient pleading.[134]

3. Data Security Enforcement

3.1 Introduction

3.1.1 Authority and Common Bases for Actions

Data security enforcement authority is divided among the FTC, the federal banking agencies, the NCUA, and, to some extent, the Consumer Financial Protection Bureau (CFPB). For many years, the FTC has been at the forefront of bringing public enforcement actions to protect consumers and the security of their sensitive financial information. The FTC relies on two primary grounds for bringing data security enforcement actions: section 5 of the FTC Act and, less frequently, the Safeguards Rule. While the Safeguards Rule applies to financial institutions, section 5 applies more broadly to any person that engages in "unfair or deceptive acts or practices" (UDAP). Lessons learned from FTC enforcement actions derive from actions against financial institutions and other companies.

The FTC regularly has used its enforcement authority under section 5 of the FTC Act to allege that companies have engaged in UDAP in connection with breaches or inadvertent disclosures of consumers' sensitive information.[135] Since 2002, the FTC

129. For example, in the FFIEC Information Security Examination Procedures, examiners are instructed as part of their evaluation of internal controls to review whether management "[h]as appropriate disposal procedures for both paper-based and electronic information." FFIEC Information Security Booklet, *supra* note 94, at 65.

130. *See* 15 U.S.C. §§ 1681n, 1681o.

131. *Id.* § 1681p; *see also* Willey v. J.P. Morgan Chase, N.A., No. 09 CIV. 1397(CM), 2009 WL 1938987, at *12 (S.D.N.Y. July 7, 2009) ("The . . . two year statute runs from the date when [Plaintiff] was on 'inquiry notice' . . . .").

132. 15 U.S.C. § 1681n.

133. *Id.* § 1681o.

134. *See Willey*, 2009 WL 1938987, at *11 (S.D.N.Y. July 7, 2009); Owens v. Dixie Motor Co., 2014 WL 12703392, at *9 (E.D.N.C. Mar. 31, 2014); Auer v. Trans Union LLC, 2015 WL 11393824, at *5 (D.N.D. Apr. 7, 2015), *appeal dismissed*, 834 F.3d 933 (8th Cir. 2016).

135. 15 U.S.C. § 45.

has brought more than seventy public enforcement actions related to weaknesses in information security programs.[136]

By contrast, the federal banking agencies and the NCUA generally rely on their supervisory functions and nonpublic enforcement actions to ensure compliance with their Safeguards Rules and data security standards. There has been, however, at least occasional public action enforcing the Interagency Guidelines.[137] In 2016, the CFPB brought its first public enforcement action related to data security against online payment platform, Dwolla.[138]

3.1.1.1 FTC Section 5 Actions

The FTC has used both the "unfairness" and "deception" prongs of section 5 of the FTC Act to challenge companies' data security practices.[139] To establish unfairness, an act or practice (1) must cause, or be likely to cause, substantial injury to consumers, (2) must not be an injury that was reasonably avoidable by the consumers, and (3) must not be outweighed by countervailing benefits to consumers or to competition.[140] To establish deception, an act or practice must be a representation, omission, or practice that is likely to mislead consumers, who act reasonably under the circumstances, to their detriment.[141] Following a data breach, for example, the FTC may allege that an unreasonable data security practice was unfair because it resulted in injury to consumers,[142] and/or allege that it was deceptive because it contradicted prior representations in the company's privacy policy, website, or advertisements.[143]

---

136. FTC, Privacy & Data Security Update (2019), at 5, https://www.ftc.gov/reports/privacy-data-security-update-2019.

137. *See, e.g.*, First Horizon Home Loan Corp., Stipulation and Consent Order for Civil Money Penalty, OCC Enforcement Decision 2005-78 (June 30, 2005), https://www.occ.gov/static/enforcement-actions/ea2005-78.pdf.

138. *See* Dwolla, Inc., No. 2016-CFPB-0007 (Feb. 27, 2016), http://files.consumerfinance.gov/f/201603_cfpb_consent-order-dwolla-inc.pdf.

139. *See, e.g.*, Compl., United States v. ChoicePoint, Inc., No. 1:06-CV-198 (N.D. Ga. Jan. 30, 2006), https://www.ftc.gov/sites/default/files/documents/cases/2006/01/0523069complaint.pdf (charging ChoicePoint with both unfair and deceptive acts or practices following a data breach exposing sensitive information of more than 163,000 customers).

140. 15 U.S.C. § 45(n).

141. Letter from James C. Miller III to Hon. John D. Dingell, Chairman, House Comm. on Energy & Commerce (Oct. 14, 1983), *available at* https://www.ftc.gov/public-statements/1983/10/ftc-policy-statement-deception.

142. *See, e.g.*, Compl., CardSystems Sols., Inc., FTC No. C-4168 (Sept. 5, 2006), https://www.ftc.gov/sites/default/files/documents/cases/2006/09/0523148cardsystemscomplaint.pdf.

143. *See, e.g.*, Compl., Life is Good, Inc., FTC No. C-4218 (Apr. 16, 2008), https://www.ftc.gov/sites/default/files/documents/cases/2008/04/080418complaint.pdf (deceptive privacy policy); Compl., Guidance Software, Inc., FTC No. C-4187 (Mar. 30, 2007), https://www.ftc.gov/sites/default/files/documents/cases/2007/04/0623057complaint.pdf (deceptive statements on website).

In addition, the FTC frequently brings actions for alleged violations of section 5 of the FTC Act in conjunction with allegations of violations of other statutes, such as the FCRA.[144]

Although the FTC frequently brings actions following large-scale data breaches, it has also pursued actions against companies for unauthorized disclosures of sensitive information affecting fewer than 1,000 consumers.[145] A data breach is not a prerequisite for FTC action. Most FTC enforcement actions lead to settlements in which the parties agree to a consent order. Consent orders typically enjoin the company from further violations of section 5 of the FTC Act or other applicable law, and may include civil money penalties and remedial measures designed to enhance the company's data security practices, including requiring independent third-party audits for up to two decades.[146]

3.1.1.2 FTC Safeguards Rule Actions

Although the FTC brings fewer actions under its Safeguards Rule, one notable recent FTC Safeguards Rule enforcement action involved TaxSlayer, LLC.[147] In August 2017, TaxSlayer settled charges that it violated the Safeguards Rule by having inadequate data security measures to prevent hackers from gaining access to 9,000 accounts, allowing the hackers to commit identity theft and obtain fraudulent tax refunds.[148] The FTC alleged that TaxSlayer failed to employ a written information security program until after the hacking had begun, failed to conduct the required risk assessment, and failed to implement adequate information security safeguards, as required by the

144. *See, e.g.*, Compl., United States v. PLS Financial Servs., Inc., No. 1:12-cv-8334 (E.D. Ill. Oct. 17, 2012), https://www.ftc.gov/sites/default/files/documents/cases/2012/11/121107plspaydaycmpt.pdf (alleging unfair and deceptive acts or practices in addition to violations of the Disposal Rule and the Safeguards Rule under the FCRA).

145. *See, e.g.*, Compl., United States v. Rental Research Servs., Inc., No. 09-CV-524 (D. Minn. Mar. 5, 2009), https://www.ftc.gov/sites/default/files/documents/cases/2009/03/090305rrscmpt.pdf.

146. *See, e.g.*, United States v. ChoicePoint, Inc., No. 1:06-CV-198 (N.D. Ga. Feb. 15, 2006), https://www.ftc.gov/sites/default/files/documents/cases/2006/01/stipfinaljudgement.pdf (requiring the company to pay a $10 million civil penalty and $5 million in consumer redress in addition to implementing other data security procedural improvements).

147. Compl., TaxSlayer, LLC, FTC. No. C-4626 (Aug. 29, 2017), https://www.ftc.gov/system/files/documents/cases/1623063_taxslayer_complaint.pdf.

148. *See* Press Release, FTC, Operator of Online Tax Preparation Service Agrees to Settle FTC Charges That it Violated Financial Privacy and Security Rules (Aug. 29, 2017), https://www.ftc.gov/news-events/press-releases/2017/08/operator-online-tax-preparation-service-agrees-settle-ftc-charges.

Safeguards Rule.[149] TaxSlayer settled the case and entered into a consent agreement with the FTC.[150]

Other examples of FTC enforcement actions under the Safeguards Rule include *United States v. PLS Financial Services* (2012)[151] and *In re: SettlementOne Credit Corporation* (2011),[152] both of which resulted in negotiated consent orders.

3.1.2 The "Common Law" of Data Security

Observers view this large and growing body of FTC enforcement activity as forming a "common law" of data security, based on the FTC's case-by-case approach.[153] The FTC relies on its prior enforcement actions, as well as external data security standards,[154] as the baseline for appropriate data security.[155] Because there have been relatively few judicial decisions on data security,[156] financial institutions must navigate FTC complaints and consent orders for guidance relating to their information security programs. In addition, since the requirements of the Safeguards Rule generally are consistent with the FTC's data security enforcement approach under section 5 of the FTC Act, FTC data security enforcement actions and guidance under both provisions are useful for assessing enforcement risk.[157]

Based on this body of FTC enforcement actions, industry observers have identified the following eight best practices regarding data security:

- Limit the collection, retention, and use of sensitive data;
- Restrict access to sensitive data;
- Implement robust authentication procedures;
- Store and transmit sensitive information securely;

149. *See id.*

150. TaxSlayer, LLC, FTC No. C-4626 (Oct. 20, 2017), https://www.ftc.gov/system/files/documents/cases/1623063_c4626_taxslayer_decision_and_order.pdf.

151. *See* Compl., United States v. PLS Financial Servs., Inc., et al., No. 12-cv-08334 (N.D. Ill. Oct. 17, 2012), https://www.ftc.gov/sites/default/files/documents/cases/2012/11/121107plspaydaycmpt.pdf.

152. SettlementOne Credit Corp. et al., FTC No. C-4330 (Aug. 29, 2011), https://www.ftc.gov/sites/default/files/documents/cases/2011/08/110819settlementonecmpt.pdf.

153. Daniel J. Solove & Woodrow Hartzog, *The FTC and the New Common Law of Privacy*, 114 Colum. L. Rev. 583, 586 (2014).

154. *See, e.g.*, FTC, *The NIST Cybersecurity Framework and the FTC* (Andrea Arias, Aug. 31, 2016), https://www.ftc.gov/news-events/blogs/business-blog/2016/08/nist-cybersecurity-framework-ftc; FTC, *Start with Security, A Guide for Business: Lessons Learned from FTC Cases* (June 2015), https://www.ftc.gov/system/files/documents/plain-language/pdf0205-startwithsecurity.pdf.

155. *See* FTC v. Wyndham Worldwide Corp., 799 F.3d 236, 243–44 (3d Cir. 2015) (describing the development of FTC enforcement under section 5 of the FTC Act).

156. Solove & Hartzog, *supra* note 153, at 583, 606.

157. *See, e.g.*, FTC, *Start with Security*, *supra* note 154.

- Implement procedures to identify and address vulnerabilities;
- Develop and test new products and services with privacy and security in mind;
- Require service providers to implement appropriate security measures; and
- Properly secure documents, media, and devices.[158]

These best practices provide a framework for understanding the FTC's data security expectations. Using these best practices as organizing principles, section 3.2 discusses the FTC's data security enforcement actions as they pertain to consumer financial services.

3.2 General Standards Derived from FTC Enforcement Actions

3.2.1 Limit the Collection, Retention, and Use of Sensitive Data

Many FTC enforcement actions involve a company failing to provide adequate protection for sensitive consumer financial information. An effective information security program limits the consumer information the entity receives to solely what is necessary to conduct its business. An entity should collect only information that is necessary, only retain such information for as long as necessary, and only use such information for a proper purpose and in a manner that aligns with its privacy policies.[159]

A financial institution that collects more information than is necessary, for example, by collecting email account passwords in addition to email addresses, can be a more appealing target to hackers and increase the potential damage to consumers from a breach.[160] Additionally, retaining sensitive data for an extended or indefinite amount of time creates an unnecessary risk that can constitute an unfair practice. For example, the FTC filed a complaint against retailer BJ's Wholesale Club for the amplified risk it posed to consumers by retaining, without a business need, credit card information it had collected from the magnetic strips of the cards for thirty days after it was used.[161] The issue was discovered when banks received customer complaints of fraudulent purchases made using counterfeit copies of cards with the

---

158. *See* Kurt Wimmer, Ashden Fein, Catlin M. Meade, & Andrew Vaden, *Data Security Best Practices Derived from FTC § 5 Enforcement Actions* 6 (Washington Legal Foundation, Working Paper No. 199, 2017), https://www.wlf.org/2017/01/13/publishing/data-security-best-practices-derived-from-ftc-%c2%a7-5-enforcement-actions/.

159. *Id.* at 7–9.

160. Compl. at 4–5, United States v. RockYou, Inc., No. 12-CV-1487 (N.D. Cal. Mar. 28, 2012), https://www.ftc.gov/sites/default/files/documents/cases/2012/03/120327rockyoucmpt.pdf.

161. Compl. at 2, BJ's Wholesale Club, Inc., FTC No. C-4148 (Sept. 20, 2005), https://www.ftc.gov/sites/default/files/documents/cases/2005/09/092305comp0423160.pdf; *see also* Compl., Life is Good, Inc., FTC No. C-4218 (Apr. 16, 2008), https://www.ftc.gov/sites/default/files/documents/cases/2008/04/080418complaint.pdf (storing consumer information indefinitely on its network in clear, readable text was an unnecessary risk).

same personal information BJ's had collected, ultimately resulting in several millions of dollars of fraudulent purchases.[162]

Financial institutions should also restrict their use of consumer information to business purposes and should not disclose unnecessary amounts of consumer data. The FTC's actions against two debt brokers, Cornerstone and Company, LLC, and Bayview Solutions, LLC, are illustrative. The companies posted on a public website Excel spreadsheets containing unnecessarily large amounts of unprotected sensitive information of more than 28,000 consumers, including bank account and credit card numbers, birth dates, contact information, and employers' names, in an effort to sell portfolios of consumer debt.[163] The FTC alleged that both companies engaged in unfair acts or practices in violation of section 5 of the FTC Act because the companies "ha[d] no business need to disclose consumers' sensitive personal information in such a public and widespread manner."[164]

Additionally, when sharing or selling consumer information, financial institutions should take reasonable steps to verify their purchasers' identities. Failure to do so has been at issue in multiple cases where companies sold sensitive information directly to identity thieves.[165] In its 2006 action against ChoicePoint, Inc., the FTC alleged that the company did not have reasonable procedures to screen prospective subscribers and consequently turned over consumer reports containing consumer names, Social Security numbers, birth dates, employment information, and credit histories, to buyers with obvious "red flags."[166] ChoicePoint's lax procedures resulted in more than 800 cases of identity theft and the exposure of more than 163,000 consumers' financial records.[167] In addition to alleging violations of the FCRA, the FTC alleged that the breach constituted a deceptive act or practice because ChoicePoint's privacy policy claimed that consumer reports would be accessed "only by those authorized under

162. *BJ's Wholesale Club, Inc.*, *supra* note 161.

163. *See* Compl., Bayview Sols., LLC, No. 1: 14-CV-1479-RC (D.D.C. Oct. 31, 2014), https://www.ftc.gov/system/files/documents/cases/111014bayviewcmp.pdf; Complaint, Cornerstone & Co., LLC, No. 1: 14-CV-1479-RC (D.D.C. Aug. 27, 2014), https://www.ftc.gov/system/files/documents/cases/141001cornerstonecmpt.pdf.

164. Compl. at 6, Bayview Sols., LLC, No. 1: 14-CV-1479-RC (D.D.C. Oct. 31, 2014), https://www.ftc.gov/system/files/documents/cases/111014bayviewcmp.pdf.

165. *See* United States v. ChoicePoint, Inc., No. 1:06-CV-198 (N.D. Ga. Feb. 15, 2006), https://www.ftc.gov/sites/default/files/documents/cases/2006/01/stipfinaljudgement.pdf; United States v. Rental Research Servs., Inc., No. 09-cv-524 (D. Minn. Mar. 5, 2009), https://www.ftc.gov/sites/default/files/documents/cases/2009/03/090305rrsorder.pdf (same); *see also* United States v. Infotrack Info. Servs., Inc., No. 1:14-CV-02054 (N.D. Ill. Mar. 25, 2014), https://www.ftc.gov/system/files/documents/cases/140409infotrackorder_0.pdf (selling consumer reports without making sure buyers have permissible reasons under the FCRA).

166. *See* Compl. at 3–4, United States v. ChoicePoint, Inc., No. 1:06-CV-198 (N.D. Ga. Jan. 30, 2006), https://www.ftc.gov/sites/default/files/documents/cases/2006/01/0523069complaint.pdf.

167. *Id.*

the FCRA."[168] The resulting consent order required ChoicePoint to pay a $10 million civil penalty and $5 million in consumer redress in addition to implementing other data security procedural improvements.[169]

3.2.2 Restrict Access to Sensitive Data

The FTC often files complaints against companies for failure to restrict access to sensitive data. Financial institutions should limit access to consumer data on a need-to-know basis, beginning with appropriate administrative controls on a financial institution's systems.[170] Further, a financial institution's privacy policies should accurately reflect its practices for restricting such access.

Financial institutions also should deploy appropriate network security to protect sensitive data. The FTC brought an action against Wyndham Worldwide after the company failed to use "readily available security measures," that is, by employing firewalls, to limit access among its various hotels' property management systems, its corporate network, and the Internet.[171] As a result, hackers gained access to sensitive information on the company's broader property management system after obtaining access to two hotel computers.[172] Wyndham experienced three separate breaches in less than two years, leading to the compromise of more than 500,000 payment card accounts, many of which were ultimately exported to a domain registered in Russia.[173]

In addition, financial institutions should ensure that their remote access processes have adequate security. Financial institutions should ensure that end users with remote access have adequate antivirus protection.[174] This practice should extend to ensuring that third-party service providers with remote access use appropriate data security measures. For example, the FTC filed a complaint against Premier Capital Lending after a hacker gained access to hundreds of credit reports through a business associate's remote login account, alleging that the company had failed to assess the

---

168. *Id.* at 10.

169. Stipulated Final Judgment and Order, United States v. ChoicePoint, Inc., No. 1:06-CV-198 (N.D. Ga. Feb. 15, 2006), https://www.ftc.gov/sites/default/files/documents/cases/2006/01/stipfinaljudgement.pdf.

170. *See* Compl. at 2–3, *In re* Twitter, Inc., FTC No. C-4316 (Mar. 2, 2011), https://www.ftc.gov/sites/default/files/documents/cases/2011/03/110311twittercmpt.pdf (claiming the company failed to "prevent unauthorized access to nonpublic user information" where it provided administrative control to "almost all" of its employees).

171. Compl. at 10, FTC v. Wyndham Worldwide Corp., No. 2:13-CV-1887-ES-JAD (D.N.J. June 26, 2012), https://www.ftc.gov/sites/default/files/documents/cases/2012/06/120626wyndamhotelscmpt.pdf.

172. *Id.*

173. *Id.* at 15.

174. *See* Compl., FTC v. LifeLock, Inc., No. 2:10-CV-00530-MHM (D. Ariz. Mar. 8, 2010), https://www.ftc.gov/sites/default/files/documents/cases/2010/03/100309lifelockstip.pdf (neglecting to install antivirus or anti-spyware programs on computers used by employees for remote access).

third party's network security and to ensure that the third party had appropriate data security measures.[175]

3.2.3 Implement Robust Authentication Procedures

Restricting access to sensitive information requires robust authentication procedures to ensure that those access privileges are not misused. Financial institutions should implement authentication measures designed to prevent unauthorized persons from obtaining and misusing access privileges. Such measures could include requiring the use of complex passwords and storing those passwords securely,[176] suspending accounts after multiple failed login attempts, and ensuring that authentication measures cannot be easily bypassed.

For instance, the FTC filed a complaint against Lookout Services, a company that contracted with employers to confirm that their new employees' I-9 information complied with immigration laws, for multiple authentication weaknesses that led to an employee of one of the company's customers gaining access to more than 37,000 Social Security numbers stored in the company's database.[177] Lookout allegedly had a number of authentication process failures, including failing to suspend user credentials after a certain number of failed login attempts.[178] The FTC also alleged that the company allowed its system authentication to be bypassed entirely because the location of sensitive information could be surmised by using standard naming conventions within the network.[179]

3.2.4 Store and Transmit Sensitive Information Securely

A frequent theme in FTC enforcement actions is the failure of companies to store and transmit sensitive consumer information securely. Sensitive information should be encrypted when collected, transmitted, and stored using industry-standard

---

175. Compl., Premier Capital Lending, FTC No. C-4241 (Dec. 10, 2008), https://www.ftc.gov/sites/default/files/documents/cases/2008/12/081206pclcmpt.pdf; *see also* Compl., SettlementOne Credit Corp., FTC No. C-4330 (Aug. 17, 2011), https://www.ftc.gov/sites/default/files/documents/cases/2011/08/110819settlementonecmpt.pdf (allowing end users with unverified or inadequate security to access consumer reports through its online portal).

176. Compl. at 4, Twitter, Inc., FTC No. C-4316 (Mar. 2, 2011), https://www.ftc.gov/sites/default/files/documents/cases/2011/03/110311twittercmpt.pdf (faulting Twitter for the use of common dictionary words as administrative passwords and for not encrypting store passwords).

177. *See* Compl. at 2, Lookout Servs., Inc., FTC No. C-4326 (June 15, 2011), https://www.ftc.gov/sites/default/files/documents/cases/2011/06/110615lookoutcmpt.pdf.

178. *Id.*

179. *Id.*

encryption.[180] Moreover, a financial institution's statements—in policies and on its website—should accurately reflect the company's practices with respect to such information. For example, the FTC brought an action against Superior Mortgage Corporation in part because the company allegedly made deceptive claims on its website that "[a]ll information submitted is handled by SSL encryption," despite the fact that once the consumer's information reached the company's server, a service provider decrypted the information and emailed it in clear text to the company.[181]

Additionally, financial institutions should incorporate information security into their web application development. The FTC has brought actions against three companies, HTC America, Credit Karma, and Fandango, because each company's mobile application developer allegedly turned off the SSL certificate validation feature, contrary to iOS and Android guidelines, which led to vulnerabilities exposing millions of consumers' sensitive information to potential "man-in-the-middle" attacks.[182]

3.2.5 Implement Procedures to Identify and Address Vulnerabilities

Financial institutions are responsible for understanding and protecting against vulnerabilities in their networks. A financial institution's lack of awareness of threats to its networks creates greater risks to the security of customer information. Therefore, financial institutions should regularly monitor network traffic and access to databases with sensitive information. For instance, following a breach that exposed information from 130,000 credit and debit cards, the FTC brought an action against restaurant and entertainment company Dave & Buster's for failing to use an intrusion detection system or monitor system logs for suspicious activity.[183] The FTC alleged that these

180. *See* Compl. at 13, United States v. ValueClick, Inc., No. CV08-1711 (C.D. Cal. Mar. 17, 2008), https://www.ftc.gov/sites/default/files/documents/cases/2008/03/080317complaint.pdf (alleging ValueClick, an online advertiser, deceived customers about its data storage practices because it stored sensitive information using "only an insecure form of alphabet substitution" that was less protective than industry standard).

181. Compl. at 3–4, Superior Mortg. Corp., FTC No. C-4153 (Dec. 14, 2005), https://www.ftc.gov/sites/default/files/documents/cases/2005/12/051216comp0523136.pdf; *see also* Compl. at 7, FTC v. 30 Minute Mortg., Inc., No. 03-60021-CIV (S.D. Fla. Nov. 26, 2003), https://www.ftc.gov/sites/default/files/documents/cases/2003/03/30mincmp.pdf (publicly claiming to use SSL encryption but failing to do so).

182. *See* Compl., HTC Am. Inc., FTC No. C-4406 (June 25, 2013), https://www.ftc.gov/sites/default/files/documents/cases/2013/07/130702htccmpt.pdf; Compl., Credit Karma, Inc., No. C-4480 (FTC Aug. 13, 2014), https://www.ftc.gov/system/files/documents/cases/1408creditkarmacmpt.pdf; Compl., Fandango, LLC, FTC No. C-4481 (Aug. 13, 2014), https://www.ftc.gov/system/files/documents/cases/140819fandangocmpt.pdf.

183. Compl. at 1–2, Dave & Buster's Inc., FTC No. C-4291 (May 20, 2010), https://www.ftc.gov/sites/default/files/documents/cases/2010/06/100608davebusterscmpt.pdf.

failures enabled a hacker to connect to the company's network multiple times without authorization and install unauthorized software to intercept the sensitive information.[184]

A financial institution's monitoring activity should also encompass application activity on employees' workstations as certain applications, particularly peer-to-peer software, can increase the risk of unauthorized disclosure of sensitive consumer information.[185] Financial institutions should also implement a process for receiving security vulnerability reports from the public, including third-party researchers and academics. The FTC has noted in multiple cases a company's failure to receive and address such reports, resulting in companies failing to detect their exposure to commonly known data security vulnerabilities.[186]

3.2.6 Develop and Test New Products and Services with Security in Mind

The FTC has emphasized that data security should be incorporated into the development of new products and services at the outset of the development process. Financial institutions should practice security-by-design across all of their products, services, websites, and applications, and security features should be tested to ensure that they protect against commonly known vulnerabilities.

The FTC has filed numerous complaints against companies that fail to test for commonly known vulnerabilities. For example, the FTC filed a complaint against retailer Guess? after it suffered an SQL injection attack in 2002 allowing hackers to gain access to databases containing consumers' credit card information.[187] The complaint pointed out that security experts had warned about such attacks since 1997. The FTC, therefore, alleged that the company's failure to routinely test for such "commonly known or reasonably foreseeable" attacks constituted a violation of section 5 of the FTC Act.[188] For web applications, financial institutions should test for the following vulnerabilities that the FTC has deemed "commonly known and

---

184. *Id.*

185. *See, e.g.*, LabMD, Inc., FTC No. 9357 (July 28, 2016), https://www.ftc.gov/system/files/documents/cases/160729labmdorder.pdf; Franklin's Budget Car Sales, Inc., FTC No. C-4371 (Oct. 3, 2012), https://www.ftc.gov/sites/default/files/documents/cases/2012/10/121026franklinautomalldo.pdf; EPN, Inc., FTC No. C-4370 (Oct. 3, 2012), https://www.ftc.gov/sites/default/files/documents/cases/2012/10/121026epndo.pdf.

186. *See, e.g.*, Compl., HTC Am. Inc., FTC No. C-4406 (June 25, 2013), https://www.ftc.gov/sites/default/files/documents/cases/2013/07/130702htccmpt.pdf; Compl., Fandango, LLC, FTC No. C-4481 (Aug. 13, 2014), https://www.ftc.gov/system/files/documents/cases/140819fandangocmpt.pdf.

187. Compl. at 3–4, Guess?, Inc., FTC No. C-4091 (July 30, 2003), https://www.ftc.gov/sites/default/files/documents/cases/2003/08/guesscomp.pdf.

188. *Id.; see also* Petco Animal Supplies, Inc., FTC No. C-4133 (Mar. 4, 2005) (allegations based on failing to take reasonable and appropriate measures to protect databases and data against "commonly known or reasonably foreseeable" third-party attacks), https://www.ftc.gov/sites/default/files/documents/cases/2005/03/050308comp0323221.pdf.

foreseeable": cross-site scripting, cross-site request forgery, buffer overflow, multiple password disclosure, and broken account and session management vulnerabilities.[189]

3.2.7 *Require Service Providers to Implement Appropriate Security Measures*

Financial institutions remain responsible for sensitive data that they make available to third parties. Therefore, prior to engaging service providers or otherwise allowing third parties access to its networks or sensitive data, a financial institution should ensure that the third party has adequate controls in place to protect that data in accordance with best practices. For example, Upromise, Inc., a membership reward service aimed at consumers saving for college, used a toolbar developed by a service provider on its website that impermissibly collected information on consumers' online activities, including account numbers and passwords, and transmitted it in unencrypted text.[190] The FTC filed a section 5 complaint against the company for failing to "ensure its service provider employed reasonable and appropriate measures to protect consumer information."[191]

3.2.8 *Properly Secure Documents, Media, and Devices*

The FTC also brings enforcement actions involving the physical security of sensitive information. Financial institutions should securely store sensitive records (whether in paper or electronic form), ensure the secure transport of such records, and properly dispose of such records when no longer needed.

The FTC has on several occasions pursued section 5 claims against companies in conjunction with alleged violations of the Disposal Rule.[192] These cases have typically involved companies that dispose of consumer report information in publicly

189. *See* Compl. at 6, United States v. RockYou, Inc., No. 12-CV-1487 (N.D. Cal. Mar. 26, 2012), https://www.ftc.gov/sites/default/files/documents/cases/2012/03/120327rockyoucmpt.pdf (cross site scripting); Compl. at 5, ASUSTeK Computer Inc., FTC. No. C-4587 (July 18, 2016), https://www.ftc.gov/system/files/documents/cases/1607asustekcmpt.pdf (cross-site request forgery, buffer overflow, and multiple password disclosure); Compl. at 3, MTS, Inc., FTC No. C-4110 (May 28, 2004), https://www.ftc.gov/sites/default/files/documents/cases/2004/06/040602comp0323209.pdf (broken account and session management vulnerabilities).

190. Compl. at 2–3, 5, Upromise, Inc., FTC No. C-4351 (Mar. 27, 2012), https://www.ftc.gov/sites/default/files/documents/cases/2012/04/120403upromisecmpt.pdf.

191. *Id.*

192. 15 U.S.C. § 1681w; *see* 16 C.F.R. § 682.3 (FTC regulation implementing the Disposal Rule).

accessible places, such as an unsecured, public dumpster.[193] The FTC also brought an action against a business owner for improperly storing boxes of consumer reports in his garage.[194]

In addition, the FTC has pursued enforcement for the improper transfer of physical documents containing sensitive information. In an action against CBR Systems, Inc. following a breach, the FTC claimed the company created unnecessary risks by allowing an employee to transport portable media containing unencrypted sensitive customer information in the employee's car between CBR facilities.[195] Backup tapes, a laptop, and a flash drive were stolen from the employee's car leading to the breach that exposed the Social Security, credit card, and debit card numbers of approximately 300,000 consumers.[196]

3.3 Enforcement by Other Agencies

As noted above, the federal banking agencies and the NCUA apply their own Safeguards Rules and Guidelines and safety and soundness authority to data security issues. These agencies tend to resolve data security deficiencies through supervisory actions or nonpublic enforcement actions, although there have been at least occasional public actions enforcing the Interagency Guidelines.[197]

In 2016, the CFPB brought its first public enforcement action involving data security against online payment platform Dwolla.[198] Following the example of the FTC's "deceptive" theory of enforcement, the CFPB invoked its authority under the Dodd-Frank Act to bring enforcement actions against entities engaged in any unfair,

193. *See* Compl., United States v. Am. United Mortg. Co., No. 07-cv-7064 (N.D. Ill. Dec. 17, 2007), https://www.ftc.gov/sites/default/files/documents/cases/2007/12/071217americanunitedmrtgcmplt.pdf; Compl., Nation's Title Agency, FTC No. C-4161 (June 19, 2006), https://www.ftc.gov/sites/default/files/documents/cases/2006/06/0523117nationstitle_complaint.pdf; Compl., FTC v. Navone, No. 2:08-cv-01842 (D. Nev. Dec. 30, 2009), https://www.ftc.gov/sites/default/files/documents/cases/2009/01/090121navonecmpt.pdf; Compl., United States v. PLS Financial Servs., Inc., No. 1:12-cv-8334 (E.D. Ill. Oct. 17, 2012), https://www.ftc.gov/sites/default/files/documents/cases/2012/11/121107plspaydaycmpt.pdf.

194. Compl., FTC v. Navone, No. 2:08-cv-01842 (D. Nev. Dec. 30, 2009), https://www.ftc.gov/sites/default/files/documents/cases/2009/01/090121navonecmpt.pdf.

195. *CBR Systems, Inc.*, 155 F.T.C. 841 (2013).

196. *Id.*

197. *See, e.g.*, First Horizon Home Loan Corp., Stipulation and Consent Order for Civil Money Penalty, OCC Enforcement Decision 2005-78 (June 30, 2005), https://www.occ.gov/static/enforcement-actions/ea2005-78.pdf.

198. *See* Consent Order, Dwolla, Inc., No. 2016-CFPB-0007 (Feb. 27, 2016), http://files.consumerfinance.gov/f/201603_cfpb_consent-order-dwolla-inc.pdf.

deceptive, or abusive act or practice (UDAAP) with regard to consumer financial products or services.[199]

The CFPB alleged that Dwolla made deceptive statements regarding its data security practices and the safety of its online payment system.[200] Specifically, the CFPB maintained that, contrary to Dwolla's claims that its data security practices "exceed industry standards," and that all data is "securely encrypted and stored," Dwolla did not encrypt all sensitive consumer information and failed to employ reasonable data protection measures.[201] The CFPB highlighted Dwolla's delayed adoption of a written data security plan, failure to conduct regular risk assessments to identify risks to consumer information, and provision of "little to no data-security training" to employees.[202] The resulting consent order required Dwolla to pay a $100,000 penalty in addition to correcting its data security practices.[203] It remains to be seen how aggressive the CFPB will be in using its UDAAP authority to enforce data security compliance.

199. Dodd-Frank Act, Title X, Subtitle C, Sec. 1031; PL 111-203 (July 21, 2010). The CFPB definitions for "unfair" and "deceptive" are nearly identical to the FTC definitions discussed in section 1. *See* CFPB, Consumer Laws and Regulations: CFPB Manual (UDAAP) v.2 (Oct. 2012), at 1, http://www.cfpaguide.com/portalresource/Exam%20Manual%20v%202%20-%20UDAAP.pdf.

200. *See* Consent Order, *Dwolla, Inc.*, *supra* note 198.

201. *Id.* at 6–7.

202. *Id.* at 7–8.

203. *Id.* at 16.

CHAPTER

6

The Fair Credit Reporting Act

Steve Forry

1. Scope of This Chapter

This chapter discusses the federal Fair Credit Reporting Act[1] (FCRA), and its implementing regulations, Regulation V.[2] The FCRA became effective on April 25, 1971, following congressional findings that (1) the banking system depends upon fair and accurate credit reporting, the absence of which undermines public confidence; (2) an elaborate mechanism had developed to investigate and evaluate credit worthiness, credit standing, credit capacity, character, and general reputation of consumers; (3) consumer reporting agencies had assumed a vital role in assembling and evaluating consumer credit and other information; and (4) consumer reporting agencies must exercise their grave responsibilities with fairness, impartiality, and a respect for consumer privacy.[3] Thus, the FCRA was intended to require that consumer reporting agencies adopt reasonable procedures to meet the needs of commerce for consumer credit, personnel, insurance, and other information in a manner that is fair and equitable to the consumer, with regard to the confidentiality, accuracy, relevance, and proper utilization of such information.[4]

---

1. 15 U.S.C. §§ 1681–1681x (2019). The FCRA protections are variously referenced by their United States Code section numbers (prefix *Id.* § 1681) and their uncodified section numbers. A crosswalk between these two references is provided at the end of this chapter.

2. 12 C.F.R. § 1022.1-1022.141 (2017).

3. 15 U.S.C. § 1681(a).

4. *Id.* § 1681(b).

Despite the title of the statute, the FCRA is not limited to consumer "credit" reporting. Instead, as discussed in more detail below, the FCRA's requirements flow from creation and use of "consumer reports," a much broader collection of consumer information that involves information bearing on a consumer's credit (including credit worthiness, credit standing, and credit capacity) as well as a consumer's character, general reputation, personal characteristics or mode of living, which information may be used for various consumer purposes.

2. The Roster

The FCRA revolves around the creation and use of consumer reports by four key players: the consumer, the furnisher of information who provides information about the consumer, the consumer reporting agency that creates the consumer report about the consumer, and the user who obtains a consumer report for use relative to the consumer. More specifically:

1. The *consumer*, defined as "an individual."[5]
2. The *consumer reporting agency*, defined as "any person[6] which, for monetary fees, dues, or on a cooperative nonprofit basis, regularly engages in whole or in part in the practice of assembling or evaluating consumer credit information or other information on consumers for the purpose of furnishing consumer reports to third parties, and which uses any means or facility of interstate commerce for the purpose of preparing or furnishing consumer reports."[7]
3. The *furnisher* of consumer information, a term that is not defined in the statute but means any person that provides consumer information to a consumer reporting agency.[8]
4. The *user* of a consumer report, a term that is not defined in the statute but means any person that uses a consumer report relative to a potential or actual transaction with a consumer.

Each consumer reporting agency, furnisher, and user has specific obligations under the statute. The statute conversely provides consumers a wide range of rights relative to each of consumer reporting agency, furnisher, and user.

5. *Id.* § 1681a(c).

6. A "person" includes individuals, entities, and governmental departments and agencies. *Id.* § 1681a(b).

7. *Id.* § 1681a(f).

8. *See, e.g., id.* § 1681s-2 (applying definition to any person who furnishes information relating to a consumer to a consumer reporting agency); Regulation V, 12 C.F.R. § 1022.41(c) (in the context of accuracy guidelines, defined as any entity that furnishes information relating to consumers to one or more consumer reporting agencies for inclusion in a consumer report).

In the typical transaction cycle, a consumer enters into a transaction with a person, which results in some information about the person's experience with the consumer. That person (a furnisher) may furnish that consumer information to a consumer reporting agency. The consumer reporting agency may convert that consumer information into a consumer report and sell that consumer report to a user who is considering entering into a transaction with the consumer. Following that user's transaction, the user may report its experiences to a consumer reporting agency, meaning the user has now become a furnisher and the consumer reporting agency now has two sets of information for consumer reports on the consumer.

3. Key Definitions

3.1 Consumer Report

A *consumer report* means

> any written, oral, or other communication of any information by a consumer reporting agency bearing on a consumer's credit worthiness, credit standing, credit capacity, character, general reputation, personal characteristics, or mode of living which is used or expected to be used or collected in whole or in part for the purpose of serving as a factor in establishing the consumer's eligibility for (1) credit or insurance to be used primarily for personal, family, or household purposes; (2) employment purposes; or (3) any other purpose authorized under Section 604 of this title.[9]

Certain information is expressly *excluded* from the definition of a consumer report—that is, if the following situations apply, the information does not qualify as a consumer report: (1) first-hand information (a report containing information solely as to transactions/experiences between the consumer and the person making the report);[10] (2) affiliate sharing (information that may be shared as between persons related by common ownership or affiliated by corporate control);[11] (3) approval of a specific extension of credit (authorization or approval of a specific extension of credit directly or indirectly by the issuer of a credit card or similar device);[12] (4) third-party decisions regarding specific extensions of credit (any report in which a person who has been requested by a third party to make a specific extension of credit directly or indirectly to a consumer conveys his or her decision with respect to such request, if the third party advises the consumer of the name and address of

9. 15 U.S.C. § 1681a(d)(1).
10. *Id.* § 1681a(d)(2)(A)(i).
11. *See* section 9.3 later in the chapter for a discussion of affiliate sharing.
12. *Id.* § 1681a(d)(2)(B).

the person to whom the request was made, and such person makes the disclosures to the consumer required under section 615);[13] or (5) certain specified communications by employment agencies engaged in procuring jobs for applicants or employees, as long as prescribed disclosures and consents are performed,[14] or consumer reports in the context of investigating employee misconduct.[15]

3.2 Investigative Consumer Report

An *investigative consumer report* is a consumer report regarding a consumer's character, general reputation, personal characteristics, or mode of living where such information is procured through personal interviews with neighbors, friends, or associates of the consumer.[16] Investigative consumer reports are more particularly discussed in section 6.3.

3.3 Consumer Reporting Agency

A consumer reporting agency is

> any person which, for monetary fees, dues, or on a cooperative nonprofit basis, regularly engages in whole or in part in the practice of assembling or evaluating consumer credit information or other information on consumers for the purpose of furnishing consumer reports to third parties, and which uses any means or facility of interstate commerce for the purpose of preparing or furnishing consumer reports.[17]

Two particular types of consumer reporting agency carry unique obligations under the statute. Nationwide consumer reporting agencies "regularly engage in the practice of assembling or evaluating, and maintaining, for the purpose of furnishing consumer reports to third parties bearing on a consumer's credit worthiness, credit standing, or credit capacity, each of the following regarding consumers residing nationwide: (1) public record information and (2) credit account information from

---

13. *Id.* § 1681a(d)(2)(C). This issue frequently arises in the context of a retailer attempting to obtain credit from an outside source for a consumer. As long as the retailer informs the consumer of the name and address of the creditor and (if the application is denied) the creditor provides appropriate adverse action notice(s) to the consumer, then the creditor's communicated decision about the credit application is not a consumer report. *See* Federal Trade Commission (FTC), *40 Years of Experience with the Fair Credit Reporting Act, an FTC Staff Report with Summary of Interpretations* 25 (July 2011), https://www.ftc.gov/reports/40-years-experience-fair-credit-reporting-act-ftc-staff-report-summary-interpretations.

14. 15 U.S.C. § 1681a(d)(2)(D), (o).

15. *Id.* § 1681a(d)(2)(D), (y).

16. *Id.* § 1681a(e).

17. *Id.* § 1681a(f).

persons who furnish that information regularly and in the ordinary course of business."[18] The most well-known nationwide consumer reporting agencies are TransUnion, LLC, Experian Information Solutions, Inc., and Equifax Information Services, LLC.

A nationwide specialty consumer reporting agency is a consumer reporting agency "that compiles and maintains files on consumers on a nationwide basis relating to (1) medical records or payments, (2) residential or tenant history, (3) check writing history, (4) employment history, or (5) insurance claims."[19] The Consumer Financial Protection Bureau (CFPB or Bureau) periodically produces a list of nationwide consumer reporting agencies and nationwide specialty consumer reporting agencies.[20]

3.4 Adverse Action

The statute defines *adverse action* in two ways. First, the statute gives the term the same meaning as in section 701(d)(6) of the Equal Credit Opportunity Act (ECOA), which is focused on credit transactions.[21] However, the FCRA is not limited to credit transactions, so the FCRA expands the definition of *adverse action* to include consumer involvement in: (1) insurance (including denials, cancellations, increased charges, reduced benefits or terms);[22] (2) employment (including denial of employment or other decisions for employment purposes[23] that adversely affect any current or prospective employee);[24] (3) license or benefit granted by government (including denials, cancellations, increased charges, or other unfavorable change in the terms of

---

18. *Id.* § 1681a(p).

19. *Id.* § 1681a(x).

20. *See* CFPB, *List of Consumer Reporting Companies* (2020), https://files.consumerfinance.gov/f/documents/cfpb_consumer-reporting-companies-list.pdf.

21. 15 U.S.C. § 1681a(k)(1)(A); 15 U.S.C. § 1691(d)(6) (2012); 12 C.F.R. § 202.2(c)(1)(i).

22. 15 U.S.C. § 1681a(k)(1)(B)(i).

23. The FTC has opined that the term "employment purposes" is broader than employment and may include persons acting as independent contractors, agents, and volunteers. *See* FTC, *40 Years of Experience, supra* note 13, at 32 (noting that the phrase "employment purposes" applies to a trucking company that obtains consumer reports on independent contractors, a title insurance company that obtains consumer reports on agents with whom it contracts, and a nonprofit organization staffed in whole or in part by volunteers) (citing Hoke v. Retail Credit Corp., 521 F. 2d 1079, 1082 (4th Cir. 1975); Fed. Trade Comm'n, Opinion Letter on Applicability of FCRA to Bona Fide Independent Contractor Relationship (Feb. 23, 1998); Fed. Trade Comm'n, Opinion Letter on Applicability of FCRA to Contractors Selling Title Insurance (Oct. 27, 1998). *See also* Fed. Trade Comm'n, Opinion Letter on Applicability of Rule Regarding Employment Purposes to Employees of a Defense Contractor (July 24, 1986). *But see* Walker, Jr. v. RealHome Services and Solutions, Inc., No. 1:18-CV-03044, 2019 WL 7944337, *1 (N.D. Ga. Aug. 9, 2019) (holding that the FCRA definition of "employment purposes" does not apply to independent contractors, citing cases).

24. 15 U.S.C. § 1681a(k)(1)(B)(ii).

any license or benefit described in section 604(a)(3)(D));[25] and (4) catch-all transactions (any action or determination that is adverse to the consumer and made in connection with a consumer-initiated application or transaction, or in connection with a review of a consumer's account per section 604(a)(3)(F)(ii)).[26]

4. Permissible Purposes to Procure a Consumer Report

The statute prescribes the circumstances under which a CRA may supply a consumer report to a user,[27] and prohibits a user from procuring a consumer report unless the circumstances for procurement fall within the prescribed list.[28] The permissible purposes are an exclusive list, and practitioners should consult the statute in each instance to confirm whether a permissible purpose is present.[29]

The most frequently cited permissible purposes to procure a consumer report are (1) in response to a court order or subpoena issued in connection with federal grand jury proceedings;[30] (2) in accordance with the written instructions of the consumer;[31] (3) if the CRA has reason to believe that the person requesting the consumer report (a) intends to use the information in connection with a credit transaction involving the consumer on whom the information is to be furnished and involving the extension of credit to or review or collection of an account of, the consumer,[32] or (b) intends to use the information for employment purposes,[33] or (c) intends to use the information in connection with the underwriting of insurance involving the consumer,[34] or (d) intends to use the information, as a potential investor or servicer, or current insurer, in connection with a valuation of, or an assessment of the credit or prepayment risks associated with, an existing credit obligation;[35] or (4) "otherwise has a legitimate business need for the information" (a) in connection with a business transaction that

25. *Id.* § 1681a(k)(1)(B)(iii).

26. *Id.* § 1681a(k)(1)(B)(iv).

27. *Id.* § 1681b(a).

28. *Id.* § 1681b(f).

29. *Id.* § 1681b(a) (A consumer reporting agency may furnish a consumer report for the listed reasons "and no other.").

30. *Id.* § 1681b(a)(1).

31. *Id.* § 1681b(a)(2).

32. *Id.* § 1681b(a)(3)(A).

33. *Id.* § 1681b(a)(3)(B). *See also* additional requirements in the context of employment, at *id.* § 1681b(b).

34. *Id.* § 1681b(a)(3)(C).

35. *Id.* § 1681b(a)(3)(E).

is initiated by the consumer,[36] or (b) to review an account to determine whether the consumer continues to meet the terms of the account.[37]

Notably, it is generally impermissible to procure a consumer report solely for purposes of marketing to the affected consumer. However, two distinct exceptions to that rule exist. First, a user may obtain information about a consumer (where the consumer has not initiated a transaction with the user) for purposes of prescreening for a firm offer of credit or insurance.[38] This opportunity is only available if all of the following are effective: (1) the consumer reporting agency must first comply with section 604(e) and its allowance for the consumer to request exclusion from prescreened lists;[39] (2) the consumer must not have elected to be removed from prescreened lists pursuant to section 604(e);[40] (3) the consumer must be more than twenty-one years old or, if younger than twenty-one, the consumer must have consented to being included in the consumer report;[41] and (4) the consumer report may only include the consumer's name and address, an identifier that is not unique to the consumer and used by the user only to verify the consumer's identity, and other information regarding the consumer that does not disclose the consumer's relationships with particular creditors or other entities.[42] Finally, effective September 2018, all consumer reporting agencies must establish a web page (in addition to other means) allowing a consumer to opt out of prescreened lists.[43]

Second, an affiliate of a user may use a consumer report for marketing purposes in certain circumstances; see discussion in section 9.3.2.

5. Adverse Actions Based in Part or in Whole on a Consumer Report

One of the FCRA's most prominent features is the protection of consumers surrounding adverse actions taken in whole or in part based upon a consumer report.[44]

36. *Id.* § 1681b(a)(3)(F)(i).

37. *Id.* § 1681b(a)(3)(F)(ii).

38. *Id.* § 1681b(c)(1)(B). *See id.* § 1681(a)(l) for a definition of "firm offer of credit or insurance."

39. *Id.* § 1681b(c)(B)(ii).

40. *Id.* § 1681b(c)(B)(iii). Section 604(e) prescribes the system that a consumer reporting agency must implement to facilitate a consumer's election to be excluded from prescreened lists, the manner in which the consumer notifies the consumer reporting agency, and how the consumer reporting agency must respond. A consumer's election to be excluded from prescreened lists lasts for five years. *See id.* § 1681b(e)(3)(A).

41. *Id.* § 1681b(c)(1)(B)(iv).

42. *Id.* § 1681b(c)(2)(A)–(C).

43. *Id.* § 1681c-1(i)(6).

44. *See* section 3.4 for a definition of adverse action.

5.1 Requirements for Adverse Action Notice

The FCRA seeks to ensure that a consumer receives notice that an adverse action may occur if the action is based, at least in part, on a consumer report.[45] Specifically, the user must give oral, written, or electronic notice: (1) of the adverse action;[46] (2) of the name, address, and telephone number of the consumer reporting agency that furnished the consumer report (including a toll-free telephone number if the consumer reporting agency is a nationwide consumer reporting agency);[47] (3) including a statement that the listed consumer reporting agency did not make the decision to take the adverse action and is unable to provide the consumer any specific reasons why the adverse action was taken;[48] (4) including notice of the consumer's right to a free copy of a consumer report under section 612, and of the consumer's sixty-day period to obtain such free copy;[49] and (5) including notice of the consumer's right to dispute the accuracy or completeness of information within the consumer report through communication to the consumer reporting agency, pursuant to section 611.[50]

Additional notices are required if the adverse action is taken based on a credit score (as defined by section 609(f)(2)(A)).[51] In that instance, the user must give specific written or electronic (i.e., not oral) notices to the consumer, as detailed in the statute.[52]

Finally, additional notice is required if a user takes adverse action against a consumer based on consumer report information received from an affiliate.[53]

5.2 Pre-Adverse Action Notices Relating to Consumer Reports for Employment Purposes

In the context of employment, section 604(b)(3) requires the user to give certain notices to the consumer "before taking any adverse action based in whole or in part on the consumer report"—the *pre-adverse action notice.* As one court described it, "the clear purpose of the pre-adverse action notice requirement is to afford employees time to discuss reports with employers or otherwise respond before action is taken."[54] Specifically, the user must provide to the consumer: (1) a copy of the consumer report

45. 15 U.S.C. § 1681m(a).

46. *Id.* § 1681m(a)(1).

47. *Id.* § 1681m(a)(3)(A).

48. *Id.* § 1681m(a)(3)(B).

49. *Id.* § 1681m(a)(4)(A).

50. *Id.* § 1681m(a)(4)(B).

51. *Id.* § 1681m(a)(2).

52. *Id.* § 1681m(a)(2)(A), (B).

53. *Id.* § 1681m(b), generally. Affiliate-sharing rules are discussed in section 9.3.

54. Goode v. LexisNexis Risk & Info. Analytics Grp., Inc., 848 F. Supp. 2d 532, 537 (E.D. Pa. 2012) (quoting Lynne B. Barr & Barbara J. Ellis, *The New FCRA, An Assessment of the First Year*, 54 Bus. Law. 1343, 1348 (1999)).

that the user relied upon and (2) a copy of the FCRA Summary of Your Rights as prescribed by the CFPB from time to time.[55]

The statute only prescribes that this pre-adverse action notice be given before adverse action is taken; the statute does not prescribe the specific period of time that a user must allow.[56] The Federal Trade Commission (FTC) has advised that the period must be a "reasonable" period depending on the particular circumstances.[57] The FTC has opined that five business days appeared reasonable in certain circumstances.[58] Courts have reached divergent results on the issue.[59]

Subsections 604(b)(2)(B) and (C) detail somewhat different requirements relative to applicants for employment in a position over which the Secretary of Transportation has supervision.[60]

6. Consumer Reporting Agency Obligations

The FCRA was founded on restraining the activities of consumer reporting agencies. It is unsurprising, then, that consumer reporting agencies retain the most obligations

55. 15 U.S.C. § 1681b(b)(3)(A)(i)–(ii). The CFPB most recently amended the Summary of Your Rights in September 2018, and users need to ensure they are using the most recent form. *See* Summaries of Rights Under the Fair Credit Reporting Act (Regulation V), 83 Fed. Reg. 47,027, 47,038 (Sept. 18, 2018) (interim final rule).

56. *See* FTC, *40 Years of Experience*, *supra* note 13, at 52–53, citing Fed. Trade Comm'n, Opinion Letter on Whether Compliance with Section 615 is Required after Compliance with Section 604 (June 27, 1997), Fed. Trade Comm'n, Opinion Letter on Compliance with FCRA for Applicants or Current Employees (Dec.18, 1997), Fed. Trade Comm'n, Opinion Letter on Application of FCRA (Feb. 11, 1998), and Fed. Trade Comm'n, Opinion Letter on Application of FCRA (June 11, 1998).

57. *Id.*

58. Fed. Trade Comm'n, Opinion Letter on Whether Compliance with Section 615 is Required after Compliance with Section 604 (June 27, 1997) (also noting that more time may be required in other circumstances).

59. *See, e.g.*, Beverly v. Wal-Mart Stores, Inc., 2008 WL 149032, at *4 (E.D. Va. Jan. 11, 2008) (denying defendant's summary judgment motion and holding that five calendar days may not be sufficient where a holiday weekend intervened); Moore v. Rite Aid Hdqtrs. Corp., 2015 WL 3444227, at *6 (E.D. Pa. May 29, 2015) (denying defendant's motion to dismiss because four business days may not suffice); Reardon v. ClosetMaid Corp., 2013 WL 6231606, at *13 (W.D. Pa. Dec. 2, 2013) (denying defendant's summary judgment motion that four business days to some plaintiffs sufficed, but granting the same motion that eight business days sufficed for other plaintiffs); Johnson v. ADP Screening & Selection Serv., Inc., 768 F.Supp.2d 979, 984 (D. Minn. 2011) (noting that a thirty-day waiting period would be an "absurd result," but ten business days was sufficient).

60. 15 U.S.C. § 1681b(b)(2)(B)(i)–(ii), (3)(B)(i). *See also* FTC, *40 Years of Experience*, *supra* note 13, at 52.

under the statute. This section discusses the consumer reporting agency's principal obligations.

6.1 Permissible Purpose to Transmit a Consumer Report to a User

One of the foundations of the FCRA's consumer protections is the requirement that a consumer reporting agency may not transmit a consumer report to a user unless the consumer reporting agency has confirmed that the user has a permissible purpose for procuring the consumer report.[61] The statute's prohibition on transmitting a consumer report in any other circumstance is patent: "Subject to subsection (c) of this section, any [consumer reporting agency] may furnish a consumer report under the following circumstances *and no other*."[62]

Consumer reporting agencies confirm the user's intent by obtaining a certification from the user that identifies the user, certifies the purposes for requesting the consumer report, and certifies that the user will not use the consumer report for any other purpose.[63] The certification may be general or specific.[64] The consumer reporting agency must maintain "reasonable procedures" designed to avoid violations of the permissible purposes requirement.[65] If the consumer reporting agency has any "reasonable grounds for believing that the consumer report will not be used for a [permissible purpose]," the consumer reporting agency may not furnish the consumer report.[66]

6.2 Content of Consumer Reports

Section 605 prescribes the content of consumer reports, and consumer reporting agencies must maintain "reasonable procedures" designed to avoid any violations of that section.[67] Section 605 begins by listing information that is prohibited from inclusion in a consumer report:[68] (1) bankruptcies more than ten years old;[69] (2) court

61. *See* discussion of permissible purposes at section 4.

62. 15 U.S.C. § 1681b(a) (emphasis added).

63. *Id.* § 1681e(a).

64. *Id.* § 1681b(f)(2).

65. *Id.* § 1681e(a).

66. *Id.*

67. *Id.*

68. The FTC has opined that these prohibitions apply only to information that casts the consumer in a negative light; neutral or positive information does not appear to be governed by these prohibitions. *See* FTC, *40 Years of Experience*, *supra* note 13, at 55.

69. 15 U.S.C. § 1681c(a)(1). If a consumer reporting agency reports bankruptcy information that falls within the ten-year period, the consumer report must identify the Title 11 Chapter under which the bankruptcy petition was filed and, if the bankruptcy petition was withdrawn before final judgment, shall note that fact upon receiving documentation sufficient to certify such withdrawal. *Id.* § 1681c(d).

records of civil suits, civil judgments, or arrest records that are either more than seven years old or past the statute of limitations;[70] (3) paid tax liens that are more than seven years old;[71] (4) accounts placed for collection or charged to profit and loss, which are more than seven years old;[72] (5) certain medical information;[73] and (6) a catch-all category (excluding criminal convictions—for which there is no time limit on reporting[74]—"[a]ny other adverse item of information . . . which antedates the [consumer report] by more than seven years.").[75]

If the consumer report is a credit report, the above prohibitions (other than the prohibition of medical information reporting, which is never exempted) are inapplicable if the credit report will be used in connection with (1) a credit transaction reasonably expected to involve a principal amount of $150,000 or more, or (2) underwriting of life insurance reasonably expected to involve a face amount of $150,000 or more, or (3) employment of an individual at an annual salary reasonably expected to be $75,000 or more.[76]

If the consumer report includes any credit score or other risk score or predictor about the consumer, and if one key factor that adversely affected the score was the number of enquiries regarding the consumer, the report must "clearly and conspicuously" give notice of that fact.[77]

If a consumer reporting agency is notified that a consumer voluntarily closed a credit account, the consumer reporting agency must indicate that fact in any consumer report involving that account.[78] If a furnisher notifies a consumer reporting agency that a consumer disputes the accuracy or completeness of information in a consumer report, the consumer reporting agency must indicate that dispute on each consumer report containing the disputed information.[79]

6.3 Investigative Consumer Reports

A consumer reporting agency is prohibited from producing an *investigative consumer report* unless the consumer reporting agency has received the user's certification

---

70. *Id.* § 1681c(a)(2).

71. *Id.* § 1681c(a)(3).

72. *Id.* § 1681c(a)(4). Section 1681c(c)(1) prescribes that the seven-year period for collections and charge offs begins *after* the 180-day period that starts on the first date of delinquency.

73. *Id.* § 1681c(a)(6).

74. *See* FTC, *40 Years of Experience, supra* note 13, at 57.

75. 15 U.S.C. § 1681c(a)(5).

76. *Id.* § 1681c(b)(1)–(3).

77. *Id.* § 1681c(d)(2) (but noting this requirement does not apply to a check services company acting as such).

78. *Id.* § 1681c(e).

79. *Id.* § 1681e(f).

pursuant to section 606(a)(2).[80] If the user intends to use the investigative consumer report for employment purposes, a consumer reporting agency may not make any inquiry if the inquiry by an employer would violate any equal employment opportunity law or regulation.[81]

Investigative consumer reports also impose additional verification requirements on consumer reporting agencies. Unless exempted under section 613, a consumer reporting agency may not include in an investigative consumer report any public record information about arrests, indictments, convictions, civil judicial action, tax liens, or outstanding judgments unless the consumer reporting agency has verified the accuracy of that information within the preceding thirty days.[82]

Although investigative consumer reports are characterized primarily by interviews of acquaintances of the consumer, a consumer reporting agency may not include adverse information about the consumer procured through personal interviews of neighbors, friends, associates, or acquaintances of the consumer unless (1) the consumer reporting agency has followed "reasonable procedures" to confirm the information, from an additional source with personal knowledge of the information, *or* (2) the person interviewed is the best possible source of information.[83]

Finally, if a consumer reporting agency prepares an investigative consumer report that contains adverse information about the consumer, the consumer reporting agency may not include that adverse information in a subsequent consumer report without verifying that the adverse information remains accurate, unless the subsequent consumer report is prepared within three months after the initial investigative consumer report was furnished.[84]

6.4 Accuracy and Completeness of Consumer Reports

The consumer reporting agency must also maintain "reasonable procedures" to "assure maximum possible accuracy" of the information concerning an affected consumer.[85] Consumers have two avenues to challenge information within a consumer report as inaccurate or incomplete—an appeal to the consumer reporting agency that produced the consumer report or appeal to the furnisher that provided the allegedly inaccurate or incomplete information. This section addresses the appeal to the consumer reporting agency; a consumer's appeal to a furnisher is addressed in section 7.4.1.

80. *Id.* § 1681d(d)(1).
81. *Id.* § 1681d(d)(2).
82. *Id.* § 1681d(d)(3).
83. *Id.* § 1681d(d)(4)(A)–(B).
84. *Id.* § 1681l.
85. *Id.* § 1681e(b).

6.5 Reinvestigation of Disputed Information

If a consumer challenges the completeness or accuracy of information contained in a consumer reporting agency's file on the consumer, the consumer reporting agency must conduct a "reasonable reinvestigation" to ascertain the accuracy and completeness of the information.[86] Following the reinvestigation, the consumer reporting agency must record the current status of the disputed information, or delete the item from the file, and do so within thirty days of the date on which the consumer reporting agency received the consumer's dispute.[87] The thirty-day period may only be extended if the consumer provides the consumer reporting agency additional relevant information during those thirty days—in that case, the period may be extended up to fifteen additional days.[88] However, the additional fifteen days does not apply if, during the initial thirty days, the consumer reporting agency determines that the consumer's dispute is meritorious.[89]

6.6 Seeking Information from the Furnisher

Part of the consumer reporting agency's reinvestigation obligation is to seek confirmation from the furnisher that provided the disputed information. To that end, the consumer reporting agency must, within five business days after receiving the consumer's dispute, give notice of the dispute to the furnisher, which notice must include the information provided by the consumer and all other relevant information that might assist the furnisher's own investigation.[90]

6.6.1 Irrelevant or Frivolous Consumer Disputes

Some consumer disputes are patently non-meritorious. A consumer reporting agency may terminate a reinvestigation if it reasonably determines that the dispute is frivolous or irrelevant, including if the consumer failed to provide sufficient information to investigate the dispute.[91] In that event, the consumer reporting agency must notify the consumer of the termination of the reinvestigation within five business days after reaching that conclusion.[92] That notice should be mailed (unless the consumer authorized other means of communication), and must include the reasons for the determination and identification of any information that is necessary to complete the reinvestigation.[93]

---

86. *Id.* § 1681i(a)(1)(A).
87. *Id.*
88. *Id.* § 1681i(a)(1)(B).
89. *Id.* § 1681i(a)(1)(C).
90. *Id.* § 1681i(a)(2)(A)–(B).
91. *Id.* § 1681i(a)(3)(A).
92. *Id.* § 1681i(a)(3)(B).
93. *Id.* § 1681i(a)(3)(C).

6.6.2 *Process Following Reinvestigation*

If, after reinvestigation, the consumer reporting agency concludes that the consumer's dispute is meritorious or the consumer reporting agency cannot verify the accuracy or completeness of the disputed information, the consumer reporting agency must promptly delete that item of information from the consumer's file or modify it (as appropriate), and promptly notify the applicable furnisher that the information has been deleted or modified.[94] The disputed information must not be reinserted into the consumer's file unless the furnisher certifies to the consumer reporting agency that item of information is complete and accurate, at which point the consumer reporting agency must give further notices to the consumer.[95] The consumer reporting agency must maintain reasonable procedures to prevent deleted or modified information from reappearing in the consumer's file.[96]

After the consumer reporting agency has completed its reinvestigation, it must give proper notice to the consumer. That notice must occur no later than five business days after the reinvestigation is done (by mail, unless the consumer otherwise authorizes communications).[97] The notice must include a statement that the reinvestigation is done, a copy of the consumer report as revised (if applicable) as a result of the reinvestigation, a statement that the consumer may request a description of the reinvestigation effort,[98] including identity of the furnisher of the disputed information, statement that the consumer has the right to add an item in the consumer's file to the effect that the consumer disputed the information.[99] Finally, the notice must include a statement that, if the dispute was meritorious, the consumer may request the consumer reporting agency to notify any users of the disputed information of the results of the reinvestigation—any users who used the consumer report for employment purpose in the preceding two years, and any users who used the report for any other purpose in the preceding six months.

6.6.3 *Expedited Dispute Resolution Process Is Available*

The FCRA forgives some of these reinvestigation requirements if the consumer reporting agency deletes the disputed information within three days of the dispute, promptly gives certain notices to the consumer, and provides written confirmation of the deletion along with a copy of the corrected consumer report within five more business days.[100]

94. *Id.* § 1681i(a)(5)(A).

95. *Id.* § 1681i(a)(5)(B).

96. *Id.* § 1681i(a)(5)(C).

97. *Id.* § 1681i(a)(6)(A).

98. If the consumer requests this summary, the consumer reporting agency must provide it within fifteen days. *Id.* § 1681i(a)(7).

99. *Id.* § 1681i(a)(6)(B), incorporating § 1681i(d).

100. *Id.* § 1681i(a)(8).

6.6.4 Consumer's Statement of Dispute Following Reinvestigation

If the reinvestigation does not end the dispute, the consumer may file a brief statement of dispute relative to the particular item of information in the consumer report.[101] The consumer reporting agency may limit the statement to one hundred words. Unless there is reasonable ground to believe the statement of dispute is frivolous or irrelevant, the consumer reporting agency shall clearly note in future consumer reports that the particular item of information is disputed and include the statement of dispute.

6.6.5 Dispute Process for a Veteran's Medical Debt

Effective May 24, 2019, the FCRA was amended to add a dispute process specific to a veteran's medical debt, if the Department of Veterans Affairs (DOVA) has submitted to a veteran a notice that the DOVA has assumed liability for part or all of a veteran's medical debt.[102] In that instance, the veteran may dispute to a consumer reporting agency the inclusion of that debt on the veteran's consumer report by submitting the DOVA's notice, proof of liability of the DOVA's payment for the debt, or documentation that the DOVA is in the process of making payments for medical services.[103] Upon receipt of that notice from the consumer-veteran, the consumer reporting agency "shall" delete all information relating to that medical debt from the consumer-veteran's file and notify the furnisher and the veteran of the deletion.[104]

6.7 Disclosures to Consumers

This section discusses the primary disclosure obligations imposed by the FCRA when a consumer requests information. A consumer reporting agency must provide its consumer file upon the consumer's express request (subject to the consumer reporting agency's ability to verify the consumer's identity).[105] The disclosure should include (1) the sources of information regarding the consumer (unless the information was the basis for an investigative consumer report);[106] (2) each person who procured a consumer report regarding the consumer for employment purposes during the

---

101. *Id.* § 1681i(b)–(c).

102. *Id.* § 1681i(g)(2). *Veteran's medical debt* means "(1) a medical collection debt of a veteran owed to a non-Department of Veterans Affairs health care provider that was submitted to the Department for payment for health care authorized by the Department of Veterans Affairs; and (2) includes medical collection debt that the Department of Veterans Affairs has wrongfully charged a veteran." *Id.* § 1681a(aa).

103. *Id.* § 1681i(g)(1).

104. *Id.* § 1681i(g)(3).

105. *Id.* § 1681g(a)(1)

106. *Id.* § 1681g(a)(2).

preceding two years, and for any other purpose during the preceding one year;[107] (3) the dates, original payees, and amount of any checks that caused reporting of any adverse information about the consumer;[108] (4) a list of all inquiries the consumer reporting agency received in the preceding one year relating to a credit or insurance transaction that was not initiated by the consumer;[109] and (5) that a credit score regarding that consumer is in the file, even if the consumer did not request the score.[110]

With any of the disclosures described above, the consumer reporting agency must include a copy of the CFPB's Summary of Your Rights,[111] a list of all federal agencies responsible for enforcing the FCRA, a statement that the consumer may have additional rights under state law, and a statement that the consumer reporting agency is not required to remove derogatory information that is accurate, unless it is obsolete or cannot be verified.[112] Prior to disclosing information to a consumer, the consumer reporting agency must require the consumer to furnish proper identification.[113] Once proper identification has been provided, the consumer reporting agency's disclosures must be in writing,[114] unless the consumer previously authorizes a different method of transmitting the disclosures.[115]

6.8 Identity Theft and Other Alerts

6.8.1 Summary of Rights Relating to Identity Theft

If any consumer notifies a consumer reporting agency that the consumer may have been the victim of fraud or identity theft involving credit, electronic fund transfer, or an account or transaction with a financial institution or creditor, the consumer reporting agency shall provide the consumer with the Summary of Identity Theft Rights created by the CFPB[116] and contact information for the CFPB.[117]

---

107. *Id.* § 1681g(a)(3)(A) (excepting from the requirement instances where the user was an agency or department of the U.S. government under certain circumstances).

108. *Id.* § 1681g(a)(4).

109. *Id.* § 1681g(a)(5).

110. *Id.* § 1681g(a)(6).

111. 15 U.S.C. § 1681b(b)(1)(B). As noted above, the CFPB amended the Summary of Your Rights document in September 2018. *See* 47 Fed. Reg. 47,038.

112. 15 U.S.C. § 1681g(c)(2).

113. *Id.* § 1681h(a)(1).

114. *Id.* § 1681h(a)(2).

115. Examples of alternative methods of giving disclosures include in-person disclosures if the consumer appears at the consumer reporting agency's place of business, or by telephone or electronic means, or by any other reasonable means. *See id.* § 1681h(b)–(d).

116. The Bureau updated this summary, titled "Remedying the Effects of Identity Theft," on September 12, 2018, and it can be accessed at: https://www.consumerfinance.gov/about-us/newsroom/bureau-consumer-financial-protection-issues-updated-fcra-model-disclosures/.

117. 15 U.S.C. § 1681g(d)(2).

6.8.2 *Identity Theft and Fraud Alerts*

Nationwide consumer reporting agencies carry special responsibilities relating to actual or suspected fraud and identity theft,[118] including initial fraud alert, extended fraud alert, active duty alert, and security freeze, discussed in later sections. For each of these, effective September 2018, all consumer reporting agencies must have established a web page (in addition to other means) allowing a consumer to request this alert.[119]

6.8.2.1 Initial Fraud Alerts

Upon the direct request from a consumer or personal representative that the consumer has been or has a good faith suspicion he or she will soon be a victim of fraud or identity theft, a nationwide consumer reporting agency that has a file on that consumer must: (1) include a fraud alert[120] in the consumer's file and provide that alert with any credit score for that consumer for a period of at least one year unless the consumer requests the alert be removed;[121] (2) inform the other nationwide consumer reporting agencies of the fraud alert, pursuant to section 621(f) (which recipients must then similarly comply with these requirements);[122] (3) inform the consumer that he or she may request a free copy of the consumer's file pursuant to section 612(d);[123] and (4) provide the consumer with all disclosures required under section 609 free of charge, within three business days after the request has been made.[124]

---

118. "Identity theft" is defined to be "a fraud committed using the identifying information of another person, subject to such further definition as the Consumer Financial Protection Bureau may prescribe, by regulation." *Id.* § 1681a(q)(3). *See also* 12 C.F.R. § 1022.3(h) ("Identity theft means a fraud committed or attempted using the identifying information of another person without authority.").

119. 15 U.S.C. § 1681c-1(i)(6).

120. "Fraud alert" is defined to include notice to users that the consumer may be a victim of fraud or identity theft, which notice must be clear and conspicuous to the user. *Id.* § 1681a(q)(2). This initial fraud alert, the extended alert (discussed in section 6.8.2.2), and the active duty alert (discussed in section 6.8.2.3) must each contain notices to users that the consumer does not authorize particular types of new credit. *See id.* § 1681c(h)(1)(A) (initial fraud alert and active duty alert) and § 1681c(h)(2)(A) (extended alerts) for details.

121. *Id.* § 1681c-1(a)(1)(A). Prior to September 2018, the period for maintaining the fraud alert was ninety days. That period was amended by the May 2018 Economic Growth, Regulatory Relief, and Consumer Act, leading to the CFPB's Interim Final Rule on September 12, 2018. *See* Press Release, CFPB, CFPB Announces Interim Final Rule (Sept. 12, 2018), https://www.consumerfinance.gov/about-us/newsroom/bureau-consumer-financial-protection-issues-updated-fcra-model-disclosures/.

122. 15 U.S.C. § 1681c-1(a)(1)(B), (e).

123. *Id.* § 1681c-1(a)(2)(A).

124. *Id.* § 1681c-1(a)(2)(B).

6.8.2.2 Extended Fraud Alerts

If a consumer or the consumer's representative files an *identity theft report*[125] with a nationwide consumer reporting agency that maintains a file on the consumer, the nationwide consumer reporting agency additionally must: (1) include a fraud alert on the consumer's file and provide the alert with any credit score generated therewith for seven years, unless the consumer requests earlier withdrawal;[126] (2) for five years after the consumer's request, exclude the consumer from any list of consumers that the nationwide consumer reporting agency provides to any third party to offer credit or insurance as part of a transaction that was not initiated by the consumer,[127] unless the consumer requests rescission of that exclusion earlier;[128] (3) notify the other nationwide consumer reporting agencies of the extended fraud alert (who must then similarly comply);[129] (4) inform the consumer that the consumer may request two free copies of the consumer's file pursuant to section 612(d) during the twelve-month period beginning when the fraud alert was added to the consumer's file;[130] and (5) give all disclosures required under section 609 free of charge within three business days after the fraud alert request.[131]

6.8.2.3 Active Duty Alerts

The FCRA also provides fraud and identity theft protection to active duty servicemen and women. Upon direct request by an active duty military consumer or personal representative, a nationwide consumer reporting agency must (1) add an active duty alert[132] to the consumer's file and include the alert in the consumer's file for any credit score generated in that file, for a period of twelve months,[133] unless the consumer requests earlier withdrawal;[134] (2) for two years, exclude the consumer from any list prepared by the nationwide consumer reporting agency to offer credit or insurance

---

125. *Identity theft report* means, at a minimum, a report (1) that alleges an identity theft, (2) that is a copy of an official, valid report filed by a consumer with the appropriate law enforcement agency, and (3) the filing of which subjects the person to criminal penalties for falsehoods. *Id.* § 1681a(q)(4). *See also* 12 C.F.R. § 1022.3(i) (lengthy definition of and required content of an identity theft report).

126. 15 U.S.C. § 1681c-1(b)(1)(A).

127. *See id.* § 1681b(c) for details on credit or insurance transactions not initiated by the consumer.

128. *Id.* § 1681c-1(b)(1)(B).

129. *Id.* §§ 1681c-1(b)(1)(C) and 1681c-1(e).

130. *Id.* § 1681c-1(b)(2)(A).

131. *Id.* § 1681c-1(b)(2)(B).

132. "Active duty alert" is defined to include notice to users that the consumer is an active duty military consumer, which notice must be clear and conspicuous to the user. *Id.* § 1681a(q)(2).

133. 12 C.F.R. § 1022.121(a).

134. 15 U.S.C. § 1681c-1(c)(1).

to the consumer as part of a transaction that was not initiated by the consumer,[135] unless the consumer requests to rescind the protection;[136] and (3) notify the other nationwide consumer reporting agencies of the active duty alert.[137]

6.8.3 Responsibilities Relating to Consumer Complaints Regarding Fraud and Identity Theft for Non-Nationwide Consumer Reporting Agencies

Although nationwide consumer reporting agencies have the most responsibility for addressing consumer notices of fraud or identity theft, all consumer reporting agencies have some responsibility. If any consumer reporting agency receives notice from a consumer that the consumer suspects fraud or identity theft, the consumer reporting agency must inform the consumer how to contact the Bureau and how to contact the nationwide consumer reporting agencies for more detailed information and to request initial and extended fraud alerts and active duty alerts.[138]

6.8.4 Blocking Identity Theft

All consumer reporting agencies have an obligation to block reporting of consumer information that the consumer has reported as resulting from identity theft. The consumer reporting agency must block the information within four business days after the consumer reporting agency receives all of the following: proof of the consumer's identity, a copy of the identity theft report, the consumer's identification of the disputed information, and the consumer's statement that is in fact not accurate relating to a transaction by the consumer.[139] The consumer reporting agency must also "promptly" notify the furnisher of the disputed information.[140] The consumer reporting agency may reject or rescind a block on consumer information if the block was requested or blocked in error, the block resulted from a material misrepresentation by the consumer, or the consumer benefited from goods, services, or money resulting from the block.[141] If the consumer reporting agency refuses a block or rescinds a block, the consumer reporting agency must notify the consumer in writing within five days.[142]

---

135. *See id.* § 1681b(c) for details on credit or insurance transactions not initiated by the consumer.

136. *Id.* § 1681c-1(c)(2).

137. *Id.* § 1681c-1(d).

138. *Id.* § 1681c-1(g).

139. *Id.* § 1681c-2(a)(1)–(4).

140. *Id.* § 1681c-2(b).

141. *Id.* § 1681c-2(c)(1)(A)–(C).

142. *Id.* § 1681c-2(c)(2), incorporating § 1681i(a)(5)(B).

6.9 National Security Freeze, National Protection of Protected Consumer Information, and Credit Monitoring

In 2018 and 2019, three amendments to the FCRA identity theft provisions were made effective: (1) creation of a national credit security freeze mechanism for consumers, (2) creation of a mechanism to protect the consumer information of minors and incapacitated persons, and (3) creation of credit monitoring obligations for active duty servicemen and women. Each is discussed below.

6.9.1 National Security Freeze

The term *security freeze* means a "restriction that prohibits a [consumer reporting agency] from disclosing the contents of a consumer report that is subject to such security freeze to any person requesting the consumer report."[143] In essence, if a consumer requests a security freeze be placed on his or her file, consumer reporting agencies may not produce a consumer report on that consumer.

A consumer must make a direct request to the consumer reporting agency,[144] the consumer reporting agency must confirm the consumer's identity,[145] then (free of charge) must place the freeze on the consumer's file within one business day (if the request comes by toll-free telephone or secure electronic means) or three business days (if the request comes by mail).[146] Within five business days after placing the freeze, the consumer reporting agency must send specific prescribed confirmations to the consumer.[147] The FCRA also details the circumstances in which a security freeze may be lifted.[148]

The FCRA also specifies numerous instances in which the security freeze will not apply, including, without limitation, using the consumer report to check on existing accounts; using credit information for a firm offer of credit or insurance; using a consumer report to provide the consumer with a copy of same; using the consumer report for employment, tenant, or background screening; and using the consumer report to assess, verify, or authenticate the consumer's identity for purposes other than granting credit, or to investigate or prevent actual or potential fraud.[149]

6.9.2 National Protection of Protected Consumer Information

The 2018 amendments to the FCRA also create protections for "protected consumers," defined to be persons under sixteen years old or incapacitated persons, or persons

143. *Id.* § 1681c-1(i)(1)(C).
144. *Id.* § 1681c-1(i)(2)(A).
145. Id.
146. *Id.* § 1681c-1(i)(2)(A)(i)–(ii).
147. *Id.* § 1681c-1(i)(2)(B)(i)–(ii).
148. *See id.* § 1681c-1(i)(3)(A)(i)–(ii), (B), and (C)(i)–(ii).
149. *Id.* § 1681c-1(i)(4).

for whom a guardian or conservator has been appointed.[150] The amendment generally provides authority for a protected consumer's representative to request a national security freeze for the protected consumer and to remove same.[151]

6.9.3 Credit Monitoring Systems

Nationwide consumer reporting agencies must implement an electronic credit monitoring service for all consumers who give notice that they are active duty military servicemen and women.[152] The credit monitoring service must be free of charge and must, at a minimum, notify the consumer of material additions or changes to the consumer's file at the consumer reporting agency.[153] The FTC is charged with rulemaking on this amendment to the FCRA.[154] There is no private cause of action for violation of this section.[155]

6.10 Credit Score Disclosures

The FCRA defines credit score to mean a "numerical value or a categorization derived from a statistical tool or modeling system used by a person who makes or arranges a loan to predict the likelihood of certain credit behaviors, including default."[156] The numerical value or categorization derived from the analysis may also be called a risk predictor or risk score.[157] The term credit score does not include mortgage scoring or rating of an automated underwriting system that considers factors in addition to credit information (e.g., the loan-to-value ratio, the amount of down payment, or the consumer's financial assets), or any other elements of the underwriting process or underwriting decision.[158]

Generally, if a consumer requests a credit score from a consumer reporting agency, the consumer reporting agency must supply a statement that the information and scoring model may be different than the credit score that a lender may use.[159] The consumer reporting agency's notice must also include the consumer's most recent credit score calculated by the consumer reporting agency relating to the extension of credit,

---

150. *Id.* § 1681c-1(j)(1)(B).
151. *Id.* § 1681c-1(j).
152. *Id.* § 1681c-1(k).
153. *Id.* § 1681c-1(k)(2).
154. *Id.* § 1681c-1(k)(3)
155. *Id.* § 1681c-1(k)(4).
156. *Id.* § 1681g(f)(2)(A)(i).
157. *Id.*
158. *Id.* § 1681g(f)(2)(A)(ii).
159. *Id.* § 1681g(f)(1).

the range of possible credit scores under the model used, all of the "key factors"[160] that adversely affected the credit score in that model (up to four key factors plus the number of inquiries with respect to the consumer report, if that number of enquiries adversely affected the credit score), the date on which the credit score was created, and the name of the person or entity that provided the credit score or credit file on which the credit score was created.[161] A consumer reporting agency that only distributes credit scores developed by others does not need to provide further explanation of the credit score, other than identifying the person or entity who developed the score or methodology, unless the consumer reporting agency modifies the other person's or entity's credit score.[162] A consumer reporting agency may charge a reasonable and fair fee for providing the credit score information.[163]

A consumer reporting agency who makes or arranges loans and uses a consumer credit score in connection with an application for a closed-end loan or establishment of an open-end loan for a consumer purpose secured by one to four units of residential real property has additional disclosure obligations set forth in section 609(g).

6.11 Reporting of Medical Information

A consumer reporting agency may not include medical information in a consumer report for employment purposes or in connection with a credit or insurance transaction unless one of three circumstances exists: (1) if the user's purpose in obtaining the consumer report is in connection with an insurance transaction and the consumer affirmatively consents to the furnishing;[164] (2) if the user intends for the consumer report to be used for employment purposes or in a credit transaction and has given specific written disclosure that clearly and conspicuously describes the use for the medical information;[165] and (3) if the medical information relates only to transactions, accounts, or balances relating to the consumer's medical debts, as long as the medical information is restricted to codes that do not identify the specific provider or nature of medical services, products, or devices.[166]

---

160. "Key Factors" means "all relevant elements or reasons adversely affecting the Credit Score for the particular individual, listed in the order of their importance based on their effect on the Credit Score." *Id.* § 1681g(f)(2)(B).

161. *Id.* § 1681g(f)(1)(A)–(E).

162. *Id.* § 1681g(f)(5)(A)–(B).

163. *Id.* § 1681g(f)(8).

164. *Id.* § 1681c(g)(1)(A).

165. *Id.* § 1681c(g)(1)(B).

166. *Id.* § 1681c(g)(1)(C).

6.12 Notices to Furnishers and Users

The FCRA requires consumer reporting agencies to give specific notices to furnishers and users, reminding them of their FCRA obligations.[167] The Bureau has prescribed template notices for this purpose.[168]

6.13 Public Record Information for Employment Purposes

The FCRA reflects concern that public record information may not be entirely reliable, particularly when used for employment purposes. To that end, if a consumer reporting agency prepares a consumer report for employment purposes based in whole or part on matters of public record, and if those items of public record information are likely to have an adverse impact on the consumer's employment, then the consumer reporting agency must do at least one of the following: (1) at the time of sending the consumer report to the employer-user, notify the consumer that public record information is being reported, along with the name and address of the impending user;[169] or (2) maintain strict procedures to ensure that the public record information used in the consumer report is complete and up to date.[170]

7. Furnisher Obligations

The Consumer Credit Reporting Reform Act of 1996 and the Fair and Accurate Credit Transactions Act of 2003 added obligations on furnishers, principally: (1) the duty to provide accurate and complete information to consumer reporting agencies,[171] (2) the duty to investigate consumer disputes relating to the accuracy and completeness of furnished information,[172] and (3) duties relating to identity theft.[173] Additional furnisher duties exist and are memorialized in section 623. These issues and other furnisher obligations are discussed below.

---

167. *Id.* § 1681e(d).

168. *See* 12 C.F.R. pt. 1022 app. M (notice to furnishers); *id.* at app. N (notice to users). A consumer reporting agency is deemed to comply with these requirements if the notices given are "substantially similar" to the template notices. 15 U.S.C. § 1681e(d).

169. 15 U.S.C. § 1681k(a)(1).

170. *Id.* § 1681k(a)(2) (Items of public record relating to arrests, indictments, convictions, suits, tax liens, and outstanding judgments are considered up to date if the current public record status of the item is reported).

171. *Id.* § 1681s-2(a).

172. *Id.* § 1681s-2(b).

173. *Id.* § 1681s-2(a)(6).

7.1 Prohibitions and Safe Harbor

A furnisher is prohibited from furnishing "information relating to a consumer to any [consumer reporting agency] if the [furnisher] knows or has reasonable cause[174] to believe that the information is inaccurate,"[175] and prohibited from furnishing information relating to a consumer to any consumer reporting agency if the consumer has notified the furnisher (at an address specified by the furnisher) that specific information is inaccurate and the information is, in fact, inaccurate.

The FCRA also offers a safe harbor: if the furnisher "clearly and conspicuously" gives an address to a consumer so that the consumer can give notice of inaccuracies, then the standard of "knows or has reasonable cause to believe" is eliminated.[176] Furnishers are thus incented (but not required[177]) to provide contact information to consumers so that consumers may report alleged inaccuracies.

7.2 Duties

All furnishers have an obligation to establish and implement reasonable written policies and procedures to protect the accuracy and "integrity" of the consumer information it furnishes to consumer reporting agencies.[178] Integrity refers to information furnished to a consumer reporting agency about the furnisher's relationship to the consumer.[179] Information has integrity if it (1) is substantiated by the furnisher's records when the information is furnished, (2) is furnished in a form and manner designed to minimize the possibility of incorrect inclusion in a consumer report, and (3) includes the information that the Bureau has announced is necessary to avoid materially misleading a reader relative to evaluating a consumer report and the information listed by the Bureau in Regulation V.[180]

The written policies and procedures should be appropriate to the nature, size, complexity, and scope of the furnisher's business, including types of business activities, nature and frequency of the information the furnisher gives to consumer reporting agencies, and the technology used.[181] The furnisher should analyze practices or activities that can compromise the accuracy or integrity of information it furnishes, through

174. *Reasonable cause to believe that the information is inaccurate* means "having specific knowledge, other than solely allegations by the consumer, that would cause a reasonable person to have substantial doubts about the accuracy of the information." *Id.* § 1681s-2(a)(1)(D).

175. *Id.* § 1682s-2(a)(1)(A).

176. *Id.* § 1681s-2(a)(1)(C).

177. *Id.*

178. 12 C.F.R. § 1022.42(a). *See also* CFPB, Compliance Bulletin 2016-01 (Feb. 3, 2016), https://files.consumerfinance.gov/f/201602_cfpb_supervisory-bulletin-furnisher-accuracy-obligations.pdf).

179. 12 C.F.R. § 1022.41(d).

180. 12 C.F.R. § 1022.41(d)(1)–(3) and app. E.

181. 12 C.F.R. pt. 1022 app. E, pt. I(a).

review of technologies used, historical records, feedback from consumer reporting agencies, consumers, and others, and internal reviews, among other considerations.[182]

Other furnisher duties are divided between duties of furnishers who "regularly and in the ordinary course of business" furnish information to consumer reporting agencies, and duties of all furnishers.

Furnishers who "regularly and in the ordinary course of business" furnish consumer information to consumer reporting agencies have a duty to correct and update information about consumers if the furnisher determines that furnished information is incomplete or inaccurate.[183] In that event, the furnisher "shall promptly" notify the consumer reporting agency and give the consumer reporting agency corrections to the information, or provide to the consumer reporting agency such additional information as is necessary to make the furnished information complete and accurate.[184] Any consumer information that remains incomplete or inaccurate may not be furnished to the consumer reporting agency any further.[185] Also, furnishers who "regularly and in the ordinary course of business" furnish consumer information to consumer reporting agencies regarding a consumer's credit account must notify the consumer reporting agency if the consumer has voluntarily closed the account with that furnisher.[186]

All furnishers have duties (1) to refrain from furnishing to a consumer reporting agency any information the accuracy or completeness of which the consumer has disputed (with the furnisher), and (2) to notify the consumer reporting agency of that dispute in conjunction with any furnishing of the information.[187] If any furnisher provides information to a consumer reporting agency regarding a delinquent account placed for collection, charged to profit or loss, or subjected to any similar action, the furnisher must, within ninety days after furnishing the information, notify the consumer reporting agency of information regarding the delinquency.[188]

7.3 Furnisher Obligations as Amended by the 2020 CARES Act

The Coronavirus Aid, Relief, and Economic Security Act (CARES Act), signed into law on March 27, 2020, amends the duties of a furnisher of information under the FCRA in light of the COVID-19 pandemic.[189] The amendment provides that if a creditor or other furnisher of information provides an accommodation to a consumer affected by COVID-19 in connection with the consumer's account or other credit obligation, and if the consumer satisfies the accommodation, then the furnisher must report the

182. *Id.* at pt. II.
183. 15 U.S.C. § 1681s-2(a)(2)(A)–(B).
184. *Id.* § 1681s-2(a)(2).
185. *Id.*
186. *Id.* § 1681s-2(a)(4).
187. *Id.* § 1681s-2(a)(3).
188. *Id.* § 1681s-2(a)(5)(A)–(B).
189. The CARES Act amends 15 U.S.C. § 1681s-2(a)(1) to add § 1681s-2(a)(1)(F).

consumer account as current. If the account of the consumer was delinquent prior to the accommodation, then the furnisher must continue to report the consumer as delinquent until the consumer brings the account current. This obligation is not applicable to charged-off accounts.

Only those consumers who have obtained an "accommodation" are covered by this amendment.[190] The CFPB issued a Policy Statement on Credit Reporting on April 1, 2020, regarding duties of furnishers and consumer reporting agencies in light of the CARES Act. Although not binding, it acknowledges the resource constraints facing furnishers a and consumer reporting agencies due to the pandemic, and that more time may be necessary to comply with existing obligations.[191] Furnishers are encouraged to work constructively with consumers in good faith to comply, and to keep furnishing information despite the pandemic.

7.4 Investigating Consumer Disputes

The FCRA creates different investigation obligations for furnishers depending on whether the consumer raises the dispute directly with the furnisher[192] or raises the dispute with the consumer reporting agency who, in turn, notifies the furnisher of the dispute.[193]

7.4.1 Dispute Raised Directly to Furnisher

Consumers may dispute the accuracy or completeness of information within a consumer report directly with the furnisher (a "direct dispute").[194] There is no private cause of action relating to the furnisher's activities following a direct dispute.[195]

---

190. The CARES Act amendment to the FCRA defines "accommodation" as "an agreement to defer one or more payments, make a partial payment, forbear any delinquent amounts, modify a loan or contract, or any other assistance or relief granted to a consumer who is affected by the coronavirus disease 2019 (COVID–19) pandemic during the covered period." 15 U.S.C. § 1681s-2(a)(1)(F)(i)(I). The term "covered period" is defined to mean the period beginning on January 31, 2020, and ending on the later of (1) 120 days after March 27, 2020, or (2) 120 days after the termination of the national emergency. *Id.* § 1681s-2(a)(1)(F)(i)(II).

191. CFPB, *Statement on Supervisory and Enforcement Practices Regarding the Fair Credit Reporting Act and Regulation V in Light of the CARES Act* (Apr. 1, 2020), https://files.consumerfinance.gov/f/documents/cfpb_credit-reporting-policy-statement_cares-act_2020-04.pdf.

192. 15 U.S.C. § 1681s-2(a)(8).

193. *Id.* § 1681s-2(b).

194. *Id.* § 1681s-2(a)(8). The phrase "direct dispute" is not a legal definition. It is offered here as a convention for ease of understanding this chapter.

195. *Id.* § 1681s-2(c)–(d).

The CFPB issued regulations governing direct disputes.[196] In general, the process is as follows: (1) The consumer must identify the account or other relationship in dispute (such as account number and the consumer's contact information), the specific information in dispute, explain the basis of the dispute, and include "all supporting documentation required by the furnisher to substantiate the basis of the dispute" (for example, a copy of the allegedly inaccurate consumer report portion, a police report, a fraud or identity theft affidavit, a court order, or account statements).[197] (2) The furnisher must conduct an investigation,[198] review all relevant information that the consumer provided,[199] and complete the investigation and report the results to the consumer within thirty days.[200] (3) If the investigation reveals that the disputed information is inaccurate, the furnisher must "promptly" send notice of that deficiency to each consumer reporting agency that received the furnisher's information and provide any correction necessary to make the information accurate.[201]

A furnisher is not required to investigate certain categories of direct disputes: (1) if the furnisher concludes that the consumer's direct dispute is "frivolous or irrelevant"[202] (for example, if the consumer failed to provide sufficient information to investigate, or previously made substantially the same dispute that had been investigated);[203] (2) if the direct dispute is "submitted by, is prepared on behalf of the consumer by, or is submitted on a form supplied to the consumer by a credit repair organization";[204] or (3) if the dispute relates to consumer identifying information, the consumer's past or present employers, inquiries or requests for a consumer report, information derived from public records, or information related to fraud alerts or active duty alerts, or information provided to a consumer reporting agency by another furnisher.[205]

---

196. *Id.* § 1681s-2(a)(8)(A); 12 C.F.R. § 1022.43.

197. 15 U.S.C. § 1681s-2(a)(8)(D)(i)–(iii); 12 C.F.R. § 1022.43(d)(1)–(3).

198. 15 U.S.C. § 1681s-2(a)(8)(E)(i).

199. *Id.* § 1681s-2(a)(8)(E)(ii).

200. *Id.* § 1681s-2(a)(8)(E)(iii) and § 1681i(a)(1); 12 C.F.R. § 1022.43(e)(3).

201. 15 U.S.C. § 1681s-2(a)(8)(E)(iv); 12 C.F.R. § 1022.43(e)(4).

202. 15 U.S.C. § 1681s-2(a)(8)(F); 12 C.F.R. § 1022.43(f).

203. 15 U.S.C. § 1681s-2(a)(8)(F)(i); 12 C.F.R. § 1022.43(f)(i)–(ii) (but note that "a direct dispute is not substantially the same as a dispute previously submitted" if the dispute includes information that was not previously provided to the furnisher).

204. 15 U.S.C. § 1681s-2(a)(8)(G). A *credit repair organization* means any person who performs or offers to perform any service in return for the payment of money or other valuable consideration, for the express or implied purpose of (1) improving a consumer's credit record, credit history, or credit rating, or (2) providing advice and assistance to any consumer with regard to any activity or service relating to improving credit record, credit history, or credit rating. *Id.* § 1679a(3).

205. 12 C.F.R. § 1022.43(b)(1).

7.4.2 *Dispute Raised Indirectly Through a Consumer Reporting Agency*

A consumer may also dispute the accuracy or completeness of information within a consumer report by initiating a dispute indirectly through a consumer reporting agency (an "indirect dispute"),[206] pursuant to section 611(a)(2). In that instance, the consumer reporting agency has obligations relating to investigation of the dispute, one obligation being notice to the applicable furnisher of the disputed information.

Upon receipt of the notice from the consumer reporting agency, the furnisher must conduct an investigation with respect to the disputed information,[207] must review all relevant information provided by the consumer reporting agency,[208] and must report the results of that investigation to the consumer reporting agency.[209] If the furnisher's investigation reveals that the furnisher's information is incomplete or inaccurate, the furnisher must report its investigation results to all nationwide consumer reporting agencies to which the furnisher supplied the same information.[210] If disputed information is inaccurate, incomplete, or cannot be verified, the furnisher must modify the information, delete the information, or permanently block the reporting of that information.[211]

The furnisher must complete its investigation within the time period the consumer reporting agency has to complete its own investigation, pursuant to section 611(a)(1) (usually thirty days).[212] Importantly, different from direct disputes, a consumer may pursue a furnisher's failure to investigate an indirect dispute through a private cause of action.[213]

7.5 Identity Theft

All furnishers must have in place reasonable procedures to respond to a consumer reporting agency's notice of a consumer's identity theft.[214] The purpose of this obligation is to ensure that the furnisher does not continue to furnish incorrect information about a consumer which results from identity theft. Similarly, a furnisher must refrain from furnishing challenged information about a consumer if the consumer notifies the furnisher directly that the information results from identity theft, unless the

206. The phrase "indirect dispute" is not a legal definition. It is offered here as a convention for ease of understanding this chapter.

207. 15 U.S.C. § 1681s-2(b)(1)(A).

208. *Id.* § 1681s-2(b)(1)(B).

209. *Id.* § 1681s-2(b)(1)(C).

210. *Id.* § 1681s-2(b)(1)(D)

211. *Id.* § 1681s-2(b)(E).

212. *Id.* § 1681s-2(b)(2).

213. *Id.* § 1681s-2(c)–(d).

214. *Id.* § 1681s-2(a)(6)(A).

furnisher determines or learns from the consumer that the challenged information is, in fact, correct.[215]

Finally, if a furnisher is a creditor of the consumer who gives notice of identity theft, the furnisher may not sell, transfer for consideration, or place for collection the debt that the consumer has identified as resulting from identity theft.[216] This prohibition does not apply to (1) the repurchase of a debt where the assignee of the debt requires such repurchase because of the identity theft, (2) the securitization of a debt as collateral for a borrowing, or (3) the transfer of the debt as a result of a merger, acquisition, purchase and assumption transaction, or transfer of assets of an entity.[217]

7.6 Special Obligations of Financial Institutions

Financial institutions[218] that extend credit and furnish consumer information to nationwide consumer reporting agencies in the regular and ordinary course of business have additional obligations under the FCRA.[219] If the financial institution provides *negative information*[220] about a consumer to a nationwide consumer reporting agency, the institution "shall provide a notice of such furnishing" in writing to the consumer.[221] Once the financial institution provides that initial notice, the institution is relieved from providing future notices each time it reports negative information on that same transaction, extension of credit, account, or consumer.[222]

The financial institution may provide the notice of negative information prior to furnishing the negative information, but must give notice no later than thirty days after furnishing the negative information to the nationwide consumer reporting agency.[223] The notice must be "clear and conspicuous" and may be sent as a stand-alone document or may be included with "any notice of default, any billing statement, or any other materials provided to the customer."[224] The Bureau has promulgated

215. *Id.* § 1681s-2(a)(6)(B).

216. *Id.* § 1681m(f)(1)–(2).

217. *Id.* § 1681m(f)(3)(A)–(C).

218. For this particular section, the FCRA imports the definition of "financial institution" from the Gramm-Leach-Bliley Act, Pub. L. 106-102, 113 Stat. 1338 (1999). *See* 15 C.F.R. § 1681s-2(a)(7)(G)(ii). By contrast, other sections of the FCRA apply the FCRA's general definition of "financial institution" found in section 1681a(t).

219. *Id.* § 1681s-2(a)(7)(A)(i).

220. "Negative information" is defined to mean "information concerning a customer's delinquencies, late payments, insolvency, or any form of default." *Id.* § 1681s-2(a)(7)(G)(i).

221. *Id.*

222. *Id.* § 1681s-2(a)(7)(A)(ii).

223. *Id.* § 1681s-2(a)(7)(B)(i).

224. *Id.* § 1681s-2(a)(7)(C)(i)–(ii).

model forms for a financial institution's use.[225] Although financial institutions are not required to use the model forms, their use is a safe harbor.[226]

The FCRA provides a second safe harbor relating to a financial institution's furnishing of negative information if, at the time of the failure to comply technically with section 623(a)(7), the institution (1) maintained reasonable policies and procedures to comply or (2) reasonably believed that the institution was prohibited by law from contacting the consumer.[227]

7.7 Special Obligations of Furnishers Furnishing Medical Information

A special notice obligation exists if a furnisher's (or its agent's or assignee's) "primary business" is providing medical services, products, or devices. In that instance, the furnisher must alert any consumer reporting agencies to whom the furnisher provides information that the furnisher is in that business, so that the consumer reporting agency is able to comply with its own obligations relative to medical information.[228]

8. User Obligations

The FCRA imposes numerous obligations on users, principally surrounding a user's right to procure a consumer report and right to use a consumer report to take adverse action against a consumer. The principal obligations imposed on users are discussed below.

225. *Id.* § 1681s-2(a)(7)(D)(i); *see* app. B to 12 C.F.R. Part 1022 (providing model notice B-1 if the financial institution gives notice before furnishing negative information to a nationwide consumer reporting agency, and model notice B-2 if the financial institution has already furnished negative information to a nationwide consumer reporting agency).

226. *Id.* § 1681s-2(a)(7)(D)(ii)–(iii).

227. *Id.* § 1681s-2(a)(7)(F).

228. *Id.* § 1681s-2(a)(9), § 1681c(g)(1) (obligations of consumer reporting agencies relating to consumer reports regarding medical information), and § 1681c(a)(6) (obligation of consumer reporting agencies to refrain from producing a consumer report containing the medical information furnisher's contact information).

8.1 Permissible Purpose to Obtain Consumer Report

A user is forbidden from procuring a consumer report unless the user has a permissible purpose for using the consumer report[229] and has given proper certifications to the consumer reporting agency regarding the user's intended compliance with the FCRA.[230]

The FCRA specifically forbids a user from procuring a consumer report under false pretenses. The statute authorizes civil liability in an action by a consumer, and authorizes the "the greater" of a consumer's actual resulting damages or $1,000, plus the potential of punitive damages and shifting of costs and reasonable attorney's fees.[231] The statute also authorizes civil liability in an action by a consumer reporting agency if a user "obtains a consumer report . . . under false pretenses or knowingly without a permissible purpose" and authorizes an award of the "the greater" of the consumer reporting agency's actual damages or $1,000.[232] Finally, the statute authorizes criminal penalties of a fine under Title 18, imprisonment for no more than two years, or both.[233]

8.2 User's Duties Surrounding Investigative Consumer Reports

A user who wants to procure an investigative consumer report on a consumer must comply with disclosure and certification requirements. First, the user must "clearly and accurately" disclose to the consumer that an investigative consumer report regarding the consumer may be made and must include certain specified information.[234] The disclosure must be in writing and mailed or otherwise delivered no later than three days after the consumer report is requested.[235] If the consumer subsequently makes written request within a reasonable period after receipt of the above disclosures, the user must make a "complete and accurate disclosure of the nature and scope of the investigation requested."[236] This second disclosure must be in writing and mailed or otherwise delivered to the consumer no later than five days after the consumer's request was received (or five days after the investigative consumer report was first requested by the user, whichever is later).[237]

Second, before procuring the investigative consumer report, the user must certify to the applicable consumer reporting agency that the user has made the initial

229. *See* section 4 for a discussion of the permissible purposes.

230. *See* section 6.1 for a discussion of the certification requirement. *See also* 15 U.S.C. § 1681b(f)(1)–(2).

231. 15 U.S.C. § 1681n(a).

232. *Id.* § 1681n(b).

233. *Id.* § 1681q.

234. *Id.* § 1681d(a)(1).

235. *Id.*

236. *Id.* § 1681d(b).

237. *Id.* § 1681d(b).

disclosure described above and will make the follow-up disclosures described above if requested by the consumer.[238]

8.3 User's Obligations Surrounding Adverse Actions

One of the users' principal FCRA obligations is the giving of proper adverse action notices and, in the context of procuring a consumer report for employment purposes, pre-adverse action notices. Those obligations are discussed in sections 5.1 and 5.2.

8.3.1 Risk-Based Pricing Notices

An alternative to a formal adverse action notice exists if a user extends credit to a consumer but on terms that are "materially less favorable" than terms the user has granted to other consumers, based at least in part on the consumer's consumer report. That alternative is the Risked-Based Pricing notice (RBPN). The RBPN option alerts consumers to possibly negative information within their consumer reports even in situations where the consumer receives credit.

If a user relies on a consumer report to make a credit decision in connection with a consumer application for credit (a grant, extension, or other provision of credit) on "material terms[239] that are materially less favorable[240] than the most favorable terms available to a substantial proportion of consumers" from or through that user, that user must provide "an oral, written, or electronic notice" in the form prescribed by the Bureau.[241] The Bureau has provided model forms for the various circumstances involving RBPNs,[242] and presented detailed information surrounding RBPN transactions.[243]

The user must issue the RBPN at the time of an application for, or a grant, extension, or other provision of, credit, or the time of communication of any approval of same.[244] Determining which consumers should receive RBPNs can be challenging,

238. *Id.* § 1681d(a)(2).

239. Regulation V defines "material terms" relative to open-end credit, credit cards, closed-end credit, and credit for which there is no annual percentage rate. *See* 12 C.F.R. § 1022.71(n)(1)–(3).

240. Regulation V defines "materially less favorable" to mean that "the terms granted, extended, or otherwise provided to a consumer differ from the terms granted, extended, or otherwise provided to another consumer" by the same user "such that the cost of credit to the first consumer would be significantly greater than the cost of credit to the other consumer." 12 C.F.R. § 1022.71(o). Relevant factors include the type of credit product, the term of the credit extension, and the extent of the differences between the material terms. *Id.*

241. *See* 12 C.F.R. § 1022.73(a)–(b) (describes in detail the content of the notice).

242. *See* 12 C.F.R. § 1022.73(b)(2) and model forms attached thereto as app. H-1 through H-7.

243. *See* 12 C.F.R. §§ 1022.70–1022.75

244. *Id.* § 1681m(h)(2); *see also* 12 C.F.R. § 1022.73(c)(1)–(3).

in light of the volume of consumers to whom a user might offer credit. The Bureau has prescribed various alternative methods for that determination.[245]

RBPNs are not required if (1) the consumer applied for specified material terms and was granted those terms (even if the terms are materially less favorable than other consumers received), unless the terms were specified only after the user procured a consumer report on that consumer,[246] or (2) the user has provided or will provide a formal adverse action notice to the consumer.[247] A safe harbor exists if, at the time of a user's failure to comply with the RBPN requirements, the user maintained "reasonable policies and procedures to comply" with the section.[248] There also is no private cause of action for failure to comply with the RBPN requirements.[249]

8.3.2 Obligations in the Context of Employment

Users who take adverse action in the context of employment have special obligations, including giving proper disclosure and consent, proper pre-adverse action notice, and proper adverse action notice.

8.3.2.1 Certification Requirement in Context of Employment

Section 604(b)(1) imposes an affirmative duty on consumer reporting agencies to obtain a certification from a user of consumer reports for employment purposes before the consumer reporting agency may transmit the consumer report. Section 604(f) in turn forbids a user from procuring a consumer report without fully complying with the permissible purposes section of the FCRA (including giving appropriate certification to the consumer reporting agency).

Pursuant to the section, a prospective user of the consumer report for employment purposes must certify that (1) the user has complied with the disclosure and consent requirements of section 604(b)(2) (*see* next section); (2) the user will comply with the pre-adverse action notice requirements of section 604(b)(3) if applicable; and (3) the user will not use the consumer report in violation of any equal employment opportunity law or regulation.[250]

8.3.2.2 Disclosure and Consent Requirements

Section 604 (b)(2)(A)(i) requires a user to disclose to the consumer that the user intends to procure a consumer report for employment purposes, and section 604(b)(2)(A)(ii)

245. 12 C.F.R. § 1022.72(b).

246. 15 U.S.C. § 1681m(h)(3)(A).

247. *Id.* § 1681m(h)(3)(B); 12 C.F.R. § 1022.74(b). Importantly, the converse is *not* true: RBPNs cannot replace adverse action notices where adverse action notices are otherwise required, because RBPNs contain different content. *Id.* § 1681m(h)(4).

248. 15 U.S.C. § 1681m(h)(7).

249. *Id.* § 1681m(h)(8)(A).

250. *Id.* § 1681b(b)(1)(A).

requires the user to obtain the consumer's consent to that procurement. Notably, a user must comply with these requirements before procuring the consumer report for employment purposes. These requirements generate a substantial amount of class action and individual litigation.

The disclosure must (1) alert the consumer that the user may procure a consumer report for employment purposes, (2) be in writing, (3) be "clear and conspicuous," and (4) be provided "in a document that consists solely of the disclosure." Frequently litigated claims regarding the disclosures include (1) that the FCRA disclosure is bundled among other disclosures that may be required by law or combined for the user's convenience (e.g., an employment packet);[251] (2) that extraneous information is included on the disclosure (e.g., state-specific credit reporting information, acknowledgement by the consumer of other employment-related rights, and waivers by the consumer).[252]

Section 604(b)(2)(A)(ii) requires that the user obtain the consumer's consent in writing after receiving the written disclosure, and permits that consent to be included on the disclosure document itself.[253] Frequently litigated claims surrounding the consent requirement are that the user failed to obtain, record, and preserve the written consent, and that consent is voided if the disclosure was invalid.

These same disclosure and consent requirements apply in the context of electronic or web-based employment application processes.

8.4 Notice Regarding Firm Offers of Credit or Insurance

Prescreened marketing lists are frequently used to solicit consumers with firm offers of credit or insurance. Users have particular disclosure obligations in that instance. With each such written solicitation, the user must "clearly and conspicuously" state that: (1) information in the consumer's consumer report was used in connection with the solicitation;[254] (2) the consumer received the firm offer because the consumer satisfied the criteria for credit worthiness or insurability under which the consumer was selected;[255] (3) if applicable, the credit or insurance may not be extended if, after the consumer responds to the solicitation, the consumer does not meet the criteria used to select the consumer or does not furnish any required collateral;[256] (4) the

251. *See* FTC, *40 Years of Experience*, *supra* note 13, at § 604(b)(2), Item 3(D); Fed. Trade Comm'n, Opinion Letter on Compliance with FCRA for Applicants or Current Employees (Dec. 18, 1997); Fed. Trade Comm'n, Opinion Letter on Application of FCRA (Sept. 9, 1998); Fed. Trade Comm'n, Opinion Letter on Application of FCRA (Feb. 11, 1998).

252. *See* FTC, *40 Years of Experience*, *supra* note 13, at § 604(b)(2), Item 3(B); Fed. Trade Comm'n, Opinion Letter on Application of FCRA (Feb. 11, 1998).

253. 15 U.S.C. § 1681b(b)(2)(A)(ii).

254. *Id.* § 1681m(h)(d)(1)(A).

255. *Id.* § 1681m(h)(d)(1)(B).

256. *Id.* § 1681m(h)(d)(1)(C).

consumer has a right to opt out of the prescreened marketing lists;[257] and (5) the consumer may exercise the opt-out right by use of a notification system established by the applicable consumer reporting agency.[258] The notice must also disclose the toll-free telephone number of the appropriate notification system.[259]

The CFPB has developed a "short notice" and "long notice" that satisfies the above requirements, and must accompany every written prescreened solicitation.[260] The written notices must be presented in a form and in a type size and manner that is simple and easy to understand.[261] The user in this circumstance must preserve the criteria used to select the consumers for at least three years from the date on which the firm offer is made.[262]

8.5 User Obligations Surrounding Identity Theft

No user of a consumer report that includes an initial fraud alert or an active duty alert may establish a new credit plan or extension of credit (other than an open-end credit plan) in the consumer's name, or issue an additional card on an existing account requested by a consumer, or grant any increase in credit limit on an existing credit account requested by a consumer unless the user exercises "reasonable policies and procedures" to form a "reasonable belief" that the user knows the identity of the person making the request.[263] A user can comply with this "reasonableness" standard by contacting the consumer via the telephone number given by the consumer when the consumer requested the alert.[264]

The same restrictions apply relative to extended fraud alerts, except that a user may only comply with its identity-confirmation obligations by contacting the user in person or via the telephone number given in the extended fraud alert.[265]

A nationwide consumer reporting agency may notify users of discrepancies in a consumer's address as part of the consumer reporting agency's procedures to identify identity theft and fraud. In such an instance, a user must develop and implement reasonable policies and procedures designed to enable the user to form

---

257. *Id.* § 1681m(h)(d)(1)(D).

258. *Id.* § 1681m(h)(d)(1)(E).

259. *Id.* § 1681m(d)(2)(A).

260. 12 C.F.R. § 1022.54(c)(1) (short notice), (2) (long notice).

261. 15 U.S.C. § 1681m(d)(2)(B). *See also* 12 C.F.R. § 1022.54(b)(1) for definition of "simple and easy to understand."

262. 15 U.S.C. § 1681m(d)(3).

263. *Id.* § 1681c-1(h)(1)(B)(i).

264. *Id.* § 1681c-1(h)(1)(B)(ii).

265. *Id.* § 1681c-1(h)(2)(B).

a reasonable belief that a consumer report relates to the consumer about whom the user has requested the report.[266]

8.6 Medical Information

In conjunction with consumer reporting agency restrictions on reporting medical information (discussed in section 6.11), users are generally prohibited from obtaining or using a consumer's medical information in connection with consumer credit.[267] The term "credit" in this context does not include (1) determination of consumer qualification or fitness for employment, insurance (other than a credit insurance product), or other noncredit products or services; (2) authorization, processing, or documenting a payment or transaction on a consumer's behalf in a manner that does not involve determining the consumer's eligibility for credit; or (3) maintaining or servicing the consumer's account in a manner that does not involve determining the consumer's eligibility for credit.[268]

Importantly, a user does not violate this prohibition if the user receives such medical information by accident.[269] In fact, a user may even use the unsolicited medical information provided to it in connection with determinations of the consumer's eligibility for credit as long as the user qualifies for at least one exception listed in Regulation V.[270]

9. Unique Issues

9.1 Free Consumer Reports

Once every twelve months, the FCRA entitles a consumer to a free copy of the consumer's consumer report from nationwide consumer reporting agencies (Equifax, Experian, and TransUnion) and nationwide specialty consumer reporting agencies.[271]

Consumers may be entitled to free consumer reports under various other circumstances. For example, a consumer reporting agency must provide a free consumer report if a consumer requests one within sixty days of receiving an adverse action notice,[272] or within sixty days of receiving notice from a debt collection agency stating

266. 12 C.F.R. § 1022.82(c). *See also* 12 C.F.R. § 1022.82(c)–(d) (describing examples of reasonable policies and procedures).

267. 12 C.F.R. § 1022.30(b)(1).

268. 12 C.F.R. § 1022.30(b)(2)(iii).

269. 12 C.F.R. § 1022.30(c)(1). *See also* 12 C.F.R. § 1022.30(c)(3) for examples of unsolicited receipt of medical information.

270. 12 C.F.R. § 1022.30(d)–(e).

271. 15 U.S.C. § 1681j(a)(1)(A)–(C).

272. *Id.* § 1681j(b).

that the consumer's credit rating has been adversely affected.[273] Also, a consumer is entitled to receive a free consumer report once every twelve months if the consumer certifies in writing that he or she is unemployed but intends to apply for a job within the next sixty days, or is a recipient of public welfare assistance, or the consumer has reason to believe that the consumer reporting agency's file contains inaccurate information due to fraud.[274] Otherwise, a consumer reporting agency may impose a "reasonable charge" to provide a consumer report on a consumer's request.[275]

9.2 Truncation of Credit Card Numbers

Amendments to the FCRA under the Fair and Accurate Credit Transactions Act included specific prohibitions relating to credit card receipts. No person that accepts credit cards or debit cards for transactions may print more than the last five digits of a card number, or the expiration date, on any receipt provided at the point of transaction.[276] The prohibition only applies to receipts that are generated through an electronic process (cash register, electronic application, etc.); it does not apply to handwritten receipts or carbon imprints of cards.[277]

9.3 Affiliate Sharing of Consumer Reports, and Sharing for Marketing Purposes

The FCRA gives unique permissions to affiliates:[278] sharing of consumer information without converting the information into a consumer report, and opportunity to use a consumer report for marketing purposes.

9.3.1 Certain Affiliate Sharing Is Permitted

The FCRA expressly allows affiliates to share two types of information. First, affiliates may share firsthand information between or among their affiliates without converting

273. *Id.*

274. *Id.* § 1681j(c)(1)–(3).

275. *Id.* § 1681j(f)(1). Effective January 1, 2020, the reasonable charge may not exceed $12.50. *See* Fair Credit Reporting Act Disclosures, 84 Fed. Reg. 65,280, 65,281 (Nov. 27, 2019) (to be codified at 12 C.F.R. pt. 1022).

276. 15 U.S.C. § 1681c(g)(1).

277. *Id.* § 1681c(g)(2).

278. For purposes of the affiliate-sharing provisions, affiliates are defined as "persons related . . . by common ownership or affiliated by corporate control." *Id.* § 1681s-3(a)(1). *See also* 12 C.F.R. § 1022.3(b) ("Affiliate means any company that is related by common ownership or common corporate control with another company. For example, an affiliate of a Federal credit union is a credit union service corporation, as provided in 12 C.F.R. Part 712, that is controlled by the Federal credit union.").

the information into a consumer report.[279] Second, affiliates may share *any* consumer information between or among affiliates but only if, before sharing the information, the fact of sharing is "clearly and conspicuously disclosed to the consumer" and the consumer is given opportunity to opt out of affiliate sharing.[280]

9.3.2 Affiliate Sharing for Marketing Purposes

Affiliates are given some permission to use consumer information for marketing purposes when the information is shared among affiliates, but only if (1) the consumer has been informed, before affiliate sharing occurs, of the basic fact that affiliate sharing might occur;[281] (2) the consumer has been given "clear and conspicuous" disclosure that the affiliate sharing of the consumer's information may occur for purposes of soliciting[282] the consumer;[283] and (3) the consumer is given an opportunity and "a simple method" to prohibit the making of such solicitations.[284]

If a consumer elects to prevent all or any form of affiliate sharing for marketing, that election lasts five years or such earlier time as the consumer revokes it.[285] At the end of the five-year period, the recipient affiliate must give the consumer notice of opportunity to extend the opt out for another period of at least five years before using the consumer report for marketing to the consumer.[286]

These additional disclosure obligations relating to marketing purposes do not apply if (1) the recipient affiliate is using the consumer information with regard to marketing to a consumer with whom the recipient affiliate has a preexisting business

---

279. 15 U.S.C. § 1681a(d)(2)(A)(ii).

280. *Id.* § 1681a(d)(2)(A)(iii).

281. *Id.* § 1681a(d)(2)(A)(iii).

282. "Solicitation" means "the marketing of a product or service initiated by a person to a particular consumer that is based on an exchange of information described in [15 U.S.C. § 1681s-3(a)], and is intended to encourage the consumer to purchase such product or service, but does not include communications that are directed at the general public or determined not to be a solicitation by the regulations prescribed under this section." *Id.* § 1681s-3(d)(2). *See also* 12 C.F.R. § 1022.20(b)(5) (solicitation means "the marketing of a product or service initiated by a person to a particular consumer that is: (A) based on eligibility information communicated to that person by its affiliate []; and (B) intended to encourage the consumer to purchase or obtain such product or service."). *See also* 12 C.F.R. § 1022.21(b)(6) for examples of making solicitations under this rule.

283. 15 U.S.C. § 1681s-3(a)(1)(A). This notice must be given by an affiliate that has, or previously had, a preexisting business relationship with the consumer; the notice may be jointly given by multiple affiliates as long as one of the affiliates has or had such preexisting business relationship. 12 C.F.R. § 1022.21(a)(3).

284. 15 U.S.C. § 1681s-3(a)(1)(B).

285. *Id.* § 1681s-3(a)(3)(A).

286. *Id.* § 1681s-3(a)(3)(B).

relationship;[287] (2) the recipient affiliate uses the consumer information to facilitate communications relating to an employee benefit plan;[288] (3) the recipient affiliate uses the consumer information to perform services on behalf of another affiliate, unless such other affiliate would be prohibited from soliciting the consumer;[289] (4) the recipient affiliate uses the consumer information in response to a consumer-initiated communication;[290] (5) the recipient affiliate uses the consumer information in response to solicitations authorized or requested by the consumer;[291] or (6) the recipient affiliate must use the consumer information to comply with any state insurance laws regarding unfair discrimination in any state in which the affiliate is lawfully doing business.[292] Regulation V provides various examples of these exceptions to the affiliate marketing rules.[293]

10. Regulatory Rulemaking

From 2003 until 2010, the FTC possessed rulemaking authority in numerous FCRA areas. Some rulemaking belonged exclusively to the FTC, other rulemaking was set for joint authority with other agencies (including the Federal Reserve and other federal financial agencies).[294]

In 2011, the Dodd-Frank Wall Street Reform and Consumer Protection Act of 2010 (Dodd-Frank Act) transferred nearly all FCRA rulemaking authority to the Bureau.[295] On December 21, 2011, the Bureau restated the FCRA regulations at 12 C.F.R. pt. 1022 (76 Fed. Reg. 79308). The Bureau frequently issues bulletins relating to the consumer laws under its supervision, and practitioners are advised to review those bulletins for regulatory guidance.[296]

287. *Id.* § 1681s-3(a)(4)(A); 12 C.F.R. § 1022.21(c)(1). *See* 15 U.S.C. § 1681s-3(d)(1) and 12 C.F.R. § 1022.20(b)(4) for definition and examples of a "pre-existing business relationship."

288. 15 U.S.C. § 1681s-3(a)(4)(B); 12 C.F.R. § 1022.21(c)(2).

289. 15 U.S.C. § 1681s-3(a)(4)(C); 12 C.F.R. § 1022.21(c)(3).

290. 15 U.S.C. § 1681s-3(a)(4)(D); 12 C.F.R. § 1022.21(c)(4).

291. 15 U.S.C. § 1681s-3(a)(4)(E); 12 C.F.R. § 1022.21(c)(5).

292. 15 U.S.C. § 1681s-3(a)(4)(F); 12 C.F.R. § 1022.21(c)(6).

293. *See* 12 C.F.R. § 1022.21(d)(1)–(4).

294. FTC, *40 Years of Experience*, *supra* note 13, at section IV.

295. CFPB, *Consumer Laws and Regulation* 1 (Oct. 2012), https://files.consumerfinance.gov/f/documents/102012_cfpb_fair-credit-reporting-act-fcra_procedures.pdf.

296. *See* CFPB, *Supervisory Guidance*, https://www.consumerfinance.gov/policy-compliance/guidance/supervisory-guidance (last visited Aug. 24, 2020).

11. Liability

11.1 Private Civil Action

The FCRA generally authorizes a private right of action against any person who fails to comply with any section of the FCRA, under two levels of culpability: willful violations[297] and negligent violations.[298]

A willful violation of the FCRA requires the consumer to prove that the defendant either knowingly or recklessly violated the statute.[299] The test involves two questions: (1) Was the defendant's conduct based on an objectively reasonable interpretation of the statute? (2) If objectively unreasonable, was the risk of violating the FCRA substantially greater than the risk associated with a merely careless reading of the statute?[300] If the consumer prevails on a willful violation theory, the consumer may recover either (1) actual damages or (2) statutory damages between $100 and $1,000.[301] A prevailing consumer may also seek punitive damages, recovery of reasonable attorneys' fees, and court costs.[302] If the civil action is based on a user's procurement of a consumer report under false pretenses or knowingly without a permissible purpose, the consumer may recover the greater of actual damages or $1,000.[303]

A negligent violation of the FCRA typically requires the consumer to prove whether the defendant acted reasonably. If the consumer prevails on a negligence theory, the consumer may recover actual damages; statutory damages are not available.[304] A prevailing consumer may also seek recovery of reasonable attorneys' fees and court costs.[305]

The FCRA removes numerous statutory violations from private civil enforcement, reserving enforcement to regulators. For example, section 623(c) removes private causes of action relating to numerous furnisher obligations.[306] Similarly, section 615(h)(8) provides that private civil liability shall not apply for failure to comply with section 615.[307] Practitioners should review the FCRA, Regulation V, and caselaw to determine whether a private cause of action exists in a given situation.

The U.S. Supreme Court decision in *Spokeo, Inc. v. Robins*[308] also emphasized a fundamental limitation on private FCRA liability, namely, that Article III standing

297. 15 U.S.C. § 1681n.
298. *Id.* § 1681o.
299. See Safeco Ins. Co. of Am. v. Burr, 551 U.S. 47, 57 (2007).
300. *Id.* at 69–70.
301. 15 U.S.C. § 1681n(a)(1)(A).
302. *Id.* § 1681n(a)(1)(2)–(3).
303. *Id.* § 1681n(b).
304. *Id.* § 1681o(a)(1).
305. *Id.* § 1681o(a)(2).
306. *Id.* § 1681s-2(c), (d).
307. *Id.* § 1681m(h)(8).
308. 136 S. Ct. 1540 (2016).

to sue for a statutory violation requires the plaintiff to have suffered an "injury in fact." An injury in fact is one that is "concrete and particularized" and "actual or imminent, not conjectural or hypothetical."[309] "For that reason, [the plaintiff] could not, for example, allege a bare procedural violation [of the FCRA], divorced from any concrete harm, and satisfy the injury-in-fact requirement of Article III."[310] The *Spokeo* decision has generated citations in thousands of decisions. All parties involved in FCRA disputes should consider how *Spokeo* might apply.

11.2 Regulatory Enforcement Authority

The CFPB and FTC retain dual primary enforcement authority for the FCRA.[311] State agencies also possess authority to enforce violations of the FCRA, subject to certain limitations on remedies and coordination with federal regulators.[312]

11.3 Statute of Limitations; Venue

Any action to enforce an FCRA violation must be filed in court before the earlier of (1) two years after the plaintiff discovers the violation, or (2) five years after the date on which the violation occurred.[313] In practice, the "discovery of violation" has been held to mean the date that the plaintiff discovered the facts that gave rise to the claim, not the date that the plaintiff discovered that those facts constitute a violation of the FCRA.[314]

Any action to enforce the FCRA may be filed in the appropriate U.S. district court or state court of competent jurisdiction.[315]

11.4 Preemption

The FCRA preempts state statutes, regulations, and common law claims that are inconsistent with the FCRA as it relates to collection, distribution, or use of consumer information or for the prevention or mitigation of identity theft, to the extent of the inconsistency.[316] The FCRA additionally forbids states from imposing requirements or prohibitions with respect to a series of specific subjects governed by the FCRA.[317]

---

309. *Id.* at 1548.

310. *Id.*

311. 15 U.S.C. § 1681s(a), (b)(1)(H).

312. *Id.* § 1681s(c).

313. *Id.* § 1681p.

314. *See, e.g.*, Rocheleau v. Elder Living Constr., LLC, 814 F.3d 398, 400–01 (6th Cir. 2016); Mack v. Equable Ascent Fin., LLC, 748 F.3d 663, 665–66 (5th Cir. 2014).

315. 15 U.S.C. § 1681p.

316. *Id.* § 1681t(a).

317. *See id.* § 1681t(b).

The FCRA also generally prohibits consumer claims against consumer reporting agencies, users, or furnishers for defamation, invasion of privacy, or negligence with respect to the reporting of information.[318] The only exception to this prohibition is if the consumer reporting agency/user/furnisher reported false information with malice or willful intent to injure the consumer.[319]

12. Crosswalk of Statutory References

U.S.C. Section	FCRA Section	FCRA Heading
§ 1681	§ 602	Congressional findings and statement of purpose
§ 1681a	§ 603	Definitions; rules of construction
§ 1681b	§ 604	Permissible purposes of consumer reports
§ 1681c	§ 605	Requirements relating to information contained in consumer reports
§ 1681c-1	§ 605A	Identity theft prevention; fraud alerts and active duty alerts
§ 1681c-2	§ 605B	Block of information resulting from identity theft
§ 1681d	§ 606	Disclosure of investigative consumer reports
§ 1681e	§ 607	Compliance procedures
§ 1681f	§ 608	Disclosures to governmental agencies
§ 1681g	§ 609	Disclosures to consumers
§ 1681h	§ 610	Conditions and form of disclosure to consumers
§ 1681i	§ 611	Procedure in case of disputed accuracy
§ 1681j	§ 612	Charges for certain disclosures
§ 1681k	§ 613	Public record information for employment purposes
§ 1681l	§ 614	Restrictions on investigative consumer reports
§ 1681m	§ 615	Requirements on users of consumer reports
§ 1681n	§ 616	Civil liability for willful noncompliance
§ 1681o	§ 617	Civil liability for negligent noncompliance
§ 1681p	§ 618	Jurisdiction of courts; limitation of actions
§ 1681q	§ 619	Obtaining information under false pretenses

318. *Id.* § 1681h(e).

319. *Id.*

§ 1681r	§ 620	Unauthorized disclosures by officers or employees
§ 1681s	§ 621	Administrative enforcement
§ 1681s-1	§ 622	Information on overdue child support obligations
§ 1681s-2	§ 623	Responsibilities of furnishers of information to consumer reporting agencies
§ 1681s-3	§ 624	Affiliate sharing
§ 1681t	§ 625	Relation to state laws
§ 1681u	§ 626	Disclosures to the Federal Bureau of Investigation for counterintelligence purposes
§ 1681v	§ 627	Disclosures to governmental agencies for counterterrorism purposes
§ 1681w	§ 628	Disposal of records
§ 1681x	§ 629	Corporate and technological circumvention prohibited

CHAPTER

7

Fair Lending

Christopher Willis, Jacqueline Parker, Lori J. Sommerfield, Sarah Pruett, Scott A. Coleman, and Reid F. Herlihy

1. Introduction

This chapter provides an overview of federal fair lending laws that were enacted by Congress in the late 1960s and early 1970s to provide fair treatment and equal access to credit and housing for certain protected class groups. In 1968, Congress passed the Fair Housing Act, which was part of the seminal federal civil rights legislation. The Fair Housing Act prohibited discrimination in all aspects of residential real estate–related transactions (including making loans to buy, build, repair, or improve a dwelling; purchasing real estate loans; selling, brokering, or appraising residential real estate; and selling or renting a dwelling) on the basis of race, color, religion, national origin, sex, familial status, or handicap. Congress then passed the Equal Credit Opportunity Act (ECOA) in 1974 to prohibit creditors from discriminating against an applicant in any aspect of a consumer or business credit transaction on the basis of race, color, religion, national origin, sex, age, marital status, receipt of public assistance, or good faith exercise of a right under the Consumer Credit Protection Act. The original purpose of ECOA was to prevent discrimination against women in obtaining access to credit and, in 1976, the law was amended to include other protected class groups. These fair lending laws provide a legal basis for prohibiting discriminatory lending practices.

This chapter also provides a brief description of two related laws—the Home Mortgage Disclosure Act and the Community Reinvestment Act (CRA)—that were enacted in the 1970s. Although these laws are not fair lending laws per se, they are designed to support the objectives of the federal fair lending laws. The Home Mortgage Disclosure Act requires covered financial institutions to collect, record, report, and disclose information about their mortgage lending activities, which is designed to help regulators determine whether financial institutions serve their communities' housing needs and assist in identifying any potential discriminatory lending patterns. The CRA requires federal financial supervisory agencies to assess the record of each insured depository institution in helping to meet the credit needs of low- to moderate-income individuals and families in its assessment area, consistent with safe and sound operations. A poor CRA record can serve as the basis for a federal regulator to decline an application for a new deposit facility or an application to merge with, or acquire, another financial institution, and it can also be taken into account in fair lending examinations. Both laws are intended to help enforce the federal fair lending laws.

2. Relevant Statutes and Regulations

2.1 The Equal Credit Opportunity Act and Regulation B

ECOA, 15 U.S.C. §§ 1691 to 1691f, enacted in 1974, prohibits *creditors* from discriminating against *credit applicants* on the basis of enumerated protected characteristics with respect to any aspect of a credit transaction.[1] Congress enacted ECOA to ensure that creditors extend credit equally to all creditworthy customers, without consideration of race, color, religion, national origin, sex, marital status, age, or other prohibited bases.[2] ECOA's implementing regulations, found in Regulation B, 12 C.F.R. part 1002, set forth procedural requirements that creditors must follow in addition to ECOA's general prohibition on discrimination.[3] The Consumer Financial Protection Bureau (CFPB or Bureau) is responsible for enforcing ECOA and administering Regulation B.[4]

Numerous federal agencies share supervision and enforcement responsibilities for ECOA, including the CFPB, Federal Reserve Board (FRB), Office of the Comptroller of the Currency (OCC), Federal Deposit Insurance Corporation (FDIC), and National

1. 15 U.S.C. § 1691(a). The terms *creditor*, *credit*, and *applicant* are specifically defined by the ECOA and discussed further in section 2.1.1.

2. Act Oct. 28, 1974, P. L. 93-495, Title V, § 502, 88 Stat. 1521.

3. ECOA expressly incorporates the requirements imposed within Regulation B; thus, a violation of Regulation B may serve as the basis for an ECOA action. *See* 15 U.S.C. § 1691a(g).

4. Title X of the Dodd-Frank Wall Street Reform and Consumer Protection Act of 2010 created the CFPB and vested it with supervisory and enforcement authority over ECOA and Regulation B. Pub. L. 111-203, 124 Stat. 1376, title X.

Credit Union Administration (NCUA).[5] Credit applicants may initiate individual or class action lawsuits against creditors for alleged violations of ECOA.[6]

2.1.1 Protected Characteristics

Like many federal laws prohibiting discrimination against protected classes, ECOA prohibits creditors from discriminating against credit applicants on the basis of race, color, religion, national origin, sex, marital status, or age.[7] ECOA also prohibits discrimination on the basis of an applicant's income deriving, in whole or in part, from a public assistance program.[8] Finally, ECOA prohibits creditors from discriminating against applicants who have, in good faith, exercised their rights under the federal consumer credit protection laws found in the Consumer Credit Protection Act, including ECOA.[9]

2.1.2 Covered Entities: Creditors and Arrangers of Credit; Potential Application to Leases in the Ninth Circuit

ECOA prohibits creditors from discriminating against credit applicants.[10] ECOA defines creditors, credit, and applicants broadly, such that the statute covers a wide

5. 15 U.S.C. § 1691c. The U.S. Department of Justice (DOJ) and the Federal Trade Commission (FTC) may also engage in enforcement measures. ECOA requires the agency responsible for administrative enforcement to refer matters to the DOJ whenever there is "reason to believe that 1 or more creditors has engaged in a pattern or practice of discouraging or denying applications for credit in violation of section 1691(a)." *Id.* at § 1691e(g).

6. *Id.* § 1691e. Damages available include equitable and declaratory relief, actual damages, punitive damages, attorney fees, and costs.

7. *Id.* § 1691(a)(1). Age is a protected category provided that the applicant has the capacity to contract.

8. 15 U.S.C. § 1691(a)(2).

9. 15 U.S.C. § 1691(a)(3). The Consumer Credit Protection Act includes, in part, laws pertaining to consumer credit cost disclosure, credit reporting, debt collection, and electronic fund transfers. *See* 15 U.S.C. §§ 1601–1693r.

10. 15 U.S.C. § 1691(a).

array of credit transactions.[11] Creditors subject to ECOA include "any person who regularly extends, renews, or continues credit; any person who regularly arranges for the extension, renewal, or continuation of credit; or any assignee of an original creditor who participates in the decision to extend, renew, or continue credit."[12] Creditors also include transferees, subrogees, and those who "regularly participate[] in a credit decision" including by negotiating, arranging, or otherwise setting the credit terms, and, in certain circumstances, those who refer applicants to creditors.[13]

2.1.3 All Aspects of Credit Transactions Covered

It is unlawful for creditors to discriminate in "any aspect of a credit transaction" and at any point in the lifecycle of the credit transaction.[14] Regulation B defines credit transaction to include "every aspect of an applicant's dealings with a creditor regarding an application for credit or an existing extension of credit (including, but not limited to, information requirements; investigation procedures; standards of creditworthiness; terms of credit; furnishing of credit information; revocation, alteration, or termination of credit; and collection procedures)."[15] Thus, every stage of a credit transaction is covered by ECOA, from an initial request for credit through payment and collection of the debt. However, a creditor is not liable under ECOA for any violation that was

---

11. ECOA defines "creditors" as "any person who regularly extends, renews, or continues credit; any person who regularly arranges for the extension, renewal, or continuation of credit; or any assignee of an original creditor who participates in the decision to extend, renew, or continue credit." 15 U.S.C. § 1691a(e). ECOA further defines "person" to include "a natural person, a corporation, government or governmental subdivision or agency, trust, estate, partnership, cooperative, or association." *Id.* at § 1691a(f). ECOA broadly defines "credit" to include "the right granted by a creditor to a debtor to defer payment of debt or to incur debts and defer its payment or to purchase property or services and defer payment therefor" and "applicant" as "any person who applies to a creditor directly for an extension, renewal, or continuation of credit, or applies to a creditor indirectly by use of an existing credit plan for an amount exceeding a previously established credit limit." *Id.* at § 1691a(b), (d). Regulation B further adds to these broad definitions.

12. 15 U.S.C. § 1691a(e).

13. 12 C.F.R. § 1002.2(l). Those persons whose sole involvement in a credit transaction is honoring a credit card are excluded from the definition of creditors. *Id.*

14. 15 U.S.C. § 1691(a).

15. 12 C.F.R. § 1002.2(m). Leases may be deemed credit transactions subject to ECOA in certain circumstances, but their treatment differs across jurisdictions. For example, the Ninth Circuit Court of Appeals determined that personal property leases covered by the Consumer Leasing Act are credit transactions in certain circumstances. *See* Brothers v. First Leasing, 724 F.2d 789 (9th Cir. 1984). Other courts have found that similar leases are not credit transactions covered by ECOA. *See, e.g.*, Liberty Leasing Co. v. Machamer, 6 F. Supp. 2d 714 (S.D. Ohio 1998).

committed by another creditor unless the person knew or had reasonable notice of the violation before becoming involved in the credit transaction.[16]

2.1.4 Prohibitions on Discrimination and Discouragement

ECOA prohibits creditors from discriminating against applicants because of a protected characteristic.[17] For purposes of ECOA, discrimination is defined in Regulation B as treating an applicant less favorably than other applicants.[18] ECOA does not prohibit creditors from distinguishing and treating higher-risk applicants differently than lower-risk applicants, regardless of the applicants' membership in any protected class.[19] Discrimination may occur directly by treating applicants differently because of a protected characteristic, or indirectly, when an action has the effect of discriminating on the basis of a protected characteristic.[20] Discouraging applicants or prospective applicants from making or pursuing a credit application is also discriminatory when the discouragement is directly or indirectly based on a protected characteristic.[21]

2.1.5 Advertising Provisions

Under ECOA and Regulation B, creditors may not directly or indirectly engage in any advertising or marketing to applicants or prospective applicants that would discourage (or selectively encourage) a reasonable person from making or pursuing an application for credit on a prohibited basis.[22]

2.2 The Fair Housing Act

The Fair Housing Act (FHA), 42 U.S.C. § 3601 *et seq.*, was enacted in 1968 as Title VIII of the seminal U.S. civil rights legislation. The FHA prohibits discrimination in the sale, rental, and financing of housing on the basis of several protected characteristics, discussed below. With regard to financing, the FHA proscribes discrimination in "residential real estate transactions," including loans to purchase or improve residential real estate. The U.S. Department of Housing and Urban Development (HUD) administers and enforces the FHA and has promulgated implementing regulations found at 24 C.F.R. part 100.

---

16. 12 C.F.R. § 1002.2(l).
17. 15 U.S.C. § 1691(a).
18. 12 C.F.R. § 1002.2(n).
19. 12 C.F.R §§ 1006(a), 1006(b)(6).
20. 12 C.F.R § 1004(a); Official Staff Interpretation to 12 C.F.R § 1004(a), Comment 4(a)-1, 2; 12 C.F.R § 1006(a); Official Staff Interpretation to 12 C.F.R § 1006(a)-2.
21. 12 C.F.R. § 1002.4(b).
22. *Id.*

2.2.1 Protected Characteristics

The FHA prohibits discrimination on the basis of race, color, religion, sex, handicap, familial status, or national origin.[23] In 2012, HUD issued a final rule entitled Equal Access to Housing in HUD Programs Regardless of Sexual Orientation or Gender Identity (Equal Access Rule).[24] HUD's Equal Access Rule prohibits discrimination based on actual or perceived sexual orientation, gender identity, and marital status, but only for those residential real estate transactions that are funded, insured, or otherwise assisted by HUD.[25]

2.2.2 Lending Transactions Covered

Section 805 of the FHA prohibits discrimination against any person, because of their protected characteristics, in making or providing loans or other financial assistance to purchase, construct, improve, repair, or maintain a dwelling.[26] The FHA defines *dwelling* to include any building that is occupied, or designed or intended for occupancy, as a residence by one or more families, as well as vacant land that is offered for sale or lease for the construction of a building that is intended or designed for occupancy as a residence.[27] The FHA also prohibits discrimination in making or providing loans or financial assistance where the loan or assistance is secured by residential real estate, regardless of the purpose for which the consumer uses the loan.[28] Lenders, brokers, agents, and any other person or entity that is involved in making or providing loans or financial assistance, as well as those who purchase loans, debts, or securities, may be subject to the FHA.[29]

Practices are discriminatory under the FHA if they are based on a person's race, color, religion, sex, handicap, familial status, or national origin.[30] Such practices include, but are not limited to, the following: (1) failing or refusing to provide information about the availability of loans, application requirements, procedures and standard for review and approval of loans, or providing inaccurate information; (2) providing, failing to provide, or discouraging loans or financial assistance in a manner that discriminates in the denial rate or availability of a loan; (3) conditioning the availability or other aspect of a loan or financial assistance on a person's response to harassment; (4) subjecting a person to harassment because of their protected characteristic such that it affects the availability of a loan or financial assistance; (5) imposing different terms

23. 42 U.S.C. § 3605(a).

24. *See* Equal Access to Housing in HUD Programs Regardless of Sexual Orientation or Gender Identity, 77 Fed. Reg. 5662 (Feb 3, 2012).

25. 24 C.F.R. § 5.105(a)(2).

26. 42 U.S.C. § 3605(b)(1); 24 C.F.R. § 100.120.

27. 42 U.S.C. § 3602(b).

28. *Id.* § 3605(b)(1).

29. *Id.* § 3605(b)(2).

30. *Id.* § 3605(a).

or conditions for loans or financial assistance; (6) using different policies, practices, or procedures to evaluate and determine creditworthiness; (7) determining the type of loan, interest rate, cost, duration, or other terms or conditions because of a protected characteristic; and (8) servicing loans in a discriminatory manner.[31]

2.2.3 Advertising Provisions

Advertising or marketing, including all written or oral notices or statements, applications, brochures, signs, or other documents and statements, must also comply with the FHA's prohibitions on discrimination.[32] Oral or written advertising may be deemed discriminatory when it expresses a preference or limitation based on race, color, religion, sex, handicap, familial status, or national origin.[33] Advertising can also be discriminatory when the location or media selected for advertising denies a protected class information about housing opportunities.[34]

Any mortgage loan–related advertising and marketing materials must include a facsimile of the Equal Housing Opportunity logo and the phrase "Equal Opportunity Lender" or a statement to the effect that the lender makes housing loans without regard to an applicant's prohibited basis characteristics.[35]

2.3 Department of Housing and Urban Development Regulations

2.3.1 Disparate Impact Rule

In 2013, HUD issued a final rule that formally recognizes the disparate impact theory under the FHA and sets forth standards for establishing such claims.[36] In the preamble to the rule, HUD stated that the rule codified its "long-held interpretation" that liability may result from a facially neutral policy or practice that has a disproportionate effect on members of a protected class, even without evidence of discriminatory intent.[37]

The rule, which is codified at 24 C.F.R. part 100, explains a three-step, burden-shifting approach to establish disparate impact liability. First, the plaintiff must prove that the challenged practice caused, or predictably will cause, a disparate impact on

31. 24 C.F.R. § 100.120(b)(1)–(4); *Id.* at §§ 100.130(a), (b)(1)–(4).

32. *Id.* § 100.75.

33. *Id.* § 100.75(a).

34. *Id.* § 100.75(c).

35. *See* 24 C.F.R. § 110.25(a), which describes fair housing posters under the FHA. State nonmember banks regulated by the FDIC and state member banks supervised by the FRB are alternatively permitted to use the "Equal Housing Lender" logo and legend. *See* 12 C.F.R. § 338.3(a); Fair Housing Advertising and Poster Requirements, 54 Fed. Reg. 11567 (March 21, 1989).

36. Implementation of the FHA's Discriminatory Effects Standard, 78 Fed. Reg. 11460 (Feb. 15, 2013). As discussed in section 2, the question of whether disparate impact claims are cognizable under ECOA is uncertain in terms of the state of current case law.

37. *Id.*

a protected class.[38] Second, the burden then shifts to the defendant to establish that the challenged practice is "necessary to achieve one or more substantial, legitimate, nondiscriminatory interests."[39] Third, the burden then shifts back to the plaintiff to prove that the challenged practice could be served by another practice with a less discriminatory effect.[40] A court will find that a "legally sufficient justification" exists where the challenged policy or practice is necessary to achieve one or more substantial, legitimate, nondiscriminatory interests of the respondent, and those interests could not be served by another practice that has a less discriminatory effect.[41] A legally sufficient justification must be supported by evidence and may not be hypothetical or speculative.[42]

Subsequently in 2015, the U.S. Supreme Court held in *Texas Department of Housing & Community Affairs v. Inclusive Communities Project, Inc.*, that disparate impact claims are cognizable under the FHA, although limits exist on its application.[43] Among other things, the Supreme Court stated that a plaintiff must demonstrate a "robust" causal connection between the challenged practice or policy and any alleged disparities.[44] Although the Supreme Court described in its opinion the use of a three-step, burden-shifting framework to analyze disparate impact claims under the FHA, the Court did not address specific standards and burdens of proof that should be used when applying the disparate impact theory. As a result, the Court did not seek to align its three-step test with HUD's disparate impact rule or to specifically validate or invalidate the rule.

HUD's disparate impact rule and its incongruity with the *Inclusive Communities* case holding have created significant compliance challenges for banks and financial institutions. To address these concerns and to attempt to align its three-part, burden-shifting test with *Inclusive Communities*, HUD issued a proposed rule in August 2019,[45] which was finalized in September 2020.[46] The final rule imposes a new five-part test to assess disparate impact claims, creates several new defenses, and clarifies certain issues with regard to HUD's disparate impact rule.[47] Some commentators claim that the

---

38. 24 C.F.R. § 100.500(c)(1).

39. *Id.* § 100.500(c)(2).

40. *Id.* § 100.500(c)(3).

41. *Id.* § 100.500(b)(1).

42. *Id.* § 100.500(b)(2).

43. Tex. Dept of Hous. & Cmty. Affairs v. Inclusive Cmtys. Project, Inc., 135 S.Ct. 2507 (2015).

44. *Id.* at 2523.

45. HUD's Implementation of the FHA's Disparate Impact Standard, 84 Fed. Reg. 42854 (Aug. 19, 2019). HUD's notice of proposed rulemaking was preceded by an advance notice of proposed rulemaking inviting comments on possible amendments to the agency's disparate impact rule. *See* Reconsideration of HUD's Implementation of the FHA's Disparate Impact Standard, 83 Fed. Reg. 28560 (June 20, 2018).

46. 85 Fed. Reg. 60288.

47. *Id.*

final rule will make it harder for plaintiffs and government agencies to bring disparate impact discrimination claims under the FHA, whereas others believe that HUD's rule closely aligns with the Supreme Court's opinion in *Inclusive Communities* while providing needed practical advice for regulators, banks and financial institutions, and attorneys who represent such institutions. The eventual status of the rule is uncertain, however, because it was the subject of lawsuits filed by consumer advocacy groups immediately after it was finalized, and a federal court in Massachusetts entered a preliminary injunction staying the effective date of the rule on October 25, 2020, pending adjudication of claims that the rule was promulgated in violation of the Administrative Procedures Act.[48]

2.4 The Civil Rights Act of 1866

ECOA and the FHA are the primary fair lending statutes at the federal level, but another federal statute comes into play in certain circumstances—the Civil Rights Act of 1866, codified at 42 U.S.C § 1981. This post-Civil War statute is broader than ECOA and the FHA in some respects, and narrower in others, and should be considered as part of any fair lending analysis.

2.4.1 Applicability to Contracts

Like ECOA and the FHA, section 1981 applies to all aspects of a credit transaction. Indeed, the statute is not limited to credit transactions at all; it broadly provides that "[a]ll persons within the jurisdiction of the United States shall have the same right in every State and Territory to make and enforce contracts . . . as is enjoyed by white citizens."[49] The statute goes on to define "make and enforce contracts" to include "the making, performance, modification, and termination of contracts, and the enjoyment of all benefits, privileges, terms, and conditions of the contractual relationship."[50] Thus, by its plain language, the Civil Rights Act of 1866 prohibits discrimination with respect to any aspect of any contractual relationship. Also, notably, because the statute applies to all contracts, it applies to relationships not covered by ECOA or the FHA, such as consumer leases of personal property, rent-to-own transactions, and ancillary products sold in connection with credit transactions.

2.4.2 Protected Characteristics: Race and Citizenship

In contrast to the lists of protected characteristics under ECOA and the FHA, section 1981 prohibits discrimination only with respect to race and citizenship.[51] With respect

48. Massachusetts Fair Housing Center v. HUD, No. 3:20-CV-11765-MGM (D. Mass. Oct. 25, 2020).

49. 42 U.S.C § 1981(a).

50. *Id.* § 1981(b).

51. *Id.* § 1981(a); *see also* Graham v. Richardson, 403 U.S. 365, 377 (1971).

to race, section 1981 is duplicative of ECOA and the FHA, but discrimination based on citizenship is uniquely prohibited by section 1981 among the federal antidiscrimination statutes applicable to lending transactions. Thus, it is a violation of section 1981 to treat non-U.S. citizens differently from U.S. citizens.[52]

This prohibition of discrimination based on citizenship appears to be contrary to ECOA, as interpreted by Regulation B. Regulation B allows a creditor to inquire about and take action on an application because of an applicant's "immigration status,"[53] and the Official Commentary to Regulation B goes on to state that "[a] denial of credit on the ground that an applicant is not a United States citizen is not per se discrimination based on national origin."[54]

This tension between ECOA and section 1981 has resulted in litigation against financial institutions, and that litigation has not yet yielded any definitive precedent for lenders to follow. Our view is that the prudent course of action is for lenders to make decisions based on immigration status (i.e., whether the applicant is permitted to legally remain in the United States for a period equal to the length of the repayment schedule on a credit transaction), but to treat permanent or long-term resident aliens in the same manner as U.S. citizens. This course of action is, as noted above, explicitly permitted by Regulation B, and also enjoys some support from case law under section 1981 that draws a distinction between discrimination based on "citizenship" and "residency" or "immigration status."[55] We caution, however, that this area is one without clear guidance, and any decisions about the treatment of citizenship or immigration status should be undertaken only after a thorough review of current case law and litigation developments.

2.4.3 Intentional Discrimination Only

Although section 1981 is broader than ECOA or the FHA in its coverage of all types of contracts, and in its prohibition of discrimination based on citizenship, it is narrower in a critical respect. Courts have definitively interpreted the statute to prohibit only

52. *Graham v. Richardson*, 403 U.S. at 377 ("The protection of this statute has been held to extend to aliens as well as to citizens.").

53. 12 C.F.R. § 1002.6(b)(7).

54. 12 C.F.R. part 1002, supp. I, § 6(b)(7)-2.

55. *See, e.g.*, Perez v. Wells Fargo & Co., No. 17-cv-00454-MMC, 2017 U.S. Dist. LEXIS 122772, at *2 (N.D. Cal. Aug. 3, 2017); Talwar v. Staten Island Univ. Hosp., No. 12-CV-0033 (CBA) (JMA), 2014 U.S. Dist. LEXIS 158953 (E.D.N.Y. Mar. 31, 2014), *aff'd in part, vacated in part, and remanded*, 610 F. app'x 28 (2d Cir. 2015); Vaughn v. City of N.Y., No. 06-CV-6547 (ILG), 2010 U.S. Dist. LEXIS 50791 (E.D.N.Y. May 24, 2010); Camara v. Schwan's Food Mfg., No. 04-121-JGW, 2005 U.S. Dist. LEXIS 44783 (E.D. Ky. Aug. 15, 2005).

intentional discrimination, and there is no disparate impact liability available under section 1981.[56]

2.5 Federal Regulatory Guidance

2.5.1 Interagency Statement on Discrimination in Lending

In 1994, several federal agencies jointly adopted the Policy Statement on Discrimination in Lending (the Interagency Policy Statement),[57] which provided foundational guidance on enforcement of the federal fair lending laws and their application.[58] The Interagency Policy Statement addresses what constitutes lending discrimination under ECOA and the FHA and provides guidance to lenders seeking to comply with these laws.[59] The CFPB subsequently adopted the Policy Statement in 2012, stating that it would "consider evidence of the disparate impact doctrine as one method of proving lending discrimination under ECOA and Regulation B."[60]

2.5.2 Side-by-Side: A Guide to Fair Lending

The FDIC issued "Side-by-Side: A Guide to Fair Lending" (the Guide) in 1996.[61] The Guide provides lenders with in-depth direction on how to use self-assessment to prevent and detect illegal discrimination under ECOA and the FHA and provides suggestions on how to correct discriminatory practices.

This Guide provides a framework for several methods of testing. For example, it suggests testing pre-application processes by utilizing trained actors to pose as applicants (which has become known as "mystery shopping"). These "testers" are given similar backgrounds in all respects other than the variable being tested (race, gender, age, etc.), but the tester for the protected class has slightly better qualifications, such

56. Guardians Ass'n v. Civil Serv. Comm'n, 463 U.S. 582, 586 n.6 (1983) (discriminatory intent is a "necessary element of a § 1981 cause of action."); *see also* Kolstad v. ADA, 527 U.S. 526, 534 (1999); Gen. Bldg. Contractors Ass'n v. Pa., 458 U.S. 375 388-91 (1982). For a discussion of the disparate impact doctrine, *see* sections 2.3 and 3.3.

57. The following agencies drafted the Policy Statement: HUD, DOJ, OCC, the now-dissolved Office of Thrift Supervision, FRB, FDIC, FTC, NCUA, Federal Housing Finance Board, and the Office of Federal Housing Enterprise Oversight.

58. Policy Statement on Discrimination in Lending, 59 Fed. Reg. 18267 (April 15, 1994).

59. *Id.*

60. CFPB Bulletin 2012-4 (Fair Lending), *Lending Discrimination* (April 18, 2012), https://files.consumerfinance.gov/f/201404_cfpb_bulletin_lending_discrimination.pdf. The Dodd-Frank Wall Street Reform and Consumer Protection Act of 2010 created the CFPB and vested it with supervisory and enforcement authority over ECOA. The CFPB likely issued this bulletin because it was a new government agency and wished to support its position that the disparate impact theory is viable under ECOA.

61. Side-by-Side: A Guide to Fair Lending, Federal Deposit Insurance Corporation, FIL-36-96 (June 6, 1996).

as a marginally better income or lower debt.[62] Similarly, an institution can use this method to test the potential validity of a complaint of illegal discrimination. In this scenario, the tester assumes a similar background to the complainant, has slightly worse qualifications, and is not a member of a protected class. The institution then compares the tester's experience with that of the complainant to see if the complainant may have experienced discrimination.[63] In addition to the methods of testing, the Guide provides information on how to select and train testers, identify discrimination, document and evaluate results, and address and correct concerns.[64]

2.5.3 CFPB Guidance on Same-Sex Marriage

On June 25, 2014, the CFPB issued guidance to ensure equal treatment for legally married same-sex couples.[65] The guidance, in the unusual form of an internal memo to Bureau staff, was intended to respond to the U.S. Supreme Court's 2013 decision in *United States v. Windsor*, in which the Court held Section 3 of the federal Defense of Marriage Act unconstitutional.[66] The act defined the word "marriage" as "a legal union between one man and one woman as husband and wife" and the word "spouse" as referring "only to a person of the opposite sex who is a husband or a wife."[67] The Court held that section 3 of the Defense of Marriage Act was unconstitutional as a deprivation of the equal liberty of persons protected under the Fifth Amendment.

The CFPB's guidance states that it will consider a person who is married under the laws of any jurisdiction to be married nationwide for purposes of enforcing, administering, or interpreting the statutes, regulations, and policies under the Bureau's jurisdiction. The guidance notes, however, that the CFPB "will not regard a person to be married by virtue of being in a domestic partnership, civil union, or other relationship not denominated by law as a marriage."[68]

---

62. *Id.* at p. 4–5.

63. *Id.* at p. 5.

64. *Id.*

65. Memorandum from CFPB Director Richard Cordray to CFPB Staff (June 25, 2014) [hereinafter "CFPB Memorandum"]. In February 2014, the DOJ issued a similar memorandum to its employees. Memorandum from the Attorney General to All Department of Justice Employees, Department Policy on ensuring Equal Treatment for Same-Sex Married Couples (Feb. 10, 2014).

66. United States v. Windsor, 570 U.S. 744 (2013).

67. *Id.* at 752 (quoting the Defense of Marriage Act).

68. CFPB Memorandum *supra* note 65, at 1.

2.5.4 Interagency Statement on the Use of Alternative Data in Credit Underwriting

In 2019, several federal agencies issued the Interagency Statement on the Use of Alternative Data in Credit Underwriting (Interagency Statement on Alternative Data).[69] The Interagency Statement on Alternative Data sets forth the agencies' recognition of the benefits of using alternative data in making credit decisions. Alternative data is data not typically found in the applicant's credit files or information customarily provided by an applicant, such as an applicant's cash flow.[70] The agencies noted that the benefits of alternative data include helping lenders evaluate the creditworthiness of applicants, increased speed and accuracy of credit decisions, and enabling applicants to obtain more favorable terms or additional credit than they would be able to obtain otherwise.[71] The agencies emphasized the continued need for compliance programs, testing, and monitoring to ensure that lenders' use of alternative data complies with applicable laws.[72]

2.6 State Laws

Although most fair lending activity has historically occurred under the federal antidiscrimination statutes described above, numerous states have antidiscrimination statutes applicable to consumer lending. Some are modeled after the federal statutes and are restricted in application to credit transactions[73] (or, sometimes, certain types of credit transactions like consumer mortgage loans), while others are broadly applicable to any kind of contract.[74] Practically, these statutes do not change a lender's fair lending analysis to any significant degree, except that several of them add protected characteristics not present in ECOA or the FHA, as discussed below.

2.6.1 Examples of Additional Protected Classes: Military Status, Familial Status, Sexual Orientation, and Gender Identity

State statutes primarily prohibit discrimination based on protected characteristics that largely overlap with those in ECOA and the FHA, but a number of states add

69. *See, e.g.*, Interagency Statement on the Use of Alternative Data in Credit Underwriting, Federal Deposit Insurance Corporation, FIL-82-2019 (December 3, 2019). The following agencies drafted the Statement on Alternative Data: The Board of Governors of the Federal Reserve System, the CFPB, the FDIC, the NCUA, and the OCC.

70. *Id.*

71. *Id.*

72. *Id.*

73. *See, e.g.*, Alaska Stat. § 18.80.250; Col. Rev. Stat. § 5-3-210; Conn. Gen. Stat. § 46a-66; N.Y. Exec. Law § 296-a.

74. *See, e.g.*, Cal. Civ. Code § 51.

protected characteristics that are not present in one or both of the federal statutes including, but not limited to the following:

- military status;[75]
- familial status (which is applicable to mortgage loans under the FHA, but is not contained in ECOA);[76]
- sexual orientation[77] and gender identity;[78]
- political affiliation;[79]
- pregnancy;[80]
- citizenship;[81] and
- immigration status.[82]

These additional protected characteristics generally lack practical import in the fair lending context because lenders are unaware of a consumer's protected status, and thus are unable to discriminate on the basis of it. However, the inclusion of "immigration status" in the California Unruh Civil Rights Act and Washington's law against discrimination is potentially problematic because plain language in both statutes appear to prohibit precisely what Regulation B allows—a lender's decision not to lend to persons who cannot legally remain in the United States to repay an extension of credit. The language about "immigration status" was added to the California statute in 2015 and Washington in 2020, and the apparent conflict with Regulation B has not yet been definitively resolved.

---

75. *See, e.g.*, N.Y. Exec. Law § 296-a(1)(a); Ohio Rev. Code Ann. § 4112.021(B)(1)(a); R.I. Gen. Laws § 34-37-4.3; Wash. Rev. Code § 49.60.030(1).

76. *See, e.g.*, N.J. Rev. Stat. § 10:5-12(i)(1); N.Y. Exec. Law § 296-a(1)(a); R.I. Gen. Laws § 34-37-4.3.

77. *See, e.g.*, Me. Rev. Stat. Ann. tit. 5 § 4595; Minn. Stat. § 363A.16, subd. 1; N.J. Rev. Stat. § 10:5-12(i)(1); N.M. Stat. Ann. § 28-1-7(H)(1); N.Y. Exec. Law § 296-a(1)(a); R.I. Gen. Laws § 34-37-4.3; Vt. Stat. Ann. tit. 8 § 10403(a).

78. *See, e.g.*, N.J. Rev. Stat. § 10:5-12(i)(1); N.M. Stat. Ann. § 28-1-7(H)(1); R.I. Gen. Laws § 34-37-4.3; Vt. Stat. Ann. tit. 8 § 10403(a).

79. *See, e.g.*, Neb. Rev. Stat. § 45-1056.

80. *See, e.g.*, Alaska Stat. § 18.80.250(a)(1); N.M. Stat. Ann. § 28-1-7(H)(1) (effective May 20, 2020); N.J. Rev. Stat. § 10:5-12(i)(1).

81. *See, e.g.*, Unruh Civil Rights Act, Cal. Civ. Code § 51(b); Wash. Rev. Code § 49.60.030(1) (effective June 1, 2020).

82. *See, e.g.*, Cal. Civ. Code § 51(b); Wash. Rev. Code § 49.60.030(1) (effective June 1, 2020). The Unruh Civil Rights Act also includes medical condition, genetic information, and primary language as protected characteristics. Cal. Civ. Code § 51(b).

2.6.2 Limited Enforcement or Litigation to Provide Clarity on State Statutes

There has been very little fair lending litigation or regulatory enforcement activity under most state antidiscrimination laws, with the consequence that there is little guidance on interpretation of those laws available.

3. Legal Theories of Lending Discrimination

Under the federal fair lending laws, courts and regulatory agencies have recognized three legal theories to demonstrate a violation of the applicable statute.[83] These parallel similar theories with respect to employment discrimination under Title VII of the Civil Rights Act of 1964, and, as a result, the terms will be familiar to those acquainted with employment discrimination law.[84]

3.1 Overt Discrimination

The most obvious—and least frequently encountered—form of discrimination under the fair lending laws is overt discrimination, sometimes referred to as "overt evidence of disparate treatment."[85] This occurs when a lender openly and intentionally treats consumers differently on the basis of a protected characteristic.

3.2 Disparate Treatment

The second legal theory under which a claim under the fair lending laws may be proven is "disparate treatment." This theory is very similar to overt discrimination, in that it rests on the ultimate conclusion that the lender engaged in intentional discrimination.[86] However, the manner in which that discrimination is proven does not require an overt policy.[87] Rather, disparate treatment can be proven by showing that the lender treated similarly situated consumers differently based on a protected characteristic, and the lender fails to offer a credible, nondiscriminatory explanation for the differential treatment.[88] When this occurs, a regulatory agency or court may

---

83. *See, e.g.*, the Interagency Policy Statement discussed in section 2.5.1.

84. 42 U.S.C. § 2000e *et seq.*

85. *See* FRB, *Consumer Compliance Handbook: Federal Fair Lending Regulations and Statutes: Overview*, 2, https://www.federalreserve.gov/boarddocs/supmanual/cch/fair_lend_over.pdf.

86. *Id.*

87. *Id.*

88. *Id.*

conclude that the lack of a credible explanation supports the inference of intentional discrimination.

3.3 Disparate Impact

The final—and most controversial—legal theory of discrimination under the fair lending laws is disparate impact. This doctrine is also borrowed from employment discrimination laws, and was originally recognized by the Supreme Court in that context in *Griggs v. Duke Power Co.*[89] Unlike disparate treatment, disparate impact does not require proof of intentional discrimination.[90] The proof in a disparate impact case proceeds in a three-stage inquiry in which the burden of proof shifts between the plaintiff (or regulator) and the lender:

1. The regulator or plaintiff must first prove that the lender applied a neutral, facially nondiscriminatory policy, and that the application of that policy disproportionately impacted members of a protected class.[91] This is typically shown by statistical evidence.
2. The defendant must then show that its policy was justified by "business necessity."[92] The amount of deference shown by regulators to lenders' business necessities has varied significantly across fair lending enforcement actions, and a number of examples are provided *infra* in section 6 of this chapter.
3. If the defendant shows a business necessity, the burden shifts back to the plaintiff or regulator to show that the business need can be served by an alternative policy or practice that results in a lesser disparate impact on members of the protected class.[93]

In the *Inclusive Communities* case, discussed in section 2.3, the U.S. Supreme Court definitively held that the disparate impact theory is available under the FHA.[94] With regard to ECOA, the federal regulators have assumed the applicability of the doctrine for several decades, and Regulation B explicitly states that the disparate impact theory applies under ECOA.[95] However, it remains unclear whether the federal courts will recognize the disparate impact theory under ECOA because of differences

89. Griggs v. Duke Power Co., 401 U.S. 424, 436, 91 S. Ct. 849, 856 (1971).

90. *See* FRB Consumer Compliance Handbook, *supra* note 85.

91. *Id.*

92. *Id.*

93. *Id.*

94. *See* Tex. Dep't of Hous. & Cmty. Affairs v. Inclusive Cmtys. Project, Inc., 135 S. Ct. 2507, 2525 (2015).

95. *See* 12 C.F.R. § 1002.6(a).

in the language of the statute as compared to federal statutes that have been held to allow for disparate impact liability.[96]

4. Fair Lending Risks Across the Loan Life Cycle

To identify fair lending risk, regulators have traditionally focused on areas of the lending process that require or permit human discretion, such as judgmental underwriting and pricing. The federal fair lending laws, however, apply to all aspects of the loan life cycle, from product development and marketing to servicing, collections, and foreclosure or repossession.[97] In recent years, the federal fair lending laws have even been applied to maintenance of residential real estate owned by banks as a result of foreclosures.

It is important to note that the fair lending laws apply to all types of consumer loans and business credit products. Consumer loans may include mortgage loans, home equity loans and lines of credit, auto loans and retail installment contracts, credit cards, student loans, unsecured loans, and overdraft lines of credit. Business loans may include small business loans and commercial loans.

This section discusses where fair lending risk lies within the loan life cycle and the importance of appropriate controls in each area to prudently manage such risks.[98]

4.1 New Product Development

Fair lending risks must be considered at the very outset of product development to ensure that any new lending products or services are developed, implemented, and maintained in compliance with the federal fair lending laws. The best way to ensure that fair lending compliance is integrated into the process is to include legal counsel and compliance professionals who are knowledgeable about fair lending in initial product discussions, design sessions, product development activities, and roll out.

Within most financial institutions, the new product or service review and approval process is usually executed through a formal new product development committee with cross-functional representatives who are needed to develop and bring the product or service to market, such as business leaders, product managers, marketing representatives, finance managers, and operational personnel, among others. Alternatively, the process may involve ad hoc meetings with similar representation, depending on the product or service at issue. In either case, it is critical that

---

96. *See* Garcia v. Johanns, 370 U.S. App. D.C. 280, 288 n.9 (D.C. Cir. 2006).

97. *See, e.g.*, 12 C.F.R. § 1002.4(a) ("A creditor shall not discriminate against an applicant on a prohibited basis regarding *any aspect of a credit transaction*.") (emphasis added).

98. *See* American Association of Bank Directors, D. Baris et al, Practical Handbook on Fair Lending for Bank Directors and Executive Officers, Ch. IV, Where Does Fair Lending Risk Lie? (2016) [hereinafter Practical Handbook on Fair Lending].

representatives from legal and compliance serve on such committees, offer fair lending advice, and provide written sign off on the new product or service. This approach demonstrates that compliance with the fair lending laws was considered and addressed as part of the process of developing and implementing the product or service.

4.2 Advertising and Marketing

As described in sections 2.1.5 and 2.2.3, both ECOA and the FHA prohibit discrimination in advertisements for extensions of credit. Before using or issuing any advertising or marketing materials, it is prudent for business units and/or marketing to request that legal and compliance representatives review and approve them to ensure that the materials comply with the fair lending laws, as well as other applicable consumer financial protection laws. In addition to reviewing advertising and marketing materials for technical compliance, legal and compliance representatives should ensure that any images used do not strictly show white non-Hispanic individuals, but depict an appropriate range of images that reflect the diversity of the financial institution's local market area and/or the U.S. population, including, among others, minorities, young people, the elderly, single men and women, and married couples. In addition, legal and compliance should ensure that any direct marketing models or other methods used to identify and select recipients of advertising or promotional materials comply with the federal fair lending laws.

4.3 Taking and Processing Applications

It is imperative that lenders treat applicants fairly and consistently when taking and processing credit applications. Such activities range from promptly and completely addressing applicant questions during the pre-application stage, providing a consistent level of assistance to similarly situated applicants during the application in-take process, and processing applications in accordance with regulatory requirements and timeframes. Regulation B contains many of the technical requirements with which lenders must comply when taking and processing applications. Among other things, lenders are required to adhere to certain rules concerning requests for information,[99] evaluate applications objectively,[100] and notify applicants of action taken on their applications within thirty days after receiving a completed application or taking adverse action.[101]

99. 12 C.F.R. § 1002.5.
100. *Id.* § 1002.6.
101. *Id.* § 1002.9.

4.4 Loan Origination

4.4.1 Credit Risk and Underwriting

In fair lending examinations, investigations, and enforcement actions, regulators often focus on the use of human judgment in the underwriting process and the adequacy of credit risk policies and underwriting procedures. If underwriting is mostly automated, it reduces fair lending risk by eliminating subjective discretion to either approve or deny a loan application. Where judgmental underwriting exists (even if it is only a small part of an automated credit decisioning process), however, it is necessary for lenders to place controls around the use of that discretion. Such controls include maintaining written underwriting guidelines, providing training to underwriters on credit risk policies and underwriting procedures, and offering periodic group "calibration training" built around underwriting scenarios to assist underwriters in decisioning loan applications consistently. This approach ensures that underwriting criteria are applied fairly and consistently to facilitate access to credit for qualified borrowers.

4.4.1.1 Use of Traditional Data in Credit Decisioning

Traditionally, lenders have used financial data and credit scores from credit reports obtained from consumer reporting agencies to decision loan applications, together with information provided on a credit application. Credit reports include various types of financial information, such as repayment history, delinquent payment data, credit limits, loan amounts, account balances, inquiries from other financial institutions, past-due accounts that have been turned over to a collection agency, and bankruptcies, among others. A credit score is a numerical representation of the creditworthiness of an individual, which is the likelihood that he or she will repay a loan. Lenders use credit scores to evaluate the potential risk posed by lending money to consumers and to predict the risk of loan default. Studies have shown that credit scores are highly predictive of risk in underwriting credit. FICO scores are commonly used in the banking industry, and lenders may also use their own proprietary scores (either alone or in combination with FICO scores) to decision credit applications.

In the United States, the use of credit reports and credit scores from the three major credit bureaus (Experian, Equifax, and TransUnion) has been widely accepted for decades as an objective method to evaluate an applicant's credit risk. New credit scores have been developed over the past decade, however, and alternative data is increasingly being used to decision and price loan applications.[102] Indeed, most lenders today use some combination of bureau scores and alternative credit scores to better understand a borrower's likelihood of repayment.

102. For example, companies such as Scorelogix, L2C, and Innovis have developed alternative scoring models. These new types of credit scores are often combined with FICO or bureau scores to improve accuracy.

4.1.1.2 Use of Alternative Data in Credit Decisioning and Pricing

Over the past several years, fintech companies have used nontraditional or alternative data in scoring models to both evaluate the creditworthiness of loan applicants and price loans. Alternative data may include, but is not limited to, financial information, such as bank account history, timeliness of paying rent, utilities, gas or cell phone bills, and even payment of insurance premiums, to underwrite a loan. Additionally, alternative data may include educational or occupational attainment data (e.g., level of education, school attended, or profession), behavioral data (such as spending and shopping habits), bank account transaction data, data from alternative credit reporting agencies, public records, and other data. By leveraging such data, these companies claim that individuals with "thin" credit files or no credit scores at all can qualify for loans, which provides needed access to credit for the unbanked or underserved. In the case of one fintech, the CFPB publicly verified that claim was true.[103] Risk-based pricing is then developed on the basis of the alternative data, and such pricing is applied based on the applicant's credit risk profile.

Banks have begun entering into partnerships with fintechs to take advantage of their innovative approaches to underwriting and pricing using alternative data, as well as their digital platforms. As noted in section 2.5.4, the Interagency Statement on the Use of Alternative Data recognizes the benefits of alternative data use in credit decisioning, subject to appropriate compliance management, testing, and monitoring programs. Advantages include lenders being able to evaluate the creditworthiness of applicants who may not meet traditional scoring requirements, increased speed and accuracy of credit decisions, and enabling applicants to obtain more favorable terms or additional credit. Nonetheless, if alternative data is based to some degree on the applicant's financial information, it will likely also exhibit protected class group disparities, just as traditional credit data does.[104] If alternative data is used in credit decisioning, then it must comply with ECOA and, unless that data represents direct

103. On August 6, 2019, the CFPB released information from its review of alternative data underwriting by Upstart Network, Inc. (Upstart), which received the Bureau's first no-action letter in 2017, on its blog. *See* Patrice Alexander Ficklin and Paul Watkins, *An Update on Credit Access and the Bureau's First No-Action Letter*, CFPB Blog, https://www.consumerfinance.gov/about-us/blog/update-credit-access-and-no-action-letter. According to the CFPB, Upstart's underwriting model resulted in 27 percent more approvals than traditional models and led to a reduction in the average annual percentage rate on approved loans by 16 percent. The Bureau found the results were distributed across all tested race, ethnicity, and sex segments and revealed no disparities that required further fair lending analysis.

104. *See* Carol A. Evans, Fed. Reserve Sys., *Keeping Fintech Fair: Thinking about Fair Lending and UDAP Risks*, Consumer Compliance Outlook, Second Issue 2017 ("[F]intech may raise the same types of fair lending risks present in traditional banking, including underwriting discrimination, pricing discrimination, redlining, and steering. Although some fintech trends may decrease certain fair lending risks, other trends could amplify old problems or create new risks.").

experience between the lender and the consumer, then the data must also comply with the federal Fair Credit Reporting Act.[105]

In summary, alternative data appears to be favorably viewed by the federal regulators at present and is beginning to be embraced by the banking industry, so the trend of using alternative data in the underwriting and pricing process is likely to continue.

4.4.2 Pricing

Discretionary pricing is another area of the loan life cycle that has drawn close scrutiny from regulators in examinations, investigations, and enforcement actions because of the potential for disparate treatment of borrowers or pricing policies that may create a disparate impact. Although lenders usually take a risk-based approach to pricing (meaning that the customer's credit risk profile drives the pricing they receive, with customers with better credit receiving more favorable pricing), discretionary pricing heightens fair lending risk because it may result in protected class borrowers being charged higher interest rates or additional fees.

It is crucial that financial institutions and nonbank lenders develop and maintain pricing policies and procedures that take into account current market conditions, competitive factors, and compliance with the fair lending laws, while reducing pricing discretion to the extent practicable. Lenders should train their loan originators and underwriters to apply such policies fairly and consistently to borrowers without consideration of any protected characteristics of the applicant. In addition, any loan fees that are imposed—and any fee waivers—should be applied fairly and consistently.

4.5 Servicing and Collections Activities

ECOA and the FHA both include servicing activities within the scope of their coverage. HUD's discriminatory effects rule expressly states that discrimination in mortgage servicing is deemed "unlawful conduct,"[106] while ECOA proscribes creditors from discriminating against any applicant on a prohibited basis regarding any aspect of a credit transaction,[107] thus implying that its prohibition extends across the entire loan life cycle.

Since the recession of 2008, regulators have set clear expectations that lenders, and any third-party providers that service lenders' loans, must appropriately manage

105. *See, e.g.*, 15 U.S.C. §§ 1681–1681x.

106. *See* 24 C.F.R. § 100.130(b): (b) Unlawful conduct under this section includes, but is not limited to: (3) Servicing of loans or other financial assistance with respect to dwellings in a manner that discriminates, or servicing of loans or other financial assistance which are secured by residential real estate in a manner that discriminates, or providing such loans or financial assistance with other terms or conditions that discriminate, because of race, color, religion, sex, handicap, familial status, or national origin.

107. *See* 15 U.S.C. § 1691(a); 12 C.F.R. § 1002.4(a).

fair lending risks in servicing activities (known as "fair servicing"). This means treating borrowers fairly and objectively and offering the same level of assistance to similarly situated borrowers. It also means identifying any areas of discretion and implementing controls to mitigate those fair servicing risks.

Payment programs (including deferrals and forbearance), application of fees or fee waivers, credit line increases and decreases, interest rate reductions, and account closures all represent decision points that can present fair servicing risks. If a financial institution's internal policies and procedures concerning those actions are applied inconsistently, protected class borrowers may end up with less favorable outcomes and thus could be disproportionately impacted. To ensure fair and consistent treatment of borrowers, loan servicers should develop and implement clear and objective policies, procedures, and controls and provide fair servicing training to all servicing and collections employees.

4.6 Loan Modifications and Loss Mitigation

In the context of mortgage lending, fair servicing risks are heightened in the context of delinquent loans and loans at risk of default because of the significant adverse consequence that a borrower could lose his or her home. For auto lending, a loan default may lead to repossession of a vehicle, which is often critically needed to commute to work and provide family support.

Frequently, loss mitigation personnel are allowed to exercise discretion in dealing with delinquent borrowers by crafting individual solutions to do what is most appropriate for the borrower. This use of judgment based on individual borrower circumstances, while well intended, can create fair servicing risk because outcomes may differ, even for similarly situated borrowers.

To mitigate fair servicing risks, lenders should ensure that their outreach programs are uniformly applied to delinquent borrowers and that borrowers receive the same information. All available loss mitigation and loan modification options for which a borrower qualifies should be offered and fully explained, together with the information that the borrower must provide for the lender to successfully process the loss mitigation option requested. Servicers should also ensure that they maintain clear policies and procedures for decision making, and that documentation is required for any exceptions that are approved. To mitigate fair servicing risks, the CFPB has issued guidance stating that mortgage servicers must conduct fair lending training for loss mitigation staff, and engage in effective and timely fair lending risk assessments, compliance monitoring, and testing of fair lending risks.[108] In addition, financial institutions should implement compensation programs that do not incent loss mitigation personnel to encourage borrowers to use options that may not be in the borrower's best interest while providing greater compensation to the employee.

---

108. CFPB, *Supervisory Highlights: Summer 2013* (August 2013), https://files.consumerfinance.gov/f/201308_cfpb_supervisory-highlights_august.pdf.

Similar fair servicing concepts apply to loan modifications.[109] A mortgage servicer could be subject to regulatory scrutiny if protected class borrowers are shown to receive loan modifications at a statistically significant lower rate than similarly situated white non-Hispanic borrowers. Although a 2010 Federal Reserve Bank study found no evidence of disparities in the rates at which minority borrowers obtained loan modifications,[110] lenders who service their own loans and third-party servicers must remain vigilant in treating borrowers fairly and consistently in a loan modification context and engage in fair servicing testing to routinely evaluate borrower outcomes.

4.7 Foreclosure

Similar to loss mitigation, foreclosure of homes poses significant fair servicing risks. To illustrate, if lenders or servicers proceed more quickly to foreclose upon homes in majority-minority neighborhoods compared to similarly situated white non-Hispanic borrowers, those actions may adversely affect protected class borrowers.

In the CFPB's Mortgage Servicing Examination Procedures,[111] the Bureau's examiners are instructed to review foreclosure policies, procedures, and complaints, and obtain a sample of servicing records of consumers whose loans have been referred to foreclosure. Examiners are also instructed to collect and review foreclosure-related information to determine whether there is any evidence of disparate treatment of borrowers in the servicer's foreclosure processing. If such evidence is present, then the examiner is instructed to consult with the Office of Supervision, Enforcement and Fair Lending to determine whether discrimination in foreclosure proceedings exists. This analysis is conducted in conjunction with loss mitigation fair lending testing to evaluate whether protected class borrowers are pushed more quickly from loss mitigation into foreclosure. Therefore, servicers must closely follow their policies and procedures to ensure equal treatment of borrowers between these two critical phases.

4.8 Real Estate Owned Property Maintenance and Municipality Litigation against Lenders

In 2011, investigations conducted by the National Fair Housing Alliance (NFHA) and other fair housing organizations into the maintenance and marketing of real estate

---

109. In auto lending, loan modifications are used less frequently; instead, payment deferrals or extensions are more common.

110. J. Michael Collins & Carolina Reid, *Who Receives a Mortgage Modification? Race and Income Differentials in Loan Workouts* (Fed. Res. Bank of San Francisco, Working Paper 2010-07, February 9, 2011), https://www.frbsf.org/community-development/files/who-receives-mortgage-modification.pdf.

111. CFPB, *Examination Procedures, Mortgage Servicing, Module 9 - Foreclosures* (June 2016), https://files.consumerfinance.gov/f/documents/11.5_Mortgage_Servicing_Exam_Procedures_June_2016.pdf.

owned (REO) properties that were foreclosed upon and then owned by banks and servicers in several major metropolitan cities revealed alleged disparate treatment.[112] Those investigations asserted that REO properties located in minority communities were not as well maintained and marketed as properties located in majority white neighborhoods. According to the reports, REO properties can often remain vacant for months or years before being sold to a homebuyer, which can create blight, foster crime, and result in other negative outcomes when not maintained responsibly.

Based on these investigations, the NFHA and HUD jointly filed complaints against several major banks and their service providers alleging differential REO property maintenance and marketing practices. Several of these complaints ended in conciliation agreements (as required for settlements under the FHA) which required the lenders and servicers to improve their marketing and maintenance practices with regard to REO properties and to invest in programs designed to support home ownership, neighborhood stabilization, property rehabilitation, and housing development.[113]

In the wake of the 2008 recession, several municipalities filed fair lending lawsuits against mortgage lenders and secondary market participants. Those cases involved allegations that a lender steered minority borrowers into less favorable or subprime loans, which in turn caused the borrowers to default and then increased foreclosure rates in the plaintiff cities. Other cases involve allegations that lenders failed to provide adequate access to credit to residents of minority communities. In such cases, the cities claimed that they were economically harmed through lower property values and decreased tax revenue, among other things.

5. Application to Models/Scorecards

Applicants for credit may be evaluated for credit using a *credit scoring system*. Regulation B defines a credit scoring system as a system that "evaluates an applicant's creditworthiness mechanically, based on key attributes of the applicant and aspects of the transaction, and that determines, alone or in conjunction with an evaluation of additional information about the applicant, whether an applicant is deemed

112. *See* Nat'l Fair Housing Alliance, Here Comes the Bank, There Goes the Neighborhood: How Lenders Discriminate in the Treatment of Foreclosed Homes (April 11, 2011), https://nationalfairhousing.org/wp-content/uploads/2017/04/There-Goes-Our-Neighborhood-REO-report-2011-for-website.pdf. The National Fair Housing Alliance subsequently issued two other reports: The Banks are Back – Our Neighborhoods are Not: Discrimination in the Maintenance and Marketing of REO Properties (April 4, 2012), https://nationalfairhousing.org/wp-content/uploads/2017/04/Banks-are-Back-Final-12.3.2012.pdf, and Zip Code Inequality: Discrimination by Banks in the Maintenance of Homes in Neighborhoods of Color (August 27, 2014), https://nationalfairhousing.org/wp-content/uploads/2017/04/2014-08-27_NFHA_REO_report.pdf.

113. *See, e.g.*, Conciliation Agreement between HUD and Wells Fargo Bank, N.A., HUD No. 00-13-001-8 (June 5, 2013).

creditworthy."[114] For example, a credit scoring system may include an applicant's payment history, late payments, total amount of outstanding credit, and the age of the oldest credit account on file. Creditors may purchase a score from a consumer reporting agency, or utilize custom scores developed by the lender or a third-party vendor. Scores are also used by lenders in other aspects of credit, such as pricing and account administration.[115]

A credit scoring system may be "empirically derived, demonstrably and statistically sound," judgmental, or a combined system. Regulation B defines a system that evaluates the creditworthiness of an applicant that is not an "empirically derived, demonstrably and statistically sound, credit scoring system" as a judgmental system.[116] Combined systems, which include aspects of a credit scoring system and a judgmental system, may also be used by creditors.

5.1 "Empirically Derived and Statistically Sound" Scoring Systems

To be an empirically derived, demonstrably and statistically sound credit scoring system, the system must be (1) based on data from an empirical comparison of sample groups or the population of creditworthy and noncreditworthy applicants who applied for credit within a reasonable preceding period of time; (2) developed to evaluate the creditworthiness of applicants with respect to the legitimate business interests of the creditor using the system (such as minimizing bad debt losses and operating expenses consistent with the creditor's business judgment); (3) developed and validated with accepted statistical principles and methodology; and (4) periodically revalidated using appropriate statistical principles and methodology and adjusted as needed to maintain predictive ability.[117]

5.2 Potentially Problematic Credit Scoring Variables

Except for the use of age under limited conditions, prohibited bases may not be used as a variable in a credit model.[118] In addition, certain variables present the risk of

---

114. 12 C.F.R. § 1002.2(p)(1).

115. *See* FDIC, *Fair Lending Implications of Credit Scoring Systems*, Supervisory Insights (Summer 2005), https://www.fdic.gov/regulations/examinations/supervisory/insights/sisum05/sisummer05-article3.pdf.

116. 12 C.F.R. § 1002.2(t).

117. *Id.* § 1002.2(p)(1). Although no specific time period for revalidation is provided in Regulation B, revalidation must be done often enough to ensure meeting recognized professional statistical standards. Creditors must periodically review the system's performance to ensure the predictive ability is maintained and make system changes as needed. Official Interpretation to 12 C.F.R. § 1002.2(p)(4), Comment 2(p)-2.

118. *See* Official Interpretation of 12 C.F.R. § 1002.2(p), Comment 2(p)-1.

disparate treatment or disparate impact in the evaluation process.[119] For example, the use of zip codes or census tracts in underwriting credit products may indicate potential disparate impact.[120] The use of absolute income levels, instead of income relative to debt, may also raise disproportionate adverse impact fair lending issues.[121]

6. Types of Fair Lending Cases

6.1 Advertising

Oral or written statements in advertising to applicants (or prospective applicants) that would discourage an application on a prohibited basis are prohibited under ECOA and the FHA. The CFPB Supervision and Examination Manual provides as an example that "a creditor may not advertise its credit services and practices in ways that would tend to encourage some types of borrowers and discourage others on a prohibited basis."[122] To illustrate, HUD recently issued a "Charge of Discrimination" against Facebook charging the company with engaging in discriminatory housing practices under the FHA.[123] HUD alleged that Facebook designed its advertising platform to show targeted housing and housing-related services advertisements "to large audiences that are severely biased based on characteristics protected by the [FHA], such as audiences of tens of thousands of users that are nearly all men or nearly all women."[124] HUD alleged that Facebook considered sex and other close proxies for other protected classes by having users disclose data about themselves when they set up a profile. Furthermore, in the ad targeting phase, Facebook would determine which users may see an ad by permitting the advertiser to select an "eligible audience" specifying required attributes of the user, such as men or women,

119. "In cases where a credit scoring system is used in conjunction with individual discretion, disparate treatment could conceivably occur in the evaluation process. In addition, neutral factors used in credit scoring systems could nonetheless be subject to challenge under the effects test." Official Interpretation to 12 CFR § 1002.2(p)(4), Comment 2(p)(4); *see also* Interagency Fair Lending Examination Procedures issued by the Office of the Comptroller of the Currency, Federal Deposit Insurance Corporation, Federal Reserve Board, Office of Thrift Supervision and National Credit Union Administration (Aug. 2009) [hereinafter "Interagency Fair Lending Examination Procedures"]; Interagency Policy Statement on Discrimination in Lending, 59 Fed. Reg. 18267, April 15, 1994; Evans, *supra* note 104, at 4–9.

120. Interagency Fair Lending Examination Procedures, *supra* note 119, appendix, 27.

121. *Id.*

122. CFPB, *Examination Procedures, Equal Credit Opportunity Act, Module 3* (April 2019).

123. Charge of Discrimination, HUD v. Facebook, Inc., HUD ALJ No. 01-18-0323-8 (U.S. Dept. of Housing and Urban Development Office of Administrative Law Judges, March 28, 2019), https://www.hud.gov/sites/dfiles/Main/documents/HUD_v_Facebook.pdf?hootPostID=da403d244cf75a732b61e6cc298bac61.

124. *Id.* at 3.

or excluding people that do not speak a certain language or lived in a specified area. In the ad delivery phase, HUD claimed Facebook selected the ad's "actual audience," the users that will be shown the ad from the eligible user population. Accordingly, HUD charged Facebook with engaging in discriminatory housing practices under the FHA and sought damages for any aggrieved person and civil money penalties.

6.2 Underwriting: Use of Discretion

Although the U.S. Supreme Court held in *Wal-Mart Stores, Inc. v. Dukes* that, under Title VII of the Civil Rights Act, a "policy" of allowing decisions to be made on a discretionary basis is "a very common and presumptively reasonable way of doing business—one that we have said should itself raise no inference of discriminatory conduct,"[125] the federal regulators have often acted upon the suspicion that the exercise of discretion in the lending context will result in less favorable outcomes for members of certain protected classes. In a series of cases involving mortgage lending, the federal regulators asserted that lenders' practice of allowing discretionary (or judgmental) evaluation of credit applications resulted in either disparate treatment or a disparate impact on the basis of race or ethnicity.[126] These cases were based primarily on statistical evidence that purportedly showed that similarly situated applicants received different decisions or interest rates, with non-Hispanic white applicants being approved for credit, while members of racial or ethnic minority groups were declined, or approved at a higher interest rate.

6.3 Underwriting: Treatment of Disability Income and Pregnancy Leave

Several fair lending regulatory enforcement actions have been based on lenders' policies requiring certain applicants to provide greater documentation in support of their loan applications. When these stricter documentation requirements coincided with a protected characteristic, the regulators have asserted that the policies violated the fair lending laws by imposing a burden on protected-class applicants that was not applied to other consumers.

For example, one mortgage lender was alleged to have required the recipients of Social Security Disability income and other disability income to provide documentation

125. Wal-Mart Stores, Inc. v. Dukes, 564 U.S. 338, 355 (2011) (internal quotation marks omitted).

126. Complaint, United States v. BancorpSouth Bank, No. 1:16-cv-118-GHD-DAS (N.D. Miss. June 29, 2016) (discretionary interest rates and application denial); Complaint, United States v. JPMorgan Chase Bank, NA, No. 1:17-cv-00347 (S.D.N.Y. Jan. 18, 2017) (discretionary interest rates).

about the expected duration of the disability.[127] The DOJ alleged that this practice violated ECOA by discriminating against applicants whose income derived from public assistance (Social Security Disability), and violated the FHA's prohibition on discrimination on the basis of "handicap."[128] Several similar examples involved mortgage lenders that allegedly declined applications because the borrower or co-borrower was a woman on maternity leave.[129] In general, the regulators in these cases asserted that the lenders' policies required women on maternity leave to return to work before becoming eligible for loans and that the application of these policies violated the prohibition on gender discrimination in ECOA and the prohibition on gender and familial status discrimination under the FHA.

Finally, the federal regulators have stated that disability income and other forms of nontaxable income must be "grossed up" to be treated equally with taxable income in evaluating loan applications.[130] The concept behind this principle is that if a loan application asks for gross income, a worker with taxable employment income will actually have less money available to repay the loan than the income figure provided on the application due to the payment of taxes. However, a person who receives disability income or other form of nontaxable income will have the full amount of income available without the impact of taxes. Treating both types of applicants equally in terms of debt-to-income or payment-to-income calculations therefore can result in a discriminatory impact on those receiving disability or other nontaxable income. The federal regulators have thus advised lenders to "gross up" disability and other nontaxable income by an assumed tax rate to equalize that income with taxable employment income. The failure to do so may give rise to discrimination on the basis of receipt of public assistance income, handicap, or age.[131]

6.4 Minimum Loan Amounts

Minimum loan amounts in credit policies can be a source for disparate impact cases. As an example, Luther Burbank Savings entered into a settlement with DOJ in 2012 to resolve allegations that the bank's $400,000 minimum residential mortgage loan amount policy for its wholesale single-family program adversely impacted minority applicants.[132] Using Home Mortgage Disclosure Act (HMDA) data, the DOJ complaint

---

127. Consent Order, United States v. Evolve Bank & Trust, Case No. 3:16-cv-02040 (W.D. Tenn. Jan. 19, 2016).

128. *Id.*

129. *See, e.g.*, Conciliation Agreement between Primary Res. Mortg., Inc. and HUD, HUD FEO Case No. 03-12-0038-8 (Mar. 28, 2013), Conciliation Agreement between PNC Mortg. And HUD, HUD Case No. 01-13-0010-8 (Feb. 6, 2013); Consent Order, United States v. First Fed. Bank of Fla., Case No. 3:16-cv-01148-J-34JBT (MD. Fla. Oct. 12, 2016).

130. *See* the Interagency Policy Statement, discussed in section 2.5.1.

131. *Id.*

132. Consent Order, United States v. Luther Burbank Savings, Case No. 2:12-cv-07809-JAK-FMO (C.D. Cal., Oct. 12, 2012).

alleged that, over a five-year period from 2006 to 2011, Luther Burbank had knowingly originated significantly fewer single-family residential mortgage loans to African American or Hispanic borrowers or in majority-minority tracts throughout California than comparable prime lenders while keeping the minimum loan amount policy in place. Based on those facts, DOJ alleged that the bank's policy violated ECOA and the FHA because it had a disparate impact on the basis of race and national origin.

6.5 Requirement to Speak English

On July 8, 2002, the United States filed a complaint and a settlement agreement against a large bank alleging a pattern or practice of discrimination in its subprime credit programs in violation of ECOA.[133] The complaint alleged that the bank had hired four service providers to market its subprime credit program without ensuring that their policies and procedures complied with the federal fair lending laws. Specifically, the complaint alleged that the bank, through the third-party service providers, had discriminated based on national origin by maintaining a policy of denying credit to credit card applicants unable to read and understand English and engaging in abusive collection practices that harassed customers on the basis of their Hispanic national origin. Other allegations included discouraging applicants who received income from public assistance from applying for credit cards, requiring all members of a household to sign an application for credit, and failing to issue credit cards in compliance with ECOA and Regulation B.

6.6 Discretionary Pricing

Discretionary pricing without appropriate written policies and other internal controls may result in disparities in pricing of retail loan products between similarly situated white non-Hispanic and minority borrowers. These cases often occur in the mortgage and auto lending context but can arise with credit card products as well. Disparities in pricing that adversely affect minority borrowers are considered a violation of ECOA for auto lending and credit card lending and a violation of both ECOA and the FHA for mortgage lending (although recovery can be sought under only one law).[134] An enforcement action brought by the DOJ, CFPB, or one of the federal banking agencies may be framed as either disparate impact or disparate treatment, but often enforcement actions do not indicate which theory was used.

In 2017, the DOJ entered into a consent order with a large bank to resolve claims of discriminatory mortgage loan pricing.[135] The DOJ alleged that the bank's wholesale

133. United States v. Fidelity Fed. Bank, Case No. 1:02-cv-03906-NG-MDG (E.D.N.Y., July 8. 2005).

134. *See* 15 U.S.C. § 1691e(i).

135. Consent Order, United States v. JPMorgan Chase Bank, Case No. 1:17-cv-00347 (S.D.N.Y., Jan. 20, 2017).

broker channel had violated the FHA and ECOA by charging African American and Hispanic borrowers higher interest rates and fees for mortgage loans than similarly situated white non-Hispanic borrowers, which resulted in adverse price disparities for minority borrowers.

Following the enactment of the Dodd-Frank Act, the first auto lending pricing discrimination consent order was entered into jointly between the DOJ and CFPB and a large bank in 2013. The consent order alleged that the bank violated ECOA by engaging in an ongoing pattern or practice of discrimination against minority borrowers in its auto lending pricing practices since 2011.[136] Specifically, the CFPB and DOJ alleged that the bank discriminated by permitting auto dealers to mark up those borrowers' interest rates, which were higher than similarly situated non-Hispanic white borrowers.[137]

In a credit card context, in 2017, the CFPB took action against two subsidiaries of a large bank for discriminating against consumers in Puerto Rico, the U.S. Virgin Islands, and other U.S. territories by providing them with credit and charge card pricing and terms that were inferior to those available to consumers in the fifty states.[138] The Bureau also alleged that the entities discriminated against certain consumers with Spanish language preferences.

6.7 Redlining

One of the most prominent series of fair lending enforcement actions by the federal regulators has involved "redlining." This theory has, thus far, been confined to mortgage lending by banks. Redlining cases are premised on the allegation that a bank mortgage lender engaged in race discrimination by seeking to avoid making mortgage loans in geographic areas with high minority populations (majority-minority areas). The regulatory complaints in these cases are typically focused on lending activity in a particular metropolitan area, and the allegations giving rise to the claim of redlining include the following:

- The lender receives significantly fewer applications from majority-minority areas than peer institutions;
- The lender originates significantly fewer mortgage loans in majority-minority areas than peer institutions;
- The lender has few or no branches in majority-minority areas;
- The lender's advertising was directed away from majority-minority areas;

---

136. Consent Order, United States v. Ally Fin. Inc. and Ally Bank, Case No. CV 13-15180 (E.D. Mich. Dec. 20, 2013).

137. Dealer mark-up is the amount by which an auto dealer may mark up the interest rate above an indirect auto lender's risk-based buy rate, based on the lender's discretionary pricing policy.

138. Consent Order, *In re* Amer. Exp. Centurion Bank, File No. 2017-CFPB-0016 (CFPB Aug. 23, 2017).

- The lender's Community Reinvestment Act service area was gerrymandered to avoid the inclusion of majority-minority areas; and
- The lender's mortgage loan officers do not include members of minority groups.[139]

There have been a large number of redlining cases brought by the federal regulators in recent years, and some cases have been brought by consumer advocacy groups.[140] One state attorney general has stated that he is investigating a redlining case.[141]

6.8 Reverse Redlining

In a few cases, the DOJ has alleged "reverse redlining" or "targeting" of consumer credit products. The theory behind these cases is that the product in question has unfavorable terms or conditions, to the point of being labeled "predatory," and that the lender preferentially marketed the product to protected groups, usually based on race. The cases also have been accompanied by allegations of direct evidence of discrimination, such as overtly discriminatory statements by the creditor.[142] There have been only a handful of these cases in recent years.

6.9 Collections

In June 2014, the CFPB and DOJ entered into a consent order with a large bank for the bank's exclusion of credit card customers from certain collection offers with a "Spanish-preferred" indicator on their accounts or a mailing address in Puerto Rico.[143] The CFPB and DOJ found the exclusion of customers with a "Spanish-preferred"

139. *See, e.g.*, Complaint, United States v. BancorpSouth Bank, No 1:16cv118-GHD-DAS (N.D. Miss. June 29, 2016); Complaint, United States v. KleinBank, No. 17-cv-136 (D. Minn. Jan. 13, 2017); Complaint, United States v. Hudson City Savings Bank, F.S.B., No. 2:15-cv-07056-CCC-JBC (D. N.J. Sept. 24, 2015); Complaint, United States v. Eagle Bank & Trust Co. of Mo., No. 4:15-cv-01492 (Sept. 29, 2015).

140. *See, e.g.*, Complaint, Conn. Fair Housing Center, Inc. v. Liberty Bank, No. 18-cv-1654 (D. Conn. Oct. 4, 2018).

141. Press Release, Office of Attorney General Commonwealth of Pennsylvania, Attorney General Shapiro Puts Spotlight on Redlining (Oct. 22, 2018), https://www.attorneygeneral.gov/taking-action/press-releases/attorney-general-shapiro-puts-spotlight-on-redlining/.

142. Consent Decree, United States v. Auto Fare, Inc., No. 3:14-cv-00008-RJC-DSC (W.D. N.C. Feb. 10, 2015).

143. Consent Order, *In re* Synchrony Bank (f/k/a GE Capital Retail Bank), File No. 2014-CFPB-0007 (CFPB Jun. 19, 2014), https://files.consumerfinance.gov/f/201406_cfpb_consent-order_synchrony-bank.pdf; Consent Order, United States v. Synchrony Bank (f/k/a GE Capital Retail Bank), Case No. 2:14-CV-00454 (D. Utah Jun. 27, 2014), https://www.justice.gov/sites/default/files/crt/legacy/2014/07/10/gecapitalbanksettle.pdf.

indicator on their accounts or with a mailing address in Puerto Rico constituted discrimination on the basis of national origin, in violation of ECOA.

6.10 Steering

Steering involves promoting different loan types, or different programs within a loan type (e.g., prime versus subprime loans), with less favorable terms, conditions, or pricing to otherwise qualified borrowers in a way that treats them differently on a prohibited basis.[144] Steering cases frequently arise in a mortgage lending context where mortgage loan originators or brokers have the opportunity to "steer" protected class borrowers from fixed-rate to adjustable-rate mortgages (in which interest rates may suddenly increase) or from conventional mortgages to more expensive FHA-insured loans.

In 2012, a large bank entered into a consent order with DOJ to resolve allegations that the bank steered minority borrowers into more expensive subprime loans with higher interest rates when they qualified for lower-interest prime mortgage loans.[145] The DOJ alleged that the bank gave its officers and third-party mortgage brokers discretion to steer African American and Hispanic borrowers into higher-interest-rate loans within the Mid-Atlantic region.

7. Enforcement: Private Rights of Action and Regulatory Enforcement

The federal fair lending statutes are enforceable by regulatory agencies, as evidenced by the numerous examples of government enforcement actions noted in section 6. Both ECOA and the FHA also carry private rights of action, allowing consumers and other private parties to bring actions in federal court.

7.1 Enforcement Actions

ECOA authorizes administrative enforcement actions by a variety of federal agencies. Banks and credit unions are subject to administrative enforcement by their prudential regulators. Nonbanks are subject to ECOA enforcement by the FTC, and all creditors subject to ECOA are subject to the enforcement authority of the CFPB.[146] In addition, these administrative agencies are permitted to refer suspected violations of ECOA to the DOJ for investigation and potential civil enforcement, and the agencies are required to make a referral to DOJ "whenever the agency has reason to believe that

144. Practical Handbook on Fair Lending, *supra* note 98, at 31.

145. Consent Order, United States v. Wells Fargo Bank, N.A., Case No. 1:12-cv-01150 (Dist. Ct. for D.C.), https://www.clearinghouse.net/chDocs/public/FH-DC-0005-0006.pdf.

146. 15 U.S.C. § 1691c.

1 or more creditors has engaged in a pattern or practice of discouraging or denying applications for credit."[147]

Enforcement of the FHA is assigned primarily to HUD. The FHA allows aggrieved consumers to file complaints with HUD and also allows HUD to conduct investigations and make findings about conduct that may violate the FHA.[148] HUD also is empowered to initiate administrative enforcement proceedings or to request that the DOJ bring an action to enforce the FHA in federal court.[149] The DOJ is authorized to bring civil actions in cases referred by HUD and may initiate enforcement actions when it has reasonable cause to believe that a pattern and practice of violation of the FHA has occurred.[150] With respect to banks, the prudential banking regulators conduct examinations under the FHA and may refer matters to HUD, which in turn may refer matters to the DOJ for enforcement proceedings.[151]

In 1996, the DOJ released a memorandum to the federal banking agencies to provide guidance on what types of cases the agencies should refer to the DOJ because they indicate a "pattern and practice" of discrimination under ECOA (DOJ Memorandum).[152] The DOJ Memorandum generally provides that an isolated ECOA violation, conduct that has already ceased, and violations where aggrieved consumers have already been made whole, should not be referred.[153] On the other hand, the DOJ Memorandum states that continuing violations, situations where consumers cannot be made whole without court action, and instances in which deterrence is desirable should be referred.[154]

7.2 Private Litigation

Both ECOA and the FHA carry explicit private rights of action, allowing private parties to bring actions in federal court.[155] Both statutes allow the recovery of actual and punitive damages, injunctive relief, and attorneys' fees.[156]

---

147. 16 U.S.C. § 1691e(g).

148. 42 U.S.C. § 3610.

149. *Id.* § 3612.

150. *Id.* § 3614(a).

151. *See* 12 U.S.C. § 1820(d) (federal banking agencies are required to examine the depository institutions they supervise); 15 U.S.C. §§ 1691e(g),1691e(k) (agencies to refer violations to the attorney general and provide notice of violations to HUD).

152. DOJ, *Identifying Lender Practices That May Form the Basis of a Pattern or Practice Referral to the Department of Justice* (1996), https://www.justice.gov/sites/default/files/crt/legacy/2014/03/05/regguide.pdf.

153. *Id.*

154. *Id.*

155. 15 U.S.C. § 1691e; 42 U.S.C. § 3613.

156. 15 U.S.C. § 1691e; 42 U.S.C. § 3613.

8. Self-Testing

A self-test is a program designed and specifically used to determine the effectiveness of a creditor's compliance with ECOA and the FHA, and the results must create data or factual information that is not otherwise available or cannot be derived from credit applications or loan files.[157] Under certain circumstances, a creditor may request prohibited basis information in connection with a self-test.[158] In addition, findings from a self-test voluntarily conducted by a creditor that meets the regulatory requirements are privileged from discovery or use by a government agency in a fair lending examination or investigation, or by a government agency or an applicant (including a prospective applicant) in any legal proceeding alleging a violation of ECOA, Regulation B, or the FHA.[159]

Privilege would apply to the self-testing report or results, data or factual information created by the test, any test analysis, opinions or conclusions, and workpapers, draft documents, and final documents.[160] The privilege would not apply to certain information, such as whether a test was conducted, the testing methodology used, the period covered by the test, and information derived from the files.[161] An additional qualification for the privilege is that appropriate corrective action is required if the test identifies that it is more likely than not that there was a violation of ECOA, Regulation B, or the FHA.[162] The privilege may be lost for several reasons, including the creditor's disclosure of the privileged information or failure to retain the records of the test for at least twenty-five months after the completion of the test.[163]

9. Use of Statistical Analysis to Assess Fair Lending Performance

For more than twenty-five years,[164] federal banking regulators and financial institutions have used statistical analysis (known as "regression analysis" by econometricians)

157. 12 C.F.R. § 1002.15(b); 24 C.F.R. § 100.141.

158. 12 C.F.R. § 1002.15(b)(1).

159. 15 U.S.C. § 1691c-1(a)(2); 12 C.F.R. § 1002.15(d)(1); 42 U.S.C. § 3614-1(a)(2); 24 C.F.R. § 100.144.

160. 12 C.F.R. § 1002.15(b)(2); 24 C.F.R. § 100.142(a).

161. 12 C.F.R. § 1002.15(b)(2); 24 C.F.R. § 100.142(b).

162. 12 C.F.R. § 1002.15(c)(1); 24 C.F.R. § 100.143(a).

163. 12 C.F.R. § 1002.15(d)(2); 24 C.F.R. § 100.145.

164. Regression analyses began being used by federal banking examiners (primarily the FRB and the OCC) following publication of the Federal Reserve Bank of Boston study on lending discrimination that was published in 1992, which purported to find evidence of discriminatory treatment of minority applicants by mortgage lenders in the Boston metropolitan area. *See* A. Munnell et al., *Mortgage Lending in Boston: Interpreting HMDA Data* (Federal Reserve Bank of Boston Working Paper, October 1992).

to identify potential fair lending risk. Such analyses can help a lender or regulator preliminarily identify differences in credit decisions or pricing outcomes for applicants and borrowers, as well as the factors that may be driving those results. Specifically, if sufficiently large and "statistically significant" disparities[165] are shown to exist in credit application denials or pricing between protected class applicants or borrowers and white non-Hispanic applicants or borrowers, it may be an indication of discrimination, especially if it appears to occur in a pattern. As a result, regression analyses play a major role in many fair lending enforcement actions brought by the federal banking agencies, the CFPB, and the DOJ.

In recent years, regression analyses have also been used in a servicing context to determine whether borrower outcomes for loss mitigation and loan modifications are consistent between protected class borrowers versus white non-Hispanic borrowers. In addition, regression analyses can be used to determine whether redlining or reverse redlining practices may exist. This section focuses on the traditional use of regression analyses to determine differences in credit decisioning and pricing, however.

Regression analysis is a statistical analysis of particular loan data (e.g., mortgage loans, auto loans, credit cards) that measures applicant and borrower credit decision and pricing outcomes by methodically comparing the variables that go into such decisions in a uniform manner. Such analyses also include an analysis of demographic data for applicants or borrowers that is either self-reported (or recorded) HMDA data for mortgage lending or proxies employed to approximate demographic data, such as race, ethnicity, and gender, for nonmortgage lending.[166] Unlike a raw statistical analysis that looks only for disparities without any explanatory variables, a regression analysis takes into account key variables that may explain how the underwriting or pricing decision was made. Factors may include, but are not limited to, credit score, loan-to-value ratio, debt-to-income ratio, property type, and any prior bankruptcies. When the results of a regression analysis show there is a statistically significant disparity in pricing or underwriting that adversely affects protected class applicants or borrowers, that does not necessarily mean that discrimination has actually occurred.[167] As a result, file reviews are typically conducted as a follow-up to the results of an initial

165. What is considered a sufficiently large and statistically significant result varies by type of analysis.

166. Since 2014, the CFPB has utilized a new proxy method called "Bayesian Improved Surname Geocoding," or BISG, to proxy for race and ethnicity of applicants and borrowers where demographic data does not exist. *See* CFPB, *Using Publicly Available Information to Proxy for Unidentified Race and Ethnicity: A Methodology and Assessment* (2014), https://files.consumerfinance.gov/f/201409_cfpb_report_proxy-methodology.pdf.

167. As a historical matter, fair lending regression analyses alone have not been considered sufficient evidence to establish a discrimination claim by the federal banking agencies or DOJ. However, during the first five years of the CFPB's existence (2011–16), the Bureau often pursued fair lending investigations of lenders based solely on regression analysis results.

regression analysis to learn more about the underwriting or pricing decision and help explain why the decision was made.[168]

The purpose of a file review is to determine whether there are any legitimate, nondiscretionary reasons for the decisions that were not captured in the regression analysis, whether certain data fields that were excluded in the initial analysis could have a material impact on the results, and whether any data integrity issues may be present. Typically, a file review involves a review of hard copy or electronic loan application files, including notes and emails kept or sent by underwriters or loan originators, as well as data stored in the loan origination system. In addition, file reviewers may need to review lending policies and procedures, or conduct interviews of underwriters or loan originators for context, particularly when file documentation is thin. It is important to provide advance training to file reviewers on file review protocols so that they know what information to look for and capture. The goal of the file review is to determine whether there is sufficient evidence in the file to support the pricing or underwriting decision.

10. The Home Mortgage Disclosure Act

The HMDA[169] and its implementing regulation, Regulation C,[170] require covered financial institutions to collect, record, report, and disclose information about their mortgage lending activities. HMDA and Regulation C are intended to serve the purposes of (1) determining whether financial institutions serve their communities' housing needs, (2) assisting public officials in distributing public investment to attract private investments, and (3) assisting in identifying potential discriminatory lending patters and enforcing the federal fair lending laws.

Regulation C applies to both depository and nondepository financial institutions, depending on certain criteria, such as asset thresholds and annual origination volume.[171] Mortgage loans covered by Regulation C include both closed-end mortgage loans and open-end lines of credit secured by a dwelling,[172] not including certain exempt transaction types.[173]

If covered by the requirements of HMDA and Regulation C, a financial institution must collect, and record on a quarterly basis, certain data points for (1) applications taken on covered loans, (2) originations of covered loans, and (3) purchases of covered loans.[174] This recorded information is compiled into a loan/application register (LAR).

168. Regulators sometimes elect to conduct a file review in lieu of regression analysis.
169. 12 U.S.C. §§ 2801–2908.
170. 12 C.F.R. part 1003.
171. 12 C.F.R. § 1003.2(g).
172. *Id.* § 1003.2(d), (e), (o).
173. *Id.* § 1003.3(c).
174. *Id.* § 1003.4(a), (f).

A covered financial institution must report its LAR data, along with certain additional accompanying information, to the institution's federal regulatory agency annually (certain high-volume institutions must also report quarterly).[175]

11. The Community Reinvestment Act

The CRA was enacted in 1977.[176] The CRA requires federal financial supervisory agencies to assess the record of each insured depository institution in helping to meet the credit needs of low- to moderate-income (LMI) individuals and families in its assessment area, consistent with safe and sound operations.[177] A poor CRA record can be the basis for a federal regulator to decline applications for new deposit facilities and for mergers or acquisitions[178] and it can also be taken into account in fair lending examinations, thus impacting both CRA and fair lending examination ratings.

On May 20, 2020, the OCC issued a final rule (to be codified, for national banks, as 12 C.F.R. part 25 and, for federal savings banks, as 12 C.F.R. part 195) to "strengthen and modernize" its CRA regulations.[179] The final rule was made effective October 1, 2020, and is applicable to national banks, federal savings banks, and uninsured federal branches of foreign banks (OCC-regulated institutions) but sets mandatory compliance dates based on the applicable performance standards.[180] OCC-regulated institutions subject to the general performance standards (which includes institutions that have $2.5 billion or more of total assets) and OCC-regulated institutions subject to the wholesale and limited-purpose bank performance standards must comply with the new CRA framework by January 1, 2023.[181] Small banks (which includes OCC-regulated institutions that have assets of $600 million or less)[182] and intermediate banks (which are OCC-regulated institutions with total assets of more than $600 million and less than $2.5 billion)[183] must comply with the rule by January 1, 2024.[184]

Until compliance with the final rule, OCC-regulated institutions must comply with the OCC's prior rule. Unless the FRB and the FDIC take action on CRA reform, state member banks and state nonmember banks will continue to

---

175. *Id.* § 1003.5(a).

176. Pub. L. No. 95-128, 91 Stat. 1147 (codified as amended at 12 U.S.C. §§ 2901–2908).

177. 12 U.S.C. §§ 2901(b), 2903(a)(1).

178. *Id.* §§ 2902(3), 2903(a)(2).

179. Community Reinvestment Act Regulations, 85 Fed. Reg. 34734 (June 5, 2020) (to be codified at 12 C.F.R. parts 25 and 195).

180. *Id.* at 34793.

181. *Id.*

182. *Id.* at 34795.

183. *Id.* at 34794.

184. *Id.* at 34793.

comply with 12 C.F.R. part 228 and 12 C.F.R. part 345, respectively, both of which are in large part identical to the OCC's prior rule.

Under the OCC's prior rule and under 12 C.F.R. part 228 (FRB Regulation BB, applicable to state member banks) and 12 C.F.R. part 345 (the FDIC version of the CRA regulations applicable to state nonmember banks), an institution is assessed under lending, investment, and services tests to ensure that it is serving the credit needs of LMI borrowers in its communities. The lending test evaluates the number and amount of residential mortgage, small business, and consumer loans made by an institution based on the location of the borrowers. An institution is evaluated based on the proportion of loans in an institution's assessment area, the dispersion of loans in its assessment area, and the number and amount of loans in low-, moderate-, middle-, and upper-income geographies in the bank's assessment area. The investment test evaluates the record of an institution in helping to meet the credit needs in its assessment areas through qualified community development investments that benefit its assessment areas or a broader state or regional area that includes the institution's assessment areas. The service test evaluates a bank's record of helping to meet the credit needs of its assessment area(s) by analyzing both the availability and effectiveness of the bank's systems for delivering retail banking services and the extent and innovativeness of its community development services.

Different performance standards are used by examiners to assess small banks and intermediate small banks than are used to evaluate larger institutions. Insured depository institutions may also be evaluated pursuant to a strategic plan developed by the institution and approved by the examining regulatory authority.[185]

An institution receives performance ratings in a CRA examination that range from substantial noncompliance to needs to improve to satisfactory (low satisfactory or high satisfactory).[186] CRA exam results are made public.[187]

The OCC's final rule: (1) clarifies and expands the list of activities that qualify for CRA credit[188] (and provides a framework by which any interested party may seek confirmation that an activity, loan, or investment qualifies for CRA credit);[189] (2) changes how an OCC-regulated institution's assessment area is delineated by requiring a bank with a significant portion of its retail domestic deposits outside of its facility-based assessment areas (such as those sourced through the Internet) to delineate additional assessment areas wherever it has a concentration of retail domestic deposits;[190] and (3) alters how CRA performance is measured by (a) instituting new general performance standards assessing both the distribution (i.e., number) of qualifying loans to LMI individuals, small farms, small businesses, and LMI geographies and the impact of

185. *See, e.g.*, 12 C.F.R. §§ 25.27, 195.27 (OCC strategic plan options for nationally chartered banks and federally chartered savings associations, respectively).

186. 12 U.S.C. § 2906(b)(2).

187. *Id.* § 2906(a)(2), (b).

188. 85 Fed. Reg. 34734, 34796 (to be codified at 12 C.F.R. § 25.04).

189. *Id.* at 34797 (to be codified at 12 C.F.R. § 25.07).

190. *Id.* at 34798 (to be codified at 12 C.F.R. § 25.09).

the bank's qualifying activities, measured by the value of such activities relative to the bank's retail domestic deposits.[191] The OCC's final rule employs presumptive ratings at the assessment area and bank levels that are adjusted based on considerations of performance context and discriminatory or other illegal credit practices.[192]

Although the prior rule required (and 12 C.F.R. part 228 and part 345 continue to require) an institution to collect, maintain, and report certain loan information, consumer loan data is optional under the prior rule, deposit data is not reported under the prior rule and, in general, the data collection and reporting requirements are less burdensome than under the OCC's final rule. The OCC's final rule requires all OCC-regulated banks to collect and maintain data and supporting information throughout the assessment period.[193] Banks evaluated under the general performance standards or a strategic plan must collect and maintain (along with supporting information) the following:

- retail lending test distribution ratios;
- CRA evaluation measures and assessment-area CRA evaluation measures;
- community development minimums and assessment-area community development minimums;
- data on qualifying loans, nonqualifying loans, community development investment, and community development services;
- retail domestic deposit data; and
- assessment area information.

Although the FDIC had joined the OCC in issuing a proposed CRA rule in 2019,[194] the FDIC decided to defer adoption of a final rule under the belief that it was not an appropriate time to impose a new regulatory regime on its state nonmember banks in the midst of the COVID-19 pandemic.[195] Despite efforts to achieve regulatory consensus, the FRB had declined to join in the proposed rule and has indicated an intent to pursue CRA reform independently at a future date.[196] Depending on whether the FDIC adopts a final rule that mirrors the OCC final rule and what action the FRB takes, it is possible that there could be two or even three different sets of CRA regulations, depending on whether the OCC, FDIC, or FRB is the primary regulator.

---

191. *Id.* at 34801 (to be codified at 12 C.F.R. § 25.13).

192. *Id.* at 34736.

193. 85 Fed. Reg. 34734, 34804 (to be codified at 12 C.F.R. part 25, subpart E).

194. 85 Fed. Reg. 1204 (Jan. 9, 2019).

195. *Anti-Redlining Revamp Best Left for 'Peacetime,' FDIC Chair Says,* Bloomberg L., June 26, 2020.

196. Testimony of FRB Chairman Jerome Powell before the House Financial Services Committee on June 16, 2020.

CHAPTER

8

Consumer Deposit Accounts and Electronic Fund Transfers

Lauren White

1. Scope of This Chapter

This chapter covers the provisions in subpart A of the Electronic Fund Transfer Act (EFTA)[1] and its implementing regulation, Regulation E,[2] that regulate deposit accounts and other types of consumer asset accounts. This chapter does not cover the following topics:

- *Gift card rules:* In 2010, the Board of Governors of the Federal Reserve System (the Board), which superintended Regulation E before the Consumer Financial Protection Bureau (CFPB) added section 205.20 (now section 1005.20) to Regulation E.[3] This section contained rules implementing the gift card provisions of the Credit CARD Act of 2009. These provisions are discussed in chapter 9 on prepaid accounts.

The views expressed in this chapter are not the views of Regions Bank, its parent corporation, or any of its affiliates or subsidiaries.

1. Electronic Fund Transfer Act, 15 U.S.C. §§ 1693–1693r (2012).
2. Regulation E, Electronic Fund Transfers (Regulation E), 12 C.F.R. pt. 1005 (2019).
3. *See* Regulation E, 12 C.F.R. § 1005.20.

- *Prepaid account regulations:* In 2016, the CFPB finalized regulations governing "prepaid accounts."[4] As described further in this chapter, these regulations provide that certain types of prepaid accounts qualify as "accounts" under Regulation E, and thus are subject to the provisions of Regulation E described in this chapter. Regulation E also imposes extensive new and special requirements on certain prepaid accounts.[5]
- *Remittance transfer provisions*: In 2013, The CFPB finalized the so-called Remittance Transfer Rule, which added subpart B to Regulation E.[6] This rule regulates consumer-initiated foreign remittances and is discussed in depth in chapter 10.

2. Authority, Purpose, and Coverage

Regulation E and its Official Interpretations[7] implement the EFTA,[8] which provides "a basic framework establishing the rights, liabilities, and responsibilities of participants in electronic fund and remittance transfer systems."[9] An electronic funds transfer (EFT) is "any transfer of funds that is initiated through an electronic terminal, telephone, computer, or magnetic tape for the purpose of ordering, instructing, or authorizing a financial institution to debit or credit a consumer's account."[10] An "account" is any asset account held by a financial institution for personal, family, or household use.[11] Today, the most common examples of accounts are checking and savings accounts held by depositary institutions (particularly banks and credit unions).

---

4. Prepaid accounts under the EFTA (Regulation E) and the Truth in Lending Act (Regulation Z), 81 Fed. Reg. 83934, 84325-6 (Nov. 22, 2016) *as modified by* Rules Concerning Prepaid Accounts Under the Electronic Fund Transfer Act (Regulation E) and the Truth in Lending Act (Regulation Z), 83 Fed. Reg. 6364 (Feb. 13, 2018) and Technical Specifications for Submissions to the Prepaid Account Agreements Database, 84 Fed. Reg. 7979 (Mar. 6, 2019) (collectively, the prepaid rule).

5. *See, e.g.*, Regulation E, 12 C.F.R. § 1005.18.

6. *See, e.g.*, *Id.* §§ 1005.30–1005.36.

7. 12 C.F.R. pt. 1005, supp. 1 (2019) [hereinafter, "Official Interpretations to Regulation E" or "Commentary"].

8. Electronic Fund Transfer Act, 15 U.S.C. §§ 1693–1693r (2012).

9. *Id.* 15 U.S.C. § 1693(b).

10. Regulation E, 12 C.F.R. § 1005.3(b)(1).

11. *Id.* § 1005.2(b)(1). When the prepaid rule became effective in April 2019, Regulation E's definition of "account" was extended to include payroll accounts, government benefit accounts, and prepaid accounts. The application of Regulation E to prepaid accounts is discussed in detail in chapter 9. *See* Regulation E, 12 C.F.R. § 1005.2(b)(2).

The primary purpose of the EFTA and Regulation E is to protect consumers engaging in EFTs.[12] Consumers generally initiate EFTs through point-of-sale (POS) terminals (i.e., swiping a debit card to make a purchase from a merchant), telephones (i.e., calling an automated telephone banking service to transfer money), or automated teller machines (ATMs).[13] EFTs also include "[t]ransfers resulting from debit card transactions, whether or not initiated through an electronic terminal."[14] This catch-all category for debit card transactions would include transactions initiated through card imprint machines, sometimes called "knucklebusters."[15]

A transaction can be an EFT though someone other than a consumer initiates it. For example, direct deposits by an employer to a consumer's account to pay wages are EFTs.[16] When a merchant initiates an automated clearing house (ACH) transaction using a consumer's check, that transaction is an EFT.[17] When a person initiates an EFT using information from a consumer's check, the regulation imposes special requirements. The person initiating the EFT must provide notice that the transaction will or may be processed as an EFT and must obtain a consumer's authorization for each transfer.[18] A consumer authorizes a one-time EFT using information from a check when the consumer receives this notice and proceeds with the underlying transaction.[19] For point-of-sale EFTs initiated using information from a check, this notice must be posted in a prominent and conspicuous location, and a copy thereof, or a substantially similar notice, must be provided to the consumer at the time of the transaction.[20]

If the EFT is a payment on an account receivable transaction, and if the payee provides a coupon book, the necessary notice can be provided once in the book rather than on every coupon.[21] To provide the notice required at a POS transaction involving an EFT initiated using a consumer's check, a merchant or other person can use model form A-6 set forth in appendix A of the Regulation.[22]

---

12. EFTA, 15 U.S.C. § 1693.
13. *See* Regulation E, 12 C.F.R. § 1005.3(b)(1).
14. *Id.* § 1005.3(b)v).
15. Official Interpretations to Regulation E, *supra* note 7, cmt. 3(b)(1)-1(iv).
16. *See, e.g., Id.* cmt. 3(b)(1)-1(ii).
17. Regulation E, 12 C.F.R. § 1005.3(b)(2).
18. Regulation E, 12 C.F.R. § 1005.3(b)(2)(ii).
19. *Id.*
20. Regulation E, 12 C.F.R. § 1005.3(b)(2)(ii).
21. Official Interpretations to Regulation E, *supra* note 7, cmt. 3(b)(2)-3.
22. Regulation E, 12 C.F.R. § 1005.3(b)(2)(iii). The information appearing in the model language is somewhat more extensive than that otherwise literally required by Regulation E. For example, the model language warns that, if the consumer's check is processed as an EFT, the consumer's account may be debited immediately and the consumer will not get a copy of the cancelled check. *See, e.g.,* Regulation E, 12 C.F.R. pt. 1005, appendix A.

3. Disclosures

The rule defines a "financial institution" as a bank, savings association, credit union, or other person that directly or indirectly holds a consumer's account.[23] An issuer of an access device[24] who agrees with a consumer to provide EFT services also is a financial institution under the rule.[25] A financial institution must provide certain disclosures when a consumer contracts to obtain EFT services or before an EFT occurs on the consumer's account.[26] If the financial institution fails to give certain elements[27] of these disclosures in a timely fashion, it cannot enforce any liability against the consumer for unauthorized transactions.[28] The prospect of being unable to enforce liability for unauthorized EFTs as a matter of law, taken together with other potential consequences of violating the regulation, supplies a strong incentive for financial institutions to provide adequate disclosures in a timely fashion.

3.1 When Initial Disclosures Must Be Provided

The Commentary addresses several practical issues regarding the provision of initial disclosures. For example, the Commentary states that a financial institution can provide disclosures at the customer level rather than the account level.[29] Thus, if a consumer contracts to receive EFT services on one account and receives disclosures covering those services, he or she need not receive another set of disclosures when subsequently opening another account on which those same services are provided so long as the terms and conditions do not differ from those previously given to the consumer.[30] The Commentary expressly provides that a financial institution can provide a comprehensive set of disclosures for all of the EFT services offered by the institution.[31] Thus, a financial institution need not customize disclosures for *every* customer, but can instead provide a set of omnibus disclosures for all EFT services offered by the institution.

Most consumers who open accounts on which EFTs can occur will enter contracts to obtain EFT services at the time they open their accounts. For example, most consumers will request and receive debit cards, along with card agreements, when

---

23. Regulation E, 12 C.F.R. § 1005.2(i).

24. Discussed in section 5, Issuance of Access Devices.

25. *Id.*

26. Regulation E, 12 C.F.R. § 1005.7(a).

27. Specifically, the initial disclosures required by Regulation E, 12 C.F.R. § 1005.7(b)(1)–(3).

28. *Id.* § 1005.6(a).

29. *See* Official Interpretations to Regulation E, *supra* note 7, cmt. 7(a)-3 (permitting such customer-level disclosure so long as the terms and conditions do not differ from those previously given).

30. *Id.*

31. *Id.* cmt. 7(a)-5.

they open consumer checking accounts. However, if a consumer does not contract to obtain EFT services at account opening, but later decides to enter such a contract with the financial institution holding his or her account, the financial institution should provide disclosures regarding the services for which the consumer contracts at the time the customer enters the contract. This is because the Commentary states that disclosures for EFT services provided pursuant to contract must be given "in close proximity" to the event requiring disclosure.[32]

Some consumers may have EFTs occur on their accounts even though the consumers never contracted with the account-holding financial institution for EFT services. Section 7 of Regulation E allows a financial institution to provide disclosures "when" the EFT occurs on the account. The Commentary would allow such a financial institution to provide disclosures as soon as reasonably possible "after" an EFT occurs if the EFT is the result of the consumer having authorized a third party to credit or debit the consumer's account and if the financial institution has not received advance notice of the EFT.[33] For a financial institution processing large quantities of EFTs every day, it may be impossible to identify the transactions that occur on accounts whose owners have not already received EFT disclosures and that have not been the subject of advance notice. Delivering a set of initial disclosures at account opening, regardless of whether the consumers on the account contract to obtain EFT services at that time, may be the most practical way of dealing with the requirement to provide disclosures on an account "when" an EFT occurs on the account. The Commentary provides that when a financial institution provides disclosures earlier than required under the regulation, assuming the terms and conditions do not differ from those previously disclosed, the disclosures "need not be repeated when a consumer later enters into an agreement with a third party to initiate preauthorized transfers to or from the consumer's account."[34]

3.2 Information Provided in the Initial Disclosures

The information required by the initial disclosures covers three general topics. First, what EFTs can a consumer make and how much will they cost? Second, how will information about the account be shared with the consumer and third parties? Third, how is liability for transfers apportioned between the consumer and the financial institution when mistakes occur? [35]

32. *Id.* cmt. 7(a)-1.
33. *Id.* cmt. 7(a)-2.
34. *Id.* cmt. 7(a)-1.
35. *See, generally*, Regulation E, 12 C.F.R. § 1005.7.

3.2.1 What Electronic Funds Transfers Can the Consumer Make and How Much Will They Cost?

The initial disclosures must describe the types of EFTs that the consumer can make, together with the frequency at which the financial institution will allow the transactions and any applicable limitations.[36] The disclosures must describe these limitations even if another regulation or law, rather than the financial institution itself, imposes the limits and even if the limits have been described in other disclosures previously given.[37] The disclosures must describe the fact that a third party can initiate transfers using information from a check.[38]

A financial institution must disclose any fees assessed for EFT services, such as those imposed on the consumer for processing debit card transactions, making a transfer at an ATM, or the right to make an EFT.[39] The disclosures must also advise that a fee may be imposed by an "automated teller machine operator" when the consumer initiates an electronic funds transfer or makes a balance inquiry and by any network used to complete the transaction.[40] An ATM operator is any person that operates an ATM who does not hold the account to or from which the transfer is made.[41]

Regulation E provides that certain other fees, such as fees for account overdrafts and stop payments, may be disclosed but are not required.[42] The Commentary specifically states that ATM balance inquiry fees imposed by the account-holding financial institution need not be disclosed because no transfer of funds occurs.[43] However, other regulations, for example Regulation DD, 12 C.F.R. Part 1030, which implements the Truth in Savings Act (TISA), may require disclosure of fees where disclosure is not required under Regulation E.[44]

3.2.2 What Information Will Be Shared about the Account and with Whom?

The initial disclosures must summarize the consumer's rights to notices of preauthorized transfers, receipts, and periodic statements.[45] In addition to advising the consumer

36. *Id.* § 1005.7(b)(4).

37. Official Interpretations to Regulation E, *supra* note 7, cmt 7(b)(4-)-2.

38. *Id.* cmt. 7(b)(4)-4.

39. Regulation E, 12 C.F.R. § 1005.7(b)(5).

40. *Id.* § 1005.7(b)(11).

41. *Id.* § 1005.16(a).

42. Official Interpretations to Regulation E, *supra* note 7, cmt. 7(b)(5)-1.

43. *Id.*

44. Regulation DD provides that initial disclosures must include "the amount of *any* fee that may be imposed in connection with [an] account . . . and the conditions under which the fee may be imposed" (emphasis added). Truth in Savings (Regulation DD), 12 C.F.R. § 1030.4(b)(4) (2011).

45. Regulation E, 12 C.F.R. § 1005.7(b)(6).

of the information he or she can expect to receive from the financial institution, the disclosures must describe the information about the consumer's account that the financial institution may provide to third parties.[46]

3.2.3 What Liability Will the Consumer and the Financial Institution Have for Unauthorized Electronics Funds Transfers?

The initial disclosures must describe the consumer's liability for unauthorized EFTs.[47] The disclosures must state the telephone number and address of the person to contact when the consumer believes an unauthorized EFT has occurred and the financial institution's business days.[48] If the financial institution chooses to impose zero liability for unauthorized transactions, the financial institution can omit these disclosures, but the omission prevents the imposition of liability for unauthorized transactions until the financial institution provides disclosures to the contrary.[49]

If the only EFTs from an account are preauthorized transfers, a consumer may be held liable for unauthorized EFTs if the consumer fails to report unauthorized transfers appearing on a periodic statement; however, before the financial institution can impose liability for those transfers it must have disclosed the potential for that liability and the telephone number and address for reporting unauthorized transfers.[50] The summary of the consumer's liability for unauthorized transfers may include advice on promptly reporting unauthorized transfers and the loss of or theft of an access device.[51]

The disclosures also must include an error resolution notice substantially similar to that prescribed by model form A-3 prescribed in appendix A of the regulation.[52] This notice must be provided in full at least annually or in an abbreviated form with each periodic statement.[53] The financial institution must describe its "business days," which are the days "on which the offices of the consumer's financial institution are open to the public for carrying on substantially all business functions," including, of course, receiving notice of error disputes.[54] In addition to summarizing the consumer's

---

46. *Id.* § 1005.7(b)(9).

47. *Id.* § 1005.7(b)(1).

48. *Id.* The financial institution can provide different numbers for (1) reporting the loss or theft of an access device or possible unauthorized transfers, (2) inquiring about the receipt of a preauthorized credit, (3) stopping payment of a preauthorized debit, and (4) giving notice of an error. Official Interpretations to Regulation E, *supra* note 7, cmt. 7(b)(2)-1.

49. Official Interpretations to Regulation E, *supra* note 7, cmt. 7(b)(1)-1; Regulation E, 12 C.F.R. § 1005.6(a).

50. Official Interpretations to Regulation E, *supra* note 7, cmt. 7(b)(1)-2.

51. *Id.* cmt. 7(b)(1)-3.

52. Regulation E, 12 C.F.R. § 1005.7(b)(10).

53. *Id.* § 1005.8(b).

54. *Id.* § 1005.2(d).

right to stop payment of a preauthorized EFT and the procedure for placing a stop payment order, the disclosures must summarize the financial institution's liability to the consumer for failing to make or to stop certain EFTs.[55]

3.3 Format

Any disclosures required under the regulation must be clear, understandable, and in a written and retainable form.[56] The disclosures may be provided electronically, subject to consumer consent and compliance with applicable provisions of the Electronic Signatures in Global and National Commerce Act (the E-Sign Act).[57] Unlike other regulations that set requirements for font size or print type, Regulation E merely provides that disclosures must be clear and readily understandable. Numbers, codes, and commonly accepted abbreviations are acceptable, though numbers and codes must be explained on the disclosure.[58] Disclosures may be made in a foreign language, provided they are made available in English at the customer's request.[59] Account disclosures required by other laws, for example, those required under the TISA, may be combined with those required under Regulation E.[60]

Where a consumer has multiple accounts, the financial institution may combine disclosures into a single statement.[61] Where an account is held by multiple consumers, the financial institution may provide the disclosures to any one of them.[62] For example, if a husband and wife open separate savings accounts and a joint checking account, the financial institution may provide Regulation E disclosures for the savings accounts and for the checking account in one statement. The financial institution may either provide both husband and wife a copy of the disclosures, or the institution, for purposes of disclosures required under Regulation E (disregarding any disclosure requirements for the savings account under TISA), could provide one set of disclosures to either the husband or the wife. As a practical matter, this could mean that some consumers may not receive initial disclosures.

When institutions offer EFT services jointly, they may contract among themselves to comply with the disclosure requirements of the regulation.[63] A financial institution need only make available initial disclosures and disclosures about error resolution

55. *Id.* §§ 1005.7(b)(7)–(8).
56. *Id.* § 1005.4(a)(1).
57. *Id.*
58. Official Interpretations to Regulation E, *supra* note 7, cmt. 4(a)-1.
59. Regulation E, 12 C.F.R. § 1005.4(a)(2).
60. *Id.* § 1005.4(b).
61. *Id.* § 1005.4(c)(1).
62. *Id.* § 1005.4(c)(2).
63. *Id.* § 1005.4(d).

that are within its knowledge and that are within the purview of its relationship with the consumer for whom it holds an account.[64]

When a financial institution joins an interchange or shared network system, disclosures are required for additional EFT services that were not previously available to consumers, if the terms and conditions previously disclosed differ from those applicable to the new service.[65] This is particularly relevant because the EFTA prohibits issuers and payment card networks from restricting the number of payment card networks over which an electronic debit transaction may be processed to one network (or two affiliated networks).[66]

4. Change in Terms

When a change in any of the terms covered by the initial disclosure will result in increased fees for the consumer, increased liability for the consumer, fewer types of available EFTs, or stricter limitations on the frequency or dollar amount of transfers, a financial institution must mail or deliver written notice to a consumer at least twenty-one days before the effective date of any such change.[67] The financial institution must also send a change in terms notice in advance if it is changing the telephone number or address used for reporting possible unauthorized transfers but only if the financial institution will impose liability on the consumer for unauthorized transfers.[68]

Regulation E provides no formatting or text requirements for a notice implementing a change in terms.[69] Thus, a financial institution may provide notice by including information on a periodic statement or sending a customer a revised disclosure statement. In any event, the notice should draw attention to the change.[70] For example, if the financial institution sends an entirely new disclosure statement, it may be appropriate to include a cover letter pointing out those terms that have changed.[71]

A financial institution may forego giving consumers any advance notice of a change in terms, if the change is temporary and necessary to maintain or restore the security of an account or an EFT system.[72] If the financial institution makes such a change permanent, and notice of the change would not jeopardize the security of the account or system, the financial institution must notify the consumer in writing

64. *Id.*
65. Official Interpretations to Regulation E, *supra* note 7, cmt. 7(a)-4.
66. EFTA, 15 U.S.C. § 1693o-2(b)(1)(A).
67. Regulation E, 12 C.F.R. § 1005.8(a)(1).
68. Official Interpretations to Regulation E, *supra* note 7, cmt. 8(a)-4.
69. *Id.* cmt. 8(a)-1.
70. *Id.*
71. *Id.*
72. Regulation E, 12 C.F.R. § 1005.8(a)(2).

on or with the next regularly scheduled periodic statement or within thirty days of making the change permanent, whichever is later.[73]

If a consumer's initial disclosure omitted dollar or use limitations on EFTs because secrecy on that subject was essential to the security of the account or system, a subsequent tightening in those limitations need not be disclosed if secrecy is still essential.[74] However, if there were no limits in place when the initial disclosures were provided, and limits are subsequently imposed, the financial institution must disclose, at a minimum, that limits have been adopted.[75] Thus, if some undisclosed limitation is further limited to protect the secrecy of the system or account, the financial institution does not have to jeopardize the security of the system to indicate that some unexplained change was made to a previously undisclosed limitation or to explain the change. However, if no such limitation existed when initial disclosures were given, but one is subsequently added to a system or an account, the financial institution must disclose that some limitation has been imposed, though the financial institution may withhold details essential to maintain the security of the system.[76]

5. Issuance of Access Devices

Under Regulation E, an access device is a card, code, or other means of access to a consumer's account that may be used by the consumer, or someone authorized by the consumer, to initiate an EFT.[77] The most common example in the experience of most consumers is a debit card issued for a checking account. In addition to debit cards, personal identification numbers (PINs), telephone transfer, and bill payment codes are access devices. One-time electronic debits initiated by means of checks can be EFTs (as can electronic images of the MICR encoding on such checks), but the checks (and the MICR lines) themselves are not access devices.[78] A preauthorized transfer[79] can be an EFT even though it can be initiated without an access device.[80]

Access devices fall into two categories: those that have been accepted and those that have not been. A financial institution can hold a consumer liable for unauthorized transactions involving an access device only if the device is an accepted

73. *Id. See also*, Electronic Fund Transfers, 44 Fed. Reg. 59464, 59467 (Oct. 15, 1979).

74. Official Interpretations to Regulation E, *supra* note 7, cmt. 8(a)-3.

75. *Id.*

76. Electronic Fund Transfers, 44 Fed. Reg. 59464, 59467 (Oct. 15, 1979).

77. Regulation E, 12 C.F.R. § 1005.2(a)(1).

78. Official Interpretations to Regulation E, *supra* note 7, cmt. 2(a). MICR refers to magnetic ink character recognition.

79. A preauthorized electronic fund transfer is "an electronic fund transfer authorized in advance to recur at substantially regular intervals." Regulation E, 12 C.F.R. § 1005.2(k).

80. Electronic Fund Transfers, 44 Fed. Reg. 18468, 18472 (Mar. 28, 1979).

access device.[81] One type of accepted device is one that the consumer requests, either orally or in writing. Another is a device issued to replace or renew a previously accepted device. A third is a device whose validation is requested by the consumer, even if the consumer did not actually request the device itself.[82]

By themselves, these rules might have the practical effect of prohibiting institutions from issuing unsolicited access devices that could be used without validation; however, the regulation goes a step further by literally prohibiting a financial institution from issuing an unaccepted access device except where the financial institution takes the steps described below. This belt-and-suspenders approach to the subject reflects a concern over fraud. If someone other than the consumer owning the account to which the device is connected obtained a device that could be used without validation, the account balance might decline sharply soon after.

A financial institution may distribute an unsolicited access device if all of the following conditions are satisfied:

- The access device is not validated, meaning the device is not capable of being used by the consumer (or recipient) to initiate EFTs;[83]
- The access device is accompanied by a clear explanation that the access device is not validated and how the consumer may dispose of the access device if validation is not desired;[84]
- The access device is also accompanied by the disclosure required by section 1005.7 of Regulation E regarding the consumer's rights and liabilities that will apply if the device is validated; and[85]
- The access device may be validated only in response to the consumer's oral or written request for validation, after the financial institution has verified the consumer's identity by reasonable means.[86]

The Commentary provides that verifying the consumer's identity by use of a photograph, fingerprint, personal visit, signature comparison, or personal information

81. Regulation E, 12 C.F.R. § 1005.6(a).

82. *Id.* § 1005.2(a)(2)(i)-(iii).

83. *Id.* § 1005.5(b)(1). Validation of the device requires the financial institution to "perform[] all procedures that would enable a consumer to initiate an EFT using the device." For example, when the access device is a debit card, a financial institution may require the card to be activated by the customer calling a toll-free number and successfully answering certain security questions. *Id.*

84. *Id.* § 1005.5(b)(2).

85. *Id.* § 1005.5(b)(3).

86. *Id.* § 1005.5(b)(4).

about the consumer may constitute "reasonable means."[87] A financial institution cannot impose any liability on a consumer for unauthorized transfers involving an unsolicited access device if the financial institution fails to correctly verify the consumer's identity and an imposter succeeds in having the device validated.[88]

6. Requirements for Overdraft Services

6.1 Background

Banks long had a practice of paying checks into overdraft on a discretionary basis generally for a fee. Those overdraft services were originally manual, and decisions to pay checks or return them were made item by item. As technology advanced, institutions began offering overdraft services for noncheck payments, such as ATM transactions, POS transactions, and ACH transactions, and decisions to pay or to return became automated. Automation reduced processing costs, ensured consistent treatment between customers, and helped institutions process a higher volume of transactions in less time.[89]

The Board found that some consumers lacked awareness of how modern overdraft services worked. For example, some consumers may not have understood that institutions would pay ATM and one-time debit card transactions into overdraft.[90] In 2009, the Board amended Regulation E to provide consumer protections for overdrafts involving ATM and one-time debit card transactions, called "covered

87. Official Interpretations to Regulation E, *supra* note 7, cmt. 5(b)-4. Presumably, "reasonable means" may entail an institution's use of Consumer Identification Program (CIP) measures to verify the customer's identity. A bank, at a minimum, must obtain each customer's name, date of birth, address, and identification number prior to opening an account. Financial Crimes Enforcement Network, Dept. of the Treasury, 31 C.F.R. § 1020.220(a)(2)(i)(A) (Mar. 1, 2011).

88. Official Interpretations to Regulation E, *supra* note 7, cmt. 5(b)-4.

89. Electronic Fund Transfers, 74 Fed. Reg. 59033 (Nov. 17, 2009) (citing *FDIC Study of Bank Overdraft Programs*. Federal Deposit Insurance Corporation, November 2008), at p. 8, *available at* http://business.cch.com/BANKD/FDIC-2008-Overdraft-Study.pdf).

90. ATM transactions include any transaction initiated at an ATM, including withdrawals and transfers between accounts. One-time debit card transactions include those made at the point of sale, online, or over the telephone. Electronic Fund Transfers 74 Fed. Reg. 59033, 59040 (Nov. 17, 2009).

transactions" in the amended rule.[91] The amended rule defines overdraft services and requires institutions to give consumers notices describing those services as they are available on any given consumer account. The amended rule prohibits financial institutions from providing overdraft services to accounts on covered transactions unless the accounts are opted in to those services in the manner required by the rule. The opt-in requirement has the practical effect of prohibiting financial institutions from charging fees for paying covered transactions unless consumers agree to pay those fees before initiating the transactions or unless the payments are made pursuant to certain exceptions from the definition of overdraft service.

6.2 Definition of Overdraft Service

An "overdraft service [is] a service under which a financial institution assesses a fee or charge on a consumer's account held by the financial institution for paying a transaction (including a check or other item) when the consumer has insufficient or unavailable funds in the account."[92] The concept of fees plays an important part in this definition: if a financial institution pays an item into overdraft but does not charge a fee, the financial institution is not providing an "overdraft service" under the rule. The fee may be a per-item or -transaction fee, a daily fee assessed for each day an item is paid into overdraft, or a sustained overdraft fee (sometimes known as a continuous negative balance fee).[93] If a financial institution charges the fee because the financial institution paid a covered transaction into overdraft, the payment is an overdraft service regardless of the type of fee charged, *unless* the payment is made pursuant to one of the arrangements excluded from the definition of an overdraft service.[94]

The arrangements excluded from the definition of an overdraft service are payments of overdrafts pursuant to a line of credit subject to Regulation Z, services

---

91. Regulators first attempted to establish parameters around overdraft services in February 2005, when the Board, along with the other federal agencies, issued The Joint Guidance on Overdraft Protection Programs. The Joint Guidance focused on three areas of consumer use of overdraft services: safety and soundness considerations, legal risk, and best practices. Then in May 2005, the Board revised Regulation DD and its staff commentary to provide uniformity in the disclosure requirements related to overdraft and returned-item fees. In May 2008, the Board, the Office of Thrift Supervision (OTS) and the National Credit Union Administration (NCUA) proposed an opt-out rule that would require institutions to give consumers the right to opt out of an overdraft service for all methods of payment, including checks, ACH, POS debit card transactions, and ATM withdrawals. The Board concurrently issued a proposal under Regulation DD which set forth requirements on delivery of the opt-out notice and model opt-out form, as well as disclosure requirements related to account balance and overdraft fees. Electronic Fund Transfers 74 Fed. Reg. 59033, 59034.

92. Regulation E, 12 C.F.R. § 1005.17(a).

93. Official Interpretations to Regulation E, *supra* note 7, cmt. 17(d)-2.

94. Regulation E, 12 C.F.R. § 1005.17(a)(1)-(4).

that transfer funds from a linked account to cover overdrafts on the deposit account (whether held individually or jointly), a line of credit or other transaction in securities of commodities in which credit is extended by a registered broker-dealer, and certain separate credit features accessed through a hybrid prepaid credit card or credit extended through a negative balance on the asset feature of a prepaid account.[95] Thus, a financial institution may charge a fee when covered transactions are paid using the arrangements described in these exclusions even if a consumer has not opted in to the institution's overdraft services for that account. It is important to note that a payment of an item into overdraft is not an overdraft service only when the payment is made pursuant to one of the arrangements excluded from the definition of overdraft service. Just because an account was linked to one of the arrangements excluded from the definition of overdraft service does not mean that all payments of overdrafts on that account are excluded from the definition of overdraft service. For example, an account may be linked to a line of credit to cover overdrafts, but if the financial institution pays an overdraft on the account, charges a fee for doing so, but never draws on the line of credit, the financial institution has provided an overdraft service.

Although these exclusions from the definition of overdraft service are important, they are relatively narrow. If a financial institution charges a fee for paying a covered transaction into overdraft under any other circumstances, the payment is an overdraft service even if the financial institution did not use its discretion in paying the item. For example, if a financial institution pays a covered transaction because it must do so (rather than because it has exercised discretion to do so), the payment is an overdraft service provided the financial institution charges a fee for making that payment (assuming the payment is not made pursuant to one of the exceptions from the definition of overdraft services). These "force pays" can occur on debit card transactions when a financial institution "either does not receive a request to authorize a transaction in advance or the final transaction amount is higher than the authorized amount, and the [institution] is required by card network rules to pay the transaction even though there are insufficient or unavailable funds in the . . . account to cover the transaction at settlement."[96]

6.3 Required Consent

A financial institution must satisfy four requirements, discussed below, before providing overdraft services on a consumer's account for covered transactions.[97] Put differently, a financial institution cannot charge a fee for paying an ATM or one-time debit card transaction into overdraft, unless the fee is assessed pursuant to an arrangement excluded from the definition of overdraft services, or unless these four conditions are satisfied. As discussed below, the four conditions require: (1) providing notice

95. *Id.*

96. Prepaid rule, *supra* note 4, at 83944.

97. *See, generally*, Regulation E, 12 C.F.R. § 1005.17.

to the consumer, (2) providing an opportunity for the consumer to consent to the overdraft service, (3) obtaining the consumer's affirmative consent, and (4) giving the consumer written confirmation of that consent.

6.3.1 Written Notice Describing the Institution's Overdraft Service

A financial institution must provide the consumer with notice describing the institution's overdraft service.[98] That notice must be in writing but can be provided electronically if the consumer has agreed to receive electronic communications.[99] The notice must be segregated from all other information.[100] The description of the overdraft service must provide the following, as applicable:

- Information regarding the financial institution's policy concerning authorization and payment of covered and noncovered transactions.[101] The description should include a statement notifying customers that they have the ability to revoke consent at any time.[102] As applicable, the description also should indicate that the financial institution pays overdrafts at its discretion and should explain that the financial institution may decline a transaction.[103]
- All fees imposed for payment of an overdraft. If the amount of the fee may vary from transaction to transaction, for instance, in the case of tiered overdraft fee structures where the amount of the fee increases based on the number of overdraft occurrences, the financial institution may indicate that a consumer may be assessed a fee "up to" the maximum fee.[104]
- Limits on fees charged, including daily fee caps and negative balance cushions. If the financial institution imposes no limit on the number of overdraft fees that may be assessed in a day, the financial institution must state that there is no limit.[105]

---

98. *Id.* § 1005.17(b)(1)(i).

99. *Id.*

100. *Id.*

101. *Id.* § 1005.17(d). As it relates to noncovered transactions, the notice may provide (1) a statement that the consumer has the right to opt in or out of the service for noncovered transactions, such as checks, ACH transactions, or automatic bill payments, and the means for the consumer to exercise this choice; (2) the amount of any associated returned item fee; (3) the fact that additional merchant fees may apply; (4) the consumer's right to revoke consent for noncovered transactions. *Id.* § 1005.17(d)(6).

102. *Id.* § 1005.17(d)(6).

103. Official Interpretations to Regulation E, *supra* note 7, cmt. 17(d)-1.

104. *Id.* cmt. 17(d)-2.

105. Regulation E, 12 C.F.R. § 1005.17(d)(3).

- Opt-in right and methods of opting in. The notice should include an explanation of the consumer's right to opt in to the overdraft service for covered transactions, including the methods by which the consumer may consent to the service.[106]
- Alternative plans for covering overdrafts, such as a line of credit subject to Regulation Z or a service that transfers funds from another account, for example a savings account, to the deposit account for the payment of overdrafts.[107]

The Regulation sets forth model form A-9 for this disclosure in appendix A. The financial institution may modify the notice but may only do so as provided in the regulation.

Some litigation has addressed whether a financial institution may adequately describe its overdraft services by relying on model form A-9 if the financial institution uses an available balance, rather than a ledger balance, to determine whether a payment would overdraw an account. The CFPB has described the difference between the two methods of balance calculation:

> A ledger-balance method factors in only settled transactions in calculating an account's balance; an available-balance method calculates an account's balance based on electronic transactions that the institutions have authorized (and therefore are obligated to pay) but not yet settled, along with settled transactions. An available balance also reflects holds on deposits that have not yet cleared.[108]

Model form A-9 does not distinguish between ledger balance and available balance.

The EFTA states that a financial institution is immune from civil or criminal liability under the EFTA arising from "any failure to make disclosure in proper form if a financial institution utilized an appropriate model clause issued by the Bureau or the Board. . . ."[109] However, courts considering this issue have reasoned that a financial institution using model form A-9 may not be protected by this safe harbor provision if the financial institution does not disclose that it calculates overdrafts on an available balance. In the view of these courts, omitting mention of the available balance method would *not* amount to a failure to make disclosure in the proper *form* but could instead be a failure to disclose proper *content*.[110] Although this may be a very narrow view of the safe harbor, a financial institution using model form A-9

106. *Id.* § 1005.17(d)(4).

107. *Id.* § 1005.17(d)(5).

108. CFPB, *Supervisory Highlights*, 8 (Winter 2015); *see also* Chambers v. NASA Federal Credit Union, 222 F.Supp.3d 1, 6 (D.D.C. 2017) (discussing the difference between ledger balance and available balance).

109. EFTA, 15 U.S.C. § 1693m(d)(2).

110. Ramirez v. Baxter Credit Union, No. 16-cv-03765-SI, 2017 WL 118859 (N.D. Cal. Jan. 12, 2017); Pinkston-Poling v. Advia Credit Union, 227 F. Supp. 3d 848 (W.D. Mich. 2016).

to disclose overdraft services based on available balance may adequately describe its services merely by referring to an "available" balance without further elaborating in the form on how the available balance is calculated.[111]

6.3.2 Reasonable Opportunity for a Consumer to Affirmatively Consent to the Institution's Overdraft Service for Covered Transactions

Where a financial institution charges a fee for paying a covered transaction into overdraft, the financial institution must always give the consumer a reasonable opportunity to opt in to overdraft services, and, as discussed below, must obtain that opt in before the consumer engages in a covered transaction that causes the financial institution to charge a fee for paying the transaction into overdraft.[112] A financial institution does not have to provide consumers with a reasonable opportunity to opt in to overdraft services on an account if the financial institution does not provide overdraft services on that account. In theory, if a financial institution were to return all items that would overdraw an account, the financial institution would never provide overdraft services, at least on that account. In practice, however, given the how the rules of payment systems work, a financial institution cannot return all ATM or debit card transactions that would overdraw a consumer's account even if the financial institution never uses its discretion to pay those transactions.[113] If a financial institution pays covered transactions into overdraft on an account, but never charges a fee for doing so, except in circumstances excluded from the definition of overdraft services, the financial institution is not providing overdraft services on that account. Thus, as a practical matter, if a financial institution provides debit card and ATM services, the financial institution must either allow consumers to opt in in the manner provided by the rule or forego overdraft fees for covered transactions.

A financial institution may require a consumer to choose whether to opt in to the institution's overdraft service as a necessary step to opening an account.[114] The Commentary provides that reasonable opportunity for and methods of opting in include mail (completing and mailing a form sent by the financial institution to the consumer), a readily available telephone line, electronic means (a form accessed at the institution's website whereby the customer clicks a button to affirm his or her consent), or in person (at a branch).[115] Other potential methods through which consumers may change their opt-in election include at an ATM, through an online banking portal, or by calling an IVR (an interactive voice response system that uses voice and keypad entry to interact with callers).

---

111. *See, e.g.*, *Chambers*, 222 F. Supp. 3d at 9–10 (holding that referring to available balance in an example on the opt-in form was an adequate description).

112. Regulation E, 12 C.F.R. § 1005.17(b)(1)(ii).

113. *See* section 6.2, regarding definition of force pay items.

114. Official Interpretations to Regulation E, *supra* note 7, cmt. 17(b)-5.

115. *Id.* cmt. 17(b)-4.

6.3.3 *Affirmative Consent to the Institution's Overdraft Service on an Account*

If a consumer initiates a covered transaction on an account before affirmatively consenting to overdraft services on that account, the financial institution cannot charge a fee for paying that transaction into overdraft.[116] Regulation E requires consent to be obtained separately from other consents or acknowledgments, ensuring that the terms of the service are not obscured by other account information.[117]

Because opt-in elections are made on an account-by-account basis, a consumer with multiple accounts must make an election for each account he or she owns. Affirmative consent to overdraft services from one owner of a joint account suffices as consent for all other owners.[118] Likewise, revocation from one owner suffices as revocation for all other owners.[119] Affirmative consent is effective until revoked or until the financial institution terminates the service.[120] A financial institution may terminate an account's overdraft service when the consumer makes excessive use of the service.[121]

A consumer must be able to revoke consent at any time and in any manner made available for providing consent.[122] Thus, a financial institution cannot allow a consumer to opt in via an ATM, an online banking portal, and an IVR system, but only allow consumers to opt out of the service by calling the IVR. Revocation must be implemented as soon as reasonably practicable.[123] If a consumer revokes consent, a financial institution is not required to waive or reverse overdraft fees assessed on the account prior to the institution's implementation of the revocation.[124] Thus, a financial institution can charge for transactions it authorized while the account was opted in to the institution's overdraft service even if the account is no longer opted in when the transactions settle into overdraft.

6.3.4 *Confirmation of the Consumer's Consent to the Institution's Overdraft Service on an Account*

Finally, the financial institution must provide the consumer with confirmation of the consumer's consent in writing, or, if the consumer agrees, electronically.[125] This confirmation must include a statement informing the consumer of the right to revoke

116. Regulation E, 12 C.F.R. § 1005.17(b)(1)(iii).
117. *Id.* § 1005.17(b)(1)(i).
118. *Id.* § 1005.17(e).
119. *Id.*
120. *Id.* § 1005.17(g).
121. *Id. See also* Official Interpretations to Regulation E, *supra* note 7, cmt. 17(g)-1.
122. Regulation E, 12 C.F.R. § 1005.17(f).
123. *Id.*
124. Official Interpretations to Regulation E, *supra* note 7, cmt. 17(f)-1.
125. Regulation E, 12 C.F.R. § 1005.17(b)(1)(iv).

such consent.[126] A financial institution does not have to provide notice to a consumer when consent is revoked. As a practical matter, a financial institution may choose to notify consumers when revocation occurs if only to avoid confusion about the status of consent on accounts owned by multiple consumers each of whom may provide and then revoke consent independently of the other(s).

6.4 Recurring Debit Card Transactions

Recurring debit card transactions are not covered transactions and are thus not subject to the opt-in rule. Accordingly, institutions may charge for paying recurring debit card transactions into overdraft regardless whether consumers opt in to overdraft services. However, some processing systems may not distinguish between recurring and one-time debit card transactions (which are, of course, subject to the opt-in rule for overdraft services). Even if a system can distinguish between the two types of transactions, the distinction may depend on a transaction having been properly identified (or coded) by a third party, such as a merchant. Thus, as a practical matter, a financial institution may not be able to discern, without input from other parties, whether a debit card transaction paid into overdraft is one for which the financial institution can charge a fee. The regulation provides a safe harbor that allows a financial institution to rely on a merchant's coding of the transaction as one time or recurring when determining whether to pay and/or charge for the payment of the item.[127]

6.5 Conditioning Payment of Other Overdrafts

The regulation requires institutions to provide consumers a reasonable opportunity to give affirmative consent to overdraft services, but a financial institution is not required to provide those services on any account, much less in connection with any particular transaction.[128] However, a financial institution cannot condition the payment of checks, ACH transactions, or any other transactions (except, of course, covered transactions) on a consumer's willingness to give affirmative consent to overdraft services for covered transactions. [129] In other words, when deciding whether to pay a noncovered transaction (into overdraft or otherwise), a financial institution cannot take into consideration whether the consumer owning the account has agreed to pay fees when the financial institution pays covered transactions into overdraft. A financial institution also cannot provide fewer or different features (e.g., free checks) on accounts because the consumer owning the account has not opted into overdraft

126. *Id.*

127. Official Interpretations to Regulation E, *supra* note 7, cmt. 17(b)-1.ii.

128. *Id.* cmt. 17(b)(2)-2.

129. Regulation E, 12 C.F.R. § 1005.17(b)(2).

services for covered transactions, relative to accounts whose consumers have opted into overdraft services.[130]

7. Documentation When an Electronic Funds Transfer Occurs

A consumer is entitled to receive two types of documentation when an EFT occurs on his or her account. The first is a receipt at the terminal when the EFT occurs. The second is the monthly periodic statement sent for each period in which an EFT occurs.[131]

Documentation of an EFT must be made available to a consumer any time an EFT occurs at an electronic terminal.[132] An "electronic terminal" is an electronic device, other than a telephone operated by a consumer, through which a consumer may initiate an EFT.[133] Common examples of an electronic terminal include ATM and POS machines.

Though the onus is on the financial institution to provide receipts, the Commentary provides that an account-holding financial institution may make terminal receipts available through third parties such as merchants or other financial institutions.[134] Merchants, card networks, and financial institutions may contract among themselves for these terms. For example, the Visa Core Rules and Visa Product and Service Rules (Visa Rules) require merchants to provide transaction receipts to consumers even though information provided on the receipt may come from a variety of sources, including the consumer's account-holding institution.[135]

A receipt must be made available in retainable form at the time the consumer initiates the EFT.[136] The receipt must display the date on which the consumer initiated

---

130. *Id.* § 1005.17(b)(3).

131. *See, generally*, *id.* § 1005.9.

132. *Id.* § 1005.9(a).This documentation is *prima facie* proof of a payment to another person, except in the case of a terminal receipt documenting a deposit. Official Interpretations to Regulation E, *supra* note 7, cmt. 9(a)(6)-2.

133. Regulation E, 12 C.F.R. § 1005.2(h).

134. Official Interpretations to Regulation E, *supra* note 7, cmt. 9(a)-2.

135. Visa Rules, § 5.10.1.1 (April 13, 2019).

136. Regulation E, 12 C.F.R. § 1005.9(a). The financial institution may program its machines such that it provides a receipt only to those consumers who elect to receive one. Official Interpretations to Regulation E, *supra* note 7, cmt. 9(a)-1.

the transfer and the amount of the transfer.[137] A transaction fee may be included in this amount, provided the amount of the fee is disclosed to the consumer.[138]

The receipt must also include the type of transfer and the type of account(s) to which, or from which, funds are transferred (e.g., "withdrawal from checking," "transfer from savings to checking," or "payment from savings").[139] If the access device used in the transaction can access only one type of account at the terminal, the account type may be omitted.[140] However, if a single access device may be used to access more than one account of the same type at the terminal where the transaction occurs, the receipt must specify which account was accessed (e.g., "withdrawal from checking II").[141] The receipt must include a number or code that identifies the consumer's account or accounts or the access device used to initiate the transfer.[142]

The receipt must provide the location or other identification, such as a code or terminal number, of the terminal where the transfer was initiated. [143] Except in limited circumstances where all terminals are located in the same city or state, if the location is disclosed, it must include the city and state or foreign country and one of the following:[144] the street address;[145] a generally accepted name for the specific location (for example, a branch of the institution, a shopping center, or an airport);[146] or the name of the owner or operator of the terminal if the terminal is not owned by the account-holding institution.[147]

The receipt must also include the name of any third party to or from whom funds are transferred.[148] The name of the payee may be provided by name or by code,

---

137. Regulation E, 12 C.F.R. § 1005.9(a)(1),(2).

138. *Id.* § 1005.9(a)(1). Official Interpretations to Regulation E, *supra* note 7, cmt. 9(a)(1)-1. Section 16 of the regulation requires an ATM operator to give notice when a transaction occurs at an ATM. The notice requirement under section 16 requires an ATM operator that imposes a fee for an electronic funds transfer or balance inquiry to provide notice that a fee will be imposed and the amount of that fee. When an ATM operator gives the notice required under section 16, that notice also satisfies the notice requirement that would otherwise be required under section 9. *See* Regulation E, 12 C.F.R. 1005.16; Official Interpretations to Regulation E, *supra* note 7, cmt. 9(a)(1)-2.

139. Official Interpretations to Regulation E, *supra* note 7, cmt. 9(a)(3)-1.

140. Regulation E, 12 C.F.R. § 1005.9(a)(3).

141. Official Interpretations to Regulation E, *supra* note 7, cmt. 9(a)(3)-3.

142. Regulation E, 12 C.F.R. § 1005.9(a)(4).

143. *Id.* § 1005.9(a)(5); Official Interpretations to Regulation E, *supra* note 7, cmt. 9(a)(5)-1.ii.

144. Regulation E, 12 C.F.R. § 1005.9(a)(5).

145. Generally, the number and street address must be provided, unless the street alone uniquely identifies the terminal location. Official Interpretations to Regulation E, *supra* note 7, cmt. 9(a)(5)(i)-1.

146. *Id.* cmt. 9(a)(5)(ii)-1.

147. *Id.* cmt. 9(a)(5)(iii)-1. *See also* Regulation E, 12 C.F.R. § 1005.9(a(5).

148. Regulation E, 12 C.F.R. § 1005.9(a)(6).

provided the code is explained on the receipt, unless the name is provided by the consumer in a way that is not machine readable.[149]

A financial institution need not provide a receipt for a transfer made at a terminal when the transfer is for fifteen dollars or less or when the transfer is not completed.[150] Further, if a bona fide, unintentional error causes a receipt to not be provided (for example, the paper jams at an ATM), the failure would not amount to a violation of the regulation provided the financial institution maintains procedures reasonably adapted to avoid such occurrences (for example, providing a phone number for the consumer to call).[151]

8. Periodic Statements

A periodic statement provides a summary of EFTs conducted over the relevant periodic cycle and provides an orderly means by which consumers may reconcile their accounts.[152] This is especially true for consumers who do not have access to electronic banking or other services that may allow them to follow real time, daily account activity. Receipt of the periodic statement serves as a key point for other provisions of Regulation E, particularly with regard to assessing liability for errors as defined under the regulation.

For an account to or from which an EFT can be made, a financial institution must send a periodic statement for each monthly cycle in which an EFT has occurred.[153] Cycles do not have to be based on calendar months provided the periodic cycles are reasonably equal, meaning the cycles do not vary by more than four days in length.[154] If no EFTs occur during a cycle, the financial institution must still send a periodic statement at least quarterly for any account on which an EFT can be made.[155] The statement may be sent electronically provided the financial institution complies with consumer consent and E-Sign Act requirements.[156] The regulation is silent on whether a financial institution may charge for providing paper statements.

149. Official Interpretations to Regulation E, *supra* note 7, cmt. 9(a)(6)-1.

150. Regulation E, 12 C.F.R. § 1005.9(e). *See also* Official Interpretations to Regulation E, *supra* note 7, cmt. 9(a)-4.

151. Official Interpretations to Regulation E, *supra* note 7, cmt. 9(a)-5.

152. Electronic Fund Transfers, 45 Fed. Reg. 8248, 8250 (Feb. 6, 1980).

153. Regulation E, 12 C.F.R. § 1005.9(b).

154. Official Interpretations to Regulation E, *supra* note 7, cmt. 9(b)-1.

155. Regulation E, 12 C.F.R. § 1005.9(b). Certain accounts have EFT access only through preauthorized transfers made to the account (e.g., recurring direct deposits). Generally, for these types of accounts, a financial institution is required to send a periodic statement at least quarterly. *Id.* Such is the case, regardless whether the account can also be accessed by other means, such as by check. Official Interpretations to Regulation E, *supra* note 7, cmt. 9(c)(1)-1.

156. Regulation E, 12 C.F.R. § 1005.4(a)(1).

The statement must include the account number and the balances of the account at the beginning and end of the statement period.[157] The periodic statement also must include transaction information that can be important to a consumer's ability to identify potential errors. For each transfer occurring during the cycle, this transaction information must include the amount of the transfer; the date the transfer was credited to or debited from the consumer's account; the type of transfer and type of account to or from which funds were transferred; for a transfer initiated by the consumer at an electronic terminal (except for a deposit of cash or a check, draft, or similar paper instrument), the terminal location; and the name of any third party to or from whom funds were transferred.[158] A financial institution need not verify each transaction that appears on the statement provided the financial institution has reasonable procedures to ensure the integrity of the data received from other institutions.[159]

The periodic statement also must include the amount of any fees assessed against the account during the statement period for making, or for the right to make, EFTs or for account maintenance.[160] Fees may be disclosed as a total sum or itemized in part or in full, and may include fees assessed for EFTs and fees assessed for other nonelectronic services, other than a finance charge imposed on the account.[161] Finally, the statement must provide the address and telephone number used for inquiries or notice of errors preceded by "Direct inquiries to" or similar language.[162] If the financial institution provides a readily available telephone line for customers to ascertain whether a preauthorized transfer to the account has occurred, the statement must also include the telephone number for that line, as discussed in section 9, Preauthorized Transfers.[163]

9. Preauthorized Transfers

9.1 Overview

A "preauthorized electronic fund transfer" (PEFT) is an EFT that is authorized in advance to recur at substantially regular intervals and that requires no further action

157. *Id.* § 1005.9(b)4).

158. *Id.* § 1005.9(b)(1). Where a consumer owns more than one account held at the institution, for example, a savings and a checking account, transfers made between those two accounts need only be documented on a periodic statement for one of the two accounts. *Id.* § 1005.9(c)(2).

159. Official Interpretations to Regulation E, *supra* note 7, cmt. 9(b)(1)-1.

160. Regulation E, 12 C.F.R. § 1005.9(b)(3).

161. Official Interpretations to Regulation E, *supra* note 7, cmt. 9(b(3)-1, 3.

162. Regulation E, 12 C.F.R. § 1005.9(b)(5).

163. *Id.* § 1005.9(b)(6).

by the consumer to initiate the transaction.[164] A monthly "paycheck" transmitted electronically is a typical PEFT to credit a consumer's account. A recurring monthly bill payment from a consumer's account is a typical PEFT to debit a consumer's account.

When a PEFT is one credited to the consumer's account, the receiving financial institution must credit the amount of the transfer to that account as of the date the funds are received.[165] A financial institution must give a consumer notice of each PEFT that a third party initiates to a consumer's account, if the PEFT occurs at least every sixty days, unless the payor gives the consumer positive notice that the transfers have occurred.[166] The financial institution may notify the consumer in one of three ways:

- oral or written notice of the transfer within two business days after the transfer occurs (positive notice),[167]
- oral or written notice, within two business days after the transfer was scheduled to occur that the transfer did not occur (negative notice),[168] or
- a readily available telephone line that a consumer may call to determine whether the transfer occurred.[169]

Institutions that use a readily available telephone line must provide the telephone number on the initial disclosure of account terms and on each periodic statement.[170] In addition, the financial institution must generally be able to verify during a consumer's initial call whether a transfer to the account occurred.[171] If the financial institution is unable to verify that a transfer occurred during the initial call, the financial institution must respond within two business days.[172] To satisfy the "readily available standard," a financial institution must provide enough telephone lines so that customers get a reasonably prompt response though the line need only be available during normal business hours.[173]

---

164. *Id.* § 1005.2(k); *see also* Official Interpretations to Regulation E, *supra* note 7, cmt. 2(k)-1.

165. Regulation E, 12 C.F.R. § 1005.10(a)(3).

166. *Id.* § 1005.10(a)(1),(2).

167. *Id.* § 1005.10(a)(1))(i). The financial institution may use different methods of notice for different types of transfers without providing the consumer a choice on which method is used. Official Interpretations to Regulation E, *supra* note 7, cmt. 10(a)(1)-1, 2. The presence of a transfer on a periodic statement sent within two business days after the transfer occurs, or the absence of a transaction on a periodic statement sent two business days after a transaction is scheduled to occur, is sufficient written notice. Official Interpretations to Regulation E, *supra* note 7, cmt. 10(a)(1)-3, 4.

168. Regulation E, 12 C.F.R. § 1005.10(a)(1)(ii).

169. *Id.* § 1005.10(a)(1)(iii).

170. *Id.*

171. Official Interpretations to Regulation E, *supra* note 7, cmt. 10(a)(1)-5.

172. *Id.*

173. *Id.* cmt. 10(a)(1)-7.

When a PEFT is one debited from a consumer's account, the transfer may be authorized only in writing, signed or similarly authenticated by the consumer.[174] The person or entity that obtains the authorization must provide a copy of the authentication to the consumer.[175]

Consumer authorization can be given electronically. The E-Sign Act generally requires consumer consent prior to using an electronic record to provide or make available information to a consumer when that information relates to a transaction required by statute, regulation, or other rule of law.[176] At least one court has held that, because obtaining authorization from a consumer for PEFTs from an account involves obtaining authorization from a consumer, authorization by means such as a recorded telephone conversation is valid under the EFTA and the E-Sign Act when confirmation of the authorization is mailed to the customer.[177]

When PEFTs from a consumer's account are initiated under a single authorization but vary in amounts, the consumer has a right to receive written notice of the amount and date of the transfer at least ten days before the scheduled date of each transfer.[178] However, the designated payee or the financial institution may inform the consumer of this right and give the consumer the option to receive notice only when a transfer falls outside a specified range of amounts or only when a transfer differs from the most recent transfer by a set, agreed-upon amount.[179] For example, if the payment is one for a utility bill, an appropriate range might be based on the highest and lowest bill of a particular season.[180]

---

174. Regulation E, 12 C.F.R. § 1005.10(b). No additional authorization is necessary when a successor financial institution begins collecting payments for the former biller, provided the former biller had the proper authorization. Official Interpretations to Regulation E, *supra* note 7, cmt. 10(b)-1. New authorization also is not required when a financial institution transitions from paper-based to electronic debiting, even if existing authorization does not specify that electronic debiting will occur. Official Interpretations to Regulation E, *supra* note 7, cmt. 10(b)-1.

175. Regulation E, 12 C.F.R. § 1005.10(b).

176. E-Sign Act, 15 U.S.C. § 7001(c)(1) (2000).

177. Blatt v. Capital One Auto Fin., Inc., 237 F. Supp. 3d 688, 692 (M.D. Tenn. 2017); CFPB Compliance Bulletin 2015-06, *Requirements for Consumer Authorizations for Preauthorized Electronic Fund Transfers* (Nov. 23, 2015).

178. Regulation E, 12 C.F.R. § 1005.10(d)(1). A financial institution holding the consumer's account from which PEFTs are made does not violate Regulation E where the designated payee fails to provide notice of varying transfer amounts. Official Interpretations to Regulation E, *supra* note 7, cmt. 10(d)(1)-1.

179. Regulation E, 12 C.F.R. § 1005.10(d)(2); Official Interpretations to Regulation E, *supra* note 7, cmt. 10(d)(2)-1.

180. Official Interpretations to Regulation E, *supra* note 7, cmt. 10(d)(2)-1.

9.2 Consumer's Right to Stop Payment

After a consumer authorizes PEFTs from his or her account, he or she must have a means to revoke the authorizations and thereby stop further payments.[181] A consumer may stop payment of a PEFT by providing oral or written notice to the financial institution that holds his or her account at least three business days before the date of the next scheduled transfer.[182] If the debit item is resubmitted, the financial institution must continue to honor the stop payment request until the consumer notifies the financial institution that the payments may resume.[183] Though it must immediately implement a stop payment requested orally, a financial institution may require a consumer to give written confirmation of a stop payment order within fourteen days of an oral notification.[184] If the financial institution requires written confirmation, it must inform the consumer of the requirement and provide the address where confirmation should be sent.[185] If the consumer fails to provide confirmation of the oral request, the request ceases to be binding fourteen days after the oral notification.[186]

9.3 Compulsory Use

A financial institution or other person may not condition the extension of credit to a consumer on the consumer's agreement to repay the debt using PEFTs.[187] However, a creditor may offer a reduced annual percentage rate or other cost-related incentive for an automatic repayment plan provided the creditor offers other loan programs that do not require repayment using PEFTs for the type of credit involved.[188] For example, a financial institution may offer a mortgage plan whereby biweekly payments are debited electronically from the consumer's account to produce a lower total finance charge.[189]

There is an important exception to the prohibition against requiring repayment by PEFTs as a condition for the extension of credit. Credit extended under an overdraft credit plan or credit extended to maintain a specified minimum balance in a consumer's account can be conditioned on the requirement that the credit is automatically repaid.[190] That condition is allowed under those circumstances even

181. *See, generally*, Regulation E, 12 C.F.R. § 1005.10(c).

182. *Id.* § 1005.10(c)(1).

183. Official Interpretations to Regulation E, *supra* note 7, cmt. 10(c)-1.

184. Regulation E, 12 C.F.R. § 1005.10(c)(2).

185. *Id.*

186. *Id.*

187. *Id.* § 1005.10(e)(1).

188. Official Interpretations to Regulation E, *supra* note 7, cmt. 10(e)(1)-4.

189. *Id.*

190. Regulation E, 12 C.F.R. § 1005.10(e)(1). This exception, however, does not apply to hybrid prepaid credit cards under Regulation Z. *Id.*

if the credit is extended pursuant to a line that can be accessed by the consumer in ways other than by overdrafts.[191]

10. Error Resolution and Consumer Liability for Unauthorized Electronic Funds Transfers

Errors can occur on any type of transaction, including EFTs. For example, the amount of an EFT can be wrong or the person who initiated an EFT may have lacked authority to do so. Regulation E sets out a framework for dealing with these and other mistakes. Section 11 of the regulation describes an institution's responsibilities with respect to investigating errors and, where appropriate, correcting them. Section 6 limits a consumer's liability for *unauthorized* EFTs, which is defined in section 2 and discussed in section 10.3. Thus, there are rules prescribing how to handle errors in general and others prescribing how to handle unauthorized transactions in particular.

10.1 Definition of an Error

Section 11 defines seven different types of errors: (1) unauthorized EFTs; (2) incorrect EFTs to or from the consumer's account; (3) the omission of an EFT from a periodic statement; (4) computational or bookkeeping errors made by a financial institution relating to an EFT; (5) EFTs improperly identified on an ATM receipt, on a periodic statement, or on a notice about a preauthorized recurring EFT; (6) a cardholder's request for documentation required on an ATM receipt, on a periodic statement or online statement, or on a notice about a preauthorized recurring EFT; and (7) a cardholder's request for additional information or clarification concerning an EFT, including a request to determine whether an error exists.[192]

Not every misunderstanding or dispute involving an EFT constitutes an error under the regulation. For example, if a financial institution simply fails to make an EFT after having been properly instructed to do so, that failure does not involve an error subject to the procedures in section 11. For example, the definition of error does not encompass what are commonly called "merchant disputes," which are disputes involving dissatisfaction with merchandise or service.[193] A financial institution may assist consumers with these disputes, but the regulation does not obligate it to do so. Although Regulation E may not be implicated in these situations, institutions that are also card issuers may have contractual obligations with the card network regarding debit card transactions. For example, a financial institution that issues Visa branded cards must adhere to the Visa Rules.[194] Generally speaking, these rules provide specific

191. Official Interpretations to Regulation E, *supra* note 7, cmt. 10(e)(1)-2.

192. Regulation E, 12 C.F.R. § 1005.11(a)(1).

193. *See id.* § 1005.11(a)(1).

194. *See, generally*, Visa Rules, *supra* note 135.

processes for resolving merchant disputes. These contractual arrangements cannot diminish a consumer's rights under Regulation E.[195]

10.2 Notice of an Error

When a mistake occurs on an EFT, a consumer's first step in having it corrected is to give the financial institution notice.[196] Whether the financial institution receives notice (which can be oral, written, or, in some instances, constructive) and when that notice is received determines what a financial institution must do to investigate and correct an error.[197] Except for errors involving unauthorized transactions, the consumer must give the financial institution notice before the financial institution has an obligation to do anything.[198]

At a minimum, notice of an error must enable the financial institution to identify the consumer's name and account number, indicate why the consumer believes an error exists, and, to the extent possible, include the type, date, and amount of the alleged error.[199] As depicted in appendix A, with some exceptions for unauthorized transactions, notice of an error is timely when it is received no later than sixty days after the financial institution sends the periodic statement on which the alleged error is first reflected.[200] A consumer who withdraws the allegation of an error may reassert the error provided he or she does so within the original sixty-day period.[201] If a consumer fails to provide timely notice, the financial institution is not required to comply with the error resolution procedures set forth in Regulation E unless the error involves an unauthorized transaction, in which case a financial institution must still follow procedures applicable to those transactions, as discussed in section 10.2.[202]

If a consumer's notice of an alleged error is timely, a financial institution must meet certain deadlines for completing an investigation. Generally, the financial institution has ten business days after receiving notice of an error to determine whether an error occurred.[203] The ten *business* days may be extended to forty-five *calendar* days from receipt of notice provided the institution, within ten business days of receiving the notice, provisionally credits the consumer's account for the amount of the disputed transaction(s) and informs the consumer within two business days

195. EFTA, 15 U.S.C. § 1693l.

196. *See, generally*, Regulation E, 12 C.F.R. § 1005.11(b).

197. *Id.*

198. *Id.*

199. *Id.* § 1005.11(b)(1)(ii), (iii).

200. *Id.* § 1005.11(b)(1)(i).

201. Official Interpretations to Regulation E, *supra* note 7, cmt. 11(e)-1.

202. *Id.* cmt. 11(b)(1)-7. Where the consumer's assertion of an error involves an unauthorized EFT, however, the financial institution must comply with section 1005.6 before imposing any liability on the consumer. *Id.*

203. Regulation E, 12 C.F.R. § 1005.11(c)(1).

of the provisional crediting of the amount and date of the credit.[204] The consumer must have full access to the provisionally credited funds during the investigation. Although the financial institution does not need grounds to extend the investigation beyond ten business days, the forty-five-calendar-day alternative is not an absolute right to take forty-five days in every case; the financial institution must investigate and make its determination promptly.[205] Similarly, though the financial institution may request additional supporting documentation of an alleged error, it cannot delay the investigation based on receipt of the supporting information.[206]

If a consumer provides oral notice of an error, the financial institution may require written confirmation within ten business days of receiving the oral notice.[207] The financial institution must begin its investigation promptly upon receipt of oral notice and cannot delay until written notice is received.[208] However, when the financial institution requests written confirmation and the consumer fails to provide such confirmation, the financial institution does not have to provide the consumer provisional credit if the investigation extends beyond the ten-day deadline.[209]

10.2.1 Investigation Scope

An investigation of error may typically include a review of the transaction history on the particular account for a reasonable time prior to the alleged error.[210] The investigation may also include a review of the location of the transaction or the payee in question relative to the consumer's residence or the habitual transaction area for the account.[211] Of course, an investigation may also include other information not only within the control of the institution, but also within the control of third-party service providers (provided the financial institution reasonably believes the third party has records that are relevant to the investigation).[212]

If an alleged error concerns a transfer to or from a third party, and if there is no agreement between the account-holding financial institution and the third party for the type of EFT involved, then the financial institution may satisfy its investigation requirement by reviewing its own internal records.[213] This concept is known as the "four walls" rule. If, however, there is an agreement between the third party and the institution, and the alleged error involves the type of transaction covered by that agreement, the financial institution must go beyond its own four walls to request

204. *Id.* § 1005.11(c)(2).
205. Electronic Fund Transfers, 45 Fed. Reg. 8248, 8255 (Feb. 6, 1980).
206. Regulation E, 12 C.F.R. § 1005.11(b)(3).
207. *Id.* § 1005.11(b)(2).
208. Official Interpretations to Regulation E, *supra* note 7, cmt. 11(c)-2.
209. Regulation E, 12 C.F.R. § 1005.11(c)(2)(i)(A).
210. Official Interpretations to Regulation E, *supra* note 7, cmt. 11(b)(1)-5.ii.
211. *Id.* cmt. 11(b)(1)-5.
212. *Id.* cmt. 11(c)(4)-5.vi.
213. Regulation E, 12 C.F.R. § 1005.11(c)(4).

additional information from the third party.[214] The type of agreement contemplated here includes those where a third party agrees to honor an access device issued by the financial institution (but not common membership in an ACH).[215]

When the error alleged is a request for documentation required by section 9 or 10 of Regulation E, and when a third party having no agreement with the financial institution possesses that information or documentation, the financial institution satisfies its investigation requirements by advising the consumer of that fact within the ten-business-day or forty-five-calendar-day timeframe.[216]

10.2.1.1 Extension of Time Periods

Regulation E extends the investigation timeframes for EFTs that are (1) initiated at POS terminals, (2) not initiated in a state,[217] or (3) initiated within thirty days of the first deposit being made in an account.[218]

These extensions balance the risk of fraud against institutions and unnecessary issuance of provisional credit, on the one hand, against consumer hardship while waiting to receive credit for the amount of an error, on the other.[219] For an error alleged on an EFT initiated at a POS terminal or outside the United States, the financial institution has ten business days either to resolve the alleged error or to give provisional credit on the account.[220] If provisional credit is issued, the financial institution has ninety calendar days to complete its investigation.[221] For errors alleged on an EFT that occurs within thirty days after the first deposit is made to the account, the general ten-business-day rule for investigation is extended to twenty business days. If provisional credit is issued, a financial institution has ninety calendar days to resolve the claim.[222]

---

214. Electronic Fund Transfers, 45 Fed. Reg. 8248, 8256 (Feb. 6, 1980). When a consumer alleges an error involving a transfer made at a POS terminal, the financial institution must verify the information previously transmitted when the transfer was initiated (e.g., the information that would appear on the sales receipt). Official Interpretations to Regulation E, *supra* note 7, cmt. 11(c)(4)-3.

215. Official Interpretations to Regulation E, *supra* note 7, cmt. 11(c)(4)-4.

216. *Id.* cmt. 11(c)(4)-1.

217. "State" is defined as any state, territory, or possession of the United States, the District of Columbia, the Commonwealth of Puerto Rico, or any political subdivisions thereof. Regulation E, 12 C.F.R. § 1005.2(l).

218. *Id.* § 1005.11(c)(3).

219. Electronic Fund Transfers, 63 Fed. Reg. 52115, 52116 (Sept. 29, 1998).

220. Regulation E, 12 C.F.R. § 1005.11(c)(3)(1). The extension related to POS transactions was established because of increased use of offline debit cards that can be used without a PIN, which may increase the risk of unauthorized access to a consumer's asset account. Electronic Fund Transfers, 63 Fed. Reg. 52115, 52116 (Sept. 29, 1998).

221. Regulation E, 12 C.F.R. § 1005.11(c)(3)(ii). *See also* 63 Fed. Reg. at 52116.

222. Regulation E, 12 C.F.R. § 1005.11(c)(3)(i), (ii). *See also* 63 Fed. Reg. at 52117.

10.2.1.2 No Error Occurred

If a financial institution finds that no error occurred or that an error occurred in a manner or amount different than that alleged by the consumer, the financial institution must provide a written explanation of its findings and must note the consumer's right to request documents the financial institution used in its investigation.[223] Upon request, the financial institution must promptly provide copies of the documents to the consumer.[224] The rule is silent as to how and in what form those copies must be provided and whether the financial institution may charge for providing those copies.

If a financial institution issues provisional credit, but finds that no error occurred or that a different error occurred than that alleged, the financial institution may debit the provisional credit in whole or in part.[225] However, the financial institution must notify the consumer of the date of the debit and that the financial institution will honor checks and other debits, without charge for an overdraft, for five business days after notification.[226] The financial institution must honor those items that would have been paid had the debit of the provisional credit not occurred.[227] Alternatively, the financial institution may notify the consumer that the provisional credit will be debited at least five business days following transmittal of the notification specifying the calendar date on which the reversal will occur.[228] This alternative allows the financial institution to close the investigation and to avoid tracking activity on the account from which the financial institution is debiting provisional credit.

10.2.1.3 Correction of an Error

If, upon completion of an investigation, the financial institution determines that an error occurred, the financial institution must correct the error within one business day and must notify the consumer regarding the results of the investigation within three business days after completing its investigation, including, if applicable, notice that the provisional credit has been made final.[229] How an error is resolved depends on the type of error. Generally, errors are corrected by crediting the amount of the error, plus interest and fees.[230] However, if an error involves one or more unauthorized

---

223. Regulation E, 12 C.F.R. § 1005.11(d)(1).
224. *Id.*
225. *See, generally*, Regulation E, 12 C.F.R. § 1005.11(d)(2).
226. *Id.*
227. *Id.*
228. Official Interpretations to Regulation E, *supra* note 7, cmt. 11(d)(2)-1.
229. Regulation E, 12 C.F.R. § 1005.11(c)(2).
230. Official Interpretations to Regulation E, *supra* note 7, cmt. 11(c)-6.

EFTs, the financial institution may be able to hold the consumer liable for part of the unauthorized transactions, depending on when the consumer notifies the institution.[231]

10.3 Consumer Liability for Unauthorized Electronic Funds Transfers

10.3.1 Basic Rule of Liability

An unauthorized EFT is one made "from a consumer's account initiated by a person other than the consumer without actual authority to initiate the transfer and from which the consumer receives no benefit."[232] Generally, the concept of unauthorized transactions applies to those made with an access device. However, a consumer can be held liable for unauthorized EFTs that do not involve an access device, but only if the unauthorized transactions occurred after the close of sixty days after transmittal of the periodic statement reflecting an unauthorized transfer and before notice to the institution.[233] To hold the consumer liable for those unauthorized EFTs, the financial institution must establish that it could have prevented the transfers had it received notice sooner.[234]

If extenuating circumstances, such as a consumer's extended travel or hospitalization, prevent the consumer from notifying the financial institution of an alleged error, the financial institution must extend notice deadlines to a reasonable period based on the circumstances.[235] In such extenuating circumstances, a third party or a person acting on the consumer's behalf may provide notice of an unauthorized transaction to the financial institution.[236] Notice may be deemed to have been given constructively when a financial institution becomes aware of circumstances leading to the reasonable belief that an unauthorized EFT to or from the consumer's account has been or may be made.[237]

From a policy perspective, an institution's ability to hold consumers liable for some unauthorized EFTs incentivizes customers to protect their card and account and to notify the financial institution promptly in circumstances when unauthorized EFTs are likely to occur. However, before a consumer can be held liable for any portion of an unauthorized transaction, the financial institution must demonstrate

231. Regulation E, 12 C.F.R. § 1005.6(b).

232. *Id.* § 1005.2(m). When an EFT is initiated by a person who was furnished the access device to the consumer's account by the consumer and the person exceeded authority in using the access device, the consumer is liable for all EFTs that occur until the consumer notifies the financial institution that transfers by that person are no longer authorized. Official Interpretations to Regulation E, *supra* note 7, cmt. 2(m)-2.

233. Regulation E, 12 C.F.R. § 1005.6(b)(3).

234. *Id.*

235. *Id.* § 1005.6(b)(4).

236. Official Interpretations to Regulation E, *supra* note 7, cmt. 6(b)(5)-2.

237. Regulation E, 12 C.F.R. § 1005.6(b)(5).

that it provided certain initial disclosures.[238] The initial disclosures that must be provided before imposing liability on a consumer for an unauthorized EFT are (1) a summary of the consumer's liability, (2) the telephone number and address of the person or office to be notified when the consumer believes that an unauthorized EFT has been or may be made, and (3) the institution's business days.[239] If the transaction involved an access device, the financial institution must show that the device was an accepted access device and that the financial institution provided means to identify the consumer to whom it was issued (for example, a PIN number or comparison of the consumer's signature).[240]

10.3.2 Tiers of Liability

Regulation E sets three tiers of liability for unauthorized transfers, each of which is dependent on when the consumer gave notice of the allegedly unauthorized transaction. The premise behind this structure is that the financial institution is not liable for transactions that could have been prevented had the initial unauthorized transaction been reported timely.[241] The first two tiers apply only when an access device is used in making the unauthorized EFTs. The third tier applies both when an access device is involved and when an access device is not involved (for example, the unauthorized transaction is an ACH).[242]

---

238. *Id.* § 1005.6(a).

239. *Id.*

240. Electronic Fund Transfers, 44 Fed. Reg. 59464, 18473. If the card was sent to the consumer, but the consumer never received and accepted it, the consumer is not liable for any charges to the card. Regulation E, 12 C.F.R. § 1005.6(a); Official Interpretations to Regulation E, *supra* note 7, cmt. 6(a)-1.

241. Consumer negligence, such as writing the PIN on a debit card or piece of paper kept with the card, does not affect a consumer's liability for unauthorized transfers. Official Interpretations to Regulation E, *supra* note 7, cmt. 6(b)(2)-2.

242. *See, generally*, Regulation E, 12 C.F.R. § 1005.6(b).

Liability Tier	Liability Tier Applicability
Liability Tier 1: $50	Consumer notifies the financial institution within two business days after learning of the loss or theft of the access device
Liability Tier 2: Up to $500	Consumer fails to notify the financial institution within two business days after learning of the loss or theft of the access device
Liability Tier 3: Unlimited	Consumer fails to notify the financial institution within sixty calendar days after transmittal of the periodic statement on which an unauthorized EFT appears (consumer faces unlimited liability for all unauthorized transfers made after the sixty-day period and before notice is given)

10.3.2.1 Timely Notice Given

If a consumer provides notice of an unauthorized EFT within two business days after learning of the loss or theft of an access device, the consumer's liability is limited to the lesser of $50 or the amount of the transaction.[243]

10.3.2.2 Timely Notice Not Given

If a consumer fails to provide notice of an unauthorized EFT within two business days after learning of the loss or theft of the access device, the consumer's liability is limited to the lesser of (1) $500, or the sum of (2) the lesser of $50 or the amount of unauthorized transfers that occur within the first two business days of the transaction, plus (3) the amount of those unauthorized transfers that occur after the close of two business days and before notice to the institution, provided the financial institution establishes that those unauthorized transactions could have been prevented had the consumer notified the financial institution within the two-day period.[244]

10.3.2.3 Periodic Statement: Timely Notice Not Given

If notice of an unauthorized EFT is not timely given under section 6, but the consumer still meets the standards for providing timely notice under section 11 (i.e., the consumer reports the unauthorized EFT within sixty days of the institution's transmittal of the periodic statement showing the unauthorized activity), the consumer may avoid liability for subsequent transfers. In such instances, a consumer's liability is limited to those transactions that occurred between the close of day sixty and the day in which notice was given provided the financial institution establishes that those transactions would not have occurred had the consumer notified the

243. *Id.* § 1005.6(b)(1).
244. *Id.* § 1005.6(b)(2).

financial institution within the sixty-day period.[245] Generally, the consumer's liability is unlimited for those transfers made after the sixty-day period.[246] However, when an access device is involved, the consumer's liability for unauthorized transfers that occur before the statement is sent and up to the sixty days following is based on the first two tiers of liability.[247]

When an access device is not involved, the first two tiers of liability do not apply.[248] A consumer can be held liable for unauthorized EFTs that do not involve an access device but only those that occur between the close of sixty days after transmittal of the periodic statement reflecting an unauthorized transfer and before notice to the institution.[249]

Consumer liability may further be limited by card network rules, state laws, and other contractual agreements provided those laws are not inconsistent with, or less protective, than what is set forth in Regulation E.[250] For example, Visa's Zero Liability Policy provides that "[a]n Issuer must limit a Cardholder's liability to zero upon notification from the Cardholder of an unauthorized Visa Transaction," unless the issuer reasonably determines that the cardholder was fraudulent or negligent in the handling of the account or card.[251] The Visa Rules appear to provide greater consumer protection than Regulation E alone, because the Visa Rules do not allow a financial institution to hold the consumer liable for any portion of an unauthorized EFT made with a Visa branded card solely because the consumer did not timely report the unauthorized transactions.

11. Electronic Funds Transfer Service Provider Not Holding Consumer's Account

11.1 Application of Electronic Funds Transfer Service Provider Provisions

The rule defines a "person" as a natural person or an organization, including a corporation, government agency, estate, trust, partnership, proprietorship, cooperative, or association.[252] If a person provides EFT services to a consumer, but does not hold the consumer's account or have an agreement regarding the service with the financial institution that does hold the consumer's account, that person is an EFT service

245. *Id.* § 1005.6(b)(3).
246. *Id.*
247. Official Interpretations to Regulation E, *supra* note 7, cmt. 6(b)(3)-1.
248. *Id.* cmt. 6(b)(3)-2.
249. Electronic Fund Transfers, 61 Fed. Reg. 19662, 19664 (May 2, 1996).
250. EFTA, 15 U.S.C. § 1693l.
251. Visa Rules, *supra* note 135 § 1.4.6.1.
252. Regulation E, 12 C.F.R. § 1005.2(j).

provider.[253] The regulation speaks of such a person as a service provider but does not specifically define that term.

For example, assume Company X, a national superstore, offers a debit card that can access a consumer's deposit account held at a financial institution. The card can be used for purchases made only at Company X. As an incentive, Company X offers a discount on purchases made using the card. Company X has an agreement with the consumer for providing the service, but Company X does not have any agreement with the consumer's account-holding institution, at least with respect to the access device or the services provided to the consumer. Company X would be an EFT service provider subject to section 14.

Where an EFT service provider issues an access device that a consumer can use to access the consumer's account held by another institution, and where no express agreement concerning the service exists between the EFT service provider and the account-holding institution, compliance duties for purposes of the rule are largely imposed on the service provider. This allocation of responsibilities reflects the fact that the account-holding financial institution would likely have no control over or knowledge of many facets of the relationship between the consumer and service provider. In addition, the account-holding financial institution may not even offer EFT services of its own and thus would otherwise have few or no compliance responsibilities under the regulation.[254]

11.2 Disclosure and Documentation Requirements of Service Providers

In what may be redundant in light of its statement that EFT service providers must comply with "this part," section 14 goes further to state that an EFT service provider must provide initial disclosures, notices of changes in terms and of error resolution, as well as receipts and periodic statements that are within the purview of its relationship with the consumer.[255]

In some instances, requiring a service provider to comply with the requirements regarding periodic statements may be a practical impossibility because the service provider may neither hold the consumer's account nor have agreements with those institutions that do. Section 14 relieves service providers from this potentially impracticable duty on the condition that the service providers satisfy five requirements.[256]

First, the debit card or access device issued to the consumer must bear the service provider's name and an address or telephone number that can be used for making inquiries or giving notice of an alleged error. Second, the consumer must receive a notice concerning the use of the access device. This notice must be substantially

253. *Id.* § 1005.14(a).

254. *Id.* §1005.14(a), (b). Electronic Fund Transfers, 45 Fed. Reg. 8248, 8258 (Feb. 6, 1980).

255. Regulation E, 12 C.F.R. § 1005.14(b).

256. *Id.* § 1005.14(b)(1)(i)–(v).

similar to model form A-4 in appendix A. Third, the consumer must receive, on or with the documentation required by section 9(a), the address and telephone number used for an inquiry, to give notice of an alleged error, or to report the loss or theft of the debit card. Fourth, the service provider must transmit to the account-holding financial institution transaction information described in section 9(b)(1) in the format prescribed by the ACH system used to clear the fund transfers. Fifth, the service provider must extend the period for notice of loss or theft of a debit card from two business days to four business days after the consumer learns of the loss or theft, and the service provider must extend the period for reporting unauthorized transfers or errors from sixty days to ninety days following the transmittal of a periodic statement by the account-holding institution.[257]

11.3 Error Resolution Requirements for Service Providers

With respect to error resolution, a consumer and an EFT service provider stand in an unusual relationship, particularly if the service provider has taken such steps as to avoid the necessity of providing periodic statements. If nothing else, a consumer might anticipate (notwithstanding instructions to the contrary) notifying the account-holding financial institution of errors rather than the entity that issued the access device. Thus, section 14 imposes special requirements on service providers with respect to this subject. The service provider is required to extend, by a reasonable time, the period in which notice of an error must be received when a consumer's delay in providing notice occurred because the consumer initially attempted to give notice to the account-holding institution.[258]

If provisional crediting of the consumer's account is necessary because an alleged error cannot be resolved within ten business days, the service provider must disclose to the consumer the date on which provisional credit is issued.[259] If the service provider determines that an error occurred, the service provider must correct the error within one business day after determining that an error occurred.[260] If funds were provisionally credited and the service provider finds that no error occurred, the service provider may debit the provisional credit.[261] Because the account-holding financial institution needs to know the relevant date regarding this requirement, the service provider must notify the account-holding financial institution of the period during which the account-holding financial institution must honor debits to the account,[262] and the account-holding financial institution must honor such debits.[263] The service

257. *Id.*
258. *Id.* § 1005.14((b)(1)(i).
259. *Id.* § 1005.14(b)(2)(ii).
260. *Id.* § 1005.14(b)(2)(iii).
261. *Id.* § 1005.14(b)(2)(iv).
262. *See Id.* § 1005.11(d)(2)(ii).
263. *Id.* § 1005.14(c)(2).

provider is responsible for reimbursing the account-holding financial institution for any overdraft fees that may result on the consumer's account during that period.[264]

11.4 Documentation Provided by Account-Holding Institution

If a service provider initiates EFTs, the account-holding financial institution has only limited error resolution duties. In particular, the account-holding financial institution must provide the consumer periodic statements describing each EFT initiated by the consumer with the access device issued by the service provider.[265] Additionally, upon request, the account-holding financial institution must provide information or copies of documentation needed by the service provider to investigate an alleged error.[266] The account-holding financial institution is also responsible for providing the consumer with copies of documents upon request.[267]

12. Disclosures at Automated Teller Machines

Just as section 14 sets forth special rules for persons who issue access devices and provide EFT services, but who do not hold the consumer's account, section 16 provides special rules for persons who operate ATMs but do not hold the consumer's account. The rule defines an "automated teller machine operator" as "any person that operates an ATM at which a consumer initiates an electronic fund transfer or a balance inquiry and does not hold the account to or from which the transfer is made or about which an inquiry is made."[268] An ATM operator that imposes a fee on consumers for initiating an EFT or a balance inquiry must post on or at the screen, in a prominent and conspicuous location, notice that a fee will or may be imposed for providing EFT services or a balance inquiry.[269] ATM operators that impose a fee on consumers for initiating an EFT or a balance inquiry must also disclose the amount of the fee.[270] This notice may be provided either on the ATM screen or on paper but must be provided *before* the consumer is committed to paying the fee.[271] The operator is prohibited from imposing a fee unless the consumer is first provided notice and then elects to continue the transaction or inquiry.[272]

---

264. *Id.* § 1005.14(b)(2)(iv).

265. *Id.* § 1005.14(c)(1). However, the financial institution is not liable for failure to comply with this requirement if the service provider fails to provide necessary information. *Id.*

266. *Id.* § 1005.14(c)(2).

267. *Id.*

268. *Id.* § 1005.16(a).

269. *Id.* § 1005.16(b).

270. *Id.*

271. *Id.* § 1005.16(c).

272. *Id.* § 1005.16(d)(1), (2).

13. Record Retention

Regulation E provides for a two-year retention period for evidence of compliance with the requirements imposed by the EFTA.[273] The two-year period begins from the date disclosures are required to be made or action is required to be taken.[274] Evidence of compliance need not include records demonstrating that a financial institution has given disclosures and documentation to each consumer. Rather, evidence of compliance is sufficient if it demonstrates that an institution's procedures reasonably ensure the consumers' receipt of required disclosures and documentation.[275]

14. Enforcement by Federal Agencies and Civil Liability

14.1 Enforcement by Federal Agencies

Compliance with the requirements of Regulation E is enforced in accordance with the EFTA.[276] Administrative enforcement of the regulation is assigned to the various federal agencies that supervise designated institutions. With respect to many large financial institutions, the requirements of Regulation E are enforced under the Federal Deposit Insurance Act.[277] National Banks, member banks of the Federal Reserve System, and banks insured by the FDIC (other than members of the Federal Reserve System) are subject to enforcement by the Comptroller of the Currency, the Board, and the Board of Directors of the FDIC, respectively.[278] Federal credit unions are subject to enforcement by the Administrator of the National Credit Union Administration under the Federal Credit Union Act.[279]

14.2 Civil Liability

If a consumer suffers a violation of his or her rights under the EFTA, section 916(a) gives him or her a remedy for "actual damage sustained by such consumer as a result of such failure."[280] This remedy may be enforced against "any person," not just financial

273. *Id.* § 1005.13(b)(1).

274. *Id.* § 1005.13(b)(2). Records involved in an ongoing lawsuit or administrative proceeding must be retained until final disposition of the matter, unless an earlier time is allowed by court or agency order. *Id.*

275. Official Interpretations to Regulation E, *supra* note 7, cmt. 13(b)-1.

276. Regulation E, 12 C.F.R. § 1005.13(a).

277. Specifically, Federal Deposit Insurance Act (12 U.S.C. 1813(q)). EFTA, 15 U.S.C. § 1963o(a)(1).

278. EFTA, 15 U.S.C. § 1963o(a)(1).

279. *Id.* § 1693o(a)(2).

280. *Id.* § 1693m(a)(1).

institutions.[281] In addition to actual damages, a consumer can recover a statutory penalty, costs, and attorneys' fees.[282] In an individual action, the penalty shall be not less than $100 and not more than $1000.[283] Actions to recover damages under section 916 are subject to important constraints, including the bona fide error defense, the safe harbor for reliance on interpretations from officials at the CFPB and the Board, and the ability of institutions to cure violations (and thereby avoid liability for penalties associated with those violations).[284]

Section 916 authorizes class actions but, for any action or series of actions arising out of the same violation, limits those penalties to $500,000 or 1 percent of the defendant's net worth, whichever is less.[285] To determine the penalty in an individual action, the court "shall consider the frequency and persistence of noncompliance, the nature of such noncompliance, and the extent to which the noncompliance was intentional."[286] In a class action, the court shall additionally consider "the resources of the defendant [and] the number of persons adversely affected."[287]

Whereas section 916(a) allows a consumer to recover actual damages resulting from any violation of the EFTA, section 908 allows a consumer to recover three times such damages from a financial institution when the violation consists of the institution's improper handling of a consumer's claims of error with respect to an EFT. A consumer can recover treble damages under section 908 when the financial institution did not issue credit to the consumer's account as required under regulations promulgated pursuant to section 908(c), and either failed to conduct a good faith investigation of the alleged error or did not have a reasonable basis for believing no error occurred, or "knowingly and willingly concluded" no error occurred when "such conclusion could not reasonably have been drawn from the evidence available to the financial institution during the time of the investigation."[288] Under the EFTA, in any action involving the consumer's liability for an unauthorized transaction, the financial institution has the burden of proving that the transaction was authorized or, if the transaction was unauthorized, that the conditions for imposing liability on the consumer have been met.[289]

An institution's failure to make an EFT or stop a preauthorized EFT would not fall within the definition of "error" for purposes of section 908.[290] Section 910

281. *Id.*
282. *Id.* § 1693m(a)(2), (3).
283. *Id.* § 1693m(a)(2)(A).
284. *Id.* § 1693m(c)-(e).
285. *Id.* § 1693m(a)(2)(B).
286. *Id.* § 1693m(b)(1).
287. *Id.* § 1693m(b)(2).
288. *Id.* § 1693f(e).
289. *Id.* § 1693g(b).
290. *Id.* § 1693f(f).

provides a remedy against financial institutions for those mistakes.[291] Under section 910, if a financial institution fails to make an EFT in accordance with the terms and conditions of the account, in the correct amount, or in a timely manner when properly instructed to, the financial institution is liable for all damages (i.e., not just actual damages) proximately caused by (i.e., not merely resulting from) the failure, unless the consumer's account has insufficient funds, the funds are subject to legal process (e.g., garnishment), the transfer would exceed an established credit limit, an electronic terminal has insufficient cash to complete the transaction, or as otherwise provided in CFPB regulations.[292] If the financial institution fails to make an EFT because the consumer's account has insufficient funds, the financial institution is still liable if it failed to credit, in accordance with the terms and conditions of the account, a deposit that would have provided sufficient funds.[293] Section 910(a) also imposes liability on financial institutions for all damages proximately caused by the failure to stop a preauthorized EFT from occurring on a consumer's account if the consumer has instructed the financial institution to stop payment in accordance with the terms and conditions of the account.[294]

The bona fide error defense allowed under section 916 is limited to actions brought to recover damages allowed under section 910. Section 910(c) states: "In the case of a failure . . . which was not intentional and which resulted from a *bona fide* error, notwithstanding the maintenance of procedures reasonably adapted to avoid any such error, the financial institution shall be liable for actual damages proved."[295] Thus, the bona fide error defense would appear to remain available against claims for penalties (and perhaps against all other remedies exclusive of actual damages).

In actions brought pursuant to section 910, financial institutions may have two defenses otherwise unavailable in actions brought to enforce liability under section 916. A financial institution has no liability under section 910 if the financial institution proves by a preponderance of evidence that (1) its failure resulted from an occurrence beyond its control and that the financial institution exercised both reasonable care to prevent such occurrence and such diligence as the circumstances required, or (2) the consumer attempted to initiate an EFT knowing a technical malfunction existed at the time the customer attempted to initiate the transaction, or, in the case of PEFTs, at the time such transfer should have occurred.[296]

Section 910(d) also provides that an ATM operator shall have no liability for the failure to provide the fee notice required under regulations promulgated pursuant to

291. *Id.* § 1693h(a)(1).
292. *Id.*
293. *Id.* § 1693h(a)(2).
294. *Id.* § 1693h(a)(3).
295. *Id.* § 1693h(c).
296. *Id.* § 1693h(b).

section 904(a)(3), if the notice ". . . has been posted by such operator in compliance with such section and the notice is subsequently removed, damaged, or altered by any person other than the operator of the automated teller machine . . ."[297]

15. Relation to Other State and Federal Laws

15.1 Relation to the Truth in Lending Act

The Truth in Lending Act, implemented by Regulation Z, promotes various consumer protections related to the extension of credit and informed use of consumer credit.[298] Regulation E regulates credit to the extent that it is offered in connection with a checking, savings, or other consumer asset account.[299] Just as Regulation E has specific requirements related to the issuance of an access device when the device gives a consumer access to an asset account, Regulation Z has specific requirements related to the issuance of an access device when the device gives a consumer access to a credit account.[300] These requirements are discussed in chapter 3A.

Generally, Regulation E governs issuance of an access device that gives access to a consumer's asset account that may be used by the consumer to initiate EFTs or issuance of an access device that may give a consumer access to incidental credit through a negative balance on the asset account or the addition of an overdraft service on an existing access device.[301] Regulation Z generally covers issuance of an access device when credit features are added to an accepted access device or when the access device is also a credit card.[302]

Governed by the Electronic Fund Transfer Act and Regulation E	Governed by the Truth in Lending Act and Regulation Z
Adding to an accepted credit card the capability to initiate EFTs[303]	Adding a credit feature to an accepted access device, even if the device is not a credit card[304]

297. *Id.* § 1693h(d).
298. Truth in Lending Act (Regulation Z), 12 C.F.R. § 1026.1(b) (2019).
299. Regulation E, 12 C.F.R. § 1005.2(b)(1).
300. *See, e.g.*, Regulation Z, 12 C.F.R. § 1026.9.
301. Regulation E, 12 C.F.R. § 1005.12(a)(1).
302. *Id.* § 1005.12(a)(2).
303. Id. § 1005.12(a)(1)(i).
304. Id. § 1005.12(b)(2)(i).

Governed by the Electronic Fund Transfer Act and Regulation E	Governed by the Truth in Lending Act and Regulation Z
Issuance of an access device that permits credit extension *only* when the consumer's account is overdrawn or to maintain a specific minimum balance in a consumer's account, or under an overdraft service[305]	Issuance of a credit card that is also an access device, except for that under which credit is extended only when the consumer's account is overdrawn or to maintain a specific minimum balance in a consumer's account, or under an overdraft service[306]
A consumer's liability for an EFT and the investigation of errors involving an extension of credit that occurs under an agreement between the financial institution and consumer to extend credit when the consumer's account is overdrawn or to maintain a specified minimum balance in a consumer's account, or under an overdraft service[307]	For transactions involving a prepaid account and a noncovered separate credit feature pursuant to Regulation Z, a consumer's liability for unauthorized use and the investigation of errors involving transactions that access the noncovered separate credit feature, as applicable[308]
Adding an overdraft service to an accepted access device[309]	

15.2 Relation to State Laws

Generally, to the extent that state law provides less protection than that set forth in Regulation E, Regulation E preempts state law.[310] Regulation E gives the CFPB the authority to determine whether the EFTA and Regulation E preempt state law.[311] As a rule, state law is deemed inconsistent with Regulation E when state law requires or permits a practice or act prohibited by federal law, provides greater consumer liability for unauthorized EFTs, allows a longer time for investigation and correction of alleged errors, or requires initial disclosures, periodic statements, or receipts that are different in content than those required by federal law.[312]

305. *Id.* § 1005.12(a)(1)(ii).
306. *Id.* § 1005.12(b)(2)(ii).
307. *Id.* § 1005.12(a)(1)(iv).
308. *Id.* § 1005.12(b)(2)(iii).
309. *Id.* § 1005.12(a)(1)(iii).
310. *Id.* § 1005.12(b)(2).
311. *Id.* § 1005.12(b)(1).
312. *Id.* § 1005.12(b)(2).

The state may apply to the CFPB for an exemption from the EFTA or Regulation E for any class of EFTs within the state.[313] Of course, an exception cannot exempt the state from the civil liability provisions of section 916 of the EFTA.[314] In other words, a state cannot receive an exemption from civil liability provisions of the EFTA, which allow for damages for individual or class action suits.[315]

Appendix A

Sufficient Notice for Unauthorized EFTs	Sufficient Notice for Other Errors
Notice may be given by the consumer or by a third party on the consumer's behalf	Notice may be given only by the consumer
The consumer need only take steps reasonably necessary to provide the financial institution with the pertinent information, whether or not a particular employee or agent of the financial institution actually receives the information	The consumer must provide notice that enables the financial institution to identify the consumer's name and account number and must indicate why the consumer believes an error exists and, to the extent possible, the type, date, and amount of the error
Notice must be provided • in writing, • by phone, • in person, or • constructively, when the financial institution becomes aware of circumstances leading to the reasonable belief that an unauthorized transfer to or from the consumer's account has been or may be made	Notice must be provided • in writing, • by phone, or • in person

313. *Id.* § 1005.12(c).

314. *Id.* § 1005.12(c)(i).

315. EFTA, 15 U.S.C. § 1963m.

CHAPTER

9

Prepaid Accounts

David L. Beam

1. Scope of This Chapter

This chapter covers the provisions of Regulation E and Regulation Z that regulate prepaid accounts and credit features associated with prepaid accounts (collectively, the prepaid rule).[1] Except as noted in this chapter, prepaid accounts are generally subject to the broader requirements of Regulation E, which govern electronic funds and remittance transfer systems, as described in chapters 8 and 10, respectively. Such broader requirements fall outside the scope of this chapter, except to the extent they apply differently to prepaid accounts. Similarly, credit features associated with prepaid accounts are governed by Regulation Z, which apply to consumer credit more broadly, as described in chapter 6. The broader provisions of Regulation Z applicable to credit products fall outside the scope of this chapter, except to the extent they apply differently to prepaid accounts.

1. The rule itself is not formally labeled the prepaid rule; this is a short-hand reference used in this chapter to describe the provisions of Regulation E and Regulation Z adopted by the Consumer Financial Protection Bureau (CFPB) in November 2016, as subsequently amended. Regulation E is codified at 12 C.F.R. §§ 1005.1 *et seq.* Regulation Z is codified at 12 C.F.R. §§ 1026.1 *et seq.*

2. Background

The Consumer Financial Protection Bureau (CFPB or Bureau) published the final version of the prepaid rule in the Federal Register on November 22, 2016.[2] The Bureau issued two extensions of the effective date, the last of which set forth an April 1, 2019, effective date, at which time the Bureau also issued various amendments to the rule.[3]

3. Scope of the Rule

The prepaid rule's provisions apply to prepaid accounts and to certain credit features associated with prepaid accounts.

Subject to some exclusions, described below, a prepaid account is a consumer asset account that is held directly or indirectly by a financial institution;[4] established primarily for personal, family, or household purposes;[5] and includes the following:

- A payroll card account;[6]

2. Prepaid Accounts Under the Electronic Fund Transfer Act (Regulation E) and the Truth in Lending Act (Regulation Z), 81 Fed. Reg. 83,934 (Nov. 22, 2016) (final rule).

3. Prepaid Accounts Under the Electronic Fund Transfer Act (Regulation E) and the Truth in Lending Act (Regulation Z); Delay of Effective Date, 82 Fed. Reg. 18,975 (April 25, 2017) (final rule delaying effective date to April 1, 2018); Rules Concerning Prepaid Accounts Under the Electronic Fund Transfer Act (Regulation E) and the Truth in Lending Act (Regulation Z), 83 Fed. Reg. 6364 (Feb. 13, 2018) (final rule delaying effective date to April 1, 2019, and amending certain provisions of the rule).

4. Regulation E defines *financial institution* as "a bank, savings association, credit union, or any other person that directly or indirectly holds an account belonging to a consumer, or that issues an access device and agrees with a consumer to provide electronic fund transfer services." 12 C.F.R. § 1005.2(i). The definition excludes auto dealers, which the Dodd-Frank Wall Street Reform and Consumer Protection Act excludes from the CFPB's jurisdiction. *Id.* (citing 12 U.S.C. § 5519).

5. These three elements (consumer asset account; held by a financial institution; and established primarily for personal, family, or household purposes) are in Regulation E's general definition of *account*. 12 C.F.R. § 1005.2(b)(1). Each prong in the definition of *prepaid account* covers only *accounts* as defined in Regulation E. Thus, a product must meet these three elements in order to be a *prepaid account*.

6. *Id.* § 1005.2(b)(3)(i)(A). *Payroll card account* is defined as "an account that is directly or indirectly established through an employer and to which electronic fund transfers of the consumer's wages, salary, or other employee compensation (such as commissions) are made on a recurring basis, whether the account is operated or managed by the employer, a third-party payroll processor, a depository institution, or any other person." *Id.* § 1005.2(b)(3)(i).

- A government benefits account;[7]
- An account that is marketed or labeled as "prepaid" and is redeemable upon presentation at multiple, unaffiliated merchants for goods or services or usable at automated teller machines (ATMs);[8] or
- An account (i) that is issued on a prepaid basis in a specified amount or capable of being loaded with funds after issuance; (ii) whose primary function is to conduct transactions with multiple, unaffiliated merchants for goods or services, or at ATMs, or to conduct person-to-person transfers; and (iii) that is not a checking account, share draft account, or negotiable order of withdrawal accounts.[9]

The last item captures many products that someone might not immediately think of as a "prepaid" product. In particular, this definition can capture digital wallet products that are capable of storing funds. However, an official interpretation explains that a digital wallet that stores payment credentials for other accounts, but that does not store funds, does not qualify as a *prepaid account*.[10] According to the interpretation, such a digital wallet would not be "issued on a prepaid basis" or "capable of being loaded with funds" after issuance.[11] The interpretation also explains that an account that acts as a "pass-through vehicle" for funds does not store funds.[12] The interpretation warns, however, that a product is "capable of being loaded with funds" if it allows a consumer to store funds before the consumer designates a destination for the funds.[13]

There are also various exclusions from the definition of *prepaid account*. Among the most notable are exclusions for checking and savings accounts,[14] health and flexible spending accounts,[15] gift card products,[16] certain reward and loyalty products,[17] and accounts established to disburse needs-tested government benefits.[18]

---

7. *Id.* § 1005.2(b)(3)(i)(B). *Government benefits account* is defined as "an account established by a government agency for distributing government benefits to a consumer electronically, such as through automated teller machines or point-of-sale terminals, but does not include an account for distributing needs-tested benefits in a program established under state or local law or administered by a state or local agency." *Id.* § 1005(a)(2).

8. *Id.* § 1005.2(b)(3)(i)(C).

9. *Id.* § 1005.2(b)(3)(i)(D).

10. 12 C.F.R. pt. 1005, supp. I, § 2(b)(3)(i)-6.

11. *Id.*

12. *Id.*

13. *Id.*

14. 12 C.F.R. § 1005.2(b)(3)(i)(D)(3). The exclusion for checking and savings accounts only applies if the account is not a payroll card account or government benefits account.

15. *Id.* § 1005.2(b)(3)(ii)(A).

16. *Id.* § 1005.2(b)(3)(ii)(D).

17. *Id.* § 1005.2(b)(3)(ii)(D)(4).

18. *Id.* § 1005.2(b)(3)(ii)(E).

4. The Pre-Acquisition Disclosures

4.1 Overview

Regulation E requires a financial institution to provide the consumer with various disclosures before the consumer acquires a prepaid account from the institution.[19]

These pre-acquisition disclosures are (1) the short form disclosure; (2) the long form disclosure; and (3) certain information that the financial institution must provide at the same time as the short form disclosure, but not in the short form disclosure itself. This chapter will refer to the disclosures in the third category as the "outside-the-box disclosures," although Regulation E itself does not use this term.

4.2 Timing of Pre-Acquisition Disclosures

4.2.1 Timing Generally

Subject to some exceptions discussed below, a financial institution must provide all the pre-acquisition disclosures before the consumer "acquires" the prepaid account.[20] An official interpretation explains that a consumer *acquires* a prepaid account "by purchasing, opening or choosing to be paid via a prepaid account."[21] For a payroll card account, the consumer *acquires* the account when the consumer chooses to receive wages via the payroll card account.[22]

4.2.2 Special Rules for Prepaid Accounts Acquired in Retail Locations

There is an exception to the requirement to provide the long form disclosure prior to the consumer's acquisition of the prepaid account if the consumer acquires the account at a retail location.[23] To qualify for this exception, the prepaid account must be contained in the packaging material, the short form disclosure must be visible on the packaging material, the short form disclosure must provide directions on obtaining the long form disclosure via telephone and online, and the long form disclosure must be provided after acquisition. [24]

19. The official interpretations state that "a consumer acquires a prepaid account by purchasing, opening or choosing to be paid via a prepaid account." 12 C.F.R. pt. 1005, supp. I, § 18(b)(1)(i)-1.i.

20. *Id.* § 1005.18(b)(1)(i).

21. *Id.* § 18(b)(1)(i)-1.i.

22. *Id.* § 18(b)(1)(i)-1.i.B.

23. 12 C.F.R. § 1005.18(b)(1)(ii).

24. *Id.* § 1005.18(b)(1)(ii).

4.2.3 *Special Rules for Prepaid Accounts Acquired Orally by Telephone*

A financial institution is not required to provide the long form disclosure prior to acquisition if the consumer acquires the prepaid account orally by telephone, provided that the long form disclosure is made available by telephone and online, the financial institution advises the consumer of this prior to the consumer acquiring the account, and the long form disclosure is provided after acquisition.[25]

5. Form of Disclosures

5.1 Written, Electronic, and Oral Disclosures

Generally, pre-acquisition disclosures must be provided in writing.[26] Further, the pre-acquisition disclosures *must* be provided in electronic form when a consumer acquires a prepaid account through electronic means.[27] This includes both through a website and via a mobile application.[28] Electronic disclosures also "must be provided in a manner which is reasonably expected to be accessible in light of how a consumer is acquiring the prepaid account, in a responsive form, and using machine-readable text that is accessible via Web browsers or mobile applications, as applicable, and via screen readers."[29] Also, as noted above, if the financial institution does not provide the long form disclosure to the consumer before acquisition of the prepaid account at a retail location, the long form disclosure must be provided electronically through a website.

When pre-acquisition disclosures are provided electronically, they "must be viewable across all screen sizes."[30] This means that the disclosures "must be provided in a way that responds to different screen sizes, for example, by stacking elements of the disclosures in a manner that accommodates consumer viewing on smaller screens."[31] Still, the responsive disclosures must meet the formatting requirements (described further in section 5.5.1), such as restrictions on the number of lines of text that certain statements in the short form disclosure may occupy.[32]

One exception to the general rule that pre-acquisition disclosures must be provided in writing is for prepaid accounts acquired via telephone. If the consumer acquires the prepaid account via telephone, then the short form disclosure and the

25. *Id.* § 1005.18(b)(1)(iii)(B).
26. *Id.* § 1005.18(b)(6)(i)(A).
27. *Id.* § 1005.18(b)(6)(i)(B).
28. *Id.*
29. *Id.*
30. *Id.*
31. 12 C.F.R. pt. 1005, supp. I, § 18(b)(6)(i)(B)-2.
32. *Id.*

outside-the-box disclosures must be provided orally before acquisition (unless they have previously been provided to the consumer in writing).[33]

5.2 Retainable Form

Like other Regulation E disclosures required to be provided in writing, pre-acquisition disclosures generally must be provided in a form that the consumer may keep.[34] This retainability requirement is described in more detail in chapter 8.

There are exceptions to this retainability requirement for pre-acquisition disclosures that are provided orally[35] and via SMS.[36]

5.3 Prominence and Size of Text

All text used to disclose information in the short form disclosure and the long form disclosure must be the same color and printed on background that provides a clear contrast.[37] All the text in these two disclosures must be printed in a single, easy-to-read type.[38] The outside-the-box disclosures are not subject to the foregoing requirements, but they are subject to Regulation E's general requirement that they be "clear and readily understandable."[39]

5.4 Foreign Language Disclosures

In certain situations, a financial institution must provide the pre-acquisition disclosures in a foreign language. These include situations where the financial institution principally uses the foreign language on the packaging materials, markets the prepaid account principally in a foreign language, or allows the consumer to acquire a prepaid account by telephone or electronically principally in a foreign language.[40]

The financial institution must still provide the information required to be disclosed in the long form disclosure in English (1) upon a consumer's request and (2) on any part of the website where it discloses this information in a foreign language.[41]

33. *Id.* § 1005.18(b)(6)(i)(C).
34. 12 C.F.R. § 1005.18(b)(6)(ii).
35. *Id.*
36. *Id.*
37. *Id.* § 1005.18(b)(7)(ii)(A).
38. *Id.*
39. *Id.* § 1005.4(a)(1).
40. *Id.* § 1005.18(b)(9)(i).
41. *Id.* § 1005.18(b)(9)(ii).

5.5 Requirements for the Short Form Disclosures

5.5.1 Formatting

As discussed in section 5.3, the text in the short form disclosure "must be in a single, easy-to-read type that is all black or one color and printed on a background that provides a clear contrast."[42] There are also specific requirements for the type size of each item in the short form disclosure (including exact type size requirements for the footnote symbols).[43] These type size requirements are both absolute (i.e., a minimum type size for each item) and relative (i.e., certain items must be larger than others).[44] Certain items must also be bolded, and some items may not be bolded.[45] A financial institution that offers prepaid accounts should review these requirements carefully, since the rule generally requires strict adherence.

Unless the short form disclosure is provided orally, the following information (the specific content of which is explained further in section 5.5.2) must be disclosed in a table:[46]

1. periodic fee;
2. per purchase fee;
3. ATM withdrawal fees;
4. cash reload fee;
5. ATM balance inquiry fee;
6. customer service fees;
7. inactivity fees;
8. statement regarding the number of additional fees charged; and
9. additional fees required to be disclosed based on revenue they generate.

The financial institution must use a short form disclosure that is "substantially similar" to one of the relevant model forms, set forth in the appendix to Regulation E (shown as figures 1 to 3).[47]

42. *Id.* § 1005.18(b)(7)(ii)(A).
43. *Id.* § 1005.18(b)(7)(ii)(B)(1).
44. *Id.* § 1005.18(b)(7)(ii)(B).
45. *Id.*
46. *Id.* § 1005.18(b)(6)(iii)(A).
47. 12 C.F.R. § 1005.18(b)(6)(iii)(A).

Figure 1: Model Short Form Disclosure for Prepaid Accounts with Single Service Plans (With Federal Deposit Insurance Corporation [FDIC] Insurance Coverage)

Monthly fee	Per purchase	ATM withdrawal	Cash reload
$5.99†	**$0**	**$0** in-network **$1.99** out-of-network	**$3.99***

ATM balance inquiry (in-network or out-of-network)	$0 or $0.50
Customer service (automated or live agent)	$0 or $0.50* per call
Inactivity (after 12 months with no transactions)	$1.00 per month

We charge 4 other types of fees. Here are some of them:

[Additional fee type]	$0.50 or $1.00
[Additional fee type]	$3.00

† No monthly fee with direct deposit or 30 transactions per month.

* This fee can be lower depending on how and where this card is used.

You may be offered overdraft/credit after 30 days. Fees would apply.
Register your card for FDIC insurance eligibility and other protections.

For general information about prepaid accounts, visit *cfpb.gov/prepaid.*
Find details and conditions for all fees and services inside the package, or call **800-234-5678** or visit ***xyz.com/prepaid***.

Figure 2: Model Short Form Disclosure for Prepaid Accounts with Single Service Plans (Without Federal Deposit Insurance Corporation [FDIC] Insurance Coverage)

Monthly fee	Per purchase	ATM withdrawal	Cash reload
$5.99*	**$0**	**$0** in-network **$1.99** out-of-network	**$3.99***

ATM balance inquiry (in-network or out-of-network)	$0 or $0.50
Customer service (automated or live agent)	$0 or $0.50* per call
Inactivity (after 12 months with no transactions)	$1.00 per month

We charge 4 other types of fees. Here are some of them:

[Additional fee type]	$1.00*
[Additional fee type]	$3.00

* This fee can be lower depending on how and where this card is used.

No overdraft/credit feature.
Not FDIC insured. Register your card for other protections.

For general information about prepaid accounts, visit *cfpb.gov/prepaid*.
Find details and conditions for all fees and services inside the package, or call **800-234-5678** or visit ***xyz.com/prepaid***.

Figure 3: Model Short Form Disclosure for Prepaid Accounts with Multiple Plans

	Pay-as-you-go plan	Monthly plan	Annual plan
Plan fee	$0	$5.99† per mo.	$39.99 per yr.
Per purchase	$0.25	$0	$0
ATM withdrawal (in-net.)	$0	$0	$0
ATM withdrawal (out-net.)	$2.50	$1.99	$1.99
Cash reload	$4.99*	$4.99*	$4.99*
ATM balance inquiry (in-net.)	$0.50	$0.50	$0.50
ATM balance inquiry (out-net.)	$1.00	$1.00	$1.00
Live customer service (per call)	$1.50	$0.50	$0.50
Inactivity (after 12 mo. w/ no trans.)	$2.50 per mo.	$2.50 per mo.	$2.50 per mo.
We charge 4 other types of fees. Here are some of them:			
[Additional fee type]	$1.00*	$1.00*	$1.00*
[Additional fee type]	$3.00	$3.00	$3.00

† $1.00 monthly fee with direct deposit.
* This fee can be lower depending on how and where this card is used.

No overdraft/credit feature.
Not FDIC insured. Register your card for other protections.

For general information about prepaid accounts, visit *cfpb.gov/prepaid.*
Find details and conditions for all fees and services inside the package, or call **800-234-5678** or visit ***xyz.com/prepaid.***

5.5.2 Fee Disclosure Requirements

Most of the short form disclosure (measured by area or text) is dedicated to disclosing information about fees in connection with the account. Generally, these fee disclosures must adhere to the rules described in the following.

5.5.2.1 Variable Fees

The short form disclosure must disclose a single figure for each fee. The financial institution may not disclose a range of fees or say something like "Fee Varies." If the amount of a fee may vary, then the financial institution must disclose the highest amount that the financial institution may impose for the fee.[48]

5.5.2.2 Third-Party Fees

With one exception, a financial institution may not disclose any "third-party fees" in the short form disclosure.[49] The exception is for cash reload fees. The financial institution must include cash reload fees that are "known" by the financial institution.[50]

5.5.2.3 Specific Fee Information Required

The short form disclosure must disclose the amounts (or indicate "N/A") for each of the following fees:

1. *Periodic fee*: The periodic fee for "holding" the prepaid account. The disclosure must use a term to describe the periodic fee that is substantially similar to "Monthly fee" or "Annual fee."[51]
2. *ATM withdrawals*: The short form disclosure must identify the fee for withdrawals from an ATM in the United States that is in the financial institution's network or a network affiliated with the financial institution, and also the fee for making a withdrawal from an out-of-network ATM in the United States outside of that network.[52]
3. *Cash reload*: Fees for making cash reloads must be disclosed using a term that is substantially similar to "Cash reload."[53]

---

48. 12 C.F.R. § 1005.18(b)(3)(i). After this amount, the financial institution must provide a symbol, such as an asterisk, that is linked to a statement that is substantially similar to the following: "This fee can be lower depending on how and where the card is used." *Id.* With one exception, the symbol that the financial institution uses must be the same for each variable fee (i.e., the symbols must all be asterisks, or all be daggers). *Id.* The exception is for variable periodic fees. The financial institution may put a symbol after a variable periodic fee that is different from the symbol after the other variable fees (the rule gives the example of a dagger) linked to one additional line of text that explains the circumstances under which the fee waiver or reduction may occur. *Id.* § 1005.18(b)(3)(ii).

49. *Id.* § 1005.18(b)(3)(iv).

50. *Id.* § 1005.18(b)(3)(v).

51. *Id.* § 1005.18(b)(2)(i).

52. *Id.* § 1005.18(b)(2)(iii). The financial institution must use a term substantially similar to "ATM withdrawal" in the heading for these fees, and it must describe the two fee amounts using terms that are substantially similar to "in-network" and "out-of-network," respectively. *Id.*

53. *Id.* § 1005.18(b)(2)(iv). The cash reload fee disclosure must reflect cash reload fees imposed by third parties that are "known" to the financial institution at the time that it prints or otherwise prepares the short form disclosure. If both a third party and the financial institution will impose fees for certain cash reloads, the financial institution should treat the sum of those fees as the cash reload fee for the transaction. *Id.* § 18(b)(2)(iv)-1.

4. *ATM balance inquiry*: The short form disclosure must disclose the fees imposed for balance inquiries at ATMs in the United States, for both in-network and out-of-network transactions.[54]
5. *Customer service fees*: The short form disclosure must disclose the fee for using an interactive voice response system, and the fee for speaking with a live customer service agent.[55]
6. *Inactivity fee*: The short form disclosure must disclose any fee for nonuse, dormancy, or inactivity of the prepaid account, using a term that is substantially similar to "Inactivity."[56] It must also disclose the conditions that trigger the fee.

5.5.2.4 Statement about the Number of Additional Fees

In addition to identifying and disclosing each of the foregoing fees (or "N/A" if the fee does not apply), the short form disclosure must state the number of additional fee types the financial institution may charge consumers in connection with the prepaid account, using a phrase that is substantially similar to the following: "We charge [x] other types of fees."[57]

The financial institution also must disclose the amounts of the two additional fee types (excluding fees already disclosed and finance charges for covered separate credit features) that (1) individually generate 5 percent or more of the total revenue from consumers for the prepaid account program or across prepaid account programs that share the same fee schedule; and (2) are the two fee types that generate the highest revenue from consumers for the prepaid account program or across prepaid account programs that share the same fee schedule.[58]

5.5.2.5 Additional Information

The short form disclosure must also disclose the following:

1. Whether the financial institution will offer any "covered separate credit features" in connection with the prepaid account.[59]

---

54. *Id.* § 1005.18(b)(2)(v).

55. *Id.* § 1005.18(b)(2)(vi). The short form disclosure for multiple-service plans is only required to disclose the fee for contacting a live customer service agent, using a term that is substantially similar to "live customer service." *Id.*

56. *Id.* § 1005.18(b)(2)(vii).

57. *Id.* § 1005.18(b)(2)(viii)(A).

58. *Id.* § 1005.18(b)(2)(ix)(B). If only one fee meets the 5 percent threshold, then the *financial institution* should disclose only that fee. *Id.* § 1005.18(b)(2)(viii)(B). If no fee meets the 5 percent threshold, then no additional fees need to be disclosed. *Id.*

59. *Id.* § 1005.18(b)(2)(x).

2. Whether the account is eligible for Federal Deposit Insurance Corporation (FDIC) or National Credit Union Administration (NCUA) insurance coverage.[60]
3. A statement that directs the consumer to the CFPB's website for general information about prepaid accounts.[61]
4. A statement that directs the consumer to the long form disclosure for complete information about the prepaid account.[62]

5.5.3 Additional Short Form Disclosure Requirements for Payroll Card Accounts and Government Benefit Accounts

The short form disclosures for payroll card accounts and government benefit accounts must contain special language that advises the consumer that he or she is not required to receive wages or benefit payments, as applicable, through the prepaid account.[63]

The financial institution also may include a statement—in one additional line of text—directing the consumer to a location outside the short form disclosure where the consumer may obtain information on ways the consumer may access payroll card account funds and balance information for free or for a reduced fee.[64]

The short form disclosure for government benefit accounts also must contain a statement at the top that notifies the consumer about other ways to receive benefit payments. There are two options, which parallel the options for payroll card accounts:

- "You do not have to accept this benefits card. Ask about other ways to receive your benefits."
- "You have several options to receive your payments: [list of options available to the consumer]; or this benefits card. Tell the benefits office which option you choose."[65]

The statement must be substantially similar to one of these options.[66]

The short form disclosure may also include a statement directing the consumer to information on ways to access government benefit account funds and balance information for free or for a reduced fee.[67]

---

60. *Id.* § 1005.18(b)(2)(xi).
61. *Id.* § 1005.18(b)(2)(xii).
62. *Id.* § 1005.18(b)(2)(xiii).
63. *Id.* § 1005.18(b)(2)(xiv)(A) (payroll card accounts); *id.* § 1005.15(c)(2)(i) (government benefit accounts).
64. *Id.* § 1005.18(b)(2)(xiv)(B).
65. *Id.* § 1005.15(c)(2)(i).
66. *Id.*
67. *Id.* § 1005.15(c)(2)(ii).

5.6 Requirements for the Long Form Disclosure

The required long form disclosure must set forth content that is segregated from other information and must comply with the particular content requirements of the rule; however, the financial institution has more latitude to present information about fees. For instance, information about fees "must be generally grouped together and organized under subheadings by the categories of function for which a financial institution may impose the fee,"[68] but the regulation does not dictate how financial institutions must organize fee disclosures beyond requiring the institution to adhere to those general principles.

The main feature of the long form disclosure is a table of fees. This table must identify all fees that the financial institution may impose in connection with the prepaid account, as well as all third-party fees that are known to the financial institution.[69] For each fee, the long form disclosure must disclose: (1) the amount of the fee[70] and (2) the conditions, if any, under which the fee may be imposed, waived, or reduced.[71] This information must be provided in close proximity to the name of the fee; the financial institution may not use symbols (like asterisks) to explain the conditions under which a fee may be imposed.[72] The financial institution may (but is not required to) disclose any service or feature that the financial institution provides at no charge to the consumer.[73]

Below the fee table are disclosures regarding certain other terms, including whether the account is eligible for FDIC or NCUA insurance coverage, whether any "covered separate credit features" (discussed further in section 5.8) may be associated with the account, and contact information for the CFPB.

If any covered separate credit features are associated with the account, then the long form disclosure must also include various disclosures required by Regulation Z, including the annual percentage rate, the date the required information was printed, and a statement that the consumer should contact the financial institution for any change in the information since it was printed.[74]

5.7 Requirements for "Outside-the-Box" Disclosures

The financial institution is required to disclose certain information (which this chapter calls outside-the-box disclosures) at the same time that the financial institution provides the short form disclosure.[75] This information includes the following:

---

68. *Id.* § 1005.18(b)(7)(i)(B).
69. *Id.* § 1005.18(b)(4)(ii).
70. *Id.*
71. *Id.*
72. *Id.*
73. *Id.*
74. *Id.* § 1005.18(b)(4)(vii).
75. *Id.* § 1005.18(b)(5).

- the name of the financial institution;
- the name of the prepaid account program;
- the purchase price for the prepaid account (if any); and
- the activation fee for the prepaid account (if any).[76]

In a setting other than a retail location, this information must be disclosed in "close proximity" to the short form disclosure.[77] If the prepaid account is acquired online, then the outside-the-box disclosures will be considered in "close proximity" to the short form disclosure if they are on the same web page as the short form disclosure.[78] If the short form disclosure is provided orally, then the information is considered to be in close proximity if it is provided immediately before or after the short form disclosure.[79]

If the prepaid account is acquired at a retail location, then all of the outside-the-box disclosures except the purchase price must be on the exterior of the product packaging.[80] If the purchase price is not disclosed on the exterior of the packaging, then it must be disclosed in close proximity to the packaging.[81]

5.8 Credit Features Associated with Prepaid Accounts

The prepaid rule imposes extensive restrictions on credit features associated with prepaid accounts. Most of these provisions are codified in Regulation Z.

5.8.1 Definitions of Key Terms

5.8.1.1 Prepaid Account Issuer

Whereas Regulation E generally refers to the "financial institution" with respect to a prepaid account, the prepaid rule provisions codified in Regulation Z generally use the term prepaid account issuer. Regulation Z defines prepaid account issuer as "a financial institution as defined in Regulation E . . . with respect to a prepaid account."[82]

5.8.1.2 Separate Credit Feature

A *separate credit feature* is defined as "a credit account or a credit subaccount of a prepaid account through which credit can be extended in connection with a prepaid card that is separate from the asset feature of the prepaid account."[83] As discussed

76. *Id.* § 1005.18(b)(4)(vii).
77. *Id.*
78. 12 C.F.R. pt. 1005, supp. I, § 18(b)(5)-2.
79. *Id.*
80. *Id.* § 1005.18(b)(5).
81. *Id.*
82. *Id.* § 1026.61(a)(5)(vi).
83. 81 Fed. Reg. at 84,371 (to be codified at 12 C.F.R. § 1026.61(a)(5)(viii)).

later, the prepaid rule divides the universe of credit features available in connection with prepaid accounts into separate credit features and negative balances on the asset feature of the prepaid account. An *asset feature* is defined as "an asset account that is a prepaid account, or an asset subaccount of a prepaid account."[84] An official interpretation explains that, for a credit feature to be set up as a "credit subaccount" of a prepaid account, "the credit feature must be set up as a separate balance on the prepaid account such that there are at least two balances on the prepaid account—the asset account balance and the credit account balance."[85]

Whether a credit feature is a *separate credit feature* or a negative balance feature is critical to the question of whether the credit feature is a *covered separate credit feature*. The definition of *covered separate credit feature* is discussed later.

5.8.1.3 Prepaid Card and Hybrid Prepaid-Credit Card

A key term in the provisions that regulate credit features associated with prepaid accounts is *prepaid card*. The term *prepaid card* is defined as "any card, code, or other device that can be used to access a prepaid account."[86] An official interpretation states that this includes a "prepaid account number or other code."[87] This definition is similar to the definition of *access device* in Regulation E.[88]

A prepaid card is a *hybrid prepaid-credit card* if either:

1. The prepaid card is "a single device that can be used from time to time to access credit extended through a negative balance on the asset feature of the prepaid account";[89] or
2. The prepaid card can be used from "time to time" to access a separate credit feature and the following two conditions are satisfied:
    i. The prepaid card "can be used to draw, transfer, or authorize the draw or transfer of credit from [a] separate credit feature in the course of authorizing, settling, or otherwise completing transactions conducted with the [prepaid] card to obtain goods or services, obtain cash, or conduct person-to-person transfers; and
    ii. The separate credit feature is offered by the prepaid account issuer, its affiliate, or its business partner."[90]

---

84. *Id.* (to be codified at 12 C.F.R. § 1026.61(a)(5)(ii)).

85. *Id.* at 84,387 (to be codified at 12 C.F.R. pt. 1026, supp. I, § 61(b)-1).

86. 12 C.F.R. § 1026.61(a)(5)(vii).

87. 12 C.F.R. pt. 1026, supp. I, § 61(a)(5)(vii)-1.

88. 12 C.F.R. § 1005.2(a)(1) ("'Access device' means a card, code, or other means of access to a consumer's account, or any combination thereof, that may be used by the consumer to initiate electronic fund transfers.").

89. *Id.* § 1026.61(a)(3)(i).

90. *Id.* § 1026.61(a)(2)(i)(A).

5.8.2 Restrictions on Negative Balances

A prepaid card will be a *hybrid prepaid-credit card* if the prepaid card is "a single device that can be used from time to time to access credit extended through a negative balance on the asset feature of the prepaid account."[91] "[S]tructuring a hybrid prepaid-credit card to access credit through a negative balance on the asset feature" is prohibited.[92]

There is an exception, however, to the general rule that a prepaid card will be a *hybrid prepaid-credit card* if the prepaid card can be used from time to time to access credit extended through a negative balance on the asset feature of the account. Because structuring a hybrid prepaid-credit card to access credit extended through a negative balance is prohibited, this exception from the definition of *hybrid prepaid-credit card* essentially delineates the circumstances under which the balance on a prepaid account may go negative.

Under the exception, a prepaid card is not a *hybrid prepaid-credit card* if:

- The prepaid card cannot access credit from a covered separate credit feature; and
- The prepaid account issuer has an established policy and practice of authorizing a transaction for which the issuer reasonably believes the consumer has insufficient or unavailable funds in the asset feature of the prepaid account to cover the transaction at the time the transaction is authorized only if: (i) the amount of the transaction will not cause the balance on the asset feature to go negative by more than $10; (ii) a transfer into the account sufficient to cover the transaction is pending; and
- No fees are imposed on the consumer for allowing the account to go negative (including higher fees for such consumer).[93]

5.8.3 Covered Separate Credit Features

5.8.3.1 Definition of Covered Separate Credit Feature

A separate credit feature is *a covered separate credit feature* if the separate credit feature can be accessed by a hybrid prepaid-credit card.[94] As explained in section 5.8.1.3, a prepaid card will be a *hybrid prepaid-credit card* with respect to a separate credit feature if the prepaid card can be used from "time to time" to access the separate credit feature and the following two conditions are satisfied:

91. *Id.* § 1026.61(a)(3)(i).
92. *Id.* § 1026.61(a)(3)(ii).
93. *Id.* § 1026.61(a)(4).
94. *Id.* § 1026.61(a)(2)(i)(A).

- The card "can be used to draw, transfer, or authorize the draw or transfer of credit from the separate credit feature in the course of authorizing, settling, or otherwise completing transactions conducted with the card to obtain goods or services, obtain cash, or conduct person-to-person transfers; and
- The separate credit feature is offered by the prepaid account issuer, its affiliate, or its business partner.[95]

A separate credit feature that is linked to a prepaid account that does not meet the foregoing requirements is referred to as a *non-covered separate credit feature*.[96]

Business partner is defined, subject to certain exceptions, as "a person . . . that can extend credit through a separate credit feature where the person or its affiliate has an arrangement with a prepaid account issuer or its affiliate."[97] There are two ways that a person can have an "arrangement" with a prepaid account issuer or its affiliate. The first is an "arrangement by agreement"—that is, "the parties have an agreement that allows the prepaid card from time to time to draw, transfer, or authorize a draw or transfer of credit in the course of authorizing, settling, or otherwise completing transactions conducted with the card to obtain goods or services, obtain cash, or conduct person-to-person transfers."[98] The second is a "marketing arrangement." A *marketing arrangement* is defined, basically, as an arrangement pursuant to which either (1) the prepaid account issuer (or its affiliates) will market the separate credit feature to prepaid account customers, or (2) the separate credit feature provider will market the prepaid accounts to its customers[99]—provided that, at the time of the marketing agreement or arrangement, the separate credit feature can be accessed through the prepaid account in connection with transactions.[100] Marketing a credit feature to holders of prepaid accounts includes marketing designed to encourage those customers to link the credit feature to the prepaid account as a backup funding source.

An exception to the definition of *business partner* provides that a credit card issuer will not be a *business partner* of the prepaid account issuer as a result of an arrangement between the two if all of the following conditions are satisfied:

- The credit card account is a "credit card account under an open-end (not home-secured) consumer credit plan";[101]

---

95. *Id.* § 1026.61(a)(2)(i)(A).
96. *Id.* § 1026.61(a)(2)(ii)(B).
97. *Id.* § 1026.61(a)(5)(iii).
98. *Id.* § 1026.61(a)(5)(iii)(B).
99. *Id.* § 1026.61(a)(5)(iii)(C)(1).
100. This last proviso addresses a situation where a prepaid account issuer and a credit provider had a joint marketing arrangement in the past, and the prepaid account issuer then releases a product to which the credit provider's products can be linked as backup funding sources.
101. 12 C.F.R. § 1026.61(a)(5)(iii)(D)(1).

- The consumer can access the credit card account "through a traditional credit card";[102]
- Either: (i) the credit card was linked to the prepaid account prior to April 1, 2019 (the effective date of the prepaid rule); or (ii) the prepaid account issuer or the card issuer "has received from the consumer a written request that is separately signed or initialized to authorize" the credit card to be accessed with the prepaid card;[103]
- The prepaid account issuer does not condition the acquisition or retention of the prepaid account on whether the consumer authorizes the credit card to be used as a backup funding source, and the same terms, conditions, and features will apply to the prepaid account regardless of whether the consumer authorizes the prepaid card to access the credit card account;[104]
- The prepaid account issuer applies the same fees to load funds with the credit card that the prepaid account issuer charges for comparable loads with a credit feature not offered by the prepaid account issuer, its affiliate, or a party that would be a business partner of the prepaid account issuer but for this exception;[105]
- The credit card issuer does not condition the acquisition or retention of the credit card account on the consumer authorizing the prepaid card to access the credit card;[106] and
- The credit card issuer applies the same terms and conditions[107] to the credit card account regardless of whether the consumer authorizes linking the prepaid card to the credit card account.[108]

5.8.3.2 Restrictions and Requirements for Covered Separate Credit Features

There are a number of restrictions and requirements applicable to covered separate credit features. Some of the most important are discussed here.

---

102. *Id.*

103. *Id.* § 1026.61(a)(5)(iii)(D)(2).

104. *Id.* § 1026.61(a)(5)(iii)(D)(3).

105. *Id.* § 1026.61(a)(5)(iii)(D)(4).

106. *Id.* § 1026.61(a)(5)(iii)(D)(3).

107. For purposes of this provision, *terms and conditions* means (1) repayment terms and conditions, (2) limits on liability for unauthorized transactions, or (3) any term or condition required to be disclosed under 12 C.F.R. § 1026.6(b) (the credit card account opening disclosures). *Id.* § 1026.61(a)(5)(iii)(D)(5).

108. *Id.* § 1026.61(a)(5)(iii)(D)(5).

5.8.3.2.1 Application of CARD Act Provisions

The Regulation Z provisions that implement the Credit Card Accountability, Responsibility, and Disclosure Act of 2009 (the CARD Act) apply to a subset of credit cards to which Regulation Z assigns the clunky label *credit card account under an open-end (not home-secured) consumer credit plan*, defined as "any open-end credit account that is accessed by a credit card," except for several excluded types of accounts.[109] The excluded accounts include overdraft lines of credit that are accessed by debit cards[110] or account numbers.[111] However, the definition of *debit card* excludes a prepaid card,[112] and the exclusion for account numbers that access overdraft lines of credit does not apply if the account number is a hybrid prepaid-credit card that accesses a covered separate credit feature.[113]

Because covered separate credit features cannot qualify for the exclusions from the definition of *credit card account under an open-end (not home-secured) consumer credit plan* that cover overdraft lines of credit associated with most types of asset accounts, a hybrid prepaid-credit card that accesses a covered separate credit feature will be a *credit card account under an open-end (not home-secured) consumer credit plan* if it otherwise meets the elements in the definition of that term. Notably, the term is limited to accounts that are *open-end credit accounts*.[114] Thus, a closed-end covered separate credit feature will not be a *credit card account under an open-end (not home-secured) consumer credit plan*, and thus will not be subject to the provisions of Regulation Z that implement the CARD Act.

5.8.3.2.2 Statements Regarding Credit Features in Pre-Acquisition Disclosures

Both the short form disclosure and the long form disclosure must contain, among other information, a statement regarding whether a covered separate credit feature "may be offered at any point to a consumer in connection with the prepaid account."[115] This statement must be substantially similar to the following: "You may be offered overdraft/credit after [x] days. Fees would apply."[116] This disclosure must be included

---

109. *Id.* § 1026.2(a)(15)(ii).

110. *Id.* § 1026.2(a)(15)(ii)(B).

111. *Id.* § 1026.2(a)(15)(ii)(C).

112. *Id.* § 1026.2(a)(15)(iv).

113. *Id.* § 1026.2(a)(15)(ii)(C).

114. Regulation Z defines *open-end credit* as "consumer credit extended by a creditor under a plan in which: (i) The creditor reasonably contemplates repeated transactions; (ii) The creditor may impose a finance charge from time to time on an outstanding unpaid balance; and (iii) The amount of credit that may be extended to the consumer during the term of the plan (up to any limit set by the creditor) is generally made available to the extent that any outstanding balance is repaid." *Id.* § 1026.2(a)(20).

115. *Id.* §§ 1005.18(b)(2)(x), (b)(4)(iv).

116. *Id.* §§ 1005.18(b)(2)(x), (b)(4)(iv).

"for all prepaid accounts that may offer such a feature, regardless of whether some consumers may never be solicited or qualify to enroll in such a feature."[117]

5.8.3.2.3 Potentially Significant Restrictions on Negative Balances

The prepaid rule has extensive restrictions on when a prepaid account issuer may allow a prepaid account balance to go negative. The provisions that lay out these restrictions are far from models of clarity. Nevertheless, the prepaid rule appears to prohibit prepaid account issuers from allowing the balance on the asset feature of the prepaid account to go negative for any reason if a hybrid prepaid-credit card can be used to access a covered separate credit feature in connection with the account—even if the prepaid account issuer cannot charge the particular transaction that will cause a negative balance to the covered separate credit feature (e.g., because the credit provider does not authorize the transaction, or the terms of the feature do not permit the particular type of transaction to be charged to it).[118] Moreover, the official interpretations suggest that if a hybrid prepaid-credit card can access a covered separate credit feature then the account cannot go negative for any reason—not just as a result of a card transaction.[119]

5.8.3.2.4 Cooling-Off Period

A prepaid account issuer must wait until thirty days after an account is registered before linking an existing credit feature to a prepaid account if the credit feature will be a covered separate credit feature after linkage.[120] Prepaid account issuers also are prohibited from soliciting or providing applications for the covered separate credit feature to accountholders during this cooling-off period.[121]

An account is not "registered" for purposes of this cooling-off provision until the prepaid account issuer has completed "its collection of consumer identifying information and identity verification in accordance with the requirements of applicable Federal and state law."[122] The thirty-day period does not begin to run when the consumer opens the account—only when the issuer successfully completes the "collection of consumer identifying information and identity verification."[123] This means that if an account can be opened with limited functionality prior to identity verification, then the thirty-day period might not begin to run when the account is first opened.

117. 12 C.F.R. pt. 1005, supp. I, § 18(b)(2)(x)-1.
118. 12 C.F.R. § 1026.61(a).
119. 12 C.F.R. pt. 1026, supp. I, § 1026.61(a)(4).
120. 12 C.F.R. § 1026.61(c).
121. *Id.* § 1026.61(c).
122. 12 C.F.R. pt. 1026, supp. I, § 1026.61(c)-1.
123. *Id.*

5.8.3.2.5 More Extensive Pre-Acquisition Disclosures

The long form disclosure for a prepaid account must include "disclosures described in Regulation Z, 12 C.F.R. 1026.60(e)(1) . . . if, at any point, a covered separate credit feature accessible by a hybrid prepaid-credit card . . . may be offered in connection with the prepaid account."[124] The "disclosures described in . . . 12 C.F.R. 1026.60(e)(1)" are the disclosures that a credit card issuer must include in applications and solicitations for the credit card.

5.8.3.2.6 Cooling-Off Period

Neither the prepaid account issuer nor the credit provider may market or make available a covered separate credit feature to a consumer within the first thirty days after the consumer acquires the prepaid account. They also may not allow the consumer to link a credit product (such as a credit card) that the consumer acquired separately from the prepaid account within the first thirty days of prepaid account acquisition if the credit product will become a covered separate credit feature upon being so linked.

5.8.3.2.7 Negative Balances Restrictions

As discussed in section 5.8.3.2.3, an issuer may authorize a transaction with a prepaid card that will cause an account to go negative only if certain requirements are met. One of these requirements is that a covered separate credit feature not be linked to the prepaid account. Thus, if a covered separate credit feature is linked to the account, a financial institution may not authorize transactions that will result in a negative balance even subject to the limitations described in section 5.8.3.2.3. Moreover, although not stated crisply, several passages in the official interpretations suggest that negative balances are completely prohibited for any reason—including reasons beyond the financial institution's reasonable control—if a covered separate credit feature is linked to the account. Some transactions that could result in a negative account balance might not be chargeable to the covered separate credit feature, however.[125] If the prepaid account balance cannot go negative, then the prepaid account issuer will be required to absorb the transaction or set up another separate credit feature to which it can charge the transaction (which might itself be another covered separate credit feature).

6. Access Device Disclosures

All physical access devices for a prepaid account must include the following information:

124. 12 C.F.R. § 1005.18(b)(2)(x).

125. Two reasons include: (1) there is not enough available credit on the covered separate credit feature to cover the transaction, and (2) the transaction that causes the negative balance is a chargeback submitted by the provider of the covered separate credit feature.

- the name of the financial institution;
- the website URL for the prepaid account product; and
- a telephone number that can be used to obtain information about the account.[126]

If a consumer does obtain a physical access device, this information must appear on the financial institution's website, mobile application, or other entry point a consumer must visit to access the prepaid account electronically.[127]

7. Submission and Posting of Prepaid Account Agreements

Prepaid account issuers must submit prepaid account agreements to the CFPB on a rolling basis.[128] Submissions must be made within thirty days of the date on which an issuer offers, amends, or stops offering any prepaid account agreement. Submissions must meet certain form and formatting requirements, but do not need to be approved by the CFPB.

Prepaid account agreements need not be submitted if an issuer has fewer than 3,000 open prepaid accounts.[129] The count refers to the total number of prepaid accounts that the issuer has—not to the number of accounts open under a particular agreement. Thus, if the issuer has more than 3,000 open prepaid accounts in total, the issuer must submit agreements for all of its prepaid account product lines.

Agreements required to be submitted to the CFPB must also be posted on the issuer's "publicly available Web site."[130] The issuer must post and update agreements on its website as frequently as the issuer is required to submit new or amended agreements to the CFPB.[131] The agreements must be "placed in a location that is prominent and readily accessible to the public."[132] The agreements must be accessible without the submission of personally identifiable information.[133]

Further, for all open accounts, the issuer must make available a copy of each individual consumer's agreement to the consumer.[134] The issuer may do this either

126. 12 C.F.R. § 1005.18(f)(3).
127. *Id.*
128. *Id.* § 1005.19(b)(1).
129. *Id.* § 1005.19(b)(4)(i), (b)(5)(i).
130. *Id.* § 1005.19(c)(1).
131. *Id.* § 1005.19(c)(3).
132. *Id.* § 1005.19(c)(4).
133. *Id.*
134. *Id.* § 1005.19(d).

by posting the account agreement on its website or by promptly providing a copy of the agreement to the consumer upon the consumer's request.[135]

8. The Alternative to Periodic Statements

8.1 Overview

As discussed in more detail in chapter 8, Regulation E requires a financial institution to provide periodic statements that contain transaction histories and other information about the account. These statements must be provided monthly (unless there have been no electronic fund transfers on the account, in which case they must be provided at least quarterly). These periodic statement requirements have not been materially updated since they were first adopted in the 1970s. Regulation E does not require a financial institution to provide online access information or access, or impose any specific rules concerning what information must be made available when a financial institution decides to provide online account access voluntarily (as virtually every—in fact, probably every—financial institution does).

As described further in the following section, Regulation E gives financial institutions the option of providing real-time electronic access to the information required to be included in periodic statements in lieu of providing such statements, provided that this online access meets certain requirements. This alternative is a slightly updated version of the alternative that Regulation E provided to providers of payroll cards when Regulation E was amended in 2006 to cover payroll cards. At the time, the alternative was dubbed "Reg E Lite," since financial institutions generally regarded the alternative requirements as less burdensome than the periodic statement requirements, at least with respect to payroll cards. This label is still often used today (although it does not appear in Regulation E). It can be a highly misleading label, however, because it might give the impression that the alternative it provides financial institutions gives consumers a less robust set of protections and rights. In 2020, however, a large number of consumers—likely most consumers—rely more on online portals to monitor account transactions and obtain other account information than on periodic statements. A set of consumer protections governing that online resource therefore does not appear—from the consumer's standpoint—to be a "lite" set of protections. Accordingly, this chapter will eschew the term "Reg E Lite" to refer to this alternative set of requirements.

8.2 General Requirements for the Alternative

A financial institution is not required to provide consumers with periodic account statements if it makes the following three things available to consumers:

135. *Id.* § 1005.19(d)(1).

- The consumer's account balance through a readily available telephone line;
- An electronic history of the consumer's account transactions, such as through a website, that covers at least twelve months preceding the date the consumer electronically accesses the account; and
- The written history of the consumer's account transactions in response to an oral or written request and that covers at least twenty-four months preceding the date the financial institution receives the consumer's request. This written history must be "provided promptly" upon receipt of the request.[136]

The transaction histories must contain all the information required to be included in periodic statements, including the fee summaries described below.[137]

The transaction histories do not need to be provided in connection with a prepaid account "for which the financial institution has not completed its consumer identification and verification process."[138] However, after an account is registered, the written histories must cover the preregistration period (up to twelve or twenty-four months, as applicable).

8.3 Modified Initial Disclosures

If an institution decides to use the online access alternative to periodic statements, it must modify the "initial disclosures" required by Regulation E as follows:

- It must provide a telephone number the consumer may call to obtain the account balance;[139]
- It must provide the means by which the consumer can obtain an electronic account transaction history;[140]
- In lieu of the initial disclosure that summarizes the consumer's right to receive a periodic statement, it must provide (in a notice substantially similar to the notice in paragraph (a) of appendix A-7 of Regulation E)[141] a summary of the consumer's right to receive

136. *Id.*

137. *Id.* § 1005.18(c)(2).

138. *Id.* § 1005.18.

139. *Id.* § 1005.18(d)(1)(i).

140. *Id.*

141. Technically, it says that the *financial institution* may, not must, provide a notice that is substantially similar to the notice in the appendix. However, providing a notice that is substantially similar to the model notice provides a safe harbor. *See* 15 U.S.C. § 1693m(d)(2).

a written account transaction history upon request (including a telephone number to call to request a history);[142] and

- In lieu of the error resolution notice required by the initial disclosure provisions, an error resolution notice that is substantially similar to the notice in paragraph (b) of appendix A-7 of Regulation E.[143]

142. 12 C.F.R. § 1005.18(d)(1)(i).

143. *Id.*

CHAPTER

10

Remittance Transfer Rule

Julia Dempewolf

1. Scope of This Chapter

This chapter covers the provisions in the Electronic Fund Transfer Act (EFTA) and subpart B of Regulation E (Remittance Transfer Rule) that regulate consumer-initiated foreign remittances. Regulation E is discussed in greater depth in chapters 8 and 9 addressing the Electronic Fund Transfer Act and prepaid cards, respectively.

2. Authority, Purpose, and Coverage

2.1 Authority and Purpose

Regulation E[1] and its Official Staff Commentary[2] implement the EFTA,[3] and in 2012, the Consumer Financial Protection Bureau (CFPB) promulgated the Remittance Transfer Rule as subpart B of Regulation E to implement the new remittance protections established by Title X of the Dodd-Frank Wall Street Reform and Consumer Protection

1. Electronic Fund Transfers (Regulation E), 12 C.F.R. § 1005 (2020).

2. 12 C.F.R. § 1005, supp. I.

3. Electronic Fund Transfer Act, Pub. L. No. 95-630, Stat. 3641 (1978) (codified as amended at 15 U.S.C. § 1693 (2018)).

Act of 2010 (CFPA).[4] The CFPA[5] amended the EFTA to establish protections for remittance transfers sent by consumers located in the United States to recipients in foreign countries.[6]

2.2 Definition of Remittance Transfer

The Remittance Transfer Rule defines *remittance transfer* as "the electronic transfer of funds requested by a sender to a designated recipient that is sent by a remittance transfer provider."[7] Thus, a remittance transfer consists of four elements: (1) an electronic transfer of funds, (2) requested by a *sender*, (3) to *a designated recipient*, (4) that is sent by a *remittance transfer provider*. Remittance transfer is defined broadly to apply "regardless of whether the sender holds an account with the remittance transfer provider, and regardless of whether the transaction is also an electronic fund transfer[.]"[8] Consequently, a remittance transfer may also constitute an *electronic fund transfer*[9] subject to subpart A of Regulation E if the transfer satisfies the elements of both definitions—but the Remittance Transfer Rule will apply to a remittance transfer even if the remittance transfer is not an electronic fund transfer under subpart A of Regulation E. Transfers of fifteen dollars or less and transfers where the primary purpose of the transfer is the purchase or sale of certain securities and commodities are excluded from the definition of remittance transfer.[10]

2.2.1 Electronic Transfer of Funds

An "electronic transfer of funds" must be involved in the transfer to constitute a remittance transfer.[11] The Remittance Transfer Rule applies the definition of *electronic* found in the Electronic Signatures in Global and National Commerce Act (the "E-SIGN Act"),[12] which defines *electronic* as "relating to technology having electrical, digital, magnetic, wireless, optical, electromagnetic, or similar capabilities."[13] Thus, the transfer

---

4. 77 Fed. Reg. 6194 (Feb. 7, 2012).

5. Dodd-Frank Wall Street Reform and Consumer Protection Act of 2010, Pub. L. 111-203, Stat. 1386 (2010) (codified as amended at 12 U.S.C. §§ 5301–5641 (2018)).

6. 12 U.S.C. § 5601.

7. 12 C.F.R. § 1005.30(e)(1).

8. *Id.*

9. Regulation E defines an *electronic fund transfer* as "any transfer of funds that is initiated through an electronic terminal, telephone, computer, or magnetic tape for the purpose of ordering, instructing, or authorizing a financial institution to debit or credit a consumer's account." 12 C.F.R. § 1005.3(b)(1). See chapter 8 for further discussion of the requirements of subpart A of Regulation E.

10. *Id.* § 1005.30(e)(2) (cross referencing 12 C.F.R. § 1005.3(c)(4)).

11. *See id.* § 1005.30(e).

12. 12 C.F.R. § 1005, supp. I, cmt. 30(e)-1.

13. 15 U.S.C. § 7006(2).

of funds must be completed using technology having electrical, digital, magnetic, wireless, optical, electromagnetic, or similar capabilities to satisfy the definition of a remittance transfer.

2.2.2 Sender

A *sender* must request the electronic transfer of funds for the transfer to constitute a remittance transfer.[14] A *sender* is a "consumer in a State who primarily for personal, family, or household purposes requests a remittance transfer provider to send a remittance transfer to a designated recipient."[15] Regulation E defines *State* as "any state, territory, or possession of the United States; the District of Columbia; the Commonwealth of Puerto Rico; or any political subdivision of the thereof[.]"[16] Generally speaking, the location of the consumer's account determines whether a consumer is "located in a State."[17]

The consumer's electronic transfer of funds must be for "personal, family, or household purposes" for the consumer to constitute a sender.[18] Generally, a remittance transfer provider may determine that the transfer is primarily for personal, family, or household purposes if the transfer is from an account established primarily for personal, family, or household purposes.[19] Conversely, when a consumer requests a transfer from an account not established primarily for personal, family, or household purposes, then the transfer is not made primarily for personal, family, or household purposes, and the requestor is not a sender.[20]

2.2.3 Designated Recipient

The consumer must request that the funds be transferred to a *designated recipient* for the transfer to constitute a remittance transfer.[21] A *designated recipient* is "any person specified by the sender as the authorized recipient of a remittance transfer to be received at a location in a foreign county."[22] A designated recipient can be either a natural person or an organization[23] and may also be the sender.[24]

14. *See* 12 C.F.R. § 1005.30(e).
15. *Id.* § 1005.30(g).
16. *Id.* § 1005.2(l).
17. *Id.*
18. *See id.* § 1005.30(g).
19. *Id.*
20. *Id.*
21. *See id.* § 1005.30(e).
22. *Id.* § 1005.30(c).
23. 12 C.F.R. § 1005, supp. I, cmt. 30(c)-1.
24. *Id.* cmt. 30(c)-3.

2.2.4 Remittance Transfer Provider

The electronic transfer of funds must be sent by a remittance transfer provider to constitute a remittance transfer.[25] A *remittance transfer provider* is "any person that provides remittance transfers for a consumer in the normal course of its business, regardless of whether the consumer holds an account with such person."[26] The Remittance Transfer Rule provides a safe harbor for determining whether a person provides remittance transfers in the "normal course of its business."[27]

2.3 Larger Participants

The CFPA grants the CFPB supervisory authority over, among others, "a larger participant of a market for other consumer financial products or services, as defined by [CFPB] rule[.]"[28] In 2014, the CFPB used this authority to establish a definition of larger participants in the "international money transfer market."[29] The CFPB defines an *international money transfer* as "the electronic transfer of funds requested by a sender to a designated recipient that is sent by an international money transfer provider" and defines *international money transfer provider* as "any nonbank covered person that provides international money transfers for a consumer, regardless of whether the consumer holds an account with such person."[30] A *nonbank covered person* is a person engaged in "offering or providing a consumer financial product or service" and an affiliate of such person acting as a service provider to such person.[31] Nonbank covered person excludes "(1) an insured depository institution with total assets of more than $10,000,000,000 and any affiliate thereof [and] (2) an insured credit union with total assets of more than $10,000,000,000 and any affiliate thereof[.]"[32]

A nonbank covered person constitutes a "larger participant of the international money transfer market" if the person "has at least one million aggregate annual international money transfers."[33] *Aggregate annual international money transfers* is defined as "the sum of the annual international money transfers of a nonbank covered person and the annual international money transfers of each of the nonbank covered person's affiliated companies."[34] *Annual international money transfers of a nonbank covered person* is defined as "the international money transfers provided by

25. *See* 12 C.F.R. § 1005.30(e).
26. *Id.* § 1005.30(f)(1).
27. *See id.* § 1005.30(f)(2)(i).
28. 15 U.S.C. § 5514(a)(1).
29. *See* 79 Fed. Reg. 56631 (Sept. 23, 2014).
30. 12 C.F.R. § 1090.107(a).
31. *Id.* § 1090.101.
32. *Id.* (citing 12 U.S.C. § 5515(a) and 5516(a)).
33. *Id.* § 1090.107(b).
34. *Id.* § 1090.101.

the nonbank covered person during the preceding calendar year."[35] The calculation of the aggregate annual international money transfers includes transfers in which another person acts as an agent on behalf of the nonbank covered person, but does not include transfers where the nonbank covered person performed activities as an agent on behalf of another person.[36] Thus, if a nonbank covered person and its affiliated companies, acting as an agent on behalf of the nonbank covered person, have at least one million aggregate international money transfers, that is, electronic transfers of funds requested by a sender to a designated recipient sent by an international money transfer provider, during the prior calendar year, then the person is a larger participant of the international money transfer market, and therefore subject to the Remittance Transfer Rule.

2.4 Agents

A person acting as an agent of a remittance transfer provider does not constitute a remittance transfer provider under the Remittance Transfer Rule.[37] Instead, the remittance transfer provider on whose behalf the agent is acting remains liable for violations of the Remittance Transfer Rule committed by the person when the person acts as an agent of the provider.[38]

3. Disclosures

Under the Remittance Transfer Rule, a remittance transfer provider must provide a sender with either (1) a "pre-payment disclosure" and a receipt, or (2) a "combined disclosure" (collectively, "disclosures").[39] Each such disclosure must generally be provided in writing, with certain alternative methodologies provided for disclosures made by telephone or a mobile application.[40] The Remittance Transfer Rule provides model forms for each required disclosure.[41]

3.1 General Disclosure Requirements

Disclosures made pursuant to the Remittance Transfer Rule must be "clear and conspicuous" and may use "commonly accepted or readily understandable abbreviations

35. *Id.* § 1090.107(a).
36. *Id.*
37. 12 C.F.R. § 1005, supp. I, cmt. 30(f)-1.
38. 12 C.F.R. § 1005.35.
39. *See id.* § 1005.31(b).
40. *Id.* § 1005.31(a)(2).
41. *See* 12 C.F.R. § 1005, app. A, model forms A-30–A-40.

or symbols."[42] Because disclosures must be provided in writing, a remittance transfer provider generally must comply with the E-SIGN Act when delivering a disclosure to a consumer.[43] Additionally, disclosures must generally be made in retainable format.[44]

Upon the sender's request, a remittance transfer provider must promptly provide to the sender a notice describing the sender's error resolution and cancellation rights, using model language or substantially similar language.[45]

3.2 Prepayment Disclosures

When the sender requests the remittance transfer, but prior to payment for the transfer, a remittance transfer provider must provide the sender with a prepayment disclosure unless the provider uses combined disclosures.[46] The prepayment disclosure must include the following information using terms prescribed in the Remittance Transfer Rule:

- *Transfer amount.* The amount that will be transferred to the designated recipient, in the currency in which the remittance transfer is funded.[47]
- *Transfer fees and transfer taxes.* Any fees imposed and any taxes collected on the remittance transfer by the remittance transfer provider, in the currency in which the remittance transfer is funded.[48] If both fees and taxes are imposed, the fees and taxes must be disclosed as separate, itemized amounts.[49] The prepayment disclosure must distinguish between fees imposed by the provider and fees imposed by a third party, which are discussed below.[50]
- *Total amount.* The total amount of the transaction, that is, the sum of the transfer amount, transfer fees, and transfer taxes, in the currency in which the remittance transfer is funded.[51]
- *Exchange rate.* The exchange rate used by the provider for the remittance transfer, rounded consistently for each currency to no fewer than two decimal places and no more than four decimal places if the designated recipient will receive funds in a currency other than the currency in

42. 12 C.F.R. § 1005.31(a)(1).
43. *Id.* § 1005.31(a)(2).
44. *Id.*
45. *Id.* § 31(b)(4).
46. *Id.* § 1005.31(e)(1).
47. *Id.* § 1005.31(b)(1)(i).
48. *Id.* § 1005.31(b)(1)(ii).
49. 12 C.F.R. § 1005, supp. I, cmt. 31(b)(1)-1.i.
50. *Id.* cmt. 31(b)(1)-1.iii.
51. 12 C.F.R. § 1005.31(b)(1)(iii).

which the remittance transfer is funded.[52] A remittance transfer provider may not state that an exchange rate is unknown, floating, or to be determined.[53]

- *Transfer amount.* The transfer amount in the currency in which the funds will be received by the designated recipient, but only if covered third-party fees are imposed.[54]
- *Other fees.* Any covered third-party fees, in the currency in which the funds will be received by the designated recipient, which must be calculated using an exchange rate rounded consistently for each currency to no fewer than two decimal places and no more than four decimal places.[55] *Covered third-party fees* are "fees imposed on the remittance transfer by a person other than the remittance transfer provider except for [noncovered third-party fees]."[56] *Noncovered third-party fees* are "fees imposed by the designated recipient's institution for receiving a remittance transfer into an account except if the institution acts as an agent of the remittance transfer provider."[57]
- *Total to recipient.* The amount that will be received by the designated recipient, in the currency in which the funds will be received, except that this amount may not include noncovered third-party fees or taxes collected on the remittance transfer by a person other than the provider regardless of whether such fees or taxes are disclosed.[58]
- *Statement regarding noncovered fees and taxes.* A statement indicating that noncovered third-party fees or taxes collected on the remittance transfer by a person other than the provider may apply to the remittance transfer and result in the designated recipient receiving less than the amount disclosed as the total to the recipient.[59] A remittance transfer provider may only include a statement regarding noncovered third-party fees or taxes if such fees or taxes do or may apply to the transfer.[60] If the provider does not know whether such fees or taxes may or will apply, the provider must include the statement.[61]

---

52. *Id.* § 1005.31(b)(1)(iv).
53. *Id.*
54. *Id.* § 1005.31(b)(1)(v).
55. *Id.* § 1005.31(b)(1)(vi).
56. *Id.* § 1005.30(h)(1).
57. *Id.* § 1005.30(h)(2).
58. *Id.* § 1005.31(b)(1)(vii).
59. *Id.* § 1005.31(b)(1)(viii).
60. *Id.*
61. 12 C.F.R. § 1005, supp. I, cmt. 31(b)(1)(viii)-1.

3.3 Receipt

The remittance transfer provider must provide the sender with a receipt when payment is made for the remittance transfer and a prepayment disclosure has been provided.[62] The receipt must contain the same information as the prepayment disclosure,[63] as well as the following information, using the specified terms:

- *Date Available.* The date in the foreign country when funds will be available to the designated recipient.[64] A provider may note that funds may be available to the designated recipient earlier than the date disclosed.[65] However, a provider must not provide a range of dates that the remittance transfer may be available or an estimate of the date on which funds will be available.[66]
- *Recipient Name and Address.* The name and, if provided by the sender, the telephone number and/or address of the designated recipient.[67]
- *Error Resolution and Cancellation Rights Statement.* A statement about the sender's error resolution and cancellation rights.[68]
- *Transfer Provider Information.* The name, telephone number(s), and website of the remittance transfer provider.[69]
- *Regulatory Agencies' Contact Information.* A statement that the sender can contact the state agency that licenses or charters the remittance transfer provider with respect to the remittance transfer and the CFPB for questions or complaints about the remittance transfer provider.[70] The disclosure must provide the state agency's name, telephone number(s), and website and the CFPB's name, toll-free telephone number(s), and website.[71]
- *Scheduled Transfer Date.* For any remittance transfer scheduled by the sender at least three business days before the date of the transfer, or the first transfer in a series of preauthorized remittance transfers, the date the remittance transfer provider will make or made the remittance transfer.[72]

62. 12 C.F.R. § 1005.31(e)(2).
63. *Id.* § 1005.31(b)(2)(i).
64. *Id.* § 1005.31(b)(2)(ii).
65. *Id.*
66. 12 C.F.R. § 1005, supp. I, cmt. 31(b)(2)-1.
67. 12 C.F.R. § 1005.31(b)(2)(iii).
68. *Id.* § 1005.31(b)(2)(iv).
69. *Id.* § 1005.31(b)(2)(v).
70. *Id.* § 1005.31(b)(2)(vi).
71. *Id.*
72. *Id.* § 1005.31(b)(2)(vii).

3.4 Combined Disclosures

In lieu of providing a prepayment disclosure and a receipt, a remittance transfer provider may provide a combined disclosure[73] to the sender when the sender requests the remittance transfer, but prior to payment for the transfer.[74] If the provider uses a combined disclosure and the sender completes the transfer, the provider must provide the sender with proof of payment when payment is made for the remittance transfer.[75] Alternatively, if a provider uses a combined disclosure for a one-time transfer scheduled five or more business days before the date of transfer or for the first in a series of preauthorized remittance transfers and payment is not processed by the remittance transfer provider at the time the remittance transfer is scheduled, then the provider may provide confirmation that the transaction has been scheduled in lieu of the proof of payment.[76] The proof of payment and confirmation of scheduling must be clear and conspicuous, provided in writing or electronically, and provided in a retainable form.[77]

3.5 Formatting

The Remittance Transfer Rule imposes specific disclosure formatting requirements concerning (1) grouping of information, (2) proximity of information, (3) prominence and size of information, and (4) segregation of information.[78]

3.5.1 Grouping

The following information must be grouped together in a Remittance Transfer Rule disclosure: (1) the transfer amount, (2) transfer fees and taxes, and (3) the transaction total.[79] Second, the following information must be grouped together in a disclosure: (1) the transfer amount, (2) other fees, (3) the total to the recipient, and (4) a statement indicating that noncovered third-party fees or taxes collected on the remittance transfer by a person other than the provider may apply to the remittance transfer and result in the designated recipient receiving less than the amount disclosed as the total to the recipient.[80]

---

73. *Id.* § 1005.31(b)(3)(i).

74. *Id.* § 1005.31(e)(1).

75. *Id.* § 1005.31(b)(3)(i).

76. *Id.* § 1005.31(b)(3)(ii).

77. *Id.* §§ 1005.31(b)(3)(i)–(ii).

78. *See id.* § 1005.31(c). The Remittance Transfer Rule provides certain formatting alternatives for disclosures made via mobile application or text message, which are not discussed here. *See id.*

79. *Id.* § 1005.31(c)(1).

80. *Id.*

3.5.2 Proximity

The exchange rate must be disclosed in close proximity to other required information.[81] Additionally, the statement regarding the sender's error resolution and cancellation rights must be disclosed in close proximity to the information required to be in the receipt.[82] Next, if applicable, the statement indicating that noncovered third-party fees or taxes collected on the remittance transfer by a person other than the provider may apply to the remittance transfer and result in the designated recipient receiving less than the amount disclosed as the total to the recipient must be included in close proximity to the total to the recipient.[83]

3.5.3 Prominence and Size

The information required or permitted to be on a disclosure must be provided on the front of the page on which the disclosure is printed.[84] Such information that is provided in writing or electronically must be in minimum eight-point font.[85] Finally, all information required or permitted to be on disclosures provided in writing or electronically must be in equal prominence to each other.[86]

3.5.4 Segregation

The information required or permitted to be on a disclosure provided in writing or electronically must be segregated from all other information on the disclosure and must only contain information that is "directly related" to the disclosure.[87]

3.6 Estimates

The remittance transfer provider must describe estimated disclosures using the term "Estimated" or substantially similar term in close proximity to the estimated term or terms.[88] Further requirements apply to estimated disclosures as described in section 4 of this chapter.

81. *Id.* § 1005.31(c)(2).
82. *Id.*
83. *Id.*
84. *Id.* § 1005.31(c)(3).
85. *Id.*
86. *Id.*
87. *Id.* § 1005.31(c)(4).
88. *Id.* § 1005.31(d).

3.7 Accuracy

The information required or permitted to be on a disclosure must be accurate when a sender makes payment for the remittance transfer, except to the extent such information is estimated.[89]

3.8 Foreign Language Disclosures

Generally speaking, the information required or permitted to be on a disclosure must be made in English.[90] Such information must also be made available in either: (1) "[e]ach of the foreign languages principally used by the remittance transfer provider to advertise, solicit, or market remittance transfer services, either orally, in writing, or electronically, at the office in which a sender conducts a transaction or asserts an error"; or (2) "[t]he foreign language primarily used by the sender with the remittance transfer provider to conduct the transaction (or for written or electronic error resolution disclosures [...], in the foreign language primarily used by the sender with the remittance transfer provider to assert the error), provided that such foreign language is principally used by the remittance transfer provider to advertise, solicit, or market remittance transfer services, either orally, in writing, or electronically, at the office in which a sender conducts a transaction or asserts an error, respectively."[91]

4. Estimates

4.1 Temporary Exception for Insured Institutions

Until July 21, 2020, certain financial institutions acting as a remittance transfer provider could estimate specific types of disclosed amounts so long as certain conditions were satisfied.[92] The EFTA established the July 21, 2020, sunset deadline and prohibited any extension beyond that date.[93]

89. *Id.* § 1005.31(f).

90. *Id.* § 1005.31(g)(1).

91. *Id.* Alternative requirements apply for transactions conducted orally, by telephone, mobile application, or text message. *See id.* § 1005.31(g)(2). These requirements are not addressed here.

92. *Id.* § 1005.32(a)(2).

93. *See* 15 U.S.C. § 1693o-1(a)(4)(B).

4.2 Permanent Exceptions

4.2.1 Transfers to Certain Countries

The Remittance Transfer Rule provides a permanent exception for transfers to certain countries. Under this permanent exception, a remittance transfer provider may estimate the following information: (1) the exchange rate, (2) the transfer amount in the currency in which the funds will be received by the designated recipient, (3) covered third-party fees in the currency in which the funds will be received by the designated recipient, and (4) the amount that will be received by the designated recipient in the currency in which the funds will be received.[94] A remittance transfer provider can estimate this information if the provider cannot determine the exact amounts for one of the following reasons: (1) the laws of the recipient country do not permit such determination, or (2) the method by which transactions are made in the recipient country does not permit such determination.[95]

The Remittance Transfer Rule provides a safe harbor in which a remittance transfer provider can rely on a list of countries published by the CFPB to determine whether a transfer to a certain country qualifies for this exception.[96] However, a remittance transfer provider cannot rely on the list if the provider has information that a country's laws or the method by which the transaction is conducted in that country permits a determination of the exact disclosure amount.[97]

4.2.2 Transfers Scheduled Before the Date of Transfer

For a one-time transfer scheduled five or more business days before the date of transfer or for the first in a series of preauthorized remittance transfers, and each subsequent preauthorized remittance transfer, the remittance transfer provider may estimate the following information: (1) the exchange rate, (2) the transfer amount in the currency in which the funds will be received by the designated recipient, (3) covered third-party fees in the currency in which the funds will be received by the designated recipient; and (4) the amount that will be received by the designated recipient in the currency in which the funds will be received.[98] If at the time the sender schedules a remittance transfer five or more business days before the date of transfer, the provider agrees to a sender's request to fix the amount to be transferred in the currency in which the remittance transfer will be received and not the currency in which it is funded, estimates may also be provided for the following amounts: (1) the amount that will be transferred to the designated recipient, in the currency in which the remittance transfer is funded; (2) any fees imposed and any taxes collected on the remittance transfer by the provider, in the currency in which the remittance transfer is funded;

---

94. 12 C.F.R. § 1005.32(b)(1).
95. *Id.* § 1005.32(b)(1).
96. *Id.* § 1005.32(b)(1)(i).
97. *Id.* § 1005.32(b)(1)(ii).
98. *Id.* § 1005.32(b)(2)(i).

and (3) the sum of the transfer amount and applicable fees and taxes in the currency in which the remittance transfer is funded.[99]

Two exceptions apply to the above.[100] First, covered third-party fees may only be estimated if the exchange rate is also estimated and the estimated exchange rate affects the amount of the fees.[101] Second, the applicable transfer fees and taxes may only be estimated if the amount that will be transferred in the currency in which it is funded is also estimated and the estimated amount affects the amount of such fees and taxes.[102]

4.2.3 Transfer Initiated by Certain Insured Institutions

Effective July 21, 2020, an insured institution may estimate the exchange rate to be used for the remittance transfer and may also estimate covered third-party fees so long as certain conditions are satisfied.[103] For purposes of the Remittance Transfer Rule, *insured institutions* are " insured depository institutions (which includes uninsured U.S. branches and agencies of foreign depository institutions) as defined in section 3 of the Federal Deposit Insurance Act (12 U.S.C. 1813), and insured credit unions as defined in section 101 of the Federal Credit Union Act (12 U.S.C. 1752)."[104]

First, an insured institution may estimate the applicable exchange rate and other disclosures that depend on the exchange rate for a remittance transfer to a particular country if the designated recipient will receive funds in that particular country's local currency and all the following conditions are satisfied:

- At the time the insured institution must provide applicable disclosures to the sender, the insured institution cannot determine the exact exchange rate for that remittance transfer;
- The insured institution made 1,000 or fewer remittance transfers in the prior calendar year to the particular country for which the designated recipients of those transfers received funds in the country's local currency; and
- The remittance transfer is sent from the sender's account with the insured institution.[105]

---

99. *Id.*

100. *See id.* § 1005.32(b)(2)(ii)–(iii).

101. *Id.* § 1005.32(b)(2)(ii).

102. *Id.* § 1005.32(b)(2)(iii).

103. 85 Fed. Reg. 34870, 34904 (June 5, 2020) (to be codified at 12 C.F.R. § 1005.32(b)(4), (5)).

104. 12 C.F.R. § 1005.32(a)(3).

105. 85 Fed. Reg. at 34904 (to be codified at 12 C.F.R. § 1005.32(b)(4)).

Second, an insured institution may estimate covered third-party fees and other disclosures that depend on covered third-party fees to a particular designated recipient's institution if all the following conditions are satisfied:

- At the time the insured institution must provide applicable disclosures to the sender, the insured institution cannot determine the exact covered third-party fees;
- Either (i) the insured institution made 500 or fewer remittance transfers in the prior calendar year to that designated recipient's institution, or (ii) federal law prohibits the insured institution from being able to determine the exact covered third-party fees; and
- The remittance transfer is sent from the sender's account with the insured institution.[106]

4.3 Bases for Estimates Generally

This section explains how estimates made pursuant to the exceptions for financial institutions and transfers to certain countries are calculated. Section 4.4 applies to estimates for transfers scheduled before the date of transfer.

Although the Remittance Transfer Rule outlines how estimates for the exceptions for financial institutions and transfers to certain countries should be calculated, it also permits a remittance transfer provider to use other methods "so long as the designated recipient receives the same, or greater, amount of funds" than the remittance transfer provider disclosed as the total to be received by the recipient in the currency in which the funds will be received.[107]

- *Estimated exchange rate.* When disclosing an estimated exchange rate, the estimate must be based on one of the following:
    - The most recent publicly available wholesale exchange rate and, if applicable, any spread that the remittance transfer provider or its correspondent typically applies to such a wholesale rate for remittance transfers for that currency;
    - The most recent exchange rate offered or used by the person making funds available directly to the designated recipient or by the person setting the exchange rate; or
    - For remittance transfers sent by an automated clearing house to countries that qualify for the exception for transfers sent to certain countries, the estimated exchange rate must be based on the most recent exchange rate set by the designated recipient

106. 85 Fed. Reg. at 34904 (to be codified at 12 C.F.R. § 1005.32(b)(5)).
107. 12 C.F.R. § 1005.32(c).

country's central bank or other governmental authority and reported by a Federal Reserve Bank.[108]

- *Transfer amount in recipient currency.* When disclosing an estimated transfer amount in the currency in which the funds will be received by the designated recipient, an estimate must be based on the estimated exchange rate, prior to any rounding of the estimated exchange rate.[109]

- *Covered third-party fees.*
    - Percentage-based fees. When disclosing covered third-party fees that are a percentage of the amount transferred to the designated recipient, an estimated exchange rate must be based on the estimated exchange rate, prior to any rounding of the estimated exchange rate.[110]
    - Fees imposed by the intermediary or financial institution. When disclosing covered third-party fees, an estimate must be based on one of the following: (i) the remittance transfer provider's most recent remittance transfer to the designated recipient's institution, or (ii) a representative transmittal route identified by the remittance transfer provider.[111]
- *Total to be received.* The total amount to be received by the designated recipient, except that this amount may not include noncovered third-party fees or taxes collected on the remittance transfer by a person other than the provider.[112]

4.4 Bases for Estimates for Transfers Scheduled before the Date of Transfer

When calculating estimates for remittance transfers scheduled before the date of transfer, the remittance transfer provider must base the estimate on the exchange rate or, where applicable, the estimated exchange rate that the provider would have used or did use that day in providing disclosures to a sender requesting such a remittance transfer to be made on the same day.[113] A provider will be deemed to be in compliance with these requirements regardless of the amount received by the designated recipient, so long as the estimation methodology is the same that the provider would have used

108. *Id.* § 1005.32(c)(1).
109. *Id.* § 1005.32(c)(2).
110. *Id.* § 1005.32(c)(3)(i).
111. *Id.* § 1005.32(c)(3)(ii).
112. *Id.* § 1005.32(c)(4).
113. *Id.* § 1005.32(d).

or did use in providing disclosures to a sender requesting such remittance transfer to be made on the same day.[114]

5. Procedures for Resolving Errors

5.1 Definition of Error

The Remittance Transfer Rule employs a different definition of error than the definition used in subpart A of Regulation E.[115] Each of the following five scenarios constitute an error for purposes of the Remittance Transfer Rule:

1. An *incorrect amount paid by a sender* in connection with a remittance transfer unless the prepayment disclosure for a transfer scheduled by a sender five or more business days before the date of the transfer stated an estimate of the amount paid by the sender and the difference results from application of the actual exchange rate, fees, and taxes, rather than any estimated amount.[116]
2. A *computational or bookkeeping error* made by the remittance transfer provider relating to a remittance transfer.[117]
3. The *failure to make available to a designated recipient the amount of currency disclosed in the prepayment disclosure and stated in the receipt or combined disclosure* for the remittance transfer unless one of the following applies: (i) the disclosure stated an estimate of the amount to be received and the difference results from application of the actual exchange rate, fees, and taxes, rather than any estimated amounts; (ii) the failure resulted from extraordinary circumstances outside the remittance transfer provider's control that could not have been reasonably anticipated; or (iii) the difference results from the application of noncovered third-party fees or taxes collected on the remittance transfer by a person other than the provider and the provider properly disclosed such fees.[118]
4. The *failure to make funds available to a designated recipient by the date of availability stated in the receipt or combined disclosure* provided to the sender unless the failure to make the funds available resulted from one of the following: (i) extraordinary circumstances outside the remittance transfer provider's control that could not have been reasonably anticipated; (ii) delays related to a necessary investigation or other special action by the remittance transfer provider or a third party as required

114. *Id.*
115. *See id.* § 1005.11(a)(1).
116. *Id.* § 1005.33(a)(1)(i).
117. *Id.* § 1005.33(a)(1)(ii).
118. *Id.* § 1005.33(a)(1)(iii).

by the provider's fraud screening procedures or in accordance with the Bank Secrecy Act, Office of Foreign Assets Control requirements, or similar laws or requirements; or (iii) the remittance transfer was made with fraudulent intent by the sender or any person acting in concert with the sender.[119] Additionally, the failure to make funds available to a designated recipient by the date of availability stated in the receipt or combined disclosure provided to the sender does not constitute an error if the sender gave the remittance transfer provider an incorrect account number or recipient institution identifier for the designated recipient's account or institution, so long as certain conditions are satisfied.[120]

5. The *sender's request for a prepayment disclosure, receipt, or combined disclosure or for additional information or clarification* concerning a remittance transfer, including a request that a sender makes to determine whether an error exists under one of the scenarios listed in items 1 to 4 of this list.[121]

5.2 Notice of Error from Sender

A remittance transfer provider must investigate and comply with the associated requirements with respect to any oral or written notice of error from a sender if the notice satisfies certain criteria. The remittance transfer provider is only obligated to investigate a notice of error received from the sender and is not obligated to do so when an error is identified by the designated recipient or by the provider and the provider corrects the error.[122]

To be valid, the notice of error must:

1. Be received by the remittance transfer provider no later than 180 days after the disclosed date of availability of the remittance transfer;
2. Enable the provider to identify: (i) the sender's name and telephone number or address, (ii) the designated recipient's name and, if known, the recipient's telephone number or address, and (iii) the remittance transfer to which the notice of error applies; and
3. Indicate why the sender believes an error exists and include, to the extent possible, the type, date, and amount of the error, except for requests for documentation, additional information, or clarification.[123]

119. *Id.* § 1005.33(a)(1)(iv)(A)–(C).
120. *Id.* § 1005.33(a)(1)(iv)(D), (h).
121. *Id.* § 1005.33(a)(1)(v).
122. 12 C.F.R. § 1005, supp. I, cmt. 33(b)-1.
123. 12 C.F.R. § 1005.33(b)(1).

The notice of error is effective so long as the remittance transfer provider is able to identify the above elements.[124]

5.3 Time Limits and Extent of Investigation

5.3.1 Time Limits to Complete Investigation after Receiving Notice of Error

Upon receiving a valid notice of error, a remittance transfer provider must investigate the asserted error "promptly" and, within ninety days of receiving such notice, determine whether an error occurred.[125] Within three business days after completing the investigation, the remittance transfer provider must report the results of the investigation to the sender and notify the sender of any remedies available for correcting the identified error.[126] The remittance transfer provider may notify the sender of the investigation findings either orally or in writing if the provider has determined that the error occurred as described by the sender.[127]

5.3.2 Remedies for Errors Identified during an Investigation

5.3.2.1 Remedies Generally

The Remittance Transfer Rule provides a specific remedy for each type of error.[128] Regardless of the type of error asserted, if the remittance transfer provider determines an error occurred, the provider must correct the error in the manner requested by the sender within "one business day of, or as soon as reasonably practicable after, receiving the sender's instructions regarding the appropriate remedy."[129] The one exception to these timing requirements is for errors involving a failure to make funds available to a designated recipient by the date of availability stated in the receipt or combined disclosure.[130] A remittance transfer provider may elect to correct an error without investigating the asserted error as directed by the sender so long as the provider complies with all provisions of the Remittance Transfer Rule provisions concerning the time limits and remedies related to error investigations.[131]

As discussed below, certain remedies require the remittance transfer provider to make an "amount appropriate to resolve the error" available to the sender or to the designated recipient.[132] Under the Remittance Transfer Rule, the "amount appropriate

124. 12 C.F.R. § 1005, supp. I, cmt. 33(b)-2.
125. 12 C.F.R. § 1005.33(c)(1).
126. *Id.*
127. 12 C.F.R. § 1005, supp. I, cmt. 33(c)-1.
128. *See* 12 C.F.R. § 1005.33(c)(2).
129. *Id.*
130. *Id.* § 1005.33(c)(2).
131. 12 C.F.R. § 1005, supp. I, cmt. 33(c)-10.
132. *See* 12 C.F.R. § 1005.33(c)(2).

to resolve the error" is "the specific amount of transferred funds that should have been received if the remittance transfer had been effected without error."[133] Other remedies require the remittance transfer provider to issue a refund to the sender.[134] The refund may be issued, in the provider's discretion, in either cash or the same form of payment initially used by the sender.[135]

5.3.2.2 Errors Involving Incorrect Amounts Paid by a Sender, Computational and Bookkeeping Errors, and Failure to Make Available the Disclosed Currency Amount

Subject to one exception, the Remittance Transfer Rule prescribes the same remedies for the following types of errors: (1) incorrect amount paid by a sender, (2) computational or bookkeeping error, and (3) failure to make available to a designated recipient the disclosed amount of currency.[136] Such errors must be remedied by either: (1) issuing a refund to the sender in the amount paid by the sender in connection with the improperly transmitted remittance or in an amount appropriate to resolve the error, or (2) making the amount appropriate to resolve the error available to the designated recipient at no additional cost to the sender or designated recipient.[137]

However, for errors involving the sender paying an incorrect amount, the sender may request that the remittance transfer provider either: (1) refund the amount appropriate to resolve the error, or (2) make the amount necessary to resolve the error available to the designated recipient at no additional cost.[138]

5.3.2.3 Errors Involving a Failure to Make Funds Available to a Designated Recipient by the Disclosed Date of Availability

Generally speaking, errors concerning a failure to make funds available to a designated recipient by the disclosed date of availability must be remedied by: (1) as applicable, either (a) refunding to the sender the amount of funds provided by the sender or the amount "appropriate" to resolve the error, or (b) making available to the designated recipient the amount "appropriate" to resolve the error at no additional cost to the sender or designated recipient; and (2) refunding to the sender any fees imposed and, to the extent allowable under law, taxes collected on the remittance transfer.[139]

As noted above, there is an exception to the general rule concerning remedies for errors involving a failure to make funds available to a designated recipient by the

133. 12 C.F.R. § 1005, supp. I, cmt. 33(c)-5.

134. *See* 12 C.F.R. § 1005.33(c)(2).

135. 12 C.F.R. § 1005, supp. I, cmt. 33(c)-6.

136. 12 C.F.R. § 1005.33(c)(2)(i).

137. *Id.*

138. 12 C.F.R. § 1005, supp. I, cmt. 33(c)-7.

139. 12 C.F.R. § 1005.33(c)(2)(ii).

date of availability stated in the receipt or combined disclosures.[140] If the failure to make funds available to a designated recipient by the date of availability stated in the receipt or combined disclosures is due to the sender providing incorrect or insufficient information in connection with the remittance transfer, then the remittance transfer provider must, within three business days of notifying the sender of the provider's error investigation determination: (1) refund to the sender the amount of funds provided by the sender or the amount "appropriate" to resolve the error; and (2) refund the sender any fees imposed and, to the extent allowable under law, taxes collected on the remittance transfer.[141] Alternatively, the remittance transfer provider may agree to the sender's request to have the funds applied to a new remittance transfer in lieu of a refund if the provider has not yet processed the refund.[142]

5.3.2.4 Errors Involving Requests for Documentation, Information, or Clarification

For errors involving a sender's request for a prepayment disclosure, receipt, or combined disclosure, or for additional information or clarification concerning a remittance transfer, the remedy is to provide the requested information.[143]

5.4 Procedures If Remittance Transfer Provider Determines No Error or Different Error Occurred

If, after investigating a notice of error, the remittance transfer provider determines that the asserted error did not occur, the provider must still provide a report to the sender notifying the sender of the provider's determination as to whether the asserted error occurred.[144] The provider must also provide such a report if the provider determines that an error occurred different from the manner or amount asserted by the sender.[145]

The report that an error did not occur or that an error occurred in a manner or amount different from that asserted by the sender must address the sender's specific complaint.[146] Such report must also provide a written explanation of the provider's findings and a notice of the sender's right to request the documents that the provider relied upon to make its final determination.[147] If a provider determines that an error occurred in a manner or amount different from that asserted by the sender, the provider may notify the sender of such determination.[148]

140. *See id.* § 1005.33(c)(2)(iii).
141. *Id.*
142. *Id.*
143. *Id.* § 1005.33(c)(2)(iv).
144. *See id.* § 1005.33(d).
145. *See id.*
146. *Id.* § 1005.33(d)(1).
147. *Id.*
148. 12 C.F.R. § 1005, supp. I, cmt. 33(d)-1.

5.5 Reassertion of Error

Generally speaking, if the remittance transfer provider has properly completed its error resolution obligations under the Remittance Transfer Rule, then the provider does not have further investigation obligations in the event that the sender reasserts the same error.[149] However, if the error asserted by the sender follows from the sender's request for documentation or additional information or clarification, then the remittance transfer provider must comply with the Remittance Transfer Rule error resolution provisions as to this error.[150]

5.6 Relation to Other Laws

An asserted error related to a remittance transfer can also implicate error resolution provisions in subpart A of Regulation E or the Truth in Lending Act and its implementing regulation, Regulation Z.[151] First, as to Regulation E, section 11 of subpart A contains a different definition of error from that found in the Remittance Transfer Rule.[152] Section 11 of subpart A imposes specific error resolution obligations for such errors.[153] One type of such error is an "incorrect electronic fund transfer to or from the consumer's account."[154] Under the Remittance Transfer Rule, if an error is alleged concerning a remittance transfer and such error involves an incorrect electronic fund transfer from a sender's account and the sender notifies the account-holding institution of the alleged error, then the account-holding institution must comply with the error resolution provisions in section 11 of subpart A of Regulation E instead of those found in the Remittance Transfer Rule unless the account-holding institution is also the remittance transfer provider.[155] If the account-holding institution is also the remittance transfer provider, then the error resolution provisions of the Remittance Transfer Rule apply to the resolution of the notice of error.[156]

Second, the error resolution provisions in section 13 of Regulation Z may be implicated when an alleged error involves one of the following: (1) an incorrect extension of credit associated with the remittance transfer; (2) an incorrect amount received by the designated recipient related to the provider's failure to make available to a designated recipient the amount of currency disclosed in the prepayment disclosure and stated in the receipt or combined disclosure; or (3) the failure to make funds available by the date of availability disclosed on a receipt or combined disclosure

149. 12 C.F.R. § 1005.33(e).

150. *Id.*

151. *See id.* § 1005.33(f).

152. *See id.* § 1005.33(f)(1).

153. *See id.* § 1005.11.

154. *Id.* § 1005.11(a)(1)(ii).

155. *Id.* § 1005.33(f)(1).

156. *Id.*

that is an extension of credit for property or services not delivered as agreed.[157] If a sender provides a notice of one such type of error to the creditor that extended the credit, then the error resolution provisions in section 13 of Regulation Z apply to the creditor regardless of whether the creditor is also the remittance transfer provider, with one exception.[158] The one exception to this rule is that if the creditor is also the remittance transfer provider, then the notice of error provisions of the Remittance Transfer Rule apply and not those of section 13 of Regulation Z.[159] However, if the sender sends a notice of error implicating one of the three types of Regulation Z-related errors described above to the remittance transfer provider, and such provider is not also the creditor, then the Remittance Transfer Rule error resolution provisions apply to the provider.[160]

Finally, both subpart A of Regulation E and Regulation Z contain resolution provisions specific to unauthorized transactions.[161] If an alleged remittance transfer error involves an unauthorized electronic funds transfer, then the provisions concerning unauthorized transfers in subpart A of Regulation E apply to the account-holding institution.[162] Consequently, a financial institution that is also the remittance transfer provider may be subject to the error resolution obligations in subpart A of Regulation E and the Remittance Transfer Rule.[163] Alternatively, if an alleged remittance transfer error involves an unauthorized use of a credit account, then the provisions concerning the unauthorized use of a credit card, if applicable, and error resolution obligations in sections 12 and 13 of Regulation Z, apply to the creditor.[164] This provision does not limit the sender's rights to assert claims and defenses against a card issuer regarding property or services purchased with a credit card under section 12 of Regulation Z.[165]

5.7 Error Resolution Standards and Recordkeeping Requirements

The Remittance Transfer Rule requires a remittance transfer provider to develop and maintain written policies and procedures designed to ensure compliance with the provider's error resolution obligations under the rule.[166] Such policies and procedures must address, at a minimum, specified recordkeeping requirements concerning documentation related to error investigations.[167] Additionally, remittance

157. *Id.* § 1005.33(f)(2).
158. *Id.*
159. *Id.*
160. *Id.*
161. *Id.* § 1005.33(f)(3).
162. *Id.*
163. 12 C.F.R. § 1005, supp. I, cmt. 33(f)-1.
164. 12 C.F.R. § 1005.33(f)(3).
165. 12 C.F.R. § 1005, supp. I, cmt. 33(f)-2.
166. 12 C.F.R. § 1005.33(g)(1).
167. *Id.* § 1005.33(g)(2).

transfer providers must comply with the record retention requirements in subpart A of Regulation E.[168] The provider is not required to maintain records of individual disclosures provided to each sender, but the provider must retain evidence demonstrating that the provider's procedures "reasonably ensure" that a consumer receives the required disclosures and documentation.[169]

6. Right of Cancellation and Refund of Remittance Transfers

The Remittance Transfer Rule provides a sender with a right to cancel a remittance transfer and obtain a refund.[170] A remittance transfer provider must cancel the transfer and issue a refund in response to the sender's request, whether oral or written, if the cancellation request: (1) is received by the provider no later than thirty minutes after the sender pays for the remittance transfer, and (2) enables the provider to identify the sender's name and address or telephone number and the particular transfer to be cancelled.[171] Additionally, the provider is only required to cancel the transfer and issue a refund if the designated recipient has not received the funds by either picking up the funds or having the funds deposited into their account.[172] Within three business days of receiving the sender's cancellation request, the remittance transfer provider must, at no additional cost to the sender, refund the total amount of funds provided by the sender, which may include any fees and, to the extent not prohibited by law, taxes imposed related to the transfer.[173]

7. Remittance Transfers Scheduled before the Date of Transfer

7.1 Timing

The Remittance Transfer Rule imposes special requirements for remittance transfers scheduled to occur at a later date;[174] however, unless otherwise specified, such transfers remain subject to all other requirements found in the Remittance Transfer Rule.[175] For a one-time transfer scheduled five or more business days before the date of transfer or

168. *See id.* § 1005.13.
169. *Id.* § 1005.33(g)(2).
170. *See id.* § 1005.34.
171. *Id.* § 1005.34(a).
172. *Id.*
173. *Id.* § 1005.34(b).
174. *See id.* § 1005.36.
175. 12 C.F.R. § 1005, supp. I, cmt. 36-1.

for the first in a series of preauthorized remittance transfers, the remittance transfer provider must provide the sender with either a prepayment disclosure and receipt or a combined disclosure pursuant to the timelines described above.[176] If a disclosure includes estimates, then the provider must mail or deliver an updated receipt to the sender no later than one business day after the date of the transfer.[177] However, if the remittance transfer involves the transfer of funds from the sender's account held by the provider, then the receipt may be included on or with the next account statement, or if a statement is not provided, then within thirty days after the date of the transfer.[178]

Additional disclosure requirements apply to subsequent preauthorized remittance transfers if there has been a change to the information contained in the most recent receipt provided to the sender other than the date of availability and transfer date or as otherwise permitted for estimates.[179] First, if there has been such a change, then the remittance transfer provider must give the sender an updated receipt.[180] The updated receipt must be mailed or delivered to the sender within a "reasonable" time before the next preauthorized remittance transfer is scheduled to occur.[181] An updated receipt is deemed to have been mailed or delivered within a "reasonable" time if the provider has mailed the receipt no later than ten business days prior to the scheduled transfer date or has delivered the receipt by hand or electronically no later than five business days prior to the scheduled transfer date.[182] This timing also applies to other updated disclosures concerning subsequent preauthorized remittance transfers.[183] The updated receipt must also "clearly and conspicuously" notify the consumer that the receipt contains updated information.[184]

Finally, unless the initial disclosure did not contain any estimates, the remittance transfer provider must mail or deliver a receipt to the sender no later than one business day after the transfer date.[185] However, if the remittance transfer involves the transfer of funds from the sender's account held by the provider, then the updated receipt may be included on or with the next account statement, or if a statement is not provided, then within thirty days after the date of the transfer.[186]

---

176. 12 C.F.R. § 1005.36(a)(1)(i).
177. *Id.* § 1005.36(a)(1)(ii).
178. *Id.*
179. *See id.* § 1005.36(a)(2).
180. *Id.* § 1005.36(a)(2)(i).
181. *Id.*
182. 12 C.F.R. § 1005, supp. I, cmt. 36(a)-3.
183. 12 C.F.R. § 1005.36(a)(2)(iii).
184. *Id.* § 1005.36(a)(2)(i).
185. *Id.* § 1005.36(a)(2)(ii).
186. *Id.*

7.2. Accuracy

For a one-time transfer scheduled five or more business days before the date of transfer or for the first in a series of preauthorized remittance transfers, the prepayment disclosure and receipt or the combined disclosure must be accurate at the time the sender pays for the transfer, except to the extent estimates are allowed.[187] For each subsequent preauthorized remittance transfer, the information on the most recent receipt must be accurate at the time of the transfer, except that the date of availability and transfer date must only be accurate if the disclosures are for the first transfer after the original disclosure was provided and, to the extent permitted, estimates.[188] Finally, the information contained in disclosures provided due to estimates in the original disclosures must be accurate at the time of the transfer to which the disclosure pertains unless the remittance transfer is eligible for the exemption for financial institutions or transfers to certain countries.[189]

7.3 Cancellation

A sender is entitled to cancel a remittance transfer scheduled at least three business days before the scheduled date of the transfer regardless of whether the transfer is a one-time transfer or part of a series of recurring transfers.[190] For such transfers, a remittance transfer provider must cancel the transfer upon the sender's oral or written request so long as the cancellation request enables the provider to identify the sender's name and address or telephone number and the specific transfer to be cancelled and the provider receives the request at least three business days prior to the scheduled transfer date.[191]

7.4 Additional Requirements for Subsequent Preauthorized Remittance Transfers

A remittance transfer provider has additional disclosure obligations as to subsequent preauthorized remittance transfers.[192] For each subsequent remittance transfer in a

187. *Id.* § 1005.36(b)(1).
188. *Id.* § 1005.36(b)(2).
189. *Id.* § 1005.36(b)(3).
190. *See id.* § 1005.36(c); 12 C.F.R. § 1005, supp. I, cmt. 36(c)-1.
191. 12 C.F.R. § 1005.36(c).
192. *See id.* § 1005.36(d).

series of preauthorized remittance transfers, the provider must disclose to the sender the following information:

- the date the provider will make the next transfer;
- a statement of the sender's cancellation rights; and
- the provider's name, telephone number, and website.[193]

A provider may describe the future transfer date as occurring in regular periodic intervals as opposed to a specific calendar date(s), but the provider must identify any future transfer date(s) that will not conform to the identified interval.[194] The information in the disclosure must be accurate as of the day on which the transfer to which the disclosure pertains occurs.[195]

The subsequent preauthorized remittance transfer disclosures must be received by the sender no more than twelve months, and no less than five business days, prior to the date of any subsequent transfer to which the disclosure pertains.[196] The disclosures may be provided in a separate disclosure or on another disclosure otherwise required under the Remittance Transfer Rule related to the same series of preauthorized remittance transfers.[197] If the transfer date of a subsequent preauthorized remittance transfer is four or fewer business days following the payment date for that transfer, then the disclosures for the subsequent transfer must be provided on or with the receipt or the disclosures provided for the initial transfer requested via telephone, mobile application, or text message.[198]

193. *Id.* § 1005.36(d)(1)(i).
194. *Id.* § 1005.36(d)(1)(ii).
195. *Id.* § 1005.36(d)(4).
196. *Id.* § 1005.36(d)(2)(i).
197. *Id.*
198. 12 C.F.R. § 1005.36(d)(2)(ii).

CHAPTER

11

Debt Collection Practices

Robert Maddox, Lee Gilley, R. Aaron Chastain,
Jonathan R. Kolodziej, and Riley Key

1. Introduction and Overview

Congress enacted the Fair Debt Collection Practices Act (FDCPA) in 1977 in response to the "abundant evidence of the use of abusive, deceptive, and unfair debt collection practices by many debt collectors."[1] Congress further found that these abusive, deceptive, and unfair debt collection practices caused a number of harms, including "personal bankruptcies, . . . marital instability, . . . the loss of jobs, and . . . invasions of individual privacy,"[2] and that "[e]xisting laws and procedures for redressing those injuries are inadequate to protect consumers."[3] Thus, the stated purpose of the FDCPA is "to eliminate abusive debt collection practices by debt collectors, to insure that those debt collectors who refrain from using abusive debt collection practices are not competitively disadvantaged, and to promote consistent State action to protect consumers against debt collection abuses."[4]

The FDCPA operates by imposing certain affirmative requirements on entities falling within the statutory definition of "debt collector," and by further restricting certain conduct by debt collectors. The FDCPA specifically bans various forms of harassment, false or misleading statements, inappropriate communications, and

---

1. Pub. L. No. 95-109, 91 Stat. 874 (1977) (codified as amended at 15 U.S.C. § 1692(a) (2018)).

2. *Id.*

3. *Id.* § 1692(b).

4. *Id.* § 1692(e).

various other unfair practices, including the collection of amounts not authorized by the agreement creating the debt or permitted by applicable law.[5] In addition to the restrictions set forth in the FDCPA, the act also requires debt collectors to provide consumers with certain information to validate the debt, including the amount of the debt and the name of the creditor to whom the debt is owed.[6] To the extent a debt collector violates the FDCPA, the law also creates a private right of action, as well as a mechanism for administrative enforcement.[7]

Prior to the enactment of the Dodd-Frank Act, Congress had not delegated to any agency the authority to issue substantive rules to interpret the FDCPA. As a result, for the first thirty years of its existence, the FDCPA's interpretation was left largely to the federal courts, which interpreted the FDCPA in small stages in the course of adjudicating lawsuits typically brought under the FDCPA's private right of action.

The Dodd-Frank Act gave the Consumer Financial Protection Bureau (CFPB) authority to issue substantive rules interpreting the FDCPA.[8] After a lengthy process, on May 7, 2019, the CFPB formally issued a Notice of Proposed Rulemaking, proposing a new and detailed Regulation F, which would include a nearly comprehensive set of regulations interpreting and implementing the FDCPA. The comment period (which the CFPB extended) closed on September 19, 2019. As of the date of this writing, the CFPB has not issued final rules or announced a timetable for finalizing the rules (which agencies generally do not do). This chapter discusses various aspects of the rules proposed by the CFPB. Significant proposed changes to current interpretations of the FDCPA are noted in the text below.

2. Who Can Sue under the FDCPA?

As with many federal consumer protection statutes, the first question is which entities have standing to enforce the provisions of the FDCPA. The FDCPA includes enforcement options for federal regulatory agencies, as well as a private right of action for consumers harmed by violations.

2.1 Administrative Enforcement

The FDCPA provides various federal agencies with the authority to enforce the FDCPA's requirements.[9] Most notably, the Federal Trade Commission (FTC) and the CFPB share enforcement powers under the law with respect to entities that may qualify as

5. *See, e.g., id.* §§ 1692c–f.
6. *Id.* § 1692g.
7. *Id.* §§ 1692k–l.
8. Pub. L. No. 111-203, 124 Stat. 1376 (2010).
9. 15 U.S.C. § 1692l(a), (c).

debt collectors under the FDCPA.[10] The FTC obtains its authority under the Federal Trade Commission Act (FTCA),[11] and the FDCPA specifically provides that a violation of the FDCPA is an unfair act or practice in violation of the FTCA.[12] The CFPB, on the other hand, obtains its authority from Title X of the Dodd-Frank Act,[13] and the FDCPA also makes clear that a violation of the FDCPA is also a violation of Title X.[14]

To facilitate the shared enforcement of the FDCPA with respect to debt collectors, the FTC and the CFPB have a formal agreement in place that outlines how the two agencies coordinate with one another. The FTC and the CFPB first signed a memorandum of understanding with a three-year term in 2012.[15] The agreement was reauthorized in 2015, and then again on February 25, 2019.[16] The most recent version is set to remain in effect "unless superseded by signed, mutual agreement of the agencies."[17] The agreement explains that "effective cooperation is critical to protect consumers, prevent duplication of efforts, provide consistency and ensure a vibrant marketplace for Consumer Financial Products or Services."[18] Among other things, the agreement between the agencies outlines how they will handle enforcement, investigations, rulemaking, providing guidance, supervision and examinations, and consumer complaints.[19]

The FTC and the CFPB actively enforce violations of the FDCPA. In 2018, for example, the FTC filed or resolved seven cases against fifty-two defendants, resulting in $58.9 million in judgments.[20] The CFPB brought six actions alleging FDCPA violations in 2018, one of which resulted in an $800,000 civil money penalty.[21]

---

10. Although various federal banking regulators, the Secretary of Transportation, and the Secretary of Agriculture also have enforcement authority over various entities, the FTC and the CFPB take the most active role in enforcing the FDCPA.

11. 15 U.S.C. §§ 41–58.

12. *Id.* § 1692l(a).

13. Pub. L. No. 111-203, 124 Stat. 1376 (2010) (codified as amended as 12 U.S.C. § 5511).

14. 15 U.S.C. § 1692l(c).

15. CFPB & FTC, Memorandum of Understanding (2012), https://www.ftc.gov/system/files/120123ftc-cfpb-mou.pdf.

16. CFPB & FTC, Memorandum of Understanding (2015), https://www.ftc.gov/system/files/documents/cooperation_agreements/150312ftc-cfpb-mou.pdf; CFPB & FTC, Memorandum of Understanding (2019), https://www.ftc.gov/system/files/documents/cooperation_agreements/ftc-cfpb_mou_225_0.pdf.

17. CFPB & FTC, Memorandum of Understanding 13 (2019), https://www.ftc.gov/system/files/documents/cooperation_agreements/ftc-cfpb_mou_225_0.pdf.

18. *Id.* at 1.

19. *Id.* at 3–10.

20. CFPB, Annual Report 2019: Fair Debt Collection Practices Act 3 (Mar. 2019), https://files.consumerfinance.gov/f/documents/cfpb_fdcpa_annual-report-congress_03-2019.pdf.

21. *Id.* at 23.

2.2 Private Right of Action

The FDCPA provides individuals with the ability to enforce the specific requirements of the law through private litigation. Specifically, a debt collector can be held civilly liable for any violation of the FDCPA. Actions can be brought in any court of competent jurisdiction, but any such claims must be made within one year from the date on which the violation occurs.[22] Actions against debt collectors may be brought individually or as a class.

Successful litigants alleging violations of the FDCPA can recover any actual damage sustained as a result of the debt collector's compliance failure, as well as the costs of the action and reasonable attorney's fees, as determined by the court.[23] Individual litigants who are successful in their suit can recover an additional amount that is determined by the court up to $1,000.[24] Unnamed members of a successful class action can recover an additional amount that is to be determined by the court, but it cannot exceed $500,000 or 1 percent of the net worth of the debt collector, whichever is less.[25] Named plaintiffs in a successful class action can recover the same additional amounts as individual litigants.[26] When determining the discretionary amounts to award to individual plaintiffs or members of a class action, the court must consider:

- the frequency and persistence of noncompliance by the debt collector;
- the nature of such noncompliance; and
- the extent to which such noncompliance was intentional.[27]

In a class action suit, the court must also consider:

- the resources of the debt collector, and
- the number of persons adversely affected.[28]

There is a circuit split as to whether an award of attorneys' fees is appropriate when the borrower prevails but fails to recover any damages. In *Johnson v. Eaton*,[29] the court held that an action without damages was not a successful action and, as a result, the debtor was not entitled to an award of attorneys' fees. However, in the Second Circuit, the prevailing plaintiff is entitled to attorneys' fees regardless of whether the plaintiff recovered any damages.[30] Moreover, the Third, Fourth, and Seventh Circuits

---

22. 15 U.S.C. § 1692k(d).
23. *Id.* § 1692k(a).
24. *Id.*
25. *Id.*
26. *Id.*
27. *Id.* § 1692k(b).
28. *Id.*
29. 80 F.3d 148 (5th Cir. 1996).
30. Emanuel v. Am. Credit Exch., 870 F.2d 805, 809 (2d Cir. 1989).

have indicated a level of agreement with the Second Circuit's position, finding an award of attorneys' fees is appropriate following even a de minis recovery.[31]

If a court determines that a suit alleging FDCPA violations was brought in bad faith and for the purpose of harassment, it can award the debt collector reasonable attorney's fees and costs.[32]

3. Who Can Be Sued under the FDCPA?

Keeping with the stated purpose of "eliminat[ing] abusive debt collection practices by debt collectors" and "promot[ing] consistent State action to protect consumers against debt collection abuses," the operative provisions of the FDCPA primarily govern "debt collectors."[33] The FDCPA gives a private cause of action to bring a lawsuit for a violation of the FDCPA against a "debt collector."[34] Thus, as the federal courts have often observed, "[t]he requirements of the FDCPA apply 'only to professional debt collectors.'"[35]

3.1 Who Is a *Debt Collector?*

Whether a party named as a defendant to an FDCPA claim qualifies as a *debt collector* is a threshold—and often dispositive—question. Section 1692a(6) defines a *debt collector* as

> any person who uses any instrumentality of interstate commerce or the mails in any business the principal purpose of which is the collection of any debts, or who regularly collects or attempts to collect, directly or indirectly, debts owed or due or asserted to be owed or due another.

---

31. *See* Zagorski v. Midwest Billing Servs., Inc., 128 F.3d 1164, 1166 (7th Cir. 1997); Carroll v. Wolpoff & Abramson, 53 F.3d 626, 628 (4th Cir. 1995) (noting that a fee award is appropriate in all but the most unusual of circumstances); Graziano v. Harrison, 950 F.2d 107, 114 (3d Cir. 1991) ("Only in unusual circumstances, however, may the court decline to award a fee").

32. 15 U.S.C. § 1692k(a).

33. *See id.* §§ 1692c–i. The only provision of the FDCPA that appears to apply more broadly is section 812(a), which renders it unlawful "to design, compile, and furnish any form knowing that such form would be used to create the false belief in a consumer that a person other than the creditor of such consumer is participating in the collection of or in an attempt to collect a debt such consumer allegedly owes such creditor." The deceptive forms provisions specifically provide a cause of action against "*any person* who violates this section." *Id.* § 1692j(b) (emphasis added).

34. *Id.* § 1692k(a).

35. Kurtzman v. Nationstar Mortg., LLC, 709 F. app'x 655, 658 (11th Cir. 2017) (quoting Crawford v. LVNV Funding, LLC, 758 F.3d 1254, 1258 n.3 (11th Cir. 2014)); *accord, e.g.*, Neff v. Capital Acquisitions & Mgmt. Co., 352 F.3d 1118, 1121 (7th Cir. 2003).

> Notwithstanding the exclusion provided by clause (F) of the last sentence of this paragraph, the term includes any creditor who, in the process of collecting his own debts, uses any name other than his own which would indicate that a third person is collecting or attempting to collect such debts. For the purposes of section 1692f(6) of this title, such term also includes any person who uses any instrumentality of interstate commerce or the mails in any business the principal purpose of which is the enforcement of security interests. The term does not include –
>
> (A) any officer or employee of a creditor while, in the name of the creditor, collecting debts for such creditor;
> (B) any person while acting as a debt collector for another person, both of whom are related by common ownership or affiliated by corporate control, if the person acting as a debt collector does so only for persons to whom it is so related or affiliated and if the principal business of such person is not the collection of debts;
> (C) any officer or employee of the United States or any State to the extent that collecting or attempting to collect any debt is in the performance of his official duties;
> (D) any person while serving or attempting to serve legal process on any other person in connection with the judicial enforcement of any debt;
> (E) any nonprofit organization which, at the request of consumers, performs bona fide consumer credit counseling and assists consumers in the liquidation of their debts by receiving payments from such consumers and distributing such amounts to creditors; and
> (F) any person collecting or attempting to collect any debt owed or due or asserted to be owed or due another to the extent such activity (i) is incidental to a bona fide fiduciary obligation or a bona fide escrow arrangement; (ii) concerns a debt which was originated by such person; (iii) concerns a debt which was not in default at the time it was obtained by such person; or (iv) concerns a debt obtained by such person as a secured party in a commercial credit transaction involving the credit.[36]

Unsurprisingly, there is an abundance of case law discussing the long and multipart statutory definition of "debt collector." The most significant areas of interpretation are discussed below.

36. 15 U.S.C. § 1692a(6).

3.1.1 "Debt Collectors" v. "Creditors"

For years, many courts interpreted the FDCPA as setting up a binary distinction between a *debt collector* regulated by the FDCPA and a first-party "creditor," which was not.[37] Courts reached this interpretation by focusing on the second part of the first sentence of the definition of *debt collector* as anyone "who regularly collects or attempts to collect, directly or indirectly, debts owed or due or asserted to be owed or due *another*."[38] By necessary implication, most courts reasoned that a party collecting debts *owed to itself* could not be collecting debts owed *another*, and thus would not qualify as a debt collector under this provision.[39] On the other hand, other courts reasoned that because Congress included a specific exception to the statutory definition that only protected "persons collecting or attempting to collect any debt owed or due or asserted to be owed or due *another* to the extent such activity . . . *concerns a debt which was not in default at the time it was obtained by such person*,"[40] the necessary implication was that a party could be a *debt collector* when it collected its own debts, if they were obtained while in default.[41]

The U.S. Supreme Court largely resolved this conflict when it issued its decision in *Henson v. Santander Consumer USA, Inc.*[42] In *Henson*, the unanimous Court reasoned that the exception in section 1692a(6) did not trump the plain language of the definition requiring a *debt collector* to be collecting debts owed "another." The Court further noted that the exception in section 1692a(6)(F)(iii) specifically referred to debts that had been "obtained," a word that signified possession without ownership, and thus did not conflict with the requirement that the debt be owed to another for one to be a debt collector.

But *Henson* was not the end of the discussion. As the Court expressly stated in its decision,[43] it was not answering the question whether a *creditor* might nonetheless qualify as a *debt collector* under the *other* part of the statutory definition: "any person who uses any instrumentality of interstate commerce or the mails in any business the principal purpose of which is the collection of any debts."[44] Since *Henson* was decided, courts have had to interpret that definition as applied to parties that purchased defaulted debts. In *Barbato v. Greystone Alliance, LLC*, the U.S. Court of Appeals for

---

37. *See, e.g.*, Simon v. FIA Card Servs., N.A., 732 F.3d 259, 267 n.4 (3d Cir. 2013); Bridge v. Ocwen Fed. Bank, FSB, 681 F.3d 355, 359 (6th Cir. 2012); Ruth v. Triumph P'ships, 577 F.3d 790, 796–97 (7th Cir. 2009).

38. 15 U.S.C. § 1692a(6).

39. *See* Davidson v. Capital One Bank (USA), N.A., 797 F.3d 1309, 1315–16 (11th Cir. 2015).

40. 15 U.S.C. § 1692a(6)(F) (emphasis added).

41. McKinney v. Cadleway Props., Inc., 548 F.3d 496, 501 (7th Cir. 2008); FTC v. Check Investors, Inc., 502 F.3d 159, 173–74 (3d Cir. 2007).

42. 137 S. Ct. 1718 (2017).

43. *Id.* at 1721.

44. 15 U.S.C. § 1692a(6).

the Third Circuit applied the principal purpose definition to an FDCPA defendant that had purchased the charged-off account in question.

3.1.2 Enforcer of a Security Interest

Another category of potential "debt collectors" are entities that are assigned a debt solely for the purposes of enforcement of a security instrument. Until 2019, the federal appellate courts were split on that question.[45] In *Obduskey v. McCarthy & Holthus LLP*, the Supreme Court resolved the split, holding that when an entity is engaged in "in any business the principal purpose of which is the enforcement of security interests," it does not qualify as a *debt collector* for the general purposes of the FDCPA.[46] The Court based its holding on the fact that section 1692a(6)(f) states that *only for the purposes of that subsection* an entity engaged in the business of enforcing security interests is considered a debt collector. The Court reasoned that, by implication, such an entity is *not* a debt collector for any of the other provisions of the FDCPA.[47]

While the *Obduskey* ruling did provide some much-needed clarification as to whether an entity engaged purely for the purpose of conducting a nonjudicial foreclosure sale qualifies as a debt collector, open questions remain. For instance, the Court left open the possibility that an entity engaged for the purposes of enforcing a security interest (such as a law firm hired to foreclose on real property, or a repossession agent) might nonetheless qualify as a debt collector if it met some other part of the statutory definition—if, for instance, it regularly attempts to collect debts from another.[48]

3.1.3 Loan Servicers

Although the FDCPA defines a debt collector as including any person who "regularly collects or attempts to collect, directly or indirectly, debts owed or due or asserted to be owed or due another," it then provides a broad exception to that definition. Under section 1692a(f)(6), a person is not a debt collector when collecting or attempting to collect a debt owed another:

> to the extent such activity (i) is incidental to a bona fide fiduciary obligation or a bona fide escrow arrangement; (ii) concerns a debt which

---

45. *Compare* Obduskey v. Wells Fargo, 879 F.3d 1216, 1223 (10th Cir. 2018), *and* Vien-Phuong Thi Ho v. ReconTrust Co., NA, 858 F.3d 568, 573 (9th Cir. 2016), *with* Kaymark v. Bank of Am., N.A., 783 F.3d 168, 179 (3d Cir. 2015), *and* Wilson v. Draper & Goldberg, P.L.L.C., 443 F.3d 373, 376 (4th Cir. 2006). The Eleventh Circuit had addressed the same issue and reached a slightly different conclusion, holding that an entity's efforts to enforce a security interest could render it a *debt collector* if the communications served a "dual purpose" of enforcing the security interest and seeking to collect on the underlying debt. Reese v. Ellis, Painter, Ratterree & Adams, LLP, 678 F.3d 1211, 1217–18 (11th Cir. 2012).

46. 139 S. Ct. 1029, 1033 (2019).

47. *Id.* at 1036–37.

48. *Id.* at 1039.

was originated by such person; (iii) concerns a debt which was not in default at the time it was obtained by such person; or (iv) concerns a debt obtained by such person as a secured party in a commercial credit transaction involving the credit.[49]

The question often arises whether a loan servicer—that is, a company assigned the duty of collecting payments on the debt, but which does not actually own the underlying debt—qualifies as a debt collector under the FDCPA. In enacting the FDCPA, Congress intended to answer that question based on the status of the debt when the servicer acquired servicing rights: for debts acquired in default, the servicer does qualify as a debt collector.[50] However, if the servicer acquired servicing rights to the debt while it was not in default, then the servicer does not qualify as a debt collector.

3.2 Vicarious Liability

When a person seeking to collect a debt qualifies as a debt collector under the FDCPA and allegedly violates the FDCPA, the consumer often seeks to hold the alleged violator's employer liable under a theory of vicarious liability.[51] The federal courts have generally held that vicarious liability is available under the FDCPA, so long as the company alleged to be vicariously liable also qualifies as a debt collector under the FDCPA.

A related issue is whether the FDCPA provides a cause of action against an individual member of a limited liability company (LLC) or shareholder of a corporation, when the LLC or corporation qualifies as a debt collector and engages in an alleged violation of the FDCPA. In *Pettit v. Retrieval Masters Creditors Bureau, Inc.*,[52] the U.S. Court of Appeals for the Seventh Circuit rejected a plaintiff's attempt to pursue FDCPA claims against the largest individual shareholder of a debt collector, holding that the shareholder's involvement in the debt collector's operations was "irrelevant to determining his liability under the FDCPA." On the other hand, in *Kistner v. Law Offices of Michael P. Margelefsky, LLC*, the Sixth Circuit held that "subjecting the sole member of an LLC to individual liability for violations of the FDCPA will require proof that the individual is a 'debt collector,' but does not require piercing of the corporate veil."[53]

The *Pettit* and *Kistner* decisions can be reconciled by recognizing that, despite articulating a disagreement, the courts of appeals actually applied the same test to each

49. 15 U.S.C. § 1692a(6)(F).

50. S. Rep. No. 95-382, at 3–4 (1977), *reprinted in* 1977 U.S.C.C.A.N. 1695, 1697–98.

51. *See, e.g.*, Kistner v. Law Offices of Michael P. Margelefsky, LLC, 518 F.3d 433 (6th Cir. 2008).

52. 211 F.3d 1057 (7th Cir. 2000).

53. 518 F.3d at 437–38.

scenario. In each case, a shareholder or member of a debt collector could not be held liable under the FDCPA *solely because of his or her role as a shareholder or member* of the debt collector—in other words, there is not a basis for imposing a "reverse" vicarious liability based on the alleged violations by the statutory debt collector. However, a member or shareholder of a debt collector is not insulated from personal liability when he or she individually qualifies as a debt collector under the FDCPA.

4. Substantive Requirements and Restrictions

4.1 Requirements for Debt Collectors

4.1.1 Debt Validation

Under the FDCPA, a debt collector generally has an obligation to provide the consumer with a debt validation notice.[54] The notice must be in writing and must be sent within five days after the initial communication with a consumer in connection with the collection of any debt.[55] If the initial communication contains the information that would otherwise have to be in the debt validation notice, then a separate notice need not be sent.[56]

Note that, for the purposes of the debt validation requirements, the initial communication in connection with the collection of a debt does not include the sending of a privacy notice as required by the Gramm-Leach-Bliley Act or any notice regarding a data security breach or privacy that is required by federal or state law.[57] A formal pleading in a civil action also cannot be considered an initial communication for purposes of the debt validation requirements.[58]

When required, the written debt validation notice must contain the following:

- The amount of the debt;
- The name of the creditor to whom the debt is owed;
- A statement that unless the consumer, within thirty days after receipt of the notice, disputes the validity of the debt, or any portion thereof, the debt will be assumed to be valid by the debt collector;
- A statement that if the consumer notifies the debt collector in writing within the thirty-day period that the debt, or any portion thereof, is disputed, the debt collector will obtain verification of the debt or a copy

54. 15 U.S.C. § 1692g(a).
55. *Id.*
56. *Id.*
57. *Id.* § 1692g(e).
58. *Id.* § 1692g(d).

of a judgment against the consumer and a copy of such verification or judgment will be mailed to the consumer by the debt collector; and

- A statement that, upon the consumer's written request within the thirty-day period, the debt collector will provide the consumer with the name and address of the original creditor, if different from the current creditor.[59]

During the thirty-day validation period, a debt collector may continue collection efforts that do not otherwise violate the FDCPA or other applicable law.[60] However, collection activities and any other communications with the consumer during the thirty-day validation period must not be inconsistent with or overshadow the disclosure of the consumer's right to dispute the debt or request the name and address of the original creditor.[61] If the consumer responds to the debt validation notice within the allotted time and disputes the validity of the entire debt or a portion of it, the debt collector must cease collection efforts with respect to the debt, or the portion that the consumer disputed.[62] The prohibition on collection activity remains in effect until the debtor obtains verification of the debt or a copy of a judgment and the verification or judgment is mailed to the consumer.[63] Similarly, if the consumer requests the name and address of the original creditor, collection activity with respect to the debt must cease until the appropriate information is mailed to the consumer.[64]

If a consumer does not dispute the validity of a debt during the thirty-day period after receiving a debt validation notice, the consumer's inaction cannot be construed by any court as an admission of liability.[65]

4.1.2 Restrictions on Communications with Debtors

The FDCPA imposes restrictions on communications with consumers in certain circumstances.[66] Specifically, a debt collector is prohibited from communicating with a consumer in connection with the collection of a debt:

- At any unusual time or place. The restriction also applies to communicating at a time or place that is known, or which should be known, to be inconvenient to the consumer. A debt collector must

59. *Id.* § 1692g(a).
60. *Id.* § 1692g(b).
61. *Id.*
62. *Id.*
63. *Id.*
64. *Id.*
65. *Id.* § 1692g(c).
66. For purposes of the restrictions on communications with consumers described in this section, the word *consumer* includes the consumer's spouse, parent (if the consumer is a minor), guardian, executor, or administrator. *See id.* § 1692g(d).

generally not communicate before 8:00 a.m. or after 9:00 p.m. in the consumer's location.[67]

- If the consumer is represented by an attorney with respect to the debt, and the debt collector knows of the representation and either knows or can determine the attorney's name and address. However, the debt collector can communicate with the consumer directly if the attorney representing the consumer consents to direct communications with the consumer or the attorney fails to respond within a reasonable period to a communication from the debt collector.[68]
- At the consumer's place of employment if the debt collector knows or has reason to know that the employer prohibits the consumer from receiving such communication.[69]

A debt collector can communicate with a consumer in any of the above-described circumstances if the debt collector obtains the consumer's prior consent or if a court of competent jurisdiction provides express permission for it to do so.[70]

Debt collectors are also generally prohibited from communicating with any person other than the consumer.[71] However, this prohibition does not apply to communications with the consumer's attorney, a consumer reporting agency if otherwise permitted by law, the creditor, the attorney of the creditor, or the debt collector's own attorney.[72] Communications with a third party in connection with the collection of a debt can occur with the consumer's prior consent given directly to the debt collector, or with the express permission of a court of competent jurisdiction.[73] Any such communications can also occur with a third party as reasonably necessary to effectuate a postjudgment judicial remedy.[74]

Finally, the FDCPA gives consumers the ability to request that a debt collector cease communicating in regards to the debt.[75] If a consumer notifies the debt collector in writing that the consumer either refuses to pay the debt or that the consumer wants the debt collector to cease further communication with the consumer, the debt collector must generally not communicate further with the consumer regarding the debt.[76] The only exceptions to the general cease communication rule is for communications that:

67. *Id.* § 1692c(a)(1).
68. *Id.* § 1692c(a)(2).
69. *Id.* § 1692c(a)(3).
70. *Id.* § 1692c(a).
71. *Id.* § 1692c(b).
72. *Id.*
73. *Id.*
74. *Id.*
75. *Id.* § 1692c(c).
76. *Id.*

- Advise the consumer that the debt collector's future collection efforts are being terminated;
- Notify the consumer that the debt collector or creditor may invoke specified remedies which are ordinarily invoked by such debt collector or creditor; or
- Notify the consumer that the debt collector or creditor intends to invoke a specified remedy.[77]

Courts have also held that consumers can waive a prior cease communication request, in which case a debt collector can then respond to a consumer's communications.[78] The concept of a waiver has also been adopted by the CFPB.[79]

4.2 What Conduct Violates the FDCPA?

The FDCPA identifies several categories of conduct by a debt collector as wrongful. In addition to the restrictions on a debt collector's communications with a debtor, the statute defines six broad categories of violations. Importantly, whether given conduct directed to a consumer constitutes an FDCPA violation is viewed under the "least sophisticated consumer standard."[80] The Seventh Circuit has noted the weakness of a literal application of a standard tailored to the least sophisticated consumer,[81] and reframed the test as the "unsophisticated consumer" standard.[82] Terminology aside, the federal courts generally apply a similar standard that tests whether conduct would violate the FDCPA from the perspective of a relatively unsophisticated consumer, who is capable of reading plain language, but not understanding specific nuances that are not made clear, or interpreting ambiguous language.

---

77. *Id.*

78. *See* Clark v. Capital Credit & Collection Servs., Inc., 460 F.3d 1162, 1172 (9th Cir. 2006).

79. *See* CFPB, Bulletin 2013-12, *Implementation Guidance for Certain Mortgage Servicing Rules* (October 15, 2013), https://files.consumerfinance.gov/f/201310_cfpb_mortgage-servicing_bulletin.pdf.

80. *See, e.g.*, Clomon v. Jackson, 988 F.2d 1314, 1319–20 (2d Cir. 1994); Bentley v. Great Lakes Collection Bureau, 6 F.3d 60, 62 (2d Cir. 1993); Smith v. Transworld Sys., Inc., 953 F.2d 1025, 1028 (6th Cir. 1992); Graziano v. Harrison, 950 F.2d 107, 111 n.5 (3d Cir. 1991); Swanson v. Southern Oregon Credit Serv., Inc., 869 F.2d 1222, 1225 (9th Cir. 1988); Jeter v. Credit Bureau, 760 F.2d 1168, 1175 (11th Cir. 1985).

81. "[S]uch a consumer would likely not be able to read a collection notice with care (or at all), let alone interpret in a reasonable fashion." Gammon v. GC Servs. Ltd. P'ship, 27 F.3d 1254, 1257 (7th Cir. 1994).

82. *Id.*

4.2.1 Harassment and Abuse

Section 1692d forbids a debt collector from "engag[ing] in any conduct the natural consequences of which is to harass, oppress, or abuse any person in connection with the collection of a debt."[83] The statute then provides a nonexclusive list of examples of conduct that are impermissible under the category of "harassment or abuse," as follows:

- "The use or threat of violence or other criminal means to harm the physical person, reputation, or property of any person.
- "The use of obscene or profane language or language the natural consequences of which is to abuse the hearer or reader.
- "The publication of a list of consumers who allegedly refuse to pay debts [other than through normal credit reporting to credit reporting agencies].
- "The advertisement for sale of any debt to coerce payment of the debt.
- "Causing a telephone to ring or engaging any person in telephone conversation repeatedly or continuously with intent to annoy, abuse, or harass any person at the called number.
- "Except as provided in section 1692b of this title [the provision addressing how a debt collector may acquire "location information" about the consumer"], the placement of telephone calls without meaningful disclosure of the caller's identity."[84]

For conduct falling outside of the enumerated examples, courts simply have to decide whether the alleged conduct is similar in kind to the named examples of harassing or abusive conduct so as to trigger liability under section 1692d. Generally, whether alleged conduct meets the standard of "harassment or abuse" is a case specific determination.

One frequent area of dispute is whether a given volume of telephone calls placed by the debt collector to the debtor violates section 1692d(5), which prohibits harassment and abuse. The FDCPA provides no definitive guidance as to what volume of telephone calls or conversations meets the standard; as a result, courts have had to make such a determination on an individualized basis.[85] For proponents of a more certain standard, Regulation F, as proposed by the CFPB, would impose specific restrictions on telephone calls, restricting calls (with certain exceptions) to seven efforts within a seven-day period, with a seven-day rest period after the debt collector engages in a conversation with the debtor.[86] As noted above, the CFPB proposed these rules in May 2019, but they had not been finalized as of the date of

83. 15 U.S.C. § 1692d.

84. *Id.*

85. *See, e.g.*, Kuntz v. Rodenburg LLP, 838 F.3d 923, 926 (8th Cir. 2016); Zarichny v. Complete Payment Recovery Servs., Inc., 80 F. Supp. 3d 610, 621 (E.D. Penn. 2015).

86. Debt Collection Practices Proposed Rule (Regulation F), 84 Fed. Reg. 23,274, 23,401–02 (May 21, 2019).

this writing. Readers should consult the CFPB's website or other resources to confirm whether the CFPB has finalized restrictions on calls by debt collectors.

4.2.2 False or Misleading Representations

Another frequently litigated part of the FDCPA is section 807, which bars a debt collector from making false or misleading representations.[87] As with section 806, the FDCPA provides a general prohibition that "[a] debt collector may not use any false, deceptive, or misleading representation or means in connection with the collection of any debt," then provides a nonexhaustive list of examples of conduct violating the section.

Perhaps unsurprisingly, section 807 appears to be the most frequently litigated part of the entire FDCPA, and there is an abundance of case law discussing all of the enumerated examples of false or misleading representations. Two of the examples merit special mention, however. Under 15 U.S.C. § 807(5), a debt collector may not make a "threat to take any action that cannot legally be taken or that is not intended to be taken." Courts have generally read section 807(5) as barring a debt collector from threatening to take or actually taking legal action on a debt, when such action would be time-barred under applicable law.[88] In addition to not permitting express threats, courts have also held that debt collectors cannot infer that legal action may be taken on a time-barred debt.[89] Given these restrictions, the CFPB has acknowledged that "[c]onsumers unfamiliar with statutes of limitations may take away from a debt collector's attempt to collect a time-barred debt the misleading impression that the debt is legally enforceable—even if the debt collector does not explicitly threaten litigation."[90] As a result of this potential consumer protection concern, the CFPB is proposing to enact specific disclosure requirements in Regulation F that would apply when a debt collector is attempting to collect on a time-barred debt.[91]

More recently, courts have had to address the more specific issue as to whether a debt collector's filing of a claim in bankruptcy for a time-barred debt also violates the FDCPA. In *Crawford v. LVNV Funding, LLC*, the Court of Appeals for the Eleventh Circuit concluded that a debt collector's filing of a proof of claim in the debtor's bankruptcy regarding a debt for which litigation would be time-barred was a "representation" or "means" used in "connection with the collection of any debt,"

---

87. 15 U.S.C. § 1692e.

88. *See, e.g.*, Phillips v. Asset Acceptance, LLC, v. 736 F.3d 1076, 1079 (7th Cir. 2013); Huertas v. Galaxy Asset Mgmt., 641 F.3d 28, 32–33 (3d Cir. 2011); Castro v. Collecto, Inc., 634 F.3d 779, 783, 787 (5th Cir. 2011); McCollough v. Johnson, Rodenburg & Lauinger, LLC, 637 F.3d 939, 949 (9th Cir. 2011); Freyermuth v. Credit Bureau Servs., 248 F.3d 767, 771 (8th Cir. 2001).

89. *See, e.g.*, Holzman v. Malcolm S. Gerald & Assocs., Inc., 920 F.3d 1264, 1272 (11th Cir. 2019); Pantoja v. Portfolio Recovery Assocs., LLC, 852 F.3d 679, 683–84 (7th Cir. 2017).

90. Debt Collection Practices (Regulation F), 85 Fed. Reg. 12672, 12673 (March 3, 2020).

91. *Id.* at 12672.

and thus constituted a violation of the FDCPA.[92] However, in *Midland Funding, LLC v. Johnson*, the U.S. Supreme Court concluded that filing a proof of claim in the debtor's bankruptcy proceeding for a stale debt did not constitute a violation of the FDCPA, as the proof of claim was neither "false, deceptive or misleading" nor "unfair or unconscionable."[93] Importantly, in *Johnson*, the Court's reasoning was rooted in the fact that the underlying state law gave the creditor the right to payment even after expiration of the limitations period.[94] After *Johnson*, the courts will have to determine whether filing proofs of claims for time-barred debts in instances where the applicable limitations period operates to actually extinguish the debt.

Second, under section 807(11), in its initial written or oral communication with a debtor, the debt collector must inform the debtor that the debt collector is attempting to collect a debt and that any information obtained will be used for that purpose.[95] This so-called "mini-Miranda" requirement stands in tension with two other parts of the FDCPA, which has frequently led to litigation. First, a party that might not consider itself a debt collector (such as a mortgage loan servicer that acquired servicing rights to a loan when it was not in default) may not wish to have its first contact with the customer include a notification that the nondebt collector is a debt collector. Aside from altering the relationship with the customer, there may be a concern that this statement can be used as evidence of the servicer's status as a debt collector. However, if the servicer does not include the mini-Miranda notice, and a court later deems it to be a debt collector based on the more generalized statutory definition, then the servicer will be in violation of section 807(11).

The mini-Miranda requirement also creates a dilemma for debt collectors seeking to contact a debtor by telephone or text message. Under section 807(11), that initial communication must include the mini-Miranda warning, which makes it clear that the communication is an effort to collect a debt. However, if that initial message is conveyed as a voicemail or text message, and a third party is able to hear or see its contents, then the debt collector has potentially violated section 805(b)'s prohibition on communications with third parties.[96] Although the proposed new Regulation F addresses this dilemma by defining a "limited content message" that a debt collector can lawfully leave on a voicemail or by text message without triggering section 807(11)'s mini-Miranda requirement, many debt collectors currently do not seek to leave voicemails or communicate by text, to avoid potential liability.

92. 758 F.3d 1254, 1261 (11th Cir. 2014).

93. 137 S. Ct. 1407, 1411–13 (2017).

94. *Id.* at 1412–13.

95. 15 U.S.C. § 1692e(11).

96. *See, e.g.*, Reich v. Van Ru Credit Corp., 191 F. Supp. 3d 668 (E.D. Tex. 2016).

4.2.3 Unfair Practices

The FDCPA establishes a general rule that debt collectors may not use unfair or unconscionable means to collect or attempt to collect any debt.[97] The law provides the following nonexhaustive list of eight examples of conduct that violates the general rule:

- Collecting any amounts that are not expressly authorized by the agreement creating the debt or permitted by law;
- Accepting a check or other payment instrument that is postdated by more than five days, unless the debt collector notifies the person that it intends to deposit the check. Notification must occur between three and ten business days prior to the deposit;
- Soliciting a postdated check or other payment instrument for the purpose of threatening or instituting criminal prosecution;
- Depositing or threatening to deposit any postdated check or other postdated payment instrument prior to the date on such check or instrument;
- Causing charges, such as collect telephone call fees, to be incurred by any person for communications by concealment of the true purpose of the communication;
- Threatening to take action, such as dispossession or disablement, with respect to property if there is no actual intent to take such action or the property is exempt by law from such action;
- Communicating with a consumer regarding a debt by post card; and
- Using any language or symbols, other than the debt collector's address, on an envelope when communicating with the consumer via mail. Business names may be included if the name does not indicate that it is in the debt collection business.[98]

Most of the restrictions in section 808 are straightforward, and debt collectors are able to comply with them by not marking their mailing envelopes with text or symbols, not soliciting (and often refusing to accept) postdated checks, not making collect telephone calls, and not using postcards to communicate with debtors. However, the first example of an *unfair practice*—"[c]ollecting any amounts that are not expressly authorized by the agreement creating the debt or permitted by law"—has proven to be an issue. Specifically, many loan servicers who qualify as "debt collectors" under the FDCPA have developed a practice of accepting debtors' payments by telephone or through an online portal. The servicers typically assess a "convenience fee" or a "phone pay fee" for providing the service, which may either be a pass-through of the fee charged by a third party for facilitating a payment or a fee calculated to cover the

97. 15 U.S.C. § 1692f.

98. *Id.*

third-party fee, plus the internal expenses incurred by the debt collector in assisting the debtor make the payment.

In recent years, debtors began challenging convenience fees under section 808(1), arguing that by collecting such fees, debt collectors were collecting an amount that was not "expressly authorized by the agreement creating the debt or permitted by law." Although at least one federal appellate court rejected such a claim by reasoning that the convenience fees were disclosed in advance, optional, avoidable by consumers, and not prohibited by state law,[99] and the FTC seemed to indicate in its commentary on the FDCPA that such fees were permissible,[100] more recent decisions have largely held that the collection of such a fee may violate the FDCPA, especially if the debt collector retains part of the fee collected.[101] In 2017, the CFPB issued regulatory guidance specifically addressing pay-by-phone fees in the context of the FDCPA, indicating that such fees were not permissible under section 808.[102] Thus, while many debt collectors have argued that section 808 states that collecting an amount not covered by the underlying agreement is a violation unless it is "permitted" by law—that is, not independently barred by applicable law—consumer groups, the courts, and the CFPB appear to have taken the provision to mean that such amounts be "*expressly* permitted by law" to be lawful under the FDCPA.

There have also been lawsuits recently under section 808(6)'s prohibition on "[t]aking or threatening to take any nonjudicial action to effect dispossession or disablement of property" if the property cannot be legally dispossessed or disabled, or the debt collector lacks a "present right" or a "present intent" to take possession of the property. Debtors often assert a "bootstrap" claim under section 808(6) when they contest the debt collector (or creditor's) substantive right to exercise a right of repossession, or contend that the debt collector violated the repossession laws in the process of repossessing.[103] Courts typically adjudicate these claims by analyzing

---

99. Lee v. Main Accounts, Inc., No. 96-3922, 1997 WL 618803, at *1 (6th Cir. Oct. 6, 1997).

100. Staff Commentary on the Fair Debt Collection Practices Act, Statements of General Policy or Interpretation, 53 F.R. 50,097, 50,107–08 (Dec. 13, 1988).

101. *See, e.g.*, Fuentes v. AR Resources, Inc., No. 15-cv-7988, 2017 WL 1197814, at *7–11 (D.N.J. Mar. 31, 2017); Johnson-Morris v. Santander Consumer USA, Inc., 194 F. Supp. 3d 757, 765 (N.D. Ill. 2016); Lindblom v. Santander Consumer USA, Inc., 1:15-cv-990-LJO-BAM, 2016 WL 2841495, at *4–7 (E.D. Cal. May 9, 2016); Campbell v. MBI Assoc., Inc., 98 F. Supp. 3d 568, 578–83, n.4 (E.D.N.Y. 2015); Liable v. Rockport Fin., LLC, No. 4:15–CV–00306–ERW, 2015 WL 4771664, at *2–3 (W.D. Mo Aug. 12, 2015); Acosta v. Credit Bureau of Napa Cnty., No. 14 C 8198, 2015 WL 1943244, *2–4 (N.D. Ill. Apr. 29, 2015); Weast v. Rockport Fin., LLC, 115 F. Supp. 3d 1018, 1023 (E.D. Mo. 2015); Quinteros v. MBI Assoc., Inc., 999 F. Supp. 2d 434, 437–39 (E.D.N.Y. 2014).

102. *See, generally*, CFPB, Bulletin 2017-01, *Phone Pay Fees* (October 15, 2013), https://files.consumerfinance.gov/f/documents/201707_cfpb_compliance-bulletin-phone-pay-fee.pdf.

103. *See, e.g.*, Goldenstein v. Repossessors Inc., 815 F.3d 142, 147 (3d Cir. 2016); Aviles v. Wayside Auto Body, Inc., 49 F. Supp. 3d 216, 225–26 (D. Conn. 2014); Krajewski v. Am. Honda Fin. Corp., 557 F. Supp. 2d 596, 618–19 (E.D. Penn. 2008).

whether the debt collector or creditor has an underlying right to repossession under applicable state law.

4.3 Lawsuits by Debt Collectors in Improper Forums

Section 811 prohibits a debt collector from bringing a legal action on a debt and against a consumer outside one of three venues.[104] If the debt collector seeks to "enforce an interest in real property securing the consumer's obligation," it must bring the legal action in the "judicial district or similar legal entity in which such real property is located."[105] In any other circumstance, the debt collector may choose to bring the legal action in either (1) the judicial district or similar legal entity "in which such consumer signed the contract sued upon" or (2) the judicial district or similar legal entity "in which such consumer resides at the commencement of the action."[106] The venue restriction is designed to prevent debt collectors from "obtain[ing] default judgments against debtors if and when debtors were unable to appear in a distant court."[107]

This relatively simple provision has spawned a significant body of case law addressing an array of questions with courts reaching different outcomes depending on the nature of the legal action, the party taking the legal action, the organization of the relevant jurisdiction, and a host of other case-specific factors.

4.3.1 What Constitutes a Legal Action on a Debt against the Consumer?

Courts, when deciding whether collection activity constitutes a legal action on a debt against the consumer, frequently look to the nature of the activity (e.g., Is the activity actually a legal action?), the nature of the debt (e.g., Is the amount at issue actually a debt as defined by the FDCPA?), and whether the collection activity is against the consumer. Unfortunately, court decisions are fact and jurisdiction specific, which can result in varied and inconsistent applications of the FDCPA.

The U.S. Court of Appeals for the Ninth Circuit, in the context of an application for writ of garnishment, held "the term 'legal action' encompasses all judicial proceedings, including those in enforcement of a previously-adjudicated right."[108] In reaching this conclusion, the court looked to precedent that essentially defined *legal action* as "a lawsuit" or "litigation."[109] A federal district court in Illinois, relying on the *Fox* definition of *legal action*, reached the opposite conclusion, finding that a

104. 15 U.S.C. § 1692i(a).

105. *Id.* § 1692i(a)(1).

106. *Id.* § 1692i(a)(2).

107. Lawson v. Mgmt. Adjustment Bureau, Inc., No. 96 C 4576, 1997 WL 283027, at *4 (N.D. Ill. May 15, 1997).

108. Fox v. Citicorp Credit Servs., Inc., 15 F.3d 1507, 1515 (9th Cir. 1994).

109. S & M Inv. Co. v. Tahoe Reg'l Planning Agency, 911 F.2d 324, 328 (9th Cir. 1990).

pre-wage-garnishment administrative hearing did not qualify as legal action because it was not litigation.[110] In reaching this conclusion, the *Lawson* court also noted that Illinois' administrative process allowed the debtor to appear by phone, thus mitigating concerns that debtors would not be able to defend themselves in a distant venue.[111]

The *Fox* court also addressed whether a postjudgment enforcement action, like a writ of garnishment, constitutes legal action *on a debt*, finding that the FDCPA's definition of debt "include[d] obligations reduced to judgment" and that "any judicial proceeding relating to such a judgment constitutes a 'legal action' on a debt."[112] However, the *Fox* court's logic may not apply when considering a postjudgment enforcement action on a mortgage deficiency debt.[113] In *Aluia*, a Florida court determined that an action to collect a mortgage deficiency did not fall within the FDCPA's definition of debt because a "deficiency proceeding, rather than being an action on a consumer debt that has been reduced to judgment, is actually an action to enforce the result of a foreclosure proceeding to obtain a money judgment."[114]

Several courts have held that, under relevant state law, garnishment proceedings are not actions against the consumer because a garnishment action is between the debt collector and the garnishee.[115] In reaching their decisions, the *Pickens* and *Smith* courts both highlighted state law indicating that garnishment actions are against a party other than the consumer (e.g., the consumer's employer) and that the consumer had already had an opportunity to contest the initial debt collection action, upon which the garnishment was based, in an FDCPA-compliant venue.[116] However, at least one Ohio court reached the opposite conclusion, finding that under Ohio's garnishment laws "[only] the judgment creditor and the judgment debtor have any beneficial interest at stake in a garnishment action. The nominal 'defendant' in a wage garnishment, the employer-debtor of the employee-judgment debtor, has no claim to the money garnished."[117]

110. Lawson v. Mgmt. Adjustment Bureau, Inc., No. 96 C 4576, 1997 WL 283027, at *4 (N.D. Ill. May 15, 1997).

111. *Id.*

112. *Id.*

113. *See* Aluia v. Dyck-O'Neal, Inc., 205 So. 3d 768 (Fla. Dist. Ct. App. 2016).

114. *Id.*

115. *See, e.g.*, Smith v. Solomon & Solomon, P.C., 887 F. Supp. 2d 334, 338 (D. Mass. 2012), *aff'd*, 714 F.3d 73 (1st Cir. 2013); Pickens v. Collection Servs. of Athens, Inc., 165 F. Supp. 2d 1376, 1380 (M.D. Ga. 2001), *aff'd*, Pickens v. Collection Servs., 273 F.3d 1121 (11th Cir. 2001).

116. *Pickens*, *supra* note 115; *Smith*, *supra* note 115.

117. Adkins v. Weltman, Weinberg & Reis Co., L.P.A., No. 2:11-CV-00619, 2012 WL 604249, at *6 (S.D. Ohio Feb. 24, 2012).

4.3.2 What Constitutes a Judicial District?

Generally, debt collection actions filed in state court must look to the state's judicial subdivisions to determine what constitutes a judicial district.[118] Similarly, debt collection actions filed in federal court must look to the federal judicial subdivisions to determine what constitutes an appropriate judicial district.[119] Although the case law requiring debt collectors to consider state judicial subdivisions when filing state law actions and federal judicial subdivisions when filing in federal court is relatively clear, there is some discussion as to what constitutes a state judicial district under the FDCPA.

Judicial district sometimes means the county court for the county in which (1) the consumer resides, (2) the consumer signed the contract, or (3) the property is located. However, at least one court has determined that judicial district refers to the state's judicial circuits even if those circuits include multiple counties.[120] Additionally, several courts have struggled to define judicial district when considering whether actions should be filed in a judicial subdivision smaller than county-wide courts of general jurisdiction.[121] The *Suesz* court, in considering how to address claims filed in smaller courts, considered three approaches but ultimately defined the relevant judicial district as "the smallest geographic area relevant to venue in the court system in which the case is filed."[122] The *Hess* court reached a similar decision.[123] However, courts have not uniformly adapted the *Suesz* and *Hess* approach, and at least one district court did not find the *Suesz* reasoning persuasive when applied to the unique facts before it.[124]

---

118. *See, e.g.*, Hess v. Cohen & Slamowitz LLP, 637 F.3d 117, 121 (2d Cir. 2011) ("We thus join the other courts that have considered this issue to conclude that the term 'judicial district,' as applied to state-court debt collection actions, must be defined in accordance with the judicial system of the state in which the debt collection action is brought."); Fox v. Citicorp Credit Servs., Inc., 15 F.3d 1507, 1515 (9th Cir. 1994) ("The fact that, as the defendants argue, the state of Arizona constitutes a single federal judicial district and has a unitary state superior court has no effect on our conclusion."); Action Prof'l Serv. v. Kiggins, 458 N.W.2d 365, 367 (S.D. 1990) ("If a debt collector files a debt collection action in state court it must be filed in the *state* 'judicial district or similar legal entity' in which the contract was signed or where the debtor resides. In South Dakota state court the 'judicial district or similar legal entity' is the circuit courts as established by state law. On the other hand, if an action is properly initiated and maintained in federal district court the term 'judicial district or similar legal entity' refers to the *federal* judicial district as established under federal law. Thus, a debt collection action initiated in federal court must be filed in the federal district in which the contract was signed or the debtor resides.").

119. *See, e.g.*, *Kiggins*, 458 N.W.2d at 367.

120. *See, e.g.*, Crawford v. Credit Collection Servs., 898 F. Supp. 699, 702 (D.S.D. 1995).

121. *See, e.g.*, Suesz v. Med-1 Sols., LLC, 757 F.3d 636 (7th Cir. 2014); Hess v. Cohen & Slamowitz LLP, 637 F.3d 117, 122 (2d Cir. 2011).

122. *Suesz*, 757 F.3d at 638.

123. *Hess*, 637 F.3d at 123.

124. Elizarov v. Equity Experts LLC, 312 F. Supp. 3d 624, 637 (E.D. Mich. 2018).

4.3.3 The FDCPA's Prohibition against Deceptive Forms

Under section 812,

> [i]t is unlawful to design, compile, and furnish any form knowing that such form would be used to create the false belief in a consumer that a person other than the creditor of such consumer is participating in the collection of or in an attempt to collect a debt such consumer allegedly owes such creditor, when in fact such person is not so participating.[125]

The FDCPA goes on to clarify that this prohibition is not limited to debt collectors: "Any person who violates this section shall be liable to the same extent and in the same manner as a debt collector is liable under section [813] of this title for failure to comply with a provision of this subchapter."[126]

Many of the cases regarding section 812 relate to a practice known as flat-rating "whereby a third-party (usually for a flat rate) sells form letters to a creditor 'which create[] the false impression that someone (usually a collection agency) besides the actual creditor is participating in collecting the debt."[127] These cases tend to revolve around the extent of the debt collectors' actual involvement in the collection process, with court's asking "whether, in consideration of all that an entity does in the collection process, [the collection entity] genuinely contributes to an effort to collect another's debt, or instead does little more than act as a mailing service for the creditor."[128] Courts, in their efforts to answer this question,

> have applied a litany of factors related to an entity's participation in the debt-collection process, including the amount of control the entity exercises over the collection letters it sends, the amount of contact the entity has with debtors, whether the entity invites and responds to debtor inquiries, whether the entity may receive or negotiate payments, whether the entity receives or retains full debtor files, and whether the entity is involved in further collection activities if the debts remain unpaid.[129]

Although each case is fact-specific, debt collectors who substantively participate in the collection process by responding to consumer correspondence, collecting payments, calling consumers, and so on, are less likely to be found in violation of section 812.

---

125. 15 U.S.C. § 1692j(a).
126. *Id.* § 1692j(b).
127. Echlin v. PeaceHealth, 887 F.3d 967, 972 (9th Cir. 2018).
128. *Id.* at 974 (citing various other cases for a similar proposition).
129. *Id.*

5. Defenses under the FDCPA

Although there are a host of substantive defenses to specific FDCPA claims, the primary restrictions on legal actions under the FDCPA are the (1) statutory scope, (2) statute of limitations, and (3) bona fide error defense. As discussed in more detail above, the FDCPA, for the most part, only applies to debt collectors seeking to collect a debt, and courts often dismiss cases because the defendant is not in fact a debt collector or was not seeking to collect a debt.

The FDCPA employs a one-year statute of limitations: "[a]n action to enforce any liability created by this subchapter may be brought in any appropriate United States district court without regard to the amount in controversy, or in any other court of competent jurisdiction, within one year from the date on which the violation occurs."[130] Until recently, circuits were split on when the FDCPA's one-year statute of limitations begins to run, with the Fourth and Ninth Circuits applying the discovery rule, and the Third Circuit holding that the statute of limitations begins to run on the date the violation occurs.[131] The U.S. Supreme Court resolved the split in December 2019 when it ruled that the discovery rule does not apply to FDCPA cases.[132]

Although the FDCPA is commonly referred to as a "strict liability statute," section 813(c) provides a substantive defense to any private action brought under the FDCPA based on lack of intent: "A debt collector may not be held liable under this subchapter if the debt collector shows by a preponderance of the evidence that the violation was not intentional and resulted from a bona fide error notwithstanding the maintenance of procedures reasonably adapted to avoid any such error."[133] Thus, to the extent a defendant in an FDCPA lawsuit is able to prove the "bona fide error defense," it can avoid any liability.

In practice, the bona fide error defense proves less helpful for defendants than it would appear. The U.S. Supreme Court has held that a debt collector's mistake of law as to whether a certain action is permissible under the FDCPA is not a basis for invoking the defense.[134] A defendant can still avoid liability by demonstrating a bona fide error as to a "factual or clerical" mistake,[135] but the defendant bears the burden of demonstrating the bona fide error defense elements by a preponderance of the

---

130. 15 U.S.C. § 1692k(d).

131. *See* Lembach v. Bierman, 528 F. app'x 297 (4th Cir. 2013) (per curiam); Mangum v. Action Collection Serv., Inc., 575 F.3d 935 (9th Cir. 2009); Rotkiske v. Klemm, 890 F.3d 422, 424 (3d Cir. 2018), cert. granted, 139 S. Ct. 1259, 203 L. Ed. 2d 271 (2019).

132. Rotkiske v. Klemm, 140 S. Ct. 355, 361 (2019).

133. 15 U.S.C. § 1692k(c).

134. Jerman v. Carlisle, McNellie, Rini, Kramer & Ulrich LPA, 559 U.S. 573, 581–82 (2010); *see also* Oliva v. Blatt, Hasenmiller, Leibsker & Moore, LLC, 864 F.3d 492, 497–98 (7th Cir. 2017) (applying *Jerman* to hold that defendant's reliance on since-abrogated precedent interpreting the "judicial district" provision in section 811 did not support a bona fide error defense).

135. *See* Owen v. I.C. System, Inc., 629 F.3d 1263, 1273 (11th Cir. 2011).

evidence.[136] Because the elements of lack of intent and the existence of procedures "reasonably adapted to avoid any such error" will rarely be established in the pleadings or even as an undisputed fact at summary judgment, defendants have a challenge invoking the defense before trial. Thus, for the small percentage of FDCPA cases that proceed all the way to trial, the bona fide error defense may have teeth, but for the majority of FDCPA cases resolved before trial, it rarely comes into play.

6. Relationship with State Laws

6.1 Preemption

Like many other federal statutes, the FDCPA contains a preemption provision that preempts state laws to the extent those laws are inconsistent.[137] The provision explains that a state law is not inconsistent with the FDCPA if the state law affords a consumer greater protection than provided by the FDCPA. As a result, where states provide greater protections than those provided by the FDCPA, those state laws remain intact.

Conflict preemption—the type of preemption implicated by the FDCPA—exists where "it is impossible for a private party to comply with both state and federal law and where the state law is an obstacle to the accomplishment and execution of Congress's full purpose and objectives."[138] As a result, preemption is often irrelevant in the FDCPA context. However, several courts have applied the FDCPA's preemption provision in the context of determining venue, finding that the FDCPA's venue provision preempts state venue law.[139]

6.2 Exemption by the Consumer Financial Protection Bureau

In addition to the preemption provision discussed above, the FDCPA provides that the CFPB may exempt certain classes of debt collection practices to the extent it has determined that state laws impose substantially similar requirements and that there is adequate provision for enforcement.[140] The CFPB has promulgated regulations where a state can apply to the CFPB for an exemption of a class of debt collection practices from the provisions of the FDCPA, including the application process, the criteria the CFPB will follow in making its determination, and notice of the exemption in the

136. *Id.* at 1271.

137. 15 U.S.C. § 1692n.

138. Arellano v. Clark Cty. Collection Serv., LLC, 875 F.3d 1213, 1218 (9th Cir. 2017); Crosby v. Nat'l Foreign Trade Council, 530 U.S. 363, 372 (2000).

139. *See, e.g.*, Martinez v. Albuquerque Collection Servs., Inc., 867 F. Supp. 1495, 1501 (D.N.M. 1994); McKnight v. Benitez, 176 F. Supp. 2d 1301, 1309 (M.D. Fla. 2001).

140. 15 U.S.C. § 1692o.

Federal Register.[141] The FTC granted an exemption to Maine in 1995 but the CFPB, as of the date of writing, has not received any applications for exemption.[142]

6.3 Relevance of State Law to Potential FDCPA Violations

Although preemption of state law and exemptions by the CFPB are rarely relevant to any FDCPA analysis, state law itself is often relevant to a potential violation of the FDCPA. For instance, as mentioned above, the FDCPA prohibits a debt collector from using false, deceptive, or misleading representations in connection with the collection of any debt, including the use of a false representation or deceptive means to collect a debt.[143] As a result, a debt collector can be held in violation of the FDCPA for threatening to take an action prohibited under state law.[144] Therefore, even if state law is not relevant in other contexts, a debt collector should be cognizant of applicable state law to avoid potential liability.

141. 12 C.F.R. § 1006.1–.8.

142. *Notice of Maine Exemption From The Fair Debt Collection Practices Act*, 60 FR 66972-01.

143. 15 U.S.C. § 1692e(10).

144. *See, e.g.*, Picht v. John R. Hawks, Ltd., 236 F.3d 446 (8th Cir. 2001) (sending a notice of intent to garnish and attempting to use a prejudgment garnishment procedure which was not authorized by state law was a violation of FDCPA); Edwards v. McCormick, 136 F. Supp. 2d 795 (S.D. Ohio 2001) (sending a letter threatening to foreclose when the state's homestead statute precluded foreclosure was a violation of state law).

CHAPTER

12

Consumer Bankruptcy Law

Robert A. Cox, Jr. and Karlene A. Archer

1. Introduction

In many instances, consumers who are facing significant financial hardship, including the potential foreclosure on a residence, repossession of a car, or harassment from debt collectors, may be compelled, sometimes as a last resort, to file for bankruptcy protection. As discussed below, the filing of a bankruptcy stops, at least temporarily, all pending foreclosures, repossessions, and other collection actions to allow the consumer debtor the opportunity to address such debt.

The concept of bankruptcy in the United States can be traced back to the U.S. Constitution, which states in Article 1, Section 8 that the Congress has the power to establish "uniform Laws on the subject of Bankruptcies throughout the United States."[1] Based on this constitutional power, Congress has adopted various bankruptcy laws since the early 1800s. Today, the bankruptcy laws are codified in Title 11 of the United States Code,[2] more commonly referred to as the *Bankruptcy Code*. This comprehensive set of statutes provides a mechanism for debtors, whether they are individuals or companies, to restructure or eliminate their debts, claims, and other liabilities. As such, filing for bankruptcy can have a substantial impact on a consumer debtor's finances. In addition to the Bankruptcy Code, bankruptcy cases are governed by the Federal Rules of Bankruptcy Procedure (the *Bankruptcy Rules*), which apply in all bankruptcy cases.

1. U.S. Const. art. I, § 8, cl. 4.
2. 11 U.S.C. § 101 *et seq.*

Although there are specific Bankruptcy Code provisions that apply to companies, as well as family farmers and fishermen (discussed briefly below), this chapter will focus on those Bankruptcy Code provisions, and related rules, applicable to individual consumer bankruptcy cases.

2. Overview of Various Bankruptcy Chapters

The Bankruptcy Code is divided into various chapters, some of which are administrative and apply in all bankruptcy cases, and some of which are specific to a particular outcome or the nature of the debtor. Below is a brief description of those specific Bankruptcy Code chapters that may be applicable to individual consumer debtors.

2.1 Chapter 7 (Liquidation)

Chapter 7 is liquidation bankruptcy and can be applicable to both individuals and business debtors.[3] Under this chapter, a trustee is appointed with duties under the Bankruptcy Code to identify all of the debtor's nonexempt assets with value, and liquidate such assets, with the proceeds from such liquidation going to pay the claims of the debtor's creditors.[4] As discussed in greater detail below, subject to certain exceptions, a debtor in Chapter 7 will receive a discharge, which will discharge the debtor from personal liability on any debts existing at the time that the debtor filed for bankruptcy and not reaffirmed.

2.2 Chapter 11 (Reorganization)

Chapter 11 bankruptcy cases typically involve business debtors. However, if an individual debtor exceeds the debt limits for filing a Chapter 13 bankruptcy case (as discussed below), the debtor may file for bankruptcy under Chapter 11. In a Chapter 11 case, the debtor typically retains its assets, and to the extent applicable, continues to operate its business.[5] The debtor will propose a Chapter 11 plan of reorganization (or liquidation) which sets forth the debtor's plan to address the claims of the debtor's creditors.[6] The Chapter 11 plan will have to comply with various requirements set forth in the Bankruptcy Code provisions addressing Chapter 11, and will be subject to a vote by the debtor's creditors.[7] In February 2020, the Small Business Reorganization Act of 2019, which created Subchapter V of Chapter 11 of the Bankruptcy Code went into effect. The new Subchapter V offers

3. *Id.* §§ 701–727.
4. *Id.* §§ 701, 704.
5. *Id.* § 1108.
6. *Id.* § 1121.
7. *Id.* §§ 1123, 1129.

a more streamlined and accelerated Chapter 11 process for both small businesses and individuals with total debt below a certain threshold level.[8]

2.3 Chapter 13 (Adjustment of Debts of Individual with Regular Income)

Chapter 13 bankruptcy cases involve individual debtors with total debt below certain threshold amounts. Under this chapter, a debtor retains his or her property and proposes a Chapter 13 plan of reorganization that provides for the debtor to make regular monthly payments, usually over a three- to five-year period, to the debtor's creditors, either through payments made to a Chapter 13 Trustee, or payments on postpetition obligations made directly to the creditor.[9] Upon completion of the payments under the chapter plan, the debtor will receive a Chapter 13 discharge, which, with certain exceptions, discharges the debtor from all their debts existing as of the bankruptcy filing date.[10] (A more thorough discussion of Chapter 13 is set forth below).

2.4 Chapter 12 (Adjustment of Debts of Family Farmer and Family Fisherman with Regular Annual Income)

Chapter 12 applies to family farmers and fishermen and provides for reorganization and repayment of debts owed to the debtor's creditors through a Chapter 12 plan.[11] Subject to certain exceptions, upon completion of the payments due under the Chapter 12 plan, the Chapter 12 debtor receives a discharge of all prepetition obligations.[12]

3. Commencement of Bankruptcy Case

Consumers may choose to file for bankruptcy protection for a number of reasons. The consumer may be facing the potential loss of their residence, through a foreclosure or eviction; or the bankruptcy may be the result of a repossession of a vehicle. Some consumers may have accumulated substantial debt in the form of credit cards, medical bills, and other expenses. The consumer may be facing a hardship, such as loss of job or a health issue, which has led to the consumer falling behind in making payments. This, in turn, may have resulted in constant calls and letters from debt collectors demanding payment. Facing such harassment and financial hardship, consumers may be left with no other choice than to file for bankruptcy.

8. *Id.* §§ 1181 *et seq.*
9. *Id.* §§ 1321, 1322.
10. *Id.* §1328.
11. *Id.* §§ 1221–1222.
12. *Id.* § 122.

Individuals can avail themselves of the protections of the Bankruptcy Code by filing a bankruptcy petition in a federal bankruptcy court in the jurisdiction where such person resides.[13] The date that the debtor files its bankruptcy petition is referred to as the "petition date," which for purposes of application of the Bankruptcy Code and Rules, separates those "prepetition" claims and matters arising prior to the bankruptcy filing, and those "postpetition" matters arising after the bankruptcy filing.

3.1 Property of the Estate

The commencement of the bankruptcy case creates an estate.[14] With certain exceptions, all legal or equitable interests of the debtor in property as of the commencement of the case is property of the estate.[15] Such property of the estate is subject to those protections provided by the Bankruptcy Code, including the automatic stay (as discussed below).

3.2 Proof of Claim

In each bankruptcy case, creditors listed in the debtor's bankruptcy schedules will receive notice of the bankruptcy case filing.[16] If a deadline has been set for filing proofs of claims, known as a "bar date," then such notice of the bankruptcy case will set forth that deadline. In Chapter 7 cases where there are no apparent assets for distribution to creditors, no bar date may be set since creditors in those cases will receive no distribution.

If a bar date is set, then creditors will usually need to file a proof of claim, using the Official Bankruptcy Form B410, to have an allowed claim and give the creditor the opportunity to receive some distribution on the claim in the bankruptcy case.[17]

4. Automatic Stay

As noted above, a driving factor for a consumer to file a bankruptcy petition may be to stop a foreclosure, repossession, or other collection action. Accordingly, one of the most important protections afforded to a debtor in bankruptcy is the automatic stay provided under section 362 of the Bankruptcy Code. As discussed below, the automatic stay, which is applicable to all bankruptcy filings, no matter the chapter, prohibits certain actions against the debtor and/or the debtor's property to collect on a debt.

---

13. *Id.* § 301.
14. *Id.* § 541.
15. *Id.*
16. *Id.* § 342.
17. *Id.* §§ 501–502.

4.1 When Does the Automatic Stay Go into Effect and When Does It Terminate

The automatic stay goes into effect at the time that the debtor files a bankruptcy petition.[18] It is effective as against all creditors and parties in interest, whether or not such creditors have notice of the bankruptcy filing.[19] Unless terminated earlier by a bankruptcy court order, the automatic stay remains in effect until the earlier of the time the bankruptcy case is closed, the case is dismissed, or a bankruptcy discharge is granted or denied; or as the stay relates to specific property, it remains in effect until such property is no longer the property of the bankruptcy estate.[20]

4.2 What Actions Are Prohibited by the Automatic Stay

Broadly speaking, section 362(a) of the Bankruptcy Code prohibits any action, or the continuation of any action, seeking to collect on a prepetition claim against the debtor or attempting to exercise control over property of the debtor. Specifically, section 362(a) operates to stay:

1. The commencement or continuation, including the issuance or employment of process, of a judicial, administrative, or other action or proceeding against the debtor that was or could have been commenced before the commencement of the bankruptcy case, or to recover a claim against the debtor that arose before the commencement of the bankruptcy case;
2. The enforcement, against the debtor or against property of the estate, of a judgment obtained before commencement of the bankruptcy case;
3. Any act to obtain possession of property of the estate or of property from the estate or to exercise control over property of the estate;
4. Any act to create, perfect, or enforce any lien against property of the estate;
5. Any act to create, perfect, or enforce against property of the debtor any lien to the extent that such lien secures a claim that arose before the commencement of the bankruptcy case;
6. Any act to collect, assess, or recover a claim against the debtor that arose before the commencement of the bankruptcy case;
7. The setoff of any debt owing to the debtor that arose before the commencement of the bankruptcy case against any claim against the debtor; and
8. The commencement or continuation of a proceeding before the United States Tax Court concerning a tax liability of a debtor that is a

---

18. *Id.* § 362(a).
19. *See In re* Smith, 876 F.2d 524, 526 (6th Cir. 1989)(citing cases).
20. 11 U.S.C. § 362(c).

> corporation for a taxable period the bankruptcy court may determine or concerning the tax liability of a debtor who is an individual for a taxable period ending before the date of the order for relief under this title.[21]

4.3 Exceptions to the Automatic Stay

Section 362(b) of the Bankruptcy Code sets forth exceptions to the automatic stay. Although many of these exceptions are unlikely to apply in a consumer bankruptcy case, there are several exceptions that may be applicable, including the following:

1. The commencement or continuation of a criminal action or proceeding against the debtor;
2. Civil actions related to child custody, child support, and other domestic support obligations, including actions to establish paternity, actions concerning child custody or visitation, actions concerning domestic support obligations, action for dissolution of marriage, withholding of income of the debtor for payment of a domestic support obligation;
3. Commencement or continuation of an action by a governmental unit to enforce policy or regulatory power;
4. Action by lessor to the debtor under lease of *nonresidential* real property that has terminated by the expiration of the stated term of the lease before commencement of or during the bankruptcy case to take possession of such property;
5. Continuation of any eviction action by a lessor against a debtor involving residential property and with respect to which the lessor obtained a prepetition judgment for possession (an eviction order) of the property against the debtor.[22]

Actions that fall under any of these exceptions can continue against the debtor or the debtor's property, notwithstanding the bankruptcy filing.

4.4 Relief from Automatic Stay

Under section 362(d) of the Bankruptcy Code, a bankruptcy court can grant relief from the automatic stay to a creditor, which will allow the creditor to proceed with an action against the debtor or the debtor's property.[23]

---

21. *Id.* § 362(a).
22. *Id.* §§ 362(b)(1), (2), (10), (22).
23. *Id.* § 362(d).

4.5 Procedure for Obtaining Relief from Automatic Stay

A request for relief from the automatic stay under section 362(d) of the Bankruptcy Code is made by motion filed with the bankruptcy court.[24] Such a motion is considered a contested matter under Bankruptcy Rule 9014, which means that certain of the procedural rules that govern lawsuits filed within a bankruptcy case, known as adversary proceedings, found in part VII of the Bankruptcy Rules, will apply to the motion seeking relief from the stay.[25] Additionally, the filing and service of a motion for relief from stay are governed by Bankruptcy Rule 4001.[26] The motion, and sometimes notice of the motion, must be served on the affected parties (the debtor, any co-debtor, any bankruptcy trustee), as well as those other parties as directed by the court or local bankruptcy rule. Although the applicable bankruptcy rules do not require a response to the motion, some courts may require, by local rule or procedure, that a response be filed for the matter to be considered contested and subject to a hearing. In these jurisdictions requiring a response, if no response is filed, the bankruptcy court may grant the motion without conducting a hearing.

In general, after a motion for relief is filed, section 362(e) of the Bankruptcy Code provides that the automatic stay will terminate thirty days after the filing, unless, after notice and hearing, the court orders the stay continued in effect pending conclusion of, or as result of, a final hearing and determination of the motion.[27] As a result, a hearing—either preliminary or final—will typically be conducted within thirty days of the filing. If the initial hearing is a preliminary hearing, the final hearing shall be concluded not later than thirty days after the conclusion of the preliminary hearing.[28] That thirty-day period may be extended with the consent of the parties or by the court based on a finding of compelling circumstances.[29]

However, in an individual case filed under Chapter 7, 11, or 13, the stay shall terminate on the sixtieth day following the filing of the motion for relief unless the court renders a final decision during the sixty-day period, or the sixty-day period is extended by consent of the parties, or by the court for good cause.[30]

4.5.1 Grounds for Granting Relief from Automatic Stay

At the hearing on the motion for relief from stay, the court may grant the motion if the grounds for the relief are shown. The grounds for relief from the automatic stay are set forth in section 362(d) of the Bankruptcy Code, and include (1) relief granted for "cause," including lack of adequate protection, (2) lack of equity in the property

---

24. *Id.* § 362(d); Fed. R. Bankr. P. 4001.
25. Fed. R. Bankr. P. 4001, 7001.
26. Fed. R. Bankr. P. 4001.
27. 11 U.S.C. § 362(e).
28. *Id.* § 362(e)(1).
29. *Id.*
30. *Id.* § 362(e)(2).

and the property is not necessary for an effective reorganization, and (3) when the bankruptcy case was filed as a scheme to delay, hinder, or defraud creditors.[31]

4.5.1.1 Cause

"Cause" for relief from the stay is not specifically defined under the Bankruptcy Code.[32] Accordingly, what constitutes "cause" for relief from stay is typically drawn from the bankruptcy case law. In these decisions, courts have broadly defined what may constitute "cause." For example, "cause" may include failure to remit payments to a creditor as required under a Chapter 13 plan, failure to maintain insurance on the property, or a bad faith filing.[33]

Additionally, as set forth in section 362(d), a lack of adequate protection may constitute cause for relief from stay. Adequate protection is not specifically defined, but section 361 of the Bankruptcy Code provides ways in which adequate protection may be provided.[34] Under section 361, adequate protection may be provided by:

1. Requiring the debtor to make a cash payment or periodic cash payments to the entity to which the stay applies;
2. Providing to the entity to which the stay applies an additional or replacement lien to the extent that such stay results in a decrease in the value of such entity's interest in the property; or
3. Granting such other relief, other than entitling such entity to compensation allowable under section 503(b)(1) (which provides for allowance of administrative expense claims, which are higher-priority claims for purposes of bankruptcy cases) as will result in the realization by such entity of the indubitable equivalent of such entity's interest in such property.[35]

For purposes of granting relief from the stay, a lack of adequate protection can be shown where the property is uninsured, or the property is depreciating in value.[36] The debtor has the burden of proving that the interest of the creditor is adequately protected.[37] If the burden cannot be met, the automatic stay may be lifted or the debtor may be ordered to provide adequate protection in some form to the creditor.

---

31. *Id.*§ 362(d).
32. *Id.* § 362(d)(1).
33. *In re* Marques, 547 B.R. 841 (Bankr. C.D. Cal. 2016) (granting stay relief based on failure to make payments); *In re* Jones, 189 B.R. 13 (Bankr. E.D. Ok 1995) (failure to maintain insurance grounds for relief); *In re* Phoenix Piccadilly, LTD, 849 F.2d 1393 (11th Cir. 1988) (bad faith filing cause for relief from stay).
34. 11 U.S.C. § 361.
35. *Id.*
36. *In re* Kowalsky, 235 B.R. 590 (Bankr. E.D. Tex. 1999).
37. 11 U.S.C. § 362(g).

4.5.1.2 Lack of Equity and Lack of Necessity of Property for Reorganization

Two grounds on which a creditor can receive relief from the automatic stay to allow the creditor to proceed against specific property are if there is a lack of equity in such property and if the property is not necessary for a successful reorganization.[38] The party moving for relief from stay has the burden of proving the lack of equity by showing that the value of the property is equal to or less than the total amount of liens against the property.[39] The party opposing relief from stay has the burden of proof on the issue of necessity to an effective reorganization, and on any other issues that may arise.[40] In a Chapter 13 case, where the debtor typically intends to retain her or his property, the debtor can usually meet their burden of establishing that the property is necessary for an effective reorganization. However, the party seeking relief from the automatic stay can establish that the property is not necessary for an effective reorganization through a showing that no reorganization is reasonably possible.[41] In a Chapter 7 bankruptcy case, where nonexempt property is liquidated for the benefit of creditors, the moving party must only show a lack of equity in the property to establish grounds for stay relief, since there is no reorganization.

4.5.1.3 Relief from Stay as to Personal Property

In most cases, an individual debtor must state their intent for the property and actually perform that intent if they would like the automatic stay to continue to apply to that property. Under section 362(h) of the Bankruptcy Code, in an individual case, the automatic stay is terminated with respect to personal property securing a claim or subject to an unexpired lease, and such property shall no longer be property of the estate, if the debtor fails (1) to timely file a statement of intention required by Bankruptcy Code section 521(a)(2) or to indicate in such statement of intention whether the debtor will surrender the property, redeem the property pursuant to section 722 (applicable in Chapter 7 cases), reaffirm the debt pursuant to section 524(c), or in the case of the lease of personal property, assume the unexpired lease if the trustee does not do so; or (2) to take timely action to surrender, redeem, reaffirm, or assume as stated in the statement of intention.[42] However, this section does not apply if the court determines that such personal property is of consequential value or benefit to the estate, orders appropriate adequate protection of the creditor's interest, and orders the debtor to deliver any such collateral in the debtor's possession to the trustee.[43]

38. *Id.* § 362(d)(2).
39. *Id.* § 362(g).
40. *Id.*
41. *In re* Cho, 164 B.R. 730 (Bankr. E.D. Va. 1994).
42. 11 U.S.C. § 362(h).
43. *Id.*

4.5.1.4 Stay of Order Granting Relief from Stay

Under Bankruptcy Rule 4001(a)(3), an order granting relief from stay is effective for a period of fourteen days after entry of the order, unless the court orders otherwise.[44] Often, parties requesting relief from the automatic stay will request a waiver of the application of this rule. Accordingly, the order granting relief from stay should be consulted to determine whether the stay provisions under this Rule have been waived.

5. The Co-Debtor Stay

To provide additional protections to consumers and their family members, section 1301 of the Bankruptcy Code provides for the automatic stay of actions by creditors to collect all or any part of a consumer debt of the debtor from any individual who is liable on such debt with the debtor, or that secured such debt.[45] This section prevents a creditor from pursuing action against a nondebtor party that co-signed or guaranteed the debt of the debtor, or pursuing action against any property provided by such nondebtor party to secure the debt of the debtor in bankruptcy.[46] The co-debtor stay does not apply if the co-debtor became liable on or secured the debt of the debtor in bankruptcy in the ordinary course of its business.[47] This exception applies to sureties or recourse lenders that guaranty or provide security to borrowers as part of their business. Additionally, the co-debtor stay does not bar a creditor from presenting a negotiable instrument or giving notice of dishonor of such an instrument.[48]

Subject to an earlier order granting relief from the co-debtor stay, the co-debtor stay expires at the time that the bankruptcy case is closed, dismissed, or converted to a case under Chapter 7 or Chapter 11.[49] A creditor can seek an earlier termination of the automatic stay by the court by filing a motion requesting such relief, which follows the procedural requirements set forth in Bankruptcy Rules 4001 and 9014, as discussed above.[50] Relief from the co-debtor stay may be granted to the extent that:

1. As between the debtor and the individual protected by the co-debtor stay, such individual received the consideration for the claim held by the creditor;

44. Fed. R. Bankr. P. 4001(a)(3).
45. 11 U.S.C. § 1301.
46. *Id.*
47. *Id.*
48. *Id.*
49. *Id.*
50. Fed. R. Bankr. P. 4001, 9014.

2. the Chapter 13 plan filed by the debtor proposes not to pay such claim; or
3. the creditor's interest would be irreparably harmed by the continuation of the stay.[51]

The grounds set forth, under (1) above for relief from the automatic stay applies when the debtor in bankruptcy is in fact the co-debtor on the loan. In other words, the party receiving the direct consideration or benefit for the claim of the creditor is the co-debtor, and the debtor in bankruptcy is the actual co-debtor on the claim.

Under section 1301(c) of the Bankruptcy Code, twenty days after filing a motion seeking relief from the co-debtor stay, such stay is terminated unless the debtor or any individual liable on such debt files and serves a written objection to the requested relief.[52] Accordingly, the debtor or co-debtor must take action in response to a motion to terminate the co-debtor stay to preserve the benefit of such stay.

6. Violations of the Automatic Stay

As noted above, the automatic stay prevents a creditor from taking or continuing action against a debtor or property of the debtor's bankruptcy estate, even if the creditor is not aware of the bankruptcy filing. Therefore, a collection action by a creditor without knowledge of the bankruptcy would constitute a technical violation of the stay. Any such action by the creditor in violation of the stay, technical or otherwise, would be void, or at least voidable.[53] However, a collection action taken by a creditor without knowledge of the bankruptcy would likely not lead to serious consequences for the creditor, provided the creditor ceases such activity on learning of the bankruptcy.

However, if a creditor takes actions against the debtor or property of the estate to attempt to collect on the debt with knowledge of the bankruptcy, it may result in serious consequences to the creditor. In such a case, the debtor or the trustee may file a motion for contempt under section 105 of the Bankruptcy Code. Section 105 gives the court broad power to take such action as necessary to carry out the provisions of the Bankruptcy Code and seek sanctions against the creditor in situations like these.[54] If the debtor or trustee shows that the violation of the automatic stay was willful, then the creditor may be accessed with the debtor's actual damages resulting from the stay violation, including costs and attorneys' fees.[55] Additionally, in "appropriate circumstances," the bankruptcy court can award punitive damages against the creditor.[56]

51. 11 U.S.C. § 1301(c).
52. *Id.* § 1301(d).
53. *In re* Richardson, 497 B.R. 546 (Bankr. S.D. Ind. 2013).
54. 11 U.S.C. § 105.
55. *Id.* § 362(k)(1).
56. *Id.*

Accordingly, it is incumbent on a creditor to cease all collection activities against the debtor and the debtor's property when the creditor learns that the debtor has filed for bankruptcy protection. Otherwise, the creditor may be subject to paying sanctions.

7. Chapter 7

Chapter 7 bankruptcy, sometimes referred to as *straight bankruptcy*, is the least complicated of the bankruptcy chapters and is available to both individuals and business debtors.[57] For purposes of individual debtors, Chapter 7 provides for the identification of all nonexempt assets with value, and the liquidation of such assets to pay the debtor's creditors.[58]

Once a debtor files, a Chapter 7 trustee is appointed to identify those assets that may be available for liquidation, to take control of and liquidate such assets, and to make distributions of the proceeds from such liquidation to the debtor's creditors.[59] Accordingly, once that bankruptcy case is filed, the Chapter 7 trustee does most of the work. The Chapter 7 trustee is granted certain avoidance powers, which allows the trustee to pursue recovery of transfers made by the debtor which may have been preferential, fraudulent, or made after the bankruptcy filing without court approval.[60]

Unless an individual has a great deal of assets in need of liquidation, or there are avoidance actions that need to be pursued, Chapter 7 cases are typically resolved in a shorter time than cases under other bankruptcy chapters.

Assuming there are no applicable exceptions and the trustee does not object to the debtor's discharge, the debtor will receive a bankruptcy discharge, which will discharge the debtor's personal liability on prepetition claims listed in the debtor's bankruptcy schedules.[61]

8. Chapter 13

Chapter 13 is one of the most commonly used chapters of the bankruptcy code. In a Chapter 13 case, the debtor proposes a plan for making periodic payments to his or her creditors out of future income pursuant to a schedule approved by the court. The periodic payments are made by the debtor to a Chapter 13 trustee, who in turn makes distributions to the debtor's creditors.

---

57. *Id.* § 109.

58. *Id.* §§ 704, 726. Although section 522 of the Bankruptcy Code sets forth exemptions, most bankruptcy courts apply the state law exemptions for the state in which the bankruptcy court is located.

59. 11 U.S.C. § 704.

60. *Id.* §§ 544, 547–550.

61. *Id.* § 727.

8.1 Eligibility

To be eligible to file a Chapter 13 case, the debtor must (1) be an individual, (2) with regular income, and (3) have debts that do not exceed the applicable debt limits.[62]

8.1.1 Individuals

Although the term *individual* is not defined in the Bankruptcy Code, bankruptcy courts have found that it is meant to refer to natural persons, such that Chapter 13 is not available to corporations, partnerships, or other business entities.[63] However, section 1304 of the Bankruptcy Code allows a debtor that is self-employed to continue to operate his or her business in the ordinary course of business, including obtaining postpetition credit, in the Chapter 13 case.[64]

8.1.2 Regular Income

Chapter 13 is often referred to as wage earner bankruptcy. To be eligible for Chapter 13, the debtor must have regular income. Section 101(30) of the Bankruptcy Code defines the term *individual with regular income* as an "individual whose income is sufficiently stable and regular to enable such individual to make payments under a plan under Chapter 13 of this title, other than a stockbroker or commodity broker."[65] *Regular income* has been defined broadly by case law and includes payments that are not work earnings, including unemployment compensation, disability income, welfare payments, social security benefits, pension income, alimony, maintenance, or child support.[66] The income must be sufficient to support payments from the debtor due under the Chapter 13 plan.

8.1.3 Debt Limits

Section 109(e) of the Bankruptcy Code sets forth the debt limits for eligibility for filing a Chapter 13.[67] As of April 1, 2019, to be eligible, an individual most owe as of the petition date, noncontingent, liquidated, unsecured debts of less than $419,275, and noncontingent, liquidated, secured debts of less than $1,257,850.[68] The dollar amounts in section 109(e) are adjusted every third year to reflect changes in the Consumer Price Index for All Urban Consumers, published by the Department of Labor.[69] In determining eligibility for filing Chapter 13, contingent and unliquidated

62. *Id.* § 109(e).
63. *In re* JAC Family Foundation, 356 B.R. 554 (Bankr. N.D. Ga. 2006).
64. 11 U.S.C. § 1304.
65. *Id.* § 101(30).
66. *In re* Robinson, 535 B.R. 437 (Bankr. N.D. Ga. 2015)
67. 11 U.S.C. § 109(e).
68. *Id.*
69. *Id.* § 104.

debts are excluded from the total amount of debt, but disputed claims are included in the determination of debt amount eligibility.[70]

8.1.4 Prior Bankruptcy Cases

Prior bankruptcy cases may also affect an individual's eligibility to file for bankruptcy, including Chapter 13 bankruptcy. An individual is not eligible to file for bankruptcy if the individual was a debtor at any time in the preceding 180 days if (1) the prior case was dismissed by the court for willful failure of the debtor to abide by orders of the court, or to appear before the court in proper prosecution of the case; or (2) the debtor requested and obtained the voluntary dismissal of the case following the filing of a request for relief from the automatic stay.[71] This provision is meant to prevent repeated filings and dismissals by a debtor in an effort to stop foreclosure proceedings and other collection actions. However, if the debtor is not eligible for filing the bankruptcy case under section 109(g) of the Bankruptcy Code, the creditor who objects to the debtor's eligibility to refile will be limited to objecting to confirmation of the debtor's plan on the grounds that the plan was not proposed in good faith or by means forbidden by law.[72]

8.1.5 Credit Counseling

Finally, for the debtor to be eligible to file for Chapter 13 bankruptcy, the debtor must have received credit counseling from an approved nonprofit credit counseling agency during the 180 days preceding the bankruptcy filing.[73]

8.2 The Chapter 13 Trustee

In each Chapter 13 bankruptcy case, a Chapter 13 trustee is appointed. The trustee will be the standing Chapter 13 trustee for the district and/or division where the case is filed.[74] The trustee's duties are set forth under section 1302(b) of the Bankruptcy Code and include the following:

- Accounting for the property of the estate;
- Investigating the financial affairs of the debtor;
- Opposing the discharge of the debtor (if appropriate);
- Furnishing information concerning the estate upon the request of interested parties;

---

70. *Id.* § 109.
71. *Id.* § 109(g).
72. *Id.* § 1325(a)(3).
73. *Id.* § 109(h).
74. *Id.* § 1302.

- Making a final report and filing a final account regarding the administration of the estate;
- Appearing and being heard at any hearing concerning the value of property subject to a lien;
- Addressing confirmation of a plan and modification of a plan after confirmation;
- Advising and assisting a debtor on nonlegal matters and in the performance of a plan; and
- Ensuring that the debtor commences timely payments as required by the plan.[75]

All payments due to the debtor's prepetition creditors will be made by the debtor to the trustee. The trustee will collect such payments and make distributions to the creditors in accordance with the debtor's confirmed Chapter 13 plan.[76]

8.3 The Chapter 13 Plan

The mechanism for a consumer debtor to address the debtor's prepetition debts is the Chapter 13 plan. Only the debtor, as opposed to a creditor or the Chapter 13 trustee, can file a Chapter 13 plan.[77] Under Bankruptcy Rule 3015, the Chapter 13 plan must be filed with the bankruptcy petition, or within fourteen days thereafter, unless that deadline is extended by the court for cause.[78]

The Chapter 13 plan must provide for the consumer to submit all or such portion of future earnings or other income as is necessary to execute the plan to the supervision and control of the Chapter 13 trustee.[79] The plan further should provide for full payment, in deferred cash payments, of all priority claims, unless the holder of a particular claim agrees to a different treatment.[80] If the Chapter 13 plan classifies claims, it must provide for the same treatment for each claim within a particular class.[81]

In addition to the mandatory requirements, the Chapter 13 plan may, among other things:

- Modify the rights of holders of secured claims, other than a claim secured only by a security interest in real property that is the debtor's principal residence, or of holders of unsecured claims, or leave unaffected the rights of holders of any class of claims;

75. *Id.* § 1302(b).
76. *Id.* § 1322.
77. *Id.* § 1321.
78. Fed. R. Bankr. P. 3015.
79. *Id.* § 1322(a).
80. *Id.* § 1322(a)(2).
81. *Id.* § 1322(a)(3).

- Provide for the curing or waiving of any default;
- Provide for payments on any unsecured claim to be made concurrently with payments on any secured claim or any other unsecured claim;
- Provide for the curing of any default within a reasonable time and maintenance of payments while the case is pending on any unsecured claim or secured claim on which the last payment is due after the date on which the final payment under the plan is due;
- Provide for the assumption, rejection, or assignment of any executory contract or unexpired lease of the debtor not previously rejected under such section;
- Provide for the payment of all or part of a claim against the debtor from property of the estate or property of the debtor;
- Provide for the vesting of property of the estate, on confirmation of the plan or at a later time, in the debtor or in any other entity; and
- Include any other appropriate provision not inconsistent with this title.[82]

The payments due from the consumer debtor under the Chapter 13 plan will be made for a period of between three to five years, but in any event, cannot last longer than five years.[83] The bankruptcy court can confirm a plan shorter than the three to five years required under the Bankruptcy Code, if the plan provides for payment in full of all allowed unsecured claims in the shorter period.[84] However, Chapter 13 plans of less than three years are not the norm.

Under section 1324 of the Bankruptcy Code, after notice to all interested parties, the bankruptcy court will hold a hearing to consider confirmation of the debtor's filed Chapter 13 plan.[85] The requirements for confirmation of the Chapter 13 plan are set forth in section 1325(a), and require that the plan provides, among other things, the following:

1. The plan must comply with all applicable provisions of the Bankruptcy Code.
2. The plan must be proposed in good faith and not by any means forbidden by law.
3. The value of property to be distributed under the plan on account of each allowed unsecured claim may not be less than the amount that would be paid on such claim in a Chapter 7 bankruptcy case. This is often referred to as the best interest test.
4. With respect to each allowed secured claim provided for by the plan, either
    a. The holder of the claim must accept the plan;

82. *Id.* § 1322(b).
83. *Id.* §§ 1322(d)(1), 1325(b)(4)(A).
84. *Id.* § 1322(b)(4)(B).
85. *Id.* § 1324.

   b. The plan must provide that:
      i. The holder of such claim retain its lien until the earlier of the payment in full of the underlying debt or the debtor's Chapter 13 discharge;
      ii. If the case is dismissed or converted prior to the completion of the plan, the secured creditor's lien will be retained in accordance with nonbankruptcy law;
      iii. The value of property to be distributed under the plan on account of such claim is not less than the amount of such claims; and
      iv. The secured claim must be paid in equal monthly payments in an amount sufficient to provide adequate protection to the secured creditor; or
   c. The debtor must surrender the property securing such claim to the holder of the claim.
5. The debtor must be able to make all payments under the plan and otherwise comply with its terms. This is often referred to as the feasibility requirement.
6. The bankruptcy case must have been filed in good faith.
7. The debtor must have filed all applicable federal, state, and local tax returns.[86]

Any party in interest may object to the confirmation of the plan within a time fixed by the court, by filing and serving a written objection to the plan.[87] The objection must set forth specifically which provision(s) under section 1325 the plan does not comply with. If the trustee or holder of an unsecured claim objects to the confirmation of the plan, then the court may not approve confirmation of the plan unless the value of the property to be distributed to such unsecured claim is not less than the amount of the claim; or the plan provides that all of the debtor's projected "disposable income" will be used to make payments to unsecured creditors under the plan for the entire period of the plan.[88] The debtor's disposable income is based on the debtor's monthly income, less amounts reasonably necessary for maintenance and support of the debtor and their dependents (or for domestic support obligation), for charitable contributions in an amount not to exceed 15 percent of gross income, and, if the debtor is engaged in business, for payments necessary for operation of the business.[89]

Assuming that the applicable provisions of 1325(a) are satisfied, and any objection is resolved or overruled, the court will enter an order confirming the

86. *Id.* § 1325.
87. *Id.* § 1324; Fed. R. Bankr. P. 3015.
88. 11 U.S.C. § 1325(b)(1).
89. *Id.* § 1325(b)(2).

debtor's Chapter 13 plan. Upon confirmation, the plan will be binding on the debtor and the debtor's creditors.

8.4 Discharge

Upon completion by the debtor of all payments due under the Chapter 13 plan, the bankruptcy court will grant the debtor a discharge. The discharge will relieve the debtor of any personal liability on any debts provided for under the plan or disallowed under section 502 of the Bankruptcy Code, with certain exceptions. For example, the discharge does not relieve the debtor from long-term debts; certain taxes; debts for restitution or criminal fines; debts arising through the debtor's false pretenses, false representation, fraud, or use of a false financial statement to obtain money, property, or services; debts not listed in the Chapter 13 schedules; debts arising from fraud or breach of fiduciary duty; claims related to embezzlement or larceny; educational loans; debtors for a domestic support obligation; or debts arising from a civil action against the debtor for willful or malicious injury by the debtor that causes personal injury or death to an individual.[90]

The bankruptcy discharge bars creditors from attempting to collect on any discharged debt personally from the debtor. Under the Fair Credit Reporting Act, the filing of the bankruptcy, and the entry of any discharge, are required to be reported by consumer reporting agencies. The bankruptcy filing will be listed on a consumer's credit report for a period of seven to ten years.[91] This may negatively affect the consumer's ability to obtain credit.

9. Secured Creditors

Creditors whose claims are secured by collateral enjoy more protections in bankruptcy than those whose claims are unsecured. However, where they have more rights, they also have more duties.

9.1 Filing a Proof of Claim

Under the 2017 amendments to the Federal Rules of Bankruptcy Procedure, secured creditors must file a proof of claim in order for the claim to be allowed.[92] Attached to that proof of claim they must include evidence of perfection of the security interest.[93]

90. *Id.* § 1328(a), 1328(d).
91. 15 U.S.C. § 1681(c).
92. Fed. R. Bankr. P. 3002(a), amended Dec. 1, 2017.
93. *Id.* P. 3001(d).

Creditors whose claims are secured by property owned by individual debtors, rather than corporate debtors, must include within the proof of claim the amount necessary to cure any prepetition default.[94]

If the property securing the claim is an individual debtor's principal residence the creditor must also include the requisite attachment to the proof of claim form and an escrow statement as of the date of the petition.[95]

In December 2015, the Judicial Conference approved form B 410A to be the requisite attachment to the proof of claim.[96] Part 1 of the attachment requires basic information about the mortgage.[97] Parts 2 and 3 of the attachment requires the secured creditor to outline for the court, and in particular the Chapter 13 trustee, all of the elements of the outstanding amount due under the loan—both the total outstanding debt and the amount necessary to cure default.[98] These elements include the principal, interest, fees, costs, escrow deficiency, and escrow shortage.[99] Part 4 of the attachment shows the monthly mortgage payment beginning the first month post-petition.[100]

Part 5 of the attachment requires the secured creditor to include a running loan payment history from the first date of default.[101] Depending on the mortgagor's payment behavior, this attachment could include a pay history several years long.[102] It is the intent of the form to have the concluding balances in part 5 to be shown on part 2.[103]

Secured creditors who file proofs of claim in accordance with Rule 3001 enjoy prima facie validity of their debt.[104] This acts as a rebuttable presumption that the claim is valid, and the debtor must overcome this presumption to disallow, or reduce the amount of, the claim.[105] Secured creditors whose proofs of claim do not comply with Rule 3001 do not enjoy this prima facie validity.[106] If a debtor objects to a

94. *Id.* P. 3001(c)(2)(B).

95. *Id.* P. 3001(c)(2)(C).

96. United States Courts, *Report of the Proceedings of the Judicial Conference of the United States* (September 17, 2015), 29–30, https://www.uscourts.gov/sites/default/files/2015-09-17_0.pdf.

97. United States Courts, *Form B 410A*, https://www.uscourts.gov/forms/bankruptcy-forms/proof-claim-attachment-0.

98. *Id.*

99. *Id.*

100. *Id.*

101. *Id.*

102. *Id.*

103. *Id.*

104. 11 U.S.C. § 502(a); Fed. R. Bankr. P. 3001(f).

105. *See In re* Allegheny Int'l, Inc., 954 F.2d 167, 173 (3d Cir. 1992), Nicholson v. eCAST Settlement Corp., 602 B.R. 295, 299 (Bankr. M.D. Pa. 2019).

106. *See* Fed. R. Bankr. P. 3001(f).

noncompliant proof of claim the court may bar the secured creditor from introducing further evidence to support its claim.[107]

If a secured creditor does not file a proof of claim at all, the debtor or trustee may file a proof of claim on their behalf.[108] The secured creditor may then be beholden to the amount claimed by the filer of the claim.[109]

Failure to file a proof of claim does not result in an extinguishment of the lien.[110] The secured creditor who did not file a proof of claim will retain their lien after the discharge.[111] Without a proof of claim the creditor will not receive any disbursements from the estate, and mortgage creditors will not receive any direct monthly payments from a trustee.[112] The creditor may still receive payments from the borrower directly.

9.2 Treatment under the Chapter 13 Plan

When a debtor has filed under Chapter 13 of the bankruptcy code, the secured creditor's treatment under the debtor's plan is dependent on the value and type of the collateral securing the claim. A creditor's claim may be only partially secured where the value of the collateral is less than the value of the claim. A claim may be oversecured where the value of the collateral is more than the value of the claim. A creditor is only entitled to security up to the value of the claim.

If the collateral securing the creditor's claim is the debtor's principal residence, the treatment of the claim will be driven by that fact.

In general, secured creditors must receive the full value of the collateral, the collateral itself, or be permitted to retain their lien after the bankruptcy has completed.

9.2.1 Non-Principal-Residence Creditors

Creditors whose claims are secured by property other than the debtor's principal residence may have their rights modified by the Chapter 13 plan.[113]

A creditor whose claim is undersecured may have their claim split in two separate claims: a secured portion and an unsecured portion.[114] The claim will be secured

107. *Id.* P. 3001(c)(2)(D).

108. 11 U.S.C. § 501(c).

109. *See In re* Walker, 526 B.R. 187, 190 (E.D. La. 2015).

110. 11 U.S.C. § 502(d)(2); Fed. R. Bankr. P. 3002(a).

111. *See In re* Batista-Sanechez, 502 B.R. 227, 230 (Bankr. N.D. Ill. 2013) (disallowed claim did not affect lien rights); *In re* Hamlett, 322 F.3d 342, 349 (4th Cir. 2003) (failure to file timely claim or failure to file claim at all did not affect lien rights).

112. *See In re Batista-Sanechez*, 502 B.R. at 230 (creditor with disallowed claim lost right to distribution under chapter 11 plan), *See also In re* Hogan, 346 B.R. 715, 720 (Bankr. N.D. Tex. 2006) ("[I]f a creditor elects not to file a claim, then it also elects not to be paid under the plan.").

113. *See* 11 U.S.C. § 1322(b)(2).

114. *Id.* § 506(a)(1).

to the extent of the value of the collateral, and the remainder will be unsecured. If the creditor receives the collateral itself, both claims will be satisfied. Otherwise the debtor must pay to the creditor the value of the collateral.

A creditor whose claim is oversecured receives not only the value of the collateral, but may also receive any interest, fees, or charges provided for under the agreement or under applicable nonbankruptcy law.[115]

The amount of security held by the creditor is established through the valuation process. This process is done either by motion or through request in the plan.[116] The collateral will be valued as of the petition date, and the replacement value will be used.[117] The debtor and creditor may introduce valuation evidence and expert witnesses to value the collateral and, accordingly, establish the extent to which the claim is secured.[118]

The lien will remain in place until the earlier of the debtor's last payment under the agreement or the debtor's discharge.[119] At either of these points, the debtor will have paid the value of the claim in full and the creditor will have received the full value of the collateral.[120]

9.2.2 Principal-Residence Creditors

A creditor whose claim is secured by a first lien on the debtor's principal residence will have their claim treated in accordance with sections 1322 and 1325 of the Bankruptcy Code.[121] The creditor's rights under such a claim cannot be modified through the plan,[122] except to allow the debtor to cure any outstanding arrearage as of the petition date without threat of immediate foreclosure.[123] Where the security instrument and note may permit the creditor to foreclose on the property upon some measure of default, the Bankruptcy Code allows the debtor to have some breathing room, and to cure the prepetition default through the life of the plan.[124] While the debtor is repaying the arrearage, they will also continue to make monthly payments to the creditor.[125] This treatment—the repayment of arrearage coupled with the payment of ongoing monthly payments—is typically called "cure and maintain."[126]

---

115. *Id.* § 506(b).
116. Fed. R. Bankr. P. 3012 (b).
117. 11 U.S.C. § 506(a)(2).
118. Fed. R. Bankr. P. 3012(a).
119. 11 U.S.C. § 1325(a)(5)(B).
120. *See id.*
121. *Id.* §§ 1322, 1325.
122. *See id.* § 1322(b)(2).
123. *See id.* § 1322(b)(5)
124. *See id., see also* § 362.
125. *See id.* § 1322(b)(5).
126. *See, e.g., In re* Stivender, 301 B.R. 498 (Bankr. S.D. Ohio 2003), *In re* Boscaccy, 442 B.R. 501 (Bankr. N.D. Miss. 2010), *In re* Dennett, 548 B.R. 733 (Bankr. N.D. Tex. 2016).

The process by which cure payments and maintenance payments are made depends on jurisdiction. Some jurisdictions are called "conduit" jurisdictions, where all mortgage payments—both arrearage and regular monthly payments—are made through the Chapter 13 trustee.[127] Others are "direct pay" jurisdictions, where the debtor pays ongoing monthly payments directly. In almost all jurisdictions, arrearage payments are made through the Chapter 13 trustee.

A debtor who cannot, or chooses not to, cure the arrearage and maintain payments on their principal residence may choose to surrender the property.[128] Under the 2017 amendments to the Federal Rules of Bankruptcy Procedure, the debtor's choice to surrender the property must be clearly indicated in the Chapter 13 plan.[129] Confirmation of the plan will result in the creditor receiving relief from the automatic stay in order to exercise their *in rem* right to foreclose on the property.[130]

9.2.3 Second Lien Creditors

Creditors who do not have a first lien on the debtor's principal residence may not enjoy the same rights and protections as first lien holders in a debtor's Chapter 13 case. Where the value of the debtor's principal residence is less than or equal to the amount of the first lien, that is, where the second lien is wholly underwater, the second lien may be stripped and the claim may be treated as an unsecured claim. The secured creditor then becomes an unsecured creditor. At the end of the case, the originally secured creditor will have received some payment on account of its unsecured claim, and will be left with no lien.

Unlike the valuation process described above, lien stripping or lien avoidance is usually completed through an adversary proceeding.[131] Under the 2017 amendments to Rule 3015.1, the debtor may also avoid or strip the creditor's lien through the plan.[132] If the debtor intends to avoid the creditor's lien through this process, the debtor must clearly indicate that intent in the Chapter 13 plan, and must serve the Chapter 13 plan as if it were an adversary complaint.[133]

---

127. *See* LBR 3015(b).2 (Bankr. D. Kan.) (requiring monthly payments made through chapter 13 trustee if debtor is delinquent as of the time of the petition or becomes delinquent post-petition), Local Rule 3015(g) (Bankr. D. Nev.) (same), Local Rule 3003-1 (Bankr. W.D.N.C.) (requiring all payments to mortgage creditors be paid through the chapter 13 trustee).

128. 11 U.S.C. § 1322(a)(5)(C).

129. *See* Fed. R. Bankr. P. 3015.1(d).

130. *See id.*

131. Fed. R. Bankr. P. 7001(2).

132. *Id.* P. 3015.1(c)(3).

133. *See id.* P. 3012(b). As the lien avoidance process is essentially a process to determine the amount of the secured claim (and determine that amount to be $0), the service of process rules under section 3012 apply.

9.3 Treatment in a Chapter 7 Case

When the debtor files Chapter 7, secured creditors will be treated in accordance with the debtor's statement of intention, filed using official form 108.[134] The debtor is required to file the statement of intention within thirty days of the filing date, or before the meeting of creditors, whichever is earlier.[135] On the form the debtor must indicate whether they intend to surrender or redeem the property or enter into a reaffirmation agreement with the secured creditor.[136] The creditor will then have thirty days after the meeting of creditors to complete that action.[137]

If the property will be "surrendered" in accordance with the statement of intention, the debtor will be required to make the property available to the creditor.[138] This does not mean the debtor must deliver the property, but it cannot interfere with the creditor's taking of the property.[139] Title does not vest in the creditor upon completion of the surrender.[140]

9.4 Mortgage Creditors' Obligations during the Case: Rule 3002.1 Notices

Creditors that have claims secured by the debtor's principal residence, and where contractual installment payments will be made during the bankruptcy case, are required to provide notice to the court, the trustee, and the debtor of changes to the debtor's regular monthly payment and any fees, expenses, or costs assessed to the debtor's account.[141]

These notices are required by Fed. R. Bankr. P. 3002.1, promulgated in December 2011.[142] The rule was enacted to ensure that debtors did not emerge from their bankruptcy in default on their mortgage because of unnoticed payment changes, fees, and costs.[143] In 2016, the rule was revised to clarify that these notices must be filed where the borrower pays their monthly mortgage payment directly, but are not required where the creditor has received relief from the automatic stay.[144]

---

134. Fed. R. Bankr. P. 1007(b)(2).

135. 11 U.S.C. § 521(a)(2).

136. *See id.*

137. *See id.*

138. *See In re* Pratt, 462 F.3d 14, 18–19 (1st Cir. 2006) (vehicle need not be delivered upon surrender, but must be made available), *In re* Tosi, 546 B.R. 487, 492 (Bankr. D. Mass. 2016) (express retention of the property for any period of time did not satisfy the completion of "surrender").

139. *See In re Pratt*, 462 F.3d at 18–29.

140. *See In re Tosi*, 546 B.R. at 493.

141. *See* Fed. R. Bankr. P. 3002.1.

142. *See id.*

143. *See* Committee Notes on Rules (2011).

144. *See* Committee Notes on Rules (2016 Amendment).

The rule by its language recognizes that the typical mortgage payment changes associated with a principal residence mortgage are escrow payment changes resulting from an annual analysis, and changes in interest rate as scheduled in the note.[145] A payment change notice is required to be filed at least twenty-one days prior to the effective date of the change.[146] The notice is recognized as a supplement to the proof of claim[147] and will be served on the trustee, the debtor's attorney, and the debtor themselves.[148]

Attorneys' fees for filing bankruptcy-related documents, nonescrowed tax or insurance amounts, and other fees or costs associated with the loan may be assessed to the account while the borrower is in bankruptcy. When such fees or costs are assessed to the account the creditor is required to notice them to the court, the trustee, and the debtor by filing a notice of postpetition fee, expense, or charge as a supplement to the proof of claim.[149] Such notices are due 180 days after the assessment of the fee or cost.[150]

9.5 Completion of the Plan

A typical Chapter 13 plan lasts between three and five years.[151] No plan may be proposed that lasts longer than five years.[152] After the plan is confirmed, it may be modified to extend or reduce the time for payments, but the maximum time still cannot exceed five years.[153]

At the conclusion of the plan, once the debtor has made all necessary payments, the parties will begin preparing for the debtor to receive a discharge. This process is largely driven by local practice but does require some standard procedures.

Once all plan payments have been made and all creditors have been paid, the trustee will file a final report and account outlining all payments made and the amount of all claims filed and allowed.[154]

145. *See* Fed. R. Bankr. P. 3002.1(b).

146. *See Id.* P. 3002.1(b)(1).

147. *See* Fed. R. Bankr. P. 3002.1(d), United States Courts, *Form Number: B410S-1*, https://www.uscourts.gov/forms/bankruptcy-forms/proof-claim-supplement-1-0.

148. *See id.*

149. *See* Fed. R. Bankr. P. 3002.1(c).

150. *See id.*

151. *See* 11 U.S.C. § 1322(d) (providing for two maximum plan lengths: three years or five years, depending on the debtor's income).

152. *See id.*

153. *See* 11 U.S.C. §§ 1329(a)(2), 1329(c).

154. *See id.* §§ 1302(b)(1), 704(a)(9).

9.5.1 Notice of Final Cure

If the debtor has a mortgage on their principal residence, and either the trustee or the debtor has been paying regular monthly payments to the creditor during the case, the trustee will also file a notice of final cure pursuant to Rule 3002.1(h).[155] This notice will state that the debtor has completed all payments required to cure the arrearage on their mortgage and is current on their postpetition mortgage payments.[156] The creditor will then have twenty-one days to respond to that notice and either agree that the debtor has completed all pre- and postpetition payments, or disagree and show what amounts are due.[157] After the response has been filed, the debtor or trustee may file a motion to determine whether the debtor's pre- and postpetition payments have been satisfied.[158]

9.6 Discharge

If the debtor is entitled to a discharge, the discharge process will begin after the completion of plan payments. In a Chapter 13 case, the debtor will be required to complete a financial management course prior to the entry of discharge.[159]

Upon entry of the discharge, all rights of most unsecured creditors to collect on the debt are terminated, and the unsecured debt is discharged, even if the creditor has not received the full value of their claim.[160]

The secured creditor whose claim has not been cured and maintained will have received either the collateral or the full value of the collateral.[161] The debtor will have completed all of their obligations under the agreement with the creditor.[162]

The secured creditor will not receive a discharge of the debt if the claim is a long-term debt that has been provided for under section 1322(b)(5).[163] Those creditors will continue to be paid after the date of discharge, as the last payment under the agreement will be due after the completion of the plan.[164] For those creditors whose claim is secured by the debtor's principal residence, any amounts past due at the time of discharge will be treated as discharged unless the creditor provided notice under Rule 3002.1(h) of those outstanding amounts, and, in some jurisdictions, if the bankruptcy court ruled that the mortgage was not current.

---

155. *See* Fed. R. Bankr. P. 3002.1(h).
156. *See id.*
157. *See id.* P. 3002.1(g).
158. *See id.* P. 3002.1(h).
159. *See id.* P. 1007(b)(7), P. 4004(c)(4).
160. *See* 11 U.S.C. § 1328(a)(outlining exceptions).
161. *See id.* § 1325(a)(5).
162. *See id.*
163. *Id.* § 1328(a)(1).
164. *Id.* § 1322(b)(5).

If the debtor has indicated an intent to surrender the principal residence, or if the creditor received relief from the automatic stay with respect to the principal residence during the case, the debtor's personal liability under the note will be discharged.[165] The mortgage, which will give the creditor the right to collect against the property only, will remain intact.[166] The creditor will be able to foreclose on the property after the discharge but will be barred from collecting any deficiency from the discharged debtor.[167]

9.7 Termination without Discharge

A debtor who has completed all payments under the plan, but has failed to complete some administrative action,[168] had received a discharge under Chapter 7, 11, or 12 fewer than four years prior to the current case,[169] or had received a discharge under Chapter 13 fewer than two years prior to the current case,[170] will have their case terminated without discharge. Under these circumstances, the case will merely be closed and creditors are free to pursue actions against the debtor.

165. *See id.* § 1328(a)(1), providing exceptions to discharge and not including these actions.

166. *See id.* § 524(a)(2) (barring actions to collect discharged debts as a personal liability of the debtor); *see also* Johnson v. Home State Bank, 501 U.S. 78, 82–83 ("[A] discharge extinguishes *only* 'the personal liability of the debtor.'") (quoting 11 U.S.C. § 524(a)(1)).

167. *See Johnson*, 501 U.S. at 84 ("Rather, a bankruptcy discharge extinguishes only one mode of enforcing a claim—namely, an action against the debtor *in personam*—while leaving intact another—namely, an action against the debtor in rem.").

168. 11 U.S.C. § 1328(g).

169. *Id.* § 1328(f).

170. *Id.*

CHAPTER

13

The Servicemembers Civil Relief Act

Robert Savoie

1. Introduction

The Servicemembers Civil Relief Act (SCRA) is a comprehensive set of legal protections and benefits afforded to members of the armed forces (servicemembers) and certain other individuals.[1] The SCRA was first enacted as a discrete set of requirements in 1940 as the Soldiers' and Sailors' Civil Relief Act, was updated and renamed in 2003, and has seen minor modifications since 2003.[2] The SCRA contains two stated purposes that gave rise to its passage. First, the SCRA was enacted to provide for, strengthen, and expedite the national defense through protections extended by the SCRA to servicemembers of the United States to allow such individuals to devote their entire

---

The views expressed in this article are those of the author and are not intended to represent the views of McGlinchey Stafford, PLLC or its clients, nor are they intended to constitute legal advice. The author recommends that readers consult their attorney to confirm the SCRA's applicability to the reader's specific facts and circumstances.

1. Soldiers' and Sailors' Civil Relief Act of 1940, ch. 888, 54 Stat. 1178, *amended by* Servicemembers Civil Relief Act, Pub. L. No. 108-189, 117 Stat. 2835 (2003) (codified as amended at 50 U.S.C. §§ 3901–4043 (2012)). Because this treatise is focused on the federal laws governing consumer financial services and products, certain provisions of the SCRA are not discussed herein. Examples of SCRA protections not discussed include protections and rights relating to termination of telephone service contracts, child custody protections, life insurance, enforcement of storage liens, taxes, public lands, professional liability, evictions, terminations of residential leases, and health insurance reinstatement, among others. Please reach out to the author if you need additional information regarding these protections.

2. *Id.*

energy to the defense needs of the United States. Second, the SCRA was enacted to provide for the temporary suspension of judicial and administrative proceedings and transactions that may adversely affect the civil rights of servicemembers during their military service.[3] The protections of the SCRA are logical ones when viewed through the prism of these dual purposes.

At its core, the portion of the SCRA discussed herein relates primarily to minimizing the burden of consumer financial products or services on servicemembers who are called to service, and protecting those servicemembers against having actions taken against them (or losing their rights to take actions against others) while they are in military service.[4] As outlined below, this includes a right to reduce the interest rate to 6 percent on certain obligations, protection against seizure of collateral or other termination of a contract, the ability to terminate certain leases early without penalty, protection against retaliation for invoking these benefits, and the ability to request and obtain a wide range of court-ordered protections. Some states have also enacted laws that grant additional protections or apply similar or identical protections to state guard and militia members.[5]

The SCRA also imposes certain obligations on the armed forces. First, the secretary of the appropriate branch of the armed forces must ensure that notice of the benefits provided under the SCRA is given in writing to any person in or entering military service.[6] Second, the secretary must also provide certain specified pertinent information on the SCRA rights and protections available to both servicemembers and their dependents.[7] The information must be provided during the initial training of the servicemember, or in the case of a member of a reserve component, during the initial orientation and when the servicemember is mobilized or otherwise individually called or ordered to active duty for a period of more than one year, and also at any other times deemed appropriate by the secretary.[8] The secretary may also decide to provide information to the adult dependents of servicemembers.[9]

2. Scope and Applicability

2.1 To Whom Does the SCRA Apply?

The SCRA applies to several categories of individuals, each of which is discussed below.

---

3. 50 U.S.C. § 3902 (2019).
4. *Id.*
5. *See, e.g.*, Cal. Mil. & Vet. Code §§ 400–409 (2019). However, state laws are outside the scope of this treatise. Please reach out to the author if you need additional information.
6. 50 U.S.C. § 3915 (2019).
7. *Id.* § 3916 (2019).
8. *Id.*
9. *Id.*

2.1.1 Servicemembers

The largest group of individuals to whom the SCRA applies is servicemembers. A *servicemember* includes any member of the uniformed services, which includes the armed forces, the commissioned corps of the National Oceanic and Atmospheric Administration, and the commissioned corps of the Public Health Service.[10] In the parlance of our times, the term *servicemember* refers to everyone entitled to protections under the SCRA, and thus this treatise refers to all such individuals as *servicemembers* except where otherwise noted (such as in the case of dependents of servicemembers). However, the following groups of protected individuals are defined separately under the SCRA.

2.1.2 Citizens Serving with Allied Forces

The SCRA also applies to a citizen of the United States who is serving with the forces of a nation with which the United States is allied in the prosecution of a war or military action.[11] However, the service must be similar to military service as defined in the SCRA, and the protections terminate on the date of discharge or release from such service.[12]

2.1.3 Reservists and Draftees

The majority of the SCRA's protections apply to any member of a reserve component (referred to herein as "reservists")[13] or a draftee who is ordered to report for military service.[14] However, financial institutions should be mindful of the fact that the timing of the extension of these protections differs from the timing for other servicemembers.[15] For reservists and draftees, these protections apply as of the date they receive orders to report for military service, not the date on which they enter military service.[16] This contrasts with nonreservist and nondraftee servicemembers, where the extension of the SCRA's protections apply from the date that military service begins. Although the special protection for reservists and draftees technically ends on the date they report for military service, this does not result in the cessation of the SCRA's protections because these individuals then become regular servicemembers and remain subject

---

10. 50 U.S.C. § 3911(1) (2019); 10 U.S.C. § 101(a)(5) (2019).

11. 50 U.S.C. § 3914 (2019).

12. *Id.*

13. The term "reservist" is not a legal definition; rather, it is used here as a convention for ease of understanding this chapter.

14. 50 U.S.C. § 3917(a), (b) (2019). Although only certain protections of the SCRA are extended to reservists and draftees (namely, the provisions in titles I, II, and III), these protections functionally include all of the protections relevant to financial institutions extending credit to, or entering into motor vehicle leases with, servicemembers.

15. *Id.*

16. *Id.*

to the SCRA's protections.[17] Further, if an order to report is revoked, the protections end on the date the order is revoked.[18]

2.1.4 Persons Secondarily Liable

Although the SCRA's primary focus is on servicemembers, the SCRA also grants certain rights to non-servicemembers who are secondarily liable on accounts established by servicemembers.[19] The difference between the SCRA's treatment of servicemembers and non-servicemembers, however, is that while servicemembers are granted certain rights and protections without the need for a court order, non-servicemembers generally must have their benefits granted expressly by court order.[20] For example, a court that stays, postpones, or suspends certain actions with respect to a servicemember may also make that action effective with respect to a non-servicemember surety, guarantor, endorser, accommodation maker, co-maker, or other person who is or may be primarily or secondarily subject to the obligation or liability subject to the court's order.[21] Those actions include the court staying, suspending, or postponing: "(1) the enforcement of an obligation or liability; (2) the prosecution of a suit or proceeding; (3) the entry or enforcement of an order, writ, judgment, or decree; or (4) the performance of any other act."[22] The SCRA grants similar protections to non-servicemembers who are secondarily liable when a court vacates or sets aside judgments, in whole or in part, and also for bail bonds where military service prevents the surety from obtaining the attendance of the principal.[23]

The protections above do not prevent a person secondarily liable from waiving these rights, provided the waiver is executed as an instrument separate from the obligation or liability to which the waiver applies.[24] However, any waiver so executed is rendered invalid by the subsequent entry of the person executing the waiver into military service.[25] A waiver is also invalidated if it is executed by a person who is a dependent of a person who subsequently enters military service.[26] Thus, the waivers must be knowing waivers executed after entry into military service.

---

17. *Id.*
18. *Id.*
19. *Id.* § 3913 (2019).
20. *Id.*
21. *Id.* § 3913(a) (2019).
22. *Id.*
23. *Id.* §§ 3913(b)–(c) (2019).
24. *Id.* § 3913(d)(1) (2019).
25. *Id.* § 3913(d)(2) (2019).
26. *Id.*

2.2 How Does a Financial Institution Determine If a Consumer Is Protected by the SCRA?

A financial institution has two primary means to determine whether a consumer is a servicemember protected under the SCRA.[27] A certificate of service signed by the secretary of the appropriate branch of the armed forces constitutes prima facie evidence as to the fact and details of a person's military service.[28] The federal government has created a website called the Defense Manpower Data Center (DMDC) through which any person may obtain such a certificate with regard to one or more persons.[29] Financial institutions should be aware, however, of the fact that a certificate of service is merely prima facie evidence and thus does not override actual knowledge. Certain SCRA protections also require specific documentation, such as written notice and a copy of any military orders, in order for a financial institution to be obligated to provide the protection.[30] Accordingly, a servicemember may also provide a copy of their military orders or other appropriate indicia of military service. Financial institutions should also be mindful that a power of attorney for a servicemember may be extended for any period when a servicemember is in a missing status.[31]

2.3 For What Period Does the SCRA Apply?

The duration of the protections should be understood in relation to the servicemember's period of *military service*.[32] Military service varies based on the category of servicemember at issue.

For a servicemember who is a member of the Army, Navy, Air Force, Marine Corps, or Coast Guard, military service includes any period of active duty.[33] *Active duty* is defined in a broad manner to include full-time duty in the active military service of the United States.[34] Active duty includes full-time training duty, annual training duty, and attendance, while in the active military service, at a school designated as a service school by law or by the secretary of the military department concerned, but does not include full-time National Guard duty.[35]

---

27. The term "financial institution" is used in this chapter to refer to a broad range of companies that offer consumer financial products and services. The SCRA does not generally distinguish between the type of institution, but rather focuses on the type of product or service offered.

28. 50 U.S.C. § 4012(a) (2019).

29. *See* Servicemembers Civil Relief Act (SCRA), https://scra.dmdc.osd.mil/scra/#/home (last visited July 2, 2020).

30. *See, e.g.*, 50 U.S.C. § 3955 (2019).

31. *Id.* § 4022 (2019). Note that certain conditions apply to this provision.

32. *Id.* § 3911(2) (2019).

33. *Id.* § 3911(2)(A)(i) (2019).

34. 10 U.S.C. § 101(d)(1).

35. *Id.*

In the case of a member of the National Guard, military service includes service under a call to active service authorized by the president or the secretary of defense for a period of more than thirty consecutive days under section 502(f) of Title 32 of the United States Code, for purposes of responding to a national emergency declared by the president and supported by federal funds.[36] For a servicemember who is a commissioned officer of the Public Health Service or the National Oceanic and Atmospheric Administration, military service includes active service.[37] For all servicemembers, military service includes any period during which a servicemember is absent from duty on account of sickness, wounds, leave, or other lawful cause.[38]

In general, the period of military service is defined based on the dates that the servicemember enters and is released from military service, but may also end upon the death of the servicemember.[39] However, the Department of Justice (DOJ) has also taken the position that the extension of the SCRA's protections during the period between the date after receipt or notification of orders, but before military service begins, does not change the applicability of the date military service begins in the substantive protections of the SCRA.[40] As a result, although counterintuitive to allow protections to begin prior to the date used to determine eligibility, financial institutions should be careful to make this distinction for reservists if they wish to avoid scrutiny.

2.4 Jurisdictional Scope

The SCRA applies broadly to proceedings in the United States, each state and their political subdivisions, and all territories subject to the jurisdiction of the United States.[41] However, the SCRA does not apply to criminal proceedings.[42] The rights and protections apply to any judicial or administrative proceeding commenced in any court or agency in any jurisdiction noted above. If a party must apply to a court for relief or permission to take certain action, the application may be made to any court that would otherwise have jurisdiction.[43]

36. 50 U.S.C. § 3911(2)(A)(ii) (2019).

37. *Id.* § 3911(2)(B) (2019).

38. *Id.* § 3911(2)(C) (2019).

39. *Id.* § 3911(3) (2019).

40. Settlement Agreement, United States v. COPOCO Cmty. Credit Union, No. 16-12756, at *2 n.1 (C.D. Cal July 5, 2017), https://www.justice.gov/opa/press-release/file/978341/download.

41. 50 U.S.C. § 3912(a) (2019).

42. *Id.* § 3912(b) (2019).

43. *Id.* § 3912(c) (2019).

2.5 Legal Representatives

The SCRA sets forth who may act as a legal representative for a servicemember with respect to requesting, receiving, or waiving SCRA rights.[44] Under the SCRA, a legal representative may include only an attorney acting on behalf of a servicemember or an individual possessing a power of attorney.[45] In any case in which an SCRA right applies to a servicemember, the term may be interpreted as including a reference to a legal representative of a servicemember.[46] Financial services companies must be careful to ensure that any waivers or other documentation requested or received in connection with the extension or denial of SCRA rights come from the servicemember or the servicemember's attorney or other individual who has been granted a power of attorney over the servicemember's affairs.

2.6 Waiver of SCRA Rights

The SCRA permits any servicemember[47] to waive any of the rights provided under the SCRA.[48] However, in certain enumerated circumstances detailed below, waivers are subject to a heightened set of requirements.[49] In these cases, a waiver must (1) be in writing, (2) be executed as an instrument separate from the obligation or liability to which it applies, (3) be executed during or after the servicemember's period of military service, (4) specify the legal instrument to which the waiver applies, and (5) specify the servicemember concerned if the servicemember is not a party to the instrument.[50] The enumerated circumstances where these heightened requirements must be followed are:

1. The modification, termination, or cancellation of (i) a contract, lease, or bailment; or (ii) an obligation secured by a mortgage, trust, deed, lien, or other security in the nature of a mortgage;[51] or
2. The repossession, retention, foreclosure, sale, forfeiture, or taking possession of property that (i) is security for any obligation; or (ii) was purchased or received under a contract, lease, or bailment.[52]

---

44. *Id.* § 3920(a) (2019).
45. *Id.*
46. *Id.* § 3920(b) (2019).
47. The SCRA specifically includes reservists and draftees as servicemembers subject to the SCRA provisions relating to waivers of SCRA rights and includes the period beginning on the date they receive their orders to report as their period of military service. *See* 50 U.S.C. § 3918(d) (2019).
48. *Id.* § 3918(a) (2019).
49. *Id.*
50. *Id.*
51. *Id.* § 3918(b)(1) (2019).
52. *Id.* § 3918(b)(2) (2019).

In any case in which a waiver of SCRA rights is in writing and relates to a contract, lease, or similar legal instrument, the waiver must be in at least twelve-point type.[53] This requirement applies to the waivers noted above as being subject to a heightened standard, as well as any other waiver that relates to a contract, lease, or similar legal instrument.[54]

As a practical matter, any financial services company seeking to have a servicemember waive his or her SCRA rights would be well advised to document that waiver in writing and comply with the twelve-point-type requirement to avoid later claims that the servicemember did not understand that he or she was waiving rights under the SCRA. The waivers should also expressly mention that the waiver relates to the SCRA and that the servicemember understands that he or she is waiving the SCRA rights at issue. In its SCRA enforcement actions, the DOJ has required various financial services companies to use a specific written SCRA waiver, and sometimes a supplemental notice specified by the DOJ.[55]

3. General Rights and Protections

The SCRA contains several rights and protections applicable to servicemembers that generally do not require court intervention. In the context of financial services, these protections consist primarily of the right to reduce the rate of interest on certain contracts to 6 percent per annum, protections against repossession, foreclosure, and other termination of contracts, the right to terminate certain lease contracts, and protections against retaliation from financial institutions relating to a servicemember's exercising of these rights and protections. Each protection is discussed below.

3.1 The 6 Percent Rate Cap

The ability of servicemembers to reduce the rate of interest owed on certain obligations to 6 percent per annum is one of the core protections granted to servicemembers under the SCRA.[56] For convenience, this chapter will refer to this protection as the "rate cap" from this point forward.[57] Financial institutions should be mindful of the rate cap, the safe harbor afforded under the SCRA, and the circumstances under which the rate cap applies.

---

53. *Id.* § 3918(c) (2019).

54. *Id.*

55. Consent Order, United States v. 3rd Generation, Inc. et al., No. 18-00523 (Mar. 6, 2019), https://www.justice.gov/opa/press-release/file/1140036/download.

56. 50 U.S.C. § 3937 (2019).

57. The term "rate cap" is not a legal definition; rather, it is used here as a convention for ease of understanding this chapter.

3.1.1 To What Obligations Does the 6 Percent Rate Cap Apply?

The rate cap generally applies to any interest-bearing obligation or liability incurred by the servicemember, either as sole obligor or co-obligor, that was entered into before the servicemember entered military service.[58] A covered obligation or liability specifically includes mortgages, trust deeds, or other security in the nature of a mortgage.[59] However, financial institutions should be mindful that this language does not exclude any other type of interest-bearing obligation or liability, as the rate cap does also apply to nonmortgage credit obligations. Further, it requires that the interest rates be reduced for different periods in the context of mortgage-related obligations versus other, nonmortgage, obligations.[60]

3.1.2 How Does a Financial Institution Become Obligated to Apply the Rate Cap to a Servicemember's Obligation or Liability?

A servicemember must affirmatively notify a financial institution in writing of his or her desire to obtain the rate cap in order for a financial institution to be obligated to apply the rate cap to the servicemember's obligation or liability.[61] A servicemember also must provide either (1) a copy of the military orders calling the servicemember to military service and any orders further extending such military service; or (2) any other appropriate indicator of military service, including a certified letter from a commanding officer.[62] Finally, a servicemember must make this request during the period of military service or within 180 days after the servicemember's termination or release from military service.[63]

The SCRA also offers an optional safe harbor verification method that a financial institution may use in lieu of the notice and documentation noted above.[64] Under the safe harbor, a financial institution may use information retrieved from the DMDC through the financial institution's normal review of the information contained in the DMDC for purposes of ascertaining whether a borrower is a servicemember on active duty.[65] Although optional, the safe harbor provides a conclusive determination that a financial institution has not failed to comply with the rate cap if the financial institution both (1) relies on information from the DMDC indicating that, on the date the financial institution retrieved the information, the servicemember was not on active duty; and (2) the financial institution has not received the written notice

58. *Id.* § 3937(a)(1) (2019).
59. *Id.* § 3937(d)(2) (2019).
60. *Id.* §§ 3937(a)(1)(A)–(B) (2019).
61. *Id.* § 3937(b)(1)(A) (2019).
62. *Id.*
63. *Id.*
64. *Id.* § 3937(b)(1)(B) (2019).
65. *Id.* § 3937(b)(1)(B)(i) (2019).

and other documentation described above during the period of military service or within 180 days thereafter.[66]

3.1.3 How Do Financial Institutions Calculate the Rate Cap?

Once a servicemember has requested the rate cap, and is eligible for its benefits, a financial institution must ensure that it grants the rate cap retroactively for the entire period of military service, starting from the initial entry into active duty through the end of military service.[67] For obligations or liabilities consisting of a mortgage, trust deed, or other security in the nature of a mortgage, a financial institution must also extend the rate cap for an additional year after the servicemember leaves military service.[68]

A financial institution must also be mindful of several other requirements. First, the calculation method used to apply the rate cap must ensure that any interest in excess of 6 percent per annum is forgiven, not deferred.[69] Second, a financial institution must ensure that the calculation method results in a reduction of the amount of the periodic payment due from a servicemember by the amount of interest forgiven that is allocable to the period for which the payment is made.[70] Third, a financial institution must ensure that it includes other fees and charges in the consideration of "interest" under the rate cap.[71] The reason for this requirement is that "interest" is defined to include service charges, renewal charges, fees, or any other charges with respect to an obligation or liability, other than bona fide insurance.[72] Depending on the interest rate at issue, financial institutions could opt to adjust these fees to ensure the all-in interest rate does not exceed 6 percent, or suppress fees other than interest to ensure that the rate cap is applied properly.[73] Although these three elements may appear simple, they can be difficult to accomplish in practice, and certain factors (such as a borrower's chronic delinquency) may complicate the analysis.

3.1.4 Financial Institution Relief and Penalties

The SCRA grants financial institutions the right to apply to a court of law for relief from the limitations of the rate cap if the court determines that the ability of the servicemember to pay interest on the obligation at a rate in excess of 6 percent per annum is not materially impacted by the servicemember's military service.[74]

66. *Id.* §§ 3937(b)(1)(B)(ii)(I)–(II) (2019).
67. *Id.* §§ 3937(a)(1)(A)–(b)(2) (2019).
68. *Id.* § 3937(a)(1)(B) (2019).
69. *Id.* § 3937(a)(2) (2019).
70. *Id.* § 3937(a)(3) (2019).
71. *Id.* § 3937(d)(1) (2019).
72. *Id.*
73. *Id.*
74. *Id.* § 3937(c) (2019).

However, financial institutions should think carefully about making such a request. The SCRA also provides for both fines and up to a year in prison, or both, as a consequence for violating the requirements of the rate cap.[75]

3.2 The Repossession Protection

The SCRA prohibits any person from rescinding or terminating certain contracts with servicemembers for a breach in terms that occurred before or during the person's military service, and similarly prohibits any person from repossessing property based on such breach, without a court order or SCRA waiver.[76] There are notable limitations to the scope of this protection. First, for a contract to be subject to this protection, the contract must be either (1) a contract for the purchase of real or personal property (including a *motor vehicle*[77]), or (2) a contract for the lease or bailment of such property.[78] Second, a servicemember must have paid a deposit or installment on the contract before the servicemember entered military service.[79] In practice, many financial institutions conduct searches of the DMDC (which operates as prima facie evidence of an individual's military status) to ensure that the individual is not a servicemember prior to conducting a repossession.

Courts are empowered to order repayment to the servicemember of all or part of the prior installments or deposits as a condition of terminating the contract and repossessing the property.[80] A court may also stay the proceedings when a servicemember's ability to comply with the contract is materially affected by military service, or may make such other disposition of the contract as is equitable.[81] A financial institution that knowingly takes possession of property in violation of the repossession protection without an effective SCRA waiver, or that knowingly attempts to do so, is subject to fines and imprisonment for up to one year, or both.[82]

75. *Id.* § 3937(e) (2019).

76. *Id.* § 3952(a)(1) (2019).

77. A motor vehicle is defined under the SCRA by reference to 49 U.S.C. § 30102(a)(6). *See* 50 U.S.C. § 33911(8) (2019). However, it is actually 49 U.S.C. § 30102(a)(7) that defines a *motor vehicle*, and does so as a vehicle driven or drawn by mechanical power and manufactured primarily for use on public streets, roads, and highways, but does not include a vehicle operated only on a rail line. 49 U.S.C. § 30102(a)(7) (2019).

78. *See supra* note 77.

79. 50 U.S.C. § 3952(a)(2) (2019).

80. *Id.* § 3952(c)(1) (2019).

81. *Id.* §§ 3952(c)(2)–(3) (2019).

82. *Id.* § 3952(b) (2019).

3.3 The Foreclosure Protection

The SCRA prohibits any person from conducting a sale, foreclosure, or seizure of property for a breach of a covered obligation while a servicemember is in military service, or within one year thereafter, without having a court order or a written SCRA waiver.[83] If a court order is obtained, it must be granted prior to the sale, foreclosure, or seizure with a return made and approved by the court.[84] The SCRA also grants special authority to courts to stay proceedings and adjust the covered obligation.[85] As long as the action is filed during military service or within one year thereafter, courts are invested with the authority to make a determination that the servicemember's ability to comply with the obligation is materially impacted by military service, and either (1) stay the proceedings for a period as determined by the court, or (2) adjust the obligation to preserve the interests of all parties.[86] The court may take these actions on its own motion after a hearing.[87]

An obligation is only covered by the above protections if it is an obligation on real or personal property owned by the servicemember that (1) was originated before the period of military service and the servicemember remains obligated for its repayment; and (2) is secured by a mortgage, trust deed, or other security in the nature of a mortgage.[88] A knowing violation of the foreclosure protection carries with it both fines and imprisonment for up to one year, or both.[89] Just as they do for the repossession protection, in practice many financial institutions conduct searches of the DMDC to ensure that the individual is not a servicemember prior to conducting a foreclosure.

3.4 The Right to Terminate a Motor Vehicle Lease

The right to terminate a motor vehicle lease before the end of its term without payment of an early termination penalty is another of the SCRA's core financial services protections.[90] A servicemember lessee may terminate a covered lease any

83. *Id.* § 3953(c) (2019).

84. *Id.*

85. *Id.* § 3953(b) (2019).

86. *Id.*

87. *Id.*

88. *Id.* § 3953(c) (2019).

89. *Id.* § 3953(d) (2019).

90. *Id.* § 3955 (2019). Note that residential leases are not discussed in this chapter because the focus of this treatise is on the laws governing the delivery of consumer financial services and products. The SCRA motor vehicle lease termination statute was amended during the editing process to include treatment of catastrophic illness and injury, the impact of a permanent separation or retirement from military service, and global stop movement orders. *See* Public Law 116-92, Div. A, Title V, §§ 545, 546, Dec. 20, 2019, 133 Stat. 1377; Public Law 116-158, § 1(a) to (d), Aug. 14, 2020, 134 Stat. 706.

time after either (1) the servicemember enters military service or (2) the date of the servicemember's eligible military orders.[91] However, the SCRA also specifically defines what constitutes a covered lease, sets forth a particular mechanism for effectively requesting a termination under the SCRA, and provides for the treatment of leases generally upon such termination.

3.4.1 A Covered Lease

There are two primary categories of covered leases. First, a lease is a covered lease if the servicemember executed the lease prior to military service and subsequently entered military service during the term of the lease under a call or order requiring a period of military service not less than 180 days.[92] The protection also applies if a servicemember receives a call or order that is for a period of less than 180 days that is subsequently extended to be a period of 180 days, as long as there is no break in service.[93]

Second, a lease may also be a covered lease when the servicemember was already in military service when they executed the lease.[94] However, in such a case the lease is only a covered lease if the servicemember receives military orders:

1. for a change of permanent station either
   (a) from a location in the continental United States to a location outside the continental United States; or
   (b) from a location in any United States municipality outside the continental United States to any other location outside that municipality[95]; or
2. to deploy with a military unit, or as an individual in support of a military operation, for a period of not less than 180 days.[96]

Accordingly, financial institutions offering motor vehicle leases must be cognizant of the fact that the lease protections may apply even when servicemembers were already in the military when they executed the lease.

---

91. *Id.* § 3955(a)(1) (2019).

92. *Id.* § 3955(b)(2)(A) (2019).

93. *Id.*

94. *Id.* § 3955(b)(2)(B) (2019).

95. *Id.* § 3955(b)(2)(B)(i) (2019). Note that the SCRA refers to municipalities outside the continental United States as a *state*, which is defined to include all possessions of the United States, including all commonwealths, territories, the District of Columbia, or any other possession of the United States. *Id.* § 3911(6) (2019).

96. *Id.* § 3955(b)(2)(B)(ii) (2019).

3.4.2 Proper Early Termination of a Motor Vehicle Lease

A servicemember must fulfill certain obligations to properly effectuate an early termination.[97] First, the servicemember must deliver written notice of the termination and a copy of the servicemember's military orders to the lessor or the lessor's agent.[98] A servicemember may deliver this notice by hand, private business carrier, or by mail.[99] If a servicemember mails the notice, he or she must do so with sufficient postage and a return receipt requested, must deposit the written notice in the United States mail, and must address the notice to the lessor or their agent.[100] Military orders include official military orders or any notification, certification, or verification from the servicemember's commanding officer with respect to the servicemember's current or future military duty status.[101] Second, the servicemember must return the motor vehicle to the lessor or the lessor's agent not later than fifteen days after the date of delivery of the written notice.[102] The effective date of the termination is the day on which both requirements are satisfied.[103]

3.4.3 Handling of Arrearages, Amounts Paid in Advance, and Other Amounts Owed

The early termination right under the SCRA does not, however, relieve servicemembers of their duty to pay any unpaid amounts owed as of the termination date.[104] Any amounts that are unpaid for the period prior to the early termination must be paid on a prorated basis.[105] Although an early termination penalty is prohibited, the servicemember must pay any taxes, summonses, title and registration fees, or other obligations and liabilities of the lessee in accordance with the terms of the lease.[106] These obligations specifically include, but are not limited to, reasonable charges to the lessee for excess wear or use and mileage that are due and unpaid at the time of termination of the lease.[107]

A financial institution offering motor vehicle leases must be careful to ensure the refund of any amounts paid in advance for a period after the effective date of the lease termination.[108] A financial institution must do so within thirty days of the

97. *Id.* § 3955(c) (2019).
98. *Id.* § 3955(c)(1)(A) (2019).
99. *Id.* § 3955(c)(2) (2019).
100. *Id.* § 3955(c)(2)(C) (2019).
101. *Id.* § 3955(i)(1) (2019).
102. *Id.* § 3955(c)(1)(B) (2019).
103. *Id.* § 3955(d)(2) (2019).
104. *Id.* § 3955(e)(2) (2019).
105. *Id.*
106. *Id.*
107. *Id.*
108. *Id.* § 3955(f) (2019).

termination date.[109] For example, any down payment made on a lease to reduce the amount of the monthly payments over the course of the lease should be refunded on a prorated basis.[110]

3.4.4 Treatment of Joint Lease and Court-Ordered Relief

A servicemember lessee's decision to terminate a lease early pursuant to the SCRA also terminates any obligation that a dependent of the servicemember lessee may have under the lease.[111] A servicemember lessor may also apply to a court before the termination date set forth in the written notice for relief as justice and equity require.[112]

3.4.5 Obligation to Return Personal Property and Penalties

Fines and imprisonment may be levied upon any person who knowingly seizes, holds, or detains any personal effects, security deposit, or other property of a servicemember or their dependent who lawfully terminates a lease early under the SCRA.[113] The same penalties may be levied upon any person who knowingly interferes with the removal of such property for the purpose of asserting a claim for rent accruing subsequent to the termination date.[114]

3.5 Antiretaliatory Provisions

Companies are prohibited from taking certain actions against a servicemember based on the servicemember's application for, or receipt of, a stay, postponement, or suspension under the SCRA in the payment of a tax, fine, penalty, insurance premium, or other civil obligation or liability of that servicemember.[115] Specifically, the application for or receipt of such a benefit may not provide the basis of any of the following:

1. A determination by a lender or other person that the servicemember is unable to pay the civil obligation or liability in accordance with its terms;[116]
2. With respect to a credit transaction between a creditor and the servicemember, (i) a denial or revocation of credit by the creditor, (ii) a change by the creditor in the terms of an existing credit arrangement,

---

109. *Id.*
110. *Id.*
111. *Id.* § 3955(a)(2) (2019).
112. *Id.* § 3955(g) (2019).
113. *Id.* § 3955(h) (2019).
114. *Id.*
115. *Id.* § 3919 (2019).
116. *Id.* § 3919(1) (2019).

or (iii) a refusal by the creditor to grant credit to the servicemember in substantially the amount or on substantially the terms requested;[117]

3. An adverse report relating to the creditworthiness of the servicemember by or to a person engaged in the practice of assembling or evaluating consumer credit information;[118]
4. A refusal by an insurer to insure the servicemember;[119]
5. An annotation in a servicemember's record by a creditor or a person engaged in the practice of assembling or evaluating consumer credit information, identifying the servicemember as a member of the National Guard or a reserve component;[120]
6. A change in the terms offered or conditions required for the issuance of insurance.[121]

The impact of these protections is sometimes misunderstood by financial services companies and servicemembers alike. It is critical to note that the antiretaliatory provisions only prohibit financial services from taking the above actions *based on the application for or receipt of SCRA protections.*[122] For example, some servicemembers have brought litigation against financial services companies for reporting accurate, but negative, information to credit reporting agencies.[123] However, courts have concluded that a financial institution's accurate reporting of a servicemember's payment history was based on the servicemember's payment history, not whether the servicemember had applied for or received any protections under the SCRA.[124] Financial services companies have received complaints or even lawsuits from servicemembers that misunderstand the function of the antiretaliatory provisions on the same and similar bases. As such, financial institutions would be well advised to understand the SCRA's applicability and the supporting case law in this regard and be prepared to explain its applicability to servicemembers, courts, and even military legal assistance personnel.

117. *Id.* § 3919(2) (2019).

118. *Id.* § 3919(3) (2019).

119. *Id.* § 3919(4) (2019).

120. *Id.* § 3919(5) (2019).

121. *Id.* § 3919(6) (2019).

122. *Id.* § 3919 (2019).

123. Rodriguez v. Am. Express, No. CVF03-5949, 2006 WL 908613 (E.D. Cal. Apr. 7, 2006); Koenig v. Waukesha State Bank, No. 05-C-255, 2006 WL 2334841 (E.D. Wis. Aug. 10, 2006); Murphy v. Bank of Am., No. 2:12-CV-2520-VEH, 2012 WL 5954144 (N.D. Ala. Nov. 28, 2012).

124. *Rodriguez*, No. CVF03-5949, 2006 WL 908613 at *7 (E.D. Cal. Apr. 7, 2006); *Koenig*, No. 05-C-255, 2006 WL 2334841 at *7 (E.D. Wis. Aug. 10, 2006); *Murphy*, No. 2:12-CV-2520-VEH, 2012 WL 5954144 at *3–4 (N.D. Ala. Nov. 28, 2012).

3.6 Protection of Personal Assets of a Servicemember in Connection with Business or Trade Obligations

The personal assets of a servicemember are not available for satisfaction of a trade or business obligation during the period of military service, even if a personal guaranty was executed by the servicemember.[125] This protection applies regardless of the form in which the trade or business is carried out.[126] However, upon application to a court of law, a court may grant relief to the holder of an obligation or liability subject to this protection as justice and equity require.[127]

4. Rights and Protections Applicable to Litigation or That Require Court Action

4.1 Protections against Default Judgments

The SCRA restricts the ability of any person or company to obtain a default judgment against a servicemember in military service.[128] A court must require any plaintiff to file a military status affidavit with the court prior to granting a default judgment in any civil action or proceeding in which the defendant does not make an appearance.[129] The military status affidavit must contain the following: (1) a statement whether or not the defendant is in military service or that the plaintiff is unable to determine whether or not the defendant is in military service, and (2) the necessary facts to support the affidavit.[130] The necessary facts to support the affidavit typically take the form of the DMDC certificate discussed earlier.[131] The form of the affidavit itself may generally be satisfied by a statement, declaration, verification, or certificate that is in writing and subscribed and certified or declared to be true under penalty of perjury.[132]

Prior to entering a default judgment against a servicemember, a court must appoint an attorney to represent a servicemember defendant.[133] However, if the appointed attorney is not able to locate the servicemember, actions by the attorney will not waive any defense of the servicemember against a plaintiff or otherwise bind the servicemember.[134] If the court is unable to determine the status of a servicemember,

---

125. 50 U.S.C. § 4026(a) (2019).
126. *Id.*
127. *Id.* § 4026(b) (2019).
128. *Id.* § 3931 (2019).
129. *Id.* §§ 3931(a)–(b)(1) (2019).
130. *Id.* § 3931(b)(1) (2019).
131. *Id.* § 4012 (2019).
132. *Id.* § 3931(b)(4) (2019).
133. *Id.* § 3931(b)(2) (2019).
134. *Id.*

the court may require that the plaintiff file a bond in an amount determined by the court to be used to indemnify the servicemember defendant against any loss or damage suffered through the judgment granted against the defendant.[135] If such a bond is issued, it will remain in effect until the expiration of the applicable period for appeal and setting aside of the judgment under applicable law.[136]

The SCRA instructs courts to grant a stay of a minimum of ninety days if a court determines that a defendant is a servicemember and (1) counsel for the servicemember defendant applies for such motion, (2) the court determines that there may be a defense to the action that cannot be presented without the presence of the servicemember defendant, or (3) counsel for the servicemember defendant has not been able to contact the servicemember after due diligence.[137] In practice, courts routinely grant the ninety-day stay on discovery of any indication that a nonappearing defendant is a servicemember.

If a default judgment is granted against a servicemember while in military service or within sixty days of termination of military service, the court may reopen the judgment upon application by or on behalf of a servicemember to permit the servicemember to defend the action.[138] However, the court may only reopen the judgment if it appears that (1) the servicemember was materially affected by reason of that military service in making a defense to the action, and (2) the servicemember has a meritorious or legal defense to the action or some part of it.[139] However, an application to reopen such a judgment must be filed within ninety days of the date that the servicemember is released from military service.[140] If a court does vacate, set aside, or reverse a default judgment under this authority, that action may not impair a right or title acquired by a bona fide purchaser for value under the default judgment.[141]

Although the text of the SCRA places the onus on courts to require military service affidavits, the DOJ has taken the position that financial institutions may be held responsible for any improper default judgments that occur against servicemembers.[142] Financial institutions may avoid scrutiny on the issue by incorporating the default judgment protections into their compliance systems. The penalties for making or

135. *Id.* § 3931(b)(3) (2019).

136. *Id.*

137. *Id.* § 3931(d) (2019). Note that a stay granted under the default judgment protections is not controlled by the general SCRA provisions governing stays when the servicemember has notice, which are found in 50 U.S.C. § 3932, unless the servicemember receives actual notice of the action and requests such a stay. *Id.* §§ 3931(e)–(f) (2019).

138. *Id.* § 3931(g)(1) (2019).

139. *Id.*

140. *Id.* § 3931(g)(2) (2019).

141. *Id.* § 3931(h) (2019).

142. *The Servicemembers Civil Relief Act*, Dept. of Justice, https://www.justice.gov/servicemembers/servicemembers-civil-relief-act-scra (last updated Oct. 1, 2019).

using an affidavit that a financial institution knows to be false include fines and imprisonment.[143]

4.2 Right to Stay Proceedings When Servicemembers Have Notice

Although the protection against default judgments deals with proceedings where the servicemember does not appear, the SCRA also grants servicemembers certain rights to stay civil actions or proceedings when the servicemember does appear.[144] The right to request a stay applies to any civil action or proceeding in which the plaintiff or defendant, at the time of filing an application for stay, is both (1) in military service or within ninety days after release from military service, and (2) has received notice of the action or proceeding.[145]

A servicemember may request a stay at any stage before final judgment in a civil action or proceeding in which the servicemember is a party, and a court may also impose such a stay on its own motion.[146] A servicemember must include the following in his or her application for a stay: (1) a letter or other communication setting forth the facts, stating the manner in which current military duty requirements materially affect the servicemember's ability to appear and stating a date when the servicemember will be available to appear; and (2) a letter or other communication from the servicemember's commanding officer stating that the servicemember's current military duty prevents appearance and that military leave is not authorized for the servicemember at the time of the letter.[147] If the court receives an application for a stay from a servicemember containing the materials noted above, a court is obligated to grant a stay for a period of not less than ninety days.[148]

A servicemember granted such a stay may also apply for an additional stay upon a showing of continuing material impact of military service on the servicemember's ability to appear.[149] A servicemember is permitted to request an additional stay at the same time that the servicemember requests his or her initial stay, but may also do so at a later time if it appears that the servicemember is unavailable to prosecute or defend the action.[150] In the event that a court denies a servicemember's request for an additional stay, the court is obligated to appoint counsel to represent the servicemember in the action or proceeding.[151]

143. 50 U.S.C. § 3931(c) (2019).
144. *Id.* § 3932 (2019).
145. *Id.* § 3932(a) (2019).
146. *Id.* § 3932(b) (2019).
147. *Id.* § 3932(b)(2) (2019).
148. *Id.* §§ 3932(b)(1)–(2) (2019).
149. *Id.* § 3932(d)(1) (2019).
150. *Id.*
151. *Id.* § 3932(d)(2) (2019).

An application for a stay by a servicemember may not be deemed an appearance in court for jurisdictional purposes, nor may it be considered to be a waiver of any substantive or procedural defense.[152] However, a servicemember who applies for such a stay and is unsuccessful may not subsequently seek the protections afforded under the SCRA's protections against default judgments, including the right to request a stay thereunder,[153] or the protections against eviction from a servicemembers' home (although those protections are not discussed herein).[154]

4.3 Treatment of Contracts Stayed Pursuant to the SCRA

No penalties may accrue for failure to comply with the terms of the contract during the period of any stay expected under the SCRA.[155] Accordingly, financial institutions should be careful to suspend the accrual of interest and refrain from charging any fees relating to the servicemember's delinquency during the term of the stay.

4.4 Settlement of Stayed Cases Relating to Property

Courts have authority to appoint three disinterested parties to appraise property when a stayed proceeding relates to a proceeding to foreclose a mortgage, or to repossess personal property, or to rescind or terminate a contract for the purchase of personal property.[156] Upon such an appraisal, the court may order that the amount of the servicemember's equity in the property may be paid to the servicemember, or the servicemember's dependents, as a condition of foreclosing the mortgage, repossessing the property, or rescinding or terminating the contract.[157] The court must, however, determine that undue hardship will not be passed to the servicemember's dependents as a result of the order.[158]

4.5 Authority of Courts to Reduce or Waive Fines and Penalties Incurred by Servicemembers

Courts are also granted certain authority to reduce or waive fines and penalties when a servicemember fails to perform an obligation arising under a contract and a fine or penalty is incurred due to a failure to comply with the terms of the contract.[159]

152. *Id.* § 3932(c) (2019).

153. *Id.* § 3932(e) (2019).

154. *Id. See id.* § 3951 (2019) for a discussion of the SCRA's protection against eviction. Those protections are not discussed herein.

155. *Id.* § 3933(a) (2019).

156. *Id.* § 3954(a) (2019).

157. *Id.* § 3954(b) (2019).

158. *Id.*

159. *Id.* § 3933(b) (2019).

A court may reduce or waive a fine or penalty if the following conditions are met: (1) the servicemember was in military service at the time the fine or penalty was incurred, and (2) the ability of the servicemember to meet his or her obligation was materially affected by that military service.[160]

4.6 Authority of Courts to Stay or Vacate the Execution of Judgments, Attachments, or Garnishments

Courts also have the ability to stay the execution of any judgment or order against any servicemember, or to vacate or stay an attachment or garnishment of the property, money, or debts in the possession of a servicemember or third party, whether before or after judgment.[161] The court may do so either on its own motion or upon the application of a servicemember when the court believes the servicemember is materially affected due to his or her military service in complying with a court order or judgment.[162] However, this protection applies only to an action or proceeding commenced in a court against a servicemember before or during the servicemember's period of military service, or within ninety days after the servicemember's release from military service.[163]

4.7 Duration of Stays and Treatment of Codefendants

A stay of an action, proceeding, attachment, or execution authorized under the SCRA may be granted for the period of the servicemember's military service and for ninety days after the servicemember's release from military service.[164] In the case of a stay granted with respect to an installment contract, the court is authorized to set the terms and amounts for installment payments as the court deems reasonable.[165] In the event that a servicemember is a codefendant with other individuals who are not in military service and not entitled to the protections of the SCRA, a plaintiff is permitted to proceed against those other defendants with the approval of the court.[166] These provisions do not, however, apply in the context of a stay of proceedings when a servicemember has notice, discussed in section 4.2, or the provisions relating to a right of a servicemember to request anticipatory relief from contracts, discussed in section 4.10.[167]

---

160. *Id.*
161. *Id.* § 3934(a) (2019).
162. *Id.*
163. *Id.* § 3934(b) (2019).
164. *Id.* § 3935(a) (2019).
165. *Id.*
166. *Id.* § 3935(b) (2019).
167. *Id.* § 3935(c) (2019).

4.8 Treatment of Statutes of Limitations and Redemption Periods

A servicemember's period of military service may not be included in computing any period limited by law, regulation, or order for the bringing of any action or proceeding in a court.[168] The same protection applies to any action or proceeding that would be brought in any board, bureau, commission, department, or other agent of a state[169] or the United States either by or against a servicemember or the servicemember's heirs, executors, administrators, or assigns.[170] Financial institutions should be mindful of the fact that this provision of the SCRA functionally tolls the statute of limitations with respect to actions the servicemember could bring, but also tolls the statutes of limitations applicable to financial institutions' claims against servicemembers, which allows for greater flexibility by a financial institution trying to avoid bringing actions against servicemembers.

A servicemember's period of military service also may not be included in computing any period provided by law for the redemption of real property sold or forfeited to enforce an obligation, tax, or assessment.[171] Despite the above, the extension of such periods does not apply to any period of limitation prescribed by or under the internal revenue laws of the United States.[172]

4.9 Extension of Protections to Dependents

A dependent of a servicemember is entitled to the protections of the SCRA only upon application to a court and a showing that the dependent's ability to comply with a lease, contract, bailment, or other obligation is materially affected due to the servicemember's military service.[173] Exceptions to this rule are generally noted in the discussion of the applicable protection.

4.10 Inappropriate Transfer of Property or Misuse of the SCRA

In the event that a court determines that, in any proceeding to enforce a civil right, any interest, property, or contract has been transferred or acquired with the intent to delay the just enforcement of such right by taking advantage of the SCRA, the court is empowered with the ability to enter a judgment or order as lawfully permitted to address such an occurrence.[174] This provision is generally designed to prevent a non-

168. *Id.* § 3936(a) (2019).

169. A *state* is defined to include a commonwealth, territory, or possession of the United States and the District of Columbia. *Id.* § 3911(6) (2019).

170. *Id.* § 3936(a).

171. *Id.* § 3936(b) (2019).

172. *Id.* § 3936(c) (2019).

173. *Id.* § 3959 (2019).

174. *Id.* § 4011 (2019).

servicemember from transferring property to a servicemember solely for the purpose of evading the lawful repercussions of that non-servicemember's actions. Although such an instance is rare, and the costs of implementing this provision are likely to be high, to the extent that a financial institution finds itself in such a position, the SCRA does provide a remedy.

4.11 Requests for Anticipatory Relief and Modification of Court Orders

A servicemember has a general right to apply to a court for relief from any obligation or liability incurred by the servicemember before the servicemember's military service.[175] The servicemember must do so during the period of military service or within 180 days of the end of such service.[176] If the ability of the servicemember to comply with the obligation has been materially impacted by military service, a court may grant certain relief after appropriate notice and hearing.[177]

In the case of an obligation payable in installments under a contract for the purchase of real estate or otherwise secured by a mortgage or similar instrument in the nature of a mortgage, the court may grant a stay of the enforcement of the obligation during the period of military service or from the date military service ends or the servicemember made the application for relief.[178] Any stay granted under this authority may be for a period equal to the remaining life of the installment contract or other instrument, plus a period of time equal to the period of military service of the servicemember, or any part of the combined period.[179] The stay must require payment of the balance of the principal and accumulated interest due and unpaid at the date of the end of military service or application for relief, but the payment may be made in equal installments during the period noted above at the rate of interest on the unpaid balance prescribed in the underlying contract, subject to equitable considerations by the court.[180]

In the case of other contracts, a court may similarly grant a stay of enforcement during the period of military service, from the date military service ends, or from the date of the application for relief.[181] Any such stay may be for a period equal to the period of military service or any part of that period.[182] The stay is again subject to payment of the balance of the principal and accumulated interest due and unpaid as of the end of military service or the application for relief, and may be paid in

175. *Id.* § 4021(a) (2019).
176. *Id.*
177. *Id.* § 4021(b) (2019).
178. *Id.* § 4021(1)(A) (2019).
179. *Id.* § 4021(b)(1)(B) (2019).
180. *Id.* § 4021(b)(1)(B)(ii) (2019).
181. *Id.* § 4021(b)(2)(A) (2019).
182. *Id.* § 4021(b)(2)(B)(i) (2019).

equal installments during the extended period at the rate of interest provided in the underlying contract.[183]

No fines or penalties may be applied under a contract subject to a stay as described above.[184] A court may revoke, modify, or extend any interlocutory order it issued upon its own motion or otherwise, as long as the court provides notice to the affected parties as required by the court.[185]

5. Penalties and Enforcement

A private right of action is afforded to any person subject to a violation of the SCRA.[186] The private right of action provides for any appropriate equitable or declaratory relief with respect to the violation, recovery of all other appropriate relief and money damages, and the payment of costs and attorney's fees to a successful claim by a person subject to such a violation.[187]

The U.S. attorney general also has authority to enforce the SCRA.[188] The attorney general may bring a civil action in any appropriate federal district court against any person who engages in a pattern or practice of violating the SCRA or who engages in a violation of the SCRA that raises an issue of significant public importance.[189] Courts are empowered to grant any appropriate equitable and declaratory relief with respect to violations, award any appropriate relief (including monetary damages) to any person subject to a violation, and to assess a civil penalty in an amount not exceeding $55,000 for a first violation and $110,000 for any subsequent violation.[190] Any person whose SCRA rights have been violated may timely apply to intervene in a civil action commenced by the attorney general, and may obtain the relief to which they are entitled under a private right of action, along with costs and attorney fees.[191]

The above penalties and remedies do not limit or restrict any other remedy available under laws other than the SCRA, such as punitive or consequential damages.[192]

---

183. *Id.*. § 4021(b)(2)(B)(ii) (2019).
184. *Id.* § 4021(c) (2019).
185. *Id.* § 4013 (2019).
186. *Id.* § 4042 (2019).
187. *Id.*
188. *Id.* § 4041 (2019).
189. *Id.* § 4041(a) (2019).
190. *Id.* § 4041(b) (2019).
191. *Id.* § 4041(c) (2019).
192. *Id.* § 4043 (2019).

CHAPTER

14

Military Lending Act

Robert Savoie

1. Scope of This Chapter

This chapter covers the provisions in 10 U.S.C. § 987 and its implementing regulations, 32 C.F.R. Part 232, collectively referred to as the Military Lending Act (MLA). This chapter does not cover state military lending laws or other federal or state laws.

2. Authority, Purpose, and Coverage

Congress enacted the MLA in 2006 as part of the John Warner National Defense Authorization Act for Fiscal Year 2007.[1] The stated purpose of the MLA as presently enacted is to impose limitations on the cost and terms of certain extensions of credit to servicemembers and their dependents and provide certain protections relating to these transactions.[2]

The views expressed in this article are those of the author and are not intended to represent the views of McGlinchey Stafford, PLLC or its clients, nor are they intended to constitute legal advice. The author recommends that readers consult their attorney to confirm the applicability of the Military Lending Act to the reader's specific facts and circumstances.

1. John Warner National Defense Authorization of Fiscal Year 2007, Pub. L. No. 109-364, 120 Stat. 2085 (2006) (codified as amended at 10 U.S.C. § 987 (2012)).

2. 32 C.F.R. § 232.1(b) (2019).

2.1 The Creation of the MLA and Its Implementing Regulations

The statutory basis for the MLA came in 2006 in the form of 10 U.S.C. § 987, a single statute that imposed a variety of requirements on certain loans made to military members and their dependents and granted the Department of Defense (DoD) rulemaking authority.[3] This statute set the parameters around the substantive protections of the MLA by prescribing its coverage to military members and their dependents, setting an interest rate limitation on covered loans, requiring certain disclosures, and imposing certain limitations on creditors who make covered loans.[4]

The following year, the DoD promulgated regulations implementing the MLA.[5] Those initial regulations have undergone substantial subsequent revisions since their initial release. Although the MLA itself had a broader potential scope, these regulations initially limited the applicability of the MLA to certain payday loans, motor vehicle title loans, and tax refund anticipation loans.[6] On July 22, 2015, the DoD issued a rule to expand the scope and protections of the MLA.[7] The majority of the provisions set forth in the 2015 rule applied to *consumer credit* transactions established on or after October 3, 2016,[8] while certain provisions applicable to credit card accounts took effect on October 3, 2017.[9]

The rule expanded the existing requirements to apply to unsecured installment lending in a broad manner and to include nonpurchase money installment lending secured by motor vehicles[10] and personal property.[11] The DoD subsequently issued two interpretive rules in a question-and-answer format with the intent of clarifying certain issues, one on August 26, 2016 (the First Interpretive Rule)[12] and a second on December 14, 2017 (the Second Interpretive Rule).[13] The DoD issued the interpretive

3. 10 U.S.C. § 987 (2019).

4. *Id.*

5. Limitations on Terms of *Consumer credit* Extended to Service Members and Dependents; Final Rule, 72 Fed. Reg. 50580 (Aug. 31, 2007).

6. *Id.* at 50585–86.

7. Limitations on Terms of *Consumer credit* Extended to Service Members and Dependents, 80 Fed. Reg. 43560 (July 22, 2015).

8. 32 C.F.R. § 232.12(c) (2019).

9. *Id.* § 232.13(c) (2019).

10. In its First Interpretive Rule the DoD clarified that a motor vehicle is defined as any self-propelled vehicle primarily used for personal, family, or household purposes for on-road transportation. The term does not include motor homes, recreational vehicles, golf carts, or motor scooters. *See* Military Lending Act Limitations on Terms of *Consumer credit* Extended to Service Members and Dependents, 81 Fed. Reg. 58840 at 58855 (Aug. 26, 2016) [Hereinafter the "First Interpretive Rule"].

11. *Id.*

12. *See, generally*, First Interpretive Rule, *supra* note 10.

13. Military Lending Act Limitations on Terms of *Consumer credit* Extended to Service Members and Dependents, 82 Fed. Reg. 58739 (Dec. 14, 2017) [Hereinafter the "Second Interpretive Rule"].

rules without notice and comment and the rules therefore do not have the same weight of authority as the regulations. Accordingly, this chapter distinguishes requirements or exceptions detailed within the interpretive rules from requirements that arise from the regulations and the statutory requirements of the MLA. As discussed below, these interpretive rules did resolve a number of concerns associated with ambiguity inherent in the 2015 amendments, but also created new uncertainties in a few areas.

2.2 Scope

The MLA governs transactions involving *consumer credit* made by *creditors* to *covered borrowers*.[14] However, the consumer credit subject to the MLA is defined more by its exclusions than by what is included.

2.2.1 Definition of Consumer Credit

Consumer credit is credit extended to a *covered borrower* primarily for personal, family, or household purposes that is either subject to a finance charge or payable by a written agreement in more than four installments.[15] However, consumer credit does not include the following: (1) a residential mortgage, including purchase money, refinancing, home equity loan or line of credit, and reverse mortgage transactions;[16] (2) transactions expressly intended to finance the purchase of a motor vehicle when secured by the vehicle being purchased;[17] (3) transactions expressly intended to finance the purchase of personal property when secured by the property being purchased;[18] or (4) any credit transaction that is exempt under Regulation Z or otherwise not subject to disclosure under Regulation Z.[19] As a result, the term consumer credit includes consumer credit transactions subject to Regulation Z as long as the transaction is not a mortgage transaction or a purchase money transaction secured by a motor vehicle or personal property.

2.2.2 Uncertainty Regarding Purchase Money Motor Vehicle and Personal Property Exclusions

As noted above, the MLA excludes from its coverage purchase money transactions secured by motor vehicles and personal property.[20] No dispute existed regarding these

14. 32 C.F.R. § 232.1(c) (2019).
15. *Id.* § 232.3(f)(1) (2019).
16. *Id.* § 232.3(f)(2)(i) (2019).
17. *Id.* § 232.3(f)(2)(ii) (2019).
18. *Id.* § 232.3(f)(2)(iii) (2019).
19. *Id.* § 232.3(f)(2)(iv) (2019). Note that the MLA does not exempt transactions specifically deemed exempt by the Consumer Financial Protection Bureau under Regulation Z pursuant to a request by a state pursuant to 12 C.F.R. § 1026.29.
20. 32 C.F.R. §§ 232.3(f)(2)(ii)–(iii) (2019).

exclusions from the statutory enactment of the MLA through the enactment of the final rule in 2015. The DoD then issued its First Interpretive Rule and created uncertainty regarding these exclusions.[21] In its First Interpretive Rule, the DoD addressed the question of whether credit extended for the purpose of purchasing personal property, where credit is simultaneously extended in an amount greater than the purchase price, is excluded from the MLA.[22] The DoD concluded that such extensions of credit were not excluded from the MLA.[23] The DoD explained that it viewed these transactions as hybrid purchase money transactions not expressly intended to finance the purchase of personal property because the transaction "provides additional financing that is unrelated to the purchase."[24] The DoD further explained that, to qualify for the exclusion, a transaction must finance only the acquisition of personal property and not be a cash-out transaction.[25]

The DoD's comments eliminated the ability of creditors to comfortably rely on a previously undisputed purchase money exclusion in any context in which additional goods or services are financed along with a core purchase or in cash-out refinancing transactions. This issue is particularly problematic because of the MLA's prohibition on nondepository lenders taking a security interest in a motor vehicle (discussed below). Consumers often purchase motor vehicles with motor vehicle warranties and other ancillary products, such as vehicle identification number etching or credit insurance (which is designed to pay off the credit in certain circumstances, such as in the event of unemployment or death of the borrower), and often wish to include those products in the financing of the motor vehicle. Because nondepository lenders are prohibited from taking a nonpurchase money security interest in a motor vehicle under the MLA, the consequence of this interpretation could have been that military members were denied the ability to finance these products through nondepository lenders. The DoD's comments resulted in the two reactions discussed below, followed by the DoD's decision to ultimately repeal a portion of its interpretation.

The Federal Financial Institutions Examination Council (FFIEC) addressed the issue in an industry outreach call on December 1, 2016, conducted by representatives of the Consumer Financial Protection Bureau (CFPB), Federal Reserve Board, Federal Deposit Insurance Corporation, and Office of the Comptroller of the Currency.[26] In that call, the FFIEC clarified that the exemption for purchase money motor vehicle extensions of credit is not voided by the financing of additional products related to the motor vehicle purchase that are included in the loan, such as an extended

21. First Interpretive Rule, *supra* note 10, at 58841.

22. *Id.*

23. *Id.*

24. *Id.*

25. *Id.*

26. Federal Financial Institutions Examination Council, FFIEC Industry Outreach (Dec. 1, 2016), https://industryoutreach.ffiec.gov/Resources/MLA_FFIEC%20Industry%20Outreach_%2012_1_16_Final%20Transcript.pdf.

warranty.[27] The DoD then issued its Second Interpretive Rule, where it amended its prior First Interpretive Rule to provide similar guidance focusing on the nature of what is financed beyond the purchase of the motor vehicle or personal property.[28] In that guidance, the DoD created two distinctions to illustrate what is included and what is excluded.

First, the DoD confirmed that financing additional costs expressly related to the motor vehicle or personal property would not cause the transaction to forfeit its exclusion from the MLA.[29] The DoD provided examples such as the financing of optional leather seats or an extended warranty.[30] However, the DoD also included several other practical examples. The DoD confirmed that financing negative equity associated with a motor vehicle trade-in would also be deemed expressly related to the motor vehicle because the trade-in of the covered borrower's current motor vehicle was expressly related to the purchase of the second motor vehicle.[31] The DoD also confirmed that the purchase of an appliance that finances the delivery and installation costs of the appliance would similarly not render the transaction subject to the MLA as the delivery and installation expressly related to the personal property being purchased.[32]

Second, the DoD confirmed that financing any credit-related product or service would cause the transaction to lose its exclusion from the MLA.[33] To this end, the DoD noted that the financing of guaranteed auto protection insurance or a credit insurance premium would cause the transaction to lose its exclusion from the MLA.[34] The DoD also observed that a hybrid purchase money and cash advance credit transaction is not exempt from the MLA because it provides financing not related to the purchase of the motor vehicle or personal property and is thus a cash-out transaction covered by the MLA.[35] The DoD was unable to give consideration to the view that many such ancillary products are intangible personal property themselves under the Uniform Commercial Code (UCC) and other state laws and thus likely subject on their own merit to the separate exemption for purchase money financing secured by personal property.[36]

27. *Id.* at 3.
28. Second Interpretive Rule, *supra* note 13, at 58740.
29. *Id.*
30. *Id.*
31. *Id.*
32. *Id.*
33. *Id.*
34. *Id.*
35. *Id.*
36. Model UCC § 9-102(42).

In 2020, however, the DoD amended its Second Interpretive Rule in 2020 yet again to address the treatment of ancillary products.[37] In its amendment the DoD expressly struck the controversial language from the Second Interpretive Rule and removed all reference to the interpretation of the purchase money exemptions for the purchase of motor vehicles and personal property.[38] The DoD asserted that the reaction to the Second Interpretive Rule necessitated additional analysis.[39] As a result, there are no longer any interpretations indicating that financing the products described by the DoD as credit related would cause an otherwise exempt transaction to become subject to the MLA.[40]

2.2.3 Definition of Creditor and Covered Borrower

A creditor subject to the MLA includes any person engaged in the business of extending consumer credit or an assignee of such a person.[41] A creditor also includes any person who meets the transaction standard for a creditor when considering the person and its affiliates as one entity.[42]

A covered borrower includes any consumer who, at the time the consumer becomes obligated on a consumer credit transaction or establishes an account for consumer credit, is a covered member or a dependent of a covered member.[43] A covered member includes any member of the armed forces who is serving on active duty under a call or order that does not specify a period of thirty days or fewer or active guard or reserve duty.[44] The term also includes any dependent of such an individual, which

---

37. Military Lending Act Limitations on Terms of Consumer Credit Extended to Service Members and Dependents, 85 Fed. Reg. 11842 (Feb. 28, 2020).

38. *Id.* at 11843.

39. *Id.*

40. *Id.*

41. 32 C.F.R. §§ 232.3(i)(1)–(2) (2019).

42. *Id.* § 232.3(i)(3) (2019).

43. *Id.* § 232.3(g)(1) (2019).

44. *Id.* § 232.3(g)(2) (2019). Note that active duty is defined in a manner to be pursuant to title 10, title 14, or title 32, and active guard and reserve duty is defined by reference to the laws governing the armed forces. However, due to the safe harbor identification process described later in this chapter, creditors generally do not bear the burden of understanding the title under which covered borrowers have been called to service, or the particular nature of the active guard or reserve duty, as long as they properly take advantage of the safe harbor identification process.

includes spouses and certain other individuals.[45] The definition of covered borrower importantly does not include a consumer who, although a covered borrower at the time he or she became obligated on a consumer credit transaction or established an account for consumer credit, is no longer a covered member or dependent of a covered member.[46] This exclusion is significant in the context of open-end credit.

2.2.4 *Treatment of Overdraft Products*

The First Interpretive Rule addressed overdraft products in detail. The MLA governs an overdraft product when the product is offered to a covered borrower, the credit is for personal, family, or household purposes, it is used to pay an item that overdraws an asset account and results in a fee or charge to the covered borrower, and the extension of credit for the item and the imposition of a fee were previously agreed upon in writing.[47] However, overdraft products that are not established pursuant to a written agreement typically are not subject to the MLA by virtue of Regulation Z's exclusion of any charge imposed by a creditor for credit extended to pay an item that overdraws an asset account and for which the borrower pays a fee or charge, unless the imposition of the fee or charge was previously agreed to in writing.[48]

45. 10 U.S.C. §§ 987(i)(2), 1072(2) (2019); 32 C.F.R. § 232.3(g)(2) (2019). In addition to spouses, dependents protected under the MLA include (1) a child who (a) is younger than twenty-one years old, (b) is younger than twenty-three and is enrolled in a course of study at an institution of higher learning approved by the administering secretary, or (c) is incapable of self-support because of a mental or physical incapacity that occurred while the person was considered a dependent of the individual; (2) a parent or parent-in-law who is or was at the time of the individual's death dependent on him or her for more than 50 percent of his support and residing in the individual's household; or (3) an unmarried person who (a) is placed in the legal custody of the member or former member as a result of an order of a court of competent jurisdiction in the United States for a period of at least twelve consecutive months; (b) either (i) has not attained the age of twenty-one, (ii) has not attained the age of twenty-three and is enrolled in a full time course of study at an institution of higher learning approved by the administering secretary, or (iii) is incapable of self-support because of a mental or physical incapacity that occurred while the person was considered a dependent of the member or former member; (c) is dependent on the member or former member for more than half of the person's support; (d) resides with the member or former member unless separated by the necessity of military service or to receive institutional care as a result of disability or incapacitation; and (e) is not a dependent of a member or a former member under any other provision above. 10 U.S.C. §§ 987(i)(2), 1072(2). However, as noted above, creditors who properly utilize the safe harbor identification method do not generally have to themselves determine whether a particular applicant is a dependent of a servicemember who qualifies as a covered borrower.

46. 32 C.F.R. § 232.3(g)(4) (2019).

47. First Interpretive Rule, *supra* note 10, at 58840.

48. *Id.* at 58841.

2.3 Examples of the Applicability of the Military Lending Act

The MLA regulations provide several examples designed to give creditors context around how to understand the applicability of the MLA. This chapter incorporates those examples below.

The first example demonstrates a circumstance in which a consumer is a covered borrower as follows:

> Consumer A is a member of the armed forces but not serving on active duty, and holds an account for closed-end credit with a financial institution. After establishing the closed-end credit account, Consumer A is ordered to serve on active duty, thereby becoming a covered borrower, and soon thereafter separately establishes an open-end line of credit for personal purposes (which is not subject to any exception or temporary exemption) with the financial institution. This part applies to the open-end line of credit, but not to the closed-end credit account.[49]

The second example demonstrates a circumstance in which a consumer is not a covered borrower as follows:

> Same facts as described [above]. One year after establishing the open-end line of credit, Consumer A ceases to serve on active duty. This part never did apply to the closed-end credit account, and because Consumer A no longer is a covered borrower, this part no longer applies to the open-end line of credit.[50]

3. Safe Harbor Identification of Covered Borrowers

The MLA's implementing regulations create a safe harbor identification method that creditors may use, although the decision not to use the safe harbor is not a violation of the MLA.[51] The safe harbor causes any transaction through which a creditor uses the safe harbor to be excluded from the scope of the MLA—even where the consumer was actually a covered borrower—thus eliminating liability under the MLA.[52]

The safe harbor is provided only if the creditor verifies the status of the applicant in one of two ways.[53] First, the creditor may verify the status of the applicant by

49. 32 C.F.R. § 232.2(a)(2)(i) (2019).
50. *Id.* § 232.2(a)(2)(ii) (2019).
51. *Id.* § 232.5(a) (2019).
52. *Id.* § 232.3(f)(2)(v) (2019).
53. *Id.* § 232.5(b)(1) (2019).

accessing a database created by the DoD referred to as the MLA database[54] using the applicant's last name, date of birth, and social security number.[55] However, a creditor may not conduct a "look back" search where it utilizes the MLA database, directly or indirectly, to determine the status of a borrower at any time after a consumer has entered into a transaction.[56] Second, the creditor may verify the status of an applicant using a statement, code, or similar indicator describing the military status, if any, contained within a consumer report obtained from a consumer reporting agency that compiles and maintains files on consumers on a nationwide basis, or a reseller of such a consumer report.[57]

For a creditor to qualify for the safe harbor under either of the two methods described above, the creditor must timely create and maintain a record of the information obtained through the chosen method.[58] A creditor may only make the determination and create the record at the time (1) a consumer initiates the transaction or thirty days prior to that time;[59] (2) a consumer applies to establish the account or thirty days prior to that time; or (3) the creditor develops or processes, with respect to a consumer, a firm offer of credit that includes the status of the consumer as a covered borrower subject to the MLA, as long as the consumer responds to the offer not later than sixty days after the offer is provided.[60]

The DoD's First Interpretive Rule notes that assignees may also rely on the original creditor's safe harbor identification as long as the assignee maintains the original creditor's record of a covered borrower check.[61]

---

54. The database website provided in the MLA's regulations is https://www.dmdc.osd.mil/mla/welcome.xhtml. 32 C.F.R. § 232.5(b)(2)(i)(A) (2019). However, the DoD's First Interpretive Rule clarifies that the DoD may modify this website over time and that such modifications do not impact the safe harbor as long as the DoD's MLA database is used. First Interpretive Rule, *supra* note 10, at 58843.

55. 32 C.F.R. § 232.5(b)(2)(i)(A) (2019).

56. *Id.* § 232.5(b)(2)(i)(B) (2019). The DoD's interpretive rule notes that the historic lookback prohibition does not prohibit creditors from accessing the MLA database for other purposes, such as determining whether a previously covered borrower retains that status. First Interpretive Rule, *supra* note 10, at 58843.

57. 32 C.F.R. § 232.5(b)(2)(ii) (2019).

58. *Id.* § 232.5(b)(3) (2019).

59. The DoD clarified in its Second Interpretive Rule that this permits a creditor to conduct the safe harbor identification process while the creditor processes the covered borrower's application for credit. Second Interpretive Rule, *supra* note 13, at 58741.

60. *Id.*

61. First Interpretive Rule, *supra* note 10, at 58842.

4. Finance Charge Limitations and the Military Annual Percentage Rate Calculation

The MLA limits the maximum allowable amount of all charges and restricts the types of charges permitted.[62] A creditor extending consumer credit to a covered borrower may not require the covered borrower to pay a finance charge except as agreed to under the terms of the credit agreement or promissory note, authorized by applicable state or federal law, and not specifically prohibited by the MLA.[63] In addition, a creditor may not impose a Military Annual Percentage Rate (MAPR) greater than 36 percent per annum for closed-end credit or in any billing cycle for open-end credit.[64]

4.1 Calculation of the Military Annual Percentage Rate

The term MAPR is a creation of the MLA itself.[65] The MAPR is the cost of the consumer credit expressed as an annual rate and calculated in the manner specified by the MLA.[66] The MLA provides that, even if otherwise excluded from the annual percentage rate (APR) under Regulation Z, the following charges must be included in the finance charge for purposes of calculating the MAPR:[67]

1. Credit insurance premiums or fees, including charges for single-premium credit insurance, fees for debt cancellation or debt suspension agreements;[68]
2. Fees for credit-related ancillary products sold in connection with the credit transaction;[69] and
3. Except for a bona fide fee (other than a periodic rate) that may be excluded, the following charges must be included in the MAPR calculation:[70]
   a. Finance charges associated with the consumer credit;[71]
   b. Any application fee charged to a covered borrower who applies for consumer credit (other than an application fee charged by a federal credit union or an insured depository institution when

62. 32 C.F.R. § 232.1(c)(1) (2019).
63. *Id.* § 232.4(a) (2019).
64. *Id.* § 232.4(b) (2019).
65. *Id.* § 232.3(p) (2019).
66. *Id.*
67. *Id.* § 232.4(c)(1)(iv) (2019).
68. *Id.* § 232.4(c)(1)(i) (2019).
69. *Id.* § 232.4(c)(1)(ii) (2019).
70. *Id.* § 232.4(c)(1)(iii) (2019).
71. *Id.* § 232.4(c)(1)(iii)(A) (2019).

making a short-term, small-amount loan,[72] provided that the application fee is charged to the covered borrower not more than once in any rolling twelve-month period);[73] and

c. Any fee imposed for participation in any plan or arrangement for consumer credit, subject to the MAPR calculation instructions for open-end credit discussed below.[74]

Although the 2015 final rule removed the prior express exclusion of late payment fees and taxes required to be paid, it did so "because these charges (as well as other charges) are not finance charges under Regulation Z."[75] These charges are excluded from the MAPR because the MLA defines a finance charge by reference to Regulation Z and nothing in the MLA expressly requires including them in the MAPR.[76] The DoD confirmed this fact as applicable to fees required by law and passed on to a covered borrower for the same reason in its First Interpretive Rule so long as such fees are not finance charges under Regulation Z.[77]

4.1.1 Closed-End Credit

For closed-end credit, the MAPR should be calculated by following the rules for calculating the traditional APR under Regulation Z, based on the charges specifically added to the MAPR beyond what would otherwise be included in the APR under Regulation Z.[78] In essence, this simply means that the general framework of the APR as contemplated under Regulation Z should still be utilized, simply with the modification of including the enumerated fees above as part of the finance charge.

72. A short-term, small-amount loan is defined as a closed-end loan that is (1) subject to and made in accordance with a federal law (other than the MLA) that expressly limits the rate of interest that a federal credit union or an insured depository institution may charge on an extension of credit, provided that the limitation set forth in that law is comparable to a limitation of an APR of 36 percent; and (2) made in accordance with the requirements, terms, and conditions of a rule, prescribed by the appropriate federal regulatory agency (or jointly by such agencies), that implements the federal law described in 32 C.F.R. section 232.3(t)(1), provided further that such law or rule contains: (a) a fixed numerical limit on the maximum maturity term, which term shall not exceed nine months; and (b) a fixed numerical limit on any application fee that may be charged to a consumer who applies for such closed-end loan. 32 C.F.R. § 232.3(t).

73. *Id.* § 232.4(c)(1)(iii)(B) (2019).

74. *Id.* § 232.4(c)(1)(iii)(C) (2019).

75. *Supra* note 7, at 43582.

76. 32 C.F.R. § 232.3(n) (2019).

77. First Interpretive Rule, *supra* note 10, at 58,841.

78. 32 C.F.R. § 232.4(c)(2)(i) (2019).

4.1.2 Open-End Credit

The MLA contains similar instructions for open-end credit. The MAPR for open-end credit should also be calculated following the rules for calculating the effective APR for a billing cycle as set forth in Regulation Z,[79] based on the charges specifically added to the MAPR beyond what would otherwise be included in the APR under Regulation Z.[80] However, regardless of Regulation Z, the MAPR calculation must also include the amount of charges related to opening, renewing, or continuing an account to the extent those charges are incorporated into the list of specifically included charges above.[81]

If the MAPR cannot be calculated in a billing cycle because there is no balance, a creditor is prohibited from imposing any fee or charge during that billing cycle, except that the creditor may impose a fee for participation in any plan or arrangement for that open-end credit so long as the participation fee does not exceed $100 per annum, regardless of the billing cycle in which the participation fee is imposed.[82] This $100 limitation on the amount of the participation fee does not, however, apply to a bona fide participation fee imposed as described below.[83] Further, the DoD's First Interpretive Rule notes that this restriction does not preclude creditors from charging permissible fees excluded from the definition of a finance charge under Regulation Z and not otherwise included in the MAPR, such as late fees, in a billing cycle where there is no balance.[84]

The DoD also clarified in its First Interpretive Rule that *creditors* are permitted to waive fees or periodic charges at the end of a billing cycle, or earlier, in order to prevent a borrower from being assessed an *MAPR* in excess of 36 percent per annum during a particular billing cycle.[85] As a result, *creditors* are able to design a system that automatically corrects the *MAPR* assessed after the fees and charges incurred during a particular billing cycle are known.

4.2 The Bona Fide Fee Exclusion Charged to Credit Card Accounts

The MLA contains provisions that exclude certain bona fide credit card fees (other than a periodic rate) from the MAPR calculation, provided certain conditions are met.[86] These conditions ensure that certain ineligible items are not mischaracterized as a bona fide fee and that the bona fide fee satisfies certain standards to be considered

79. Specifically, 12 C.F.R. § 1026(c) and (d) as if a creditor must comply with that section.
80. 32 C.F.R. § 232.4(c)(2)(ii)(A) (2019).
81. *Id.*
82. *Id.* § 232.4(c)(2)(ii)(B) (2019).
83. *Id.*
84. First Interpretive Rule, *supra* note 10, at 58841.
85. *Id.*
86. 32 C.F.R. § 232.4(d)(1) (2019).

a bona fide fee. [87] The conditions also establish the like-kind fee standards used to determine whether the credit card fee is bona fide and reasonable for that type of fee.[88]

4.2.1 Ineligible Charges

The following credit card fees may not be excluded from the MAPR under the bona fide fee exclusion:

1. Credit insurance premiums or fees, including charges for single premium credit insurance, fees for debt cancellation or debt suspension agreements;[89] and
2. Fees for credit-related ancillary products sold in connection with the credit transaction.[90]

As a result, creditors should be careful to make sure any such charges are not excluded from the MAPR calculation.

4.2.2 Standards for Bona Fide Fees

The like-kind fee must be compared to fees that other creditors typically impose for the same or substantially similar product or service.[91] For example, when the creditor assesses a bona fide cash advance fee, it must be compared to fees charged by other *creditors* for transactions in which consumers receive extensions of credit in the form of cash or its equivalent. The MLA clarifies that the creditor, when assessing a foreign transaction fee, may not compare it to a cash advance fee because the foreign transaction fee involves the service of exchanging the consumer's currency for the local currency demanded by a merchant for a good or service, and thus does not involve the provision of cash to the consumer.[92]

The creditor may use a safe harbor calculation to determine whether a bona fide fee is reasonable. To qualify for the safe harbor and be presumed reasonable, the creditor must determine whether the amount of the fee is less than or equal to an average amount of a fee for the same or a substantially similar product or service charged by five or more creditors, each with active U.S. credit card accounts that total at least $3 billion in outstanding balances (or at least $3 billion in loans on U.S. credit card accounts initially extended by the creditor) at any time during the

87. *Id.* §§ 232.4(d)(2)–(3) (2019).
88. *Id.*
89. *Id.* § 232.4(d)(2)(i) (2019).
90. *Id.* § 232.4(d)(2)(ii) (2019).
91. *Id.* § 232.4(d)(3)(i) (2019).
92. *Id.*

three-year period before the average is computed.[93] A bona fide fee that exceeds the average amount calculated under the safe harbor may also be reasonable depending on other factors relating to the credit card account.[94] A fee is not unreasonable solely because other creditors do not charge a fee for the same or substantially similar product or service.[95]

The amount of a bona fide fee the creditor charges for participation in a credit card account may also be deemed reasonable if it reasonably corresponds to (1) the credit limit in effect or credit made available when the fee is imposed, (2) the services offered under the credit card account, or (3) other factors relating to the credit card account.[96] For example, a creditor's $400 annual fee may be reasonable, even where other creditors typically charge a $100 annual fee, if (relative to other accounts carrying participation fees) the creditor makes significantly higher credit available or offers additional services or other benefits under that account.[97] The DoD noted in its First Interpretive Rule that a creditor may consider the benefits provided by credit card rewards in determining the eligibility for the safe harbor and overall reasonableness of the fee.[98]

The DoD also clarified in its First Interpretive Rule that a minimum interest charge the creditor assesses for an open-end credit card account, when disclosed in the account-opening table under Regulation Z, may qualify as a bona fide fee that can be excluded from the MAPR,[99] if it otherwise qualifies as a bona fide fee and is reasonable for that type of fee.[100]

4.2.3 Effect of Charging Non-Bona Fide Fees on Bona Fide Fees

The MLA generally treats bona fide fees separately from other fees but incorporates a harsh penalty for a creditor that charges a non-bona fide fee—namely, by requiring the creditor to include even bona fide fees in the MAPR calculation if it elects to assess a non-bona fide fee.[101] To wit, if a creditor imposes any fee during a particular billing cycle (other than a periodic rate and the fees expressly included in the MAPR), and

---

93. *Id.* § 232.4(d)(3)(ii) (2019). The DoD clarified in its First Interpretive Rule that creditors may rely on commercially compiled sources of information in conducting calculations necessary for the conditional reasonable bona fide credit card fee safe harbor. First Interpretive Rule, *supra* note 10, at 58842. However, the DoD noted that the safe harbor is only available if the amount of the fee actually meets the mathematical test, so creditors should ensure such databases are accurate. *Id.*

94. 32 C.F.R. § 232.4(d)(3)(iii) (2019).

95. *Id.*

96. *Id.* § 232.4(d)(3)(iv) (2019).

97. *Id.* § 232.4(d)(3)(iv) (2019).

98. First Interpretive Rule, *supra* note 10, at 58842.

99. *Id.*

100. *Id.*

101. *Id.* § 232.4(d)(4) (2019).

that fee is not a bona fide fee and a finance charge is assessed, the total amount of those fees and any bona fide fees must be included in the MAPR.[102] The MLA contains two examples to clarify how this consequence will occur. First, if Creditor A imposes on a covered borrower a fee for a debt cancellation product, a finance charge, and a bona fide foreign transaction fee that qualifies for the bona fide fee exclusion, only the fee for the debt cancellation product and the finance charge must be included when calculating the MAPR.[103] Second, if Creditor B imposes on a covered borrower a fee for a debt cancellation product, a finance charge, a bona fide foreign transaction fee, and an unreasonable bona fide fee for a cash advance, then Creditor B must now include all of the fees (including the otherwise bona fide foreign transaction fee) in the MAPR calculation.[104]

5. Mandatory Disclosures

A creditor must provide certain disclosures in connection with any extension of consumer credit subject to the MLA that is made to a covered borrower.[105] Although the MLA specifies three discrete written disclosures, two of the three written disclosures are typically satisfied by the Truth in Lending Act disclosures. In addition, the MLA requires that two of the three disclosures also be made orally. Each disclosure and the method of delivery are discussed below.

5.1 The Statement of the Military Annual Percentage Rate

A creditor must provide a statement of the MAPR applicable to the extension of consumer credit.[106] The MLA contains certain guidance regarding the obligation to describe the charges the creditor may impose and the fact that the statement of the MAPR does not require a numerical description.[107] However, the MLA also sets forth a specific form of disclosure that satisfies the obligation, rendering most of that guidance largely immaterial.[108] The following model statement, or one substantially similar to it, may be used to satisfy the statement of the MAPR disclosure requirement:

> Federal law provides important protections to members of the Armed Forces and their dependents relating to extensions of *consumer credit*. In general, the cost of *consumer credit* to a member of the Armed Forces

102. *Id.* § 232.4(d)(4)(ii) (2019).
103. *Id.* § 232.4(d)(4)(iii)(A) (2019).
104. *Id.* § 232.4(d)(4)(iii)(B) (2019).
105. *Id.* § 232.6(a) (2019).
106. *Id.* § 232.6(a)(1) (2019).
107. *Id.* § 232.6(c) (2019).
108. *Id.* § 232.6(c)(3) (2019).

and his or her dependent may not exceed an annual percentage rate of 36 percent. This rate must include, as applicable to the credit transaction or account: the costs associated with credit insurance premiums; fees for ancillary products sold in connection with the credit transaction; any application fee charged (other than certain application fees for specified credit transactions or accounts); and any participation fee charged (other than certain participation fees for a credit card account).[109]

5.2 The Regulation Z Disclosures and Clear Description of the Payment Obligation

Two other written disclosures must be provided, both of which are typically satisfied through the Truth in Lending Act disclosures otherwise being provided. First, a creditor must provide any disclosure required by Regulation Z.[110] A creditor complies with this disclosure requirement simply by making the requisite Truth in Lending Act disclosures.[111]

Second, a creditor must provide a clear description of the payment obligation of the covered borrower.[112] However, a payment schedule for closed-end credit, or an account-opening disclosure for open-end credit, provided pursuant to Regulation Z also satisfies this disclosure requirement.[113]

5.3 Timing and Delivery of the Written Disclosures

Although there are several ways MLA disclosures may be made, a creditor who provides a copy of the loan agreement or contract and the Truth in Lending Act disclosures to the consumer to keep should be able to satisfy the MLA's written disclosure obligations by incorporating the disclosures into those documents. However, the MLA may require a separate disclosure form depending on a creditor's practices.

The three written disclosures must be made before or at the time the borrower becomes obligated on the transaction or establishes an account for the consumer credit.[114] Further, a creditor must provide the written statement of the MAPR and the clear description of the payment obligation disclosures in a form the covered borrower may keep, with the Regulation Z disclosures simply required to be made in accordance with Regulation Z.[115] However, a creditor may include the statement of

109. *Id.*
110. *Id.* § 232.6(a)(2) (2019).
111. *Id.*
112. *Id.* § 232.6(a)(3) (2019).
113. *Id.*
114. *Id.*
115. *Id.* § 232.6(d)(1) (2019).

the MAPR applicable to the consumer credit within the loan agreement or contract.[116] The statement of the MAPR also need not be provided in any advertisements relating to the credit.[117]

In its First Interpretive Rule, the DoD addressed the timing of the disclosures in the context of transactions where Regulation Z allows a creditor to provide disclosures after the borrower has become obligated on the transaction, such as in the case of purchase orders or requests for credit made by mail, telephone, or facsimile.[118] The DoD confirmed that any disclosure required by Regulation Z shall be provided only in accordance with the requirements of Regulation Z applicable to such disclosure.[119] Accordingly, the DoD agreed that the MLA's specific timing requirement does not override more specific disclosure timing requirements in Regulation Z.[120] To that end, the DoD agreed that all the MLA required disclosures (the statement of the MAPR, the Regulation Z disclosures, and the clear description of the payment obligation) may be provided at the time prescribed by Regulation Z.[121]

5.4 Oral Disclosure Obligation

A creditor must also provide orally the statement of the MAPR and the clear description of the payment obligation.[122] The oral disclosures may be delivered in person to the covered borrower, but also may be delivered through the use of a toll-free telephone number.[123] If the creditor opts to use the toll-free number, the number must be included on a form the creditor directs the consumer to use to apply for credit or on a written disclosure provided to the borrower.[124]

The DoD also clarified how the oral disclosure of the clear description of the payment obligation may be made in its First Interpretive Rule.[125] In that guidance, the DoD noted the difficulty of providing the payment schedule or account opening disclosures under Regulation Z in an oral manner.[126] The DoD confirmed that a creditor may satisfy this requirement by providing a general description of how the payment obligation is calculated or a description of what the borrower's payment obligation would be based on an estimate of the amount the borrower may borrow.[127]

---

116. *Id.* § 232.6(c)(2) (2019).
117. *Id.*
118. First Interpretive Rule, *supra* note 10, at 58844.
119. *Id.*
120. *Id. See also* 32 C.F.R. § 232.6(a)(2) (2019).
121. First Interpretive Rule, *supra* note 10, at 58844.
122. 32 C.F.R. § 232.6(d)(2)(i) (2019).
123. *Id.* § 232.6(d)(2)(ii) (2019).
124. *Id.* § 232.6(d)(2)(iii) (2019).
125. First Interpretive Rule, *supra* note 10, at 58843.
126. *Id.*
127. *Id.*

As an example, the DoD noted that a creditor could generally describe how minimum payments are calculated on open-end credit plans issued by the creditor and then refer the covered borrower to the written materials the borrower would receive in connection with opening the plan.[128] As another example, the DoD noted that a creditor could choose to describe generally borrowers' obligations to make a monthly, bimonthly, or weekly payment as the case may be under the borrower's agreements.[129] The DoD noted that a disclosure may be the same for borrowers with a variety of consumer credit transactions or accounts.[130]

The DoD also clarified the timing as to when the oral disclosures must be provided to covered borrowers when the toll free number is used as the means of delivery.[131] Like the written disclosures, the toll-free number must be provided on either (1) a form the creditor directs the consumer to use to apply for the transaction or account, or (2) the other written disclosures being provided in a form the covered borrower may keep.[132] The oral disclosures provided through the toll free number must, of course, be available from the time the toll free number is initially provided.[133] However, the toll-free number need only be maintained for a duration of time reasonably necessary to allow a covered borrower to contact the creditor for the purpose of listening to the disclosure.[134]

5.5 Disclosure Requirements for Renewals, Refinancing Transactions, and Transactions with Multiple Creditors

In general, the MLA disclosures need only be provided once for each transaction or account established for consumer credit with respect to a specific borrower.[135] The refinancing or renewal of consumer credit does require new disclosures under the MLA, however, but only when the transaction for that credit would be deemed a new transaction that requires disclosures under Regulation Z.[136] If a transaction involves more than one creditor, the MLA disclosures need only be provided by one creditor.[137] The creditors may determine which creditor will provide the disclosures.[138]

128. *Id.*
129. *Id.*
130. *Id.* at 58843–44.
131. *Id.* at 58844.
132. *Id.*
133. *Id.*
134. *Id.*
135. 32 C.F.R. § 232.6(b)(1) (2019).
136. *Id.* § 232.6(e) (2019).
137. *Id.* § 232.6(b)(2) (2019).
138. *Id.*

6. Substantive Limitations on Loans to Covered Borrowers

A creditor must comply with numerous substantive restrictions on the terms of consumer credit that may be offered to covered borrowers.[139] These restrictions include a ban on arbitration, restrictions on the use of motor vehicles as security, and others.[140]

6.1 Arbitration, Notice, and Waiver Requirements

A creditor may not require a covered borrower to submit to arbitration or impose other onerous legal notice provisions in the case of a dispute.[141] A creditor also may not demand unreasonable notice from a covered borrower as a precondition to legal action.[142] Last, a creditor may not require a covered borrower to waive their right to legal recourse under any otherwise applicable provision of law, including the Servicemembers Civil Relief Act.[143]

6.2 Ban on the Use of a Motor Vehicle as Collateral

The MLA curiously incorporates a prohibition on nondepository creditors taking a security interest in the title of a motor vehicle.[144] The decision to ban *nondepository* creditors from this market is a strange decision given that more than half of motor-vehicle-secured financing is provided by nonbanks, including the captive auto finance companies of many major auto manufacturers.[145] The ban was added in the 2015 final rule expanding the scope of the MLA, but it was not included in the initial proposed rule—an administrative agency surprise that denied the public the ability to comment on the effects of this provision and the DoD any opportunity to consider the effect of this decision in light of the public's comments.[146] However, it is possible that this particular provision was drafted in error. The reason is that, prior to the 2015 amendments, the MLA had a specific inclusion of motor vehicle title loans within its scope.[147] A motor vehicle title loan is a form of non-purchase-money consumer credit

139. *Id.* § 232.8 (2019).

140. *Id.*

141. *Id.* § 232.8(c) (2019).

142. *Id.* § 232.8(d) (2019).

143. *Id.* § 232.8(b) (2019).

144. *Id.* § 232.8(f) (2019).

145. Ralf R. Meisenzahl, Auto Financing during and after the Great Recession FEDS Notes (Board of Governors of the Federal Reserve System, June 22, 2017), https://doi.org/10.17016/2380-7172.2015.

146. Limitations on Terms of Consumer credit Extended to Service Members and Dependents; Proposed Rule, 79 Fed. Reg. 58602, 58640 (Sept. 29, 2014).

147. Limitations on Terms of *Consumer credit, supra* note 5, at 50,593.

whereby the lender typically takes physical possession of the motor vehicle's title and only returns it upon payment in full.[148] In this context, the particular phrasing of the prohibition (prohibiting a creditor that "uses the title of a vehicle as security for the obligation" rather than a more conventional prohibition on the use of a motor vehicle as collateral) appears to continue the focus on vehicle title loans.[149]

However, in oral remarks made after the final rule was announced, Marcus Beauregard, the official contact designated in the 2015 final rule regarding this issue, asserted that the provision did have the impact of prohibiting any nondepository entity from taking any type of non-purchase-money security interest in a motor vehicle, and thus was not limited in applicability to motor vehicle title loans.[150] As a result, the prohibition on any entity other than a depository institution using a motor vehicle's title as collateral effectively prohibits nonbank entities from offering non-purchase-money installment loans, including motor vehicle refinance financing, secured by motor vehicles, to covered borrowers.

6.3 Prohibition on the Use of a Check or Other Method of Access to a Deposit, Savings, or Other Financial Account

The MLA prohibits a creditor from using a check or other methods to access a deposit, savings, or other financial account maintained by the covered borrower.[151] However, creditors are granted three exceptions from this requirement.[152] First, a creditor may require an electronic funds transfer (EFT) to repay a consumer credit transaction, unless otherwise prohibited by law.[153] Second, a creditor may require direct deposit of the consumer's salary as a condition of eligibility for consumer credit, unless otherwise prohibited by law.[154] Third, if not otherwise prohibited by applicable law, a creditor may take a security interest in funds deposited after the extension of credit in an account established in connection with the consumer credit transaction.[155]

---

148. Fed. Trade Comm'n, *Car Title Loans* (Jul. 2014), https://www.consumer.ftc.gov/articles/0514-car-title-loans.

149. 32 C.F.R. § 232.8(f) (2019).

150. The 2015 final rule provided an official contact, Marcus Beauregard, to receive and respond to inquiries relating to the Rule. *Supra* note 7, at 43,560. At the time, Mr. Beauregard was a retired colonel in the U.S. Air Force and was the chief of the DoD-State Liaison Office within the Office of the Deputy Assistant Secretary of Defense for Military Community and Family Policy. Mr. Beauregard responded orally to the author's inquiry on August 31, 2015.

151. 32 C.F.R. § 232.8(e) (2019).

152. *Id.* Note that the MLA provides that these three exceptions apply for transactions that comply with the MAPR restrictions built into the MLA.

153. *Id.* § 232.8(e)(1) (2019).

154. *Id.* § 232.8(e)(2) (2019).

155. *Id.* § 232.8(e)(3) (2019).

6.3.1 Single and Recurring Payments from Financial Accounts

The DoD clarified in its First Interpretive Rule, however, that this prohibition does not prohibit a borrower from repaying a credit transaction by check or EFT.[156] To that end, covered borrowers may use a check or otherwise authorize access to a deposit, savings, or other financial account to repay a creditor.[157] These permitted payment methods include authorizing automatically recurring payments that comply with the Electronic Fund Transfer Act or any other applicable laws.[158]

6.3.2 Remotely Created and Postdated Checks

The DoD also clarified in its First Interpretive Rule, however, that a creditor is prohibited from using the borrower's account information to create a check or similar payment order remotely.[159] The use of a postdated check provided at or around the date of origination is similarly prohibited, as the DoD believes this payment mechanism removes control over the timing of payment from the covered borrower.[160]

6.3.3 Security Interests in Checking, Savings, or other Financial Accounts

The MLA's regulatory treatment of security interests in checking, savings, or other financial accounts was initially unclear. As noted above, the MLA prohibits a creditor from using a check or other method of access to a deposit, savings, or other financial account maintained by the covered borrower.[161] However, the MLA states that, if not otherwise prohibited by applicable law, a creditor may take a security interest in funds deposited after the extension of credit in an account established in connection with the consumer credit transaction.[162] Questions arose regarding whether a security interest could be taken in funds deposited prior to the extension of credit in a previously existing checking, savings, or other financial accounts.

In both its First Interpretive Rule and its Second Interpretive Rule, the DoD appeared to clarify that this prohibition does not prohibit covered borrowers from granting a security interest to a creditor in the covered borrower's checking, savings, or other financial account so long as that security interest is not otherwise prohibited by applicable law when the creditor otherwise complies with the MLA.[163]

---

156. First Interpretive Rule, *supra* note 10, at 58844.

157. *Id.*

158. *Id.*

159. *Id.*

160. *Id.*

161. 32 C.F.R. § 232.8(e) (2019).

162. *Id.* § 232.8(e)(3) (2019).

163. First Interpretive Rule, *supra* note 10, at 58,845; Second Interpretive Rule, *supra* note 13, at 58,740.

Although the DoD continued to use as an example the taking of a security interest in funds deposited after the extension of credit, in both rules, the DoD further emphasized its discussion of remotely created checks and payment orders as the focus of this prohibition, rather than an attempt to limit the ability of creditors to take such a security interest.[164] Last, in the context of a contractual right to setoff, discussed below, the DoD clarified in its Second Interpretive Rule that this prohibition "does not prohibit a *creditor* from exercising rights to take a security interest in funds deposited into a *covered borrower*'s account at any time," and confirmed that creditors should not interpret the timing requirement in the exception to the general prohibition as imposing a timing requirement on the prohibition itself.[165] As a result, it appears that the taking of such a security interest should be permissible. The DoD did clarify, however, that this permission does not impact any other state or federal law, rule, or regulation that provides greater protections to borrowers, including provisions limiting offsets and security interests.[166]

6.3.4 *Right to Setoff*

In both its First Interpretive Rule and its Second Interpretive Rule, the DoD noted that the MLA does not prohibit a creditor from exercising a statutory right, or a right arising out of a security interest granted by the covered borrower to the creditor, to take a security interest in funds deposited within a covered borrower's account at any time.[167] As an example, the DoD noted that federal credit unions are granted a statutory right to enforce a lien upon the shares and dividends of any member to pay off a loan made to that member, or any dues or charges owed by said member.[168] The DoD then confirmed that the MLA would not impact such a statutory right.[169]

6.4 Prepayment, Refinancing, and Allotments

A creditor may not prohibit a covered borrower from prepaying the consumer credit, nor charge a penalty fee for such prepayment.[170] A creditor also may not require that the covered borrower establish an allotment to repay the obligation.[171] Last, a creditor may not renew, roll-over, refinance, or consolidate any existing consumer credit with

---

164. *Supra* note 163.

165. Second Interpretive Rule, *supra* note 13, at 58740.

166. *Id.*

167. First Interpretive Rule, *supra* note 10, at 58845; Second Interpretive Rule, *supra* note 13, at 58740.

168. Second Interpretive Rule, *supra* note 13, at 58741.

169. *Id.*

170. 32 C.F.R. § 232.8(h) (2019).

171. *Id.* § 232.8(g) (2019). An allotment is a federal government mechanism through which federal employees, including servicemembers, may direct funds directly from their paycheck.

additional credit, when the original credit and the new credit were both extended by that same creditor.[172] However, this prohibition does not apply to a transaction when the same creditor extends credit to a covered borrower to refinance or renew an extension of credit that was not covered by the MLA because the consumer was not a covered borrower at the time of the original transaction.[173] Although this exception is potentially helpful to creditors and covered borrowers alike, it has the effect of simply permitting a creditor to convert preexisting credit not governed by the MLA into a new transaction entirely subject to the MLA. This single prohibition does contain two exclusions. First, this prohibition limits the definition of a "creditor" to those persons engaged in the business of extending consumer credit subject to applicable law to engage in deferred presentment transactions or similar payday loan transactions.[174] Second, this prohibition also limits the definition of "creditor" to exclude a person chartered or licensed under federal or state law as a bank, savings association, or credit union.[175]

6.5 The Use of a Single Credit Agreement and a Savings Clause

The DoD addressed the use of a savings clause in its First Interpretive Rule.[176] The DoD noted that creditors may use a single credit agreement for both covered and noncovered borrowers that utilizes a savings clause that excludes covered borrowers from the prohibited notice, waiver, arbitration, and other terms otherwise applicable to noncovered borrowers.[177] As a result, the inclusion of a proscribed term under the MLA within a credit agreement used with respect to a covered borrower is not a violation per se of the MLA, provided that the agreement has a savings clause limiting the applicability of the proscribed term to only noncovered borrowers.[178]

7. Enforcement by Federal Agencies and Civil Liability

The MLA sets forth specific penalties for violations of its terms.[179] A creditor who knowingly violates the MLA is subject to misdemeanor enforcement consisting of a fine as provided under Title 18 of the United States Code or imprisoned for not more than one year, or both.[180] The administrative enforcement authority of the MLA

172. *Id.* § 232.8(a) (2019).
173. *Id.*
174. *Id.*
175. *Id.*
176. First Interpretive Rule, *supra* note 10, at 58844.
177. *Id.*
178. *Id.*
179. 32 C.F.R. § 232.9 (2019).
180. 10 U.S.C. § 987(f)(1) (2019); 32 C.F.R. § 232.9(a) (2019).

is vested in the various prudential regulatory agencies referenced in the Truth in Lending Act,[181] and this authority includes all penalties and remedies other than the enforcement of the criminal misdemeanor penalties noted just above.[182]

The MLA also states that a person who violates the MLA is civilly liable to the individual whose rights were violated for (1) any actual damages sustained as a result, but not less than $500 for each violation; (2) appropriate punitive damages; (3) appropriate equitable or declaratory relief; and (4) any other relief provided by law.[183] In a successful action to enforce liability under the MLA, the costs of the action and reasonable attorney's fees may be recovered.[184] The MLA also provides that, in a successful action by a defendant, the court may make a finding of bad faith and harassment on the part of a plaintiff, and may hold a plaintiff liable for the defendant's legal fees, although this burden would likely be very high.[185]

Further, any credit agreement, promissory note, or other contract prohibited under the MLA is void from the inception of the contract.[186] The status of the contract as void applies where the contract fails to comply with a single requirement of the MLA or its implementing regulations.[187] Last, the penalties and remedies provided under the MLA are not exclusive, and thus do not preclude any other remedy otherwise available under federal and state laws, including awards for consequential or punitive damages.[188]

An action for civil liability may be brought in any appropriate U.S. district court, regardless of the amount in controversy, not later than the earlier of (1) two years after the date of discovery by the plaintiff of the violation that is the basis for such liability, or (2) five years after the date on which the violation that is the basis for such liability occurs.[189]

A person may not be held civilly liable if he or she shows by a preponderance of the evidence that the violation was not intentional and resulted from a bona fide error notwithstanding the maintenance of procedures reasonably adapted to avoid any such error. Examples of such a bona fide error include clerical, calculation, computer

181. 10 U.S.C. § 987(f)(6) (2019). These agencies include the Federal Deposit Insurance Corporation, Consumer Financial Protection Bureau, Office of the Comptroller of the Currency, Board of Governors of the Federal Reserve System, National Credit Union Administration, and others. *See* 15 U.S.C. § 1607(a) (2018).

182. 32 C.F.R. § 232.10 (2019).

183. 10 U.S.C. § 987(f)(5)(A) (2019); 32 C.F.R. § 232.9(e)(1) (2019).

184. 10 U.S.C. § 987(f)(5)(B) (2019); 32 C.F.R. § 232.9(e)(2) (2019).

185. 32 C.F.R. § 232.9(e)(3) (2019).

186. 10 U.S.C. § 987(f)(3) (2019); 32 C.F.R. § 232.9(c) (2019). Because of this potentially catastrophic result, the scope of the motor vehicle purchase money exclusion was hotly debated.

187. 32 C.F.R. § 232.9(c) (2019).

188. *Id.* § 232.9(b) (2019).

189. 10 U.S.C. § 987(f)(5)(E) (2019); 32 C.F.R. § 232.9(e)(5) (2019).

malfunction and programming, and printing errors, except that an error of legal judgment with respect to a transaction subject to the MLA is not a bona fide error.[190]

The federal banking regulatory agencies have created updated MLA examination manuals to facilitate MLA compliance through supervisory examinations.[191] However, the CFPB has determined that it does not have authority to conduct supervisory examinations with respect to the MLA and has requested that Congress grant it such authority.[192]

8. Relation to Other State and Federal Laws

The MLA expressly preempts any state or federal law, rule, or regulation, including any state usury law, to the extent that such law is inconsistent with the MLA and its implementing regulations.[193] However, those laws that provide greater protections than set forth in the MLA are not preempted.[194] States also may not authorize creditors to charge covered borrowers rates of interest for any credit transaction that are higher than the legal limit for residents of that state.[195] Further, the MLA requires that states grant covered borrowers the protections of their laws even where a covered borrower may be a permanent resident of another state—a protection designed to consider the mobile nature of military members on deployment.[196] The prohibition itself provides that a state may not permit the violation or waiver of any state consumer lending protection covering consumer credit that is for the benefit of residents of the state solely on the basis of a covered borrower's nonresident or military status, regardless of the covered borrower's domicile or permanent home of record, where such protection would otherwise apply.[197]

One issue addressed directly by the DoD is the fact that the DoD intentionally prohibited the offering of credit with terms that did not comply with the MLA. The DoD acknowledged the effect of the MLA when it first published its regulation in 2007 by stating that the "Department (of Defense) understands *creditors* may otherwise decline offering beneficial credit products to *covered borrowers* as a result of concerns over

---

190. 10 U.S.C. § 987(f)(D) (2019); 32 C.F.R. § 232.9(e)(4) (2019).

191. *See, e.g.*, OCC, *Comptroller's Handbook: Military Lending Act* (May 2019), https://www.occ.gov/publications/publications-by-type/comptrollers-handbook/military-lending-act/pub-ch-mla.pdf.

192. CFPB, *Consumer Financial Protection Bureau Asks Congress for Clear Authority to Supervise for Compliance with the Military Lending Act* (Jan 17, 2019), https://www.consumerfinance.gov/about-us/newsroom/consumer-financial-protection-bureau-asks-congress-clear-authority-supervise-compliance-military-lending-act/.

193. 32 C.F.R. § 232.7(a) (2019).

194. *Id.*

195. *Id.* § 232.7(b)(1) (2019).

196. *Id.* § 232.7(b)(2) (2019).

197. *Id.*

potential violations."[198] In its most recent final rule, the DoD maintained this position, stating that the "Department (of Defense) continues to believe that, consistent with the MLA, there may be a need to limit access to high cost borrowing."[199] Accordingly, the DoD's commentary confirms that the MLA intentionally prohibits some lenders from being able to offer any products to covered borrowers under the MLA and that the MLA should therefore be viewed as preempting any state laws that could require the extension of credit to covered borrowers or otherwise prevent creditors from declining to extend credit to covered borrowers.

198. 72 Fed. Reg. at 50588.

199. 80 Fed. Reg. at 43565.

CHAPTER

15

Real Estate Settlement Procedures Act and Regulation X

Andy Arculin, Peter S. Frechette, and Makalia A. Griffith

1. Overview and General Provisions

The Real Estate Settlement Procedures Act (RESPA)[1] is intended to ensure that consumers receive timely settlement cost disclosures during a home purchase or sale transaction and protect consumers from abusive practices associated with these transactions.[2] In enacting RESPA, Congress set out to provide four settlement process reforms aimed at protecting consumers: (1) provide homebuyers and sellers with effective disclosures of settlement costs, (2) eliminate kickback and referral fees that increased settlement costs, (3) reduce the amount homebuyers are required to place

1. Pub. L. No. 93-533, § 2, 88 Stat.17242 (1974) (codified as amended at 12 U.S.C. §§ 2601–2617 (2018)).

2. 12 U.S.C. § 2601(a). As defined by § 2602, "settlement services" include "any service provided in connection with a real estate settlement including, but not limited to, the following: title searches, title examinations, the provision of title certificates, title insurance, services rendered by an attorney, the preparation of documents, property surveys, the rendering of credit reports or appraisals, pest and fungus inspections, services rendered by a real estate agent or broker, the origination of a federally related mortgage loan (including, but not limited to, the taking of loan applications, loan processing, and the underwriting and funding of loans), and the handling of the processing, and closing or settlement."

in escrow accounts for real estate taxes and insurance, and (4) reform and modernize local record keeping of land title information.[3]

Since its 1974 enactment, RESPA has governed the settlement process for residential real estate transactions involving *federally related mortgage loans*. The statute was expanded in 1991 to include servicing of *federally related mortgages*.[4] Over the years the statute has been amended to require detailed disclosures if a mortgage is transferred or sold, or if mortgage servicing rights are assigned. Another amendment required itemized disclosures for mortgage escrow accounts at closing and annually. Aspects of RESPA were overhauled following the 2008 financial crisis. The Dodd-Frank Wall Street Reform and Consumer Protection Act of 2010 (Dodd-Frank Act) further amended RESPA in response to what Congress viewed as abusive consumer practices in the mortgage market.[5] Thus, modern RESPA is a product both of its long history and fundamental shifts in the mortgage industry.

1.1 Administration

RESPA is implemented through Regulation X, 12 C.F.R. part 1024. Prior to 2010, the U.S. Department of Housing and Urban Development (HUD) administered and enforced RESPA and was the agency authorized to interpret RESPA under Regulation X. The Dodd-Frank Act transferred these activities to the Consumer Financial Protection Bureau (CFPB or Bureau).[6]

The CFPB has not always deferred to previous HUD interpretations and guidance to RESPA's requirements as "rules, regulations, or interpretations thereof" and industry participants should proceed with caution before relying on any such materials without express CFPB guidance.[7] However, HUD's interpretations remain instructive on RESPA interpretation, and courts and administrative agencies "may use previous opinions to determine the validity of conduct under the previous Regulation X."[8]

1.2 Overview

RESPA is generally applicable to all federally related mortgage loans, as that term is defined in the statute, with certain exceptions.[9] The term federally related mortgage

---

3. *Id.* § 2601(b).

4. Cranston-Gonzalez National Affordable Housing Act of 1990, Pub. L. No. 101-625, § 941, 104 Stat. 4079, 4405 (1990).

5. Dodd-Frank Wall Street Reform and Consumer Protection Act, Pub. L. No. 111-203, 124 Stat. 1376 (2010).

6. *See* 12 U.S.C. § 2617(a).

7. *See* 12 C.F.R. § 1024.4(b); *see also* discussion *in* section 4.2.

8. *Id.* § 1024.4(b).

9. 12 U.S.C. § 2602(1).

loan is defined broadly to include any loan that meets both of the following provisions. The loan must:[10]

- First, be secured by a first or subordinate lien on residential real property, including a refinancing of any secured loan on residential real property, located within a state upon which there is either:
    - A one- to four-family structure designed principally for occupancy (including individual units of condominiums and cooperatives and including any related interests, such as a share in the cooperative or right to occupancy of the unit) using the proceeds of the loan; or
    - A manufactured home that is located or will be placed following settlement using the proceeds of the loan; and
- Second, fall within one or more of the following categories:[11]
    - Be made in whole or in part by a federally regulated lender or lender whose deposits or accounts are insured by any agency of the federal government;
    - Be made in whole or in part, or be insured, guaranteed, supplemented, or assisted in any way by HUD or an agency of the federal government;
    - Be made and intended to be sold by the originating lender or creditor to the Federal National Mortgage Association (FNMA or Fannie Mae), Government National Mortgage Association (GNMA or Ginnie Mae), or the Federal Home Loan Mortgage Corporation (FHLMC or Freddie Mac) (or the successor to one of the entities);
    - Be made in whole or in part by a "creditor," as defined in section 103(g) of the Consumer Credit Protection Act;[12]
    - Be originated either by a dealer or mortgage broker, if the obligation is to be assigned to any maker of mortgage loans listed in this section; or
    - Be subject to a reverse mortgage issued by a lender or creditor of mortgage loans listed in this section.

---

10. 12 C.F.R. § 1024.2(b).

11. 12 U.S.C. § 2602(1).

12. 15 U.S.C. § 1602(g). The statue defines "creditor" as "a person who both (1) regularly extends, whether in connection with loans, sales of property or services, or otherwise, consumer credit which is payable by agreement in more than four installments or for which the payment of a finance charge is or may be required, and (2) is the person to whom the debt arising from the consumer credit transaction is initially payable on the face of the evidence of indebtedness or, if there is no such evidence of indebtedness, by agreement." *Id.* § 1602(g).

Federally related mortgage loans also include any installment sales contracts, land contracts, or contracts for deeds if the contract is funded in whole or in part by proceeds of a loan made by any maker of mortgage loans specified above.[13] If the loan is covered by RESPA, all parties to the transaction must comply with the statute to the extent applicable.

1.3 Exemptions

As the definition of "federally related mortgage loan" is expansive, most residential mortgage transactions fit the definition and are subject to RESPA requirements. However, RESPA exempts the following transactions:[14]

- Business, commercial, or agricultural purpose loans, as defined by Regulation Z.[15]
- Temporary financing, such as construction loans. The exemption does not apply if the loan is used as, or may be converted to, permanent financing by the same lender or is used to finance transfer of title to the first user. If the lender issues a commitment for permanent financing, with or without conditions, the loan is covered. These loans are still subject to the Truth in Lending Act (TILA)-RESPA Integrated Disclosure Rule (TRID).[16]
- Loans secured by vacant or unimproved property, unless a structure or a manufactured home will be constructed or placed on the real property using the loan proceeds within two years from the date of the settlement of the loan. The transaction is not exempted if the loan for a structure or manufactured home to be placed on vacant or unimproved property will be secured by a lien on that property.
- An assumption in which the lender does not have the right expressly to approve a subsequent person as the borrower on an existing federally related mortgage loan. An assumption in which the lender's permission is both required and obtained is not exempt.

13. 12 C.F.R. § 1024.5(a).

14. *Id.* § 1024.5(b).

15. 12 C.F.R. part 1026. Regulation Z is the implementing regulation of the Truth in Lending Act (TILA).

16. CFPB, *TILA-RESPA Integrated Disclosures for Construction Loans: Guide for Combined, One-Transaction Disclosures* (Dec. 2019), https://files.consumerfinance.gov/f/documents/cfpb_trid-combined-construction-loan-guide.pdf.

- A conversion of a federally related mortgage loan to different terms where a new loan is not required.
- A bona fide secondary market transfer (not including *table funded transactions*).[17] However, the mortgage servicing disclosure requirements of sections 1024.30 through 1024.41 of Regulation X still apply.[18]

1.4 Relation to State Law

Although issues of preemption are complex, and often fact-specific, generally, lenders or servicers that comply with RESPA timing, content, and notification procedure requirements are considered to be in compliance with similar state laws.[19] RESPA preempts state law requirements that are inconsistent with the statute to the extent of the inconsistency,[20] but RESPA does not "annul, alter, or affect, or exempt any person" from complying with state laws.[21] The state law is not preempted if it provides borrowers with greater protections than RESPA and is not preempted under some other federal law that is not inconsistent with RESPA.[22] The CFPB is authorized to determine if inconsistencies exist.[23]

---

17. *Table funding* means a settlement at which a loan is funded by a contemporaneous advance of loan funds and an assignment of the loan to the person advancing the funds. 12 C.F.R. § 1024.2.

18. *Id.* In determining what constitutes a bona fide transfer, the CFPB will consider the real source of funding and the real interest of the funding lender. A secondary market transfer does not include the creation of a dealer loan or dealer consumer credit contract, or the first assignment of the contract to a lender.

19. *Id.* § 1024.5(c)(1).

20. *Id.* § 1026.28(a); 12 U.S.C. § 2616; *see also* Ervin v. JP Morgan Chase Bank, No. GLR-13-2080, 2014 WL 4052895, at *3–4 (D. Md. Aug. 13, 2014).

21. 12 U.S.C. § 2616.

22. 12 C.F.R. § 1026.28(a).

23. One example of this type of inconsistency would be a state law that allows a servicer to make the first notice or filing in a foreclosure action prior to the borrower being 120 days delinquent, which would conflict with the prohibition in section 1024.41(f)(1) on initiating a foreclosure action unless the borrower is 120 days delinquent. According to the CFPB, section 1024.41(f)(1) "preempts state foreclosure procedures to the extent that they allow an earlier commencement of foreclosure proceedings." *See* Mortgage Servicing Rules Under the Real Estate Settlement Procedures Act (Regulation X), 78 Fed. Reg. 10,696, 10,833 (Feb. 14, 2013) (Section-by-Section Analysis, 12 C.F.R. § 1024.41(f)) ("The Bureau understands and intends that any such requirement will preempt State laws to the extent such laws permit filing of foreclosure actions earlier than after the 120th day of delinquency."). This section is the exception to the rule that Regulation X and RESPA do not preempt state common-law claims. However, a state law that prohibits the first notice or filing prior to the borrower being 180 days delinquent would not be preempted by section 1024.41(f)(1).

1.5 RESPA Naming Convention

Because industry stakeholders generally refer to RESPA provisions according to their sections, rather than the implementing statute, the list below provides a short summary of the relevant RESPA sections. Subsequent sections refer to the statute by section number throughout this chapter.

- RESPA section 2 outlines Congress's goal in creating the rule. As detailed earlier in the chapter, in creating RESPA, Congress set out to provide four settlement process reforms aimed at protecting consumers. 12 U.S.C. § 2601.
- RESPA section 3 provides definitions applicable to the statute. 12 U.S.C. § 2602.
- RESPA sections 4 and 5 outline the mortgage loan disclosure requirements lenders must provide to applicants of transactions covered by RESPA. Section 4 directs the CFPB to "publish a single, integrated disclosure for mortgage transactions, which includes mortgage disclosure requirements under the Truth in Lending Act (TILA) and Sections 4 and 5 of RESPA." 12 U.S.C. §§ 2603–2604.
- RESPA section 6 pertains to mortgage servicing and imposes certain duties on servicers. Regulation X, 12 C.F.R. part 1024 is the implementing regulation. 12 U.S.C. § 2605(e).
- RESPA section 7 details transactions that are exempted from the statute. RESPA does not apply to extensions of credit "primarily for business, commercial, or agricultural purposes; or to government or governmental agencies or instrumentalities." 12 U.S.C. § 2606.
- RESPA section 8 prohibits certain practices by real estate settlement service providers, such as kickbacks in exchange for referrals or unearned fee splits. These add-on fees can add to the settlement costs for home buyers. 12 U.S.C. § 2607.
- RESPA section 9 prohibits a seller from requiring the home purchaser to purchase title insurance, either directly or indirectly, from a particular title company as a condition of the sale. 12 U.S.C. § 2608.
- RESPA section 10 addresses escrow accounts. The statute limits the amounts a lender may require a borrower to place into an escrow account at settlement or hold for purposes of paying taxes, hazard insurance, and other charges related to the property. 12 U.S.C. § 2609.

2. Brief Overview of TRID

One of the fundamental purposes of RESPA is to ensure that home buyers and sellers receive pertinent and timely disclosures regarding the nature and costs of the real estate settlement process.[24] The Dodd-Frank Act directed the CFPB to integrate the mortgage loan disclosures under TILA and RESPA. The CFPB promulgated rules to integrate the various disclosures required under TILA and RESPA, known as the TILA-RESPA Integrated Disclosure rules or TRID—also called the "Know Before You Owe" Mortgage Disclosure Rule—on December 31, 2013.[25] The TRID rules, as they have been updated and amended to correct and clarify elements of the rules, are codified in Regulation Z.

As noted above, the TRID rules apply to most closed-end consumer loans secured by real property or a cooperative unit, but does not apply to home equity lines of credit (HELOCs), reverse mortgages, or mortgages secured by a mobile home or by a dwelling that is not attached to real property.[26]

2.1 Good Faith and Tolerances

When reviewing mortgage loan applications, creditors are required to provide certain disclosures regarding the costs and fees associated with the loan. Creditors must provide an initial set of estimated fees in a loan estimate (or LE) form, and then must provide the actual costs and fees in a closing disclosure (or CD). The estimates in the LE must be made in good faith and consistent with the best information reasonably available to the creditor at the time.[27] Good faith is measured by comparing the LEs with the actual charge or charges paid by or imposed on the consumer in the CD.[28] If the actual fees are higher, the original estimate is not considered to be in good faith. However, for certain types of fees and charges, the TRID rules allow for a tolerance (meaning that the estimate can be slightly higher than the actual costs in certain situations). Many charges are subject to zero tolerance, some may vary by up to 10 percent of the fee amount, and other charges may change without regard to a tolerance limitation.[29]

2.2 Loan Estimate

The LE form is designed to provide disclosures that will be helpful to a consumer in understanding the key features, costs, and risks of the mortgage loan for which the consumer is applying. The LE must be provided to the consumer no later than the third business day after he or she submits a loan application. The term *application*

---

24. *See* 12 U.S.C. § 2601(b)(1).

25. Integrated Mortgage Disclosures Under the Real Estate Settlement Procedures Act (Regulation X) and the Truth in Lending Act (Regulation Z), 78 Fed. Reg. 80,225 (Dec. 31, 2013).

26. 12 C.F.R. §§ 1026.19(e), (f).

27. *Id.* §§ 1026.17(c)(2)(i), 1026.19(e)(3); Cmts. 1026.19(e)(3)(iii)-1, -2, -3.

28. 12 C.F.R. § 1026.19(e)(3).

29. *See id.*

is defined under the TRID rules to consist of six elements—all of which must be received from the consumer or otherwise obtained by the borrower. These include:

- the consumer's name;
- the consumer's income;
- the consumer's social security number to obtain a credit report;
- the property address;
- an estimate of the value of the property; and
- the mortgage loan amount sought.[30]

Under the TRID rules, the LE must contain the creditor's *good faith estimate* (GFE) of credit costs and transaction terms, based on "the best information reasonably available at the time the disclosure is provided to the consumer," and use due diligence in obtaining the information.[31]

TRID sets out the information required to be disclosed on the LE.[32] When providing the LE, creditors must use the model form found in Regulation Z, including all of its elements, such as various font sizes, bolding, shading, and underscoring.[33]

The timing of the LE controls certain other elements of the application process. Generally, the creditor may not charge fees to a consumer before the consumer has received the LE and indicated an intent to proceed with the transaction.[34] Written estimates of terms or costs specific to consumers that are provided before the LE must be accompanied by a written statement informing the consumer that the terms and costs may change.[35] Further, creditors may not require submission of documents verifying information related to the consumer's application before providing the LE.[36]

---

30. *Id.* § 1026.2(a)(3). The definition of "application" under the TRID rules is similar to the definition under Regulation X, but excludes the catch-all of "any other information deemed necessary by the loan originator." *See* 12 C.F.R. § 1024.2(b). This reduces the creditor's ability to control when it receives an application.

31. *Id.* § 1026.19(e)(1)(i); Cmt. 1026.19(e)(1)(i)-1.

32. *Id.* §§ 1026.37(a)–(n).

33. *Id.* § 1026.37(o)(3)(i); *see also* § 1024.2(b). The model forms are provided in appendix H to Regulation Z (specifically, H-24(A) and (G) and H28(A) and (I)). Using the LE sample forms (H-24(B) through (F) and H-28(B) through (E)) provides a safe harbor if properly completed with accurate content.

34. 12 C.F.R. § 1026.19(e)(2)(i). TRID provides one exception to this prohibition, for a bona fide and reasonable fee for obtaining a consumer's credit report. *Id.* § 1026.19)(e)(2)(i)(B); Cmts. 1026.19(e)(2)(i)(A)-1, -3, -5; Cmt. 19(e)(2)(i)(B)-1.

35. *Id.* § 1026.19(e)(2)(ii).

36. *Id.* § 1026.19(e)(2)(iii).

2.3 Revised Loan Estimate Scenarios

A creditor may provide a consumer with a revised LE at any time before it provides the CD; however, the creditor is bound by the estimates contained in the initial LE unless an exception applies. Such exceptions include the following:

- Changed circumstances that cause an estimated charge to increase beyond what is permitted under TRID;[37]
- Changed circumstances that affect the consumer's creditworthiness or the value of the property securing the loan, which in turn causes a consumer to be ineligible for an estimated charge previously disclosed to the consumer;[38]
- Changes to the credit terms or the settlement requested by the consumer that cause an estimated charge to increase;[39]
- Locking the applicant's rate, if the rate lock causes the points, lender credits, and any other interest-rate-dependent charges or terms to change;[40]
- The consumer indicates an intent to proceed with the transaction more than ten business days after the LE was originally provided, unless the creditor set a different deadline for the consumer's intent to proceed;[41]
- Certain delays in construction loan settlements longer than sixty days.[42]

Although a revised LE may be provided any time before the CD, there are certain dates controlled by the final LE provided by the creditor. The creditor may not provide a revised LE on or after the date it provides the CD.[43] Because of this, and the CD timing rules, the consumer must receive the revised LE no later than four business days prior to consummation of the loan.

2.4 Closing Disclosure

The CD is intended to provide information that will be helpful to consumers in understanding the costs of the transaction. This form must be provided to consumers at least three business days before consummation of the loan.[44]

---

37. *Id.* § 1026.19(e)(3)(iv)(A).
38. *Id.* § 1026.19(e)(3)(iv)(B).
39. *Id.* § 1026.19(e)(3)(iv)(C).
40. *Id* § 1026.19(e)(3)(iv)(D).
41. *Id.* § 1026.19(e)(3)(iv)(E).
42. *Id.* § 1026.19(e)(3)(iv)(F).
43. *Id.* § 1026.19(e)(4)(ii).
44. A loan is consummated when the consumer becomes contractually obligated to the creditor on the loan, which depends on applicable state law. *Id.* § 1026.2(a)(13); Cmt. 1026.2(a)(13)-1.

Similar to the LE, a creditor can provide a corrected CD if there has been a triggering event, such as a changed circumstance. If the creditor provides a corrected disclosure, it may also be required to provide the consumer with an additional three-business-day waiting period prior to consummation.[45]

To accomplish these goals, the CD generally must contain the actual terms and costs of the transaction, rather than estimates.[46] The CD must contain only the specific information set forth in 12 C.F.R. sections 1026.38(a) to (s), and follow the model form (H-25).[47]

3. Brief Overview of RESPA Mortgage Disclosures

For most mortgage loans covered by RESPA, the required disclosures are set out in the TRID rules that were promulgated under the TILA and RESPA following the 2008 financial crisis. The rules apply to most closed-end consumer credit transactions secured by real property (i.e., most residential mortgage loans). These rules combined separate mortgage loan disclosure requirements contained in the two statutes to provide a uniform set of rules and model disclosures. However, RESPA contains mortgage disclosure requirements separate from TRID. Any loan subject to the TRID rules is exempt from RESPA's requirement to provide a HUD-1 settlement statement, a GFE, a mortgage servicing transfer statement, and the settlement costs booklet.[48] This exemption applies to most closed-end consumer mortgages; however, HELOCs and reverse mortgages are not subject to the TRID rules and, therefore, are not eligible for this exemption. For these and other loans subject to RESPA but not to the TRID rules, the RESPA disclosures provide the operative requirements. This section provides a brief overview of the primary RESPA mortgage disclosures.

3.1 Good Faith Estimate

Lenders must provide an applicant with the GFE disclosure not later than three business days after a lender receives an application or information sufficient to complete an application.[49] Regulation X specifies timing requirements and other restrictions with regard to providing the GFE. Generally, the estimate of the charges and terms for all settlement services must be available for at least ten business days from when the GFE is provided.[50] In many ways, the GFE fulfills the same role as the LE under the

45. *Id.* § 1026.19(f)(2).

46. *Id.* § 1026.19(f)(1)(i).

47. *Id.* § 1026.38(t). Using the CD sample forms (H-25(B) through (G) and H28(G) and (H)) provides a safe harbor if properly completed with accurate content.

48. *Id.* § 1024.5(d).

49. *Id.* § 1024.7(a).

50. *Id.* § 1024.7(c).

TRID rule; for example, the originator is bound, within specified tolerances, to the settlement charges and terms listed on the GFE provided to the borrower, unless a revised GFE is provided prior to settlement.[51]

3.2 HUD-1 Settlement Statement

RESPA requires that applicants for covered loans for which TRID is not applicable receive the HUD-1 or HUD-1A (Shortened) Settlement Statement at or before settlement.[52] The statement itemizes all charges imposed on the buyer and the seller in connection with the settlement. Transactions that include both a borrower and a seller will receive HUD-1. If the transaction does not include a seller, the HUD-1 may be completed by using only the borrower's side of the settlement statement, or the HUD-1A may be used.[53] Examples of these transactions may include refinancing and subordinate lien loans. Inadvertent or technical errors in connection with completing the HUD-1 or HUD-1A are not RESPA violations if a revised statement is provided within thirty calendar days after settlement.[54]

4. RESPA Regulation and Enforcement

4.1 Overview

In addition to the CFPB, other regulators also have the authority to enforce RESPA. The Dodd-Frank Act provides state enforcement and regulatory authorities with broad authority to bring cases under the act's enumerated consumer laws, including RESPA. State attorneys general, therefore, maintain the authority to enforce RESPA compliance. RESPA also expressly authorizes HUD, state attorneys general, and state insurance commissioners to enforce certain violations.[55] These sections also provide private rights of action, allowing private plaintiffs to bring lawsuits based on a violation of the statute. Prudential banking regulators also separately review for RESPA compliance in their examinations of supervised entities.

The CFPB administers RESPA through a combination of enforcement actions, consent orders, and supervisory guidance, including compliance bulletins, and

51. *Id.* § 1024.7(f). The GFE form and instructions are set out in appendix C. *Id.* part 1024, app. C.

52. *Id.* § 1024.8(a).

53. *Id.* § 1024.8(c).

54. *Id.* § 1024.8(b)(2)(i).

55. 12 U.S.C. § 2607.

maintains an active consumer complaint database.[56] CFPB RESPA enforcement has generally focused on violations of the antikickback provision. Recent RESPA enforcement has also focused on failure to send or timely send loss mitigation evaluation notices to borrowers.[57]

The CFPB's rulemaking activities have focused on the mortgage application and origination process and rules related to servicing mortgage loans. For other areas of RESPA, principally the anti-kickback provisions, the CFPB has relied heavily on enforcement actions and consent orders to announce the Bureau's policies.

4.2 Formal and Informal Guidance

The CFPB provides industry stakeholders with formal RESPA interpretive guidance through regulations and official interpretations. Informal guidance is provided through reports, preambles to proposed and final rules, frequently asked questions, webinars, oral statements, and other sources.[58] The CFPB also provides RESPA guidance through no-action letters (NALs) issued to parties that submit formal NAL applications requesting assurances that the CFPB, in issuing the letter, will not make supervisory findings or bring an enforcement action against the applicants for the products or services described in the application. The NALs are not binding and are revocable at any time. Although the NAL is not a legal conclusion nor an endorsement of the activities, it may provide the requestor with a legal safe harbor from enforcement for the specified activities during the period the NAL is effective.

In January 2020, the CFPB granted a NAL application submitted by a bank regarding its funding arrangements with HUD-approved housing counseling agencies. The CFPB granted the request, indicating that it would not make supervisory findings or bring an enforcement action under RESPA section 8 or Regulation X section 1024.14, even if the arrangements could be construed as payments for referrals.[59]

56. CFPB, Consumer Complaint Database, https://www.consumerfinance.gov/data-research/consumer-complaints/search/?dataLens=Overview&dataNormalization=None&dateInterval=Month&dateRange=3y&date_received_max=2020-06-07&date_received_min=2017-06-07&from=0&page=1&searchField=all&size=25&sort=created_date_desc&tab=Map.

57. 12 C.F.R. § 1024.41(c)(1).

58. The CFPB designates such regulatory guidance as "Compliance Aids." According to the CFPB's Compliance Aids policy, "Compliance Aids present the requirements of existing rules and statutes in a manner that is useful for compliance professionals, other industry stakeholders, and the public," but "[r]egulated entities are not required to comply with the Compliance Aids themselves. Regulated entities are only required to comply with the underlying rules and statutes." *Policy Statement on Compliance Aids*, 85 Fed. Reg. 4579 (Jan. 27, 2020).

59. Bank of America No Action Letter, Consumer Financial Protection Bureau (Jan. 10, 2020), https://files.consumerfinance.gov/f/documents/cfpb_bank-of-america_no-action-letter.pdf.

RESPA provides a safe harbor for actions done in "good faith conformity" with any rule, regulation, or interpretation of the CFPB or the attorney general.[60] Regulation X defines a "a rule, regulation or interpretation of the Bureau" to include all regulation, appendices, and supplements, as well as any document published by HUD in the Federal Register that states that it is an "interpretation," "interpretive rule," "commentary," or a "statement of policy."[61]

The effect and import of regulatory guidance and policy is highly fact-specific and often evaluated on a case-by-case basis. However, one example, the D.C. Circuit's due process analysis in *PHH Corporation v. CFPB*, supports the assertion that stakeholders who follow or implement CFPB nonbinding RESPA guidance may rely on RESPA's good faith safe harbor. In 2014, the CFPB issued a fine against a mortgage lender, PHH Corp., alleging that captive reinsurance programs were kickbacks and a violation of RESPA section 8.[62] PHH argued that it had relied upon a HUD letter, which stated that the arrangements were permissible as long as reinsurance services are actually furnished, and any payments were "bona fide compensation that does not exceed the value of such services."[63] According to the CFPB, PHH could not invoke the safe harbor because the HUD letter that PHH relied upon was not a formal interpretation under Regulation X.[64] Regarding the allegation, the court held that the CFPB violated the Due Process Clause of the Constitution by disregarding informal guidance issued by HUD and could not retroactively apply a new agency interpretation to proscribe past conduct.[65] The PHH case is thus a helpful example of the considerations of parties, and of courts, when relying on agency guidance involving RESPA issues.

4.3 RESPA Claims

RESPA is a consumer protection statute and should be "construed liberally in order to best to serve Congress' intent."[66] Although courts will generally construe the

60. 12 U.S.C. § 2617(b).

61. 12 C.F.R. § 1024.4(a)(1).

62. Notice of Charges, In the Matter of PHH Corp., File No. 2014-CFPB-002 (Jan. 29, 2014), https://files.consumerfinance.gov/f/documents/201402_cfpb_0002_notice-of-charges.pdf.

63. Letter from N. Retsinas, Ass't Sec'y for Hous.-Fed. Hous. Comm'r, HUD, to S. Samuels, Countrywide Funding Corp. (Aug. 6. 1997).

64. Decision of the Director, In the Matter of PHH Corp., File No. 2014-CFPB-0002, at 17 (June 4, 2015), http://files.consumerfinance.gov/f/201506_cfpb_decision_by_director_cordray_redacted_226.pdf.

65. PHH Corp. v. CFPB, 839 F.3d 1, 44 (2016) ("[t]he CFPB violated due process by retroactively applying that new interpretation to PHH's conduct that occurred before the date of the CFPB's new interpretation.") *rev'd on other grounds*, 881 F.3d 75 (D.C. Cir. 2018) (en banc).

66. McLean v. GMAC Mortg. Corp., 398 F. App'x 467, 471 (11th Cir. 2010).

statute broadly, a plaintiff must have standing to bring the claim.[67] Standing does not include a "bare procedural violation divorced from any concrete harm."[68] Courts applying this standard have required that a causal link exists between the servicer's or lender's noncompliance and the plaintiff's damages.[69] Therefore, a RESPA claim will not survive based on mere procedural violations.[70]

Parties involved in home purchase and home sale transactions may be liable for statutory violations under sections 6, 8, 9, and 10 of RESPA. Lawsuits for violations of section 6, 8, or 9 may be brought in any federal district court in the district in which the property is located or where the violation is alleged to have occurred. Because section 8 violations are the most frequently encountered, we dedicate an entire segment to explaining the statue.

5. Escrow Accounts

RESPA establishes rules and disclosure requirements related to escrow accounts associated with federally related mortgage loans. An escrow account is an account established or controlled by a servicer or lender on behalf of a borrower to pay taxes, insurance premiums (including flood insurance), or other charges with respect to a federally related mortgage loan, including charges that the borrower and servicer have voluntarily agreed that the servicer should collect and pay.[71]

5.1 Initial Escrow

At settlement, a *servicer*[72] may establish an escrow account and fund the account with the borrower's funds.[73] RESPA and Regulation X limit the amount of escrow funds a servicer may place into the account at settlement or at account creation.[74]

---

67. Spokeo, Inc. v. Robins, 136 S. Ct. 1540, 1547 (2016). The court stated that "the plaintiff must have (1) suffered an injury in fact, (2) that is fairly traceable to the challenged conduct of the defendant, and (3) that is likely to be redressed by a favorable judicial decision."

68. *Spokeo*, 136 S. Ct. at 1549.

69. Renfroe v. Nationstar Mortg., LLC, 822 F.3d 1241, 1244 (11th Cir. 2016); Diedrich v. Ocwen Loan Servicing, LLC, 839 F.3d 583, 591–93 (7th. Cir. 2016); Baehr v. Creig Northrop Team, P.C., 953 F.3d 244, 258 (4th Cir. Mar. 13, 2020).

70. *Baehr*, *supra* note 69.

71. 12 C.F.R. § 1024.17(b); 12 U.S.C. § 2605(g).

72. The term "servicer" includes an entity that "makes or holds such loan if such person also services the loan," so may also include the lender. *Id.* § 1024.2.

73. The servicer may fund the account, if the terms of a federally related mortgage loan require the borrower to make payments to the servicer for deposit into an escrow account to pay taxes, insurance premiums, and other charges for the mortgaged property. *See* 12 C.F.R. §§ 1024.17(k), 1024.34(a).

74. *Id.* § 1024.17(b).

Under these regulations, servicers may only place an "amount sufficient" to pay charges for the mortgaged property. The deposit should be computed "so that the lowest month end target balance projected for the escrow account computation year is zero."[75] The servicer may also add a cushion of one-sixth of the estimated total annual payments from the account.[76]

The term *cushion* means an amount allotted in excess of federal or state law to cover increases in insurance premiums or property tax. The escrow deposit ceilings prohibit servicers from requiring excessive cushion. The amount of permissible cushion is found in the mortgage documents, as follows:[77]

- If the documents provide for lower cushion limits, then the documents control.
- If the documents provide for higher payments than under the statute, then the statute controls.
- If the documents do not "specifically establish" an escrow account, then federal or state law controls. Where the mortgage documents do not provide escrow account limits and the servicer establishes an escrow account under federal or state law, the servicer is limited to the amounts under the statute unless the federal or state law provides for a lower amount.
- If the documents cross-reference RESPA, then RESPA controls (unless state law is more restrictive).

Servicers are required to conduct an initial escrow analysis to determine the borrower's initial escrow deposit and periodic payment amounts. Servicers are also required to prepare and deliver an initial escrow account statement to the borrower. For escrow accounts that are established as a condition of the loan, the servicer must deliver the escrow account statement at settlement or within forty-five calendar days of settlement.[78] The initial statement must include the amount of the monthly mortgage payment, the amount of the monthly mortgage payment that is going into escrow, itemized estimated taxes, insurance premiums, other charges that the servicer reasonably anticipates to be paid from the escrow account during the escrow account computation year and the anticipated disbursement dates of those charges, the amount of cushion, and a trial running balance for the account.[79]

---

75. *Id.*
76. *Id.* § 1024.17(c)(1).
77. *Id.* § 1024.17(c)(8).
78. *Id.* § 1024.17(g).
79. *Id.*

5.2 Escrow Funds throughout the Life of an Account

The escrow account computation year is a twelve-month period established by the servicer for the escrow account, beginning with the borrower's initial payment date and continuing every year after unless the servicer issues a *short year statement* (see the next section for more information about short year statements).[80] Throughout the life of an account, the servicer may charge the borrower one-twelfth of the total annual escrow payments that the servicer reasonably anticipates paying from the account as a monthly payment. The servicer may also add a cushion of one-sixth of the estimated total annual payments from the account. Therefore, the servicer may add a cushion of two months of the borrower's escrow payments or a lesser amount specified by state law or the mortgage document. If the servicer determines a shortage or a deficiency, the servicer may then require the borrower to pay an additional amount.[81]

Servicers must also conduct subsequent escrow account analyses and deliver an annual escrow statement to borrowers within thirty days of an escrow account computation year. The escrow account analysis is a review of the account to determine whether there is a surplus, shortage, or deficiency of funds. A servicer is not required to deliver an annual account analysis if (1) at the time the servicer conducts the escrow account analysis, the borrower was more than thirty days overdue; (2) there is an action for foreclosure; or (3) the borrower is in an action for bankruptcy.[82]

The servicer must adjust the escrow account based on the results of the escrow account analysis. In reviewing the account, the servicer must determine the appropriate target balances, compute the borrower's monthly payments for the next escrow account computation year and any deposits needed to establish or maintain the account.

5.2.1 Short Year Statements

A *short year statement* is an annual escrow account statement that is issued before the twelve-month period that the servicer established. The short year escrow account changes the escrow account computation year to another term by ending the escrow account computation year and establishing the beginning date of the new escrow account computation year. Servicers must provide borrowers with short year statements if the account is transferred from one servicer to another, within sixty days of the effective date of transfer. Additionally, if borrowers pay off their mortgage loan during the escrow account computation year, the servicer must submit a short year statement to the borrower within sixty days after receiving the payoff funds.

---

80. *Id.* § 1024.17.

81. This amount is limited by § 1024.17(f).

82. *Id.* § 1024.17(i)(2). If the account is subsequently "reinstated or otherwise becomes current," the servicer must provide the statement within ninety days of the date the account was brought current.

5.2.2 Escrow Accounts and Transfer of Servicing

If a borrower's account is transferred to a new servicer, the borrower's unpaid escrow balance must also be transferred to the new servicer. The new servicer may continue to use the same escrow account computation year established by the old servicer if it retains the monthly payments and accounting method used by the old servicer. However, if a transfer occurs and the new servicer changes either the escrow monthly payment amount or the accounting method used to calculate the escrow payment, the new servicer must provide the borrower with an initial escrow account statement within sixty days of the date of servicing transfer.[83]

5.2.3 Shortages, Surpluses, and Deficiencies

RESPA provides servicers certain flexibilities regarding the servicer's response to shortages, surpluses, or deficiencies discovered during the annual account analysis.[84] For surpluses, the servicer must refund the surplus or credit the amount to the borrower's account, depending on the surplus amount.[85] For shortages and deficiencies, servicers generally have the option to allow the shortage or deficiency, require it to be repaid in thirty days, or require it to be repaid over a certain number of monthly payments.[86]

Regulation X distinguishes between a shortage and a deficiency. A shortage is defined as "an amount by which a current escrow account balance falls short of the target balance at the time of escrow analysis."[87] For example, a shortage exists if the escrow analysis projected a balance at the end of the twelve-month computation year and the account actually had a lower balance than initially projected. A deficiency is defined as "the amount of a negative balance in an escrow account."[88] A deficiency exists when the servicer has advanced funds for the borrower to cover disbursements; the advance creates a negative balance in the account.

Additionally, servicers must notify borrowers at least once during the escrow account computation year if there is a shortage or deficiency in the escrow account through a separate document to the annual escrow account statement. The statement is required for borrowers in default, foreclosure, or bankruptcy.

5.2.4 Timely Payments

Regulation X requires servicers to make timely escrow disbursements. Specifically, servicers must pay escrow disbursements in a timely manner on or before the deadline to avoid a penalty, as long as the borrower's payment is not more than thirty days

83. *Id.* § 1024.17(e).
84. *Id.* § 1024.17(f).
85. *Id.* § 1024.17(f)(2).
86. *Id.* §§ 1024.17(f)(3), (f)(4).
87. *Id.* § 1024.17(b).
88. *Id.*

overdue. The servicer may then seek repayment from the borrower. Regulation X defines a "penalty" as a "late charge imposed for paying after the disbursement is due."[89]

Property taxes are subject to a special rule. If property taxes are paid from the escrow account and the taxing jurisdiction offers a choice between annual and installment disbursements and does not provide a discount for lump sum annual payments or impose an additional charge or penalty for installment payments the servicer is required to make payments on an installment basis.[90] If the taxing authority provides a discount for lump sum annual payments, or imposes additional charges for installment payments, the servicer may make a lump sum annual payment at its discretion.[91]

5.3 Escrow Account Enforcement

RESPA section 10 limits the amounts a lender may require a borrower to place into an escrow account at settlement or hold for purposes of paying taxes, hazard insurance, and other charges related to the property.[92] Section 10 authorizes the secretary of HUD to impose civil penalties of fifty dollars on servicers for each failure to submit initial or annual escrow account statements to borrowers. Because of the omission of an express private right of action, courts have generally held that a private right of action does not exist.[93]

6. RESPA Section 8

Purchasing a home, likely using a mortgage loan, is by far the most expensive and most complicated transaction in which most consumers will ever engage. The home-buying process includes many different stages, with different entities providing services at each stage. In an effort to protect consumers during the home-buying process, section 8 of RESPA prohibits certain practices by real estate settlement service providers, such as kickbacks in exchange for referrals or unearned fee splits, which can add to the settlement costs for home buyers. Section 8 is enforceable by private litigants as well as state and federal regulators under RESPA.

Accordingly, interpretations and applications of section 8 are derived from judicial precedent, guidance and enforcement actions issued by HUD during its time as the primary enforcer of RESPA, CFPB guidance (including its Real Estate

---

89. *Id.* § 1024.17(b).

90. *Id.* § 1024.17(k)(3).

91. *Id.*

92. *Id.* §§ 2609(a)–(b).

93. Campbell v. Machias Sav. Bank, 865 F. Supp. 26 (D. Me. Oct. 7, 1994); Brophy v. Chase Manhattan Mortg. Co., 947 F. Supp. 879, 882–83 (E.D. Pa. 1996).

Settlement Procedures Act FAQs[94]) and enforcement activity since taking over the statute following the Dodd-Frank Act, and state actions.

Since the CFPB began enforcing RESPA, the agency has been especially active in enforcing section 8, bringing actions against various types of service providers, resulting in consent orders that have created new section 8 precedent and, in some instances, changed long-standing industry-accepted views of section 8. It is important to note here that most CFPB actions result in negotiated consent orders, which are often limited in terms of facts and legal analysis. Although the CFPB's policies and approaches may shift, these consent orders form the basis of the CFPB's read of RESPA as it was taken over from HUD and integrated into the CFPB regulatory framework.

6.1 Section 8(a)—Anti-Kickback Provision

> No person shall give and no person shall accept any fee, kickback, or thing of value pursuant to any agreement or understanding, oral or otherwise, that business incident to or a part of a real estate settlement service involving a federally related mortgage loan shall be referred to any person.[95]

RESPA section 8(a) prohibits the "giving or receiving" of any "fee, kickback, or thing of value pursuant to any agreement or understanding" for the referral of settlement business involving federally related mortgages. RESPA prohibits accepting or paying a fee or any thing of value for a referral, defined as any act that "affirmatively influences the selection by any person of a particular settlement service provider."[96] An agreement or understanding does not need to be written, but may be established by a practice, pattern, or course of conduct.[97] Examples of prohibited actions include compensating a realtor for merely completing an application, compensating services for merely providing a forum for a borrower's application, and brokers providing incentives for sales agents to refer consumers to loan officers. However, section 8(a)

94. The FAQs are were published pursuant to the CFPB's Policy Statement on Compliance Aids and are available on the CFPB's website. CFPB, Real Estate Settlement Procedures Act FAQs (updated Oct. 7, 2020), https://www.consumerfinance.gov/policy-compliance/guidance/mortgage-resources/real-estate-settlement-procedures-act/real-estate-settlement-procedures-act-faqs/ [hereinafter RESPA FAQs].

95. 12 U.S.C. § 2607(a).

96. 12 C.F.R. § 1024.14(f).

97. *In re* Zillow Grp., Inc. Sec. Litig., No. C17-1387-JCC, 2019 U.S. Dist. LEXIS 67197, at *1, *15–17 (W.D. Wash. Apr. 19, 2019); Freeman v. Quicken Loans, Inc., 566 U.S. 624, 132 S. Ct. 2034, 2043 (2012) ("[A] settlement-service provider who agrees to exchange valuable tickets to a sporting event in return for a referral of business would violate § 2607(a), but not § 2607(b)."

provides that a "payment for a good, service, or facility provided" is not a violation as long as the payment reflects reasonable market value.[98]

6.1.1 Thing of Value

RESPA defines the term *thing of value* broadly as "any payment, advance, funds, loan, service or other consideration."[99] Regulation X adds examples to the definition of a thing of value to include, among others, money, goods, discounts, commissions, increased earnings, reduction in credit against an existing obligation, and the opportunity to participate in a money-making program.[100]

Beyond the regulatory text, a thing of value has been interpreted broadly and can include such things as:

- money, salaries, commissions, fees;
- stock, dividends, profit distributions, franchise royalties;
- retained or increased earnings, increased equity in a parent or subsidiary entity;
- products or services at special or free rates;
- payment of another's expenses or reduction of an existing debt or obligation (e.g., "defraying marketing expenses");
- the opportunity to participate in a money-making program; and
- tickets, favors, paid vacations.

The CFPB has, with some controversy, taken the position that a contract (specifically, a marketing services agreement) could itself be a thing of value given in exchange for referrals, triggering the section 8 kickback prohibition.[101] The CFPB expanded on this reasoning in subsequent actions, finding, for example, that an individual mortgage loan officer received illegal kickbacks for escrow referrals when certain applicants were offered a discount upon the loan officer's request, while escrow costs to other applicants allegedly were increased.[102] The CFPB alleged that the discounts were a *thing of value* to the mortgage loan officer, because they enabled him to offer certain customers "no cost loans," thereby allowing him to ultimately make more loans.

---

98. PHH Corp. v. CFPB, 839 F.3d 1, 44 (D.C. Cir. 2016), *reh'g en banc granted, order vacated* (Feb. 16, 2017), *on reh'g en banc*, 881 F.3d 75 (D.C. Cir. 2018) *abrogated* on other grounds by *Seila Law LLC v. CFPB*, 140 S. Ct. 2183 (2020).

99. 12 U.S.C. § 2602(2).

100. 12 C.F.R. § 1024.14(d).

101. In the Matter of Lighthouse Title, Inc., File No. 2014-CFPB-0015 (Sept. 30, 2014), https://files.consumerfinance.gov/f/201409_cfpb_consent-order_lighthouse-title.pdf.

102. In the Matter of David Eghbali, File No. 2016-CFPB-0011 (May 25, 2015), https://files.consumerfinance.gov/f/documents/201605_cfpb_consent-order-david-eghbali.pdf.

In response to these consent orders, the mortgage industry expressed concern that the broad construction of the term thing of value nullified the RESPA section 8 safe harbor for bona fide payments.[103] Given the breadth of the definition, construing the term thing of value in certain situations may ultimately come down to satisfying the safe harbor, but there is not unanimous agreement as to how the substantive prohibition of section 8(a) and the safe harbor of section 8(c)(2) work together.

The U.S. Court of Appeals for the District of Columbia Circuit, in *PHH Corporation v. CFPB*, addressed the interplay between RESPA's kickback prohibition and the bona fide compensation safe harbor, reiterating that section 8(c)(2) is an exemption to the section 8(a) prohibitions, effectively rolling back some of the CFPB's administrative precedent to the contrary.[104] Thus, while contracts, agreements, and other intangible items that present a quid pro quo could be deemed to be things of value, parties will need to closely examine the RESPA safe harbors when analyzing conduct for compliance with the statute.

6.1.2 Referral

The term *referral* is defined as any action that has the effect of affirmatively influencing the selection by any person of a particular settlement service provider or business, incident to or part of a settlement service.[105] A referral also occurs when a person paying for a settlement service or business incident to a settlement service is required to use a particular provider of a settlement service.[106]

What may constitute a referral typically has been construed broadly by regulators, and the CFPB has stated in non-binding guidance that "referrals include a settlement service provider directly handing clients the contact information of another settlement service provider that happens to result in the client using that other settlement service provider."[107] Further, any activities that "steer" consumers to a particular service provider, through recommendations, encouragement, or economic coercion may be considered referrals that implicate RESPA. As one example, in *In the Matter of Prospect Mortgage, LLC*, the Bureau alleged that a mortgage lender violated

---

103. For a discussion of the RESPA section 8 safe harbors, see section 6.3.

104. *PHH Corp. v. CFPB*, 839 F.3d 1, 44 (D.C. Cir. 2016), *reh'g en banc granted, order vacated* (Feb. 16, 2017), *on reh'g en banc*, 881 F.3d 75 (D.C. Cir. 2018). See also the discussion of section 8(c)(2)in section 6.3.

105. 12 C.F.R. § 1024.14(f).

106. *Id.* The term "required use" means a situation in which a person must use a particular provider of a settlement service in order to have access to some distinct service or property, and the person will pay for the settlement service of the particular provider or will pay a charge attributable, in whole or in part, to the settlement service. *Id.* § 1024.2. However, a packaged combination of settlement services or a true discount or rebate, if optional is not a required use. *See id.*

107. *See* RESPA FAQS, *supra* note 94, at RESPA Section 8: Marketing Services Agreements (MSAs) Question 2.

RESPA when it "selectively imposed economic measures to coerce consumers into using Prospect, such as fees that would be waived if the consumer used Prospect, or credits that would be given only if the consumer used Prospect."[108]

On the other hand, regulators have determined that certain activities, like the sale of leads to mortgage lenders, providing information about various lenders to consumers, or performing bona fide marketing services on behalf of a service provider at fair market value for those services, are not considered referral activity. For example, prior to the transfer of RESPA to the CFPB, HUD had long taken the position that a sale of leads or "prospects" did not constitute a referral.[109] However, the CFPB distinguished between the sale of prospects/leads and paid referrals in *Prospect Mortgage*.[110] The CFPB explained that real estate brokers that entered into lead sale agreements with the mortgage lender, Prospect Mortgage, "went beyond simply transferring information about prospective buyers" by actively referring prospective buyers.[111]

6.1.3 Settlement Service

RESPA broadly defines a real estate *settlement service* as "any service provided in connection with a real estate settlement."[112] Mortgage origination is deemed a settlement service under RESPA, as well as any activity performed by mortgage bankers/lenders, mortgage brokers, real estate agents, title agents, and attorneys. Regulation X provides examples of specific real estate settlement services including the following:

- Origination of a federally related mortgage loan (including, but not limited to, the taking of loan applications, loan processing, and the underwriting and funding of such loans);
- Rendering of services by a mortgage broker (including counseling, taking of applications, obtaining verifications and appraisals, and other loan processing and origination services, and communicating with the borrower and lender);

---

108. In the Matter of Prospect Mortgage LLC, File No. 2017-CFPB-0006 (Jan. 1, 2017), https://files.consumerfinance.gov/f/documents/201701_cfpb_ProspectMortgage-consent-order.pdf.

109. HUD Advisory Letter from Grant E. Mitchell, dated March 24, 1994 ("Prospects List Letter").

110. *Prospect Mortgage*, File No. 2017-CFPB-0006, at 5–6.

111. *Id.*

112. 12 U.S.C. § 2602. The definition includes "title searches, title examinations, the provision of title certificates, title insurance, services rendered by an attorney, the preparation of documents, property surveys, the rendering of credit reports or appraisals, pest and fungus inspections, services rendered by a real estate agent or broker, the origination of a federally related mortgage loan (including, but not limited to, the taking of loan applications, loan processing, and the underwriting and funding of loans), and the handling of the processing, and closing or settlement." *Id.*

- Provision of any services related to the origination, processing, or funding of a federally related mortgage loan;
- Provision of title services, including title searches, title examinations, abstract preparation, insurability determinations, and the issuance of title commitments and title insurance policies;
- Rendering of services by an attorney;
- Preparation of documents, including notarization, delivery, and recordation;
- Rendering of credit reports and appraisals;
- Rendering of inspections, including inspections required by applicable law or any inspections required by the sales contract or mortgage documents prior to transfer of title;
- Conducting of settlement by a settlement agent and any related services;
- Provision of services involving mortgage insurance;
- Provision of services involving hazard, flood, or other casualty insurance or homeowner's warranties;
- Provision of services involving mortgage life, disability, or similar insurance designed to pay a mortgage loan upon disability or death of a borrower, but only if such insurance is required by the lender as a condition of the loan;
- Provision of services involving real property taxes or any other assessments or charges on the real property;
- Rendering of services by a real estate agent or real estate broker; and
- Provision of any other services for which a settlement service provider requires a borrower or seller to pay.[113]

The term settlement services is expansive, and covers a wide array of activities connected with the sale and financing of residential real estate. For example, in addition to the statutory and regulatory examples, courts have ruled that finding or brokering such services itself constitutes a settlement service, as well as advertising, marketing, and promotional services. However, activities that occur after the purchase of a property (also called post-closing activities) do not constitute a settlement service.[114]

113. 12 C.F.R. § 1024.2.

114. *See* Arnett v. Bank of Am., N.A., 874 F. Supp. 2d 1021, 1040 (D. Or. 2012) (holding that RESPA did not apply to mortgagee's alleged forced placement of flood insurance on mortgagors' property approximately two years after the mortgagors closed on their home loan). This also includes a variety of services and service providers, such as lawn care/gardening companies, interior design firms, moving companies, and home improvement contractors.

6.2 Section 8(b)—Fee Splitting

> No person shall give and no person shall accept any portion, split, or percentage of any charge made or received for the rendering of a real estate settlement service in connection with a transaction involving a federally related mortgage loan other than for services actually performed.[115]

RESPA section 8(b) prohibits any fee splitting fees for unperformed services.[116] Any fees split must be payment for actual services rendered and cannot be earned without providing a service to consumers. For example, RESPA allows for payments in the "amount of a bona fide salary or compensation or other payment for goods or facilities actually furnished or for services actually performed."[117]

In *Freeman v. Quicken Loans*, the U.S. Supreme Court held that a plaintiff must show that a charge for a real estate settlement service was divided between two or more persons.[118] Therefore, section 8(b) does not prohibit a service provider from charging an unearned fee if the provider retains the fee and does not share the fee with anyone.

Courts have held that RESPA is not a price-control statute, and section 8(b) cannot be used to regulate "overcharges." However, the statute prohibits "markups" where one party receiving a fee split adds onto a charge but does not render actual services for a bona fide fee.[119]

6.3 Section 8(c)—Safe Harbors

The broad application of sections 8(a) and 8(b) of RESPA is moderated by the safe harbors provided in section 8(c), which expressly permit certain transactions between providers of settlement services that otherwise could be construed as things of value in exchange for referrals in violation of RESPA section 8(a) or fee splits in violation of RESPA section 8(b).

The section 8(c) safe harbors allow (1) payments to attorneys, payment by a title company to its duly appointed agent, or payments by a lender to its duly appointed agent for services actually rendered or performed; (2) payment of a bona fide salary or compensation or other payment for goods or facilities actually furnished or for services actually performed; (3) payments pursuant to cooperative brokerage and referral arrangements or agreements between real estate agents and brokers; or (4)

115. 12 U.S.C. § 2607(b).

116. *Id.* §§ 2607(a)–(b).

117. *Id.* § 2607(c)(2).

118. Freeman v. Quicken Loans, Inc., 566 U.S. 624, 132 S. Ct. 2034, 2043 (2012).

119. *See, e.g.*, Chultem v. Ticor Title Ins. Co., 46 N.E.3d 340, 343 (Ill. App. 2015); Snellgrove v. Common Bond Title, LLC, No. 1:17-CV-500-WKW-SRW, 2019 WL 5067562, *4 (M.D. Ala. July 31, 2019) *report and recommendation adopted as modified*, No. 1:17-CV-500-WKW, 2019 WL 4781599 (M.D. Ala. Sep. 30, 2019).

payments pursuant to affiliated business arrangements that otherwise meet RESPA requirements.[120]

The exceptions to section 8's broad anti-kickback and fee-splitting provisions were subject to interpretation and guidance from HUD, which the CFPB adopted when it obtained ownership of Regulation X. However, CFPB guidance and consent orders have since raised questions about the reliability of some of the exemptions. For example, in *In the Matter of PHH Corporation*, the CFPB took the position that section 8(c)(2) merely "clarifies section 8(a), providing direction as to how that section should be interpreted, but does not provide a substantive exemption from section 8(a)."[121]

However, the D.C. Circuit in *PHH Corporation v. CFPB* reinforced the viability of the section 8(c) safe harbors in light of several CFPB enforcement actions that had asserted the theory that a contract for services awarded to a potential referral partner could constitute a kickback in violation of section 8(a) even where those services were legitimate and payments were made at fair market value for services rendered. The D.C. Circuit rejected the CFPB's position that section 8(c)(2) is intended to "clarify the application of section 8(a), not [to act] as a substantive exemption to liability,"[122] holding instead that "[S]ection 8(a) and 8(c) do not prohibit bona fide payments by the mortgage insurer to the lender for other services that the lender (or the lender's subsidiary or affiliate) actually provides to the mortgage insurer."[123]

Specific safe harbors under section 8(c) include those described in the following sections.

6.3.1 Attorneys and Agents (Section 8(c)(1))

RESPA section 8 does not prohibit certain services actually rendered by attorneys, as well as agents of title companies and lenders providing services related to issuing title insurance or making loans, respectively.[124]

6.3.2 Bona Fide Payments for Services Actually Performed (Section 8(c)(2))

6.3.2.1 Overview

RESPA section 8 does not prohibit "the payment to any person of a bona fide salary or compensation or other payment for goods or facilities actually furnished or for services actually performed."[125] Determining whether a payment is bona fide often

120. 12 U.S.C. § 2607(c).

121. In the Matter of PHH Corp., Decision of the Director, File No. 2014-CFPB-0002 at 15–16 (Jun. 4, 2015), http://files.consumerfinance.gov/f/201506_cfpb_decision-by-director-cordray-redacted-226.pdf.

122. *Id.*

123. *PHH Corp.*, 839 F.3d at 41.

124. 12 U.S.C. § 2607(c)(1).

125. *Id.* § 2607(c)(2).

involves quantifying the fair market value of the services to ensure that the payment amount matches the value of the services provided. A discrepancy in payment to value could indicate to a regulator that part of the payment was actually intended to serve as a kickback or payment for a referral.

Regulation X states that "[i]f the payment of a thing of value bears no reasonable relationship to the market value of the goods or services provided, then the excess is not for services or goods actually performed or provided."[126]

Bona fide payments and services under section 8(c)(2) may take many forms, but the CFPB has scrutinized advertising and marketing agreements and other arrangements where the Bureau may suspect purported bona fide service agreements could be disguised quid pro quo arrangements in the form of overpayments for services, payments for services not actually rendered, or other means of exchanging value for referrals.

It is important, therefore, for settlement service providers to ensure that they pay market value for legitimate services rendered by potential sources of referrals and that contracts are never structured around the value or amount of business received in connection with these contracts. Overpayment for services rendered also could result in an excess amount that could be deemed to be a thing of value, creating an inference that the overpayments were intended to compensate for referrals. Similarly, offering free or below market rate services could constitute a subsidy that would be a thing of value that could be scrutinized as being given in exchange for referrals.

Since both over and underpayment could be viewed as a thing of value, settlement service providers will often choose to determine the fair market value of specific services through a neutral and unrelated third party. Detailed third-party valuations can support the parties' assertion of the section 8(c)(2) safe harbor and show that the payments made for the services rendered were bona fide. As the value of services fluctuates, service providers should periodically audit and review fair market value determinations to ensure that the pricing on contracts and services agreements remain demonstrably bona fide.

6.3.2.2 Marketing Services Agreement

Marketing services agreements (MSAs) are contracts, typically between lenders and real estate agents (as well as other settlement services providers) whereby an entity will provide certain advertising and marketing services on behalf of the other for a fee. Often these arrangements involve two or more settlement service providers, with the party being paid for marketing services also acting as a referral source for the other provider. Thus, the lines between conducting marketing services on behalf of a service provider and referring business to a service provider are not always clear, so MSAs must be structured and implemented carefully around the available RESPA safe harbors.

126. 12 C.F.R. § 1024.14(g)(2).

The CFPB has periodically espoused the view that MSAs between service providers inherently carry risk under RESPA, as they can be used to disguise payments for referrals as payments for "marketing services" where few if any marketing services are actually being performed, or the payments are not commensurate with fair market value for the services rendered; however, the CFPB has never flatly prohibited MSAs or set specific requirements prohibitions related to such agreements.[127] For example, in *In the Matter of Lighthouse Title*, the CFPB found, among other things, that fees paid to Lighthouse were not based on the fair market value for services rendered.[128] Instead the CFPB found, "marketing fees set by considering the amount of business received from the counterparty are connected with the volume or value of the business referred, and therefore are evidence that the payments are made pursuant to an agreement or understanding for the referral of business."[129]

6.3.2.3 Desk Rental Agreements

Renting office space, facilities, and accompanying services, also called desk licensing or rental agreements, have typically been analyzed by looking at the fair market value of the rented space. Entities face RESPA risk if the rental payment exceeds the fair market value of the space, or if the provider does not use the space.

HUD interpretations and guidance that predate the transfer of RESPA to the CFPB help clarify how desk rental agreements and similar arrangements are viewed under RESPA. Under this guidance, rental payments must bear a reasonable relationship to the general market value (i.e., the market rate among non-settlement-service providers that would receive no value from renting from a mortgage lender) of the rental facilities provided.[130] The market value of the rental space may include an appropriate proportion of the cost for office services actually provided to the

---

127. Current guidance from the CFPB states that "[w]hether a particular MSA violates RESPA Section 8 will depend on specific facts and circumstances, including the details of how the MSA is structured and implemented," and indicates that MSAs continue to be subject to scrutiny. Press Release, CFPB, CFPB Provides Clearer Rules of the Road for RESPA Marketing Service Agreements (Oct. 7, 2020), https://www.consumerfinance.gov/about-us/blog/cfpb-provides-clearer-rules-road-respa-marketing-service-agreements/. On October 7, 2020, the CFPB rescinded its prior regulatory guidance regarding MSAs. CFPB Compliance Bulletin 2015-05, *RESPA Compliance and Marketing Services Agreements* (Oct. 8, 2015), https://files.consumerfinance.gov/f/201510_cfpb_compliance-bulletin-2015-05-respa-compliance-and-marketing-services-agreements.pdf (Noting that "[c]onsistent with the rescission, the Bulletin has no force or effect"). The CFPB replaced the prior compliance bulletin with the RESPA FAQs, which address MSAs and other issues under section 8.

128. In the Matter of Lighthouse Title, Inc., File No. 2014-CFPB-0015 (Sept. 30, 2014), https://files.consumerfinance.gov/f/201409_cfpb_consent-order_lighthouse-title.pdf.

129. *Id.*

130. Office of the Assistant Secretary for Housing-Federal Housing Commissioner; Real Estate Settlement Procedures Act (RESPA); Statement of Policy 1996-3, Rental of Office Space, Lock-outs, and Retaliation, 61 Fed. Reg. 29,264 (June 7, 1996).

tenant, such as secretarial services, utilities, telephone, and other office equipment. Importantly, no part of the rent may be calculated based on a multiple of the number or value of referrals made.[131]

Issues with desk rental agreements can be clear and direct, such as requirements to make referrals, exclusivity agreements, or other activities beyond an arm's length office lease. However, less direct evidence, such as higher-than-typical rent for the geographic area can raise red flags. The CFPB has addressed some of these issues in its enforcement actions. In *Prospect Mortgage*, the CFPB indicated that promises to endorse the lessor or market it as a "preferred partner" or "preferred lender" may violate RESPA, even where rental price is commensurate with fair market value.[132] In *In the Matter of Fidelity Mortgage Corporation*, the CFPB found a violation because the rental arrangement involved "an exclusive quid pro quo" relationship and monthly rent that was $200 to $1,100 over comparable rental space "not located in the middle of a bank."[133]

6.3.2.4 Strategic Partnerships/Co-Marketing Agreements

Joint advertising between partners that may be in a position to refer business to one another also raises potential RESPA issues. Although "[n]othing in RESPA prevents joint advertising . . . if one party is paying less than its pro rata share for the brochure or advertisement, there could be a RESPA violation where the other party may be subsidizing its advertising costs and, in turn, getting *referrals* of business."[134] A co-marketing agreement between potential referral partners thus must divide all costs on a pro rata basis to ensure that no party is subsidizing the advertising of the other. Imbalances in the advertising costs and co-marketing value can push the agreement out of the safe harbor.

For instance, in *Genuine Title*, the CFPB alleged that a title company purchased leads and sent marketing letters to the leads on behalf of banks and specific loan officers in violation of section 8.[135] The CFPB alleged that Genuine Title "provided and paid for a variety of marketing services to loan officers," including the following:

---

131. *Id.* HUD acknowledged that renting desks or office space to a settlement servicer provider could result in competing settlement service providers being "locked-out" of a referral source. This can raise the question of whether the rental payment is bona fide, but HUD stated that RESPA did not give it the authority to "regulate access to the offices of settlement service providers or to require a company to assist another company in its marketing activity." *Id.* at 29,266. HUD also stated that section 8 does not prohibit disincentives for failing to make a referral.

132. *Prospect Mortgage*, File No. 2017-CFPB-0006.

133. In the Matter of Fidelity Mortgage Corp., File No. 2014-CFPB 0001 (Jan. 16, 2014), https://files.consumerfinance.gov/f/201401_cfpb_consent-order_fidelity.pdf

134. HUD, *FAQs About RESPA for Industry*, https://www.fdic.gov/news/conferences/otherevents/2019-11-19-hud-faqs-about-respa-for-industry.pdf.

135. Complaint, CFPB v. Genuine Title, LLC, No. 1:15-cv-01235-JFM (D. Md. filed Apr. 29, 2015).

- Purchasing marketing leads from a third-party vendor and providing them to loan officers;
- Providing marketing analytics servicers; and
- Paying for marketing letters directed to the consumer leads to be printed, folded, stuffed into envelopes, and mailed.[136]

The CFPB maintained that "Genuine Title offered loan officers valuable services to increase their profits in a competitive environment."[137] The CFPB argued that the entities that received the benefit of the marketing did not pay their full share of the marketing costs.

6.3.2.5 Promotions and Sponsorships

Regulation X provides that RESPA permits "[n]ormal promotional and educational activities that are not conditioned on the referral of business and that do not involve the defraying of expenses that otherwise would be incurred by persons in a position to refer *settlement services* or business incident thereto."[138] Thus, activities likely do not violate RESPA as long as costs and fees are bona fide and charged at fair market value. However, sponsoring an event or similar activity for an organization that refers the sponsor settlement service business could nevertheless be scrutinized under RESPA section 8 to the extent that the sponsorship is provided in expectation of referrals or defrays the referring party's expenses.[139]

6.3.2.6 Mutual Contracts for Services

Mutual contracts, or mutual agreements, through which settlement service providers agree to exchange obligations, can constitute a thing of value for each party—and thus are subject to section 8(a). Accordingly, both agreements must satisfy the section 8(c)(2) safe harbor to ensure the parties do not violate RESPA.

6.3.3 Real Estate Broker/Agent Cooperative Agreements (Section 8(c)(3))

RESPA and Regulation X permit payments pursuant to cooperative brokerage and referral arrangements or agreements between real estate agents and real estate brokers.[140] This safe harbor (also called the "broker-to-broker" exception) broadly allows fee-division arrangements between parties both acting in a real estate broker capacity.

136. *Id.* at 10.
137. *Id.* at 11.
138. 12 C.F.R § 1024.14(g)(1).
139. HUD RESPA Q&A (2005).
140. 12 U.S.C. § 2607(c)(3); 12 C.F.R. § 1024.14(g)(v).

The broker-to-broker statutory exception is narrowly applicable only to splits between two real estate brokers both acting in a real estate broker capacity,[141] and makes clear that it does not extend to arrangements between real estate brokers and other parties who are operating in non-real-estate-broker capacities.

6.3.4 Affiliated Business Arrangements (Section 8(c)(4))

Affiliated business arrangements (called ABAs or AfBAs) are a common method of consolidating services for consumers to streamline the mortgage application and home-buying process.[142] The term "affiliated business arrangement" means an arrangement in which a person who is in a position to refer business incident to or a part of a real estate settlement service involving a federally related mortgage loan, or an associate of such person,[143] has either an affiliate relationship with or a direct or beneficial ownership interest of more than one percent in a provider of settlement services, and either of such persons directly or indirectly refers such business to that provider or affirmatively influences the selection of that provider.

AfBAs are not a violation of section 8 of RESPA if certain terms of the arrangement are disclosed and certain conditions are satisfied.[144] The person making the referral must provide an affiliated business arrangement disclosure statement to each person whose business is referred prior to the referral and the disclosure statement must evidence:

- The nature of the relationship and must explain the ownership and financial interest between the provider and the person making the referral; and
- The estimated charge or range of charges generally made by the provider that describes the charge using the same terminology.

The disclosure must be provided on a separate piece of paper at the time of loan application, with the LE, or at the time of the referral.[145] Further, the person making the referral is prohibited from requiring the use of an AfBA, except:

141. 12 C.F.R. § 1024.14(g)(1)(v) ("The [cooperative brokerage exemption] refers only to fee divisions within real estate brokerage arrangements when all parties are acting in a real estate brokerage capacity . . . .").

142. 12 U.S.C. § 2602(f).

143. An "associate" is defined to include a corporation or business entity that controls, is controlled by, or is under common control with the institution; an employer, officer, director, partner, franchisor, or franchisee of the institution; or anyone with an arrangement with the institution that enables the person to refer settlement business and benefit financially from the referrals. 12 U.S.C. § 2602(8).

144. 12 C.F.R. § 1024.15.

145. *Id.*

- The person is a lender who requires a buyer, borrower, or seller to pay for the services of an attorney, credit reporting agency, or real estate appraiser chosen by the lender to represent its interest; or
- The person is an attorney or law firm used for arranging issuance of a title insurance policy for a client, directly as agent or through a separate corporate title insurance agency that may be operated as an adjunct to the law practice of the attorney or law firm, as part of representation of that client in a real estate transaction.[146]

The referring affiliate may only receive a return on ownership or franchise interest, or payment otherwise permitted by RESPA.[147] This excludes payments based on referrals with no other apparent business motive, payments tied to the number of referrals, or payments based on an ownership, partnership, or joint venture share that has been adjusted based on previous referral activity.[148]

HUD guidance includes four factors that companies may use to help assess whether a payment is a return on ownership interest or a payment for referrals of settlement service business:

1. Has each owner or participant in the new entity made an investment of its own capital, as compared to a "loan" from an entity that receives the benefits of referrals?
2. Have the owners or participants of the new entity received an ownership or participant's interest based on a fair value contribution? Or is it based on the expected referrals to be provided by the referring owner or participant to a particular cell or division within the entity?
3. Are the dividends, partnership distributions, or other payments made in proportion to the ownership interest (proportional to the investment in the entity as a whole)? Or does the payment vary to reflect the amount of business referred to the new entity or a unit of the new entity?
4. Are the ownership interests in the new entity free from tie-ins to referrals of business? Or have there been any adjustments to the ownership interests in the new entity based on the amount of business referred?[149]

The CFPB and HUD have indicated that some types of AfBAs—particularly joint ventures between two settlement service providers that allow the referring party to share in the profits from the joint venture—may be subject to the challenge that the arrangement is not a legitimate business arrangement, but rather a "sham." The agencies have maintained that any joint venture party must be a "bona fide provider

---

146. *Id.*

147. *Id.* § 1024.15(b)(3).

148. *Id.* § 1024.15(b)(3)(ii).

149. HUD, Statement of Policy 1996-2 Regarding Sham Controlled Business Arrangements, 61 Fed. Reg. 29,258, 29,262 (Jun. 7, 1996) [hereinafter "HUD Policy 1996-2"].

of settlement services" (for example by having its own office space, email addresses, or phone numbers) and developed a ten-point test for determining the legitimacy of an AfBA.[150] Under this guidance, ten different factors must be considered and balanced to determine whether, in light of the specific facts, an entity is a bona fide provider. The factors measure the independence and legitimacy of the affiliate as a going business concern, such as whether the business has its own capital, resources, employees and managers, and office space; determines its own business goals and directions; conducts its own work, or subcontracts with independent third parties; and actively competes in the marketplace.[151]

However, some courts have rejected this guidance and held that no bona fide requirement applies to section 8(c)(4).[152] In particular, the U.S. District Court of the Western District of Kentucky rejected the CFPB's arguments regarding sham business arrangements and held, without detailed discussion, that section 8(c)(4) provided an exemption from RESPA liability without reference to the HUD ten-point test or other analysis of the actual business arrangement, focusing instead on the fact that the settlement service provider delivered the AfBA notice as required under the rules.[153]

6.4 Enforcement, Penalties, and Liabilities

As previously mentioned, RESPA imposes civil and criminal liability for section 8 violations. Violators may be subject to a criminal penalty of $10,000 and may be imprisoned for up to one year or both. Violators are also liable to the affected person for a civil fine of three times the amount of any charge paid for such settlement service. In private actions, the court may also award the prevailing party the cost of reasonable attorney's fees.[154]

---

150. *See, e.g.*, Complaint, CFPB v. Borders & Borders PLC, No. 3:13CV01047, ¶¶ 29–30, 2013 WL 5816580 (W.D. Ky., Oct. 24, 2013); HUD Policy 1996-2, *supra* note 149, at 29262. HUD guidance issued prior to the transfer of authority to the CFPB includes ten factors companies can review to evaluate whether a provider is bona fide.

151. HUD Policy 1996-2, *supra* note 149, at 29,262–63.

152. CFPB v. Borders & Borders, PLC, No. 3:13-CV-01047-CRS-DW, 2017 WL 2989183, at *5 (W.D. Ky. July 13, 2017) (citing Carter v. Welles-Bowen Realty, Inc., 736 F.3d 722, 725 (6th Cir. 2013) (holding that section 8(c)(4) does not contain a "bona fide" requirement and that neither HUD nor the CFPB has the authority to add such a requirement through a policy statement or other nonbinding guidance)).

153. Note that on reconsideration, the court instead based its decision on section 8(a), and found that the referrals at issue did not constitute a thing of value, and in any event would have been exempt under section 8(c)(2). CFPB v. Borders & Borders, No. 13-cv-01047, 2018 U.S. Dist. LEXIS 46906 (W.D. Ky. Mar. 21, 2018). Although the court did not expressly overturn the prior decision, the precedential value of the initial ruling is unclear.

154. 12 C.F.R. § 1024.12.

The CFPB, the secretary of HUD, a state attorney general, or a state insurance commissioner may bring an action to enjoin violators.[155] RESPA section 8(d) provides a private right of action for a plaintiff who is "charged for the settlement service involved in the violation."[156] For example, plaintiffs have standing to sue a settlement service provider under section 8 of RESPA even if the individual was not "overcharged" for settlement services.[157]

7. Title Insurance Company Selection

Under Section 9 of RESPA, sellers that hold legal title to the property being sold are prohibited from requiring borrowers, either directly or indirectly, as a condition to selling the property, to use a particular title insurance company.[158] Sellers who violate the provision are liable to the buyer for an amount equal to three times all charges made for the title insurance. This section also provides a private right of action for section 9 violations.[159]

8. Mortgage Servicing

This section addresses the applicability of the Mortgage Servicing Rules and sets out key terms and definitions. Sections 8.1 and 8.2 provide an overview of the Mortgage Servicing Rules and their applicability. Section 8.3 discusses the general requirements and limitations of the Mortgage Servicing Rules. Section 8.4 reviews the requirements for handling delinquent borrowers or providing loss mitigation. Section 8.5 discusses mortgage servicing transfers. Section 8.6 covers enforcement, penalties, and liabilities.

8.1 Overview of the RESPA Mortgage Servicing Rules

The CFPB succinctly outlines the mortgage servicing industry as follows:

> A mortgage servicer typically collects and processes loan payments on behalf of the owner of the mortgage note, conducts escrow-related processes, and handles loss mitigation, as appropriate. Servicing transfers

155. 12 U.S.C. § 2607.

156. *Id.* § 2607(d)(2).

157. For example, in Carter v. Welles-Bowen Realty, Inc. (*In re* Carter), 553 F.3d 979, 989 (6th Cir. 2009), the plaintiffs alleged that a portion of the fees they were charged was used to pay a kickback for referral of business. The plaintiffs did not allege that they suffered "individual harm" but instead alleged "collective harm." *See* Halaburda v. Bauer Publ. Co., LP, 2013 U.S. Dist. LEXIS 109954, *1, *18–19 (E.D. Mich. 2013).

158. 12 U.S.C. § 2608; 12 C.F.R. § 1024.16.

159. 12 U.S.C. § 2608.

> are common and may occur in several ways. The mortgage owner may sell the rights to service the loan, the owner of the loan may hire a vendor—typically called a sub-servicer to take on the servicing duties—or the entity that owns the loan may outright sell the mortgage loan as an asset.[160]

Requirements applicable to the mortgage servicing process were added to RESPA through the Dodd-Frank Act in the wake of the 2008 financial crisis, which saw a wave of foreclosures, borrower complaints, and confusion about the servicing process. RESPA and Regulation X require mortgage servicers to maintain policies and procedures to ensure that the servicer follows certain general servicing practices and standards, responds to borrower inquiries and corrects account errors, discloses information relating to the transfer of servicing operations, and makes timely payments out of escrow accounts. RESPA also includes requirements regarding force-placed insurance procedures and notices, early intervention efforts for delinquent borrowers, and loss mitigation processes.

The federal mortgage servicing rules are comprised of specific requirements in RESPA and Regulation X, as well as certain requirements codified in TILA and Regulation Z.[161] The current rules were issued by the CFPB on January 17, 2013, and amended in July 2013, September 2013, October 2013, October 2014, and August 2016 (collectively, the Mortgage Servicing Rules).[162] Although this chapter focuses on rules and requirements under RESPA, certain servicing rules codified under TILA and Regulation Z are discussed herein and noted accordingly.

8.2 Applicability

The Mortgage Servicing Rules apply to federally related mortgage loans. Open-end lines of credit, such as HELOCs, are not covered by the Mortgage Servicing Rules. The Mortgage Servicing Rules also do not apply to reverse mortgage loans, temporary or bridge loans, the construction phase of a construction to permanent loan, commercial loans (meaning loans for business purposes secured by a consumer's dwelling), or

---

160. Press Release, CFPB, Consumer Financial Protection Bureau Outlines Mortgage Loan Transfer Process to Prevent Consumer Harm (Apr. 24, 2020), https://www.consumerfinance.gov/about-us/newsroom/cfpb-outlines-mortgage-loan-transfer-process-prevent-consumer-harm/.

161. 78 Fed. Reg. 10,695 (Feb. 14, 2013); 78 Fed. Reg. 44,685 (July 24, 2013), 78 Fed. Reg. 60,381 (Oct. 1, 2013), 79 Fed. Reg. 65,299 (Nov. 3, 2014). Mortgage servicers must also comply with the requirements and prohibitions of other applicable laws and regulations, including the Equal Credit Opportunity Act (ECOA) and Regulation B; Electronic Fund Transfer Act (EFTA) and Regulation E; the Fair Debt Collection Practices Act (FDCPA); the Homeowners Protection Act (HPA); the Fair Credit Reporting Act (FCRA) and Regulation V; and the Gramm-Leach-Bliley Act (GLBA).

162. 78 Fed. Reg. 44,685 (July 24, 2013); 78 Fed. Reg. 60,381 (Oct. 1, 2013); 79 Fed. Reg. 65,299 (Nov. 3, 2014); 81 Fed. Reg. 72,160 (Oct. 19, 2016).

mortgages secured by farm or agricultural properties where the lender is a qualified lender under the Farm Credit Act of 1971.

Most of the requirements in the Mortgage Servicing Rules apply specifically to servicers. A *servicer* is defined as the person responsible for the servicing of the loan, which can be the maker or holder of the loan if such entity also services the loan.[163] The statute defines the term *servicing* as "receiving any scheduled periodic payments from a borrower pursuant to the terms of any loan, including amounts for escrow accounts . . . and making the payments of principal and interest and such other payments with respect to the amounts received from the borrower as may be required pursuant to the terms of the loan."[164]

Small servicers, a term defined in Regulation Z, but carried over in Regulation X, are exempt from certain provisions of the Mortgage Servicing Rules.[165] Small servicers comprise those entities that service 5,000 or fewer consumer mortgages that they or an affiliate own or originated, entities that service mortgages for certain nonprofit entities where the servicer is not compensated, and entities that service seller-financed mortgages (for which the servicer may be compensated).[166] Among other areas, small servicers are exempt from sections 1024.38, 1024.39, and 1024.40, consisting of the general servicing policy and procedures requirements, early intervention requirements, and continuity of contact rules.[167] Small servicers are also exempt from some (but not all) of the loss mitigation obligations, as well as the periodic statement rules.[168]

The Mortgage Servicing Rules generally apply to mortgage loan borrowers but may also apply to a borrower's *successor in interest*. Amendments to the Mortgage Servicing Rules adopted in 2018 define a consumer's successor in interest and provide that confirmed successors in interest are considered borrowers for the purposes of Regulation X's mortgage servicing provisions.[169] *Confirmed successor in interest* means a successor in interest once a servicer has confirmed the successor in interest's identity and ownership interest in a property that secures a mortgage loan. The CFPB states that the agency adopted the successor in interest provisions after learning about difficulties that some surviving spouses, children, or other successors in interest experienced in attempting to communicate with servicers.[170]

163. 12 U.S.C. § 2605(i)(2).

164. *Id.* § 2605(i)(3).

165. 12 C.F.R. § 1026.41(e)(4)(ii).

166. *Id.*

167. *Id.* § 1024.30(b).

168. CFPB, *Real Estate Settlement Procedures Act (Regulation X) and Truth in Lending Act (Regulation Z) Mortgage Servicing Rules: Small Entity Compliance Guide* (Apr. 19, 2018), https://files.consumerfinance.gov/f/documents/cfpb_mortserv_guide_v3.2.1.pdf.

169. *See* 81 Fed. Reg. 72,160 (Oct. 19, 2016).

170. CFPB Bulletin 2013-12, *Implementation Guidance for Certain Mortgage Servicing Rules* (Oct. 15, 2013), https://files.consumerfinance.gov/f/201310_cfpb_mortgage-servicing_bulletin.pdf.

8.3 General Duties of Mortgage Servicers

The Mortgage Servicing Rules generally set out the rights of borrowers with respect to federally related mortgage loans and the responsibilities of the servicer. Servicers' responsibilities include providing various disclosures; processing payments from the borrower and to third parties on behalf of the borrower, including escrow account payments; communicating with the borrower, responding to inquiries, and investigating (and as necessary, correcting) errors made on borrowers' accounts. Servicers must also comply with specific limitations on certain activities, such as force-placed insurance, and maintain a complete servicing file and other records.

In general, RESPA prohibits covered servicers from engaging in the following activities:

- Obtaining force-placed hazard insurance unless there is a reasonable basis to believe the borrower has failed to comply with the loan contract's requirements to maintain property insurance;
- Charging fees for responding to valid qualified written requests (as defined in CFPB regulations);
- Failing to take timely action to respond to a borrower's requests to correct errors relating to allocation of payments, final balances for purposes of paying off the loan, or avoiding foreclosure, or other standard servicer's duties;
- Failing to respond within ten business days to a request from a borrower to provide the identity, address, and other relevant contact information about the owner or assignee of the loan; or
- Failing to comply with any other obligation found by the CFPB, by regulation, to be appropriate to carry out the consumer protection purposes of RESPA.[171]

Of course, the requirements and limitations on mortgage servicers are subject to a detailed set of rules codified in Regulation X. The Mortgage Servicing Rules interpret and implement the RESPA servicing requirements, and are themselves further interpreted through the Official Commentary, CFPB regulatory and supervisory guidance, and agency and judicial precedent. Key aspects of the Mortgage Servicing Rules requirements that apply to servicers' everyday practices are discussed below.

8.3.1 Servicer Policies and Procedures

Servicers are required to maintain policies and procedures that are reasonably designed to achieve objectives set by the Mortgage Servicing Rules, which are set out in five categories:

- Accessing and providing timely and accurate information;

171. 12 U.S.C. § 2605(k).

- Properly evaluating loss mitigation applications;
- Facilitating oversight of, and compliance by, service providers;
- Facilitating transfer of information during servicing transfers; and
- Informing borrowers of the written error resolution and information request procedures.[172]

Included in these requirements, the Mortgage Servicing Rules mandate that servicers maintain and regularly update a servicing file. The servicing file must contain, at least, a schedule of all credits and debits to the account (including escrow accounts and suspense accounts); a copy of the security instrument establishing the lien securing the mortgage; any notes created by servicer personnel concerning communications with the borrower, a report of the data fields created by the servicer's electronic systems relating to the borrower's account (if applicable); and copies of any information or documents provided by the borrower in connection with error notices or loss mitigation.[173]

Specifically regarding successors in interest, a servicer must have policies and procedures reasonably designed to ensure that, upon notification of the death of a borrower, the servicer promptly identifies and facilitates communication with a successor in interest of the deceased borrower with respect to the property that secures the deceased borrower's mortgage loan.[174]

8.3.2 Mortgage Servicing Disclosures

In general, servicing disclosures required by the Mortgage Servicing Rules must be clear and conspicuous, provided in writing,[175] and provided in a form that a recipient may keep. When drafting disclosures, servicers may use commonly accepted or readily understandable abbreviations. Disclosures may be made in a language other than English, provided that they are made in English upon a recipient's request.[1761]

---

172. 12 C.F.R. § 1024.38(b).

173. *Id.* § 1024.38(c)(2).

174. Cmts. 1024.38(b)(1)(vi)-2-3; CFPB Bulletin 2013-12, *supra* note 170. The CFPB's mortgage servicing bulletin sets out examples of servicer practices the CFPB would consider to be components of policies and procedures that are reasonably designed to achieve the objectives of the successor in interest provision.

175. Including electronic disclosures, subject to consumer consent and the provisions of the Electronic Signatures in Global and National Commerce (E-SIGN) Act, Pub. L. 106-229, § 101 (2000) (codified as amended at 15 U.S.C. §§ 7001–7008 (2018)).

176. 12 C.F.R. § 1024.32(a)(2).

8.3.2.1 Periodic Statements

The Mortgage Servicing Rules mandate certain requirements related to borrowers' periodic statements, which are contained in Regulation Z, 12 C.F.R. section 1026.41.[177] Each billing cycle, a periodic statement must be delivered or placed in the mail within a reasonably prompt time after the payment due date or the end of any courtesy period provided for the previous billing cycle.[178] Section 1026.41 specifies the content, details, and positioning of items required to be included on the periodic statement. The regulation also provides sample forms for periodic statements at appendix H-30, and the proper use of these forms complies with the periodic statement requirements.

8.3.2.2 Successors in Interest Notice

As an optional notice, servicers may provide a confirmed successor in interest[179] with a disclosure and acknowledgment form.[180] The disclosure sets out the successor's rights with regard to the mortgage and the property, as well as the right to receive certain notices and communications from the servicer. To receive such notices and communications, the successor must execute an acknowledgment form.

If the successor does not execute and return the acknowledgment form, the servicer is not required to provide to the confirmed successor in interest any written disclosure required by enumerated Mortgage Servicing Rules (including 12 C.F.R. §§ 1024.17, 1024.33, 1024.34, 1024.37, or 1024.39) or to comply with the live contact requirements with respect to the successor in interest until the successor either assumes the mortgage loan obligation under state law or executes an acknowledgment form and provides it to the servicer.[181]

8.3.2.3 Adjustable-Rate Mortgage: Initial Rate Adjustment Notice

The Mortgage Servicing Rules require a disclosure regarding an initial interest rate adjustment on an adjustable-rate mortgage (codified under Regulation Z).[182]

---

177. *Id.* § 1026.41. The periodic statement requirements are codified in Regulation Z. The Mortgage Servicing Rules include certain requirements that are codified under TILA and Regulation Z, the bulk of which goes beyond the scope of this chapter. However, certain TILA and Regulation Z requirements are included herein to ensure continuity in the descriptions of the servicing requirements.

178. *Id.* § 1026.41(a), (b). Among other exemptions under section 1026.41(e), certain exceptions apply for consumers in bankruptcy or who have discharged personal liability for a mortgage loan through bankruptcy. 12 U.S.C. § 1026.41(e)(5).

179. 12 C.F.R. § 1024.31.

180. *Id.* § 1024.32(c).

181. *Id.* § 1024.32(c)(2).

182. *Id.* § 1026.20(d).

8.3.3 Mortgage Servicing Activities and Responsibilities

8.3.3.1 Timely Escrow Payments and Treatment of Escrow Account Balances

Servicers must comply with RESPA and Regulation X requirements concerning the treatment of escrow funds, including adhering to the requirement to make payments from the escrow account in a timely manner.[183] For additional discussion of escrow requirements, see section 5 of this chapter.

8.3.3.2 Error Resolution

RESPA provides borrowers with the right to file disputes and request information related to RESPA-covered mortgages. RESPA requires that consumers be able to obtain information about the servicing of covered loans and escrow accounts by providing a written inquiry to the servicer. A borrower inquiry must be a *qualified written request* in order to trigger RESPA's response requirements. A qualified written request is an inquiry by the identified borrower and "includes a statement of the reasons for the belief of the borrower, to the extent applicable, that the account is in error or provides sufficient detail to the servicer regarding other information sought by the borrower."[184]

Regulation X expands RESPA's qualified written request framework to add response requirements for error notices and requests for information. Regulation X requires servicers to follow error resolution procedures that are triggered when a borrower submits an error notice to the servicer. An error notice must be in writing and identify the borrower's name, information that allows the servicer to identify the borrower's account, and the alleged error.[185] A request for information, covered separately by Regulation X, can consist of an error notice if the borrower asserts an error relating to the servicing of a mortgage.[186] It is up to the servicer to determine, based on the content and nature of a borrower's communication, whether the communication is an error notice or a request for information.

The Official Commentary cautions that "[a] servicer should not rely solely on the borrower's description of a submission to determine whether the submission constitutes a notice of error under § 1024.35(a), an information request under § 1024.36(a), or both" to be considered an error notice.[187] To be considered a notice of error, inquiries must generally state the reasons why the borrower believed that the account was in error.[188] Regulation X lists the types of errors that trigger the response requirements, including various actions or omissions by the servicer set out in section 1024.35(b).

183. *Id.* § 1024.34.

184. 12 U.S.C. § 2605(e).

185. 12 C.F.R. § 1024.35(a).

186. *See id.*

187. Cmt. 1024.35(a)-2.

188. *See* Gorham-Dimaggio v. Countrywide Home Loans, Inc., No. 108-CV-00019LEK/RFT, 2010 WL 883683 (N.D.N.Y. Mar. 8, 2010), *aff'd*, 421 Fed. Appx. 97 (2d Cir. 2011).

Regulatory guidance from the CFPB (CFPB Bulletin 2013-12) states that a servicer's communications with a borrower regarding an error notice are not subject to the "cease communication" provision of the Fair Debt Collection Practices Act (FDCPA) unless the borrower specifically withdraws the request for action regarding the error.[189]

8.3.3.3 Requests for Information

Servicers must respond to any written request for information from a borrower that "states the information the borrower is requesting with respect to the borrower's mortgage loan."[190] Requests for information are defined broadly to include any information concerning the borrower's mortgage loan. In the preamble to the 2013 Final Rule, the CFPB stated that section 1024.36 "requires servicers to provide to borrowers upon their request information about their mortgage loan accounts, including their servicing files, which includes a complete payment history, a copy of their security instrument, collection notes, and other valuable information about their accounts."[191] The servicer's obligation, however, is limited to information accessible by the servicer.

Servicers that receive a written request for information that meets the conditions of the Mortgage Servicing Rules must provide an acknowledgment of receipt and a response to the information request within the timing requirements under the Mortgage Servicing Rules. The acknowledgement consists of a written response acknowledging receipt of the information request, which must be provided within five days (excluding legal public holidays, Saturdays, and Sundays) of a servicer receiving an information request.[192]

The servicer's response must consist of the requested information and the servicer's contact information, including a telephone number, for further assistance in writing; or a written notification that states that the servicer has determined, based on a reasonable search, that the requested information is not available to the servicer, provide the basis for the servicer's determination, and provide contact information, including a telephone number, for further assistance.[193] The Official Commentary explains that information is not available when it is not in the servicer's control or possession, or the information cannot be retrieved in the ordinary course of business through reasonable efforts.[194]

---

189. CFPB Bulletin 2013-12, *supra* note 170.

190. 12 C.F.R. § 1024.36(a).

191. 78 Fed. Reg. 10,781 (Feb. 14, 2013).

192. *Id.* § 1024.36(c).

193. *Id.* § 1024.36(d)(1).

194. Cmt. 12 C.F.R. § 1024.36(d)(1)-1. Comment 2 to this section provides examples in which information is available or not available to the servicer.

For potential successors in interest, servicers are required to respond to any written request by providing a written description of the documents that the servicer reasonably requires to confirm the person's identity and ownership interest.[195]

Servicers must complete any required investigation and provide a response:

- No later than ten days (excluding legal public holidays, Saturdays, and Sundays) after the servicer receives an information request for the identity of, and address or other relevant contact information for, the owner or assignee of a mortgage loan; and
- No later than thirty days (excluding legal public holidays, Saturdays, and Sundays) after the servicer receives the information request for all other requests for information.[196] This deadline may be extended by fifteen days with notice to the borrower.[197]

Investigations sufficient to meet the reasonable search requirement can be costly in time and resources. However, the Mortgage Servicing Rules prohibit servicers from charging a fee or requiring a borrower to make any payment that may be owed on a borrower's account, as a condition of responding to an information request.[198] The Mortgage Servicing Rules do provide exceptions to reduce the burden on servicers for responding to requests that cannot reasonably be met. Certain types of requests are excluded from the rules, and do not trigger response requirements, including requests for:

- Duplicative information (information previously requested by the borrower for which the servicer has previously complied with its obligation to respond);
- Confidential, proprietary, or privileged information;
- Irrelevant information (information not directly related to the borrower's mortgage loan account);
- Overbroad or unduly burdensome information request; or
- Untimely information request (requests delivered more than one year after the mortgage loan was transferred or discharged).[199]

---

195. 12 C.F.R. § 1024.36(i).

196. *Id.* § 1024.36(d)(2).

197. *Id.* § 1024.36(d)(2)(ii).

198. *Id.* § 1024.36(g). The Mortgage Servicing Rules do not prohibit charging a fee for providing a beneficiary notice under applicable state law, if such a fee is not otherwise prohibited by applicable law. *Id.* § 1024.36(g)(2).

199. *Id.* § 1024.36(f). The Commentary to this section provides examples of each of the exclusions from the request for information requirements. *See* Cmts. 1024.36(f)(1)(i)-1–1024.36(f)(1)(iv)-1.

8.3.3.4 Limitations on Force-Placed Insurance

Mortgage lenders and servicers (and investors) regularly require that the borrower obtain and maintain insurance coverage for the property that collateralizes the mortgage loan. Such insurance must comply with the requirements in the loan contract to be considered adequate.[200] When borrowers fail to obtain or maintain insurance coverage as required under the contract, the Mortgage Servicing Rules allow servicers, in certain contexts, to obtain insurance on behalf of the borrower and pass the costs on to the borrower. This is called *force-placed insurance.*

The force-placed insurance rules apply to hazard insurance obtained by a servicer on behalf of the owner or assignee of a mortgage loan that insures the property securing such loan, but exclude certain types of insurance, including the following:

- Hazard insurance required by the Flood Disaster Protection Act of 1973 (FDPA);[201]
- Hazard insurance obtained by a borrower but later renewed by the borrower's servicer; and
- Hazard insurance obtained by a borrower but renewed by the borrower's servicer at its discretion, if the borrower agrees.[202]

A servicer's force-placed insurance charges must be bona fide and reasonable.[203] This means that the charges must be reasonably related to the servicer's cost of providing the service and not otherwise prohibited by law. Force-placed insurance may be retroactive to the start of any period in which the borrower did not maintain hazard insurance.[204]

To force-place hazard insurance, servicers must first have a *reasonable basis* to believe that the borrower has failed to maintain required hazard insurance.[205] A reasonable basis may be formed from information about a borrower's hazard insurance

---

200. *See* Wilson v. Deutsche Bank Tr. Co. Americas, 2019 WL 5840325 (N.D. Tex. Nov. 7, 2019) (RESPA claims must allege that a borrower's current insurance "complies with the loan contract's requirements").

201. 42 U.S.C. §§ 4001–4129. Accordingly, FDPA-mandated flood insurance does not fall under the RESPA force-placed insurance rules, and should be evaluated under the force-placed insurance provisions of the FDPA. In the preamble to the 2013 Final Rule, the Bureau stated that "overlapping regulatory restrictions would be unduly burdensome and produce little consumer benefit." *See* 78 Fed. Reg. 10,696, 10,723 (Feb. 14, 2013).

202. 12 C.F.R. § 1024.37(a).

203. *Id.* § 1024.37(h).

204. Cmt. 1024.37(c)(1)(i)-1. The CFPB provides that, if not prohibited by state or other applicable law, a servicer may charge a borrower for force-placed insurance the servicer purchased, retroactive to the first day of any period in which the borrower did not have hazard insurance in place.

205. 12 C.F.R. § 1024.37(b).

received by the servicer from the borrower, the borrower's insurance provider, or the borrower's insurance agent, as well as through reasonable diligence.[206]

When determining if there is a reasonable basis to believe that a borrower failed to maintain insurance as required by the mortgage contract, servicers must accept "any reasonable form of written confirmation from a borrower of existing insurance coverage."[207] Such evidence includes the existing policy number and insurance company information. Servicers may also require:

- a copy of the borrower's hazard insurance policy declaration page;
- the borrower's insurance certificate, the borrower's insurance policy; or
- other similar forms of written confirmation.

Servicers may reject evidence if neither the borrower's insurance provider nor insurance agent provides confirmation of the insurance information submitted by the borrower, or if the terms and conditions of the borrower's hazard insurance policy do not comply with the borrower's loan contract requirements.[208] A servicer placing insurance may only be required pursuant to the following rules.

- *Initial notice requirements*: Prior to placing insurance, the servicer must mail (via first-class mail) or deliver an initial written notice to the borrower at least forty-five days before assessing a charge or fee related to force-placed insurance. The notice must comply with content and formatting requirements, which are included in 12 C.F.R. part 1024, appendix MS-3(A). The initial notice must state that hazard insurance is required on the borrower's property, request up-to-date hazard insurance information, and inform the borrower that the servicer has purchased or will purchase insurance at the borrower's expense. The servicer must send a reminder notice at least thirty days after the initial notice is mailed or delivered and at least fifteen days before the servicer assesses charges or fees. Initial notices and reminders cannot contain information other than the specific statements listed above and, at the servicer's option, the loan account number.
- *Renewal/replacement notice requirements*: Servicers must follow a similar process for renewing or replacing existing force-placed insurance. A renewal notice must be sent at least forty-five days before assessing a premium charge or fee. Servicers must mail or deliver the renewal notice before each anniversary of purchasing *force-placed insurance*, though the servicer need not send the renewal notice more than once each year.[209]

---

206. Cmt. 1024.37(b)-1.
207. 12 U.S.C. § 2605(l)(2).
208. Cmt. 1024.37(c)(1)(iii)-2.
209. 12 C.F.R. § 1024.37(e).

- *Escrow exception*: For borrowers with escrow accounts administered by the servicer, the servicer must disburse funds from the escrow account to pay the borrower's current insurance policy, and may not force-place insurance, even if the borrower's mortgage payment is more than thirty days overdue or there are not sufficient funds in the escrow account.[210]
- *Cancellation*: Servicers must cancel force-placed insurance no later than fifteen days after the servicer receives evidence of hazard insurance coverage.[211] The servicer must also refund force-placed insurance premium charges and fees for the period of overlapping insurance coverage and remove all force-placed charges and fees from the borrower's account for the relevant period.[212]

8.4 Delinquent Borrower and Loss Mitigation Requirements

The Mortgage Servicing Rules also contain requirements for the treatment of delinquent borrowers and loss mitigation requests. These rules apply to servicers when borrowers miss payments, become delinquent, or affirmatively request relief.[213] The Mortgage Servicing Rules do not mandate that servicers provide any particular form of assistance (referred to as *loss mitigation* throughout this chapter), but the rules require servicers that offer loss mitigation options to do so equitably and fairly, and in accordance with certain standardized procedures. The Mortgage Servicing Rules also contain restrictions on servicers' post-default activities to protect borrowers who have sought loss mitigation.

8.4.1 Early Intervention

8.4.1.1 Overview and Applicability

The Mortgage Servicing Rules require mortgage servicers to attempt to establish contact with the borrower at the beginning stage of delinquency to inform the borrower about available options to avoid foreclosure.[214] Under the rules, the term *delinquency* for

---

210. *Id.* §§ 1024.17(k)(5)(i), 1024.17(k)(5)(ii)(B).

211. 12 U.S.C. § 2605(l)(3)(A); 12 C.F.R. § 1024.37(g)(1).

212. *Id.* § 1024.37(g)(2).

213. *See* Smith v. Wells Fargo Bank, No. 18 CV 7979, 2019 WL 2189285 (N.D. Ill. May 21, 2019) (servicer remained responsible for servicing after default); Buyea v. Select Portfolio Servicing, Inc., No. 9:16-CV-80347, 2016 WL 5904502, at *3 (S.D. Fla. Oct. 11, 2016) ("Whether or not Defendant was actively servicing the loan, Defendant remained responsible for servicing the loan at the time it received Plaintiff's RFI.").

214. 12 C.F.R. § 1024.41.

purposes of 12 C.F.R. section 1024.39 (and certain other sections in Regulation X) means a period of time beginning on the date a periodic payment sufficient to cover principal, interest, and, if applicable, escrow, becomes due and unpaid, until such time as no periodic payment is due and unpaid.[215] Borrowers who are performing as agreed under a loss mitigation agreement designed to bring the borrower current on a previously missed payment are not considered delinquent.[216]

The Mortgage Servicing Rules' early intervention requirements, as well as the loss mitigation requirements, apply only to covered loans secured by a property that is the borrower's principal residence.[217]

8.4.1.2 Live Contact

Servicers must make good faith efforts to establish live contact with the borrower within thirty-six days after each time the borrower became delinquent.[218] Under the Mortgage Servicing Rules, "[p]romptly after establishing live contact with a borrower, the servicer shall inform the borrower about the availability of loss mitigation options, if appropriate."[219] Servicers must continue to attempt to contact the borrower within thirty-six days of each subsequent missed payment for as long as the borrower remains delinquent.[220] Note that payment in full by the borrower prior to the end of the thirty-six day period negates the live contact requirements.[221] Additionally, servicers must attempt to reestablish contact if the borrower becomes delinquent again.[222] Live contact established through other means (such as through a loss mitigation application) satisfies the requirement.

The Official Commentary to section 1024.39 states that good faith efforts to establish live contact consist of "reasonable steps under the circumstances to reach a borrower and may include telephoning the borrower on more than one occasion or sending written or electronic communication encouraging the borrower to establish live contact with the servicer."[223] CFPB guidance also indicates a greater degree of leniency from regulators for servicers attempting to contact unresponsive borrowers "where there is little or no hope of home retention, such as when all applicable loss mitigation possibilities have been exhausted."[224]

When the servicer establishes live contact with the borrower, the servicer must promptly inform the borrower of any loss mitigation options that might be available.

215. *Id.* § 1024.31.
216. Cmt. 1024.39(a)-1.ii.
217. 12 C.F.R. § 1024.30(c)(2).
218. *Id.* § 1024.39(a).
219. *Id.*
220. 12 C.F.R. § 1024.39(a).
221. Cmt. 1024.39(a)-1.iv.
222. Cmt. 1024.39(a)-6.
223. Cmt. 1024.39(a)-2; CFPB Bulletin 2013-12, *supra* note 170, at 4–5.
224. CFPB Bulletin 2013-12, *supra* note 170, at 6.

Information on loss mitigation options may be provided orally, in writing, or through electronic communication.[225]

8.4.1.3 Written Notice

Servicers must send a written notice within forty-five days of a borrower becoming delinquent.[226] Similar to the timing rules regarding establishment of live contact, the written notice must be resent every forty-five days after each payment due date. However, the written notice need only be sent once every 180 days—functionally, this means that a servicer has 180 days after providing the written notice before it must provide the notice again.

Delinquencies that occur immediately before, during, or after a mortgage servicing transfer present additional challenges and disclosure requirements. In servicing transfers,[227] the transferee servicer must comply with section 1024.39(b), regardless of whether the transferor servicer provided a written notice within the preceding 180-day period.[228] However, the transferee servicer is not required to send a written notice if the transferor servicer sent the notice within forty-five days of the transfer, but must continuing sending notices within forty-five days of each missed payment if the delinquency progresses.[229]

Servicers are exempt from the written notice requirements for borrowers: (1) in bankruptcy; (2) who do not qualify for any loss mitigation options; or (3) where loan servicing was transferred while the loan was in default, which may be subject to the FDCPA, where any borrower on the mortgage loan has provided a cease communication notice under the FDCPA with respect to that mortgage loan.

Servicers must send a modified written notice to borrowers in bankruptcy, assuming the exceptions above are not met. The modified written notice cannot request payment and need only be sent once (i.e., the 180-day rule may be ignored). The letter must be sent:

- For a preexisting delinquency, forty-five days after the borrower files a bankruptcy petition;
- For a delinquency subsequent to a bankruptcy filing, forty-five days after the borrower's delinquency.

---

225. Cmt. 1024.39(a)-4.i.
226. 12 C.F.R. § 1024.39(b).
227. Servicing transfers are discussed in further detail below; *see* section 8.5.
228. Cmt. 1024.39(b)(1)-5.
229. *Id.* The Commentary provides the following example:

> [A]ssume a borrower has monthly payments, with a payment due on March 1. The transferor servicer provides the notice required by § 1024.39(b) on April 10. The loan is transferred on April 12. Assuming the borrower remains delinquent, the transferee servicer is not required to provide another written notice until 45 days after May 1, the first post-transfer payment due date—i.e., by June 15.

If the borrower discharges personal liability for the mortgage loan in bankruptcy, the servicer is not required to continue to comply with the live contact rules, but must send written notices under the Mortgage Servicing Rules if the borrower made a partial or periodic payment after commencing a bankruptcy proceeding. For other outcomes, standard compliance with the regulation resumes when (1) the bankruptcy case is dismissed, (2) the bankruptcy case is closed, or (3) the borrower reaffirms personal liability for the mortgage loan.[230]

Borrowers may also have certain rights vis-à-vis debt collectors under the FDCPA related to their mortgage loans if servicing is transferred while the loan is in default. For mortgages subject to the FDCPA, where borrowers invoke their FDCPA cease communication protections,[231] servicers are exempt from the live contact requirements.[232] Servicers may be exempt from the written notice requirement as well, if: (1) no loss mitigation option is available or (2) any borrower on the mortgage loan is a debtor in bankruptcy.[233] If no exemption applies, servicers must give a modified written notice even when the borrower becomes delinquent. The modified written notice must only be provided once in a 180-day period. Servicers governed by the FDCPA may provide the written early intervention notice even after the borrower requests a cease of communications.[234] Despite the rules set out above, loss mitigation information may be provided in response to a borrower-initiated request.[235]

8.4.2 Continuity of Contact

Servicers must maintain policies and procedures reasonably designed to assign personnel to a delinquent borrower by the time the written early intervention notice was provided or within forty-five days after the borrower became delinquent.[236] Under the servicer's policies and procedures, assigned personnel must be available, via telephone, to answer the borrower's questions and (as applicable) assist the borrower with available loss mitigation options until the borrower has made two consecutive, on-time (i.e., without incurring a late charge) mortgage payments in accordance with the terms of a permanent loss mitigation agreement.[237] If the borrower does not immediately receive a live response, the servicer's policies and procedures must ensure that the servicer can provide a live response in a timely manner.

Under the continuity of contact rules, a delinquent borrower excludes borrowers that have refinanced the mortgage loan, paid off the mortgage loan, brought the

---

230. 12 C.F.R. § 1024.39(c)(2).

231. 15 U.S.C. § 1692c.

232. 12 C.F.R. § 1024.39(d).

233. *Id.* § 1024.39(c)(1); *see also* Cmt. 1024.39(d)-1.

234. Cmt. 1024.39(d)-2; *see also* 2016 FDCPA Interpretive Rule (81 Fed. Reg. 71,977, 71,979–81).

235. Cmt. 1024.39(d)-2.

236. 12 C.F.R. § 1024.40(a).

237. *Id.* § 1024.40(a)(2).

mortgage loan current by paying all amounts owed in arrears, or transferred title to the property to a new owner through, for example, a deed in lieu of foreclosure, a sale of the borrower's property, including, as applicable, a short sale, or a foreclosure sale.[238] For this subsection of the Mortgage Servicing Rules, the term *borrower* includes a person authorized by the borrower to act on the borrower's behalf.

Many servicers assign a single point of contact to assist borrowers handling delinquency. However, the Official Commentary to the Mortgage Servicing Rules provides servicers "discretion to determine whether to assign a single person or a team of personnel to respond to a delinquent borrower."[239]

Assigned personnel must be able to, among other things:

- Provide the borrower with accurate information about available loss mitigation options, including the steps the borrower must take to be evaluated for such options, including how to complete a loss mitigation application or appeal a denial of a loan modification option (if applicable);
- Provide the borrower with accurate information about the status of any loss mitigation application submitted;
- Provide the borrower with accurate information about the circumstances under which the institution may refer the account to foreclosure;
- Provide the borrower with accurate information about applicable loss mitigation deadlines;
- Timely retrieve a complete record of the borrower's payment history and all written information the borrower has provided to the institution (or the institution's predecessors) in connection with a loss mitigation application, and provide these documents to other persons required to evaluate the borrower for available loss mitigation options; and
- Provide the borrower with information about submitting a written error notice or written request for information.[240]

8.4.3 Loss Mitigation

8.4.3.1 Overview and Applicability

The Mortgage Servicing Rules do not require servicers to offer or provide loss mitigation or any particular loss mitigation option. Rather, the rules provide a framework of *how* servicers must offer any loss mitigation options available through the servicer, lender, or investor. The loss mitigation requirements apply only to a mortgage loan that is secured by a property that is the debtor's principal residence.

238. Cmt. 1024.40(a)-1.

239. Cmt. 1024.40(a)-2.

240. 12 C.F.R. § 1024.40(b).

Fair lending principles and the requirements of the Equal Credit Opportunity Act (ECOA)[241] and Fair Housing Act (FHA)[242] apply to loss mitigation, specifically regarding activities that may indicate disparate treatment or practices with a disparate impact on consumers in violation of ECOA on the basis of race, color, religion, national origin, sex, marital status, or age; because all or part of the applicant's income derives from any public assistance program; or because the applicant has in good faith exercised any right under the Consumer Credit Protection Act and/or the FHA on the basis of race, color, national origin, religion, sex, familial status, or disability.

8.4.3.2 Loss Mitigation Procedures

The Mortgage Servicing Rules do not require that loss mitigation applications be in any particular form.[243] The term loss mitigation application is considered expansively—an application requires only that "the borrower expresses an interest in applying for a loss mitigation option and provides information the servicer would evaluate in connection with a loss mitigation application."[244] Under the Mortgage Servicing Rules, a loss mitigation application "means an oral or written request for a loss mitigation option that is accompanied by any information required by a servicer for evaluation for a loss mitigation option."[245]

Servicers may establish requirements for determining when a "completed application" that may be decisioned is received, based on the information that the servicer needs to evaluate an application for loss mitigation options. However, in gathering information from the borrower and other parties, servicers must exercise reasonable diligence in obtaining documents and information to complete a loss mitigation application. Servicers must provide a written notice within five days (excluding legal public holidays, Saturdays, and Sundays) after receiving the borrower's completed loss mitigation application. The notice informs the borrower that the loss mitigation application is complete as of a certain date and sets out the borrower's rights and next steps in the loss mitigation process.

If the servicer receives a loss mitigation application forty-five days or more before a scheduled foreclosure sale, the servicer must notify the borrower in writing within five days (excluding legal public holidays, Saturdays, and Sundays) that it has received the application and state whether it is complete or incomplete. If the application is incomplete, the notice must advise (1) what additional documents or information

241. 15 U.S.C. § 1691(a).

242. 42 U.S.C. § 3604.

243. Cmt. 1024.41(b)(1)-2.

244. Cmt. 1024.41(b)-2.

245. *Id.* In its *Winter 2020 Supervisory Highlights*, the CFPB focused heavily on failure of servicers to recognize verbal loss mitigation applications. CFPB, *Supervisory Highlights*, Issue 21, Winter 2020, 5–6 (Feb. 2020), https://files.consumerfinance.gov/f/documents/cfpb_supervisory-highlights_issue-21_2020-02.pdf.

are needed, and (2) a "reasonable date" by which the borrower must submit them.[246] Where no foreclosure sale has been scheduled, servicers must treat the application as received more than forty-five days from a foreclosure sale.

A servicer that receives an incomplete loss mitigation application must take reasonable steps to collect the information needed to make a decision regarding a borrower's eligibility for loss mitigation options offered by the servicer, such as by promptly contacting the borrower to obtain missing information or determining whether information already exists in the servicer's files that may provide the information missing from the borrower's application.[247] A servicer must continue to exercise reasonable diligence to obtain documents and information from the borrower that the servicer requires to evaluate the borrower as to all other loss mitigation options available to the borrower.[248]

If the servicer determines that additional information or corrected documents are required after informing the borrower that an application was complete, the servicer must promptly request such information or documents from the borrower and treat the application as complete under 12 C.F.R. sections 1024.41(f)(2) and (g) until the borrower is given a reasonable opportunity to complete the application. Notifying the borrower that a servicer has received a completed application sets the operative date for the timing requirements in the loss mitigation rules, even if the servicer later determines that updated or additional information is necessary.[249]

---

246. The Official Commentary indicates that thirty days from the date the servicer provides the written notice is a "reasonable date." Cmt. 1024.41(b)(2)(ii)-1. Additionally, the reasonable date must be no later than the earliest of (1) the date by which any document or information submitted by a borrower will be considered stale or invalid pursuant to any requirements applicable to any loss mitigation option available to the borrower; (2) the date that is the 120th day of the borrower's delinquency; (3) the date that is ninety days before a foreclosure sale; or (4) the date that is thirty-eight days before a foreclosure sale. Cmt. 1024.41(b)(2)(ii)-2.

247. 12 C.F.R. § 1024.41(b)(1).

248. Cmt. 1024.41(b)(1)-1.

249. 12 C.F.R. § 1024.41(c)(2)(iv). A loss mitigation application is facially complete when (1) the servicer's initial notice under § 1024.41(b) advised the borrower that the application was complete, (2) the servicer's initial notice under § 1024.41(b) requested additional information from the borrower to complete the application and the borrower submits such additional information, or (3) the servicer is required to provide the borrower a written notice of a complete application under § 1024.41(c)(3)(i). The date of the facially complete application serves as the date the application was actually complete in the event that a servicer requests missing or corrected documents and the borrower provides them in a reasonable period.

The servicer must evaluate the borrower for all loss mitigation options available to the borrower from the owner or investor of the borrower's mortgage loan.[250] The servicer must provide the borrower with a written notice stating which loss mitigation options, if any, the servicer will offer to the borrower. The notice must state the amount of time the borrower has to accept or reject an offered loss mitigation option and, if applicable, that the borrower has the right to appeal a denial of a loan modification option, as well as the time period and any requirements for making an appeal.[251]

If a servicer receives the information and documentation necessary to constitute a complete loss mitigation application more than thirty-seven days before a foreclosure sale, the servicer must (1) evaluate the borrower for all loss mitigation options available to the borrower; and (2) within thirty days of receiving the complete loss mitigation application, provide the borrower with a notice in writing stating the servicer's determination of which loss mitigation options, if any, it will offer to the borrower on behalf of the owner or assignee of the mortgage.[252] The evaluation need not "meet any standard other than the discretion of the servicer."[253]

As discussed above, generally, a servicer may not offer a loss mitigation option based on an evaluation of an incomplete application. The Mortgage Servicing Rules, however, provide the following exceptions to this general principle:

- Servicers may offer loss mitigation without receiving a complete application if the offer is not based on an evaluation of information submitted by the borrower in connection with such application;
- Servicers may offer loss mitigation based on an incomplete application if the application still remains incomplete for a significant period of time without further progress by the borrower;[254] or
- Servicers may offer a short-term payment forbearance program or a short-term repayment plan to a borrower based on an evaluation of an incomplete loss mitigation application.[255]

250. 12 C.F.R. § 1024.41(c)(1)(i). However, the Commentary explains that, where an owner or assignee has established an evaluation criterion that sets an order ranking for evaluation of loan modification options (or a "waterfall") and a borrower has qualified for a particular loan modification option in the ranking, the servicer may deny "any other loan modification options below the option for which the borrower is eligible in the ranking." *See* Cmt. 1024.41(d)-1.

251. 12 C.F.R. § 1024.41(c)(1).

252. *Id.* § 1024.41(c)(1).

253. Cmt. 1024.41(c)(1)-1.

254. 12 C.F.R. § 1024.41(c)(2)(ii).

255. *Id.* § 1024.41(c)(2)(iii). The CFPB issued guidance regarding short-term forbearance or repayment plans under the Mortgage Servicing Rules and explained the use of short-term loss mitigation options for addressing emergencies or other scenarios in which a large number of borrowers may need relief. *See* CFPB, *The Bureau's Mortgage Servicing Rules FAQs related to the COVID-19 Emergency*, v.1 (April 3, 2020), https://files.consumerfinance.gov/f/documents/cfpb_mortgage-servicing-rules-covid-19_faqs.pdf.

A servicer must not deny a complete loss mitigation application solely because the servicer lacks required documents or information not in the borrower's control, unless the servicer has been unable to obtain the documents and information for a significant period following the thirty-day evaluation period provided under section 1024.41(c)(1) and is unable to make a determination on the complete application. However, a servicer is permitted to offer a borrower a loss mitigation option, even if the servicer does not obtain the requested documents or information.[256]

8.4.3.3 Loss Mitigation Denials and Appeals

The Mortgage Servicing Rules require an appeal process for denials of a loss mitigation application for a trial or permanent modification option. The notice must include the servicer's specific reason or reasons for denying each trial or permanent loan modification option, and, if applicable, a statement that the borrower was not evaluated on other criteria. Specific disclosures are required in certain instances, including the following:

- *Investor criteria/waterfall.* For loan modification denials based on investor criteria, the servicer must identify the owner or assignee of the mortgage loan and the specific criteria that the borrower failed to satisfy. For ordered loss mitigation waterfalls, the notice can explain that the investor's requirements include the use of such a waterfall and that an offer of a loan modification option necessarily results in a denial for any other loan modification options below the option for which the borrower is eligible in the ranking.[257]
- *Net present value calculation.* If the denial was based on a net present value calculation, the servicer must disclose the inputs used in the calculation.[258]
- *Necessary criteria.* If a servicer follows a hierarchy of eligibility criteria and does not consider other criteria beyond the denial reason the servicer need only provide the specific reason or reasons why the borrower was actually rejected, and notify the borrower that the borrower was not evaluated on other criteria.

For applications completed ninety days or more before a foreclosure sale, the servicer must give the borrower at least fourteen days to decide. For applications completed fewer than ninety but more than thirty-seven days before a foreclosure sale, the servicer must give the borrower at least seven days to decide. If a borrower does not respond to an offer of loss mitigation within the timeframes above, the failure

256. 12 C.F.R. § 1024.41(c)(4).
257. Cmt. 1024.41(d)-1.
258. Cmt. 1024.41(d)-2.

to respond can be treated as a rejection.[259] If a borrower makes a payment under a trial modification plan (implicitly accepting the offer), the servicer must provide the borrower a reasonable time to fulfill any remaining requirements of the servicer for acceptance of the trial loan modification plan.

Borrowers that submit a complete application ninety days or more before a scheduled foreclosure sale have a right to appeal a denial of or any trial or permanent loan modification program available to the borrower.[260] For appeals, borrowers have until fourteen days after the servicer provides notice of its determination regarding resolution of that appeal to decide whether to accept any offered loss mitigation option.[261] No later than thirty days after the appeal, the servicer must provide a notice to the borrower stating the following:

- Whether it will offer the borrower a loss mitigation option based on the appeal; and
- How long the borrower has to accept or reject this loss mitigation option or a previously offered loss mitigation option (if applicable).[262]

Loss mitigation appeals must receive independent evaluations, meaning that appeals cannot be reviewed by the same personnel responsible for evaluating the borrower's complete loss mitigation application.[263] If the appeal results in an offer of loss mitigation, the servicer must provide the borrower at least fourteen days to decide whether to accept the offered loss mitigation option.

Servicers do not need to comply with the loss mitigation rules twice for the same borrower during the same delinquency—if the borrower has already submitted a complete application and the servicer complied with the Mortgage Servicing Rule's requirements. The regulation provides that "[a] servicer is only required to comply with the requirements of this section for a single complete loss mitigation application."[264]

8.4.3.4 Prohibition on Dual-Tracking Foreclosures

The Mortgage Servicing Rules prohibit a practice known as *dual tracking*. The practice entails proceeding with the foreclosure process while evaluating a borrower for loss mitigation options. Under the anti-dual tracking provisions, a servicer cannot make

---

259. 12 C.F.R. § 1024.41(e).

260. *Id.* § 1024.41(h)(1).

261. *Id.* § 1024.41(h)(2).

262. *Id.* § 1024(h)(4).

263. *Id.* § 1024(h)(3).

264. *Id.* § 1024.41(I). Courts have agreed that the loss mitigation requirements only apply to the first application; thereafter, the regulation imposes no obligation to respond to further duplicative requests. *See, e.g.*, Houle v. Green Tree Servicing, LLC, No. 14-14654, 2015 WL 1867526, at *3 (E.D. Mich. Apr. 23, 2015).

the first foreclosure notice or filing for any judicial or nonjudicial process[265] until (1) the borrower is more than 120 days delinquent,[266] (2) the foreclosure is based on a borrower's violation of a due-on-sale clause, or (3) the servicer is joining a superior or subordinate lienholder's foreclosure action.[267]

If a borrower submits a completed loss mitigation application before the 120th day of delinquency or before the servicer makes the first foreclosure notice or filing, then the servicer cannot make the first foreclosure notice or filing unless one of the following occurs: (1) the servicer sends a notice to the borrower stating that the borrower is ineligible for any loss mitigation option and, if an appeal is available, either the borrower did not timely appeal or the appeal has been denied; (2) the borrower rejects all the offered loss mitigation options; or (3) the borrower fails to perform under a loss mitigation agreement.

The loss mitigation rules also protect borrowers who apply for relief after the servicer has initiated the foreclosure process, but more than thirty-seven days before the foreclosure sale.[268] If the borrower submits a complete loss mitigation application more than thirty-seven days before the foreclosure sale, the servicer must take steps to suspend the foreclosure process and proceedings. These steps may include promptly instructing foreclosure counsel not to make a dispositive motion for foreclosure judgment or order of sale. The Official Commentary states that no action may be

265. The Official Commentary to the rule explains that the "first foreclosure notice or filing" consists of the earliest required to be filed with a court or other judicial body to commence the action or proceeding (judicial foreclosure), required to be recorded or published to initiate the foreclosure process (nonjudicial foreclosure), or that establishes, sets, or schedules a date for the foreclosure sale (nonjudicial foreclosure). A notice to the borrower that does not constitute one of these types of documents is not a "first notice or filing," even if providing the notice is a necessary step in the foreclosure process. Cmt. 1024.41(f)-1.

266. The 120-day rule is a strict bar to the commencement of a foreclosure proceeding, and preempts state foreclosure timelines to the extent that they allow an earlier commencement of foreclosure. *See* 78 Fed. Reg. 10,696, 10,833 (Feb. 14, 2013).

267. 12 C.F.R. § 1024.41(f).

268. *Id.* § 1024.41(g). The loss mitigation rules do not apply to application made thirty-seven days or less before a foreclosure sale. However, the servicers are required to maintain general policies and procedures to, among other things, properly evaluate a borrower who applies for loss mitigation for all options available to the borrower pursuant to any requirements established by the owner or assignee of the borrower's mortgage loan. *See* Cmt. 1024.41(g)-1; 12 C.F.R. § 1024.38(b)(2)(v). The timing requirements form a distinct element of RESPA/Regulation X claims under the loss mitigation rules. To allege a violation of the anti-dual tracking rules, a borrower must plead that he or she submitted a complete loss mitigation application no later than thirty-seven days before the foreclosure sale. *See* Gresham v. Wells Fargo Bank, N.A., 642 F. App'x. 355 (5th Cir. 2016); Forscht v. Select Portfolio Servicing, Inc., No. CV H-17-2659, 2018 WL 1757610 (S.D. Tex. Apr. 12, 2018).

taken if it would "cause or directly result" in the issuance of a foreclosure judgment, order of sale, or sale of the property.[269]

The foreclosure proceedings may only move forward if:

- The servicer sends a notice to the borrower stating that the borrower is ineligible for any loss mitigation option and the appeal process is inapplicable, the borrower did not timely appeal, or the appeal has been denied;
- The borrower rejects all the offered loss mitigation options; or
- The borrower fails to perform under a loss mitigation agreement.

The anti-dual tracking protections apply until a servicer determines that the borrower does not qualify for any loss mitigation option, regardless of the borrowers stated preference.[270]

It is important to note that the Mortgage Servicing Rules provide that servicers are responsible for controlling foreclosure counsel and other agents. The Official Commentary expressly states that "[a] servicer is not relieved of its obligations because foreclosure counsel's actions or inaction caused a violation."[271]

8.5 Mortgage Servicing Transfers

Mortgage loans are rarely static. Mortgage loans are assigned and sold frequently, and an individual borrower's loan is typically sold several times during its term—and such transactions are often accompanied by a transfer to a new servicer. Moreover, a mortgage loan may be owned or held by one entity but serviced by another. The borrower has no control over when or how the servicing of a loan is transferred, and such transfers can result in disruptions to the borrower's repayment of the loan, create confusion, and interrupt servicing processes (such as loss mitigation applications). To combat these issues, the Mortgage Servicing Rules mandate certain disclosures and

269. Cmt. 1024.41(g)-2; *see also* Tripicchio v. Seterus, Inc., No. 16-CV-4967, 2016 WL 7374273 (N.D. Ill. Dec. 20, 2016). The Eleventh Circuit has held that rescheduling a preexisting foreclosure sale does not violate § 1024.41(g), since it is not an order of sale. *See* Landau v. RoundPoint Mortg. Servicing Corp., 925 F.3d 1365, 1371 (11th Cir. 2019); Hevia v. Ocwen Loan Servicing, L.L.C., No. 1:18-CV-25463-KMM, 2019 WL 3000761 (S.D. Fla. June 25, 2019), *appeal dismissed*, No. 19-13556-GG, 2019 WL 6790019 (11th Cir. Dec. 2, 2019).

270. The CFPB has been particularly active with regard to enforcement actions against servicers that violate the dual tracking prohibitions. *See, e.g.*, In the Matter of Specialized Loan Servicing, LLC, File No. 2020-BCFP-0002 (May 11, 2020), https://files.consumerfinance.gov/f/documents/cfpb_specialized-loan-servicing_consent-order_2020-05.pdf; In the Matter of Fay Servicing, LLC, File No. 2017-CFPB-0014 (June 7, 2017), https://files.consumerfinance.gov/f/documents/062017_cfpb_Fay_Servicing-consent_order.pdf.

271. Cmt. 1024.41(g)-3.

require that servicers maintain appropriate procedures to ensure loans are transferred completely and accurately.

8.5.1 Policies and Procedures

The Mortgage Servicing Rules require transferor servicers to maintain policies and procedures that are reasonably designed to achieve the objective of the timely transfer of all information and documents in the possession or control of the servicer relating to a transferred mortgage loan to a transferee servicer in a form and manner that ensures the accuracy of the information and documents transferred and that enables a transferee servicer to comply with the terms of the transferee servicer's obligations to the owner or assignee of the mortgage loan and applicable law. However, the rules do not prescribe any specific policies or procedures that a servicer must implement; the rule says that the policies and procedures must be "reasonably designed" to achieve the goal of facilitating the transfer of information during servicing transfers.[272] Thus, servicers have the flexibility to determine their own policies and procedures and methods in light of the size, nature, and scope of their operations, including, for example, the volume and aggregate unpaid principal balance of mortgage loans serviced, the credit quality, including the default risk, of the mortgage loans serviced, and the servicer's history of consumer complaints.[273]

The CFPB has identified key information and areas important to the servicing transfer process. CFPB Bulletin 2020-02, *Compliance Bulletin and Policy Guidance: Handling of Information and Documents During Mortgage Servicing Transfers* identifies critical considerations at each stage of the transfer.[274] The CFPB recommends that servicers adopt the practices below, among others:

- *Planning and pretransfer testing.* The CFPB identifies processes that help ensure that information and records are transferred fully and completely, creating a seamless experience for the consumer. These steps include planning and preparation well in advance of the transfer to identify and correct data integrity issues. Importantly, transferor servicers should identify any loans in default, active foreclosure, or bankruptcy, as well as identify and collect documentation regarding loss mitigation activity.
- *Post-transfer monitoring.* The CFPB recommends that servicers conduct a post-transfer review to identify any gaps or errors in the transfer of servicing data and loan records, that is, monitoring consumer complaints

272. 12 C.F.R. § 1024.38(b)(4)(i).

273. *See* CFPB Bulletin 2020-02, *Compliance Bulletin and Policy Guidance: Handling of Information and Documents During Mortgage Servicing Transfers* (May 1, 2020), https://files.consumerfinance.gov/f/documents/cfpb_policy-guidance_mortgage-servicing-transfers_2020-04.pdf.

274. 85 Fed. Reg. 25,281 (May 1, 2020).

and loss mitigation performance metrics, such as borrower engagement rate, approvals of trial modifications, repayment plans, non-home retention options, and completed workouts for at least four to six months post-transfer. This would also include monitoring for delinquencies, foreclosures, and bankruptcies to detect trends, including for month-to-month increases after transfer.

Further, in a consent order with Service One, Inc., the CFPB highlighted alleged failures in handling mortgage servicing transfers with incomplete or inaccurate loss mitigation information, resulting in errors with pending loss mitigation applications, in-process loan modifications, and permanent loan modifications, as well as failures in handling mortgage servicing transfers with incomplete or inaccurate escrow information resulting in untimely escrow disbursements.[275]

8.5.2 Servicing Transfer Disclosure

When a covered loan is assigned, sold, or transferred, the transferor servicer generally must provide a disclosure at least fifteen days before the effective date of the transfer, and the transferee servicer must provide a disclosure at least fifteen days after the effective date of the transfer.[276] The disclosures may be combined if delivered at least fifteen days before the effective date of the transfer.

8.5.3 Payments during Transfer

Servicers may not charge a late fee or other penalty on a borrower who has made a timely payment to the transferor servicer. If the transferor servicer receives any incorrect payments on or after the effective date of the transfer, the transferor servicer must either transfer the payment to the transferee servicer or return the payment and inform the payor of the proper recipient of the payment.

8.5.4 Loss Mitigation Compliance during Transfer

A mortgage servicing transfer does not eliminate a borrower's protections under the Loss Mitigation Rules. If a transferee servicer acquires the servicing of a mortgage

---

275. *See* In the Matter of Service One, Inc. d/b/a BSI Financial Services, File No. 2019-BCFP-006 (May 29, 2019), https://files.consumerfinance.gov/f/documents/cfpb_servis-one-inc-BSI-financial-services_consent-order_2019-05.pdf.

276. 12 U.S.C. § 2605(a). This requirement is limited to the transfer of servicing, and does not apply to transfers of ownership of the note and mortgage. TILA, however, requires that if ownership is transferred, the new owner or assignee of a mortgage loan must notify the borrower within thirty days after the loan is sold or assigned of its identity, address, and telephone number, as well as information about any agent or party with authority to act on behalf of the new owner and other relevant information. 15 U.S.C. § 1641(g). Although it is not part of RESPA, this requirement forms part of the broader Mortgage Servicing Rules.

loan for which a loss mitigation application is pending as of the transfer date, the transferee servicer must comply with the Loss Mitigation Rules for that application within the timeframes that were applicable to the transferor servicer based on the date the transferor servicer received the loss mitigation application.[277]

The rights of borrowers with incomplete applications, facially complete applications, completed applications, and any rights to appeal a loss mitigation decision must be assumed by the transferor servicer subject to section 1024.41(k). However, the transferor servicer is typically not required to provide loss mitigation notices or disclosures that the borrower already received from the transferee servicer.[278]

8.6 Enforcement, Penalties, and Liabilities

8.6.1 Administrative Enforcement

Since the enactment of the Dodd-Frank Act, the CFPB is authorized to write rules and regulations and otherwise interpret the RESPA mortgage servicing requirements. The authority provided to the CFPB under RESPA, such as to investigate violations, issue civil investigative demands, and conduct hearings, extends to the servicing requirements as well.[279]

CFPB enforcement of the RESPA Mortgage Servicing Rules has generally focused on ensuring borrowers are notified of available loss mitigation options, and failure by servicers to timely evaluate borrowers' loss mitigation applications. For example, in *In re Specialized Loan Servicing*, the CFPB alleged that the servicer failed to send or timely send evaluation notices to borrowers who were entitled to the notices.[280] The CFPB also made similar allegations in *In Fay Servicing, LLC*.[281] RESPA and Regulation X require that federally related mortgage loan servicers comply with certain loss mitigation procedures.[282] The statute's plain terms place this responsibility on servicers rather than lenders. As such, a lender is not vicariously liable for the alleged RESPA violations of its servicers.[283] The CFPB also has enforced RESPA against servicers who fail to establish and maintain a comprehensive data

277. 12 C.F.R. § 1024.41(k)(1)(i).

278. Cmt. 1024.41(k)(1)(i)-3.

279. For further information on RESPA enforcement, *see* section 5 of this chapter; *see* 12 U.S.C. § 2617.

280. In the Matter of Specialized Loan Servicing, File No. 2020-BCFP-0002 (May 11, 2020), https://files.consumerfinance.gov/f/documents/cfpb_specialized-loan-servicing_consent-order_2020-05.pdf.

281. In the Matter of Fay Servicing, LLC, File No. 2017-CFPB-0014 (June 7, 2017), https://files.consumerfinance.gov/f/documents/062017_cfpb_Fay_Servicing-consent_order.pdf.

282. 12 U.S.C. § 2605; 12 C.F.R. § 1024.41.

283. Christiana Tr. v. Riddle, 911 F.3d 799, 805 (5th Cir. 2018).

integrity program that ensures the "accuracy, integrity, and completeness of the data for loans that [they] service."[284]

8.6.2 Private Enforcement

Certain sections of the Mortgage Servicing Rules are privately enforceable, both individually and on a class basis.[285] Section 2605(f) of RESPA provides a statutory private right of action, stating "[w]hoever fails to comply with any provision of this section shall be liable to the borrower for each such failure in the following amounts . . ."

- Individual Action: (A) any actual damages to the borrower as a result of the failure; (B) any additional damages, as the court may allow, in the case of a pattern or practice of noncompliance with the requirements of this section, in an amount not to exceed $2,000; and (C) costs and attorney's fees.
- Class Action: (A) any actual damages to each of the borrowers in the class as a result of the failure; (B) any additional damages, as the court may allow, in the case of a pattern or practice of noncompliance with the requirements of this section, in an amount not greater than $2,000 for each member of the class, except that the total amount of damages under this subparagraph in any class action may not exceed the lesser of (i) $1,000,000; or (ii) one percent of the net worth of the servicer; and (C) costs and attorney's fees.[286]

However, the CFPB did not promulgate all of the Mortgage Servicing Rules pursuant to section 2605 in an effort to reduce private enforcement of the rules. By opting to use its general rulemaking authority for certain regulations, the

284. In the Matter of BSI Financial Services, File No. 2019-BCFP-0006 (May 5, 2019), https://files.consumerfinance.gov/f/documents/cfpb_servis-one-inc-BSI-financial-services_consent-order_2019-05.pdf.

285. Lage v. Ocwen Loan Servicing L.L.C., 839 F.3d 1003, 1007 (11th Cir. 2016) ("If the servicer fails to respond adequately to the borrower's notice of error, then the borrower has a private right of action to sue the servicer under RESPA."); Lucas v. New Penn Fin., L.L.C., No. 17-CV-11472-ADB, 2019 WL 404033 (D. Mass. Jan. 31, 2019); Sutton v. CitiMortgage, Inc., 228 F. Supp. 3d 254, 271 (S.D.N.Y. 2017); *see also* 78 Fed. Reg. at 10,714, n.64 ("regulations established pursuant to [12 U.S.C. § 2605] are subject to [12 U.S.C. § 2605(f)], which provides borrowers a private right of action to enforce such regulations.").

286. 12 U.S.C. § 2605(f).

Bureau made these provisions enforceable only through administrative enforcement or supervision.[287]

For example, the following provisions of the Mortgage Servicing Rules allow for private remedies:

- *Transfer notice.* Failure to provide the borrower with a transfer notice or the grace period for payments.[288]
- *Loss mitigation procedures.* Failure to comply with the loss mitigation procedure requirements can result in private liability.[289]

Additionally, some courts have held that the early intervention rules allow for a private right of action, because the rules were promulgated under section 6 of RESPA.[290] Varying judicial opinions indicate that question is unsettled.[291]

The following provisions of the Mortgage Servicing Rules do not provide for private remedies and are subject only to administrative enforcement and supervision:

- *Servicing policies and procedures.* The requirement that servicers adopt reasonable policies and procedures on many routine servicing activities is not enforceable through private action.[292]
- *Continuity of contact.* The continuity of contact rules are not enforceable through private action, because the rules require servicers to maintain policies and procedures, rather than directly mandate compliance with a particular requirement.[293]

---

287. *See* Mortgage Servicing Rules Under the Real Estate Settlement Procedures Act (Regulation X), 78 Fed. Reg. 10,696, 10,779 (Feb. 14, 2013) ("the Bureau is restructuring the final rule so that it neither provides private liability for violations of § 1024.38" nor "relies on its authorities under Section 6 of RESPA to issue § 1024.38. Instead, the Bureau is adopting § 1024.38 pursuant to its authority under Section 19(a) of RESPA[,] . . . Section 1022(b) of the Dodd-Frank Act[, and] . . . Section 1032(a) of the Dodd-Frank Act.").

288. 12 U.S.C. § 2605(f).

289. 12 C.F.R. § 1024.41(a) ("A borrower may enforce this provision of this section pursuant to Section 6(f) of RESPA (12 U.S.C. 2605(f).").

290. *See* Vance v. Wells Fargo Bank, N.A., 291 F. Supp. 3d 769, 773 (W.D. Va. 2018) ("Because the Bureau promulgated Section 1024.39 under the authority of RESPA Section 6 and Section 6 confers a private right of action, Section 1024.39 authorizes a private right of action."). *But see* Gresham v. Wells Fargo Bank, N.A., 642 F. App'x 355, 359 (5th Cir. 2016) (citing Miller v. HSBC Bank U.S.A., N.A., No. 13 CIV. 7500, 2015 WL 585589, *11 (S.D.N.Y. Feb. 11, 2015)).

291. *Supra* note 290.

292. *See* Smith v. Nationstar Mortg., No. 15-13019, 2015 WL 7180473 (E.D. Mich. Nov. 16, 2015) (holding that violations of § 1024.38 are not privately enforceable).

293. *See* Final Rule, 78 Fed. Reg. 10,696, 10,808 (Feb. 14, 2013) (stating that "private liability is not compatible" with the continuity of contact requirements).

8.6.3 *Vicarious Liability under Mortgage Servicing Rules*

The Mortgage Servicing Rules apply to all RESPA-covered loans.[294] However, the plain language of most provisions applies only to servicers. The U.S. Court of Appeals for the Fifth Circuit recently confirmed that those obligations are only applicable to the servicer, and that an originating lender or assignee of the loan is not "vicariously" liable for any such violations by the servicer.[295]

8.6.4 *Defenses to Liability*

The Mortgage Servicing Rules include a safe harbor from liability under RESPA for servicers who timely correct an account error.[296] A servicer can avoid liability by making an appropriate adjustment to an account within sixty days of discovering an error. The correction must also occur before commencement of an action under section 2605(f) and the receipt of a written notice of the error from the borrower. However, RESPA, unlike its TILA counterpart, does not set out a bona fide error defense. This means that servicers may be liable for unintentional violations of the Mortgage Servicing Rules even when the servicer maintained reasonable procedures to prevent errors.

294. 12 C.F.R. § 1024.30(a).

295. *See Riddle*, 911 F.3d at 805 (5th Cir. 2018); *see also, e.g.*, Hawk v. Carrington Mortg. Servs., LLC, No. 3:14-CV-1044, 2016 WL 4433665, at *2 (M.D. Pa. Aug. 17, 2016); Green v. Cent. Mortg. Co., 148 F. Supp. 3d 852, 876–77 (N.D. Cal. 2015); Bennett v. Nationstar Mortg., LLC, No. CV 15-00165-KD-C, 2015 WL 5294321, at *10 (S.D. Ala. Sept. 8, 2015); McAndrew v. Deutsche Bank Nat'l Tr. Co., 977 F. Supp. 2d 440, 445 (M.D. Pa. 2013). *But see* Rouleau v. US Bank, N.A., No. 14-CV-568-JL, 2015 WL 1757104 (D.N.H. Apr. 17, 2015).

296. 12 U.S.C. § 2605(f)(4).

Table of Cases

Index

B

C

E

F

G

M

N

O

P

Q

R

S

T

U

V

W

Z